The Waite Group's

MICROSOFT QUICKBASIC™ BIBLE

THE WAITE GROUP

Mitchell Waite, Robert Arnson, Christy Gemmell, and Harry Henderson

PUBLISHED BY
Microsoft Press
A Division of Microsoft Corporation
One Microsoft Way
Redmond, Washington 98052-6399

Library of Congress Cataloging-in-Publication Data

The Waite Group's Microsoft QuickBASIC bible / Mitchell Waite ... [et al.].
p. cm.
Includes index.
ISBN 1-55615-262-0
1. BASIC (Computer program language) 2. Microsoft BASIC (Computer program) I. Waite, Mitchell. II. Waite Group.
QA76.73.B3W333 1990
005.26'2--dc20 90-43927
CIP

Printed and bound in the United States of America.

3 4 5 6 7 8 9 RARA 5 4 3 2 1

Distributed to the book trade in Canada by Macmillan Publishing, a division of Canada Publishing Corporation.

Distributed to the book trade outside the United States and Canada by Penguin Books Ltd.

Penguin Books Ltd., Harmondsworth, Middlesex, England
Penguin Books Australia Ltd., Ringwood, Victoria, Australia
Penguin Books N.Z. Ltd., 182-190 Wairau Road, Auckland 10, New Zealand

British Cataloging-in-Publication Data available

As used in this book, DOS refers to the Microsoft MS-DOS operating system and the IBM version of the MS-DOS operating system, also known as PC-DOS.

For Microsoft Press:
Project Editor: Karen Marcus
Technical Editor: Mary DeJong
Manuscript Editor: Gary Masters
Acquisitions Editor: Dean Holmes

For The Waite Group:
Developmental Editor: Mitchell Waite
Editorial Director: Scott Calamar
Editor: Kay Nelson
Editorial Assistant: Joel Fugazzotto

CONTENTS

Foreword

BASIC was Microsoft's first product back in 1975, but its history goes back even further, to an Ivy League math department in the early 1960s. BASIC's inventors imagined a general-purpose, easy-to-use, low-overhead programming language that would make computers accessible to their liberal arts students. They created it, and BASIC has been a strategic key to success for virtually every major computer platform since then.

How did BASIC go from Ivy League to PC major league? In 1975, Bill Gates and his school buddies found a way to squeeze the BASIC they had conceived into a tiny, 4-KB interpreter for the MITS Altair 8800 (the first microcomputer to achieve real commercial fame). This somewhat inconspicuous event suddenly made it possible for everyone to write software for the world's first microcomputer. Shortly after the development of the interpreter for the Altair, dialects of Microsoft BASIC propelled the successes of the Tandy TRS-80, the Commodore PET, the Apple II, and the IBM PC. Soon Microsoft BASIC was shipped by every personal computer manufacturer, and the useful applications that determined the success or failure of a new platform were written in BASIC.

Because of these beginnings, 25 years later nearly all of 100 million worldwide microcomputer users know about Microsoft BASIC. And while BASIC's gentle syntax has guaranteed its popularity, its simplicity and power have made it a productive, serious tool for a wide range of professional programmers, consultants, and users.

But why does Microsoft care so much about BASIC now? Isn't it time to put this doddering language out to pasture, given that we now have exciting dialects of the structured teaching language, Pascal, for students, and friendly versions of that serious developer's language, C, to whet beginners' appetites?

The answer is apparent if you take a look at a modern dialect of BASIC such as Microsoft QuickBASIC. While QuickBASIC is faithful to the original spirit of BASIC (easy to learn and easy to use, with low overhead), successive versions of QuickBASIC illustrate BASIC's advances in modern language technology and on computing platforms. No longer a line-oriented dialect of BASIC designed for 8-bit microcomputers, the BASIC interpreter has been replaced by a powerful new model that combines the instantaneous response of a compiler with the interactiveness of an interpreter. BASIC now has all the speed, capacity, and structured programming features of a modern, compiled language. Today more than a quarter of a million professional programmers work with modern, structured, compiled BASIC, and BASIC is still the most widely taught language in all of academia.

But Microsoft's vision for BASIC extends far beyond these accomplishments. In the future, we at Microsoft Corporation see BASIC being used for the visual programming, rather than coding, of large portions of applications; as a central control language for specifically focused BASIC programs that treat multiple applications as though their data and capabilities were libraries; and as a common macro language across programmable applications. We think that BASIC, with its universal popularity, will remain the language of choice for the professional programmers, consultants, and power users who know it so well.

I was pleased to learn that The Waite Group would turn their painstaking, comprehensive attention to QuickBASIC. Their language bibles and DOS developer guides line our programmers' bookshelves, and I expected great things of this book. Now that I have the final galleys in hand, I am very pleased because The Waite Group has done their job and more. They have written the definitive programmer's reference guide to QuickBASIC.

Tutorials in distinct categories speak to the learners' and the professionals' needs. Detailed examples illustrate the use of every QuickBASIC keyword, function, and statement. The compatibility box format The Waite Group introduced in their C bibles tells the reader quickly whether a QuickBASIC keyword works in all versions of QuickBASIC, in GW-BASIC, in BASICA, in Microsoft's BASIC Professional Development System, and so forth. Detailed descriptions of third-party products, information from the QuickBASIC KnowledgeBase, and tips on public domain programs round out the most comprehensive reference book on QuickBASIC I've ever seen.

This remarkable book belongs on every serious BASIC programmer's desk.

Tom Button
Microsoft BASIC Program Manager

Preface

Our Approach

We wrote this book with a special approach in mind. The idea is to allow you to access the most general information first, followed by more specific information. For example, if you are just getting started with QuickBASIC, you might want a general overview of the entire language—its advantages over other languages and its limitations, its power and its potential. The Introduction, "A Task-Oriented Overview of QuickBASIC," gives you this information in a style that is both comprehensive and readable.

If you already know a version of BASIC, you probably want to identify those areas of QuickBASIC that are new and different. To this end, you can read the tutorials that introduce each chapter of the book; these sections summarize and discuss the usage of any commands and keywords that might be new to you.

Finally, if you understand the big picture and you need to use a command, you'll want to read about it in greater detail. The reference sections of each chapter in this book discuss the purpose, syntax, and usage of every statement and function; they provide authoritative information about each entry, including programming tips and warnings; and they supply compatibility information that lets you immediately recognize which versions of BASIC support the statement or function. The discussions of statements and functions are arranged by subject area rather than alphabetically, as they are in most reference books. This organization lets you understand the relationships of the statements in a specific area, so you can quickly grasp their interactions rather than having to search for scattered entries throughout the book. We've also provided two alphabetic "jump" tables of keywords and concepts on the inside front and back covers of this book so that you can quickly focus on a specific topic.

How We Wrote This Book

We developed the outline of this book by organizing all QuickBASIC keywords into 22 groups of related keywords. Next, we thoroughly studied each statement and function and agreed on the best example for it. Then we wrote the reference pages for each command. Short sample programs for the keywords were designed specifically to showcase the commands in an interesting, helpful, and useful manner.

We then used the reference pages to produce the tutorial for each chapter. We condensed the most important elements of the 22 command categories into succinct, instructive summaries that show how you use the commands together. Then we further condensed the 22 tutorials into the Introduction, "A Task-Oriented Overview of QuickBASIC."

Each step of this process further refined the information, pulling out the most salient facts and filtering out the finer details. Finally, we produced the "jump" tables that you see on the inside front and back covers. The front jump table is a conceptual listing of tasks you can perform with QuickBASIC and the pages on which you can find the relevant information; this critical listing is frequently omitted from reference books and manuals. The back jump table lists the QuickBASIC keywords alphabetically within categories and the page numbers on which the keywords are found.

Refinement and the Microscope Analogy

Think of this book as a microscope with different powers of magnification. You can start at the lowest level, inside front and back covers, examine more details in the "Task-Oriented Overview of QuickBASIC," study the interrelationships of commands in the tutorials, and, finally, view each element of QuickBASIC under the powerful magnification of the reference entries. The index is a final lens that gives you a finely detailed list of all the topics that form this language.

The Compatibility Box

✲ QB2	■ QB4.5	✲ PowerBASIC
✲ QB3	■ ANSI	GW-BASIC
■ QB4	■ BASIC7	■ MacQB

Each keyword in the reference sections has a special compatibility box like the one shown above. The box quickly lets you know whether the keyword works with the different versions of QuickBASIC from version 2.0 through version 4.5, ANSI BASIC, Microsoft BASIC 7.0 Professional Development System, PowerBASIC, GW-BASIC, and Microsoft QuickBASIC for the Macintosh—which appears in the box as "MacQB." Note that the Microsoft BASIC 7.0 Professional Development System supports all code written in Microsoft BASIC 6.0. PowerBASIC is the upgraded version of Turbo BASIC 1.1, which was distributed by Borland International, Inc. PowerBASIC is now being published by SPECTRA Publishing under an agreement with Robert Zale, the developer of Turbo BASIC and PowerBASIC.

If the keyword is fully supported by a version, a square bullet (■) appears in the space beside the version name in the compatibility box. If the keyword is not supported, the space is empty. And if differences in compatibility exist between QuickBASIC 4.5 and the listed version, an asterisk (✲) in the space refers you to a note in the reference section under the heading "Compatibility" that explains what you need to know. These boxes will make your programming more professional: They let you see how easy (or difficult) it is to port your program from one version to another, and they alert you to any trade-offs you must make if you run the program under another version of BASIC.

What We Left Out

We intentionally omitted coverage of the compiler options, the linker, and the library manager. We felt that these programs (as well as the finer points of program development) deserve their own, more advanced, book, and we hope to write that book someday soon.

We hope you find this book helpful and practical as you learn and use QuickBASIC. If you have any suggestions for improvements or other comments, please fill out the card included at the back of this book and return it to The Waite Group.

Mitchell Waite, Robert Arnson,
Christy Gemmel, Harry Henderson
The Authors, Winter 1989

Acknowledgments

Publishing a book such as this requires a monumental effort on the part of the authors, editors, publisher, and others involved in the process.

First and foremost, The Waite Group would like to thank our authors for their superhuman work. Mitch Waite immersed himself in developing and designing this book, in addition to his writing. Coauthors Christy Gemmel, Robert Arnson, and Harry Henderson virtually slept and ate QuickBASIC during this process. All were incredibly creative, responsive to our comments and direction, and a pleasure to work with. The combined talents of these BASIC afficionados have created a true milestone for The Waite Group. Thanks to Ethan Winer of Crescent Software for his time and work putting together the Third-Party Routines appendix. Thanks also to Kay Nelson for her very helpful editing and to Joel Fugazzotto for his ongoing, amiable assistance.

This book would not have been possible without the support of Microsoft Press. Our special thanks to Jim Brown and Dean Holmes for once again bringing together The Waite Group and Microsoft. Beaucoups thanks to Gary Masters for his editing, which fit our more than 3000 pages of manuscript into this book, to Mary DeJong for her thorough technical editing of every facet of the book's content, including its example programs, and to Karen Marcus, for her editing and her professional and good natured management of this project for Microsoft Press. Our appreciation to Darcie Furlan, for coming up with a very elegant and readable design that enabled us to shoehorn thousands of facts into these pages. Thanks also to Jean Zimmer and the eagle-eyed, ace proofreaders. And, finally, thanks to David Rygmyr, Eric Stroo, and Suzanne Viescas. Microsoft Press's editorial and technical staff always goes above and beyond the call of duty.

Scott Calamar
Editorial Director, The Waite Group

INTRODUCTION

A Task-Oriented Overview of QuickBASIC

How to Use This Overview

As we explained in the Preface, *The Waite Group's Microsoft QuickBASIC Bible* was designed with four specific levels of information access in mind. Each level provides vital help for different situations that arise when you work with the QuickBASIC compiler.

This chapter, the Introduction, is the "big picture" section of the book—it gives you an overview of the QuickBASIC language from the perspective of a grizzled, professional programmer who has wrestled QuickBASIC to the ground several times but still loves it. This overview presents practical information that answers questions such as, "What can I do with this statement?" and "What, if anything, should I watch out for?" If you are moving to QuickBASIC from another language (such as Pascal, FORTRAN, or Cobol) or from other versions of BASIC, such as GW-BASIC or BASICA, read this chapter first to get a complete feeling for what QuickBASIC can and can't do.

The organization of this chapter parallels that of the book itself so that you can easily find an introduction to a particular category of QuickBASIC statements. As you read this overview, you can at any time jump to the corresponding tutorial for a more detailed explanation. If you are interested in the most technical explanation of a particular statement or function (for example, if you are an advanced programmer who merely needs to see the syntax), you can jump to the first page of the reference entry for that statement or function. We have numbered each main heading so that you know which chapter we are referring to. Let's begin.

I. Core

Variables and Types (Chapter 1)

Variables

Although all programming languages provide ways to handle information, what's really important is how they represent that information. Traditionally, programming languages organize data in a fairly primitive manner, much like the way an advanced scientific calculator manipulates numbers. Numbers and other data are represented in QuickBASIC as "types." QuickBASIC offers several numeric data types and one type for ASCII characters (letters, and so on). QuickBASIC also lets a programmer combine these primitive types into more sophisticated, user-defined types.

QuickBASIC, like all programming languages, lets you use descriptive names to define variables. Variables are symbolic names, such as *dollarsOwed!*, *flowerColor$*, *maxRads%*, or *emptyTank&*, that can be assigned values. In QuickBASIC, the last character of the variable can indicate what type of variable the name represents, but you can also define a type in other ways, as you will see. Assignment statements look like this:

```
dollarsOwed! = 123.34
flowerColor$ = "Red"
maxRads% = 0
emptyTank& = -128,000
```

There are rules for using variable names, but QuickBASIC is very flexible. The first character of a variable name must be a letter. A variable cannot contain more than 40 characters and cannot have the same name as a reserved word, such as the name of a statement or function. After the first letter you can use any character or number in a name (even a period, although periods can cause problems in certain circumstances).

Types

You can represent two fundamental types of data in QuickBASIC—numbers and characters. QuickBASIC has five identifiers that tell the program what type of data a variable can contain: INTEGER, LONG, SINGLE, DOUBLE, and STRING. (See the entries in Chapter 1, "Variables and Types," for more details about these types.)

For whole numbers (numbers that have no fractional portion), QuickBASIC offers the 16-bit integer type, which includes numbers in the range –32768 through 32767, and the long-integer type, which includes numbers in the range –2147483648 through 2147483647. The long-integer type is useful for representing money (in terms of cents) so that no rounding errors occur, as they would with fractional representation. This lets you manipulate a value as great as $21,474,836.48 without generating an error.

For numbers with decimals, QuickBASIC provides the single-precision type, which represents floating-point numbers in the range –1.401298E-45 through

3.402823E+38 with seven digits of precision, and the double-precision type, which represents floating-point numbers in the range –4.940656458412465D-324 through 1.797693134862315D+308 with 16 digits of precision. This probably is enough precision for any application, especially when you consider that 1.797693134862315D+308 is greater than the number of all the atoms in the universe!

QuickBASIC supports two types of strings—the variable-length string and the fixed-length string (STRING *). Each type can contain as many as 32767 characters. Fixed-length strings are a recent development; variable-length strings are a much older structure. (See the section about strings in this chapter for more details about fixed-length and variable-length strings.)

Constants

You can think of variables as read-write value holders. The values held by variables can be numbers, letters, or strings of characters. When you change a variable you "write" a new value to it. When you access a variable you "read" its contents. Sometimes you want variables in your program that don't change—that are "read only." For example, you might want to represent an important mathematical constant that should never be changed, such as pi or Avogadro's Number, or perhaps you want to represent the width of the EGA screen, and you don't want a subprogram to be able to change that value. For such cases, QuickBASIC provides the CONST statement. This statement lets you protect the value of a variable; if your program tries to change the value of a constant, QuickBASIC displays an error message—a useful safety feature. The CONST statement also lets you change the value of a constant at the beginning of the program in which it is declared and thereby change it throughout the program. This lets you easily change, for example, your EGA-width constant to a VGA-width constant in a later version of your program.

Default types

In some early computer languages, such as FORTRAN, the letters I through N can be used as integer variables and the remaining letters of the alphabet can be used as floating-point variables. QuickBASIC includes the DEFINT statement, which enables it to handle variables as an old-fashioned language does. The statement *DEFINT I-N*, for example, makes every variable that starts with a letter I through N an integer variable. DEFLNG, DEFSNG, DEFDBL, and DEFSTR let you define variables as the other types.

Hexadecimal and octal numbers

QuickBASIC uses the decimal (base 10) numbering system, but you might need to display values in hexadecimal (base 16) or octal (base 8) notation, especially when you use assembly-language routines. For such purposes QuickBASIC provides the HEX$ and OCT$ functions, which convert decimal numbers to strings containing their hexadecimal and octal equivalents.

SWAP

Suppose your program uses the variables *A* and *B*, and you need to exchange the values held by these variables so that *A* contains the value of *B* and *B* contains the value of *A*. You can write the QuickBASIC code to do this by using a temporary variable and three assignment statements. An easier method, however, is to use the SWAP statement, which exchanges the values in a single operation and doesn't require an interim variable. SWAP is especially useful for algorithms that perform sorts.

User-defined types

Although it might be easier for programmers if all data were naturally organized into decimals, strings, or long integers, the truth is that the world is a much richer place because data is rarely so homogenized. For example, consider something as simple as your birthday. In a humdrum and unambiguous world we could say you were born on day 693,908.314159 (the day a typical 44-year-old might have been born, in days and fraction of a day, with 1 A.D. being the starting point). However, it is more "human" to refer to dates as month, day, and year—as in May 3, 1946.

So how do you store such complex information as birthdays in QuickBASIC, which doesn't have a date data type? The answer is the TYPE...END TYPE statement, which was introduced in QuickBASIC 4.0. This structure lets you combine different types of variables into a single unit (often referred to as a "record"), which works much like a regular variable. You access the individual elements of such a "user-defined" type by using a period to separate their names, as in *myDay.month* or *myDay.year*.

For example, you might have a variable named *customer* that is of a user-defined data type including several different elements—strings representing the names and addresses of the customer, integers holding amounts owed, a long integer holding a 16-digit account number, and so on. Each element of the record, or user-defined type, has its own name, but to access an element, you must specify the name *customer*. One convenient use of record variables is easily writing them to a random-access file; before the TYPE...END TYPE statement, this operation required a complex setup using the FIELD statement. Unfortunately, user-defined types can't hold arrays. You can create arrays of user-defined types, and user-defined types can contain other user-defined types as members. However, QuickBASIC will not let you use arrays inside a user-defined type, period.

Flow Control (Chapter 2)

Programs don't do anything powerful until they make decisions, change the direction of their processing based on such decisions, and perform a single task repeatedly. The area of programming concerned with the direction and path of program operation is referred to as "flow control."

The flow-control statements in QuickBASIC conduct the overall direction of the program—they determine where it jumps to next, the branches it makes, and so on. If you think of the group of statements that operate on strings, numbers, files, sounds, and pixels as the "threads" of a QuickBASIC program, you can then envision the flow control statements as the "weave" of a program: The statements are the means by which all the threads of a program are woven into the pattern of the flow of execution.

GOTO

The GOTO statement, which is followed by the line number or label of the statement you want to execute, can be used in your main program and inside subprograms or functions. You can jump from any location in a module to any other location in the main code of the same module by using GOTO. However, you can't use GOTO to jump from the main code to a location in a subprogram or a function in the module. Nor can you use it to jump to another module. After you branch to a location with GOTO, there is no turning back; the program continues from that location and does not return, as it would with a subroutine, subprogram, or function call. Avoid using GOTO statements because programs containing GOTO tend to become unstructured and difficult to debug; in short, too many GOTO statements produce "spaghetti" code, which causes programs to jump haphazardly from one location to another. Furthermore, QuickBASIC's other flow-control statements usually make GOTO unnecessary.

You can also use the ON...GOTO statement as a conditional statement that branches to one of several locations, depending on the value of a specified variable. This lets you set up a table of labels or line numbers to jump to. Although this use of ON...GOTO might result in code that is difficult to decipher, both GOTO and ON...GOTO can be useful. (See the tutorial in Chapter 2, "Flow Control," for a tip that shows you how to use 255 line numbers or labels in an ON...GOTO statement.)

QuickBASIC also provides an ON...GOSUB statement, which jumps to a specified subroutine based on the value of a specified variable and lets you build jump tables of routines. Both the ON...GOTO and ON...GOSUB statements can be replaced with the new QuickBASIC SELECT CASE statement. SELECT CASE is more flexible and has none of the limitations that ON...GOTO and ON...GOSUB have.

Loops

A loop is a sequence of statements that your program executes more than once. A loop might comprise statements that compute the factorial of a number, that search a file for a value in a record, or that play the rising and falling notes of a siren. The simplest loop statement is the FOR...NEXT loop, which is found in every version of BASIC. This loop directs the program to repeat a group of statements the number of times you specify in the FOR...NEXT statement. The statements to be repeated begin after the FOR keyword and end at the NEXT keyword. The FOR...NEXT loop also offers a STEP option that lets you control the amount by which QuickBASIC increments the loop index at each pass.

In another kind of loop, the number of iterations is not known when the loop begins, and the length of the loop is determined by a test that QuickBASIC performs during every pass. This structure is called a WHILE...WEND loop, and it was introduced in BASICA.

WHILE...WEND is an "entry-condition" loop because the test that determines whether its statements execute is performed at the start of the loop—in the WHILE clause. If the test fails, the loop does not execute, but if the test succeeds, the loop executes the statements that follow until it reaches the WEND keyword. WHILE...WEND is most useful for statements that should be skipped unless a certain criterion is met. A typical use of WHILE...WEND would be reading a sequential file of unknown length; by using the clause *WHILE NOT EOF(1)*, you can be sure the loop will stop executing as soon as it reaches the end of the file.

WHILE...WEND is not an ANSI standard loop statement. Instead, ANSI specifies the DO...LOOP statement, which is much more powerful and flexible. You can create DO...LOOP as either an entry-condition loop or an exit-condition loop. In addition to the WHILE modifier, it also offers the UNTIL modifier, which lets you simplify a loop's syntax; for example, the DO...LOOP equivalent of *WHILE NOT EOF(1)* is *DO UNTIL EOF(1)*—a much clearer statement. The DO...LOOP lets you put the test at its end; for example, you can use the keyword DO, followed by your loop body statements, followed by the clause *LOOP UNTIL ready$ = "P"*. In this case the loop is always executed at least once before the test is performed.

EXIT DO and EXIT FOR

Sometimes a program must exit from a loop before the loop limits are reached. For example, perhaps you are running a loop that searches every record of a sequential file for a certain value. It might even use the test used in the previous example, *DO UNTIL EOF(1)*. However, when you find the correct value, you don't want the loop to continue; you want to exit from it immediately and perform the next step. The EXIT DO statement breaks out of any DO...LOOP—exit or entry—and begins executing the next statement after LOOP. EXIT FOR exits a FOR...NEXT loop in the same manner. Although you can also prematurely exit a user-defined function or procedure, the WHILE...WEND loop has no corresponding EXIT statement.

Decisions and Operators (Chapter 3)

IF...THEN...ELSE

Wouldn't it be nice if all programs started at the beginning and continued to the end with no changes, departures, sidetracks, or tangents? That would certainly make programming easier. However, the nature of a program is exactly the opposite; programs are constantly changing direction, altering the behavior of their processing based on certain criteria. QuickBASIC handles changes in processing with several statements, the most common being the IF statement. IF lets you set up a test condition and then do something based on the result of that test. For example, you can use it to branch to a new location in the program, compute a complex formula, or execute a subprogram or a function. The statement *IF score% = 10 THEN PRINT "Game Over"* specifies that if the value of the integer variable *score%* equals 10, the program displays "Game Over."

In BASICA, the IF statement is quite simple; it can be only a single line long, as in the following example:

```
IF amountDue# > 10000.00 THEN GOTO creditHold
```

The IF statement in BASICA cannot span several lines to compute several operations if a condition is true. Also, some early versions of BASIC (such as Applesoft BASIC) have no way of dealing with a test condition that is false; in other words, execution always skips to the next statement line if the condition is false. To do any kind of sophisticated decision making with IF, you have to use clever tricks with GOTO statements. The solution to the multi-statement problem is QuickBASIC's "block form" IF statement, identified by the IF...END IF structure. The block form IF statement performs a group of statements if the condition is true.

The second problem—how to handle a test that is false—is solved by the ELSE and the ELSEIF clauses. In the case of the single line IF statement, you can use the syntax

IF *condition* THEN *statement1* ELSE *statement2*

and in the case of the block form, you can use the syntax

IF *condition* THEN
[*statements*]

ELSEIF *condition* THEN
[*statements*]

ELSE
[*statements*]
END IF

There are elaborate ways to nest block IF statements. If your nested blocks become too complex, you can replace them with a simpler SELECT CASE structure.

Be careful when using anything other than an integer or a long integer as the condition in an IF statement that tests for truth or falsehood. QuickBASIC is picky—if you use a floating-point expression, it evaluates 0.0 as false; any other value is considered true. (This is not true for integers and long integers, of course, and that's why these types are better for IF conditions.) In formulas that have rounding errors, it's difficult to avoid spurious decimals at 0.0. Another limitation is that the expression must evaluate to the range of a long integer, which means scientific numbers greater than 10^{10} or less than -10^{10} will not return correct results.

Logical operators

The expression in an IF statement can be very simple, such as "if A is true, then do Z," or it can be more complex, such as "if A is true, and B is also true, but C is false, and D is anything but X, then do Z." To handle all these situations QuickBASIC offers six logical operators: AND, OR, NOT, XOR, EQV, and IMP. These operators let you set up complicated conditions to combine expressions in an IF statement.

Keep in mind, however, that these are also "bitwise" operators; that is, they operate on the bits that make up the numbers you are comparing. Therefore, although all expressions that evaluate to false are 0, all expressions that evaluate to true are not necessarily equal.

SELECT CASE

The SELECT CASE statement can simplify a mess made from the poor application of nested IF statements. SELECT CASE greatly simplifies the syntax for comparing a variable with several constants or with ranges of numbers or strings and then executing statements based on those comparisons. In other words, it lets you compare an expression to a range of possible results.

Procedures (Chapter 4)

The programming community long disdained BASIC because the language often produced spaghetti code, usually due to a multiplicity of and overreliance on GOTO and GOSUB statements and the limitations of the required line-number format. The spaghetti code of a typical fragment of BASICA statements might look like that shown in Figure I-1.

This section of code is from an earlier BASIC book written by The Waite Group. At that time, this program represented the best you could do in BASICA to process a keystroke and branch to a particular subroutine. The lines in the figure show where the program changes direction and branches. Note that many of the statements return to line 160, while many branch to scattered subroutines whose purposes are not readily apparent.

Another early criticism of the BASIC language was that its programs run slowly because it is an interpreted language. Its final death knell as a serious programming language was that the largest program you could write was only 64 KB, a pathetic figure compared with the size of today's multi-megabyte applications.

Through its reincarnation as QuickBASIC, BASIC has managed to requalify as a "serious" programming language. QuickBASIC is now both an interpreted and a compiled language, so although it can still execute a statement instantly in the Immediate window, it can also compile the program code to produce a fast, stand-alone program.

QuickBASIC now lets you link separate modules to make as large a program as you can fit in the 640 KB of memory of an IBM PC or compatible computer. (This size

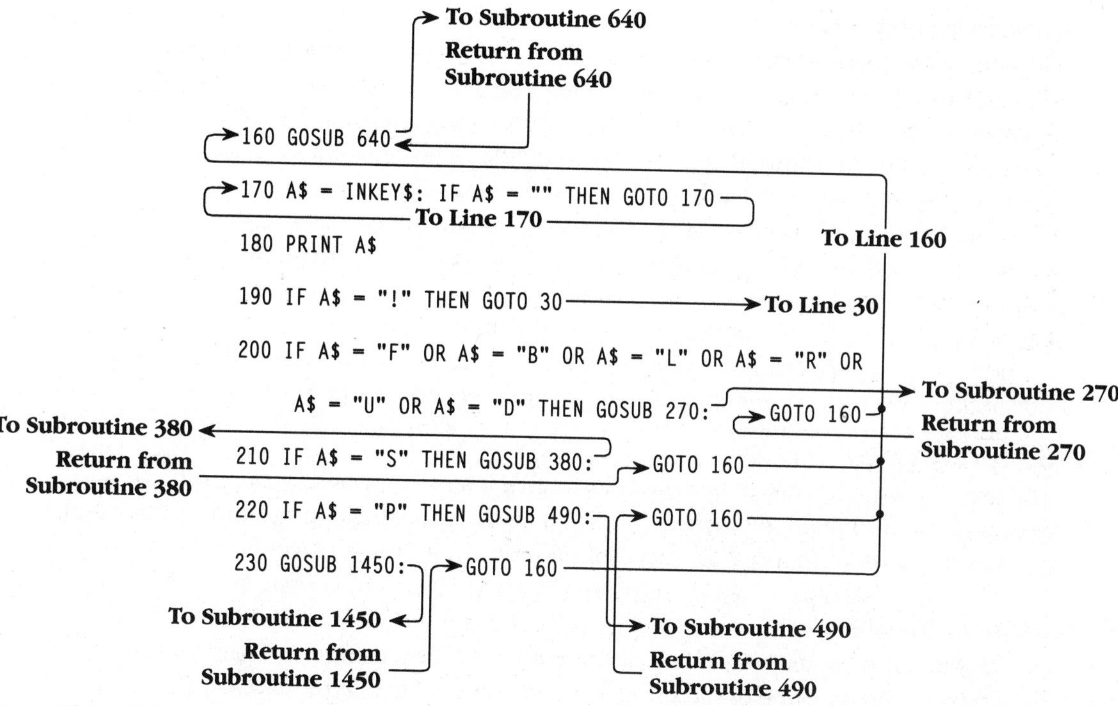

Figure I-1.
An example of BASICA code.

varies between 100 and 250 KB and is determined by whether you compile the program from the environment or you use the BC.EXE command-line compiler.) If your program is larger than available memory, QuickBASIC lets you chain additional modules from the disk into memory.

A second module has access to the same memory space as the original module that specified the chain. However, some space might still be occupied by variables from the original module, thus reducing the space available to the new module.

QuickBASIC now has features found in other professional languages such as C and Pascal. You can define and call functions and procedures across modules and pass variables and arguments to them. You can control the scope of variables—for example, you might make them visible to only the current module, share them with other procedures, or make them common to the entire program or even to other programs. Let's examine a few of these features of QuickBASIC.

Organizing your program in modules

The new way to write moderate to large QuickBASIC programs requires the use of "modules," which are independent files that contain program fragments called by a "main" QuickBASIC module. Splitting a program into modules forces you to handle data carefully and to pay judicious attention to the flow of information. It also lets several programmers work independently on different parts of a single program. Perhaps most importantly, modular programming allows a module to be used by different parts of one program and by future programs that need the same capability.

Memory problems with the IBM PC and compatibles running under DOS continue. A QuickBASIC program in a single file still can't occupy more than 64 KB, the same limit that BASICA had. To make programs larger than 64 KB, you must use separate modules. This limitation is created by DOS itself; however, Microsoft has enabled QuickBASIC to let a program use as many 64-KB modules as it needs. QuickBASIC also includes a host of special new statements and keywords that let you take advantage of the modular, procedure-oriented, structured approach to programming.

Subprograms

Microsoft added a feature to QuickBASIC to give it a more professional polish: the subprogram, a self-contained block of code that performs a single programming task and handles its variables in a special way. Subprograms not only replace the subroutines of BASICA; they also offer much more power and flexibility. (Of course, for compatibility reasons, subroutines still exist.) A subprogram does not need a RETURN statement. Instead, you call it as you would call a procedure in C, by using the CALL keyword, or merely by using the name of the subprogram. Instead of using the statement

```
IF task$ = "Print" THEN GOSUB 1000
```

you can now use the statement

```
IF task$ = "Print" THEN PrintChecks(amount, name$)
```

With subroutines, all parts of the program have access to the variables. A subprogram's variables, however, are private, or local, to the subprogram; you can use variable names in other modules and their values won't replace variables of the same name in the subprogram. (Subprograms also let you override this privacy so that the module can share specified variables.)

Module-level code and the main module

If a program is based on multiple executable files, or modules, which one is running and which one starts the program? Microsoft designed modules so that only one of them is directly executable by QuickBASIC. This is called the "main" module, and it is the only module of a multi-module program that executes if you select Start from the Run menu or type the name of an executable file on the command line. The "support" modules hold subprograms and functions, all of which are called from the main module. Of course, a support module can also call a subprogram that is in another support module.

The statements in support modules can be written in QuickBASIC, or they can be written in another language, such as C, Pascal, or assembly language. Understand that you can't use GOTO or GOSUB to access any of these subprograms—you must call them by name or by using the CALL statement.

The main module can also contain subprograms and functions. When you write simple programs, like most of the examples in this book, you can use a single main module until your compiled code reaches 64 KB. However, subprograms and user-defined functions in the main module are not considered part of the main code that is executed by QuickBASIC. Microsoft somewhat bafflingly calls the code of any module that is not part of a subprogram or function the "module-level code." So, although a support module can also have module-level code, its code differs from the main module's module-level code because it is not directly executable. Module-level code in a support module can hold metacommands; DIM, SHARED, and COMMON statements; user-defined type definitions; and event-handling and error-handling routines. However, no module can compile to more than 64 KB of object code.

Scope

In earlier versions of BASIC, when you created a variable, such as *a$*, it was a "global" variable; no matter what part of the program was running—a subroutine or a few lines at the end—the variable was always available. Any part of the program could change the value of any variable. But this led to problems, especially if your program was large. If you accidently used a variable name that was already defined somewhere else in the program, BASIC could not differentiate between the two, and it would alter your earlier definition and value. This created all kinds of havoc in programs. Programmers needed a way to make a variable private, or local, to a particular part of the program.

The "visibility" of a variable (including an array or user-defined type) is called its "scope." In QuickBASIC, you can control the scope of your variables by using the DIM, SHARED, and COMMON statements. You can dimension and declare variables and arrays in the module-level code of both main and support modules. If you want all the subprograms and functions in a module to be able to use these variables, define them by using the DIM statement with the SHARED keyword. (As you will see, DIM declares the type of a variable, as in the statement *DIM customerName AS STRING * 12.*) You can also make these variables and arrays visible in a specific subprogram or function by specifying them in a SHARED statement within that subprogram or function. However, doing this does not make these variables visible to other subprograms or functions unless their variables are defined in a SHARED statement as well.

To make variables accessible across all modules, you must specify them in a COMMON statement. This enables every module that contains a similar COMMON statement to share the variables. (That is, they are global.) Common variables are not visible to all subprograms or functions in the module unless you specify them in a COMMON statement with the SHARED keyword.

Variables that are local to a subprogram or function are created each time the subprogram or function is called; they are destroyed (removed from memory) each time control returns to the calling module. Because each call to the subprogram results in a new set of variables, subprograms and functions can call themselves; this recursive ability is useful in many programming situations. However, in many cases you want a subprogram or function to retain its values even after it has completed its operation. For example, you might have a subprogram that calculates a value by using successive approximation. The STATIC statement lets you define a variable as static so that its value is retained. You can also use the keyword STATIC in the first line of a subprogram or function so that none of its variables are destroyed when the procedure exits.

Declarations

You call a subprogram by using the CALL statement. If you want to call a subprogram located in another module, you must use the DECLARE statement to declare the subprogram in the module so that when you call it, QuickBASIC knows where it is. For example, you would use the declaration

```
DECLARE SUB ListPeople (names AS STRING)
```

in the main module code to be able to call a subprogram named *ListPeople*, which requires a variable-length string parameter called *names*. Merely replace the word SUB with FUNCTION to declare a user-defined function. Note that when you create a subprogram or function in the QuickBASIC environment, the editor produces the DECLARE statement for you. If you used DECLARE to declare a subprogram, you do not need to use the CALL keyword when you call the subprogram. You can simply type

```
ListPeople names
```

to call the subprogram *ListPeople* and pass the *names* parameter.

Subroutines

Ho-hum. That's how people feel about using subroutines, which is the traditional way of writing code in BASIC. To branch to a subroutine in QuickBASIC, you use the syntax GOSUB *line*, in which *line* is the line number or label of the beginning of the subroutine. The end of the subroutine is marked by the RETURN statement, which directs QuickBASIC to return to the statement immediately following the one that made the call. Subroutines have limited value, and it is best to avoid using them now that subprograms are available. In QuickBASIC you can use GOSUB to branch only to a routine in the current module. Also, you can't pass parameters to subroutines. In fact, subroutines might someday be eliminated from the ANSI standard, so use them at your own risk.

Function procedures

Unlike a subprogram, a function returns a value. If your program requires a specialized function that is not part of QuickBASIC, you can create your own, "user-defined" function. QuickBASIC supports two kinds of user-defined functions; DEF FN functions, like subroutines, are a holdover from earlier versions of BASIC; function procedures, defined by the FUNCTION statement, are much more powerful and flexible.

User-defined functions follow the same rules as subprograms, and you must declare them in a DECLARE statement. (However, you can't call them by using the CALL statement.) A function always returns a value, so you must use it in a statement—for example

```
decimal& = BinDec&(binaryNumber$)
```

Here, *decimal&* is a variable and *BinDec&* is a function. The scope of variables follows the same rules in functions as it does in subprograms: All variables in a function are local to the function unless you first specify them in a SHARED or COMMON statement.

Chaining

If your system doesn't have enough memory to contain all your program's modules or if you need to execute more module-level code than fits in the main module, you can use the CHAIN statement to call another program. CHAIN always starts a second program and can be used in conjunction with the COMMON statement to enable programs to share variables. However, only programs run in the QuickBASIC environment and executable programs that use BRUN45.EXE, the QuickBASIC runtime module, can pass common variables when chaining. Stand-alone programs can't use common variables, although the example program in the COMMON entry illustrates a way around this. Chaining to non-BASIC programs is also permitted, but sharing variables with such programs is not.

Strings (Chapter 5)

String essentials

Strings—collections of characters stored as the string variable type—are a vital aspect of all computer languages. Without strings, a computer couldn't display messages on the video display, hold names and addresses in a database, or manipulate letters of the alphabet.

Although a language such as C is blessed with a large and comprehensive set of character-manipulation routines, it is cursed by a rigid syntax. In fact, C doesn't even recognize strings; everything in C is done with characters and arrays of characters. QuickBASIC, on the other hand, has only a few character-manipulation routines. However, its excellent string statements, functions, and operators do almost everything found in the C library, and they do it with a lot less programming effort.

QuickBASIC allows a string to have as many as 32,767 characters, and a string character can be any character in the IBM PC set of 256. (However, because a PC has only 64 KB of space in which to store regular strings, you usually cannot use more than one string that fills all 32,767 locations with characters.) Still, you can store huge amounts of text in a QuickBASIC string—up to 30 KB. If you designed a text editor, for example, you could put an entire paragraph into a string, and it's unlikely the paragraph would ever be too long. (At an average of five letters plus one white-space character per word, the program would let you store up to 5461 words per paragraph! Of course, you could store only 12 such paragraphs in 64 KB.)

The characters in a string consist of selections from a set of 128 different symbols in the ASCII code that represent letters, numbers, and punctuation symbols. Another 128 special graphics characters (defined in the IBM PC's ROM) are available from the IBM extended character set, and you can assign these to any string character using the keyboard or the CHR$ string function. You declare string variables in QuickBASIC by attaching the dollar sign ($) suffix to a variable name, by using the DEFSTR statement, or by using the DIM statement with the AS STRING clause. You can create string constants, which hold unchangeable values, with the CONST statement. String constants are useful in large programs, where it is likely that you'll use the constant throughout the code in many locations. Changing the value in the CONST statement changes the value of the constant in all parts of the program.

Sometimes you need to manipulate strings independently but store them as some sort of organized unit. For this, QuickBASIC offers string arrays. An array can hold many strings, each of which can be accessed by an index number. You create an array by using the DIM statement.

Fixed-length vs. variable-length strings

In all versions of QuickBASIC earlier than version 4.0, strings had a variable length of up to 32,767 characters. If you created a string and added to its length later in the program, QuickBASIC found room for the new part of the string and manipulated memory to find space for the larger string. The problem with this approach is that QuickBASIC variable-length strings are stored in an area of memory called DGROUP, which can contain only 64 KB; this severely limits the operations QuickBASIC can perform before the program runs out of string space.

In QuickBASIC 4.0, Microsoft introduced the fixed-length string. You declare these strings differently (by using STRING * *numChars* as the type in a DIM statement) to distinguish them from variable-length strings. Any empty part of a fixed-length string is filled, or "padded," with spaces, and once you set the length of a fixed-length string, it maintains that length for the life of the running program. Therefore, if you create a large fixed-length string but fill only a small part of it with useful text, this type of string will waste memory. However, what you give up in storage space inefficiency you gain in memory management; QuickBASIC stores fixed-length strings outside DGROUP, in an area of memory called the "far heap." The size of the far heap varies with the amount of memory installed in your computer, but on the average it's between 200 and 300 KB. So, using the previous example, in which paragraphs are represented as regular, 32,767-byte variable-length strings, you can store only two 32,767-byte paragraphs before running out of memory. By using fixed-length strings and setting the length of the paragraphs to 1500 characters, you can store as many as 200 paragraphs of the same length before the hypothetical editor uses up its allotted memory.

String utilities

Because the empty part of a fixed-length string is filled with spaces, controlling how the string appears when it is stored or displayed is more difficult than managing regular strings, which are not padded with spaces. The RSET and LSET statements let you control the justification of the text inside a fixed-length string. The LTRIM$ and RTRIM$ functions let you remove spaces from the beginning or end of a string.

Often you have to know how long a string is before you can use it. For example, to find the position of the first period in a string that holds a paragraph, you need to write a loop that examines each character until it either finds a period or reaches the end of the string. The LEN function returns the number of characters in a variable-length string and the defined size of a fixed-length string.

QuickBASIC supports several functions that are useful for analyzing strings, for searching for and replacing strings, or for converting a string from one format to another. QuickBASIC's statements and functions for manipulating groups of characters inside strings are generally adequate, but the clarity and consistency of their syntax leave something to be desired. For now, though, you'll just have to wrestle to get characters in and out of strings in QuickBASIC.

For example, the functions for extracting a contiguous number of characters from the beginning or the end of a string—LEFT$ and RIGHT$—are fairly straightforward. It also seems logical that to extract characters from inside a string you use the MID$ function. However, to replace part of a string with another string, you must use a statement that is also (confusingly) called MID$. The differences between the MID$ function and the MID$ statement can trip up even the most seasoned QuickBASIC expert.

Number to string

QuickBASIC lets you easily convert strings to numbers by using the VAL function and numbers to strings by using the STR$ function. These functions help you avoid the problems associated with inputting numbers. If you allow the user to type a string in response to an INPUT statement that expects a number, the program might "bomb," causing QuickBASIC to display a "Redo from start" error message on the user's screen—a frustrating event. However, if you let the user enter numbers in the form of a string (for example, you use *INPUT a$* as your input statement), QuickBASIC will never stop your program because a user entered the wrong type of data. You then can write code that analyzes the input string carefully and responds to the information it finds. You—not QuickBASIC—are in control. The STRING$ function lets you create any number of single characters, and SPACE$ lets you create a string of spaces.

Case operators

Rounding out QuickBASIC's repertoire of string-manipulation routines are the LCASE$ and UCASE$ functions. The former converts a string to all lowercase characters, the latter converts to all uppercase.

The comparison operators you use on numbers, such as >, <, <=, >=, =, and so on, work for strings, too. QuickBASIC merely compares the value of the ASCII, or IBM extended, codes of each character in the string. For example, the ASCII value for the letter b (98) is greater than the ASCII value for the letter a (97). That seems right, but the ASCII value for the letter A (65) is smaller than the ASCII value for the letter a (97). The space character has the least value of all the characters, and the value for the period is not much greater. After you get used to using the ASCII codes, manipulating strings is easy. (The ASCII characters and IBM extended characters are listed in Appendix H, "ASCII Characters.") You can also combine strings by using the string concatenation operator (+), but you must insert spaces to separate the individual sections of the resulting string.

Arrays and Data (Chapter 6)

Programmers spend a lot time thinking about the data they need to manipulate. Data is any organized collection of information—all the letters of the alphabet, the files used by the Department of Motor Vehicles, the number of beans in a beanbag, and so on. Data can be very abstract, like the statistical analysis of the average income of first-time car-buyers, or it can be very simple, like the price of the car. However, no matter how data is arranged, QuickBASIC provides a simple structure to manipulate lists of data—the array. The array in QuickBASIC (and in most programming languages, for that matter) is a collection of values stored in elements that you access by "indexing" into the array. You use the DIM statement to create an array that has a specific number of elements, and you access the contents of the array by using a special syntax: For example, you use *movie$(5)* to access the sixth element of a string array called *movie$* (if *movie$(0)* is the first element of the array).

An array can hold only one type of variable, so you can't define an array as a string array and then store integers in it. However, QuickBASIC lets you create custom data structures, called "user-defined" types, that contain more than one data type, and you can store collections of these data structures in an array; the type of the array is the same as the type of the custom data structure.

Dimensioning arrays

You can specify the number of elements an array can hold by using the DIM statement. More precisely, you can control the number of elements in each "dimension" of an array by specifying the number of elements in each dimension, separated by commas. Each dimension represents a set of elements (like rows or columns in a spreadsheet), and you can cascade them in a single DIM statement. For example, the statement *DIM num%(2,3)* creates an array of 12 elements; each of the three elements in the first dimension has four subelements in the second dimension. Note that the elements of arrays are numbered by default from 0, so the array defined by the statement *DIM a(1)* consists of two elements—*a(0)* and *a(1)*. (This is why the previous example has 12 elements.) You can change the starting number of an array to 1 by using the OPTION BASE statement. An array can have as many dimensions as can fit into the syntax of a single statement. (The QuickBASIC documentation claims an array can have 60 dimensions, but this isn't true.) However, avoid creating arrays of more than three dimensions; they are difficult to conceptualize.

DATA and READ statements

Data is inconsistent in that it is modified at different levels. Some data, such as the number of signs in the Zodiac and the value of pi, never change. Other data, such as the number of people on the earth and the volume of activity on the New York Stock Exchange at 9 A.M., change frequently. When writing code, you'll often run into situations in which you want to store data in the program, but not one variable at a time. In such cases, you can use the DATA and READ statements. Often used with arrays, DATA statements are program lines containing values (separated by commas) that you want to read into variables. The READ statement reads the lists in the DATA statements as if it were reading the contents of a file. Placing these values directly into your program gives you the convenience of later being able to modify them easily with an editor.

Sharing arrays

When you use QuickBASIC, you must constantly ask yourself, Is this variable local or global? Will any other routines need to access it? Frequently you'll need to share the contents of arrays because by default an array is local to module-level code in which it is declared but not local to subprograms or functions. You can make the array accessible to subprograms and functions by using the SHARED clause in a DIM or COMMON statement. A subprogram or function can also specify an array in a SHARED statement, which makes an array declared in module-level code accessible to the subprogram or function.

Perhaps the most straightforward way of sharing an array is to pass it to a subprogram or function as a parameter. Passing an array keeps the information it contains completely private between the caller and subprogram or function, so other routines can't change it. Passing arrays also invokes QuickBASIC's parameter-checking mechanisms, which further safeguard against unsound data. Using the SHARED statement provides similar privacy but less checking.

Dynamic and huge arrays

Recall that QuickBASIC once had only variable-length strings, which had to fit in less than 64 KB of memory. The fixed-length string type in QuickBASIC lets you store strings in far memory, which makes available a much larger string space. The tradeoff, however, is that a fixed-length string wastes memory space because the empty part of the string is filled with blank spaces.

Arrays present a different problem. Early versions of BASIC offered only fixed-size arrays, called "static" arrays. Whatever array size you defined when the program was compiled or interpreted became the final size in the program; no expansion or contraction of the array size was permitted. This meant that sometimes you had to define an array to hold the greatest *potential* number of elements, thus wasting space in these arrays much as space is wasted in fixed-length strings. Furthermore, like variable-length strings, all static arrays had to fit within a single 64-KB memory segment, which limited their size to a small number of elements (32,767 maximum elements for an integer array type). QuickBASIC now supports "dynamic" arrays, which let you redefine the size of an array (but not the number of dimensions) as the program is running, and make the array "huge," that is, occupying more than 64 KB.

To use huge arrays, you must specify a special command-line option (/AH) when starting QuickBASIC. Using huge arrays has one small pitfall. An element of an array can't cross the boundary between one 64-KB segment and another, and if the element size doesn't divide evenly into 64 KB, a portion of memory is not used, which creates a gap. Because QuickBASIC allows only one gap, it would seem that you can only have 128 KB of space for the huge array; however, the tutorial in Chapter 6, "Arrays and Data," offers a solution to this problem.

Math (Chapter 7)

You need to use math for many programming operations, but if you are at all familiar with a scientific calculator, you already know most of the math features of QuickBASIC.

Trigonometric functions

Trigonometric functions, for example, are important for forming shapes and calculating curves in graphics programs, for figuring where to wrap text around an object, for calculating how far the planet Pluto is from Earth, or for figuring how many feet of wood you need to build a slanted roof. QuickBASIC provides the ATN, COS, SIN, and TAN functions for finding arctangents, cosines, sines, and tangents. You can derive many other trigonometric functions from these basic four. (See the tutorial in Chapter 7, "Math," for a table containing other trigonometric functions.) Nearly all of QuickBASIC's math routines support single-precision and double-precision floating point numbers, although a few accept only integer parameters.

Be careful when using the trigonometric functions; their angle parameter value must be specified in radians, not in degrees as you might expect. A radian is a measurement of an angle in multiples of the constant pi. There are 2 * pi (6.2831852) radians in 360 degrees. Be sure to convert from angles to radians before using the trigonometric functions.

Logarithms

Heavy-duty math usually involves the logarithm function, a function commonly found in financial interest-rate programs, simulations of population growth, science and engineering formulas, and generally whenever you need to deal with one parameter that varies in a large way while another changes a little. A typical example is the Richter scale, used for measuring earthquakes. The LOG function works with natural logarithms, which are logarithms to the base *e*, and the EXP function raises *e* to a specified exponent. Often you need to convert the natural logarithm QuickBASIC computes to a base 10 logarithm.

Truncation

In QuickBASIC, you will often have to chop off the decimal fraction part of a number. For example, although the RND function returns fractions between 0 and 1, you usually want the random number to be within a range of integers such as 1 through 10. You multiply the random fraction by 10 and add 1 to get a number in the range 1 through 10.999999. To delete the .999999 part, use the INT function. The CINT function converts a value to the closest integer when rounding is important; the FIX function returns the next higher integer. Consult the entries for the INT and CINT functions before you use them; they truncate even numbers and odd numbers differently.

Random numbers

Random numbers are useful in game programs when you want to create objects at different locations on the screen, in statistics when you test probabilities, or whenever you need a series of numbers that follow no pattern. The QuickBASIC RND function returns a pseudo-random floating-point number between 0 and 1. Actually, RND returns the same sequence of random numbers each time you run it. Therefore, QuickBASIC also includes the RANDOMIZE statement, which "seeds" the random number generated by RND so that it begins with a different value. (This certainly makes games more interesting.)

Simple I/O (Chapter 8)

The most active area of software development technology is the "interface," the environment that a program presents to a user. What is important these days is the ease with which commands flow from the user to the computer and back. Interfaces that offer modern pull-down menus, dialog boxes, scroll bars, and the mouse cursor are referred to today as GUIs (pronounced "goo-eeys"), which stands for Graphical User Interfaces. The QuickBASIC interface is an example of a GUI that runs under DOS. Microsoft Windows is another example of a DOS-based GUI.

The QuickBASIC environment is a competent example of how a modern interface should work and what its components should do, and QuickBASIC provides all the raw statements and keywords you need to build such an interface yourself. However, be aware that the programs that construct menus, dialogs, or scroll bars from pure QuickBASIC code are not simple. Fortunately, several third-party companies sell QuickBASIC-compatible libraries that contain many kinds of interface tools. One package offers a complete editor that you can easily graft onto your programs; the result looks like an editor created by your program. Microsoft's BASIC 7.0 PDS (Professional Development System) also contains a complete set of interface-related modules that you can link to your code.

As you read the following sections about QuickBASIC's statements for working with screen input and output, keep in mind that—with some effort—you can construct a graphical interface in the text mode by using the graphics characters of IBM's extended character set. That is how QuickBASIC conjures its slick look.

Creating your own interface

QuickBASIC includes statements that let you prompt for and accept text and numeric data entered from the keyboard, check for keypresses without interrupting program execution, respond to the function and arrow keys, and correctly process other characters such as î or Æ. It also includes statements for displaying text and messages at any location on the screen, for putting text on the display using a variety of formats, and for changing the number of rows and columns displayed. More sophisticated interface control is possible with statements that let you define a text viewport, selectively erase a rectangular section of the screen, and control the size and visibility of the cursor.

Keyboard input

If you merely want to accept a numeric value or string from the keyboard, use the INPUT statement. This statement pauses the program until the user enters values for the specified variables and presses Enter. The LINE INPUT statement accepts a stream of characters and assigns them to one string variable. Both INPUT and LINE INPUT allow the user to edit and correct characters by using the cursor keys before pressing Enter. The INPUT$ function also accepts keyboard input, but it requires you to specify the number of characters it accepts.

INKEY$

The INKEY$ function reads the keyboard but does not stop the program while it waits for a keypress. If no key is in the keyboard buffer, INKEY$ returns a null (empty) string. This statement lets you respond to keys that don't generate printable characters, such as the Alt and Ctrl keys. You'll often see the INKEY$ function used in a menu subprogram or a fragment that loops until the user presses a key. After calling INKEY$, you can use a SELECT CASE statement to process the character obtained from the keyboard.

Reading files by using INPUT, LINE INPUT, and INKEY$

Sometimes you want your program to be able to accept input from a file rather than from the keyboard. Or perhaps you want it to read input from the serial port. If you run your program outside of the QuickBASIC environment, you can use the DOS input redirection operator (<) to let your program read input from a file.

Displaying characters on the screen: PRINT, WRITE, and TAB

Perhaps the most often used statement in the QuickBASIC language is PRINT, which displays alphabetic, numeric, and graphic characters on the screen. PRINT sends its output to the screen starting at the current cursor position. The cursor is set to the top of the screen when you clear the screen by using the CLS statement, but you can move the cursor anywhere on the display by using the LOCATE statement. With PRINT, the characters you want to display must be specified after the keyword and can be separated by commas, semicolons, or spaces. Each of these separators has a different effect on the horizontal spacing of the output.

PRINT works like an old Teletype machine; that is, it leaves the cursor at the last place it printed so that the output of the next PRINT statement begins there. When the cursor is on the bottom line of the screen, the screen scrolls up 1 line each time you execute a PRINT statement.

Another form of PRINT is PRINT USING. This statement lets you create a template string into which the variables you print are fitted before they are displayed. This, for example, lets you align the decimal point in a column of figures. PRINT USING is a powerful method for formatting output—one that QuickBASIC programmers should be sure to investigate. QuickBASIC also includes the TAB function for moving the cursor to the specified position in a line, letting you control indention.

You use the WRITE # statement to send sequential output to a disk file; if you don't name a file, WRITE without the # symbol displays output on the screen. WRITE displays its output enclosed in double quotation marks, and the variables that are output are separated with commas. QuickBASIC uses this format so that the information is organized into "fields" separated by commas and "records" separated by carriage return/linefeed combinations—perfect for handing disk file I/O.

Moving the cursor

You can move the cursor to any text location on the screen by using the LOCATE statement and specifying the row and column for the cursor. Subsequent output begins from that position. You can also use the LOCATE statement to control the size of the cursor—

from a single underline to a solid block. You use the POS function to determine the column of the cursor and CSRLIN to determine the row of the cursor if your program doesn't keep track of them internally.

Display width

The WIDTH statement lets you adjust the number of rows and columns in your display. In a standard, 80-column-by-25-row text screen, you can also use WIDTH to switch to 40 columns, which results in double-width characters. If your computer uses an EGA adapter, you can use WIDTH to change the default number of rows from 25 to 43. If your computer has a VGA adapter, you can switch to 50 rows. Note that the characters shown on an 80-by-43 or an 80-by-50 display format are quite small; indeed, in the VGA 80-by-50 mode, the characters are one half the size of their standard counterparts. Because the dot matrix for each character remains the same, the result is a display of rough characters that is not especially easy to read. A VGA or MCGA display can also present 80-by-30 and 80-by-60 formats, but only in graphics screen modes 11 and 12. (See the SCREEN statement entry for details.)

VIEW PRINT

Suppose you want to reserve several rows at the bottom of your display for graphics information (such as a series of graphics dials or similar figures) and you want the program's text output to scroll above this area instead of overwriting it. You can use the VIEW PRINT statement to restrict displayed text to specific rows on the screen. When a PRINT statement reaches the bottom row you specify, it causes the text in the window to scroll and leaves the screen below that point untouched.

Clearing the screen

QuickBASIC provides an enhanced CLS statement for clearing the screen of graphics, text, or both. CLS can be restricted so it clears only the text viewport and leaves the graphics intact. Or you can use CLS to clear a graphics viewport of only the graphics and leave the text alone.

Trapping and Errors (Chapter 9)

Let's face it, computer programs can generate errors. Because QuickBASIC is a forgiving language (letting you avoid defining variables before using them, for example), it is capable of generating lots of errors. You will see two principal kinds of errors when you use QuickBASIC—compiler errors and runtime errors. Compiler errors occur when QuickBASIC doesn't understand what you typed or when you didn't use the correct syntax for a statement or function. Runtime errors occur when a QuickBASIC program is running and something goes wrong—for example, the program tries to print when no printer is connected, divides by 0, or tries to read from a disk file when the disk-drive door is open.

Enabling error trapping

When an error occurs at the DOS level, it is passed to QuickBASIC, which responds with an internal error-handling routine and then halts the program. If you are running the program in the QuickBASIC environment, an error message is displayed in a dialog box; if you are running a stand-alone QuickBASIC application, an error message is displayed on the screen. You can use error trapping in your programs to prevent errors from halting the program. The ON ERROR GOTO statement directs QuickBASIC not to stop the program but rather to branch to a line specified by a line number or label where an error-handling routine can process the error and prevent the program from crashing. This error handler might display a specific message about the error to the user, produce a sound to signal the error, or take corrective action.

Handling errors

After an error occurs and QuickBASIC branches to an error-handling routine, your program must find out what caused the error. The ERR function returns the error code, and the ERDEV and ERDEV$ functions return the status and name of the device in which a hardware error occurred. If you use line numbers in your program, the ERL function tells you the line number of the statement in which the error occurred.

Your error handler must determine whether the error is a fatal one (for example, a division by 0), which stops the program, or a recoverable one, from which the program can continue. If the error is a fatal one (one that doesn't let you restart the program easily), use the RESUME *line* statement to send the program to a routine that shuts down the program gracefully. For recoverable errors, your error handler must tell the user how to fix the problem—turn on the printer, close the disk drive door, enter new values, and so on. To resume the program at the statement that caused the error (assuming the user has corrected the problem that caused the error), use the RESUME statement. To continue with the statement following the one that caused the error, use RESUME NEXT.

When testing your error routines, you can use the ERROR statement to simulate an error. This saves you from having to create the real-world error condition each time you want to test your handler. When the program encounters an ERROR statement, execution jumps to the error handler.

User events

QuickBASIC offers several statements that let you trap different types of events. These include the ON TIMER GOSUB statement, which enables timer event trapping, and the ON COM GOSUB statement, which enables serial port trapping. QuickBASIC 4.5, Microsoft BASIC 6.0, and Microsoft BASIC 7.0 (PDS) all let you create your own custom event handler by using the UEVENT statement. Event-handling routines are useful when your computer uses a custom hardware device, such as a scanner or D/A converter board. You write an assembly-language routine that responds to the device and then sets QuickBASIC's uevent flag, thus signaling to the QuickBASIC program that an external event has occurred.

Time (Chapter 10)

Date and Time

Every IBM PC and compatible computer includes a built-in, standard clock that keeps track of the date and time while the computer is running. (The user can set the date and time from the DOS command line by using the DATE and TIME commands.) When you turn off the computer, the date and time are abandoned unless, in addition to the standard clock, your computer is equipped with a real-time clock. If it is, your computer continues to keep track of the date and time after you turn it off.

QuickBASIC lets you manipulate the date and time features of the PC by using the DATE$ statement and function and the TIME$ statement and function. The DATE$ function returns the current date, and the DATE$ statement lets you change the date. Valid dates range from the year 1980 through 2099. The TIME$ function returns the time, and the TIME$ statement lets you change the time. QuickBASIC works with time in the 24-hour format *hh:mm:ss.*

You can use these statements and functions to insert dates in your program, to time-stamp files, to seed a random-number generator, to control a real-time clock on the screen, and so on.

Pausing a program

The SLEEP statement lets you pause a program for a specified number of seconds. If the user presses a key during this QuickBASIC respite, the program immediately continues executing, beginning at the first statement following SLEEP. You use the SLEEP statement when you want to display a screen for a short time or when you want a brief lull in the program, such as at the start-up screen of your program. You can set the pause length as a variable that the program progressively lowers as it runs, so that after the program has been used for a while, the delay is minimal.

Timing

QuickBASIC can use the standard PC hardware clock to time specific operations. The TIMER function returns the number of seconds that have elapsed since midnight. You can use this number for innumerable operations, such as recording when a file was opened, seeding the random-number generator, or timing how long a simulated object takes to reach the end of a simulated racetrack. For example, to find out how long your program takes to run some code, insert a TIMER statement at the beginning of the code. Assign the number of seconds since midnight to a variable called, for example, *start.* Then, at the end of your tested code, use TIMER once again to read the number of seconds into another variable, *end.* Subtracting *start* from *end* tells you how many seconds your code took to run.

Timer event trapping

QuickBASIC offers the timer-event statements to let you create a subroutine that execution will repeatedly branch to after a specified number of seconds.

The ON TIMER GOSUB statement specifies the number of seconds and the location to which execution will branch, and the TIMER ON, TIMER OFF, and TIMER STOP statements enable, disable, and suspend timer event trapping. Timer event trapping is a powerful feature because it lets you set up a simple subroutine that comes to life at predetermined intervals. This feature has many uses; for example, it lets you create a subroutine that displays the time on the screen every 60 seconds. You can also use TIMER in games to display waves of sprites after a predetermined number of seconds have elapsed, to make macabre sound effects, or to update a player's score.

The good news about timer event trapping is that you do not need to restrict your program to a skintight loop that merely counts the number of seconds gone by. The bad news about timer event trapping is that it consumes additional time between every program statement, so if you set the interrupts too often, your program might run sluggishly.

Here is a programming trick everyone should know: Although the smallest segment of time you can specify in ON TIMER GOSUB is 1 second, you can use ON PLAY GOSUB with short musical notes and maximum tempo to specify an interval as small as 1/30 of a second. Merely direct the music subroutine to play a rest, so there's no sound, and then use the subroutine to perform whatever operation you need.

II. Multimedia

Graphics (Chapter 11)

Since 1983, GW-BASIC and BASICA have furnished keywords that let you draw pictures on the screen. In fact, these BASIC languages offer a rich graphical environment and contain statements for drawing points, lines, and circles; creating animation; painting; and more. The more modern QuickBASIC builds on these features, adding statements for drawing within windows, controlling a viewport, and supporting high-resolution displays.

The two worlds of graphics

There are two ways to program graphics in QuickBASIC on the PC. One way is to use the keywords defined by Microsoft for treating the screen as an array of dots and for specifying which color each dot will be. These simple statements give you an easy-to-manipulate interface to the screen dots, or pixels. The interface is called the "graphics mode."

The other way to program graphics is to use the IBM-PC character set. This is called "text-mode graphics programming." The 128-character IBM extended character set contains symbols and a fixed set of graphics characters. These characters are best suited for drawing forms, boxes, and block shapes, but they offer enough variety that you can use them to design some ingenious screens. You access this character set from QuickBASIC in a rather obtuse manner—you must use the CHR$ function. To see these characters, enter and run the following program in QuickBASIC:

```
CLS
PRINT
FOR char% = 128 TO 255
    PRINT CHR$(char%); "   "; ' use 3 spaces between quote marks
NEXT char%
```

Figure I-2 shows the output as it appears on the screen. As you can see, this program produces international symbols, such as those of the English pound, the Japanese yen, Greek letters, and an assortment of accented letters, blocks, and line and corner characters for drawing boxes.

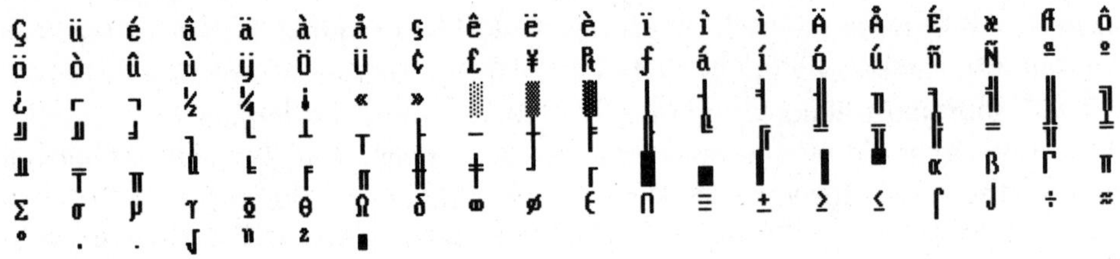

```
Ç   ü   é   â   ä   à   å   ç   ê   ë   è   ï   î   ì   Ä   Å   É   æ   Æ   ô
ö   ò   û   ù   ÿ   Ö   Ü   ¢   £   ¥   ₧   ƒ   á   í   ó   ú   ñ   Ñ   ª   º
¿   ⌐   ¬   ½   ¼   ¡   «   »   ░   ▒   ▓   │   ┤   ╡   ╢   ╖   ╕   ╣   ║   ╗
╝   ╜   ╛   ┐   └   ┴   ┬   ├   ─   ┼   ╞   ╟   ╚   ╔   ╩   ╦   ╠   ═   ╬   ╧
╨   ╤   ╥   ╙   ╘   ╒   ╓   ╫   ╪   ┘   ┌   █   ▄   ▌   ▐   ▀   α   ß   Γ   π
Σ   σ   µ   τ   Φ   Θ   Ω   δ   ∞   φ   ε   ∩   ≡   ±   ≥   ≤   ⌠   ⌡   ÷   ≈
°   ∙   ·   √   ⁿ   ²   ■
```

Figure I-2.
The 128 characters of the IBM extended character set.

You must use PRINT statements to draw in text mode. Although drawing in text mode is simple to understand and program, it is tedious and requires a lot of typing. Furthermore, you can't access all the dots on the screen in a straightforward manner, so drawing something as simple as a diagonal line can be staggeringly time consuming. However, some third-party tools on the market greatly simplify the creation of these screens. (Crescent Software, for example, offers QuickScreen for this purpose.)

A useful feature of the IBM PC (and compatibles) is that these computers let you change the graphics character set to a completely different set of characters. The characters in Figure I-2 are those that the IBM-PC ROM contains; these are loaded into video memory by a small routine during boot-up. However, you can alter this default and load your own custom character set, which can contain anything that fits into the 5-by-7-pixel map. When your program stops running, however, it must reload the default set; otherwise, the QuickBASIC screen will be unreadable. (For more information, see *Graphics Primer for the IBM PC,* by Mitchell Waite and Christopher Morgan, Berkeley, Calif.: Osborne-McGraw Hill, 1985.)

Display adapters

The IBM PC and compatibles have many standards for their displays. As of this writing, six different displays have been used with the PC and have attained a status of "standard." Each of these displays, or display adapters, has a different screen and color resolution; in fact, most have several different modes, which further complicates the number of possibilities. Therefore, when you write a QuickBASIC program for the PC, you must decide what and how many adapters and display modes you want your program to support.

The crudest display adapter is the original Monochrome Display Adapter (MDA). All display adapters support this mode. Because this mode uses the IBM-PC character ROM, many programs use it as the default. IBM also developed the CGA, or Color Graphics Adapter. Once considered state of the art, its low resolution (320 by 200 pixels) and limited colors (in the bit-mapped mode, a maximum of four colors at one time) makes it an unattractive alternative today. The Hercules Graphics Card (HGC) was one of the first high-resolution (720-by-348-pixel) monochrome adapters for the PC that not only offered crisp displays but also contained a custom graphics character set, referred to as a "font." An HGC adapter can display true italics. Although the HGC is no longer as popular as it was, Microsoft still provides a QuickBASIC driver for accessing this display.

The fourth display adapter for the IBM PC was the first display that extended the resolution and range of colors over what was previously available. The Enhanced Graphics Adapter (EGA) sports a resolution of 640 by 350 pixels and supports 16 colors at a time. It also supports all the earlier CGA graphics modes, letting IBM maintain compatibility among all its adapters.

When IBM introduced the PS/2 line of computers, it created two new standard display adapters, called the MCGA and the VGA. The MCGA, or Multi-Color Graphics Array, is like the CGA in resolutions, but it adds a 320-by-200-pixel, 256-color mode and a 640-by-480-pixel, 2-color mode, which is similar to the CGA 640-by-200 mode. The MCGA is used only on models 25 and 30 of the PS/2. The VGA, or Video Graphics Array, is the most powerful of the commonly used graphics adapters supported by QuickBASIC to date. It takes advantage of analog (RGB) monitors to create a richer variety of colors. In addition to the modes supported by the MCGA, the VGA has a 640-by-480-pixel, 16-color mode suitable for painting programs, CAD (Computer-Aided Design) packages, and high-quality bit-mapped graphics.

Pixels and pictures

You'll find that all the graphics commands in QuickBASIC treat the screen as a collection of dots, or pixels, that can be turned on or off or made a specific color. These points are arranged in rows and columns, like the elements on a piece of graph paper. The number of pixels on a CGA screen is only 64,000, but a VGA or MCGA screen can have as many as 307,200 pixels.

Screen modes

Because some of the six graphic adapters support multiple graphics modes, QuickBASIC lets you switch to any of 10 different graphics modes. You use the SCREEN statement to enable the various modes. The modes are numbered from 1 through 13. (The reason they are not numbered 1 through 10 is that QuickBASIC doesn't support some modes used by the Tandy 1000 and the now defunct PCjr.)

The easiest way to determine the highest graphics mode available to your program is to use the SCREEN statement to try to switch to the highest mode (13). Then, if the statement results in an error, use error trapping to switch to successively lower resolutions until no error occurs.

Using SCREEN to change graphics modes clears the screen by executing a CLS in the new mode. Sometimes you might want to retain what is displayed on the screen when you switch modes, such as when you create an explosion effect. You can accomplish this by using the CALL INTERRUPT statement, as described in the "Tips" section in the SCREEN (Statement) entry.

Using coordinates

Pixels are organized in row-and-column format in QuickBASIC, with columns numbered from left to right and rows numbered from top to bottom. To access pixels, think of them as having *x*- and *y*-coordinates—*x* being the column number and *y* being the row number. For example, the coordinates (0, 0) specify the upper left corner of the screen. Mathematicians, engineers, and scientists might dislike this arrangement, so you can use the WINDOW statement to flip the row direction, which makes the coordinates (0, 0) represent the lower left corner.

Plot pixels

You turn on (color) a pixel by using the PSET statement. PSET sets the pixel to a specified foreground color. The PRESET statement, on the other hand, resets the specified pixel to the background color. You use PSET whenever you are plotting a curve, drawing a rule, or performing similar tasks. You can use PRESET to erase that line. (Of course, you can erase the entire display by using CLS.) Plotting points specified by *x*- and *y*-coordinates is a common use of PSET and PRESET.

You can also draw complex shapes by using QuickBASIC. The CIRCLE statement, for example, can be used to draw circles, ellipses, curves, and arcs. The LINE statement lets you draw a line or a box of any color, and you can also fill the box with any color by specifying the parameters B and F in the LINE statement. Both CIRCLE and LINE can specify the pixel pattern, or style, of the line. However, making and programming a pattern for the line is rather tedious because you must convert your pixel pattern to a numeric representation and then put these numbers in the statement. (The example program in the LINE entry shows you how to do this.)

The PAINT statement lets you fill with any color or pattern any closed shape you draw. You must seed the image by giving the PAINT statement *x*- and *y*-coordinates inside the object to be filled (not on the object's boundary). The fill continues to the boundary of the shape. The technique of filling with a pattern is called "tiling" and is explained in detail in the PAINT entry. Tiling can result in the appearance of a much higher resolution of color; that is, more colors seem to appear because it allows color mixing, which is also called "dithering." For example, if you add white dots around some of the dots that make up a default color, and if the white dots are repeated regularly across the screen, you'll see a new color.

Relative addressing

One useful feature of QuickBASIC's graphics statements is their ability to address *x*- and *y*-coordinates as relative locations rather than as absolute locations. With relative addressing, the specified *x* and *y* values represent the relative distance from the last pixel referenced. This means that QuickBASIC saves the *x* and *y* values of the previous plot; if there was no previous plot, QuickBASIC uses the center of the screen. To use relative addressing, simply follow the name of the statement with the keyword STEP. Relative addressing is a powerful technique because it lets you construct complex images and then move them to various locations on the screen by simply changing the first point referenced.

Controlling colors

Although you can control the color of pixels by using a parameter in a graphics statement, QuickBASIC also provides the COLOR statement, which lets you set the default foreground and background colors. Some screen modes also let you set the border or the display color. The PALETTE and PALETTE USING statements were designed for the EGA, MCGA, and VGA displays; they let you change any or all of the colors currently on the display to a different color or set of colors without changing the graphics on the screen. It is worth learning to use palettes because they enable you to produce powerful animation special effects. (The example program in the PALETTE entry shows how the manipulation of colors can simulate motion.)

Most people know that the CGA has two color palettes. You can also access a third color mode, which comprises the colors cyan, red, and white. Although this additional palette is not a much better choice than the normal color palettes, the COLOR entry explains how to access it.

Viewports

Suppose you are designing an interface for a jet simulator that must display text and graphics on the screen at the same time. You want a square window in the upper right corner of the screen to display the ground as you pass over it. It's easy to figure out how to use graphics statements to simulate the ground moving by. But how do you prevent the graphics from overwriting the text outside the window? The trick is to use the VIEW statement, which sets up a pair of *x*- and *y*-coordinates that represent the limits of a rectangular viewport. QuickBASIC clips any values outside this viewport so they don't appear on the screen. Although you can create multiple viewports, you can draw in only one at a time.

Magnifying, panning, and zooming

Remember the problem of the coordinate system appearing upside down for scientists? You can turn it right side up by using the WINDOW statement. Merely define a set of logical coordinates and map them into the physical viewport. This procedure lets you use a plotting equation, for example, that produces values between –1000 and 1000. QuickBASIC then scales the values to fit the proper points on a 640-by-400-pixel screen. (The example program in the WINDOW entry demonstrates how to accomplish this.)

If you use WINDOW to define a logical window that has a range of coordinates smaller than the physical dimensions of the screen, images plotted in that window will be larger than they would be if plotted in the physical coordinates. By contracting, expanding, or displacing a window's coordinates, you can create panning (sideways motion) and zooming special effects. You can easily simulate panning by plotting a stationary foreground object on the physical page and then using PMAP to redraw a moving background. (The example program in the PMAP entry demonstrates how to do this. The example program in the WINDOW entry shows how to zoom in on an image.)

Animation

You can create animation in QuickBASIC by using the GET and PUT statements. GET lets you capture a rectangular area of a graphics screen in an integer array. You can then use PUT to display that array of pixels anywhere on the screen. PUT also lets you control how the pixels in the array interact with the pixels already on the screen. You specify this by using specific keywords—PSET, PRESET, AND, OR, NOT, IMP, and XOR. Calculating the size of the array that will hold the pixels is a little complicated, but it works. The "bouncing ball" routine in the *Microsoft QuickBASIC Programmer's Toolbox*, by John Clark Craig (Redmond, Wash.: Microsoft Press, 1988), shows you how to place objects on the screen and detect when they hit other objects. (The example program in the PUT entry demonstrates simple animation produced by using GET and PUT.)

Screen pages

Certain display modes let you produce and store multiple screen pages simultaneously, but you can view only one page at a time. Thus you can write to one screen while displaying another—an operation that can make animation much smoother. The SCREEN statement lets you choose the screen page, and the PCOPY statement lets you copy the contents of one screen page to another. Using this method, you can create a set of complex screens that load instantly when the user presses a specific key. (The example program in the PCOPY entry shows how to set up a "help screen" that you can access by pressing a key.)

QuickBASIC also includes a SCREEN function in addition to the SCREEN statement; the purpose of this function is to return the ASCII code of the character that is displayed at a specified row and column. The SCREEN function can be useful for reading characters directly from formatted data-entry screens.

Vector graphics

QuickBASIC also provides a complex sublanguage for drawing "vector graphics," which are lines and shapes specified by endpoints that are relative to the most recent point referenced. The DRAW statement lets you use this sublanguage. The statement accepts a complex string that contains commands that tell DRAW how to execute. DRAW's commands control the movement of an invisible cursor that can draw in different directions, different colors, different styles, and so on.

One useful feature of DRAW is that it enables you to scale the final drawing with a single command, so magnification and graphics zooming are simple procedures. DRAW tends to be slow, however, when the image to be drawn requires a large number of commands. (The example program in the DRAW entry shows how to draw *fractals*, shapes defined by complex mathematical formulas that are used to demonstrate chaos theory, consume lots of computer time when being drawn, and look beautiful.)

Sound (Chapter 12)

The PLAY sublanguage

QuickBASIC also contains a sublanguage for playing music. The PLAY statement contains an extensive language that consists of characters and sequences of characters that generate musical notes and specify how these notes are played. The PLAY language is deep—you can specify notes ranging from a hemidemisemiquaver (a 64th note) through a whole note, play over a range of seven octaves, and dictate tempo, flats, sharps, staccato, legato, and more. You can create a command string in this language and assign it to a variable, thereby letting you play long passages of often-used tunes by specifying simple names.

The biggest drawback to the PLAY statement is the limited number of voices and channels in the PC hardware. Sound for the QuickBASIC PLAY statement is based on a simple, single-frequency tone generator. Although this single tone is well suited for beeps and warning sounds, a single distorted sine wave voice coupled with the placement of the tiny speaker at the back of a PC makes the sound characterless and often inadequate for music. (Note that the IBM PS/2 line has much better speaker placement, but the sound hardware is just as poor as that of the original PC.)

However, even with these limitations, the PLAY statement can be awesome. One feature of QuickBASIC's music language is that you can set it up to play music in the background by using the statement *PLAY "MB"*. This means that you don't have to stop your program while PLAY produces the notes; you can use music event trapping (with the ON PLAY GOSUB statement) to place notes in an internal 32-note buffer. After you enable music event trapping with the PLAY ON statement, QuickBASIC checks the buffer after it executes each statement; it then plays the notes it finds in the buffer before executing the next statement. By carefully "trimming" the number of notes loaded into the buffer by music event trapping, you can easily control your music so it plays during an active animation or text display. (However, the background sound driver is quite large.)

The PLAY ON statement enables the event trapping of music notes, which executes the subroutine specified in the ON PLAY GOSUB if fewer than a specified number of notes remain in the music buffer. The PLAY OFF statement disables the checking of the music buffer, and PLAY STOP checks the buffer but doesn't execute the subroutine until another PLAY ON statement is executed. PLAY STOP is most useful when a critical section of code needs to run at maximum speed, but later you want to resume the music where you left off. The PLAY function returns the number of notes left in the buffer, but it is easier to let music event trapping do this checking for you.

BEEP and SOUND

Not remarkably, the BEEP statement produces a beep of fixed duration and frequency. It generates the same sound produced by *PRINT CHR$(7)*, which outputs the bell character in ASCII code.

The SOUND statement lets you play a tone of an arbitrary frequency and duration. You can specify a frequency between 32 and 32,767 Hz (although these extremes are inaudible) and a duration in "ticks," which occur 18.2 times each second. Although SOUND is more flexible than PLAY because it is not limited to the notes of the musical scale, SOUND cannot play its tones in the background.

Light Pen and Joystick (Chapter 13)

Although the mouse has become the most popular input device other than the keyboard, the light pen and joystick are still used in point-of-sale operations, flight simulations, education, games, and programs that require on-screen navigation. Both devices transfer the physical motion of the device into x and y graphics or row and column text information on the screen. The light pen can be a physical strain to use for a long time because you must hold it up to the screen, and it also can scratch the glass that covers the screen. Nevertheless, the light pen provides an intuitive connection between the user and the program and avoids the mental and physical translation that the user must perform with the mouse or joystick. (Sometimes these devices require great hand-eye coordination.) For this reason, you often see light pens being used in situations in which the public uses the computer to guide them through a museum or tell them what subway to take. You use the light pen by touching its tip to the screen and pressing it, thereby engaging a switch, or by pressing a button on the side of the pen barrel. You use a joystick by maneuvering its arm in a right-left-forward-backward manner. One button can be located on top of the joystick's stick, and one or more other buttons are located on its base. In either location, the buttons are easy to press by using your thumb. With a little practice, you can manipulate this interface like Chuck Yeager.

Device interrupts

Like many QuickBASIC devices, the light pen and joystick peripherals use the interrupt approach. A button press on either device interrupts your program and causes it to branch to a subroutine previously set up by an ON PEN GOSUB (for light pens) or ON STRIG GOSUB (for joysticks) statement. You then use the PEN or STRIG functions to read the *x,y* or row,column positions of the device. Note that the program does not receive an interrupt if someone merely moves the light pen or joystick; therefore, any program that uses these devices in the event-driven mode must rely on a crude polling loop to determine the current pointing position.

Be sure to scale any values that the joystick returns because a joystick's maximum value for an axis can be any number in the range 80 through 200.

Because Microsoft does not supply a mouse driver for QuickBASIC for the IBM PC, many third-party companies have flourished by selling these routines. However, Microsoft BASIC 7.0 (PDS) does contain support for the mouse. It's a little known fact that you can use the PEN function to read the mouse *x*- and *y*-coordinates or row and column coordinates if the user presses both buttons on the mouse; so you do have a way to support the mouse in QuickBASIC.

III. Devices

Keyboard (Chapter 14)

GW-BASIC and BASICA display a list of abbreviated statements and associated keys at the bottom of the screen. These are called "soft keys," and each links a BASIC keyword with a function key. When you press a function key, the associated keyword is inserted into your statement line. Of course in QuickBASIC, with its sophisticated environment, no set of soft keys exists—or is really needed. However, you can add the soft-key feature to your QuickBASIC programs by using the KEY statement.

The KEY ON statement displays the first 6 characters of the first 10 strings corresponding to soft keys at the bottom of the screen. You can turn off the display with the KEY OFF statement; however, this merely disables the display—your keys still operate. To list all your soft-key assignments, use the KEY LIST statement.

Keyboard event trapping

Most programmers write their QuickBASIC input routines as polling loops based on the INKEY$ function. While the program is waiting for keyboard input, it is stuck in a cycle of examining characters. Sometimes you might want your program to do something while it is waiting for user input. For example, after a user types a value, you might want it to play a background tune and calculate a spreadsheet value while waiting for the next value to be entered. QuickBASIC provides the ON KEY(*n*) family of statements to let you handle this type of keyboard event trap. For example, you might set up keyboard event trapping with the statement

```
ON KEY(1) GOSUB CalculateNext
```

The program can then perform its calculations and play a tune without paying any attention to the keyboard. However, when the user presses the F1 function key, QuickBASIC will immediately branch to the subroutine *CalculateNext* and execute that code.

As with other QuickBASIC event-trapping statements, you can't call subprograms from them; you can call only subroutines. You must therefore be careful about the scope and visibility of your variables. (They probably will be global, because subroutine variables are not protected like those in a subprogram.) To enable event trapping for the keyboard, use the KEY(*n*) ON statement; to disable event trapping, use the KEY(*n*) OFF statement; to suspend the trap temporarily, use the KEY(*n*) STOP statement.

Although event-trapping statements seem like a great idea, they are not always worth the overhead they create. Turning on event trapping for the keyboard slows your program considerably because it forces QuickBASIC to check for keyboard activity after each program statement executes. Some third-party routines perform similar operations without using event trapping. For example, some routines can read the state of the Shift, Caps Lock, and Num Lock keys; see whether a key is pending without removing it from the buffer; or even insert keystrokes into the buffer for the next program.

Printer (Chapter 15)

Although the printer is an essential output device, it gets paltry attention from the programming community. This is too bad because today's printers have many built-in routines and features and can be programmed extensively. QuickBASIC has several routines that let you manipulate the printer. The LPRINT and LPRINT USING statements send output directly to the printer instead of to the screen. (The L stands for line printer, which means a printer that prints one line at a time. Today's printers print characters differently—laser printers print an entire page at a time—but Microsoft kept the statement's original name.) LPRINT works with the printer as PRINT does with the screen, letting you print strings, numbers, and so on as easily as displaying them on the monitor. LPRINT USING lets you create a special template string that filters and formats the values your program outputs; it works much as PRINT USING does with the screen.

Manipulating the printer

The LPOS function returns the column at which the print head is positioned. That information is useful if you want to print something at a specific location on a line. The WIDTH LPRINT statement lets you specify the width of a printed line, that is, the column at which characters output with LPRINT will wrap to the next line.

When all printers were line printers, it was impossible to address the printer with the same flexibility that you use to address the screen. For example, to move to anywhere on the screen vertically or horizontally before printing, you merely use the LOCATE statement; no equivalent statement exists for maneuvering around the printed page. Using a line printer and LPRINT for output also makes operations such as plotting graphs more difficult because you need to compute the output of your graph in vertical slices. Most printers today, such as the popular Epson and IBM dot-matrix machines and the Hewlett-Packard LaserJet laser printer, contain a built-in set of commands that can shift the paper, set the margins, change the color of the printer ribbon, and so on. (However, it's still difficult to move the print head to an arbitrary location on a page.) QuickBASIC lets you use these printer commands by sending an escape sequence via the LPRINT statement. Many printers can generate different styles of text—compressed, expanded, bold, underlined, and so on—and LPRINT lets you access these features too.

Communications Port (Chapter 16)

Information transfer

When you program, it is frequently necessary to transfer information between computers; the computers can be in the same office, connected by a cable, or they can be in different countries, connected by a modem and telephone lines. QuickBASIC offers several statements for handling this transfer of information. These statements are designed to work with data moving through the serial ports of your PC. These ports contain the electronics necessary to send and receive data to a similar serial port on a peripheral device. The peripheral is usually a printer, but it also can be another computer, in which case the other computer must have a similar serial port. The computers can be connected directly (with a cable) or indirectly (through modems and phone lines). Both these configurations—cable and modem—send and receive characters through the serial-port electronics into a register connected to an I/O port, which is a collection of registers in the computer's memory. It is through these registers that QuickBASIC lets computers read and write characters.

Accessing the serial port

You can handle serial communications from QuickBASIC in two ways. One way involves directly accessing the serial port registers by using the INP (input) or the OUT (output) function. You can use INP to monitor the bits in the serial register that tell whether a modem carrier signal is present, whether a character has arrived in the send/receive register, and so on. This method is complicated because your program must constantly "poll," or test, the port for activity; therefore, your program is tied up doing one operation in a continuous loop. Also, you have the grueling job of deciphering the technical aspects of the serial port standard.

The more modern approach uses the communications event-trapping statements. In the case of communications event trapping, characters arriving at the serial port cause your program to branch to a specified subroutine that processes the character and then returns to the statement following the one at which the interrupt occurred. This approach eliminates polling; however, there are tradeoffs. Your program is slower because the interrupt mechanism uses a slice of time after every statement QuickBASIC processes. If characters arrive too quickly, the program also slows down.

A device as a file

To make serial I/O easier, QuickBASIC treats the serial communications (COM) port much like a disk file. You can also manipulate the port just as you can a file. The OPEN COM statement sets up the serial port by associating a transmit-and-receive buffer area in memory for the specified serial port. You can then write to and read from the port. You can also set up communications event trapping so that your program executes a subroutine when a communications event occurs. OPEN COM is powerful—it lets you set the transmission speed (baud rate), parity, and so on—but it makes your program larger when you compile with it enabled. With OPEN COM you can even tell the program to handle the incoming or outgoing data stream as a random-access file (the default) or a sequential file. You can also control the size of the buffer, treatment of the data as ASCII or binary, and more.

Note that the buffer won't overflow if it is not read, but you have to be sure that you use input statements often enough or you'll lose data. Fortunately, that's easy because in communications event trapping, the subroutine specified by the ON COM GOSUB statement can perform the input.

To use the COM buffer for input, you treat it like a sequential file, reading the buffer in a loop using INPUT$. Your loop ends when it reaches the end-of-file (EOF) marker, which indicates that the buffer contains no more characters to process. To output characters to the COM port, merely write to the buffer by using PRINT # or PUT #.

Files (Chapter 17)

Files are to a programmer what bowls are to a cook—they hold the essential ingredients called for by a recipe. In the case of the QuickBASIC programmer, the recipe is the program, and the ingredients contained in the bowl are information (data) of some kind contained in the file. A file is a collection of letters, words, numbers, or other data, arranged in a format that can be stored on the magnetic media of a floppy or hard disk. QuickBASIC offers a flexible and powerful set of statements and functions for accessing and manipulating files. These commands let you store program data on disk and read data from disk files into your program. Variables hold the data that you read from or write to the file. There are two approaches to file I/O in QuickBASIC—sequential access and random access.

Sequential files

Sequential files are the simplest files to use. In this mode, a file is like a cassette tape: the information in the file is ordered sequentially, so to get to one piece of data, you must read through all the information that precedes it.

You open a sequential file with the OPEN statement, and you close it with the CLOSE statement. (It is good programming practice to always close open QuickBASIC files, even though when you end a program, QuickBASIC closes any files that are still open.) You can open a sequential file in one of three ways—for output, input, or appending. In the output mode, you empty the contents of a file and insert new information; in the input mode, you retrieve the contents of a file; and in the append mode, you add information to the current contents. When you program in QuickBASIC, you must explicitly enable one of these three modes when you open a sequential file.

Reading from and writing to sequential files

You read information from sequential files using the INPUT #, LINE INPUT #, or INPUT$ statement. You write information to sequential files with the PRINT # or WRITE # statement. PRINT # works much like PRINT for the screen. Opened files need an identification number because you can open many of them at one time. (You can open either as many files as the number specified in your FILES= statement in the AUTOEXEC.BAT file, or 20 per program, whichever is smaller.)

The WRITE # statement writes the contents of variables to a sequential file using a set format; PRINT # lets you control the format. WRITE # handles a file as a series of "records," each separated by a carriage return/linefeed. Each record consists of a series of "fields," which are items separated by commas. When you use WRITE #, strings are stored within a set of quotation marks, but numbers require no quotation marks.

The LINE INPUT # statement is best for files filled with the WRITE # statement because it reads the contents of a sequential file a line at a time, using a carriage return/linefeed as the separator. You use WRITE # and LINE INPUT # in programs that need to manipulate lines of text, such as a text editor.

The INPUT # statement works much like the LINE INPUT # statement, but it reads one field at a time instead of one record at a time. Again, a field is a data item separated by commas (if WRITE # was used) or separated by a white-space character such as tab (if PRINT # was used). You can use INPUT # and LINE INPUT # together, one to read one record at a time, the other to read the individual fields of that record.

The INPUT$ statement reads a specified number of characters from a file. It can also be used to read characters from the keyboard. (Microsoft QuickBASIC's designers seem to like to give the same command a dual role. So, to use INPUT$ to read from a file, merely include parameters—specifying the file number and the number of bytes to read—in the syntax.) The beauty of the INPUT$ statement is that it reads everything in the file, even the carriage-return/linefeed sequences. The LINE INPUT # statement doesn't read past the carriage-return/linefeed sequence, and INPUT # doesn't read past double quotation marks and commas.

Sequential files can have variable-length records, each containing a different number of fields, which can expand and contract to fit the data. That is useful if the format of your data is not consistent. Having data of inconsistent format also means, however, that your program will need to use parsing and interpretation routines to determine what the data means.

Random-access files

A random-access file is more effective than a sequential file for storing and retrieving some forms of data. Like a sequential file, the random-access file consists of a sequence of records, each record consisting of a sequence of fields. However, a random-access file needs no wasteful record or field separators such as carriage returns or commas; instead, each record in the file has the same specified length and the same number of fields. However, a different kind of waste occurs in the random-access file—each record has the same length, even if it is only partially full of data.

Another difference between sequential and random-access files is that QuickBASIC stores numbers in a sequential file as pure ASCII text. In a random-access file, QuickBASIC stores numbers in the same binary format that it uses internally. Although this prohibits you from directly viewing the contents of a random-access file (for example, by using the DOS TYPE command), it lets QuickBASIC store numbers in less space than they would need in a sequential file. For example, a 5-digit integer in a sequential text file requires 5 bytes (one for each character). That same number in a binary file requires only 2 bytes. A single-precision number can require as many as 12 characters in a sequential file; in a binary file, it needs only 4 characters. Another advantage of the binary approach is that it is more precise: If you must convert from the text form of a number to its binary format, precision is lost due to round-off errors.

Two more major differences between sequential and random-access files are that you can open a random-access file for both reading and writing at the same time and, most important, you can access the records of a random-access file in any order you want.

Reading to and writing from random-access files

Before QuickBASIC 4.0, the significance of random-access files was seriously compromised by the complicated technique that was needed to use them. You had to create a special template, called a "field" variable, that defined the lengths of the various elements that made up the record. This syntax is complex. You also needed to convert numbers to binary-encoded string representations to work with fielded variables. The MK*type* functions performed this conversion. Then you had to use LSET and RSET to load these strings with the proper justification in the field variable. Finally, you had to use PUT to write the field variable to the file.

With the advent of QuickBASIC 4.0, using random-access files became much easier. You still need to use PUT to write a copy of the record to the file and GET to read a record, but now you can easily create a record by using QuickBASIC's TYPE...END TYPE statement to create a user-defined type. This straightforward approach lets you simply specify *typename.fieldname* to refer to the field you want. Fields can be of any data type, but not an array. (Microsoft BASIC 7.0 lets a user-defined type contain an array.) Accessing records in a random-access file is now much clearer because each field of the record is defined in the variable name, as in the following example:

```
LINE INPUT #1, client.who.lastName
```

Binary files

In addition to sequential and random-access files, you can also create binary files. These are accessed in the same way as random-access files except that they are a succession of bytes rather than a succession of records. Binary files are suitable for storing non-text files that are not collections of records. Word processors that add complex formatting codes to a document often store the document as a binary file. Binary files are the most powerful, versatile approach to files because they give you random access to every byte in a file. However, their lack of structure (specifically, the absence of records) usually requires you to do more programming.

IV. Development

DOS and Program Management (Chapter 18)

Using DOS from QuickBASIC

It's easy to think of QuickBASIC as a rich collection of statements and functions that let you manipulate numbers, letters, graphics, sound, and other complex data. Indeed, QuickBASIC's syntax is a world unto itself; after using it for a while, you begin to think of even more things it can do. And that is the problem—you can become myopic, seeing the world through QuickBASIC-colored glasses.

Actually, QuickBASIC is a programming language with an impressive set of commands that exists inside a larger and more specialized environment called the operating system, which has its own set of special-purpose commands for manipulating and running programs. For QuickBASIC 4.5, the operating system is DOS.

DOS is powerful. It has its own set of file-management and directory-management commands, such as DIR for displaying the contents of a directory, CHDIR for changing directories, and so on. It can change the time on the system clock, format disks, compare files, set up configuration routines and run programs. All these functions of DOS can be lumped under the heading "program management." The good news is that QuickBASIC has a similar set of commands for dealing with program management at the DOS level, and these can embrace all the power of DOS. Indeed, you can run DOS itself from your own QuickBASIC program.

SHELL—starting a new command processor

Perhaps the most useful of the program-management commands is the SHELL statement. Executing SHELL causes a QuickBASIC program to run a second copy of the DOS command processor, COMMAND.COM (the program that is running when you are at the DOS prompt). The first copy of COMMAND.COM begins running when you turn on your computer. SHELL accepts a command string that contains the DOS command you want to run. It can be the name of a program (with a COM, EXE, or BAT extension) or a DOS command string, such as "DIR > LIST.TXT", which redirects the contents of the directory into a file called LIST.TXT. Imagine the operations this allows. You could write your own custom interface to DOS that runs under QuickBASIC. You could set up a more modern interface, like the one on the Apple Macintosh or Microsoft Windows, and create your own commands for manipulating DOS so that instead of having to type a command, the user could merely press a function key or click the mouse on an icon. Internally, QuickBASIC would reinterpret the user command into a SHELL statement that uses the proper DOS command. Although it might not be as fast as typing at the DOS command line, this is the way to go if you want to simplify operations for the user and control everything from your interface. (See the SHELL entry in Chapter 18, "DOS and Program Management," for an example program that shows you how to use the DOS commands DIR, TYPE, PRINT, and COPY from a QuickBASIC program.)

SHELL also lets your QuickBASIC program run a utility or large commercial application program. So, for example, you could write a program in QuickBASIC that collects data from the user through a simple interface, stores the results in a text file, and then uses SHELL to run a copy of a Microsoft Excel spreadsheet. The Excel spreadsheet could then open the data file, read the values, manipulate them, and then plot the results. When the user quits Excel, the new copy of COMMAND.COM would also terminate, and the user would be back in the original QuickBASIC program. QuickBASIC could then present the Excel-processed values or display the chart.

Chaining programs

In some ways, the QuickBASIC CHAIN statement is similar to SHELL. CHAIN lets you run another QuickBASIC program and includes a mechanism that enables these programs to share variables through the COMMON statement. Although this sharing ability is lacking in the SHELL statement, the example program in the COMMON entry shows a technique that lets your program use the Intra-Application Communication area for passing variables through DOS. One drawback to the CHAIN statement is that it doesn't return to the original program; you must execute another CHAIN statement or a RUN statement to return to it.

The RUN statement also lets you start another QuickBASIC program from your main QuickBASIC program. Although RUN doesn't let programs share variables as CHAIN does, RUN can restart the current program at a specified line number (but not at a label). This is a trick that you can employ to simulate a "controlled warm start" to your program—resetting all your variables, and so on. Splitting your programs into separately run and tested modules is one of the more advanced approaches to programming and leads to great program flexibility.

Accessing the DOS environment

If you are going to use CHAIN or RUN to execute QuickBASIC programs, you should know that DOS uses an area of memory called the "environment string table." This area holds the definitions for several variables (called environment variables) that DOS uses and any variables that you create with the DOS SET command. QuickBASIC's ENVIRON$ function and ENVIRON statement let you read and modify the variables in this area. You'll find that the environment area contains things such as the PATH and INCLUDE variables, the specifications for the active command processor, and so on, all set up by your AUTOEXEC.BAT file.

Other QuickBASIC program management commands are MKDIR, CHDIR, RMDIR, and KILL. The SYSTEM statement lets you exit QuickBASIC and return to DOS.

Making programming easier

QuickBASIC has a few other statements that help you with your programming chores. END and STOP halt processing of a QuickBASIC program. REM and the single-quote character let you insert comments into your program. QuickBASIC's CLEAR statement reinitializes all variables and sets all string variables to null. You can also set the size of the program stack by using CLEAR so that programs that use recursive techniques have enough memory to store values during successive calls.

Port and Memory (Chapter 19)

You can tap many powerful features by taking control of your PC's memory and its ports directly from QuickBASIC. With direct access to memory, your programs can perform operations that are not possible using the built-in QuickBASIC statements. For example, if you know how DOS utilizes memory to store its status information, you can directly read this information and find out more about your running environment than even QuickBASIC knows. The PC uses ports to communicate directly with peripheral devices such as the keyboard, disk drive, serial port, and serial mouse. By manipulating these ports, you can control your peripherals in ways that even designers of QuickBASIC did not anticipate.

However, directly accessing memory is a risky and complex process. The IBM-PC standard uses an Intel family of microprocessors that divides memory into complicated sections called "segments." Microsoft designed QuickBASIC to use these segments in specific ways. For example, by default a single segment called DGROUP (data group) holds the data from your program. (Note, however, that you can put "dynamic" data elsewhere. See Figure 19-2 in Chapter 19, "Port and Memory.") The existence of segments complicates the accessing of specific memory locations: You must first specify a segment, and then you must tell QuickBASIC which offset within the segment to access.

PEEK and POKE

The QuickBASIC PEEK statement lets you examine the contents of memory. PEEK returns the value of the byte (0 through 255) located at an address specified as an integer in the range 0 through 65,535. This address represents the offset of the byte measured from the start of the current segment. The default segment is always DGROUP, QuickBASIC's default data segment. Conversely, the POKE statement lets you place an 8-bit value in a specified address. Because QuickBASIC stores variable-length strings in DGROUP, you can use POKE to modify them in memory. The VARPTR and SADD statements help you find the addresses of your variables.

Because QuickBASIC has such good string-handling routines, the real value of PEEK and POKE are not apparent until you leave the default data segment and access other areas of memory. For example, the low areas of memory contain the status of various equipment attached to your PC—the initial mode of your video adapter and even the state of the special keys on the keyboard, such as Shift, Ctrl, and so on. The DEF SEG statement lets you change the current segment to a value in the range 0 through 65535 so that you can use PEEK and POKE anywhere in memory. Note that because a QuickBASIC integer is in signed format, you need to use a long integer to access a segment whose value is greater than 32767. QuickBASIC will internally convert this value to an unsigned integer for PEEK and POKE. DEF SEG also affects the segment that the BLOAD, BSAVE, and CALL ABSOLUTE statements use.

SETMEM—allocating far heap space

Whenever you use dynamic arrays or fixed-length strings, QuickBASIC locates them outside the DGROUP segment—in an area of memory called the "far heap." Unlike DGROUP, this area is larger than 64 KB; the function call FRE(−1) returns the size of the far heap. Although normally you don't have to think about this area of memory, whenever you use non-BASIC procedures that require memory from the far heap, you must set that memory aside with SETMEM. (SETMEM is equivalent to the C function *malloc*.)

Ports—INP, OUT, and WAIT

The Intel family of PC microprocessors contain a separate 64-KB area of memory called the "port I/O memory." The peripheral devices of the IBM PC use this area for communicating with DOS and programs. Because these peripheral devices usually send and receive information in single bytes, each device needs only one or two ports. Sometimes a device uses one port for input, one for output, and a third for control status.

The INP and OUT statements perform the same operations on port memory that PEEK and POKE perform on regular memory. The WAIT statement works like INP except that it waits for a specific bit pattern from the port before it returns a value. You use WAIT to delay an operation until a device connected to the port of the PC sends a specific value.

Mixed Language (Chapter 20)

External routines

Suppose you developed a QuickBASIC routine that you also want to use in the other QuickBASIC programs you are writing. It might be a menu or window support system, a statistics package, or a set of sound effects. The simplest approach to reusing the routine is to specify the $INCLUDE metacommand to merge the source code of your external module into any new program you write. Unfortunately, this approach will *not* let you use subprograms or user-defined functions in the code of the merged file; it limits you to old-fashioned subroutines and DEF FN statements. This method also limits the file to 64 KB of code and data per module, as described earlier.

The best way to use your QuickBASIC routine in a new QuickBASIC program is to combine it with your main program through the compiling and linking process. In this approach, you compile both the main module and the routines you want to attach to it by using the BC.EXE command-line compiler. While this procedure is not as easy as compiling from the QuickBASIC environment, you can simplify the entire process by creating a short DOS batch file. Compiling with BC.EXE results in an "object code" file—a collection of instructions that QuickBASIC can access. However, before you can use the routines in this object code file, you must attach it to the object code of the new program you are creating. To accomplish this, you must also compile the new program as an object file with BC.EXE and then combine the two object files with the Microsoft object linker, LINK.EXE. (Of course, although you compile the new program with BC.EXE, you can still use the QuickBASIC editor to work on the code.) For example, the statement

```
LINK MAINPROG PANEL
```

combines the object files MAINPROG.OBJ and PANEL.OBJ and produces a single executable file called MAINPROG.EXE. That's all there is to it.

Using source files from other languages

The same method for including compiled QuickBASIC code into your program can be used to include object code from Microsoft C, FORTRAN, Pascal, Cobol, and assembly language. The only requirement is that this other language must produce a Microsoft-compatible object code module. When you compile your non-BASIC object module, you must be sure to specify the medium memory model; QuickBASIC accepts no other.

Declaring non-BASIC routines

Before you can use any newly made object-code module in your program, you must insert the appropriate DECLARE statement to define the number and type of parameters that the external function or procedure requires. (The QuickBASIC editor inserts the needed DECLARE statements for subprograms and functions defined in your program as you work.) The DECLARE statement also tells QuickBASIC how your program should pass variables. To pass variables to a C function, you must use the CDECL keyword in the declaration. This keyword tells QuickBASIC to pass the variables in the format C requires. If the DECLARE line contains the BYVAL keyword, QuickBASIC passes the following variables "by value." This means that a copy of the variable's value instead of the variable's actual address is passed to the program. For example, if you used Microsoft QuickC to create a C function called *CopyBlock*, you might use the following statement at the top of the main QuickBASIC module:

```
DECLARE SUB CopyBlock CDECL (seg1%, off1%, seg2%, off2%, BYVAL bytes%)
```

Later in the program, you could call the function with the following statement:

```
CopyBlock 21185, 0, 22954, 0, 10000
```

After declaring *CopyBlock*, you can think of it as being part of QuickBASIC; you don't need to define it again in subprograms or associated modules. If you have a collection of these external routines, you should create a single file to hold all the DECLARE statements for these routines. Then you merely need to place the $INCLUDE metacommand at the top of the program to include all the declarations in one statement.

Libraries

This book does not discuss LIB.EXE, LINK.EXE, or BC.EXE in any detail. If you want to learn how to use these tools, see the Microsoft QuickBASIC documentation. However, let's briefly look at what these tools do and how they are used to create and manage a QuickBASIC library.

A "library" is a collection of object modules combined into one file; you should use a library when you are linking many modules to your main program. QuickBASIC has two kinds of libraries: Link libraries are stand-alone libraries that you use with LINK.EXE, and Quick libraries are libraries that you use in the QuickBASIC environment.

Link libraries

To build link libraries, run the library manager, LIB.EXE, with the names of your object modules. (They can be from mixed languages.) LIB.EXE produces a file with the LIB extension that contains your object modules and another file, with the CAT extension, that contains a list of the modules, names, symbols, offsets, and code and data sizes. You use this file as a catalog of your library.

After you create the link library file, you merely specify it on the LINK.EXE command line along with the name of the program that will use the library. Again, you must compile all QuickBASIC modules into object code with BC.EXE.

When you use LINK.EXE with a link library, the linker loads only those modules that contain routines that you have specified with DECLARE statements in the main module. The declarations serve as inclusion flags, telling QuickBASIC what code to transfer from the library. This means there is no wasted overhead or unwanted code from modules that the program doesn't use. The LIB.EXE program also includes features that let you add to existing libraries and replace or delete modules.

Quick libraries

The Quick libraries used by the QuickBASIC environment are made differently than the link libraries used with stand-alone programs. You still need to compile your routines as Microsoft-compatible object code modules. However, instead of using LIB.EXE to create the library, you use LINK.EXE. To complicate the matter, you must also include the special file BQL45.LIB in the LINK command line. Instead of the extension LIB, QuickBASIC assigns the Quick library the extension QLB. Next you start QuickBASIC with the name of your main program, and the /L option, followed by the name of your Quick library. The DECLARE statements in your main module code enable only those routines of the Quick library that your program will use. However, because you are in the QuickBASIC environment, the size of the resulting program will not change as it does with link libraries. (Note that most third-party QuickBASIC software is supplied in both QLB and LIB formats.)

Storing machine-language routines in variables

In GW-BASIC and BASICA, the only way to use machine-language routines in your program was to store the code in a variable and then execute the code using the CALL ABSOLUTE statement. This approach is not as good as using Quick or link libraries because it accepts only machine-language code. The other problem with this approach is that you have to convert the machine-language code into DATA statements before you can store it in a variable; this can be an arduous process. CALL ABSOLUTE is an external routine that functions like any other object-code module. The QB.LIB or QB.QLB library must be linked to your program with LINK.EXE or LIB.EXE before you can use the CALL ABSOLUTE statement. The QB.LIB and QB.QLB libraries also contain the code for the CALL INTERRUPT and the CALL INT86OLD routines (discussed later in this book). When you use CALL ABSOLUTE, you must be sure to declare it using the QuickBASIC include file, QB.BI.

To execute a machine-language routine, you need to specify the address in memory of the variable that holds the routine. To find the address, use either the VARPTR or SADD statement. VARPTR returns the address of a numeric variable, an array, or a fixed-length string. SADD returns the address of a variable-length string. If you use a dynamic array to hold your machine-language routine, in addition to specifying the address with VARPTR, you must also change to the correct segment by using DEF SEG. After you properly specify the address, you can load the machine language into memory by using the POKE statement.

Be careful when using CALL ABSOLUTE to call machine-language routines. If your program defines a variable and then executes a few statements, QuickBASIC might move the variable, and the address you specify will be wrong. The safest procedure is to use a dynamic array to hold your string; QuickBASIC does not move these in memory.

The most tedious part of writing routines that can be used with CALL ABSOLUTE is converting the assembled and tested code into DATA statements. An example program in the tutorial in Chapter 20, "Mixed Language," shows a simple QuickBASIC program that converts a binary file containing machine code into a set of DATA statements.

Using BIOS and DOS interrupts

Both the IBM-PC ROM and DOS contain large sets of routines that QuickBASIC can access through the "interrupt" technique. The PC ROM BIOS contains a table of 256 4-byte addresses, each of which points to a specific low-level routine. When signaled by a hardware device or a software instruction, an interrupt causes the processor to stop what it is doing, execute the interrupt routine, and then restart where it left off. Interrupts are numbered from 1 through 256, but each interrupt number can have many associated "subservices" that you can access by placing a value in one of the microprocessor's registers before calling the interrupt. To call these interrupt services from QuickBASIC, you use the CALL INTERRUPT statement, which is found in the libraries QB.LIB and QB.QLB. QB.BI also contains the type definition for *RegType*, a special variable that holds the values for setting up the registers when you make an interrupt call.

The example in the tutorial in Chapter 20, "Mixed Language," shows how to call an interrupt that specifies the default disk drive. QuickBASIC also provides the CALL INT86OLD statement to provide compatibility with QuickBASIC versions 2.0 and 3.0, which used the INT86 statement.

Metacommands (Chapter 21)

QuickBASIC has three commands whose functions differ from all others in the language; in fact, they are not really QuickBASIC statements but rather commands that give the compiler instructions. The $DYNAMIC and $STATIC metacommands specify whether memory for dimensioned arrays is allocated at runtime ($DYNAMIC) or at compile time ($STATIC), so they are either alterable or fixed in length. The $INCLUDE metacommand merges external source code into your module. This lets you split your programs into smaller, more manageable units.

Debugging (Chapter 22)

Writing QuickBASIC code is only the first step to creating a program—getting the program to work appropriately is the rigorous job. There are many reasons a program might not work. Some mistakes are obvious: For example, you typed a variable name incorrectly, so that although QuickBASIC finds the program to be logical and compiles it, a variable somewhere is not correctly initialized. Or the error can result from your misunderstanding of QuickBASIC: Perhaps you made a mistake in the logic of an IF or DO...LOOP statement, or you used a string operator incorrectly. These errors are called "bugs." Whatever the reason for your bug, to fix it you need to apply some clever reasoning and determine why the program isn't doing what it is supposed to do. To do this you need debugging tools, and QuickBASIC provides many of these. Understand, however, that the chief debugging features of QuickBASIC are implemented in menus, dialog boxes, and windows and not in statements (although there are two statements used for debugging), so the chapter that discusses debugging is slightly different from the others.

Tracing—the old-fashioned way

GW-BASIC and BASICA include the TRON and TROFF statements. These statements display the line numbers of a program as it is running, thereby giving a list of the line numbers the program is using. When the program stops due to some error, you can see the last line number it executed and then look at your listing to find out what was the matter. To further isolate the problem, you can place PRINT statements in strategic spots in the program to print the values of variables you suspected were not holding the right values. This is a long and tedious process. You can accomplish all this and much more by using the QuickBASIC environment's Debug menu. (Note: This means that debugging must be done in the environment, not in the stand-alone mode.)

Animated tracing

The Debug menu Trace On command lets you perform tracing in a much more sophisticated way than TRON and TROFF do. When Trace On is active, QuickBASIC runs your program in the Edit window, highlighting each line number as it executes. You can stop this animated trace at any time by pressing Ctrl-Break. If the program generates output, it switches to the Output window, displays its data, returns to the Edit window, and then continues with the tracing.

Watch variables

Earlier, we mentioned using PRINT statements to display the values of potentially troublesome variables in the program. Debug provides the "watch" mechanism to help you accomplish the same result without cluttering and touching the code itself.

A watch variable is a variable whose value you want to monitor as the program is running. To monitor a variable, you must first select the Add Watch command from the Debug menu. QuickBASIC displays a dialog box in which you can enter the name of the variable you want to monitor. QuickBASIC then opens the Watch window below the menu bar and displays the value of the watch variable as the program runs. You can also monitor expressions; for example, if you specify *a! = 1.1* in the Add Watch dialog box, QuickBASIC displays in the Watch window TRUE or FALSE rather than a numeric value.

Watchpoints

Watchpoints let you test a program by running it until a certain variable or expression becomes true. When the program stops, you can use the Immediate command to monitor the value of the expression window, and then resume execution by pressing the F5 key. You enter your Watchpoint variable in a dialog box, and QuickBASIC displays it and the name of the module under the menu bar in the Watch window. QuickBASIC evaluates the expression or variable in the Watchpoint window after every statement, and this slows your program considerably. When the expression becomes true (nonzero), the program stops. You can set as many as eight watchpoints in QuickBASIC. If you switch to a different module, QuickBASIC can't evaluate the watchpoint until you return to the module in which it was defined.

Instant watch

If you position the cursor on a variable and press Shift-F9, QuickBASIC displays a dialog box that shows the selected variable's name and value. This is called the Instant Watch command because it saves you the trouble of switching to the Immediate window and typing a variable's name after a PRINT statement to find out its present value. You use Instant Watch when you have stopped at a breakpoint and want to examine the values of critical variables on the fly. A button in the Instant Watch dialog box lets you convert the variable you are examining into a watch variable so that you can monitor its operation as the program runs.

History

When enabled, the History On command lets you step forward or backward through the last 20 statements that your program executed. This is useful for programs that use a lot of complex branching to different labels. History On is valuable when you want to review the statements that led up to a particular runtime error or that triggered a watchpoint. When the program stops with History On enabled, press Shift-F8 to step the cursor backward, and press Shift-F10 to step forward. Only the statements the program executed are shown. (Note that when you enable Trace On, QuickBASIC enables History On.)

Breakpoints

During debugging, you often want your program to stop at a certain statement, subprogram, or function so that you can check the value of variables at that point or determine that the program is still executing properly. A "breakpoint" is a line in the program at which execution stops. You can set a breakpoint in QuickBASIC with the Toggle Breakpoint command in the Debug Menu or by pressing F9 when the cursor is on the desired line. QuickBASIC then highlights the line to remind you that it is a breakpoint line. The actual statement on the line is not executed when you run the program. You can resume program execution at the breakpoint by pressing F5.

Single-stepping through a program

After your program has stopped, perhaps from a breakpoint or an error, you can run the program one line at a time by pressing the F8 key. Each time you press the key, QuickBASIC executes the next statement. If you come to a procedure and you don't want to single-step through it, you can execute the entire procedure by pressing the F10 key. The F7 key lets you execute the program from its beginning to the line containing the cursor, so it acts as a shortcut breakpoint.

Break On Errors

The Break On Errors command is new in QuickBASIC 4.5. It suspends any error trapping that your program might have, so that any runtime error halts the program and stops at the first line of your error handler. This lets you examine the conditions that led to the error and then test the operation of the handler. You can use the Immediate window or Watch window to view the values of your variables, and if History On is enabled, you can use Shift-F8 and Shift-F10 to move backward and forward through the statements that led to the error.

Set Next Statement

The Set Next Statement command lets you specify at which statement line QuickBASIC should begin executing when a halted program is restarted or single-stepped. You set the statement line by placing the cursor on the statement from which you want to resume and then enabling Set Next Statement from the Debug menu. QuickBASIC highlights the specified line.

SECTION I

CORE

CHAPTER 1

Variables and Types

Introduction

QuickBASIC programmers are lucky: They can let QuickBASIC manage the details of their programming while they concentrate on problem solving and program design. QuickBASIC lets you use symbolic names for the locations at which QuickBASIC stores values. These locations are known as *variables*. You can name a variable to describe the meaning of the value you want to store. You might, for example, choose the variable name *pastDueAmount* to store the past-due amount a customer owes.

Select self-describing variable names so that you and others who read your programs will immediately recognize the meaning of the values stored in the variables. Some people abbreviate variable names to save typing time. That's acceptable up to a point; however, variable names can be confusing if they're abbreviated too much. If you abbreviate the variable name *pastDueAmount* to *pastAmt*, for example, its purpose is still clear. However, if you further abbreviate the variable name to *pamt*, you might later think that it means "payment amount."

QuickBASIC variable names must conform to the following conventions:

- The first character of a variable name must be a letter (A–Z), either uppercase or lowercase.
- The remaining characters of a variable name can be letters (A–Z), either uppercase or lowercase, the digits 0–9, or periods (.).
- The last character of a variable name may be a special character (%, &, !, #, or $) that indicates the type of value to be stored in the variable.
- A variable name can be up to 40 characters in length.
- A variable name must not be the same as a QuickBASIC reserved word.

You can think of a variable name as the title on an office door. The title tells you the function of the person inside but not the person's name. In fact, the person who does the job can change without the title changing. The variable *president$*, for example, might contain the value "Smith." However, in the future the value in the variable *president$* might be "Jones." The variable name hasn't changed, yet its contents have.

When you create a program's variables, you must choose between two distinct types of variables—numeric and character. In QuickBASIC, as in most other computer languages, a numeric variable can be one of several types. Each type defines a range of values the variable can contain. A numeric variable can be an integer, a long integer, a single-precision value, or a double-precision value. A character variable can be one of two types: a variable-length string or a fixed-length string. You use the statements and functions described in this chapter to define variables and to convert values to different types of variables. Chapter 5, "Strings," discusses string management.

This tutorial summarizes variables and types and offers some suggestions for their use. Table 1-1 lists in alphabetic order the keywords, statements, and functions used to define and work with variables.

Keyword, statement, or function	Description
CONST	Defines a mnemonic name for values that don't change
DEF*type*	Defines characters that specify default variable types
DOUBLE	Creates a double-precision variable
HEX$	Returns a string containing the hexadecimal value of an integer value
INTEGER	Creates an integer variable
LET	Assigns a value to a variable
LONG	Creates a long-integer variable
OCT$	Returns a string containing the octal value of an integer value
SINGLE	Creates a single-precision variable
STRING	Creates a string variable
SWAP	Exchanges values between two variables
TYPE...END TYPE	Defines a new variable type

Table 1-1.
Variable-typing keywords, statements, and functions.

Defining Mnemonic Names for Constant Values

Because much programming involves numeric codes, QuickBASIC provides the CONST statement to let you assign meaningful names, called constants, to these codes. The COLOR statement, for example, accepts parameters that are values in the range 0 through 31. Each number specifies a different color. Values 16 through 31 specify the same colors as 0 through 15, but with the blinking attribute. You can define constants to represent some of those values, as shown in the following statements:

```
CONST BLACK = 0, BLUE = 1, GREEN = 2, CYAN = 3
CONST RED = 4, MAGENTA = 5, BROWN = 6, WHITE = 7
CONST BLINKING = 16
```

These statements let you easily change colors on the screen without having to memorize the entire code table—for example,

```
COLOR WHITE, BLUE
PRINT "This text is white on a blue background."

COLOR BLINKING + RED, WHITE
PRINT "This text is blinking red on a white background."
```

The CONST statement is also useful for providing names for constant values you might later want to change. Although the standard screen has a height of 25 characters, EGA adapters also support screens 43 characters high. VGA adapters support screens 25, 43, and 50 characters high. To enable users with those adapters to take advantage of more lines on the screen, you can define a constant *HEIGHT* that should be set to 25 for a standard screen, 43 for an EGA screen, and 50 for a VGA screen.

In QuickBASIC, a constant's value can be either a *constant value* or a *constant expression.* Any literal number or string of characters is a constant value. For example, the literal number 69 is a constant-integer value, and the string of characters "QuickBASIC Bible" is a constant character-string value. An expression that contains only constant elements is called a constant expression—for example,

```
69 + 128 * 2
```

is a constant expression because each element is a constant value. However, the expression

```
69 + 128 * FACTOR
```

is a constant expression only if *FACTOR* has been defined as a constant value. If *FACTOR* is a variable, the above expression is not a constant expression.

Constants that are defined with an expression can contain only literal numbers, literal strings, and other constants; they cannot contain variables or functions. For example, you may define the constant *BLINKINGRED* as shown below because it is a combination of other constants:

```
CONST RED = 4, BLINKING = 16
CONST BLINKINGRED = RED + BLINKING
```

Variable Types

QuickBASIC provides five simple variable types—integer, long integer, single precision, double precision, and string. You can declare a variable as one of these types in an AS clause in the QuickBASIC statements listed in Table 1-2 on the following page.

COMMON
DECLARE SUB
DECLARE FUNCTION
DEF FN
DIM
FUNCTION
REDIM
SHARED
STATIC
SUB
TYPE...END TYPE

Table 1-2.
QuickBASIC statements in which variables can be declared.

The statements DECLARE SUB, DECLARE FUNCTION, DEF FN, FUNCTION, and SUB declare variables only if a parameter list is included in the statement. You use the remaining entries in the above table only to declare variables. You can use the DIM statement to dimension arrays or to define the type of a variable. See the entries of those statements for more details.

You can declare a variable's type in one of two ways: either with an AS clause or with a type-declaration character. To declare a type by using an AS clause, follow the variable name with the AS keyword and the keyword of the desired type. For example, the statement

```
COMMON total AS DOUBLE
```

declares the variable *total* as double precision. Table 1-3 lists the AS clauses for the five simple types:

Type declaration	Purpose
AS INTEGER	Declares an integer variable
AS LONG	Declares a long-integer variable
AS SINGLE	Declares a single-precision variable
AS DOUBLE	Declares a double-precision variable
AS STRING	Declares a string variable

Table 1-3.
Type declarations with the AS keyword.

To declare a variable's type by using a type-declaration character, follow the variable name with one of the type-declaration characters: %, &, !, #, or $. When you do this, QuickBASIC assigns that variable a type according to Table 1-4.

Type-declaration character	Purpose
%	Declares an integer variable
&	Declares a long-integer variable
!	Declares a single-precision variable
#	Declares a double-precision variable
$	Declares a string variable

Table 1-4.
Type-declaration characters.

For example, the statement

```
total# = 128.69
```

assigns the value 128.69 to the double-precision variable named *total#*. Remember, the type-declaration character is part of the variable name, and you must always include it in references to the name. For example, consider the following statements:

```
total# = 128.69
total = 100.55
```

Note that the variable *total* without the # type-declaration character is a different variable from *total#*. In fact, you can use a single name for five different variables:

```
total%        ' an integer variable
total&        ' a long-integer variable
total!        ' a single-precision variable
total#        ' a double-precision variable
total$        ' a string variable
```

The type-declaration character is useful for reminding you what type a variable is. You know, for example, that a variable named *total#* holds a double-precision value.

Creating Default Types for Variables

QuickBASIC, unlike most other traditional programming languages, does not require you to explicitly declare a variable. Instead of using AS or a type-declaration character, you can use a DEF*type* statement that sets the default data type. The first time you use a new variable, QuickBASIC assigns it whatever type is specified by a DEF*type* statement.

DEF*type* statements specify letters or letter ranges. Any variable names that begin with the specified letters are immediately assigned the type specified by the DEF*type* keyword. The DEF*type* keyword can be DEFINT, DEFLNG, DEFSNG, DEFDBL, or DEFSTR.

Some older programming languages, such as FORTRAN, define variables beginning with the letters I through N as integers and the rest as double precision. You can do the same thing with the following QuickBASIC statements:

```
DEFINT I-N
DEFDBL A-H, O-Z
```

Now you can use the variable *number*, for example, in FOR...NEXT loops, which use integer values, and you don't need to specify types for variables that require double precision if you give them names such as *total* and *subtotal*.

Converting Decimal to Hexadecimal or Octal

When you display the value of a variable using the PRINT statement, QuickBASIC displays it as a decimal (base 10) number. However, QuickBASIC provides two functions that let you display numbers in other bases. The HEX$ function converts a decimal number to a string that represents the value in base 16 (hexadecimal), and OCT$ converts a decimal number to a string that represents the value in base 8 (octal).

Representing numbers in hexadecimal and octal can be useful when you work with assembly-language routines. Most likely, you will not often use these functions. After all, very few invoices or balance sheets must be printed with hexadecimal or octal values.

Assigning Values to Variables

Variables wouldn't be of much use if you couldn't assign values to them. In old versions of BASIC (such as TRS-80 Level I BASIC) you had to use the LET statement to assign values to variables. Modern versions of BASIC no longer require you to use the LET statement; now you can assign a value by using an equal sign (=).

Often, for example, you will need to increment a variable that acts as a counter. Old versions of BASIC required you to use the following statement:

```
LET counter = counter + 1
```

With QuickBASIC, you can omit the LET keyword:

```
counter = counter + 1
```

You can assign values to string variables by using string constants or other string variables. You can also assign to a string variable the result of a concatenation operation:

```
language$ = "QuickBASIC "
title$ = language$ + "Bible"
```

After a program executes these statements, the variable *title$* contains the value "QuickBASIC Bible."

Exchanging Values Between Two Variables

The SWAP statement exchanges the values of two different variables and is especially useful in some sorting algorithms. The SWAP statement is equivalent to three assignment statements organized into a single statement. For example,

```
SWAP currentTotal, subTotal
```

exchanges the values of the variables *currentTotal* and *subTotal* and is equivalent to the following statements:

```
temp = subTotal
subTotal = currentTotal
currentTotal = temp
```

Defining a Compound-Variable Type

Some items are usually grouped together: for example, month, day, and year form a date; and honorific, first name, middle name, and last name form a title. Perhaps the most natural way to store the three separate elements of today's date would be to use three variables: *month*, *day*, and *year*. Computer languages such as Pascal and C support record structures that can be used to create a variable that contains more than one variable. QuickBASIC version 4.0 introduced the TYPE...END TYPE statement to enable programmers to create types that accommodate record variables consisting of several elements.

To create a record structure for the parts of a person's name, you might use a TYPE...END TYPE statement, as in the following statement:

```
TYPE CompleteName
    honorific AS STRING * 4
    first AS STRING * 16
    middle AS STRING * 16
    last AS STRING * 20
END TYPE
```

After you create the above structure, you could define a new variable as that structure type, as in the following statement:

```
DIM customerName AS CompleteName
```

Now you can assign values to the variables in the record variable *customerName*, as in the following statements:

```
customerName.honorific = "Mr."
customerName.first = "John"
customerName.middle = "Q."
customerName.last = "Public"
```

Variables of a type defined by a TYPE...END TYPE statement are often used to combine all the variables of one record in a file into a single variable. That way, you need write only a single variable into the file. (This method has replaced the practice of using the FIELD statement.)

You can also create arrays of record variables. The following program segment first declares an array of record variables that are defined by the *CompleteName* type and then assigns values to the variables:

```
TYPE CompleteName
    honorific AS STRING * 4
    first AS STRING * 16
    middle AS STRING * 16
    last AS STRING * 20
END TYPE

DIM customerName(2) AS CompleteName

customerName(1).honorific = "Mr."
customerName(1).first = "John"
customerName(1).middle = "Q."
customerName(1).last = "Public"

customerName(2).honorific = "Ms."
customerName(2).first = "Jane"
customerName(2).middle = ""
customerName(2).last = "Doe"
```

Figure 1-1 shows a graphic representation of the array of record variables declared above.

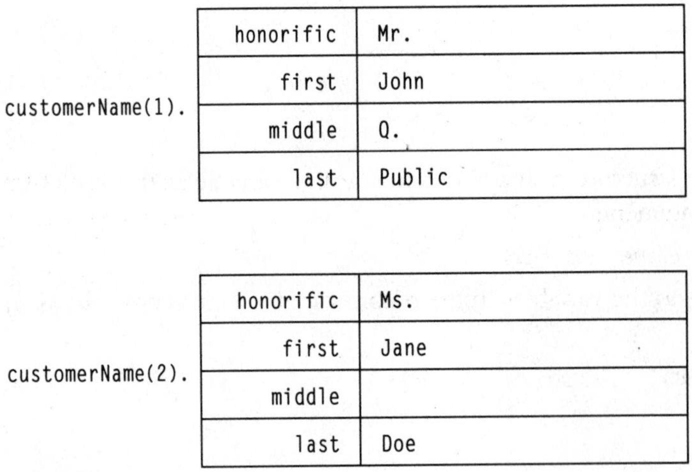

customerName(1).	honorific	Mr.
	first	John
	middle	Q.
	last	Public

customerName(2).	honorific	Ms.
	first	Jane
	middle	
	last	Doe

Figure 1-1.
Values in an array of record variables.

You can also define structures that contain other structures as members. This is a useful technique for reusing basic structures you have already defined, such as the previous structure for names. Other, more complicated, structures might contain these basic structures. The following program segment, for example, declares an array of record variables of the defined type *Patients.* The structure *Patients* contains the variable *patientName,* which is a record variable of type *CompleteName.*

```
TYPE CompleteName
    honorific AS STRING * 4
    first AS STRING * 16
    middle AS STRING * 16
    last AS STRING * 20
END TYPE

TYPE Patients
    patientName AS CompleteName
    address AS STRING * 128
END TYPE

DIM patient(100) AS Patients

patient(1).patientName.honorific = "Ms."
patient(1).patientName.first = "Anna"
patient(1).patientName.middle = "Marie"
patient(1).patientName.last = "Smith"
patient(1).address = "1695 Park Street"

patient(2).patientName.honorific = "Mr."
patient(2).patientName.first = "George"
patient(2).patientName.middle = "John"
patient(2).patientName.last = "Jones"
patient(2).address = "1024 Disk Drive"
```

Figure 1-2 on the following page shows a graphic representation of the structure within a structure of the above record variables.

The TYPE...END TYPE statement allows you to specify a wide variety of types for the elements. QuickBASIC provides programmers the flexibility to define types with the TYPE...END TYPE statement. However, QuickBASIC doesn't yet allow you to define arrays within structures. You can have arrays of structures, as in the two preceding examples, but you cannot use arrays in your structures. For example, QuickBASIC does not permit the following structure:

```
TYPE IdealPatientType
    patientName AS CompleteName
    address(4) AS STRING * 32     ' generates a compile-time error
END TYPE
```

The BASIC Compiler Professional Development System version 7.0, however, does allow you to define arrays within structures.

patient(1).	patientName.	honorific	Ms.
		first	Anna
		middle	Marie
		last	Smith
	address	1695 Park Street	

patient(2).	patientName.	honorific	Mr.
		first	George
		middle	John
		last	Jones
	address	1024 Disk Drive	

Figure 1-2.
Values in a structure within a structure.

Related Reading

Lafore, Robert. *The Waite Group's Microsoft C Programming for the PC,* rev. ed. Indianapolis, Ind.: Howard W. Sams and Co., 1989.

Norton, Peter, and Richard Wilton. *The* New *Peter Norton Programmer's Guide to the IBM PC and PS/2.* Redmond, Wash.: Microsoft Press, 1988.

CONST

QB2	■ QB4.5	PowerBASIC
■ QB3	ANSI	GW-BASIC
■ QB4	■ BASIC7	MacQB

Purpose

The CONST statement lets you give symbolic, meaningful names to numeric and string constant values. For example, you could use the CONST statement to assign the name PI to the number 3.141592653.

Syntax

CONST *NAME* = *expr* [, *NAME* = *expr*]...

NAME is a constant's name. It must be distinct from any keyword, variable, or subprogram name.

expr is a numeric or string expression containing only a constant value or a constant expression.

Usage

```
CONST PI = 3.141592653
```

Assigns the name PI to the value 3.141592653.

```
CONST FALSE = 0, TRUE = NOT FALSE
```

Defines two symbolic constants, FALSE and TRUE.

Description

Programming in QuickBASIC often requires the use of numeric codes, which can represent everything from screen colors to keyboard keys. The CONST statement lets you assign meaningful names to these codes and is comparable to the #define directive in C and the CONST statement in Pascal.

The constant is the word to which you want to assign the specified expression. You can use a type-declaration character (%, &, !, #, or $) at the end of the name to specify the constant's type, but this character is not considered part of the name. For example, if you specify

```
CONST ARRAYSIZE% = 2500
```

you can use the constant in statements without the ending type-declaration character, as in the following statements:

```
DIM patients(100 TO ARRAYSIZE)
```

```
FOR i% = 1 TO ARRAYSIZE
```

If you omit a type-declaration character, QuickBASIC assigns a type to the constant that matches the type of the specified expression. If the expression is the value "gobbledygook," for example, QuickBASIC types the constant as a string. If the expression is numeric, QuickBASIC determines the smallest type that can hold it and assigns a type of integer, long integer, single precision, or double precision. For example, in the statement

```
CONST ANNUALSALES = 298500
```

QuickBASIC first determines that 298500 is not in the range of the integer type; and then it checks whether the value is in the range of the long-integer type. Because it is in the range, *ANNUALSALES* is typed as a long-integer constant.

In the following statement, 0.015 is a floating-point number:

```
CONST SERVICECHARGE = 0.015
```

Because the constant cannot be an integer or a long integer, QuickBASIC checks only the ranges of the single-precision and double-precision types. Because it fits in the range of the single-precision type, SERVICECHARGE becomes a single-precision constant.

The specified expression is a QuickBASIC expression that contains string or numeric constants, other constants defined by a CONST statement, and arithmetic and logical operators. It cannot contain variables, program-defined functions, or QuickBASIC functions and statements such as CHR$, SIN, and SEEK.

Before you use a constant, you must define it with a CONST statement. The following statement, for example, generates a runtime error because you used the constant FALSE before you defined it.

```
CONST TRUE = NOT FALSE, FALSE = 0
```

The proper way to define these symbolic constants TRUE and FALSE is

```
CONST FALSE = 0, TRUE = NOT FALSE
```

If you define a constant by using a CONST statement inside a subprogram or a user-defined function, you can use the constant name only within the subprogram or function (that is, it is a *local* constant). Use local constants for constants that are applicable to only one subprogram or function. If, for example, you create a subprogram to track the number of transactions completed, you need to include the following statement in the subprogram to make the constant local:

```
CONST MAXTRANSACTIONS = 1024
```

If you define a constant by using a CONST statement in the main program (outside a subprogram or a user-defined function), you can use the constant name throughout the module (that is, it's a *global* constant). Use global constants, such as TRUE and FALSE, for constants that are applicable throughout a program.

You can use a constant anywhere you would normally use a variable or an expression.

Comments

The type of a constant is not affected by DEF*type* statements (DEFDBL, DEFINT, DEFLNG, DEFSNG, and DEFSTR). You can determine the type of a constant by adding a type-declaration character to the end of the constant or by merely assigning a value of that type to *expr*—for example,

```
DEFDBL A-Z

CONST MINAMOUNT = 125.50
maxAmount = 9999.99
```

MINAMOUNT is a single-precision constant, and *maxAmount* is a double-precision variable.

Errors

If you create an expression that cannot be used as a CONST constant, QuickBASIC returns an "Invalid constant" error message. If you attempt to modify the name of a constant defined in a CONST statement, QuickBASIC returns a "Duplicate definition" error message. If you use the exponentiation operator (^) in an expression in a CONST statement, QuickBASIC returns an "Illegal function call" error message.

Tips

Using the CONST statement offers several advantages over using variables or literals:

- Using constants lets you see the meanings of specific values rather than the values themselves. Using the constant *F1* to represent the value for the F1 function key, for example, is clearer than using the value 59.
- When you define a constant outside a subprogram or user-defined function, it is available to the entire module; a variable declared outside the subprogram or function can be accessed only with a SHARED statement.
- The value of a constant defined in a CONST statement cannot be accidentally changed; a variable's value can be changed easily.
- When you compile programs to create executable files by using the BC.EXE compiler, programs that use CONST are smaller and run faster than those that use variables.
- Using CONST constants lets you make changes to a program more easily than if you use literals. If you originally designed a program to work with a screen height of 25 characters, for example, you might declare the constant *SCREENLINES* as follows:

  ```
  CONST SCREENLINES = 25
  ```

  Later, to expand the program to work with a VGA screen with a height of 50 characters, you need only make the following change to the program:

  ```
  CONST SCREENLINES = 50
  ```

It is common practice to capitalize the names of constants. This practice helps show you when your program is using a constant instead of a variable.

Warnings

When you compile programs using the BC.EXE compiler, the CONST statement must *follow* statements that are position dependent (such as COMMON). The CONST statement is an executable statement; if it precedes a COMMON statement, QuickBASIC returns a "COMMON and DECLARE must precede executable statements" error message. Note that this error does not occur in the QuickBASIC environment.

Example

The following program uses the CONST statement to provide symbolic names for the ASCII codes of certain keystrokes.

```
' define constants that contain the ASCII codes of some keystrokes
CONST ESC = 27, ENTER = 13, CTRLBACKSPACE = 127

CLS
PRINT "Type something... (press Ctrl - Backspace to quit)."
PRINT
LOCATE , , 1                        ' turn on cursor

DO
    DO                              ' loop until a key is pressed
        inky$ = INKEY$
    LOOP WHILE inky$ = ""

    SELECT CASE ASC(inky$)
        CASE ENTER                  ' if key is Enter, print [ENTER]
            PRINT " [ENTER]"

        CASE ESC                    ' if key is Esc, print [ESC]
            PRINT " [ESC] ";

        CASE CTRLBACKSPACE          ' if key is Ctrl-Backspace, exit loop
            PRINT " [CTRL-BACKSPACE] ";
            EXIT DO

        CASE ELSE                   ' otherwise, print the key
            PRINT inky$;
    END SELECT
LOOP
```

DEF*type*

See also: DIM, DOUBLE, INTEGER, LONG, SINGLE

✲ QB2	■ QB4.5	■ PowerBASIC
✲ QB3	ANSI	✲ GW-BASIC
■ QB4	■ BASIC7	■ MacQB

Purpose

QuickBASIC's DEF*type* statements set the default type for variables and user-defined functions that don't include a type-declaration character or that aren't specifically declared by an AS clause.

Syntax

DEFDBL *letters* [, *letters*]...
DEFINT *letters* [, *letters*]...
DEFLNG *letters* [, *letters*]...
DEFSNG *letters* [, *letters*]...
DEFSTR *letters* [, *letters*]...

letters is either a single letter or a range of letters specified by two letters separated by a hyphen.

Usage

```
DEFLNG S, T
```

Declares all variables that begin with the letter S or T to be long integers.

```
DEFINT A-Z
```

Declares all variables to be integers.

Description

Unlike most other computer languages, QuickBASIC does not require you to define the type and size of variables and functions before you use them. If you don't specify a type, QuickBASIC assigns a type to a variable the first time you use it. This gives you the freedom to create a new variable whenever you need it without having to first declare it. The DEF*type* statements set the default types that are used when QuickBASIC automatically assigns a type to a variable.

A DEF*type* statement sets variables to a specific type. The type depends on which DEF*type* keyword you use. The five DEF*type* keywords are shown in Table 1-5 on the following page.

Any variable that hasn't already been defined and whose name begins with any letter specified in a DEF*type* statement is assigned the type specified by the DEF*type* keyword. (See Table 1-5.)

DEF*type* affects variables that begin with the specified letters in lowercase or in uppercase. QuickBASIC arranges in alphabetic order the letters given in a range.

With the DEF*type* statement	The default variable type is
<none>	Single precision
DEFDBL	Double precision
DEFINT	Integer
DEFLNG	Long integer
DEFSNG	Single precision
DEFSTR	String

Table 1-5.
*DEF*type *keywords.*

Comments

Because the types of all elements in a record variable defined by a TYPE...END TYPE statement are explicitly defined by AS clauses, they are not affected by QuickBASIC's DEF*type* statements.

Adding a type-declaration character (%, &, !, #, or $) to a variable name defines the variable as a specific type. Adding an ampersand (&) to the end of a variable, for example, defines it as a long integer. Also, if you declare a variable or a function by using an AS clause, that variable or function is defined as the type you specify. For example, in the following statement

```
DIM freeSpace AS LONG
```

the variable *freeSpace* is a long integer. This explicit typing overrides any defaults created by DEF*type* statements.

Tips

- Because they are of different types, *i%*, *i&*, *i!*, *i#*, and *i$* are distinct variable names, and each can hold a different value. However, using different variables with such similar names can be confusing, so you should avoid doing so.
- If you use a DEF*type* statement to set the type of a function defined by a DEF FN statement, remember that the name of the function begins immediately to the right of the letters FN. If you create a function named *FNAverage*, for example, you use the statement *DEFDBL A* to define *FNAverage* as double precision.

Compatibility

QuickBASIC 2.0, QuickBASIC 3.0, GW-BASIC, and BASICA

QuickBASIC versions 2.0 and 3.0, GW-BASIC, and BASICA do not support long integers; therefore, they do not implement the DEFLNG statement.

GW-BASIC and BASICA

The GW-BASIC and BASICA interpreters assign a type to a variable each time the variable in a statement is encountered. If you change the default type and then return to a statement, the variable's type is changed and its contents are erased. QuickBASIC, as a compiler, assigns a variable in a statement its type only once. If you change the default and then return to a statement, the variable's type and contents are not changed. Table 1-6 demonstrates how this might occur.

Statements	GW-BASIC and BASICA	QuickBASIC
1 DEFINT X	Sets default variable type	Sets default variable type
2 x = 10	Defines *x* as an integer	Defines *x* as an integer
3 PRINT x	Displays 10 on screen	Displays 10 on screen
4 DEFDBL x	Redefines *x* as double precision and resets contents to 0	This statement is ignored and not executed
5 GOTO 3	Goes back to line 3 and begins displaying zeros	Goes back to line 3 and continues to display 10s

Table 1-6.
*GW-BASIC and BASICA versus QuickBASIC with DEF*type.

Example

The following program uses DEF*type* statements to set the default variable type for loop variables, total amounts, and prompt strings.

```
DEFDBL A, G      ' amt, grandTotal are double precision
DEFINT I         ' i is an integer
DEFLNG X         ' x is a long integer
DEFSNG S         ' subTotal is single precision
DEFSTR Y         ' yesNo is a string

CLS

' initialize variables
grandTotal = 0#
x = 1

DO
    PRINT "How many items on receipt"; x;    ' get number of items on the receipt
    INPUT itemsOnReceipt

    subTotal = 0!                            ' initialize subtotal
    FOR i = 1 TO itemsOnReceipt              ' for each item on receipt
        PRINT "Enter amount of item"; i;
```

(continued)

continued

```
        INPUT ; amt                          ' get item amount
        subTotal = subTotal + amt            ' add item amount to subTotal
        grandTotal = grandTotal + amt        ' add item amount to grandTotal
        PRINT TAB(70); USING "##,###.##"; subTotal
    NEXT

    PRINT TAB(70); "---------"               ' print current grand total
    PRINT TAB(70); USING "##,###.##"; grandTotal
    PRINT

    INPUT "Do you want to add up more receipts"; yesNo  ' prompt if user
    x = x + 1                                           ' wants more receipts
LOOP UNTIL UCASE$(yesNo) = "N"                          ' else quit program
```

DOUBLE

See also: COMMON, DECLARE, DEF FN, DIM, FUNCTION, INTEGER, LONG, REDIM, SHARED, SINGLE, STATIC, STRING, SUB, TYPE...END TYPE

QB2	■ QB4.5	PowerBASIC
QB3	ANSI	GW-BASIC
■ QB4	■ BASIC7	MacQB

Purpose

The DOUBLE keyword specifies in an AS clause the type of a variable or function as double precision floating point. Use the DOUBLE keyword when you must use large, accurate numbers, as in scientific and business calculations.

Syntax

var AS DOUBLE

var is the name of a variable; the exact syntax depends on the statement in which you use the variable.

Usage

```
DIM total AS DOUBLE
```

Defines *total* as a double-precision variable.

```
DECLARE FUNCTION CubeRoot# (number AS DOUBLE)
```

Declares a function that takes a double-precision argument.

Description

The DOUBLE keyword is used in the AS clause of many QuickBASIC declaration statements. Table 1-7 lists the statements that use the AS clause. (For details, see the entries of the statements in the table.)

COMMON
DECLARE SUB
DECLARE FUNCTION
DEF FN
DIM
FUNCTION
REDIM
SHARED
STATIC
SUB
TYPE...END TYPE

Table 1-7.
QuickBASIC statements that use the AS clause.

Variables declared as double precision can hold floating-point values (values that have numbers after a decimal point) accurately to 15 significant digits. This means that although a double-precision variable can hold much larger values, only 15 digits are accurate. Because double-precision variables can use exponential notation (that is, scientific notation), they can hold extremely large values. Values for positive double-precision numbers range from 4.940656458412465D−324 through 1.797693134862315D+308. Values for negative double-precision numbers range from −1.797693134862315E+308 through −4.940656458412465D−324.

Exponential notation for double-precision numbers is expressed as follows:

±*mantissa*D±*exponent*

An example of this format is the number 4.107D+6, which is equivalent to

4.107×10^6 and to 4,107,000.

Note that, in keeping with the mathematical definition of scientific notation, when the exponent is negative, the overall value of the expression is fractional—not negative—as in the following example:

$4.107D-6 = 4.107 \times 10^{-6} = 0.000004107$

Tips

Rather than declaring a variable using the clause AS DOUBLE, you can add the type-declaration character # to the end of the variable name. Remember, however, that the pound sign (#) becomes part of the name and that you must include it every time you use the variable.

Also, you can use a DEFDBL statement to declare that all variables whose names begin with certain letters be double precision. (See the DEF*type* entry.)

Errors

If you assign to a double-precision variable a value outside the range of the double-precision type, QuickBASIC returns an "Overflow" error message.

HEX$

See also: OCT$

■ QB2	■ QB4.5	■ PowerBASIC
■ QB3	ANSI	■ GW-BASIC
■ QB4	■ BASIC7	■ MacQB

Purpose

The HEX$ function converts an integer or long-integer expression to a string that contains the hexadecimal (base 16) value of the expression. You might use the HEX$ function if you work with assembly-language routines.

Syntax

HEX$(*num*)

num is the numeric variable or expression that HEX$ converts.

Usage

```
PRINT HEX$(65536)
```

Displays the hexadecimal value of the integer 65536, which is 10000.

Description

People are most comfortable using decimal numbers (base 10). But other base systems, such as binary (base 2), octal (base 8), and hexadecimal (base 16) work better for digital processing. QuickBASIC provides the HEX$ function to convert decimal numbers to strings containing the representation of the numbers in hexadecimal.

The specified value is a numeric variable or expression of any numeric type; QuickBASIC converts it to an integer or a long integer. Note that QuickBASIC ignores any fractional part of the value.

Errors

If the specified value is not in the range –2147483648 through 2147483647, QuickBASIC returns an "Overflow" error message.

Example

The following example uses the PEEK and HEX$ functions to print the hexadecimal representation of some memory-status variables.

```
CLS
DEF SEG = 0             ' access the "BIOS data area"

PRINT "Press the Shift keys, Ctrl keys, Alt keys, "
PRINT "    Num Lock, Caps Lock, and Scroll Lock."
PRINT "Press Esc to quit."

DO
    LOCATE 4, 1     ' position the cursor

    ' get the data at address 0417 hexadecimal, convert it to hexadecimal
    PRINT RIGHT$("0" + HEX$(PEEK(&H417)), 2)
LOOP UNTIL INKEY$ = CHR$(27)
```

INTEGER

See also: COMMON, DECLARE, DEF FN, DIM, DOUBLE, FUNCTION, LONG, REDIM, SHARED, SINGLE, STATIC, STRING, SUB, TYPE...END TYPE

QB2	■ QB4.5	PowerBASIC
QB3	ANSI	GW-BASIC
■ QB4	■ BASIC7	MacQB

Purpose

The INTEGER keyword specifies in an AS clause the type of a variable or function as integer. Use the INTEGER keyword when you need to use only small whole numbers (integers) for operations such as accessing screen coordinates.

Syntax

var AS INTEGER

var is the name of a variable; the exact syntax depends on the statement in which you use the variable.

Usage

```
DIM age AS INTEGER
```

Defines *age* as an integer variable.

```
DECLARE FUNCTION Cube (number AS INTEGER)
```

Declares a function that takes an integer argument.

Description

The INTEGER keyword is used in the AS clause of many QuickBASIC declaration statements. Table 1-7 in the DOUBLE entry lists the statements that use the AS clause. (See the entries of the statements in the table for details.)

Variables declared as INTEGER can hold whole numbers in the range −32768 through 32767. If you need to use a larger range of whole numbers, you must use the LONG integer keyword. (See the LONG entry.)

Comments

Mathematical operations on integer and long-integer variables are executed much faster than they are executed on single-precision and double-precision variables. Integer and long-integer variables can be directly represented in the registers of the CPU; however, the three parts of single-precision and double-precision variables (sign, mantissa, and exponent) must be calculated, causing slower mathematical operations. Use integer or long-integer variables whenever possible.

Errors

If you assign to an integer variable a value outside the range of the integer type, QuickBASIC returns an "Overflow" error message.

Tips

Rather than declaring a variable using the clause AS INTEGER, you can add the type-declaration character % to the end of the variable name. Remember, however, that the percent sign (%) becomes part of the name and that you must include it every time you use the variable.

Also, you can use a DEFINT statement to declare that all variables whose names begin with certain letters be integers. (See the DEF*type* entry.)

LET

See also: LSET, TYPE...END TYPE

✲ QB2	■ QB4.5	✲ PowerBASIC
✲ QB3	✲ ANSI	✲ GW-BASIC
■ QB4	■ BASIC7	✲ MacQB

Purpose

The LET statement assigns the value of an expression to a variable, an array element, or a user-defined TYPE...END TYPE variable or element. Use LET to initialize variables or to change their current value.

Syntax

[LET] *var* = *expr*

var is the name of the variable that is assigned the value of *expr*.

The LET keyword is optional.

Usage

```
LET a = 0
```

Assigns the value 0 to the variable *a*.

```
x = x + 1
```

Increments the variable *x* by 1.

```
item(5) = 4.8
```

Assigns the value 4.8 to element 5 of the array *item.*

```
item.partnum = "26-3004B"
```

Assigns the string "26-3004B" to the element *partnum* in the user-defined record variable *item.*

Description

The LET statement is the QuickBASIC assignment operator; it lets you assign values to variables. You can use it to assign the initial values of the variables in a program or to change the values of variables later in the program. For example, programmers often assign initial values at the beginning of a program:

```
x = 0
y = 0
z = 0
```

QuickBASIC lets you use the same variable on both sides of the equal sign. This lets you make changes relative to the variable's current value. The statement *x = x + 1,* for example, increments the value of *x* by 1. In the statement *y = 5 *y,* QuickBASIC calculates the expression *5 *y* and then assigns the resulting value to *y.*

Both the variable and the expression in a LET statement can be record variables defined by a TYPE...END TYPE statement; however, both must be defined as the same user-defined type. For example, the DIM statements

```
DIM newItem AS Inventory
DIM item AS Inventory
```

let you execute the following assignment statement:

```
item = newItem
```

Note that this works only when the AS clause is the same for both record variables. If the AS clauses are different, you can use the LSET statement to assign the contents of one record variable to the other. (See the LSET entry in Chapter 17, "Files," for details.)

Compatibility

QuickBASIC 2.0, QuickBASIC 3.0, ANSI BASIC, PowerBASIC, BASICA, GW-BASIC, and QuickBASIC for the Macintosh

These versions of BASIC support the LET statement but do not support the TYPE...END TYPE statement; therefore, the LET statement does not support record variables.

Example

The following example uses the LET assignment statement to build a table of the square and square root of the numbers 1 through 20.

```
CLS

PRINT "         Number   Square root"
PRINT "Number  Squared  of Number"
PRINT

FOR i% = 1 TO 20
    LET square# = i% ^ 2           ' assign square# the square of i
    LET squareRoot# = SQR(i%)      ' assign squareRoot# the square root of i
    PRINT USING "##      ####     #.#####"; i%; square#; squareRoot#
NEXT
```

LONG

See also: COMMON, DECLARE, DEF FN, DIM, DOUBLE, FUNCTION, INTEGER, REDIM, SHARED, SINGLE, STATIC, STRING, SUB, TYPE...END TYPE

QB2	■ QB4.5	PowerBASIC
QB3	ANSI	GW-BASIC
■ QB4	■ BASIC7	MacQB

Purpose

The LONG keyword specifies in an AS clause the type of variables and functions as long integers. Use the LONG keyword when you need to use large whole numbers (without decimals) in operations that include whole-dollar amounts.

Syntax

var AS LONG

var is the name of a variable; the exact syntax depends on the statement in which you use the variable.

Usage

```
DIM deficit AS LONG
```

Defines *deficit* as a long-integer variable.

```
DECLARE FUNCTION Cube (number AS LONG)
```

Declares a function that takes a long-integer argument.

Description

The LONG keyword is used in the AS clause of many QuickBASIC declaration statements. Table 1-7 in the DOUBLE entry lists the statements that use the AS clause. (See the entries of the statements in the table for details.)

Variables declared as LONG can hold whole numbers that are in the range –2147483648 through 2147483647. If you need to use a larger range of whole numbers, you must declare the variable with the DOUBLE keyword. Double-precision variables hold floating-point numbers (values that have numbers after a decimal point), but, of course, you can use the variable to hold whole numbers as well. (See the DOUBLE entry.)

Comments

Mathematical operations on integer and long-integer variables are executed much faster than they are executed on single-precision and double-precision variables. Integer and long-integer variables can be directly represented in the registers of the CPU; however, the three parts of single-precision and double-precision variables (sign, mantissa, and exponent) must be calculated, causing slower mathematical operations. Use integer or long-integer variables whenever possible.

Errors

If you assign to a long-integer variable a value outside the range of the long-integer type, QuickBASIC returns an "Overflow" error message.

Tips

Rather than declaring a variable using the clause AS LONG, you can add the type-declaration character & to the end of the name. Remember, however, that the ampersand (&) becomes part of the name and that you must include it every time you use the variable.

Also, you can use a DEFLNG statement to declare that all variables whose names begin with certain letters be long integers. (See the DEF*type* entry.)

OCT$

See also: HEX$

■ QB2	■ QB4.5	■ PowerBASIC
■ QB3	ANSI	■ GW-BASIC
■ QB4	■ BASIC7	■ MacQB

Purpose

The OCT$ function converts an integer or long-integer expression to a string that contains the octal (base 8) value of the expression. You might use the OCT$ function if you work with assembly-language routines.

Syntax

OCT$(*num*)

num is the numeric variable or expression that OCT$ converts.

Usage

```
PRINT OCT$(511)
```

Displays the octal value of the integer 511, which is 777.

Description

People are most comfortable using decimal numbers (base 10). But other base systems, such as binary (base 2), octal (base 8), and hexadecimal (base 16) work better for digital processing. QuickBASIC provides the OCT$ function to convert decimal numbers to strings containing the representation of the numbers in octal.

The specified value is a numeric variable or expression of any numeric type; QuickBASIC converts it to an integer or a long integer. Note that QuickBASIC ignores any fractional part of the value.

Errors

If the specified value is not in the range –2147483648 through 2147483647, QuickBASIC returns an "Overflow" error message.

Example

The following example uses the OCT$ function to print the octal representation of decimal numbers input by the user.

```
CLS

PRINT "To quit, press Enter or enter 0."
PRINT

DO
    INPUT "Enter a decimal integer"; dec%
    IF dec% <= 0 THEN EXIT DO

    PRINT dec%; "decimal is "; OCT$(dec%); " octal"
    PRINT
LOOP UNTIL dec% = 0
```

SINGLE

See also: COMMON, DECLARE, DEF FN, DIM, DOUBLE, FUNCTION, INTEGER, LONG, REDIM, SHARED, STATIC, STRING, SUB, TYPE...END TYPE

QB2	■ QB4.5	PowerBASIC
QB3	ANSI	GW-BASIC
■ QB4	■ BASIC7	MacQB

Purpose

The SINGLE keyword specifies in an AS clause the type of a variable or function as single precision floating point. Use the SINGLE keyword when you need to use decimal numbers, such as small dollar amounts.

Syntax

var AS SINGLE

var is the name of a variable; the exact syntax depends on the statement in which you use the variable.

Usage

```
DIM total AS SINGLE
```

Defines *total* as a single-precision variable.

```
DECLARE FUNCTION CubeRoot# (number AS SINGLE)
```

Declares a FUNCTION that takes a single-precision argument.

Description

The SINGLE keyword is used in the AS clause of many QuickBASIC declaration statements. Table 1-7 in the DOUBLE entry lists the statements that use the AS clause. (See the entries of the statements in the table for details.)

Variables declared as single precision can hold floating-point values (values that have numbers after a decimal point) accurate to seven significant digits. This means that although a single-precision variable can hold much larger values, only seven digits are accurate. Because single-precision variables can use exponential notation (that is, scientific notation), they can hold large values. Values for positive single-precision numbers range from 1.401298E–45 through 3.402823E+38. Values for negative single-precision numbers range from –3.402823E+38 through –1.401298E–45.

An example of exponential notation is the number 4.107E+4. This number is equivalent to $4.107 * 10^4$ and to 41,070. Note that, in keeping with the mathematical definition of scientific notation, when the exponent is negative, the overall value of the expression is fractional—not negative—as in the following example:

$$4.107E\text{-}4 = 4.107 \times 10^{-4} = 0.0004107$$

Errors

If you assign to a single-precision variable a value outside the range of the single-precision type, QuickBASIC returns an "Overflow" error message.

Tips

Rather than declaring a variable using the clause AS SINGLE, you can add the type-declaration character ! to the end of the name. Remember, however, that the exclamation mark (!) becomes part of the name and that you must include it every time you use the variable.

You can use a DEFSNG statement to declare all variables whose names begin with certain letters as single precision. (See the DEF*type* entry for details.)

Remember that the default variable type in QuickBASIC is single precision. You can change the default by adding DEF*type* statements to your program.

STRING

See also: COMMON, DECLARE, DEF FN, DEF*type*, DIM, FIELD, FUNCTION, REDIM, SHARED, STATIC, STR$, SUB, TYPE...END TYPE

QB2	■ QB4.5	PowerBASIC
QB3	ANSI	GW-BASIC
■ QB4	■ BASIC7	MacQB

Purpose

The STRING keyword specifies in an AS clause the type of a variable or function as string. A variable of the type string contains a series of characters. Use the STRING keyword when you need to use character strings for operations such as reading a user's name.

Syntax

var AS STRING

var is the name of a variable; the exact syntax depends on the statement in which you use the variable.

Usage

```
DIM name AS INTEGER
```

Defines name as a string variable.

```
DECLARE FUNCTION InKey$ (key AS STRING)
```

Declares a function that takes a string argument and returns a string value.

Description

The STRING keyword is used in the AS clause of many QuickBASIC declaration statements. Table 1-7 in the DOUBLE entry lists the statements that use the AS clause. (See the entries of the statements in the table for details.)

Variables declared as STRING can hold any of the 128 characters in the ASCII character set or the 128 characters in the IBM extended character set. A string can contain up to 32,767 characters.

Errors

If you assign to a string variable a string with more than 32,767 characters, QuickBASIC returns an "Out of string space" error message.

If you attempt to assign a numeric value to a string variable, QuickBASIC displays a "Type mismatch" error message.

Tips

Rather than declaring a variable using the clause AS STRING, you can add the type-declaration character $ to the end of the variable name. Remember, however, that the dollar sign ($) becomes part of the name and that you must include it every time you use the variable.

You can use a DEFSTR statement to declare that all variables whose names begin with certain letters are strings. (See the DEF*type* entry for details.)

SWAP

See also: TYPE...END TYPE

■ QB2	■ QB4.5	■ PowerBASIC
■ QB3	ANSI	■ GW-BASIC
■ QB4	■ BASIC7	■ MacQB

Purpose

The SWAP statement exchanges the values of two variables, array elements, record variables defined by a TYPE...END TYPE statement, or record-variable elements. Use the SWAP statement to swap values between variables quickly, such as during a sort.

Syntax

SWAP *var1*, *var2*

var1 and *var2* are variables that contain the values the SWAP statement exchanges.

Usage

```
SWAP currentTotal, subTotal
```

Exchanges the values of *currentTotal* and *subTotal*.

Description

QuickBASIC's SWAP statement combines a three-step operation into one step. For example,

```
SWAP currentTotal, subTotal
```

is equivalent to the following statements:

```
temp = subTotal
subTotal = currentTotal
currentTotal = temp
```

Note that the latter operation requires the use of a temporary variable.

The two variables can be simple variables, array elements, record variables defined by a TYPE...END TYPE statement or record-variable elements, but they must be of the same type. If they are not, QuickBASIC returns a "Type mismatch" error message.

Warnings

QuickBASIC 4.5 contains a bug that causes your computer to lock up if you attempt to use the SWAP statement to swap two fixed-length strings that are elements of record variables defined by a TYPE...END TYPE statement. Instead, you must manually exchange the two strings.

Example

The following example uses the SWAP statement to perform a "bubble sort" on a 10-element integer array. A bubble sort is so named because values rise to their proper positions just as bubbles float to a surface. Although a bubble sort is one of the easiest sort algorithms to program, it is a bit slow. (Run the QuickBASIC SORTDEMO program to see how various sort programs execute.)

```
CLS

DEFINT A-Z

CONST FALSE = 0, TRUE = NOT FALSE          ' define TRUE and FALSE

DIM array(1 TO 10) AS INTEGER              ' declare a 10-element array

PRINT "Enter 10 integer values, pressing Enter after each value."
PRINT

FOR i = 1 TO 10
    INPUT array(i)        ' assign integers to the elements of array
NEXT
PRINT

' perform a bubble sort
DO
    switch = FALSE
    FOR i = 1 TO 9
        'check whether two adjacent numbers are out of order
        IF array(i) > array(i + 1) THEN
            SWAP array(i), array(i + 1)     ' if out of order, swap
            switch = TRUE
        END IF
    NEXT
LOOP WHILE switch

PRINT : PRINT "Here they are, sorted:": PRINT

FOR i = 1 TO 10
    PRINT array(i);
NEXT
```

TYPE...END TYPE

See also: COMMON, DECLARE, DEF FN, DIM, FUNCTION, REDIM, SHARED, STATIC, SUB, SWAP

QB2	■ QB4.5	PowerBASIC
QB3	ANSI	GW-BASIC
■ QB4	■ BASIC7	MacQB

Purpose

QuickBASIC's TYPE...END TYPE statement lets you create a data type (sometimes referred to as a record type) that is a structure consisting of one or more variables. You can use TYPE...END TYPE statements to simplify data management. For example, you could create a variable named *inventory* that holds several different variables relating to inventory data.

Syntax

TYPE *Structure*
    element AS *type*
    ⋮
END TYPE

Structure is the name of the record.

element is the name of a variable that is of type *type*.

Usage

```
TYPE Patients
    first AS STRING * 15
    last AS STRING * 20
    birthdate AS STRING * 6
END TYPE
```

Creates a user-defined type named *Patients*.

```
TYPE Family
    address AS STRING * 30
    patient1 AS Patients
    patient2 AS Patients
    patient3 AS Patients
END TYPE
```

Creates a user-defined type named *Family* that contains elements that are of the user-defined type named *Patients*.

Description

Almost all modern computer languages let you create new data types; usually, you create a *record type* that enables a single variable to hold several variables at once. For example, in developing a program for doctors to handle their insurance billing, you probably would want a single variable to contain the patient's name, address, social security number, medicare number, and so on. In Pascal, you create a type that can contain these variables by using the keyword RECORD; in C, by using the keyword *struct.* In QuickBASIC you use the TYPE...END TYPE statement.

The first thing you must do when you define a type with the TYPE...END TYPE statement is give the type a name. This is the name you must refer to when you later define variables to be of this new type. The type name must be a legal QuickBASIC identifier and must not be used by any other variable.

Then you define each element of the record type. The element name *can* be the same as another variable, type, element, function, or subprogram name, but it cannot be the name of another element in the same TYPE...END TYPE statement; also, it cannot be the name of an array or contain periods.

You must then assign each element a type. This can be the keyword DOUBLE, INTEGER, LONG, or SINGLE, a fixed-length string (STRING*x) type, or the name of another record type, but it cannot be a standard, variable-length string.

You can define a particular type only once in a module, and you cannot use TYPE...END TYPE statements in subprograms or program-defined functions. Therefore, the best place to put a TYPE...END TYPE statement is at the beginning of a module.

Defining a record type does not create any variables; you must create variables of the record type by using the COMMON, DIM, REDIM, SHARED, or STATIC statements. You can also use the AS clause in a DECLARE SUB, DECLARE FUNCTION, DEF FN, FUNCTION, or SUB statement to indicate that a variable you are passing is of a certain record type.

Figure 1-3 on the following page shows an example of a TYPE...END TYPE statement and a record-variable declaration.

You must use a special syntax to access an element in a record variable: Specify the record-variable name followed by a period (.) and then the element name. For example, in the record variable *birth,* which is declared in Figure 1-3, you would use the following statement to set the value of the element *month* to 9:

```
birth.month = 9
```

Use the same syntax to use an element of a record variable in the condition of an IF statement; for example,

```
IF 1990 - birth.year >= 18 THEN
    PRINT "OK to vote"
END IF
```

```
TYPE Dates ——————————— Dates is the type name.
    month AS INTEGER ┐
    day AS INTEGER   ├── month, day, and year are element names.
    year AS INTEGER  ┘   INTEGER is the type of the elements.
END TYPE

DIM birth AS Dates ——— birth is a record variable of type Dates.
```

Figure 1-3.
An example TYPE...END TYPE statement and record-variable declaration.

Comments

Although you cannot use arrays in a TYPE...END TYPE statement, you can create arrays that contain records defined by a TYPE...END TYPE statement. (See the program in the "Example" section below.)

Errors

If you create an element name that contains periods, QuickBASIC returns an "Identifier cannot include period" error message.

Warnings

QuickBASIC 4.5 contains a bug that causes your computer to lock up if you attempt to use the SWAP statement to swap two fixed-length strings that are elements of record variables defined by a TYPE...END TYPE statement. Instead of using the SWAP statement, you must manually exchange the two strings.

Example

The following example uses a TYPE...END TYPE statement to create a record type that holds information about the planets in a single variable. You can use the program to write information to and then to read information from the data file SOL.DAT.

```
TYPE Planets                        ' type to hold planet information
    nam AS STRING * 20              ' planet name
    diameter AS LONG                ' planet diameter
    perihelion AS DOUBLE            ' orbital point closest to sun
    aphelion AS DOUBLE              ' orbital point farthest from sun
    highTemp AS SINGLE              ' highest surface temperature
    lowTemp AS SINGLE               ' lowest surface temperature
    yearDiscovered AS INTEGER       ' year planet was discovered
END TYPE

DIM planet AS Planets               ' define the variable planet

CLS
OPEN "SOL.DAT" FOR RANDOM AS #1 LEN = 50     ' open the data file
```

(continued)

continued

```
DO
   PRINT : PRINT : PRINT
   INPUT "Information on which planet [1-9]"; planetNum%  ' get number

   ' if out of range or user presses Enter, then exit the loop
   IF planetNum% < 1 OR planetNum% > 9 THEN EXIT DO

   GET #1, planetNum%, planet                ' get data from file

   PRINT : PRINT "Information on planet "; planet.nam     ' print header
   PRINT STRING$(79, 45): PRINT

   ' if the record is empty, then get all the information from the user
   IF planet.nam = STRING$(20, 0) THEN
      INPUT "Name"; planet.nam
      INPUT "Diameter (km)"; planet.diameter
      INPUT "Perihelion (km)"; planet.perihelion
      INPUT "Aphelion (km)"; planet.aphelion
      INPUT "High temperature (Celsius)"; planet.highTemp
      INPUT "Low temperature (Celsius)"; planet.lowTemp
      INPUT "Discovered in"; planet.yearDiscovered

      ' write the information to the file
      PUT #1, planetNum%, planet

      PRINT : PRINT "Information saved": PRINT : PRINT

   ' if record is not empty, then display it on the screen
   ELSE
      PRINT "Diameter is"; planet.diameter; "kilometers"
      PRINT "Perihelion is"; planet.perihelion; "kilometers"
      PRINT "Aphelion is"; planet.aphelion; "kilometers"
      PRINT "High temperature is"; planet.highTemp; "xC"
      PRINT "Low temperature is"; planet.lowTemp; "xC"
      PRINT "Discovered in"; planet.yearDiscovered
   END IF
LOOP            ' go back to beginning of loop

CLOSE
```

CHAPTER 2

Flow Control

Introduction

Few programs execute in one continuous sequence from the first statement to the last. Typically, a program performs different tasks; the tasks it performs depend upon the data it generates or the instructions it receives from the user. A well-structured program contains a separate section of code for each task, and execution branches to the appropriate section whenever the associated task must be performed.

Often a program must also perform a single task repeatedly. One program might execute a global search-and-replace on a 1000-page novel, changing every occurrence of the heroine's name from "Cindy" to "Sue." Another might print all the payroll checks for a company's employees. These types of operations, in fact, make computers particularly useful in business: Computers execute the same sequence of statements again and again without complaint, performing those boring and repetitive jobs that humans dislike.

This chapter discusses the ways that QuickBASIC lets you control the sequence in which statements are executed. Table 2-1 lists these flow-control statements in alphabetic order.

Statement	**Description**
DO...LOOP	Repeats a block of statements while or until a given logical condition is true.
EXIT	Transfers control from a subprogram, user-defined function, or loop structure before the normal exit conditions are met.
FOR...NEXT	Repeats one or more program statements a specified number of times.
GOTO	Executes an unconditional branch to a specified program line.
ON...GOSUB	Executes a subroutine at one of several specified lines. On completion of the subroutine, control returns to the statement following the ON...GOSUB statement.
ON...GOTO	Branches to one of several specified lines.
WHILE...WEND	Repeats program statements while a given logical condition is true.

Table 2-1.
Flow-control statements in alphabetic order.

Branching

If a program consists of several sections, each of which performs a particular task, the program must be able to transfer control from one section to another. One way to transfer control in QuickBASIC is to use a statement that performs branching. Branching unconditionally always transfers control; branching conditionally transfers control only if a certain condition is met.

Unconditional Branching

The simplest way to direct the flow of execution to another part of the program is to use an unconditional branch. You can use the GOTO statement for this; for example,

```
GOTO Finish
```

transfers control to the line that contains the label *Finish*. You can also use GOTO with a line number (if your program uses line numbers). The target line must be in the same module as the GOTO statement; you cannot use GOTO to branch to another program module or to branch into a subprogram or user-defined function in the same module. You can, however, use GOTO inside functions and subprograms, provided the target line is in the same function or subprogram.

GOTO differs from a function call: After the branch is made, the program executes statements following the target line either until it encounters another branching statement or until the program ends. Program execution doesn't return to the line following the GOTO statement, as it does with GOSUB. (See Chapter 4, "Procedures.") Note the one exception—when you use GOTO with the ON ERROR statement (defined in Chapter 9, "Trapping and Errors") to define an error-handling routine. In this case, when a subsequent RESUME statement is encountered, control returns to the section of the program from which the branch was made.

Although the use of GOTO runs counter to current programming practice, the statement itself, unlike GOSUB, has not been tagged for removal from the ANSI standard for BASIC. The main criticism of GOTO is that unrestricted branching obscures a program's logic; this makes it difficult to understand and debug the program. Moreover, because QuickBASIC now supports structured-programming control statements, such as DO...LOOP, WHILE...WEND, and SELECT CASE, and because it lets you call user-defined subprograms and functions, you rarely need to use GOTO. Occasionally, however, situations arise in which using an unconditional branch is simply the most efficient way of directing program flow. In these circumstances, there is nothing wrong with using a GOTO statement.

Conditional Branching

Although by itself GOTO is unconditional, it can be used as part of a conditional statement. For example, the following statements cause the program to branch to line 1000 only when the string variable *response$* contains a "Y":

```
240 INPUT "Report to printer"; response$
250 IF UCASE$(LEFT$(response$, 1)) = "Y" THEN 1000
```

Note that the keyword GOTO is implicit when you use an IF...THEN statement. However, if the target statement has a label rather than a line number, you must include the GOTO keyword, as shown in the following statement:

```
250 IF UCASE$(LEFT$(response$, 1)) = "Y" THEN GOTO Print
```

Another version of the GOTO statement is also conditional. The ON...GOTO statement can direct the program to branch to one of several lines; the value of a variable or an expression determines which line. In the example

```
900 ON selection% GOTO 1000, 2000, 3000, Start, Finish
```

control branches to one of five line numbers or labels in response to the value of the integer variable *selection%*. If *selection%* contains the value 1, the program branches to line 1000; if *selection%* contains the value 2, the program branches to line 2000; and so on. If *selection%* is 0 or, in this case, is greater than 5, no branching occurs, and control continues with the statement following line 900. Always be sure the variable *selection%* is either 0 or greater. If the variable is negative, QuickBASIC returns an "Illegal function call" error message.

The list of target lines in an ON...GOTO statement is called a "jump table." Notice that you can use both line numbers and labels as destinations for a jump.

You can use ON...GOTO to branch to as many as 60 different line numbers or labels. You will find it is difficult to insert 60 different labels into a single QuickBASIC line. However, because control falls through to the next statement in the program if the value of the variable is greater than the number of entries in the jump table, you can extend the jump table by using several successive ON...GOTO statements, as in the following example:

```
TakeAim:
    target% = INT(RND * 13) + 1

100 ON target% GOTO One, Two, 300, Four, Five
110 ON target% - 5  GOTO Six, Seven, 800, Nine, Ten
120 ON target% - 10 GOTO 1100, Twelve, Thirteen
```

If you need to make many branches, this method is much cleaner than using a single line that extends off the screen. However, always be sure the initial value of *target%* does not evaluate to 0; if it does, QuickBASIC generates an "Illegal function call" error message when control falls through to the second ON...GOTO statement.

Subroutines

QuickBASIC also lets you use a jump table to conditionally execute subroutines. The ON...GOSUB statement is similar to the ON...GOTO statement except that control returns to the statement following the ON...GOSUB statement after the subroutine finishes. Do not, therefore, try to extend the jump table to multiple lines by writing successive ON...GOSUB statements with the same argument. The following example demonstrates the problems that writing successive ON...GOSUB statements creates:

```
150 ON dispatch% GOSUB 10000, 11000, 12000, 13000, 14000
160 ON dispatch% - 5 GOSUB 15000, 16000, 17000, 18000, 19000
```

If, for example, *dispatch%* has a value of 3, the ON...GOSUB statement in line 150 sends control to the subroutine at line 12000. When control returns from this subroutine, however, the program executes the ON...GOSUB statement in line 160, which subtracts 5 from the original value of *dispatch%* before applying the value to the next jump table. Because 3 minus 5 equals –2, the statement generates an "Illegal function call" error message, and QuickBASIC interrupts the program.

The ON...GOTO and ON...GOSUB statements are provided only to preserve compatibility with previous versions of BASIC. In QuickBASIC, the preferred method of conditionally executing blocks of statements is to use the SELECT CASE statement. (See Chapter 3, "Decisions and Operators.") The SELECT CASE statement is more flexible than and has none of the limitations of ON...GOTO and ON...GOSUB.

Loops

A loop is a sequence of statements that a program executes more than once in succession. QuickBASIC provides two kinds of loops. The first, which is controlled by the FOR...NEXT statement, is a loop that repeats a fixed number of times. (The program specifies the number of repetitions when the loop begins.)

In the second type of loop, the actual number of iterations is not specified in advance—it is determined by the result of a logical test that is made during every pass through the loop. Execution continues until a certain condition is met. In early versions of BASIC you can create this kind of loop only with a WHILE...WEND statement. (QuickBASIC retains this statement to maintain compatibility with the earlier versions.) However, QuickBASIC now provides the more powerful DO...LOOP statement.

The FOR...NEXT Statement

In a FOR...NEXT statement, QuickBASIC repeats the statements between the keywords FOR and NEXT a specified number of times. You determine the number of repetitions by assigning a range of values to the variable that is the loop counter; for example,

```
FOR count% = 1 TO 10
    PRINT count%;
NEXT count%
```

sets the initial value of the counter to 1 and then executes the loop. The loop increments the counter on each iteration until the counter reaches its maximum value, which in this case is 10. Because the single statement in the body of the loop prints only the value of the counter, the output of the program is a series of numbers, 1 through 10.

QuickBASIC lets you use the STEP clause to specify the value of the increment of the FOR...NEXT loop. The default increment is 1. For example, the following loop counts to 10 by twos:

```
FOR count% = 1 TO 10 STEP 2
    PRINT count%;
NEXT count%
```

This loop generates the output

```
1 3 5 7 9
```

You can also use the STEP clause to decrement the loop counter. The following program counts backward by threes:

```
FOR count% = 10 TO 1 STEP -3
    PRINT count%;
NEXT count%
```

This loop generates the output

```
10 7 4 1
```

You can use as many statement lines as you want in the body of the loop; the entire sequence repeats until the value of the counter is outside the specified range. When this happens, the program continues with the statement that follows the NEXT keyword.

The WHILE...WEND Statement

You can use the WHILE...WEND statement for those situations in which your program must execute a series of statements an indeterminate number of times. When QuickBASIC first encounters the WHILE keyword, it tests the value of the associated logical expression or variable, and if the value of the expression or variable is true (nonzero), it executes the subsequent statements. When the program finds the matching WEND keyword, it returns control to the top of the loop and tests the value of the associated expression or variable again. If the value is still true, the process is repeated; if it is false (zero), program execution continues with the statement that follows the WEND keyword. (See Chapter 3, "Decisions and Operators," for an explanation of what makes an expression logically true or false.) The following program, for example,

```
count% = 1
WHILE count% <= 10
    PRINT count%;
    count% = count% + 1
WEND
```

generates the output

```
1 2 3 4 5 6 7 8 9 10
```

This kind of loop is called an "entry-condition" loop because the test is made at the top of the loop. If the test expression is already false when the WHILE keyword is first encountered (for example, if *count%* is initially 11), the program bypasses the loop completely and no statements within it are executed.

Because all QuickBASIC numeric variables and functions return values that can be interpreted logically as well as numerically, the WHILE...WEND statement has many applications. The following example opens a sequential access file of unknown length and uses a WHILE...WEND statement to read from the file until the end of the file is encountered:

```
OPEN file$ FOR INPUT AS #1
WHILE NOT EOF(1)
    LINE INPUT #1, record$
    PRINT record$
WEND
```

The DO...LOOP Statement

Despite its usefulness, the WHILE...WEND statement is not included in the ANSI standard for BASIC. It has been replaced by the DO...LOOP statement, a statement that is more powerful and flexible than WHILE...WEND. You can easily rewrite the previous example by using a DO...LOOP statement:

```
OPEN file$ FOR INPUT AS #1
DO WHILE NOT EOF(1)
    LINE INPUT #1, record$
    PRINT record$
LOOP
```

This is almost identical to the WHILE...WEND version, including the rudimentary test for the end of the file. In addition to repeating a series of statements while a condition is true, a DO...LOOP statement can also repeat statements only while a condition is false; that is, it loops until the condition is true. The syntax of the DO...LOOP statement, in fact, lets you state this explicitly by using the keyword UNTIL in the DO...LOOP statement, as shown in the following example:

```
OPEN file$ FOR INPUT AS #1
DO UNTIL EOF(1)
    LINE INPUT #1, record$
    PRINT record$
LOOP
```

Both loops in the two previous DO...LOOP examples are, like WHILE...WEND statements, entry-condition loops; this means that if the test fails when the loop is first entered (if the file is empty, for example), the statements inside the loop are never executed. However, a loop created by a DO...LOOP statement can also be an "exit-condition" loop, in which the body of the loop is always executed at least once; for example,

```
DO
    PRINT SPACE$(81 - POS(0))
LOOP WHILE CSRLIN < 23
```

always clears to the end of the current line, even if the cursor is already on or below line 23 of the display. You can also use UNTIL in place of WHILE in an exit-condition loop, as shown in the following example:

```
PRINT "Ready printer, press P to continue"
DO
    ready$ = UCASE$(INPUT$(1))
LOOP UNTIL ready$ = "P"
```

The preceding examples show that the DO...LOOP statement is far more versatile than the WHILE...WEND statement. Because of its versatility, the DO...LOOP statement has become the preferred method of constructing loops that involve logical tests.

Breaking Out of Loops

QuickBASIC lets you exit a loop at a statement within the body of a loop in addition to exiting at its usual exit point, even if the normal exit condition has not been met. An EXIT DO statement interrupts the execution of a DO...LOOP statement from any point between the keywords DO and LOOP and resumes execution at the statement following the keyword LOOP. The EXIT FOR statement performs the same operation in a FOR...NEXT loop.

The following set of statements uses a FOR...NEXT loop to scan for a character that has been set at a random location in a string of blank spaces. If the character is found, the program uses an EXIT FOR statement to exit the loop; this leaves the *i%* counter indicating the location of the target character.

```
RANDOMIZE TIMER

a$ = SPACE$(10000)
x% = INT(RND * 10000) + 1
MID$(a$, x%, 1) = CHR$(INT(RND * 223) + 32)

FOR i% = 1 TO 10000
    IF MID$(a$, i%, 1) <> " " THEN EXIT FOR
NEXT i%
IF i% > 10000 THEN
    PRINT "Not found!"
ELSE
    PRINT i%; MID$(a$, i%, 1)
END IF
```

In earlier versions of BASIC, the only way to exit a FOR...NEXT loop prematurely was to set the counter to a value outside the iteration range. The following example performs the same task the FOR...NEXT statement performed in the previous example:

```
FOR i% = 1 TO 10000
    IF MID$(a$, i%, 1) <> " " THEN i% = 10001
NEXT i%
```

However, now the counter no longer contains the position of the nonblank character, and the test for success or failure in the subsequent line is more difficult to code.

QuickBASIC provides similar EXIT statements for escaping from user-defined functions and subprograms. EXIT DEF, for example, lets a program exit a DEF FN function call before the END DEF statement is executed; EXIT SUB and EXIT FUNCTION do the same thing for subprograms and user-defined functions. (See Chapter 4, "Procedures," for details of subprograms and functions.) No equivalent exit statement exists for the WHILE...WEND statement.

DO...LOOP

See also: EXIT, FOR...NEXT, WHILE...WEND

QB2	■ QB4.5	■ PowerBASIC
QB3	■ ANSI	GW-BASIC
■ QB4	■ BASIC7	MacQB

Purpose

The DO...LOOP statement repeats the execution of a block of statements while (or until) an exit or entry condition is met. Use DO...LOOP to count up or down, iterate a value, or repeat a procedure while a given condition is true or until it becomes false.

Syntax

The DO...LOOP statement has two possible syntaxes; the syntax depends on whether you test for the exit condition at the beginning or at the end of the loop.

To test at the beginning of a loop, use the following syntax:

DO [{WHILE|UNTIL} *expr*]
[*statements*]
LOOP

If the exit condition is already met on entry into the structure, the loop is not executed.

To test at the end of a loop, use the following syntax:

DO
[*statements*]
LOOP [{WHILE|UNTIL} *expr*]

The body of the loop is always executed at least once, whether or not the exit condition is met on entry into the structure.

statements are the one or more QuickBASIC program statements that are repeated. Notice that they are optional—empty loops, which do nothing until an external event (such as a keypress) occurs, are permissible.

expr is any logical expression; that is, it must evaluate to either true (a nonzero value) or false (a value of zero).

If you use the WHILE keyword, the loop repeats while the expression remains true. If you use UNTIL, the loop repeats while the expression remains false (that is, until the expression is true).

Usage

```
DO
LOOP WHILE INKEY$ = ""
```

Suspends program execution until a key is pressed.

```
DO UNTIL PLAY(1) = 0
LOOP
```

Suspends program execution until the background music buffer is empty.

```
DO
    x% = INT(RND * 80) + 1
    y% = INT(RND * 24) + 1
    LOCATE y%, x%
    PRINT "*";
LOOP UNTIL INKEY$ = CHR$(27)
```

Prints asterisks at random locations on the screen until the user presses Esc.

Description

The DO...LOOP statement lets you execute a loop either while a given condition is true or until the condition is true. The DO...LOOP statement also lets you test for the exit condition at either the beginning or the end of the loop. If you place the test condition at the beginning of the loop and if the exit condition is already met, the loop is not executed. If, however, you place the test condition at the end of the loop, the body of the loop is always executed at least once, even if the exit condition is already met.

Be sure that any loop you create will eventually end. If you create a loop whose exit condition is never met, the program will run indefinitely.

You can use the EXIT DO statement in the middle of a loop to exit the loop before the exit condition is met. EXIT DO transfers control to the first statement after the keyword LOOP.

Although QuickBASIC returns –1 to represent a true expression, in practice any nonzero value evaluates as true; therefore, you can use any numeric variable or function as the expression in a DO...LOOP statement.

Errors

Every DO statement in a program must have a corresponding LOOP statement, just as every LOOP must have a preceding DO. If the program executes a LOOP statement without having encountered a previous DO, QuickBASIC returns a "LOOP without DO" error message. Conversely, an unmatched DO statement causes QuickBASIC to display a "DO without LOOP" error message.

Tips

Although QuickBASIC does not require indention, indenting the lines that are repeated makes them stand out in a program listing and is a useful aid to debugging the program. This practice is particularly important when you nest loops within other loops or structures because it lets you immediately determine the level of a specific instruction.

Warnings

Although the GOTO statement does not produce an immediate error, do not use it to exit the body of a DO...LOOP statement. When QuickBASIC starts the loop, it pushes the address of the instruction that follows the LOOP keyword onto the stack, to be retrieved on exit. (See Chapter 19, "Port and Memory," for details about the stack.) If you repeatedly exit a loop with GOTO, the program stack will grow uncontrollably, eventually producing an "Out of stack space" error message. If you must exit a loop prematurely, use the EXIT DO statement.

Example

The following program uses a DO...LOOP statement to create a game. The program displays a character representing a skier. The skier moves down the screen between two lines of a "track"; if the skier hits either edge of the track, the program ends. The user can avoid ending the program by moving the skier left and right with the left and right arrow keys.

```
CLS : RANDOMIZE TIMER

ySkier% = 21: xSkier% = 55                       ' coordinates for the skier
yTrack% = 24: xTrack% = 51                       ' coordinates for the track
rightArrow$ = CHR$(0) + CHR$(77): leftArrow$ = CHR$(0) + CHR$(75)
track$ = CHR$(176) + "         " + CHR$(176)

DO
    LOCATE 1, 1: PRINT "Score ="; score&         ' print score
    score& = score& + 1

    LOCATE yTrack%, xTrack%: PRINT track$        ' print track
    change% = INT((RND * 3) - 1)
    xTrack% = xTrack% + change%                  ' change position of track

    r$ = INKEY$
    IF r$ = leftArrow$ THEN xSkier% = xSkier% - 1    ' move skier left
    IF r$ = rightArrow$ THEN xSkier% = xSkier% + 1   ' move skier right

    LOCATE ySkier%, xSkier%: PRINT CHR$(2);      ' print skier
LOOP WHILE SCREEN(ySkier% + 1, xSkier%) <> 176   ' exit loop if skier hits track

END
```

EXIT

See also: DEF FN, DO...LOOP, FOR...NEXT, FUNCTION, SUB

✲ QB2	■ QB4.5	✲ PowerBASIC
✲ QB3	■ ANSI	GW-BASIC
■ QB4	■ BASIC7	✲ MacQB

Purpose

EXIT transfers control out of a loop or procedure either before the exit condition is met or before the end of the procedure is reached. Use this statement if you want your program to respond to a separate event that might occur before the loop finishes executing.

Syntax

EXIT {DEF¦DO¦FOR¦FUNCTION¦SUB}

Use EXIT with one of the five QuickBASIC keywords in the preceding syntax line. You must include one of the keywords in braces; the keyword you must include depends on the type of loop or procedure in which you use the EXIT statement.

Usage

```
DO WHILE x% < 100
    PRINT x%, x% ^ 2
    IF INKEY$ = "Q" THEN EXIT DO
    x% = x% + 1
LOOP
```

Uses EXIT DO to exit a loop if the user types the letter Q.

```
SUB AddInventory
    INPUT "Enter part number", partnum%

    IF partnum% > 1000 THEN
        PRINT "Invalid part number"
        EXIT SUB
    END IF

    INPUT "Enter part description", desc$
END SUB
```

Uses EXIT SUB to exit a subprogram if the user enters an invalid part number.

Description

The EXIT DO and EXIT FOR statements can be used to exit a loop defined by either a DO...LOOP statement or a FOR...NEXT statement. When a program executes either of these statements, control transfers to the first statement after the loop. (If a program uses EXIT FOR in a FOR...NEXT loop, the loop's counter variable retains the value set on entry into the most recent iteration of the loop.)

If a program contains nested FOR...NEXT or DO...LOOP statements, EXIT exits only the current loop. Statements in any loop outside of the one in which the EXIT instruction occurs continue to execute until that loop terminates or another EXIT statement is encountered.

The EXIT DEF, EXIT FUNCTION, and EXIT SUB statements can be used to exit a procedure defined by a DEF FN, a FUNCTION, or a SUB statement. When a program uses any of these statements, control returns to the statement following the call to the procedure. If a program uses EXIT DEF or EXIT FUNCTION before an assignment has been made to the function, the function returns an indeterminate value.

Compatibility

QuickBASIC 2.0 and QuickBASIC3.0

QuickBASIC versions 2.0 and 3.0 include only the EXIT SUB and EXIT DEF statements. You can use EXIT SUB to exit subprograms and EXIT DEF to exit functions defined with the DEF FN statement.

PowerBASIC

PowerBASIC supports all the EXIT variations in QuickBASIC. In PowerBASIC, however, EXIT DO is called EXIT LOOP. EXIT LOOP can also be used to exit a WHILE...WEND loop. In addition, PowerBASIC provides EXIT IF to exit multi-line IF statements and EXIT SELECT to exit SELECT CASE blocks.

QuickBASIC for the Macintosh

QuickBASIC for the Macintosh provides only EXIT SUB, which can be used to exit user-defined subprograms.

Example

The following QuickBASIC program calls a function that checks a string the user entered to see whether the string is a valid filename. The function tests the characters in the string and the length of the string. The string can be a filename with or without an extension. If any test fails, the function uses the EXIT FUNCTION statement to return prematurely; this sets a validation flag to false.

```
DECLARE FUNCTION ValidName% (fileSpec$)

CONST FALSE = 0, TRUE = NOT FALSE

CLS
PRINT "Enter a filename for testing: ";
LINE INPUT f$
PRINT : PRINT "That is a";

IF ValidName%(f$) THEN
    PRINT " legal filename."
ELSE
    PRINT "n illegal filename."
END IF
END

' test filename for invalid characters and length
FUNCTION ValidName% (fileSpec$) STATIC
    length% = LEN(fileSpec$)
    invalid$ = ""
    ValidName% = FALSE
```

(continued)

continued

```
    FOR i% = 0 TO 32          ' create string of all invalid characters
        invalid$ = invalid$ + CHR$(i%)
    NEXT
    invalid$ = invalid$ + "/\[]:|<>+=;," + CHR$(34)

    FOR i% = 1 TO length%     ' check for any invalid characters
        IF INSTR(invalid$, MID$(fileSpec$, i%, 1)) > 0 THEN
            EXIT FOR
        END IF
    NEXT i%

    IF i% < length% + 1 THEN EXIT FUNCTION  ' string has an invalid character
    ValidName% = TRUE                        ' string has no invalid characters

    dot% = INSTR(fileSpec$, ".")             ' check for an extension
    IF dot% = 0 THEN
        IF length% > 8 THEN                  ' check length of string
            ValidName% = FALSE
        END IF
    ELSEIF dot% > 9 OR dot% < (length% - 3) THEN  ' check length of extension
       ValidName% = FALSE
    END IF
END FUNCTION
```

FOR...NEXT

See also: DO...LOOP, EXIT, WHILE...WEND

■ QB2	■ QB4.5	■ PowerBASIC
■ QB3	■ ANSI	✲ GW-BASIC
■ QB4	■ BASIC7	■ MacQB

Purpose

A FOR...NEXT loop executes a sequence of program statements a specified number of times. Use the FOR...NEXT statement to specify the number of times you want the statements to be repeated—for example, to print the numbers 1 through 100.

Syntax

FOR *cntr* = *initval* TO *finalval* [STEP *incr*]
[*statements*]
NEXT [*cntr* [,*cntr*...]]

cntr is a numeric variable that counts the number of times the loop executes. It can be of type integer, long integer, single-precision, or double-precision and can be an element of an array. However, it must not be a record variable that has been assigned a type defined by a TYPE...END TYPE statement.

inital is the value assigned to the counter when the loop begins; *inital* can be a constant, a variable, or an expression.

finalval is the value for which the loop tests *cntr* at the beginning of each pass. If the counter value is greater than *finalval*, execution of the loop ceases and control transfers to the statement following the keyword NEXT. *finalval* can be a constant, a variable, or an expression.

incr is the amount by which the counter variable is increased (or decreased, if *incr* is a negative value) after every iteration of the loop. It can be a constant, a variable, or an expression; if you omit it, QuickBASIC uses a value of 1.

When FOR...NEXT loops are nested within each other, you can combine the NEXT statement of each loop into a single NEXT statement by including after the keyword NEXT the name of every counter.

Usage

```
FOR i% = 1 TO 10000
NEXT
```

This "do-nothing" loop simply pauses execution while the program counts to 10,000. (The amount of time this operation takes to execute depends on the speed of your computer.)

```
FOR third! = 1 TO 10 STEP 1 / 3
    PRINT third!;
NEXT third!
```

This loop counts from 1 to 10 in steps of ⅓. The loop terminates after 28 iterations.

```
FOR counter% = 20 TO 1 STEP -1
    PRINT TAB(5); counter%
NEXT counter%
PRINT TAB(5); counter%
PRINT "BLAST OFF!"
```

This loop executes 20 times; the STEP instruction decrements the value of the counter variable by 1 at each iteration. (Note that when the loop terminates, the counter contains the value 0, not 1.)

Description

The FOR...NEXT statement repeats execution of a block of statements a specified number of times. On entry into a FOR...NEXT loop, QuickBASIC first stores the value of the specified final value and then sets the counter variable to the value of the specified initial value. QuickBASIC also checks for a STEP instruction to see whether the loop counter is to be incremented or decremented on successive iterations of the loop. If no STEP instruction is given, QuickBASIC increments the counter variable by 1.

If, at this preliminary stage, the counter value is greater than the final value and the increment is positive, QuickBASIC does not execute the loop. Instead, control transfers to the statement following the NEXT statement. Similarly, if the increment is negative and the initial counter value is less than the final value, the loop is not executed.

If the counter value is within the range specified by the initial and final values, QuickBASIC executes the program lines following the FOR statement until it encounters the NEXT statement. Then it adjusts the counter variable by the value given in the STEP instruction. If the increment is positive, the value is added to the counter variable; if it is negative, the value is subtracted from the counter variable.

Note that the actual test is always made after the FOR keyword, at the beginning of the loop. The NEXT statement merely adjusts the counter value before it returns control to the FOR statement. This means that on completion of the loop, the counter value is always greater (if the increment is positive) or less (if the increment is negative) than the specified final value.

If, when control returns to the original FOR statement, the value of the counter is greater than the final value, control transfers to the statement that follows the loop. Otherwise, the loop executes again.

You can nest FOR...NEXT loops within each other. For example, if you nest a loop that counts from 1 to 10 in a loop that counts from 1 to 5, the program counts from 1 to 10 five times. By including in one NEXT statement the name of the counter of each loop in a nested FOR...NEXT loop, you can combine the NEXT statements of the loops. The following two segments of code, for example, are syntactically equivalent:

```
FOR row% = 1 TO 24
    LOCATE row%, 1
    FOR stripe% = 1 TO 20
        FOR colors% = 9 TO 12
            COLOR colors%
            PRINT "*";
        NEXT colors%
    NEXT stripe%
NEXT row%
```

```
FOR row% = 1 TO 24
    LOCATE row%, 1
    FOR stripe% = 1 TO 20
        FOR colors% = 9 TO 12
            COLOR colors%
            PRINT "*";
NEXT colors%, stripe%, row%
```

Errors

Each FOR statement must have a corresponding NEXT statement just as every NEXT statement must have a preceding FOR. If you omit the NEXT statement, QuickBASIC returns a "FOR without NEXT" error message. If QuickBASIC encounters a NEXT statement without a previous FOR, it displays a "NEXT without FOR" error message. The "NEXT without FOR" error also occurs if you inadvertently cross loops. The following code fragment shows a typical mistake that produces such an error:

```
FOR i% = 1 TO 20
    PRINT i%
    FOR j% = 1 TO 10
        PRINT j%;
    NEXT i% ─┐
    PRINT    ├──────── These two lines have been transposed.
NEXT j% ─────┘
```

Tips

Note that QuickBASIC sets the final value for the loop before it initializes the counter to the starting value. The following program fragment, for example, prints the numbers 1 through 10 (not 1 through 6, as you might suppose):

```
i% = 5
FOR i% = 1 TO i% + 5
    PRINT i%;
NEXT
```

You must close nested loops in the reverse order from that in which you opened them. You cannot close a FOR...NEXT loop until you've closed all other loops nested inside it.

If you do not specifically name a variable in the NEXT statement, QuickBASIC uses the counter specified by the most recent FOR statement.

Compatibility

GW-BASIC and BASICA

GW-BASIC and BASICA permit only integer and single-precision values to be used for the counter of FOR...NEXT loops. QuickBASIC lets you use long-integer and double-precision values as well. You should, however, use integers whenever possible because they require less storage space and speed program execution.

Example

FOR...NEXT loops are ideal for tasks that repeat a series of actions an exact number of times. The following program prints large text for title screens and banners. The displayed text is encoded into DATA statements that are read into the program by a series of FOR...NEXT loops. Figure 2-1 shows the output of the program.

```
CONST FALSE = 0, TRUE = NOT FALSE
DEF SEG = &H40: IF PEEK(&H49) = 7 THEN mono% = TRUE  ' check for monochrome

CLS : DEF SEG : RESTORE Text

READ row%, column%, hue%, numColumns%
IF NOT mono% THEN COLOR hue%

' print each letter of the banner one column at a time
FOR newColumn% = 1 TO numColumns%
    READ item$
    IF item$ = "F" THEN item$ = "12345678"          ' if "F," fill the column
    FOR i% = 1 TO LEN(item$)
        IF MID$(item$, i%, 1) = "*" THEN EXIT FOR   ' if "*," start next letter
        space% = VAL(MID$(item$, i%, 1))            ' index of the space to fill
        LOCATE row% + space%, column%
        PRINT CHR$(219);                            ' fill the space
    NEXT i%
    IF i% = 1 THEN                  ' change color for the next letter
        hue% = hue% + 1
        IF hue% = 7 THEN hue% = 9
        IF hue% > 14 THEN hue% = 1
        IF NOT mono% THEN COLOR hue%
    END IF
    column% = column% + 1
NEXT newColumn%
COLOR 14, 0: LOCATE 15, 32: PRINT "B I B L E"
END

' Data Division
Text:
DATA    3, 6, 9, 67
DATA    F, F, 1238, 168, 1678, 18, F, F, *                    ' "Q"
DATA    45678, 45678, 8, 8, 45678, 45678, *                   ' "u"
DATA    245678, 245678, *                                     ' "i"
DATA    45678, 45678, 48, 48, 4578, 4578, *                   ' "c"
DATA    F, F, 5, 345, 35678, 35678, 3, *                      ' "k"
DATA    F, F, 1248, 148, 148, 148, F, 1235678, *              ' "B"
DATA    F, F, 124, 14, 14, F, F, *                            ' "A"
DATA    123478, 123478, 148, 148, 1245678, 1245678, *         ' "S"
DATA    F, F, *                                               ' "I"
DATA    F, F, 18, 18, 1278, 1278                              ' "C"
```

Figure 2-1.
Output of the FOR...NEXT example program.

GOTO

■ QB2 ■ QB4.5 ■ PowerBASIC
■ QB3 ■ ANSI ■ GW-BASIC
■ QB4 ■ BASIC7 ■ MacQB

Purpose

The GOTO statement can be used to branch to a particular section of code. In QuickBASIC, you rarely need to use GOTO; it is retained to provide compatibility with programs written in earlier versions of BASIC.

Syntax

GOTO {*line* | *label*}

line or *label* is the destination of the GOTO statement. The destination must be a line in the current module. Execution branches to the statement at *line* or *label* and continues until either another GOTO statement is encountered or until the program ends.

Usage

```
GOTO 1000
```

Branches to the statement at line 1000 in the current module.

```
GOTO PrintOut
```

Branches to the line labeled *PrintOut* and continues execution from there.

Description

GOTO forces QuickBASIC to branch to the line number or label specified; control always transfers to the destination line. If the destination line contains a remark or a DATA statement, control passes to the next executable statement.

The destination line must be in the same module as the GOTO statement that names it; you cannot use a GOTO statement to transfer to a statement in a separately compiled module. Nor can you use GOTO to branch into or out of a subprogram or user-defined function stored in the same module; you can, however, use GOTO to direct control flow within these procedures.

IF...THEN statements (described in Chapter 3, "Decisions and Operators") can include an implied GOTO statement after the THEN clause, as in the following example:

```
IF y% = 50 THEN 1000
```

In this case, execution branches to line 1000 when *y%* equals 50. This implicit GOTO works only with line numbers, however; if the destination line has a label, you must insert the GOTO keyword:

```
IF x% >= 100 THEN GOTO OverFlow
```

Example

QuickBASIC control structures, such as multi-line IF statements and DO loops, have lessened the need for GOTO statements. The following example uses a GOTO statement to check that the user entered a valid name. The subprogram following the example uses structured programming to perform the same task. Structured programming produces compact and efficient code and is much easier to maintain.

```
10  lc$ = "abcdefghijklmnopqrstuvwxyz "
20  uc$ = UCASE$(lc$)
30  nu$ = "0123456789-+/."
40  valid$ = uc$ + lc$          ' a string containing all valid characters
50  buffer$ = ""                ' buffer for name
60  max% = 30                   ' maximum number of characters

70  CLS : LOCATE 10, 1, 1: PRINT "Type your name > ";
```

(continued)

continued

```
80  length% = 0
90  keyStroke$ = INKEY$
100 IF keyStroke$ = "" THEN 90          ' loop until user types a character
110 IF keyStroke$ = CHR$(13) THEN 230   ' exit when user presses Enter

120 IF keyStroke$ <> CHR$(8) THEN 180   ' branch if user does not press Backspace
130 IF length% = 0 THEN 90
140 PRINT CHR$(29); " "; CHR$(29);
150 length% = length% - 1
160 buffer$ = LEFT$(buffer$, length%)
170 GOTO 90

180 IF length% = max% OR INSTR(valid$, keyStroke$) = 0 THEN 90
190 buffer$ = buffer$ + keyStroke$
200 PRINT keyStroke$;
210 length% = length% + 1
220 GOTO 90

230 LOCATE 20, 1: PRINT buffer$
240 END
```

```
' this program does the same as previous program using structured programming
SUB GetInput (max%, buffer$) STATIC
    SHARED valid$
    length% = 0
    DO
        DO
            keyStroke$ = INKEY$
        LOOP WHILE keyStroke$ = ""      ' loop until user types a character
        IF keyStroke$ = CHR$(8) THEN   ' check whether user pressed Backspace
            IF length% > 0 THEN
                length% = length% - 1
                PRINT CHR$(29); " "; CHR$(29);
                buffer$ = LEFT$(buffer$, length%)
            END IF
        ELSE
            IF length% < max% AND INSTR(valid$, keyStroke$) THEN
                buffer$ = buffer$ + keyStroke$
                PRINT keyStroke$; : length% = length% + 1
            END IF
        END IF
    LOOP UNTIL keyStroke$ = CHR$(13)   ' exit when user presses Enter
END SUB
```

ON...GOSUB

See also: GOSUB...RETURN, ON...GOTO, SELECT CASE

■ QB2	■ QB4.5	■ PowerBASIC
■ QB3	✲ ANSI	■ GW-BASIC
■ QB4	■ BASIC7	■ MacQB

Purpose

The ON...GOSUB statement branches control to one of several QuickBASIC subroutines; the value of an expression determines the subroutine to which the statement branches. It is similar to the ON...GOTO statement except that control eventually returns to the section of the program from which it branched.

Syntax

ON *expr* GOSUB {*line1* ¦ *label1* [, {*line2* ¦ *label2*}]...}

expr is a numeric variable or expression. QuickBASIC converts *expr* to an integer and then applies the value to the list of line numbers or labels. The list is used as a jump table that specifies the line to which the program branches. If *expr* evaluates to 1, control branches to the line specified by *line1* or *label1*; if *expr* evaluates to 2, control branches to the line specified by *line2* or *label2*; and so on. Note that the list can be a mixture of labels and line numbers.

Usage

```
ON go% GOSUB North, South, East, West
```

Branches to one of four subroutines; the subroutine to which it branches depends on the value of the variable *go%*. If *go%* is 2, for example, the program branches to the subroutine labelled *South*.

```
ON INT(RND*2) + 1 GOSUB Heads, Tails
```

Branches to one of two subroutines; which subroutine depends upon the value of a random number.

Description

ON...GOSUB is an alternative to the ON...GOTO statement. Like ON...GOTO, it lets your program branch to one of several line numbers or labels; the line number or label to which it branches depends on the value of an expression. Execution continues from there. Unlike ON...GOTO, the target address is the start of a QuickBASIC subroutine. When the program encounters the RETURN statement that marks the end of the subroutine, control returns to the statement following the ON...GOSUB statement.

If the expression evaluates to 0 or is a number greater than the number of entries in the jump table, control passes to the statement that follows ON...GOSUB and none of the subroutines are executed.

You do not need to use a different line number or label for every entry in the jump table; the same line number or label can serve in several entries. In the following example, the program branches to line number 200 when the variable *where%* contains the value 2, 4, or 7:

```
ON where% GOSUB Start, 200, 300, 200, File, Printer, 200, Finish
```

Comments

Although QuickBASIC accepts integers within the range 0 through 255 as the value of the expression in an ON...GOSUB statement, you cannot branch to more than 60 line numbers and labels in the list of addresses. In practice, you are even more limited because you must fit the entire statement—line or label list included—into a single program line. With the ON...GOSUB statement you cannot branch to more subroutines by writing successive ON...GOSUB statements that use the same expression in the same way that you can with ON...GOTO. (See the ON...GOTO entry.) On return from one subroutine, the program would encounter the next ON...GOSUB statement in the sequence and, because the expression is out of range, QuickBASIC would return an "Illegal function call" error message.

Errors

If the expression used in the ON argument evaluates to a number less than 0 or greater than 255, QuickBASIC returns an "Illegal function call" error message.

Compatibility

ANSI BASIC

ANSI adds an ELSE clause to the ON...GOSUB statement. If the value of the conditional argument is less than 1 or greater than the number of line numbers or labels in the list, the statement that follows ELSE executes, as shown in the following example:

```
ON choice% GOSUB Add, Edit, Delete ELSE GOTO Menu
```

Example

Because ON...GOSUB can branch to different subroutines in response to different values of an expression, it's ideal for programming multiple-choice tests and menus. The following program displays a multiple-choice question and then uses an ON...GOSUB statement to execute the routine that corresponds to the response it receives.

```
COLOR 0, 2: CLS : COLOR 14, 4: PRINT SPACE$(240)
LOCATE 2, 30: PRINT "****MULTIPLE CHOICE****";
LOCATE 4, 1: PRINT STRING$(80, "_"); : COLOR 0, 2
LOCATE 10, 25: PRINT "Are you enjoying this program?";
```

(continued)

continued

```
DO
    PLAY "L62 04 T250 D G G D G# A A 03 D G G D A A# A# 02 D G G D A# B B"
    LOCATE 13, 29, 1: PRINT "<Y>es,  <N>o,  <M>aybe";
    LOCATE 15, 40
    r$ = UCASE$(INPUT$(1))                        ' get input from user
    ON INSTR("YNM", r$) GOSUB Yes, No, Maybe      ' branch to Yes, No, or Maybe
LOOP WHILE response$ = ""
LOCATE 18, 40 - (LEN(response$) \ 2)
PRINT response$;
PLAY tune$
END

Maybe:
    tune$ = "T255 L15 01 A D C E F A 02 D E F A E C"
    response$ = "You sound undecided!"
    RETURN
Yes:
    tune$ = "L8 02 T240 D.. E. P16 ML A G B."
    response$ = "You sound very positive!"
    RETURN
No:
    tune$ = "T200 0314 G C D E L2 F L4 E C L2 D P64 D L4 E L1C"
    response$ = "You sound very negative!"
    RETURN
```

ON...GOTO

See also: GOTO, ON...GOSUB, SELECT CASE

■ QB2	■ QB4.5	■ PowerBASIC
■ QB3	✲ ANSI	■ GW-BASIC
■ QB4	■ BASIC7	■ MacQB

Purpose

The ON...GOTO statement branches control to one of several lines. A program often needs to perform one of a set of different tasks, the event that occurs while the program is executing determines the task. This event might be the result of a test or input from the user. The ON...GOTO statement is the traditional means of testing an event and transferring control to the appropriate address.

Syntax

ON *expr* GOTO {*line1* | *label1* [, {*line2* | *label2*}]...}

expr is a numeric variable or expression. QuickBASIC converts it to an integer value and then applies the value to the list of line numbers or labels. The list is used as a jump table that specifies the lines to which the program branches. If *expr* evaluates to 1, control branches to the line specified by *line1* or *label1*; if *expr* evaluates to 2, control passes to the line specified by *line2* or *label2*, and so on. Note that the list can be a combination of labels and line numbers.

Usage

```
ON choice% GOTO 100, 200, 300, Four
```

Branches to one of four possible destinations; the destination depends on the value of the variable *choice%*. If *choice%* is 3, for example, the program branches to line 300 and continues from there.

```
ON INT(RND * 3) + 1 GOTO One, Two, Three
```

Randomly branches to a destination routine starting at the label *One*, *Two*, or *Three*.

Description

Using the ON...GOTO statement is the traditional way of creating jump tables in BASIC. The value of the expression supplied to it is an index to the list of line numbers or labels that follow the GOTO keyword. When the statement executes, QuickBASIC evaluates the expression and then transfers control to the line specified by the corresponding table entry. If the expression evaluates to 0 or is greater than the number of entries in the table, no branch is made and control passes to the next statement after the ON...GOTO statement.

You do not need to use a different line number or label for every entry in the jump table; the same line number or label can serve as several entries. In the following example, the program branches to line number 200 when *where%* contains the value 2, 4, or 7:

```
ON where% GOTO Start, 200, 300, 200, File, Printer, 200, Finish
```

ON...GOTO can branch only to a line number or label that is inside the same module as the ON...GOTO statement itself. You cannot use this statement to transfer execution into or out of either a subprogram or a user-defined function.

Beginning with version 4.0, QuickBASIC provides a more flexible way of constructing jump tables with the SELECT CASE statement. One benefit of SELECT CASE is that it lets you specify a range of values that causes the program to branch to a single address. (See Chapter 3, "Decisions and Operators," for more details.)

Comments

Although QuickBASIC accepts integers in the range 0 through 255 as the value of the expression in an ON...GOTO statement, you cannot branch to more than 60 line numbers or labels in the list of addresses. In practice, you are even more limited because you must fit the entire statement—line or label list included—into a single program line. Because control falls through to the next statement in the program if the value of the expression is greater than the number of entries in the jump table, you can extend the jump table by using successive ON...GOTO statements, as in the following example:

```
ON where% GOTO North, South, East, West
ON where% - 4 GOTO Northeast, Southeast, Northwest, Southwest
```

You must always be sure that the initial value of the expression (*where%*, in this example) is not 0. If it is 0, QuickBASIC generates an "Illegal function call" error message at the second ON...GOTO statement after control passes over the first one.

Errors

If the expression used in the ON argument evaluates to a number less than 0 or greater than 255, QuickBASIC returns an "Illegal function call" error message.

Compatibility

ANSI BASIC

ANSI adds an ELSE clause to the ON...GOTO statement. If the value of the conditional argument is less than 1 or greater than the number of line numbers or labels in the list, the statement that follows ELSE executes, as shown in the following example:

```
ON a% GOTO 1000, 2000, 3000 ELSE PRINT "OUT OF RANGE!"
```

Example

In games or computer-aided instruction software, you need to be able to reward a successful player. The following program uses an ON...GOTO statement to instruct your computer to play a piece of music whose duration corresponds to the size of the score obtained by a call to the RND function.

```
RANDOMIZE TIMER:  ' force a new random number each time

CLS : LOCATE 10, 30: PRINT "YOUR SCORE ...";
score% = RND * 5000
PRINT score%

ON (score% \ 1000) + 1 GOTO Shortest, Shorter, Longer, Longest

Shortest:
    PLAY "L4 T200 ML O2 G E G F D O1 B O2 C.. MN"
    SYSTEM
Shorter:
    PLAY "P32 L4 T200 ML O1 G O2 C D E2 C E O2 D C D E F"
    SYSTEM
Longer:
    PLAY "L4 T200 ML O1 G O2 C D E.. P16 MS E ML E D C D. D"
    SYSTEM
Longest:
    PLAY "L4 T200 ML O1 G O2 C D E.. P16 MS E ML E D C D C O1 A P48"
END
```

WHILE...WEND

See also: DO...LOOP, FOR...NEXT

■ QB2	■ QB4.5	✲ PowerBASIC
■ QB3	ANSI	■ GW-BASIC
■ QB4	■ BASIC7	■ MacQB

Purpose

The WHILE...WEND statement repeats a series of statements only while a given condition is true (for example, until the end of a file is reached).

Syntax

WHILE *logicalexpr*
[*statements*]
WEND

logicalexpr is any numeric variable or expression that evaluates to true (a nonzero value) or false (zero). While *logicalexpr* is true, QuickBASIC executes the statements in the loop between the WHILE and WEND keywords. When *logicalexpr* becomes false, control transfers to the statement that follows WEND. Execution continues from there.

Usage

```
WHILE INKEY$ = ""
WEND
```

Loops continuously until the user presses a key.

```
WHILE NOT EOF(1)
   LINE INPUT #1, buffer$
   PRINT buffer$
WEND
```

Reads successive lines from the sequential file in buffer #1 into the string variable *buffer$* and displays the lines on the screen. This continues until the loop reaches the end of the file.

Description

WHILE...WEND is called an entry-condition loop because the logical test is performed at the beginning of the loop. If the expression is already false when the WHILE statement is first encountered, QuickBASIC bypasses the loop and does not execute the statements within it.

The body of a WHILE...WEND loop can contain any number of statements. WHILE...WEND loops can also include other WHILE...WEND loops; these can be nested to any level. Newer versions of BASIC include the DO...LOOP statement, which provides greater flexibility than the WHILE...WEND statement.

Errors

Every WHILE in a program must have a corresponding WEND, just as every WEND must have a preceding WHILE. If a program executes a WEND statement without having encountered a previous WHILE, it returns a "WEND without WHILE" error message. Conversely, an unmatched WHILE statement causes QuickBASIC to display a "WHILE without WEND" error message.

Compatibility

PowerBASIC

The PowerBASIC implementation of the WHILE...WEND statement is similar to the QuickBASIC version except that it requires you to use an integer expression for the test. PowerBASIC also provides the EXIT LOOP statement, which lets you exit a loop before the specified test condition is met. QuickBASIC does not include the EXIT WHILE statement.

Example

Because it executes until a specified condition becomes true, a WHILE...WEND loop is particularly suitable for procedures that need to monitor external events, such as user input. The following program uses WHILE...WEND statements to switch between two graphics displays; one display changes to the other in response to a keypress. Figure 2-2 shows the output of this program.

```
' this program requires at least a Color Graphics Adapter
SCREEN 1: LINE (0, 0)-(320, 200), 1, BF
VIEW (32, 4)-(288, 196), 0, 15
CLS 1
esc$ = CHR$(27)
WHILE keyPress$ <> esc$
    LINE (78, 75)-(178, 75), 3                    ' draw top line
    LINE (78, 125)-(178, 125), 3                  ' draw bottom line
    PSET (78, 75), 3: DRAW "C3 H8 BD16 E8"        ' draw arrows
    PSET (178, 75), 3: DRAW "C3 E8 BD16 H8"
    PSET (86, 125), 3: DRAW "C3 BU8 G8 F8"
    PSET (170, 125), 3: DRAW "C3 BU8 F8 G8"
    keyPress$ = ""
    WHILE keyPress$ = ""
        keyPress$ = INKEY$
    WEND
    IF keyPress$ <> esc$ THEN
        PSET (78, 75), 0: DRAW "C0 H8 BD16 E8"    ' erase arrows
        PSET (178, 75), 0: DRAW "C0 E8 BD16 H8"
        PSET (86, 125), 3: DRAW "C0 BU8 G8 F8"
        PSET (170, 125), 3: DRAW "C0 BU8 F8 G8"
        keyPress$ = ""
```

(continued)

continued

```
        WHILE keyPress$ = ""
            keyPress$ = INKEY$
        WEND
    END IF
WEND
END
```

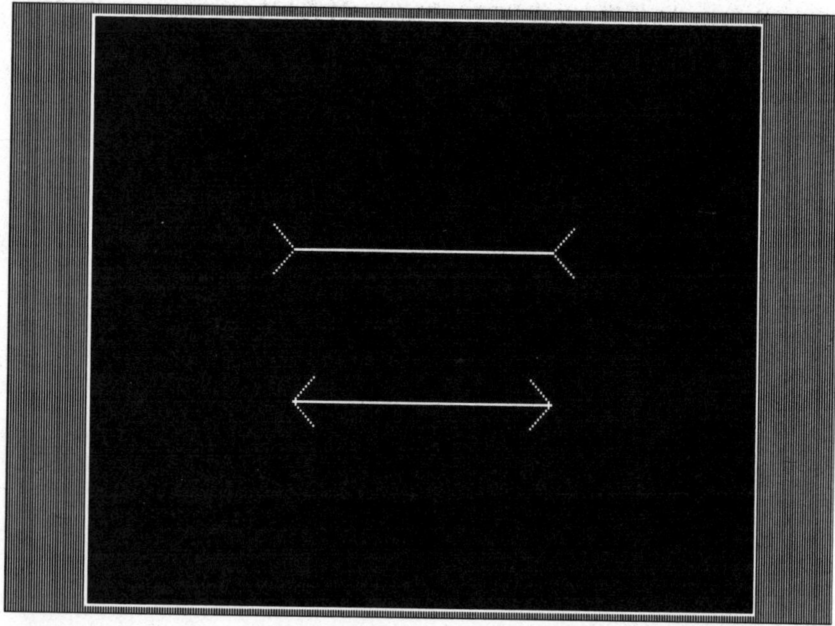

Figure 2-2.
Output of the WHILE...WEND example program.

CHAPTER 3

Decisions and Operators

Introduction

Decisions. The average person makes thousands of decisions every day. Changing situations and new stimuli force everyone into constantly shifting actions and reactions. Programs, too, must confront new information and alter their performance accordingly. Computers would be of little use if their responses were always fixed and unalterable.

Decision-making structures are vital to programming. Something as simple (yet important) as accepting a user's choice from a menu requires decision making. For example, if the user enters an "A" (for Add), the program adds new information; however, if the user enters a "Q" (for Quit), the program ends. The statements, functions, and operators of the "Decisions" category of QuickBASIC let you create programs that can make these important decisions.

This tutorial summarizes QuickBASIC's decision-making abilities and offers some suggestions for their use. Table 3-1, below, is a list of QuickBASIC's decision-making statements, functions, and operators.

Statement, function, or operator	Description
AND	Logical conjunction operator
+	String concatenation operator
EQV	Logical equivalency operator
IF	Conditional statement
IMP	Logical implication operator
MOD	Arithmetic modulo operator
NOT	Logical negation operator
OR	Logical disjunction operator
SELECT CASE	Conditional comparison statement
XOR	Logical "exclusive or" operator

Table 3-1.
QuickBASIC decision-making statements, functions, and operators.

IF—The General-Purpose Decision Maker

In QuickBASIC, as in English, you use the IF statement to make general-purpose decisions. Consider the following sentence:

> If the sun is shining, I will go on a picnic; otherwise, I will stay inside.

You can rephrase the sentence to include the words "then" and "else":

> If the sun is shining, then I will go on a picnic; else, I will stay inside.

Now you can translate this phrase into QuickBASIC statements:

```
IF sunShining THEN
    GOTO Picnic
ELSE
    GOTO Indoors
END IF
```

The expression that follows the IF keyword (in this case, *sunShining*) is called the *antecedent.*

The actions of the IF statement are straightforward. If the antecedent is true, the statements following the THEN keyword are executed; if the antecedent is false, however, the statements following the ELSE keyword are executed. In the example, if the expression *sunShining* is true, the program branches to *Picnic.* If the expression is false, the program branches to *Indoors.*

How does QuickBASIC know what is "true" and what is "false"? For QuickBASIC, true and false are merely numbers—false is 0, and true is any number except 0. In the previous example, *sunShining* could be a variable that is 0 when the sun isn't shining and any other number when it is. Internally, QuickBASIC generates the value –1 for true; however, any number other than 0 will work.

Relational Operators

Let's look at QuickBASIC's relational operators, which are =, <>, >, <, >= and <=. Table 3-2 defines these operators.

Relational operator	Math symbol	Example	Meaning
=	=	x = y	Equal to
<>	≠	x <> y	Not equal to
>	>	x > y	Greater than
<	<	x < y	Less than
>=	≥	x >= y	Greater than or equal to
<=	≤	x <= y	Less than or equal to

Table 3-2.
Relational operators.

With QuickBASIC's idea of true and false in mind, let's examine how the relational operators work. Remember that QuickBASIC returns the value –1 if an expression is true and 0 if an expression is false. All of these operators compare one value to another.

Equality

When QuickBASIC encounters the expression

$x = y$

it compares *x* with *y*. If *x* equals *y*, the expression is true; otherwise, the expression is false. For example, the expression *150 = 200* is false.

Inequality

The operator <> checks for inequality. When QuickBASIC encounters the expression

$x <> y$

it compares *x* with *y*. If *x* does not equal *y*, the expression is true; otherwise, the expression is false. For example, the expression *150 <> 200* is true.

Greater Than

The operator > checks for relative values. The expression

$x > y$

is true if *x* is greater than *y*. If *y* is greater, the expression is false.

Less Than

Like the greater-than operator, the operator < checks for relative values. The expression

$x < y$

yields a result of true if *x* is less than *y*; if *y* is less than *x*, the expression is false. So the expression *150 < 200* evaluates as true.

Greater Than or Equal To

The operator >= checks for relative values and equality. The expression

$x >= y$

compares the values of *x* and *y*. If *x* is greater than or equal to *y*, the expression is true; otherwise, the expression is false. For example, the expression *150 >= 200* is false and the expression *100 >= 100* is true.

Less Than or Equal To

Like the operator >=, the operator <= checks for relative values and equality. The expression

$x <= y$

is true if *x* is less than or equal to *y*. Otherwise, the expression evaluates as false.

Examples Using Relational Operators

Let's assume that *temp* is a variable that contains the temperature. To be sure that you don't go on a picnic unless the temperature is higher than 75 degrees Fahrenheit, you might use the following IF statement:

```
IF temp > 75 THEN
    GOTO Picnic
ELSE
    GOTO Indoors
ENDIF
```

If you want to go to the health club's spa whenever the water temperature at the beach is 60 degrees or less, you could make your decision with the following IF statement:

```
IF waterTemp <= 60 THEN
    GOTO Spa
ELSE
    GOTO Beach
END IF
```

You might want to vary your activities depending on the weather. Let's assume the following: If it's raining, you'll stay inside; if the sun is shining, you'll go to the beach; if it's snowing, you'll build a snowman; and if you can't do any of these things, you'll merely take a nap. You can represent this in QuickBASIC by using the ELSEIF keyword in an IF...THEN statement:

```
IF weather = sunny THEN
    GOTO Beach
ELSEIF weather = raining THEN
    GOTO Inside
ELSEIF weather = snowing THEN
    GOTO BuildSnowMan
ELSE
    GOTO TakeNap
END IF
```

In this statement, the variable *weather* represents one of many possible values for the weather. QuickBASIC evaluates each IF and ELSEIF statement and tries to find a match. This example contains only three statements; however, if you use many ELSEIF statements, your program might be hard to read and understand. Fortunately, QuickBASIC offers an alternative—the SELECT CASE statement. (See the SELECT CASE entry later in this chapter.)

The Logical Operators—AND, EQV, IMP, NOT, OR, and XOR

One of the virtues of QuickBASIC is that it lets you combine simple expressions to create complex expressions. You combine simple expressions with the logical operators AND, EQV, IMP, NOT, OR, and XOR. The operators you will use most often are AND and OR.

Let's expand the previous picnic example to include more details. For example, let's specify that the sun must be shining and the temperature must be more than 75 degrees before you go on a picnic:

```
IF sunShining AND temp > 75 THEN
    GOTO Picnic
ELSE
    GOTO Indoors
ENDIF
```

Notice that the AND operator works in almost the same way as it does in an English sentence. You must include one operand on each side of the AND, as in the following example:

```
this AND that
```

The AND operator returns a value of true only when both operands are true. In the previous example, the sun must be shining *and* the temperature must be greater than 75 degrees before you can go on the picnic.

The OR operator returns a value of true if either operand is true. For example, if the temperature of the water at the local beach is below 60 degrees *or* the sun isn't shining, you will go to the health club's spa. The following QuickBASIC IF statement expresses those conditions:

```
IF waterTemp < 60 OR sunNotShining THEN
    GOTO Spa
ELSE
    GOTO Beach
END IF
```

The NOT operator is different from the other logical operators—it is a unary operator, which means that it requires only one operand. The NOT operator, as its name implies, "reverses" the value of the operand. If the operand is true, the result of a NOT operation is false; if the operand is false, the result of a NOT operation is true. Thus you can rephrase the previous example as follows:

```
IF waterTemp < 60 OR NOT sunShining THEN
    GOTO Spa
ELSE
    GOTO Beach
END IF
```

The EQV, IMP, and XOR logical operators let you construct complex expressions because they test two expressions at once. The EQV operator returns true if both its operands have a value of true or both have a value of false. The IMP operator returns a result of false only if the first operand is true and the second is false. Finally, the XOR operator returns true when only one of the operands is true; if both of the operands are true (or both are false), XOR returns false.

SELECT CASE

QuickBASIC's SELECT CASE statement doesn't do anything that the IF statement can't—it merely uses a clearer format. For example, the following statements use a SELECT CASE statement to perform the same task as a previous example that used the IF statement:

```
SELECT CASE weather
    CASE sunny
        GOTO Beach
    CASE raining
        GOTO Inside
    CASE snowing
        GOTO BuildSnowMan
    CASE ELSE
        GOTO TakeNap
END SELECT
```

Suppose that you also want to go inside if it is windy. To specify this, you need to change an ELSEIF clause in the IF statement as follows:

```
ELSEIF weather = raining OR weather = windy THEN
    GOTO Inside
```

However, with SELECT CASE you can simply add *windy* to the appropriate case clause:

```
CASE raining, windy
    GOTO Inside
```

The MOD Operator

The MOD operator is related to the integer division operator (\). MOD returns the remainder from an integer division operation. For example, *5 MOD 2* is 1, because 5 divided by 2 is 2 with a remainder of 1.

Programmers often use the MOD operator as an "evenly divisible" operator. For example, to determine whether a year is a leap year, you must know whether it is divisible by 4 but not by 100 (unless it's also divisible by 400). You can use the MOD operator to check for divisibility, as the following statements illustrate:

```
CLS
DIM year AS INTEGER, by4 AS INTEGER, by100 AS INTEGER, by400 AS INTEGER

INPUT "Enter a year in four digits (for example: 1989)"; year

by4 = year MOD 4            ' evenly divisible by 4?
by100 = year MOD 100        ' evenly divisible by 100?
by400 = year MOD 400        ' evenly divisible by 400?

IF (by4 = 0 AND by100 <> 0) OR by400 = 0 THEN
    PRINT "Yes,"; year; "is a leap year."
ELSE
    PRINT "No,"; year; "is not a leap year."
END IF
```

The + (Concatenation) Operator

BASIC is well known for its advanced string-handling capabilities. For example, QuickBASIC has built-in support for combining (or concatenating) two strings. Not only can QuickBASIC's + operator add two numbers, it can also "add" two strings. Concatenation is often used to combine the separate elements of a name into a single string. For example, after the following statements,

```
title$ = "Dr."
first$ = "Heywood"
last$ = "Floyd"

whole$ = title$ + " " + first$ + " " + last$
```

the value of *whole$* is "Dr. Heywood Floyd". Note that the statement also concatenates spaces in the string in order to separate the parts of the name.

Related Reading

Bergmann, Merrie, et al. *The Logic Book.* New York, N.Y.: Random House, 1980.

Prata, Stephen, with Harry Henderson. *The Waite Group's Microsoft QuickBASIC Primer Plus.* Redmond, Wash.: Microsoft Press, 1990.

AND

See also: EQV, IF, IMP, MOD, NOT, OR, XOR

■ QB2 ■ QB4.5 ■ PowerBASIC
■ QB3 ■ ANSI ■ GW-BASIC
■ QB4 ■ BASIC7 ■ MacQB

Purpose

The AND operator is both a logical and an arithmetic operator. As a logical operator, it returns a value of true only if both its operands have a value of true. As an arithmetic operator, it performs AND operations with the corresponding bits of two values.

Syntax

IF *op1* AND *op2* THEN ...

or

result% = *op1* AND *op2*

The *op1* and *op2* operands can be of any numeric type (integer, long integer, single precision, or double precision), but the result is always an integer or a long integer.

result% is the variable that contains the result of an arithmetic AND operation.

Usage

```
IF rich% AND famous% THEN
    PRINT "Are you single?"
END IF
```

If the variables *rich%* and *famous%* are both true, the message is displayed.

Description

QuickBASIC's AND operator can be used in a logical expression to tell you whether both operands are true. For example,

```
var1 > 2 AND var2 < 4
```

is true only when the expressions *var1 > 2* and *var2 < 4* are both true.

The AND operator can also be used arithmetically to perform a bit-by-bit comparison of the operands. If the corresponding bits in the operands are 1, the resulting bit is 1; otherwise (if one or both of the bits is 0), the result is 0. See the truth table in Table 3-3.

p	q	p AND q
1	1	1
1	0	0
0	1	0
0	0	0

Table 3-3.
AND truth table.

Figure 3-1 demonstrates the use of the arithmetic AND operator.

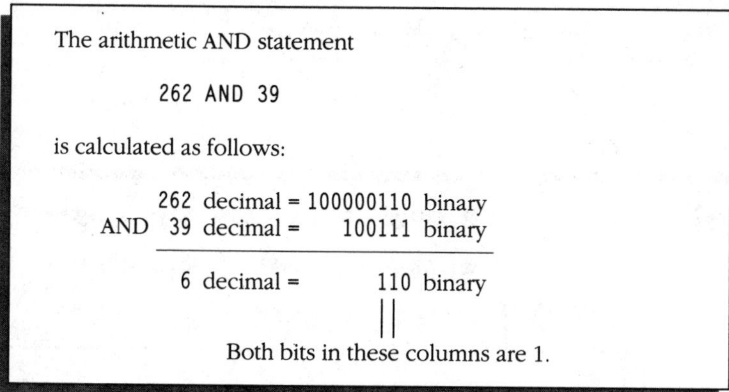

The arithmetic AND statement

```
262 AND 39
```

is calculated as follows:

```
    262 decimal = 100000110 binary
AND  39 decimal =    100111 binary
    ------------------------------
      6 decimal =       110 binary
                        ||
```

Both bits in these columns are 1.

Figure 3-1.
Arithmetic AND.

The AND operator accepts single-precision and double-precision operands; however, it converts them to either an integer or a long integer before processing them. The result of the AND operation is always an integer or a long integer.

Errors

The operands in an AND operation can be of any numeric type (integer, long integer, single precision, or double precision) in the range –2147483648 through 2147483647. If either operand is out of range, QuickBASIC returns an "Overflow" error message.

Example

The following example shows how you can use the AND operator to determine eligibility for a loan.

```
CLS
PRINT "Loan Application": PRINT

INPUT "Amount of desired loan"; amt#
INPUT "Does the applicant have a good credit history (Y/N)"; goodCreditHistory$
INPUT "Is the applicant working full-time (Y/N)"; fullTime$

PRINT
IF UCASE$(goodCreditHistory$) = "Y" AND UCASE$(fullTime$) = "Y" THEN
    PRINT "Because the applicant has a good credit history and ";
    PRINT "is working full-time,"
    PRINT "the application for"; amt#; "is approved."
ELSE
    PRINT "The applicant does not meet our qualifications;  ";
    PRINT "the application is denied."
END IF
```

+ (Concatenation)

See also: CONST, FRE

■ QB2	■ QB4.5	■ PowerBASIC
■ QB3	✲ ANSI	■ GW-BASIC
■ QB4	■ BASIC7	■ MacQB

Purpose

The + operator, when used with strings, combines (concatenates) two or more strings into one string. Use the + operator, for example, to combine a first name and a last name into a single string.

Syntax

result$* = *string1$ + *string2$* [+ *string3$*] ...

result$* is a string variable that contains the concatenation of *string1$, *string2$*, *string3$*, and so on.

Usage

```
overall$ = prefix$ + baseName$
```

Combines the contents of *prefix$* and *baseName$* into *overall$*.

```
fullName$ = firstName$ + " " + lastName$
```

Combines the contents of *firstName$* and *lastName$* (separated with a space) into *fullName$*.

Description

QuickBASIC's + operator lets you perform string concatenation, the process of combining several strings or string expressions into a single, longer string. For example,

```
"ABCDE" + "FGHIJ"
```

results in the single string "ABCDEFGHIJ". The + operator enables you to combine many strings in a single operation; for example,

```
"ABCDE" + "FGHIJ" + "KLMNO" + "PQRST" + "UVWXYZ"
```

results in the single string "ABCDEFGHIJKLMNOPQRSTUVWXYZ".

Comments

QuickBASIC doesn't permit string concatenation in a CONST statement. (See the CONST entry in Chapter 1, "Types and Variables," for details.)

When you concatenate a variable-length string with another string, QuickBASIC creates a new string containing the original two strings. This is true even if you merely add characters to the same string. For example, with the following string concatenation:

```
longString$ = longString$ + "*-*-*-*-*"
```

QuickBASIC creates a new string, copies the previous contents of *longString$* to it, adds "*-*-*-*-*" to it, gives the new string the name *longString$*, and then deletes the old *longString$* to make room for other strings. However, during the process QuickBASIC needs enough string space for two copies of *longString$*. For example, assume you have 20,000 bytes of free string space and that *longString$* is 10,000 bytes long. If you try to concatenate "*-*-*-*-*" to *longString$*, the compiler returns an "Out of string space" error message because QuickBASIC makes another copy of *longString$*, leaving no room for "*-*-*-*-*".

Compatibility

ANSI BASIC

ANSI BASIC uses the ampersand (&) as its concatenation operator. For example, to add the strings contained in the variables first$ and second$ and to assign the result to third$, you use the following statement:

```
third$ = first$ & second$
```

Example

The following example uses the + operator to combine the three parts of an employee's name.

```
CLS
LINE INPUT "Enter the employee's first name:     "; firstName$
wholeName$ = firstName$ + " "

LINE INPUT "Enter the employee's middle initial: "; middleInitial$
wholeName$ = wholeName$ + middleInitial$ + ". "
```

(continued)

continued

```
LINE INPUT "Enter the employee's last name:       "; lastName$
wholeName$ = wholeName$ + lastName$

INPUT "Enter the amount of the employee's salary:   "; amt#

PRINT
PRINT "Pay to the order of "; wholeName$; TAB(60);
PRINT USING "##,###.##"; amt#
END
```

EQV

See also: AND, IF, IMP, MOD, NOT, OR, XOR

■ QB2	■ QB4.5	■ PowerBASIC
■ QB3	ANSI	■ GW-BASIC
■ QB4	■ BASIC7	■ MacQB

Purpose

The EQV operator is both a logical and an arithmetic operator. As a logical operator, it returns a value of true only if both its operands have a value of true or both have a value of false. As an arithmetic operator, it performs EQV operations with the corresponding bits of two values.

Syntax

IF *op1* EQV *op2* THEN …

or

result% = *op1* EQV *op2*

The *op1* and *op2* operands can be of any numeric type (integer, long integer, single precision, or double precision), but the result is always an integer or a long integer.

result% is the variable that contains the result of an arithmetic EQV operation.

Usage

```
IF amt1# > 100# EQV amt2# > 2000# THEN
    PRINT "The amounts are in range"
END IF
```

Tests two double-precision values. If *amt1#* is greater than 100 and *amt2#* is greater than 2000, the expression is true; if *amt1#* is less than 100 and *amt2#* is less than 2000, the expression is also true. The expression is false if one value is true and the other is false.

Description

QuickBASIC's EQV operator can be used in a logical expression to tell you whether both operands are true or both are false. For example,

```
var1 > 2 EQV var2 < 4
```

is true only when the expressions *var1 > 2* and *var2 < 4* are either both true or both false.

The EQV operator can also be used arithmetically to perform a bit-by-bit comparison of the operands. If the corresponding bits in the operands are both 1 or both 0, the result is 1; otherwise, the result is 0. See the truth table in Table 3-4.

p	q	p EQV q
1	1	1
1	0	0
0	1	0
0	0	1

Table 3-4.
EQV truth table.

QuickBASIC's EQV operator is rarely used in arithmetic expressions. More often it is used in logical expressions.

The EQV operator accepts single-precision and double-precision operands; however, it converts them to either integer or long integer before processing them. The result of the EQV operation is always an integer or a long integer.

Errors

The operands in an EQV operation can be of any numeric type (integer, long integer, single precision, or double precision) in the range –2147483648 through 2147483647. If either operand is out of range, QuickBASIC returns an "Overflow" error message.

Example

This example shows how you can use the EQV operator to determine eligibility for a loan.

```
CLS
PRINT "Loan Application"
PRINT

INPUT "Amount of desired loan"; amt#
INPUT "What is the applicant's annual salary"; salary#
```

(continued)

continued

```
PRINT
IF amt# > 1000 EQV salary > 15000 THEN
    PRINT "Because the applicant is requesting an amount ";
    PRINT "appropriate for his or her salary,"
    PRINT "the application for"; amt#; "is approved."
ELSE
    PRINT "The applicant does not meet our qualifications; ";
    PRINT "the application is denied."
END IF
```

IF

See also: DO...LOOP, ON...GOSUB, ON...GOTO, SELECT CASE

✲ QB2	■ QB4.5	✲ PowerBASIC
■ QB3	■ ANSI	✲ GW-BASIC
■ QB4	■ BASIC7	■ MacQB

Purpose

The IF statement uses the value of an expression to control the order in which statements are executed. The expression IF statement can test the equivalence of two variables; these comparisons can be combined by using the logical operators AND, OR, NOT, XOR, EQV, and IMP.

Syntax

Single line:

IF *expr* THEN *true* ELSE *false*

Block form:

IF *expr1* THEN
[*true*]

[ELSEIF *expr2* THEN
[*true*]]
⋮

[ELSEIF *exprx* THEN
[*true*]]

[ELSE
[*false*]]
END IF

expr is an expression that yields a result of true or false. The expression can use QuickBASIC's relational operators (=, <>, >, <, >=, <=) and logical operators (AND, OR, NOT, XOR, EQV, IMP) to yield a value of true or false. Your program can represent false by 0 and true by any nonzero value. Therefore, *expr* can be an integer expression; it doesn't have to yield a value of true or false.

true is a block of statements to be executed if *expr* is true. In the single-line IF statement, multiple statements must be on the same line, separated by colons. In the block-form IF statement, multiple statements can be on the same line (separated by colons) or on separate lines. If you must include more than a few statements, use the block-form IF statement and put the statements on separate lines. The block-form IF statement is easier to read than the single-line IF statement.

The statements following the ELSEIF clause, which can appear only in a block-form IF statement, are executed only if *expr1* is false and *expr2* is true. ELSEIF lets you test for many different conditions within a single IF statement.

QuickBASIC executes *false*, which is a block of statements that follow the keyword ELSE, if all preceding IF and ELSEIF expressions are false. The ELSE clause is the catchall clause—if all else fails, QuickBASIC executes the statements following the ELSE keyword.

Usage

```
IF age% < 18 THEN status$ = "Minor"
```

If the value of the variable *age%* is less than 18, the statement sets *status$* to "Minor."

```
IF memSize& < 250 THEN
    PRINT "Sorry, not enough memory."
    BEEP
    SYSTEM
END IF
```

Prints a message, beeps, and then exits the program if the variable *memSize&* is less than 250.

```
IF answer$ = "Y" THEN 10 ELSE 20

IF answer$ = "Y" THEN GOTO 10 ELSE GOTO 20

IF answer$ = "Y" THEN
    GOTO 10
ELSE
    GOTO 20
END IF
```

These three statements are equivalent—all jump to line 10 if the value of the variable *answer$* is equal to "Y" and to line 20 if it is not.

```
IF age% >= 16 AND license$ = "NO" THEN
    PRINT "Take your driver's test...and drive carefully."
    GOTO GetDriversLicense
ELSEIF age% > 16 AND license$ = "YES" THEN
    PRINT "Renew your license."
    GOTO RenewLicense
ELSE
    PRINT "Sorry, but you'll have to wait..."
    GOTO TooYoung
END IF
```

Checks the value of the variables *age%* and *license$* and prints the message that corresponds to the combination of those values.

Description

QuickBASIC's IF statement checks to see whether a certain condition has been met. If the condition has been met, QuickBASIC executes the given statements; if the condition has not been met, QuickBASIC executes different statements. The IF statement provides the lowest level of decision making in QuickBASIC; unlike control flow loops, IF statements are executed only once.

When an IF statement branches to another *numbered* line in the program, you can omit the keyword GOTO. If the line has a label, however, you must use GOTO. The following statements illustrate valid usages of the IF statement:

```
IF amountDue# > 1000.0 THEN GOTO CreditHold

IF amountDue# > 1000.0 THEN GOTO 10000

IF amountDue# > 1000.0 THEN 10000
```

You should use a single-line IF statement when the set of statements that are executed when the expression is true includes only a couple of statements. In fact, when there is only one statement, a single-line IF is more concise and easy to read than a block-form IF, as shown in the following example:

```
IF amountDue# > 1000.0 THEN 10000

IF amountDue# > 1000.0 THEN
    GOTO 10000
END IF
```

The block-form syntax is a response to recent programming developments. The block-form IF statement lets you include whatever statements are needed rather than forcing you to fit statements (separated by colons) on a single line.

QuickBASIC evaluates the IF statement from the top, starting at the first expression and working down. Each block-form IF statement must end with a matching END IF clause. Whenever an expression evaluates to true, QuickBASIC executes the statements on the line following the keyword THEN. If the expressions corresponding to the

IF clause and all the ELSEIF clauses are false, QuickBASIC executes the statements following the keyword ELSE. Remember that including statements in the IF, ELSEIF, and ELSE clauses is optional—if you omit statements, QuickBASIC executes nothing if the expression is true. The following block-form IF statement, for example, is legal:

```
IF age% >= 21 THEN
ELSE
    PRINT "You're under arrest!"
END IF
```

Also note that the ELSEIF and ELSE clauses are optional—if the IF expression is false and there are no ELSEIF or ELSE clauses, QuickBASIC continues execution at the first statement following the END IF clause.

A block-form IF can include other block-form statements, such as IF and DO...LOOP statements; a single-line IF cannot. The IF, ELSEIF, ELSE, and END IF clauses of the block-form IF must be the first statements on each line; however, you can precede them with a line number or line label if you must branch to them from another part of the program.

Because QuickBASIC looks at what follows the THEN clause to determine whether the IF statement is a block-form or single-line statement, you cannot add anything except a comment after the THEN keyword in a block-form IF statement.

Errors

You must compare like values (numeric to numeric or string to string). If you attempt to compare different types of values (for example, numeric to string), QuickBASIC returns a "Type mismatch" error message.

If you use a numeric expression as the expression in an IF statement, it must evaluate to a number in the range of a long integer, –2147483648 through 2147483647; if you use a floating-point expression that exceeds this range, QuickBASIC returns an "Overflow" error message.

Tips

To see whether a variable is 0, simply use

```
IF NOT variable%
```

If *variable%* is 0, then *NOT variable%* is true. The simple expression *variable%* in the following statement is true if *variable%* equals any integer value except 0:

```
IF variable%
```

Floating-point operations sometimes generate inaccurate results; therefore, floating-point numbers that appear equal when printed might actually be minutely different. If you round the floating-point numbers before you compare them, the differences do not affect the comparison.

Compatibility

QuickBASIC 2.0

QuickBASIC version 2.0 allows you to conditionally use the NEXT or WEND statement to close a FOR or WHILE loop in a single-line IF statement. For example, the following statement increments count only if *done%* is true.

```
IF done% THEN NEXT count
```

(See Chapter 2, "Flow Control," for details about FOR...NEXT.)

PowerBASIC

PowerBASIC can extend QuickBASIC's block-style IF statement in two ways.

- You can optionally use a comma after an expression in an IF or ELSEIF clause. This usage mirrors English syntax and improves readability, as shown in the following example:
  ```
  IF age% = 16, THEN PRINT "Celebration!"
  ```
- PowerBASIC includes the EXIT IF keyword to transfer control from a block-style IF. (See Chapter 2, "Flow Control," for details about the EXIT statement.) In QuickBASIC you can simulate this EXIT IF statement by using a GOTO statement, as in the following example:

```
IF age% >= 16 THEN
    PRINT "You may take the driver's test."

    INPUT "Did you pass the test"; passedTest$
    IF UCASE$(passedTest$) = "N" THEN GOTO ExitIf

    ' in PowerBASIC, you could use:
    ' IF UCASE$(passedTest$) = "N" THEN EXIT IF

    PRINT "You passed the test."
END IF

ExitIf:
    PRINT "COMPLETE"
```

GW-BASIC and BASICA

GW-BASIC and BASICA support only the single-line style of IF.

Example

The following example sounds the speaker (from low to high frequencies) and displays the frequency and range of the tones.

```
CLS
FOR freq% = 100 TO 1000 STEP 10
    IF RND <= .5 THEN dur% = 1 ELSE dur% = 2   ' pick a random duration

    SOUND freq%, dur%
    LOCATE 1, 1
    PRINT USING "#####  "; freq%;

    IF freq% < 200 THEN
        PRINT "Very low frequency "
    ELSEIF freq% < 400 THEN
        PRINT "Low frequency      "
    ELSEIF freq% < 600 THEN
        PRINT "Average frequency  "
    ELSEIF freq% < 800 THEN
        PRINT "High frequency     "
    ELSE
        PRINT "Very high frequency"
    END IF
NEXT
END
```

IMP

See also: AND, EQV, IF, MOD, NOT, OR, XOR

■ **QB2**	■ **QB4.5**	■ **PowerBASIC**
■ **QB3**	**ANSI**	■ **GW-BASIC**
■ **QB4**	■ **BASIC7**	■ **MacQB**

Purpose

The IMP operator is both a logical and an arithmetic operator. As a logical operator, it returns a value of false only if its first operand is true and its second operand false. As an arithmetic operator, it performs IMP operations with the corresponding bits of two values.

Syntax

IF *op1* IMP *op2* THEN ...

or

result% = *op1* IMP *op2*

The *op1* and *op2* operands can be of any numeric type (integer, long integer, single precision, or double precision), but the result is always an integer or a long integer.

result% is the variable that contains the result of an arithmetic IMP operation.

Usage

```
IF amount > 1000 IMP safetyGoggles$ = "YES" THEN
    PRINT "Ready to proceed"
END IF
```

The expression in the IF statement is false only if *amount* is greater than 1000 and *safetyGoggles$* is not equal to "YES".

Description

QuickBASIC's IMP operator can be used in a logical expression when you want to check for implication. The expression is true if the value of the first operand implies the value of the second one. An expression that uses the IMP operator is true except when the first operand is true and the second is false. For example,

```
var1 > 2 IMP var2 < 4
```

is false only when the expression *var1 > 2* is true and the expression *var2 < 4* is false.

The IMP operator can also be used arithmetically to perform a bit-by-bit comparison of the operands. If a bit in *op1* is 1 and the corresponding bit in *op2* is 0, the result is 0; otherwise, the result is 1. See the truth table in Table 3-5.

p	q	p IMP q
1	1	1
1	0	0
0	1	1
0	0	1

Table 3-5.
IMP truth table.

QuickBASIC's IMP operator is rarely used in arithmetic expressions. More often it is used in logical expressions.

The IMP operator accepts single-precision and double-precision operands; however, it converts them to either integer or long integer before processing them. The result of the IMP operation is always an integer or a long integer.

Errors

The operands in an IMP operation can be of any numeric type (integer, long integer, single precision, or double precision) in the range –2147483648 through 2147483647. If either is outside the range, QuickBASIC returns an "Overflow" error message.

Example

This example shows how you can use the IMP operator to determine eligibility for a loan.

```
CLS
PRINT "Loan Application": PRINT

INPUT "Amount of desired loan"; amt#
INPUT "Is the applicant working full-time (Y/N)"; fullTime$

PRINT
IF amt# > 1000 IMP UCASE$(fullTime$) = "Y" THEN
    PRINT "Because the applicant is requesting an amount ";
    PRINT "appropriate for his or her work status,"
    PRINT "the application for"; amt#; "is approved."
ELSE
    PRINT "The applicant doesn't meet our qualifications; "
    PRINT "the application is denied."
END IF
```

MOD

■ QB2	■ QB4.5	■ PowerBASIC
■ QB3	■ ANSI	■ GW-BASIC
■ QB4	■ BASIC7	■ MacQB

Purpose

The MOD operator is an arithmetic operator that returns the remainder of division between two integers. Use MOD, for example, to start a new page of a report every 55 lines.

Syntax

remainder% = *op1* MOD *op2*

The *op1* and *op2* operands can be of any numeric type (integer, long integer, single precision, or double precision), but the result is always an integer or a long integer.

remainder% is the variable that contains the result of the MOD operation.

Usage

```
IF line% MOD 55 = 0 THEN
    LPRINT CHR$(12);
END IF
```

If the MOD operation generates no remainder, the program sends a formfeed character to the printer.

Description

QuickBASIC's MOD operator divides two operands and returns the remainder of that division. Before the division, the operands are rounded to integers; the result of the division is also rounded to an integer before the remainder is calculated. The result of the MOD operation is always an integer or a long integer.

Errors

The operands in a MOD operation can be of any numeric type (integer, long integer, single precision, or double precision) in the range –2147483648 through 2147483647. If either is outside the range, QuickBASIC returns an "Overflow" error message.

Example

This example uses the MOD operator to stop displaying output at the end of each screenful.

```
x = 1
DO
    PRINT TAB(x MOD 55); "QuickBASIC Bible"

    IF x MOD 23 = 0 THEN
        PRINT "Press [Esc] to end the program or any other key to continue...";
        DO
            wait$ = INKEY$
        LOOP WHILE wait$ = ""
        IF wait$ = CHR$(27) THEN EXIT DO
    END IF
    x = x + 1
LOOP
```

NOT

See also: AND, EQV, IF, IMP, MOD, OR, XOR

■ **QB2**	■ **QB4.5**	■ **PowerBASIC**
■ **QB3**	■ **ANSI**	■ **GW-BASIC**
■ **QB4**	■ **BASIC7**	■ **MacQB**

Purpose

The NOT operator is both a logical and an arithmetic operator. As a logical operator, NOT returns a value of true if its operand has a value of false. As an arithmetic operator, it reverses the bit values of its operand. Use the NOT operator to reverse the truth value of a variable.

Syntax

IF NOT *op* THEN ...

or

result% = NOT *op*

The *op* operand can be of any numeric type (integer, long integer, single precision, or double precision), but the result is always an integer or a long integer.

Usage

```
IF NOT printerReady% THEN
    PRINT "Please load paper in the printer and press Enter."
END IF
```

Displays a message when the printer is not ready. The variable *printerReady%* represents the status of the printer, and returns true when the printer is ready. Because you need to know when the printer is *not* ready, you simply apply the NOT operator to *printerReady%*.

Description

QuickBASIC's NOT operator can be used in a logical expression to tell you whether an operand is false. For example,

```
NOT var1 > 2
```

is true only when the expression *var1 > 2* is false.

The NOT operator can also be used arithmetically to reverse the bits of the operator. If a bit in the operator is 1, the resulting bit is 0. If it is 0, the result is 1. See the truth table in Table 3-6.

p	NOT p
1	0
0	1

Table 3-6.
NOT truth table.

The NOT operator examines each bit in the operand before it returns a value. If the bit is 1, the resulting bit is 0. If the bit is 0, the resulting bit is 1. Because of the way QuickBASIC stores integers and long integers, using the NOT operator on them is the same as adding 1 to the value and making it negative.

The NOT operator accepts single-precision and double-precision operands; however, it converts them to integer or long-integer values before processing them. The result of the NOT operation is always an integer or a long integer.

Errors

The operand in a NOT operation can be of any numeric type (integer, long integer, single precision, or double precision) in the range –2147483648 through 2147483647. If the operand is outside the range, QuickBASIC returns an "Overflow" error message.

Example

This example uses the NOT operator to reverse the value of the user-defined function *Ok* so that the program doesn't end until the function returns a true value.

```
DECLARE FUNCTION Ok% (prompt$)
CONST FALSE = 0, TRUE = NOT FALSE

CLS
DO WHILE NOT Ok("Ready to end program.  ")   ' call the Ok function
LOOP                                         ' loop while Ok returns true

SYSTEM

' The Ok function returns TRUE if the user enters "Y"

FUNCTION Ok% (prompt$) STATIC
    LOCATE , , 1                             ' turn on cursor
    PRINT prompt$; "Is this OK?  ";

    DO
        keyboard$ = UCASE$(INKEY$)           ' get a character
    LOOP WHILE NOT (keyboard$ = "N" OR keyboard$ = "Y")

    SELECT CASE keyboard$
        CASE "N"
            PRINT "No"
            Ok% = FALSE

        CASE "Y"
            PRINT "Yes"
            Ok% = TRUE
        END SELECT
END FUNCTION
```

OR

See also: AND, EQV, IF, IMP, MOD, NOT, XOR

■ QB2	■ QB4.5	■ PowerBASIC
■ QB3	■ ANSI	■ GW-BASIC
■ QB4	■ BASIC7	■ MacQB

Purpose

The OR operator is both a logical and an arithmetic operator. As a logical operator, it returns a value of true if either or both its operands have a value of true. Use the logical OR operator to guarantee that at least one variable is true. As an arithmetic operator, it performs OR operations with the corresponding bits of two values.

Syntax

IF *op1* OR *op2* THEN ...

or

result% = *op1* OR *op2*

The *op1* and *op2* operands can be of any numeric type (integer, long integer, single precision, or double precision), but the result is always an integer or a long integer.

result% is the variable that contains the result of an arithmetic OR operation.

Usage

```
IF rich% OR famous% THEN
    PRINT "That's good enough--are you single?"
END IF
```

If either or both of the variables *rich%* and *famous%* are true, a message is displayed on the screen.

Description

QuickBASIC's OR operator can be used in a logical expression to tell you whether either or both of the operands are true. For example,

```
var1 > 2 OR var2 < 4
```

is true when the expression *var1 > 2* is true, when the expression *var2 < 4* is true, or when both are true.

This or operation is an "inclusive or"—it is true if either or both of the operands are true. If you need to check whether only one and not both the operands is true, use XOR. (See the XOR entry for details.)

The OR operator can also be used to perform a bit-by-bit comparison of the operands. If either or both of the corresponding bits in the two operands are 1, the resulting bit is 1; otherwise, the resulting bit is 0. See the truth table for OR in Table 3-7.

p	q	p OR q
1	1	1
1	0	1
0	1	1
0	0	0

Table 3-7.
Logical OR truth table.

Figure 3-2 on the following page demonstrates the use of the arithmetic OR operator.

The arithmetic OR statement

```
262 OR 39
```

is calculated using binary as follows:

```
      262 decimal = 100000110 binary
OR     39 decimal =    100111 binary
   ---------------------------------
      295 decimal = 100100111 binary
                      |  | |||
```

One or both of the bits in these columns are 1.

Figure 3-2.
Arithmetic OR.

The OR operator accepts single-precision and double-precision operands; however, it converts them to integers or long integers before processing them. The result of the OR operation is always an integer or a long integer.

Errors

The operands in an OR operation can be of any numeric type (integer, long integer, single precision, or double precision) in the range –2147483648 through 2147483647. If either is outside the range, QuickBASIC returns an "Overflow" error message.

Example

The example following shows how you can use the OR operator to determine eligibility for a loan.

```
CLS
PRINT "Loan Application": PRINT

INPUT "Amount of desired loan"; amt#
INPUT "Is the applicant working full-time (Y/N)"; fullTime$
INPUT "Does the applicant have sufficient collateral (Y/N)"; collateral$
PRINT

IF UCASE$(fullTime$) = "Y" OR UCASE$(collateral$) = "Y" THEN
    PRINT "Because the applicant requested a loan that is reasonably secured,"
    PRINT "the application for"; amt#; "is approved."
ELSE
    PRINT "The applicant doesn't meet our qualifications; ";
    PRINT "the application is denied."
END IF
```

SELECT CASE

See also: IF

QB2	■ QB4.5	■ PowerBASIC
✲ QB3	■ ANSI	GW-BASIC
✲ QB4	■ BASIC7	■ MacQB

Purpose

The SELECT CASE statement provides a readable method of comparing an expression to several constants and then executing statements based on the comparison. Use SELECT CASE when you must execute different statements depending on the value of an expression. The SELECT CASE statement offers a readable and more structured alternative to complex IF...ELSE statements.

Syntax

SELECT CASE *expr*
    CASE *comp* [,*comp* ...]
        [*statements*]
    CASE *comp* [,*comp* ...]
        [*statements*]
    CASE ELSE
        [*statements*]
END SELECT

expr is any numeric or string expression. Unlike the IF statement, this expression must be a constant rather than a true or false value.

comp is an expression that represents a range of values to which *expr* is compared. *comp* must use one of the following forms:

expr	A single expression
lowexpr TO *highexpr*	A value range
IS *relationexpr*	A range comparison

statements is one or more QuickBASIC statements. You can either place the statements on separate lines or separate them with colons on a single line.

Usage

```
SELECT CASE menu&
    CASE 1
        AddCustomers
    CASE 2
        AddTransactions
END SELECT
```

If *menu&* equals 1, the program executes the subprogram *AddCustomers*; if *menu&* equals 2, the program executes the subprogram *AddTransactions.*

```
SELECT CASE ok$
    CASE "Y", "y"
        DoIt
    CASE "N", "n"
        Cancel
END SELECT
```

If the variable *ok$* equals "Y" or "y", the program executes the subprogram *DoIt*; if *ok$* equals "N" or "n", the program executes the subprogram *Cancel*.

```
SELECT CASE year%
    CASE 1901 TO 1930
        PRINT "Early twentieth century..."
    CASE 1931 TO 1960
        PRINT "Mid-twentieth century..."
    CASE IS > 1961
        PRINT "Late twentieth century or beyond..."
END SELECT
```

If the variable *year%* is between 1901 and 1930, or between 1931 and 1960, or greater than 1960, an appropriate message is displayed.

```
SELECT CASE number%
    CASE 0, 2 TO 8, IS > 99, IS < max%
        PRINT "Valid range"
        GOTO Valid
    CASE ELSE
        PRINT "Invalid range"
        GOTO Invalid
END SELECT
```

Shows a complex combination of SELECT CASE options: If *number%* is 0, 2, 3, 4, 5, 6, 7, 8, greater than 99, or less than the value of *max%*, the program prints the message "Valid range" and transfers control to the line with the label *Valid*. Otherwise, the program prints the message "Invalid range" and transfers control to the line labeled *Invalid*.

Description

The IF statement (discussed in the IF entry) is the lowest level of decision making in QuickBASIC. QuickBASIC's SELECT CASE, like Pascal's CASE statement and C's *switch* statement, offers enhancements to the simple IF statement. IF operates on logical comparisons; SELECT CASE is more efficient in working with range and relational comparisons. Because QuickBASIC's SELECT CASE accepts relational operators, you can make any comparisons with either SELECT CASE or a combination of IF, ELSEIF, and ELSE statements.

The expression in the SELECT CASE clause can be any integer, floating-point, or string expression. For example, in the following clause the value of the expression *LOG(e)* is compared to the constants in the CASE clauses:

```
SELECT CASE LOG(e)
```

SELECT CASE compares the value of the expression to the values or range of values in the CASE clauses. If the expression matches the value or range of values, the statements of that CASE clause are executed. After the block of statements executes, control continues at the first statement following the END SELECT clause.

Following are some examples of valid values for the comparison expression.

A single expression:

CASE 3.141592653# * arc#	Matches the value of pi times *arc#*
CASE pastDueAmount!	Matches the variable *pastDueAmount!*
CASE 1000&	Matches the long integer 1000
CASE patientName$	Matches the string variable *patientName$*

A value range (*lowexpr* TO *highexpr*, where *lowexpr* must be less than *highexpr*, either numerically smaller or earlier in ascending ASCII order):

CASE 1 TO 10	Matches 1.0 through 10.0
CASE "A" TO "Z"	Matches all capital letters
CASE 10 TO 1	Invalid—must be 1 TO 10

A range comparison:

CASE IS = 1	Matches numbers equal to 1
CASE 1	Matches numbers equal to 1
CASE IS <= 10	Matches numbers less than or equal to 10
CASE IS <> 255	Matches all numbers not equal to 255
CASE IS <= "Z"	Matches all strings less than or equal to Z

The IS keyword gives SELECT CASE all the functionality of the IF statement by letting you use QuickBASIC's relational operators (=, <>, >, <, >=, and <=). Note that a CASE clause using an equal sign is equivalent to a CASE clause that uses a single expression.

If none of the CASE statements' values or ranges of values match the expression, QuickBASIC executes the statements of the CASE ELSE clause (if one exists). To maintain compatibility between the versions of QuickBASIC that support SELECT CASE, include a CASE ELSE statement even if your program doesn't require it.

You can make several comparisons (separated by commas) in each CASE clause. If you use multiple comparisons, QuickBASIC executes the associated statements if any of the comparisons match. The commas act like the logical operator OR in the IF statement. However, you cannot simulate the logical operator AND.

Tips

Because you cannot use logical operators with SELECT CASE, the IF statement is a better choice when your program must make logical comparisons (using the logical operators AND, OR, NOT, XOR, EQV, and IMP).

Because floating-point operations can be inaccurate, floating-point numbers that appear equal when printed might actually have minute differences. If you round floating-point numbers before you compare them, the differences will not affect the comparison.

Warnings

In versions of QuickBASIC earlier than 4.5, if you use a GOTO statement to branch into a SELECT CASE statement, the statements of the CASE ELSE clause will be executed.

Compatibility

QuickBASIC 3.0

QuickBASIC version 3.0 does not permit you to use variables in the CASE comparison clause—only string and numeric literals can be used. For example, you can use the literal string "YES" or the literal number 1000&, but not the variable *firstName$* or *pastDueAmount!*.

QuickBASIC 3.0 and QuickBASIC 4.0

QuickBASIC versions 3.0 and 4.0 return a runtime error message "CASE ELSE expected" if you use a SELECT CASE statement without a matching CASE clause and without a CASE ELSE clause. QuickBASIC version 4.5 merely ignores the entire SELECT CASE statement and continues execution at the first statement following END SELECT.

Example

The following example uses the SELECT CASE statement to determine how many characters in a sentence are vowels, consonants, and punctuation marks.

```
CLS
LINE INPUT "Enter a sentence: "; sentence$

vowels = 0: consonants = 0: punctuation = 0   ' initialize counter variables

FOR X = 1 TO LEN(sentence$)                   ' loop through the string
    char$ = UCASE$(MID$(sentence$, X, 1))     ' get a single character

    SELECT CASE char$
        CASE "A", "E", "I", "O", "U"          ' check for vowels
            vowels = vowels + 1
        CASE "A" TO "Z"                       ' consonants
            consonants = consonants + 1       ' includes the vowels, but they
                                              ' are counted first
        CASE ELSE
            punctuation = punctuation + 1     ' all others are punctuation marks
    END SELECT
NEXT

' print totals
PRINT "In the sentence containing"; LEN(sentence$); "characters,"
PRINT "there are"; vowels; "vowels,"; consonants; "consonants and";
PRINT punctuation; "punctuation marks"
```

XOR

See also: AND, EQV, IF, IMP, MOD, NOT, OR

■ QB2	■ QB4.5	■ PowerBASIC
■ QB3	ANSI	■ GW-BASIC
■ QB4	■ BASIC7	■ MacQB

Purpose

The XOR operator is both a logical and an arithmetic operator. As a logical operator, it returns a value of true if either, but not both, of its operands has a value of true. Use the XOR operator to guarantee that only one variable is true; this prevents conflicting options from being true. As an arithmetic operator, it performs XOR operations with the corresponding bits of two values.

Syntax

IF *op1* XOR *op2* THEN ...

or

result% = *op1* XOR *op2*

The *op1* and *op2* operands can be of any numeric type (integer, long integer, single precision, or double precision), but the result is always an integer or a long integer.

result% is the variable that contains the result of an arithmetic XOR operation.

Usage

```
IF hardDisk% XOR floppyDisk% THEN
    PRINT "You can now install the program."
END IF
```

If either (but not both) of the variables *hardDisk%* or *floppyDisk%* is true, the message is displayed.

Description

QuickBASIC's XOR operator can be used in a logical expression to tell you whether one (but not both) of the operands is true. For example,

```
var1 > 2 XOR var2 < 4
```

is true only when the expression *var1 > 2* is true and *var2 < 4* is false or when the expression *var1 > 2* is false and *var2 < 4* is true.

The XOR operator can also be used to perform a bit-by-bit comparison of the operands. If the corresponding bits in the operands have different values, the resulting bit is 1; if they have the same values, the resulting bit is 0. See the truth table in Table 3-8 on the following page.

p	q	p XOR q
1	1	0
1	0	1
0	1	1
0	0	0

Table 3-8.
XOR truth table.

Figure 3-3 shows an example of an arithmetic use of the XOR operator.

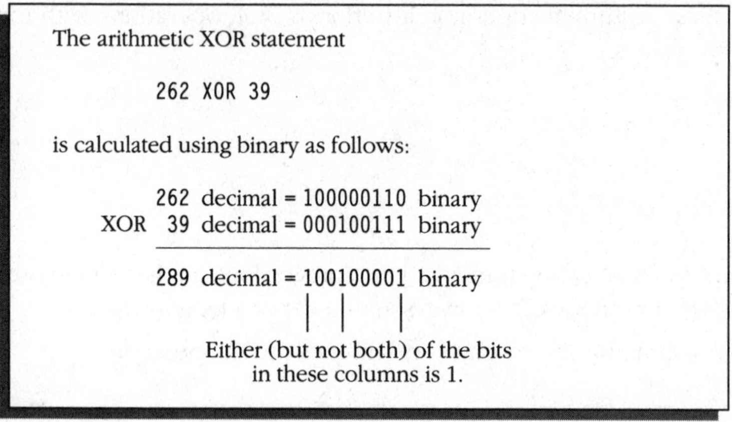

Figure 3-3.
Arithmetic XOR.

The XOR operator accepts single-precision and double-precision operands; however, it converts them to integers or long integers before processing them. The result of the XOR operation is always an integer or a long integer.

Errors

The operands in an XOR operation can be of any numeric type (integer, long integer, single precision, or double precision) in the range –2147483648 through 2147483647. If either is outside the range, QuickBASIC returns an "Overflow" error message.

Example

The following example shows how to use the XOR operator in the UNTIL clause of a DO...LOOP statement to loop until the user chooses only one of the two types of loans.

```
CLS
PRINT "Type of Loan": PRINT

DO
    DO
        INPUT "Would you like a fixed-interest-rate loan (Y/N)"; fixed$
        INPUT "Would you like an adjustable-interest-rate loan (Y/N)"; adj$
        PRINT
    LOOP UNTIL UCASE$(fixed$) = "Y" XOR UCASE$(adj$) = "Y"

    IF UCASE$(fixed$) = "Y" THEN
        PRINT "You have chosen a fixed-interest-rate loan."
    ELSE
        PRINT "You have chosen an adjustable-interest-rate loan."
    END IF
    INPUT "Have you changed your mind (Y/N)"; change$
LOOP UNTIL UCASE$(change$) = "N"
```

CHAPTER 4

Procedures

Introduction

Early versions of BASIC don't offer structured features; if programmers aren't careful, their programs can become difficult to read and maintain. Also, programs that use early versions of BASIC are limited to the size of the largest source file that the interpreter can process.

QuickBASIC has neither of these problems. It contains all the structured features of the structured programming languages such as C and Pascal. You can define your own functions and subprograms, use them in separately compiled modules, and pass them the variables and arguments that they require. You can also control the scope of variables—making them visible only to the current module, sharing them with other procedures, or making them common to the entire program.

QuickBASIC also lets you link together individual modules to create a program whose size is limited only by the amount of memory in your computer. If your application uses more memory than you have available, QuickBASIC lets you build a set of programs and chain between them in whatever sequence you require.

This chapter discusses the structured features of QuickBASIC in detail. Table 4-1 lists the QuickBasic procedure statements and functions in alphabetic order.

Statement or function	Description
CALL	Transfers control to a QuickBASIC subprogram or a mixed-language procedure in a separately compiled module
CHAIN	Transfers control to another program
COMMON	Declares variables that can be passed to other modules of the same program or to a separate, chained program
DECLARE	Defines the name and parameter list of a procedure specified by a SUB or FUNCTION statement
DEF FN	Defines a user-defined function compatible with those written in early versions of QuickBASIC
FUNCTION	Defines a QuickBASIC function
GOSUB...RETURN	Branches to a subroutine in the current program module
SHARED	Specifies variables that can be shared by functions, subprograms, and statements in the module-level code

Table 4-1.
Procedure statements and functions.

(continued)

Table 4-1. *(continued)*

Statement or function	Description
STATIC	Specifies the local variables that retain their values between calls to a function or a subprogram
SUB	Defines a subprogram

Program Organization

A QuickBASIC program does not need to be a single source-code file. A program is often easier to construct from a number of independent sections, called modules, each of which contains code dedicated to a specific part of the program's overall task. Modules are self-contained and can be developed and tested apart from the body of the program. In fact, different modules in a single program are often written by different programmers, and one module can often be used in several unrelated programs.

Modules enable programmers to create large programs. Because the memory in IBM PCs and PC compatibles has a maximum segment size of 64 KB, a single-module program cannot have more than 64 KB of code. However, when QuickBASIC links a program with several modules, each module is given its own code segment; therefore, multiple-module programs easily overcome the 64-KB limit. (See Chapter 19, "Port and Memory," and Chapter 20, "Mixed Language," for more information about memory segments.)

It is important to distinguish between programs, modules, and subprograms. A program, which is a series of statements that instruct your computer to perform a task, can consist of one or more modules. A module is a separate source file that performs either all or a portion of the program's task. Each module of a program can contain subprograms and user-defined functions.

Only one of the files that make up a program can contain the module-level code that QuickBASIC directly executes when a user runs the program. This is called the "main module." The other files are "support modules"; they can hold functions and subprograms that are called from the main module. The statements in a support module can be written in QuickBASIC or in another programming language, such as FORTRAN, Pascal, C, or assembly language. You must *call* these procedures, however; you cannot use GOTO or GOSUB to jump to a separately compiled module. (See Chapter 20, "Mixed Language," for details.)

Support Modules

In addition to subprograms and functions, a support module can contain its own module-level code; however, this code cannot be executed from the main program. The module-level code in a support module is restricted to the following:

- Metacommands
- DIM, SHARED, and COMMON statements
- TYPE...END TYPE statements
- ON *event* GOSUB and ON ERROR GOTO statements

Metacommands

You can use any compiler metacommand in a support module. Use $INCLUDE, for example, to insert additional source code into the program when the program is compiled; however, you cannot include subprograms or functions in the inserted file.

Use the $DYNAMIC metacommand to make all the module's arrays dynamic. If an array is dynamic, you can redimension it when the program runs. If you use $STATIC, QuickBASIC allocates memory for the arrays when the program is compiled, and the arrays cannot be redimensioned. (For more information see Chapter 21, "Metacommands.")

DIM, SHARED, and COMMON Statements

You can dimension variables and arrays in the module-level code of a support module. If you want the variables and arrays to be available to all the procedures in the module, use the DIM statement with the SHARED keyword. Without the SHARED keyword, the dimensioned variables are visible to the subprograms and functions only if you specify the variables in a SHARED statement in each procedure that uses them. The DIM statement that includes the SHARED keyword does not make these variables available to procedures in other modules; only a COMMON statement can do that.

The COMMON statement makes specified variables accessible in all modules that contain a matching COMMON statement. If the variable that you declare in a COMMON statement is a dynamic array, you need to dimension it only once (in the main module) after the COMMON statement for that module. However, you must dimension a static array in every module that uses it (before the corresponding COMMON statement).

Variables specified by a COMMON statement are not visible to the subprograms and functions in the module. To make them visible, either you must include the keyword SHARED in the COMMON statement or you can include a separate SHARED statement in every procedure that needs to access variables specified in the COMMON statement.

Variable Type Definitions

You can define complex variable types by using the TYPE...END TYPE statement. (See Chapter 1, "Types and Variables," for information about user-defined types.) In the DIM statement that declares a variable of a user-defined type, you must include the SHARED keyword if you want the variable to be visible to procedures in the module—for example,

```
DIM SHARED stockRecord AS RecordType
```

If the module doesn't include this statement, the subprograms and functions themselves must include the statement

```
SHARED stockRecord AS RecordType
```

to access the contents of the variable *stockRecord*.

ON *event* GOSUB and ON ERROR GOTO

The module-level code of support modules can include event-trapping as well as error-trapping statements. These two types of statements, however, are handled in different ways.

Error trapping is local to the module in which it takes place. This means that if a support module includes an ON ERROR GOTO statement, the line number or label to which the GOTO refers must be in the same module as the ON ERROR GOTO statement.

Event trapping is global to the entire program. If you define a subroutine to handle events specified by an ON KEY(*n*) GOSUB, ON COM GOSUB, or ON UEVENT GOSUB statement or another event handler in one module, and the named event occurs while the program is executing another module, control still branches to the handling routine in the first module and then returns to the second at the end of the operation. Therefore, unless you want to enable events only in a specific module, you probably should place your event-trapping statements in the main module.

See Chapter 9, "Trapping and Errors," for more information about error trapping. Event-handling statements are discussed in the chapters that describe the events to which they refer.

Scope of Variables

Because QuickBASIC lets you build programs from separate modules, it also provides a means for these modules to access common data. The DIM statement with the SHARED keyword makes specific variables available to all functions and subprograms in a single module. The COMMON statement permits access to variables in any module in the current program that includes a matching COMMON statement. It also lets you pass variables when you chain one program to another. The extent to which a variable is visible to different parts of a program is called its "scope." Figure 4-1 shows the relationship of variables between programs, modules, and procedures.

In Figure 4-1, the integer variable *a%* is declared common in the main module of Program 1. Because *a%* is also declared common in Modules 1 and 3 of Program 1, it can be used by statements in those modules as well. Module 2, however, has no variables declared in a COMMON statement. If you declare a variable named *a%* in a procedure in Module 2, it will be a completely different variable from the *a%* used in other parts of the program.

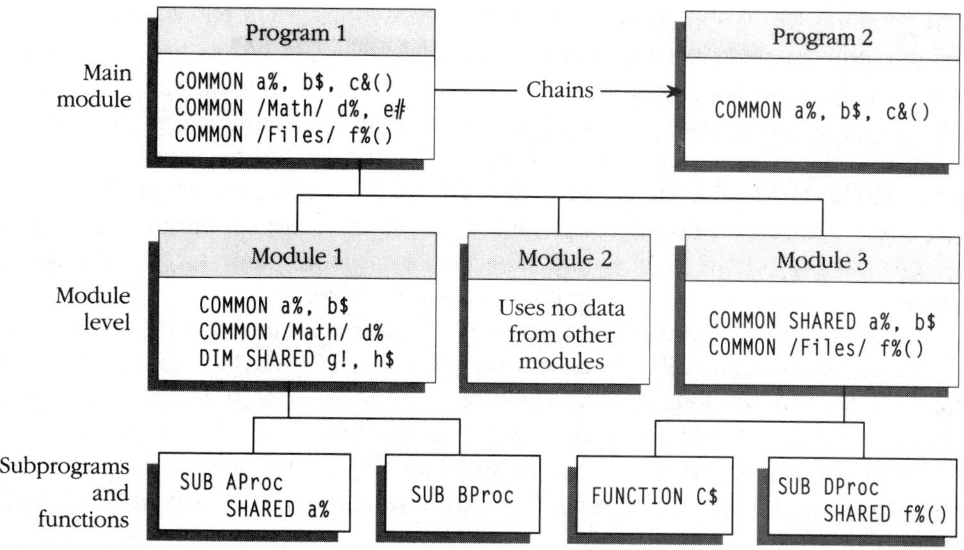

Figure 4-1.
Relationships between programs, modules, and procedures.

The variable *a%* in Module 1, although visible to the main module and Module 3, is not visible to the subprograms or functions in Module 1 unless it is specified in a SHARED statement, as is the case in the subprogram *AProc*. In Module 3, however, *a%* is declared in a SHARED statement in the module-level code so that the function *C$* and the subprogram *DProc* can use it.

Finally, because *a%* is declared common in the main module of Program 1, its contents can be passed to Program 2, which is chained when Program 1 finishes.

Subprograms

A subprogram is a type of procedure. Because it is a self-contained block of code that performs a single programming task, it can easily be transferred from one module to another; indeed, you can use the same subprogram in many different programs.

Unlike the traditional BASIC subroutine, which it is intended to replace, a subprogram defined by a SUB statement has only one entry point—at the first executable statement of the procedure. However, a subprogram can have more than one exit point because, in addition to the END SUB statement that marks the normal exit point, QuickBASIC also provides an EXIT SUB statement that forces an early termination of the subprogram.

You can place subprograms either in the main module of a program or in one of the support modules. You can also store them in an external library or in a Quick

Library for use in the QuickBASIC environment. No matter where you place a subprogram, it is not considered part of the module-level code, and its variables (except those passed to it or specified in a SHARED statement) are local to the subprogram.

By default, variables that are local to a subprogram (or to a function, as explained below) are created each time the procedure is called and are destroyed each time control returns to the line that called the procedure. Local variables are unique to the procedure that uses them and cannot be accessed by any other subprogram, even if it contains variables of the same name. This enables subprograms to call themselves recursively, with each iteration using its own set of variables.

In some cases, however, you might want a subprogram to retain the values of its local variables between calls. To do so, use QuickBASIC's STATIC statement. If you define the entire procedure as static, none of its variables is destroyed when the procedure completes; if you make only one or two variables static, the rest remain transient. Note, however, that two types of variables are always static—those that are passed to the subprogram as arguments and those that are specified in a SHARED statement.

Calling Subprograms

You can execute a subprogram by issuing a CALL (BASIC procedures) statement. The following statement, for example, is a call to a subprogram named *VGASave*:

```
CALL VGASave(picName$)
```

picName$*, the variable in parentheses, is a string argument that is passed to the called subprogram. Any changes made to *picName$ in the subprogram are returned to the calling module when *VGASave* completes.

If *VGASave* is not located in the current module, you must tell QuickBASIC what kind of variables will be used in a call to it by using a DECLARE statement. Here is a DECLARE statement for *VGASave*:

```
DECLARE SUB VGASave (pictureName AS STRING)
```

This statement tells the compiler that when you call *VGASave* you are calling a subprogram (and not a function) and that the subprogram requires a single argument, which must be a string.

It is good practice to include DECLARE statements for every subprogram or function you call, even if they are called from the same module. Indeed, if you write a program in the QuickBASIC environment, the "smart" editor generates these statements. Using DECLARE, in fact, makes the CALL statement unnecessary and lets you call *VGASave* merely by naming it:

```
VGASave picName$
```

Notice that if you omit the CALL statement, you must not use parentheses around the argument list.

Subroutines

Subroutines are the traditional way of storing code that must be executed repeatedly during the course of a program. To branch to a subroutine, you use the following statement syntax:

GOSUB *location*

In this statement, *location* is the line number or label of a statement in the subroutine code. It does not need to be the first statement in the subroutine, although entering at some other point is poor programming style. The program continues from the entry point until it encounters a RETURN statement, which causes execution to resume with the statement following the GOSUB statement.

You can use GOSUB only to branch to a routine in the current module. You cannot branch to a subroutine in another module as you can with a subprogram, nor can you pass arguments to a subroutine. In fact, all the variables in the module-level code are available to a subroutine and may be changed by it.

Avoid using the GOSUB statement. In QuickBASIC, subroutines have been largely replaced by the more powerful subprograms; however, they still have their uses, particularly in event trapping. (See the various ON *event* GOSUB statements.)

User-Defined Functions

Functions are merely procedures that return a value. QuickBASIC not only provides many built-in functions; it also lets you design your own. The two types of QuickBASIC functions are the functions defined by DEF FN (a carryover from BASICA) and the more powerful function procedure, which is defined by the FUNCTION statement.

FUNCTION Procedures

A procedure defined by a FUNCTION statement is similar to a subprogram except that it returns a value. It also must be named as though it were a variable of the same type as the returned value. For example, you might declare a function that returns a long integer as follows:

```
DECLARE FUNCTION BinDec& (binry AS STRING)
```

The DECLARE statement lets you call *BinDec&* from anywhere in the program, even from a separately compiled module or a library. You don't use a CALL statement; instead, you must assign the value returned by the function to another variable, as in the following example:

```
decimal& = BinDec&(binaryNumber$)
```

You can also use a procedure defined by FUNCTION in a QuickBASIC statement or as an argument to another function or statement—for example,

```
PRINT BinDec&("01010011")
OUT speaker%, CINT(BinDec&(mask$))
```

Like subprograms, procedures defined by FUNCTION take arguments and use local variables (except for those designated by a SHARED statement). You must make variables static with the STATIC statement if you want to preserve their values between calls. Because variables are local to each function and because a function can be used as an argument to another function, you can call functions recursively.

DEF FN Functions

Functions defined by a DEF FN statement are to procedures defined by FUNCTION what subroutines are to subprograms. QuickBASIC includes them for compatibility with older versions of BASIC, in which DEF FN is the only user-defined function.

DEF FN statements must appear in the module-level code of the main program module. You cannot put them in support modules or store them in libraries, nor can they be called by procedures in these modules. Variables named in a DEF FN statement are not local by default, as they are in a FUNCTION statement. To isolate DEF FN variables, you must make them static; otherwise, their scope extends to the entire main module. In short, DEF FN statements do nothing more than FUNCTION statements, and they are more difficult to use.

Use subprograms and functions rather than subroutines and DEF FN functions; their modular nature makes them easy to develop and test in isolation. Also, because subprograms and functions are completely self contained, you can easily incorporate them into libraries, where they are ready to be linked to any program that needs them.

Chaining

Instead of returning control to DOS, a QuickBASIC program can transfer control to another program when it finishes. You can accomplish this in one of two ways. Simply use the RUN statement to execute a second program or, if you don't specify a filename, to start the same program again. Or, use the CHAIN statement to start a second program. The difference between these two commands is that CHAIN lets you pass selected variables to the new program.

To pass information to another program, you must use CHAIN in conjunction with the COMMON statement. As well as being available to different modules within the same program, variables specified by a COMMON statement can be transferred to any program that contains a matching COMMON statement. However, only programs that run in the QuickBASIC environment and executable programs that use the BRUN45.EXE runtime library can pass common variables when chaining. Stand-alone executable programs cannot do this. (See the entry for the COMMON statement for a method of circumventing this restriction.)

In a stand-alone executable program, you can also use the CHAIN statement to chain to programs written in other languages.

CALL (BASIC procedures)

See also: CALL ABSOLUTE, CALL (Non-BASIC procedures), DECLARE, FUNCTION

■ QB2	■ QB4.5	■ PowerBASIC
■ QB3	■ ANSI	GW-BASIC
■ QB4	■ BASIC7	■ MacQB

Purpose

The CALL statement for BASIC procedures lets you execute subprograms from anywhere in your program. The subprograms can be stored in separately compiled support modules or in libraries that you link to a program.

Syntax

[CALL] *name* [[(] *arg* [, *arg* ...] [)]]

name can contain up to 40 characters and must match the name of the subprogram being called.

arg is one or more optional arguments (variables, constants, or expressions), separated by commas, that are passed to the subprogram.

CALL is a keyword that is optional if you use a DECLARE statement to define the types of variables for the call to the subprogram. If you omit CALL, you must also omit the parentheses around the argument list.

Usage

```
CALL ShutDoor
```

Executes the procedure *ShutDoor*, which does not take any parameters.

```
CALL Scan(UCASE$(COMMAND$))
```

Executes the subprogram *Scan*, which receives an argument that is the result of a call to the QuickBASIC function UCASE$.

```
VerMenu 8, 28, menu%
```

Executes the subprogram *VerMenu*, which has been previously declared in the module-level code or has a related DECLARE statement.

Description

This version of the CALL statement can be used only to execute subprograms written in QuickBASIC. The extended version, which is described in the entry CALL (Non-BASIC procedures) in Chapter 20, "Mixed Language," can be used to transfer control to procedures written in other programming languages.

Subprograms are self-contained blocks of statements and, as such, are not part of the module-level code, even when you include them in the current source file. Because they are separate entities, you cannot branch to them with GOTO and GOSUB statements. Instead, you must use a CALL statement, which transfers control to a subprogram, even if the subprogram is in a library or a support module.

Using the DECLARE statement to define how a subprogram is called removes the need for the CALL keyword and lets you execute the subprogram using only its name. If you omit CALL, you must also omit the parentheses around the argument list. In effect, the subprogram becomes an extension of the QuickBASIC language.

If an argument is a variable, it must be of the type that the subprogram expects.

By default, any variables in the CALL statement's argument list are *passed by reference.* This means that QuickBASIC passes to the subprogram the address of the variables—not the values—so that any changes made to the variables in the subprogram are maintained when control returns from the subprogram. You can prevent this by enclosing in parentheses each variable that you don't want modified, as in the following statement:

```
QuickSort observations%(), (day1%), (day6%)
```

This causes QuickBASIC to evaluate the variable in parentheses and to copy the result to a temporary variable, the address of which is then passed to the procedure, leaving the original variable unaffected. This is often called *passing by value*; however, it is not the same as using the BYVAL keyword, which is available in calls to non-BASIC procedures. BYVAL achieves true passing by value by placing the contents of parameter variables on the program stack.

Warnings

If you call a subprogram by its name alone, QuickBASIC might mistake the reference for a line label. This can happen if the subprogram name is the first statement on the line and the call does not include any parameters, as in the following example:

```
PrintScreen: LOCATE 24, 65: PRINT "Press a key >";
```

In this line, QuickBASIC will probably mistake the call to the procedure *PrintScreen* as a line label, even if *PrintScreen* has previously been declared as a subprogram.

This mistake does not produce an error message. However, the subprogram never executes, and this might result in long hours of debugging time before you understand why. In such circumstances, always include the CALL keyword, even if you previously used a DECLARE statement.

Example

The following program uses a procedure to draw outlined boxes on the text screen, exactly as the LINE statement does on the graphics screen. You can store the procedure in a library so that you can use it with other programs.

```
DECLARE SUB Panel (switch%, row%, col%, numrows%, numcols%)

CLS
FOR i% = 1 TO 7
    COLOR 15, i%
    Panel 1, i% * 2, i% * 2, 8, 20          ' draw a single-border panel
    Panel 2, i% * 2, 40 + i% * 2, 8, 20     ' draw a double-border panel
NEXT i%
COLOR 7, 0
END

SUB Panel (switch%, row%, col%, numrows%, numcols%) STATIC
    IF numcols% > 81 - col% THEN numcols% = 81 - col%
    IF numrows% > 24 - row% THEN numrows% = 24 - row%

    IF switch% = 1 THEN     ' characters for single-border panel
        top$ = CHR$(218) + STRING$(numcols% - 2, CHR$(196)) + CHR$(191)
        mdl$ = CHR$(179) + STRING$(numcols% - 2, " ") + CHR$(179)
        bot$ = CHR$(192) + STRING$(numcols% - 2, CHR$(196)) + CHR$(217)

    ELSE                    ' characters for double-border panel
        top$ = CHR$(201) + STRING$(numcols% - 2, CHR$(205)) + CHR$(187)
        mdl$ = CHR$(186) + STRING$(numcols% - 2, " ") + CHR$(186)
        bot$ = CHR$(200) + STRING$(numcols% - 2, CHR$(205)) + CHR$(188)
    END IF
    LOCATE row%, col%, 0: PRINT top$;                ' print top of square
    FOR i% = 1 TO numrows% - 2
        LOCATE row% + i%, col%: PRINT mdl$;          ' print middle of square
    NEXT i%
    LOCATE row% + i%, col%: PRINT bot$;              ' print bottom of square
END SUB
```

CHAIN

See also: CALL (BASIC procedures), COMMON, SHELL

■ QB2	■ QB4.5	✲ PowerBASIC
■ QB3	✲ ANSI	✲ GW-BASIC
■ QB4	■ BASIC7	✲ MacQB

Purpose

When one program's task is finished, the CHAIN statement lets you pass control to another program. Use CHAIN when a programming task is divided among several programs.

Syntax

CHAIN *filename*

filename is the name of the program to which you are chaining. Like all DOS filenames it can be no more than 8 characters long; you can also include a drive letter, directory path, and filename extension. If you enter the name literally, you must enclose it in quotation marks; otherwise, you can use any valid string variable or expression to hold the filename.

Usage

```
CHAIN "A:\BIN\PROGRAM2"
```

Transfers control to the PROGRAM2 program in drive A and directory BIN.

```
CHAIN drive$ + path$ + program$(choice%)
```

Transfers control to the program specified by the concatenation of the variables *drive$*, *path$*, and *program$(choice%)*.

Description

QuickBASIC is a modular language. On the lowest level are the subprograms and functions that are included in the main module. In addition, you can group subprograms and functions into separately compiled support modules, which are called from the main module, but are linked to it only when the program executes. Finally, for large applications, you might find it convenient to divide the task among several different programs, each devoted to one particular aspect of the job. The CHAIN statement lets you transfer control from one such program to another.

You can pass variables that are specified in a COMMON statement in the "chaining" program to the "chained-to program," provided that both have matching COMMON statements. This applies only to programs run in the QuickBASIC environment and to those compiled for use with the runtime library, BRUN45.LIB. Stand-alone programs that don't use BRUN45.LIB cannot pass variables during chaining. (See the entry for the COMMON statement for an alternative method of passing variables.)

CHAIN handles programs run in the QuickBASIC environment in a manner different from the way it handles programs run from the DOS command line. When you chain programs in the QuickBASIC environment, the target program must be in source-code format. QuickBASIC assumes a BAS file extension unless another is specified. When you chain from a program compiled with BC.EXE, the command-line compiler, the target program must be in the same executable format. If no filename extension is supplied, compiled programs assume an EXE file extension.

Tips

When you chain to stand-alone programs (outside of the QuickBASIC environment), the chained-to program does not have to be written in QuickBASIC or even another Microsoft language. However, if you want to chain to anything other than a file with the EXE extension (for example, an assembly-language program in COM format), you must include the file extension in the program name, as in the following statement:

```
CHAIN "C:\TOOLS\RAMPAGE.COM"
```

If you don't use the COM extension, QuickBASIC tries to chain to an EXE file; when it doesn't find the EXE file, it generates a "File not found" error message.

Warnings

Note that when you chain between programs in the QuickBASIC environment or between programs compiled for use with the BRUN45.LIB runtime library, any files left open by the chaining program remain open when the chained program starts. Because QuickBASIC lets you open the same file more than once, you could accidently reopen files until you generate a "Too many open files" error message. Chaining between stand-alone executable programs (those compiled with the BC.EXE /O switch) always closes any currently open files.

Compatibility

ANSI BASIC

ANSI BASIC uses a different method for passing variables between programs. Instead of using the COMMON statement, ANSI suggests a syntax with the form "CHAIN *filename* WITH (*argument_list*)," which passes parameters to the chained program exactly as they are passed to a subprogram or function.

PowerBASIC

PowerBASIC does not let you CHAIN between programs from within its own environment. You can chain only from programs run at the DOS command line and from programs that have been compiled as executable files or special modules. Aside from these restrictions, the syntax and usage of the CHAIN statement in PowerBASIC is identical to that of CHAIN in QuickBASIC.

GW-BASIC and BASICA

The GW-BASIC and BASICA versions of the CHAIN statement have several options that are not supported by QuickBASIC. The MERGE option lets you overlay the chained-to file (saved in ASCII format) onto the current program without removing the current program from memory. (The QuickBASIC environment lets you merge another file with the currently loaded program, but not while the program is running.) The DELETE option of the CHAIN command lets you delete a range of line numbers in the current program. This option is often used to delete the lines of one overlay before another overlay is merged with the program. The ALL option saves all the current program's variables in memory for use by the chained-to program, thus eliminating the need for the COMMON statement. In addition, GW-BASIC and BASICA offer the line-number option, which lets you specify the line number at which the chained-to program should start execution. In QuickBASIC, chained programs always start at the first executable statement.

QuickBASIC for the Macintosh

QuickBASIC for the Macintosh has two versions of the CHAIN statement. The first lets you chain to source files within the QuickBASIC environment; this version is identical to the GW-BASIC and BASICA CHAIN statement, which supports the MERGE, ALL, DELETE, and line-number options. The second version is the same as the CHAIN statement in QuickBASIC 4.5 and is used for transferring control between executable programs. In both cases the target file must be another QuickBASIC program; QuickBASIC for the Macintosh does not let you chain to programs written in another language.

Example

To simplify programming, large applications are often split into several smaller programs or overlays. The following program presents the top-level menu for such an application. It is flexible enough that you can use it for a variety of applications. After the user chooses a menu option, the program uses a CHAIN statement to execute the program corresponding to the option.

```
' $DYNAMIC

CLS : RESTORE
READ options%                   ' get the number of options in the menu
DIM menu(options%) AS STRING    ' declare an array of strings
READ menu(0)                    ' get the string containing possible choices

FOR i% = 1 TO options%
    READ menu(i%)
    IF i% = 1 THEN column% = 40 - (LEN(menu(i%)) \ 2)
    LOCATE 8 + i%, column%: PRINT menu(i%);                  ' print menu option
NEXT i%

LOCATE 9 + i%, column%: PRINT "Press <Esc> to quit";
LOCATE 12 + i%, column% + 3: PRINT "< Your choice";

DO
    LOCATE 12 + i%, column%, 1
    choice$ = INPUT$(1): IF choice$ = CHR$(27) THEN EXIT DO
    choice$ = UCASE$(choice$)
    selection% = INSTR(menu(0), choice$)   ' find the index of the choice
    IF selection% THEN
        PRINT choice$;
        CHAIN "PROG" + LTRIM$(RTRIM$(STR$(selection%)))   ' chain to a program
    END IF
    BEEP
LOOP WHILE 1
END

DATA    6, "CAEDSP"
DATA    "C.  Create a data file", "A.  Add a new record"
DATA    "E.  Edit a record     ", "D.  Delete a record "
DATA    "S.  Sort the file     ", "P.  Print reports   "
```

COMMON

See also: CALL (BASIC procedures), CHAIN, $DYNAMIC, FRE

✲ QB2	■ QB4.5	✲ PowerBASIC
✲ QB3	✲ ANSI	✲ GW-BASIC
■ QB4	■ BASIC7	■ MacQB

Purpose

The COMMON statement determines the scope of variables in the list that follows it. By default, variables named in a program module are available to only that module. They cannot be accessed by other modules or even by subprograms and functions in the same module. COMMON extends the scope of the listed variables to other modules and chained programs that have a matching COMMON statement.

Syntax

COMMON [SHARED][/*Blockname*/] *var*[()][AS *type*][,*var*[()][AS *type*]] ...

SHARED is an option that extends the scope of the variables in the list by making them available to the subprograms and functions in the module as well as to other modules. Variables that are declared in a COMMON statement that includes the SHARED keyword in the module-level code can be examined or changed by all subprograms and functions in that module; therefore, you don't have to declare each as shared inside the subprograms and functions that use them.

Blockname is a legal QuickBASIC identifier of up to 40 characters that identifies the variable list as a unique block; the block is called a *named common block*. You must enclose the name in a pair of slash characters to distinguish it from other items in the variable list. Named blocks let you selectively pass variables between modules. Using them, a module must only specify the COMMON block (or blocks) that it actually needs, rather than maintain all common variables for the entire program. However, you cannot pass a named block to another (chained) program.

var is any legal QuickBASIC variable name and can include a type-declaration character (such as % for integers) to define the type of variable. Using the AS clause instead, however, is more flexible because it lets you include user-defined structures in addition to the types integer, long, single, double, and string. Array variables are identified in the COMMON statement by parentheses. Although you do not need to list the number of dimensions inside the parentheses, QuickBASIC accepts the number in order to maintain compatibility with earlier versions of BASIC.

Usage

```
COMMON wealth#
```

Declares a double-precision global variable.

```
COMMON wealth AS DOUBLE
```

Declares a double-precision global variable.

```
COMMON balance, surName AS STRING
```

Declares a single-precision variable and a variable-length string.

```
COMMON SHARED ages() AS INTEGER
```

Declares a global dynamic integer array and makes it available to all subprograms and functions in the current module.

```
DIM lightYears(1 TO 50) AS LONG
COMMON lightYears()
```

Declares a static, long-integer array of 50 elements and makes it available to other modules and chained programs.

```
TYPE CityType
    name AS STRING * 30
    population AS LONG
    latitude AS SINGLE
    longitude AS SINGLE
END TYPE

DIM capitals(1 TO 50) AS CityType
DIM seaPorts(1 TO 100) AS CityType

COMMON /Cities/ capitals() AS CityType, seaPorts() AS CityType
```

Declares a named common block containing two structures of type *CityType*.

Description

COMMON statements assign storage for global data (data that can be used by more than one module) during program initialization. Therefore, you must place them at the top of the main program, before any executable code. The only statements that can precede COMMON are the metacommands ($INCLUDE, $DYNAMIC, and $STATIC), the declarations of constants and procedures (CONST, DATA, and DECLARE), data type declarations using DEF*type*, or the statements TYPE...END TYPE, SHARED, STATIC, OPTION BASE, and DIM. Static arrays named in the variable list of the COMMON statement must be declared with DIM statements before the COMMON statement. Arrays in the COMMON statement that are not declared before COMMON are considered dynamic; this enables you to use the DIM or REDIM statement to dimension them anywhere in the current module.

All common variables declared without a block name occupy the same storage block in DGROUP, the root data segment. This is called the *blank* common block and is the only block that can be passed to chained programs. Named blocks, which have been given a block name, are stored separately in DGROUP and cannot be chained.

You must include matching COMMON statements in all modules that need to access global data. Note, however, that QuickBASIC does not preserve variable names across modules. Consequently, you can use different names to refer to the same variables in different modules. It is important only that you maintain the type and position of the variables in the COMMON statement, as shown in Figure 4-2.

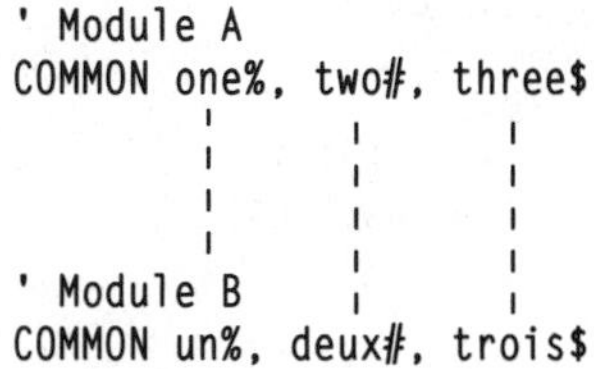

```
' Module A
COMMON one%, two#, three$
        |     |      |
        |     |      |
        |     |      |
        |     |      |
' Module B    |      |
COMMON un%, deux#, trois$
```

Figure 4-2.
Matching common variables.

If you declare a common array in the main program module as static, you must also declare it static in all other modules that use it. Similarly, a dynamic array must be dynamic in all participating modules because QuickBASIC stores static and dynamic arrays in different segments of memory.

The blank common block does not have to be the same size in each module that shares it. If, for example, Module A declares four common variables and Module B uses only the first two, you need declare only two variables in Module B:

```
' Module A
COMMON one AS INTEGER, two AS DOUBLE, three AS STRING, four AS LONG

' Module B
COMMON one AS INTEGER, two AS DOUBLE
```

If, however, Module B needs to access variables *one* and *four*, you must declare all four as common in Module B as shown below, even though *two* and *three* are not used:

```
' Module A
COMMON one AS INTEGER, two AS DOUBLE, three AS STRING, four AS LONG

' Module B
COMMON one AS INTEGER, x#, y$, four AS LONG
```

A more efficient way of selectively sharing variables with other modules is to use named blocks. (See Figure 4-3 on the following page.) You could, for example, group the variables used for specific programming tasks in different named blocks. Then the module that performs a particular task need only declare the appropriate block so that it doesn't have to maintain all the common variables in the program.

Remember, however, that named blocks can be shared only between modules of the same program; they cannot be passed to another program with the CHAIN statement. Only data declared in a blank common block can be chained.

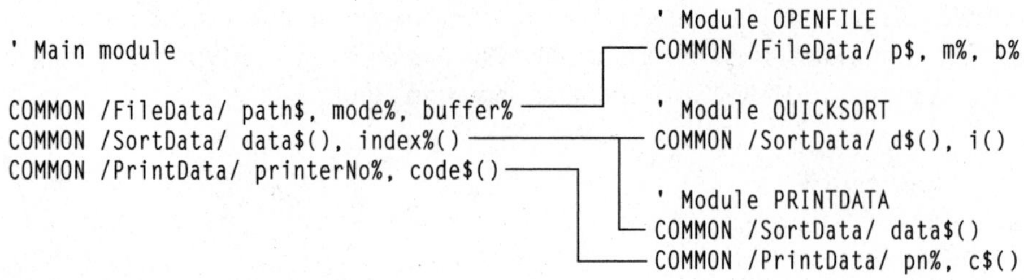

```
                                                 ' Module OPENFILE
' Main module                                  ┌─COMMON /FileData/ p$, m%, b%
                                               │
COMMON /FileData/ path$, mode%, buffer% ───────┘ ' Module QUICKSORT
COMMON /SortData/ data$(), index%() ─────────┬── COMMON /SortData/ d$(), i()
COMMON /PrintData/ printerNo%, code$() ──┐   │
                                         │   │   ' Module PRINTDATA
                                         │   └── COMMON /SortData/ data$()
                                         └────── COMMON /PrintData/ pn%, c$()
```

Figure 4-3.
Named blocks in program modules.

Comments

There is no arbitrary limit to the number of variables that you can declare as common; however, because common blocks are allocated to DGROUP, you must leave enough of this 64-KB space for the other variables your program uses. Use the statement *FRE("")* to determine the number of free bytes remaining in DGROUP.

Dynamic numeric arrays are an exception to this because they use only enough space in DGROUP for the array names. The contents of dynamic arrays are stored as far data (outside DGROUP) and are limited only by the amount of available memory in RAM (random-access memory). The statement *FRE(-1)* returns the number of bytes available for dynamic arrays.

Passing common data between chained programs is subject to one serious restriction: If you compile outside the QuickBASIC environment, the resulting executable files require the runtime library (BRUN45.EXE in QuickBASIC 4.5) to be present at runtime if you use COMMON statements. This means that you cannot compile with the /O switch to produce a truly stand-alone program. If you distribute programs commercially, you must either ensure that your customer has the correct version of the runtime library or avoid the use of common variables between programs.

You can partially avoid this restriction by using the MS-DOS Intra-Application Communication area (IAC), an area of memory reserved by the operating system that programs can use to communicate with each other. The IAC is 16 bytes long and is located in low RAM, at addresses 0040:00F0 through 0040:00FF (hexadecimal). The operating system retains a value set in the IAC until you reset it or the computer is rebooted. The following programs demonstrate this method of passing data.

```
' FLAGS1.BAS
DECLARE SUB SetFlag (flag%, setting%)

CLS
FOR i% = 1 TO 8
    j% = i% ^ 2
```

(continued)

continued

```
    PRINT j%; "  ";
    SetFlag i%, j%      ' i% is the index to the data, j% is the value
NEXT i%
CHAIN "FLAGS2"

SUB SetFlag (flag%, setting%) STATIC
    IF flag% > 0 AND flag% < 9 THEN
        offSet% = &HF0 + ((flag% - 1) * 2)
        hiByte% = setting% \ 256: loByte% = setting% MOD 256
        DEF SEG = &H40
        POKE offSet%, loByte%        ' place low byte of data in memory
        POKE offSet% + 1, hiByte%    ' place high byte of data in memory
        DEF SEG
    END IF
END SUB
```

```
' FLAGS2.BAS
DECLARE FUNCTION GetFlag% (flag%)

PRINT : PRINT
FOR i% = 1 TO 8
    PRINT GetFlag%(i%); "  ";
NEXT i%
END

FUNCTION GetFlag% (flag%) STATIC
    setting% = -1
    IF flag% > 0 AND flag% < 9 THEN
        offSet% = &HF0 + ((flag% - 1) * 2)  ' find offset of data
        DEF SEG = &H40
        setting% = PEEK(offSet%) + PEEK(offSet% + 1) * 256  ' get value of data
        DEF SEG
    END IF
    GetFlag% = setting%
END FUNCTION
```

A more advanced technique is to start the system with a small TSR (terminate-and-stay-resident) program that establishes a block of memory for shared data, writes the address of this block into the IAC, and then transfers control to the first program in the chain. Using this method, you can pass quantities of data larger than 64 KB, subject only to the memory available in your computer after you load your programs.

Errors

If a common variable has a type different from that of the variable occupying the same position in the common block of a chained-to program, QuickBASIC returns a "Type mismatch" error message at runtime.

Tips

Do not give the same name to variables declared in different COMMON statements in the same module. Doing this does not always produce the expected "Duplicate definition" error message at runtime and can result in incorrect data being passed between modules. This is a bug that can be very difficult to track down. To avoid this error, you can list declarations of common variables in a separate file that you include with the $INCLUDE metacommand in each module that uses them.

You should also keep in mind that common variables are not global to the module in which they are declared unless you specify the SHARED option.

Compatibility

QuickBASIC 2.0 and QuickBASIC 3.0

QuickBASIC versions 2.0 and 3.0 do not support named common blocks, nor do they contain the AS clause for defining variable types.

ANSI BASIC

The ANSI technique for passing variables to chained programs is different from the QuickBASIC method of using common blocks. The ANSI syntax for the CHAIN statement includes the WITH clause, in which the chaining program passes an argument list to its successor; for example,

```
CHAIN "NEXTONE" WITH (a%, b$)
```

would transfer control to the program NEXTONE, passing the contents of the variables *a%* and *b$* in the process.

PowerBASIC

Array variables declared in COMMON statements in PowerBASIC must be dynamic. PowerBASIC does not support named common blocks or the SHARED option. Otherwise, the syntax is the same as in QuickBASIC version 4.5.

GW-BASIC and BASICA

GW-BASIC and BASICA use the COMMON statement only for passing data to chained programs. They do not support named common blocks or the AS clause. As in QuickBASIC, you need not declare the number of subscripts in arrays; however, you do need to specify the number of dimensions if there are more than one. In GW-BASIC and BASICA, COMMON statements can occur anywhere in the program; in QuickBASIC, they must occur at the beginning of the program. Unlike QuickBASIC, GW-BASIC and BASICA do not require you to redimension arrays in the chained-to program.

The CHAIN statement in GW-BASIC and BASICA provides the (ALL) option, which lets you pass all your variables to the chained program without using COMMON declarations. QuickBASIC does not offer this option.

Example

The following two modules demonstrate the use of the COMMON statement. The first module prompts for the user's name and then calls the subprogram *InTake*, which is in the second module. *InTake* is a subprogram that accepts and validates keyboard input. The procedure generates its own cursor so that it can be used in both graphics and text modes, and it can be compiled and linked separately from the modules that use it. Therefore, it uses COMMON variables to receive and pass data.

```
DECLARE SUB InTake (Buffer$)

COMMON SHARED abort AS INTEGER
COMMON SHARED /InputData/ maxLen AS INTEGER, validKeys AS STRING

CONST FALSE = 0, TRUE = NOT FALSE                ' constants used by module

lc$ = "abcdefghijklmnopqrstuvwxyz": uc$ = UCASE$(lc$)
nu$ = "0123456789": punc$ = " .,;:'"

COLOR 14, 0: CLS
LOCATE 12, 1: PRINT "Enter your name > ";        ' prompt for name
COLOR 0, 7
maxLen = 40
validKeys = uc$ + lc$ + punc$                    ' string containing valid keys

InTake yourName$

LOCATE 15, 1
IF abort THEN
    PLAY "T255 L24 01 A A A 02 B B B 03 C C C 04 D D D 05"
    COLOR 12, 0: PRINT "You pressed Esc"
ELSE
    PLAY "T240 03 L8 G F L4 E L8 E E D E L3 F L4 E"
    PLAY"L8 E L4 D L8 D D C D L3 E L4 C L8 D L4 E"
    PLAY "L8 E E D E L4 F L8 G L4 A L8 A L4 G L8 F L4 E L8 D L4 C"
    COLOR 11, 0: PRINT "Hello, "; yourName$
END IF
LOCATE , , 1
END
```

```
COMMON SHARED abort AS INTEGER
COMMON SHARED /InputData/ maxLen AS INTEGER, validKeys AS STRING

CONST FALSE = 0, TRUE = NOT FALSE     ' constants used by module

SUB InTake (buffer$) STATIC
```

(continued)

continued

```
    bSpace$ = CHR$(8): cr$ = CHR$(13): esc$ = CHR$(27)     ' special keys
    cLeft$ = CHR$(29): cursor$ = CHR$(95): cFlag% = FALSE ' variables for cursor
    ptr% = 0: buffer$ = "": done% = FALSE: abort% = FALSE
    tick& = 0: start% = POS(0)

    PRINT SPACE$(maxLen);
    LOCATE , start%, 0
    DO
        DO                                       ' print a blinking cursor
            IF ABS(TIMER - tick&) > .3 THEN
                tick& = TIMER
                IF cFlag% THEN
                    PRINT " "; cLeft$;           ' erase cursor
                    cFlag% = FALSE
                ELSE
                    PRINT cursor$; cLeft$;       ' draw cursor
                    cFlag% = TRUE
                END IF
            END IF
            key$ = INKEY$                        ' get a character from the user
        LOOP WHILE key$ = ""

        SELECT CASE key$
            CASE esc$           ' if character is Esc
                abort = TRUE
                done% = TRUE
            CASE cr$            ' if character is Enter
                done% = TRUE
            CASE bSpace$        ' if character is Backspace
                IF ptr% > 0 THEN
                    PRINT " "; cLeft$; cLeft$;
                    ptr% = ptr% - 1
                    buffer$ = LEFT$(buffer$, ptr%)
                END IF
            CASE ELSE           ' check validity of character
                IF INSTR(validKeys, key$) AND ptr% < maxLen THEN
                    PRINT key$;
                    ptr% = ptr% + 1
                    buffer$ = buffer$ + key$
                END IF
        END SELECT
    LOOP UNTIL done%
    PRINT " "; cLeft$;
END SUB
```

DECLARE (BASIC procedures)

QB2	■ QB4.5	■ PowerBASIC
QB3	✲ ANSI	GW-BASIC
■ QB4	■ BASIC7	MacQB

See also: CALL (BASIC procedures), CALL (Non-BASIC procedures), CALLS (Non-BASIC procedures), DECLARE (Non-BASIC procedures), FUNCTION, SUB

Purpose

The DECLARE statement for BASIC procedures defines how QuickBASIC function and subprogram procedures are called. The DECLARE statement specifies the name of a procedure and defines the number and type of variables that are passed to it as arguments. Using the DECLARE statement saves you from having to specify this information every time you call the procedure and makes the CALL keyword unnecessary.

Syntax

DECLARE FUNCTION *Name* [([*params*])]
DECLARE SUB *Name* [([*params*])]

Name is the name of the procedure to be called. It can contain as many as 40 characters and must correspond to the name of the procedure in the module in which it resides.

params is the list of variables that are the parameters of the procedure. The types of the variables must be specified in the list.

Usage

```
DECLARE SUB Warble ()
```

Declares that references to the subprogram *Warble* are calls to a subprogram that takes no arguments.

```
DECLARE SUB Verify (prompt$, ok%)
```

Defines a subprogram named *Verify* and specifies the types of arguments passed to it.

```
DECLARE FUNCTION Center$ (text AS STRING, maxWidth AS INTEGER)
```

Declares that *Center$* is a user-defined function that takes as arguments a string and an integer.

Description

DECLARE statements can appear only in module-level code and are usually listed at the top of the program, before any executable statements. They define the names of procedures that are called by statements in the current module, and they specify the number and type of the variables to be passed as arguments. DECLARE statements are often called *prototypes* of the procedures they refer to.

If the called procedure returns a value, you should define it with the FUNCTION statement, in which case *Name* is interpreted as a variable. Use a type-declaration character (%, &, !, #, or $) to specify the type of the value returned by a FUNCTION statement. If the procedure doesn't return a value, declare the procedure with the SUB keyword.

The names of the variables in the argument list are not passed to the external procedure and do not need to match the names of the variables used in the called procedure. However, it is important that the types of the variables used in the call to the procedure be the same as those in the corresponding positions of the DECLARE statement's parameter list. You can specify variable types by including a type-declaration character or by using an AS clause with INTEGER, LONG, SINGLE, DOUBLE, STRING, or a user-defined type to declare that the variable is of a particular type. Do not, however, use fixed-length strings as arguments; only variable-length strings may be passed to functions and subprograms.

You can also pass complete arrays to a procedure (to be sorted, for example). In such cases you do not need to specify the number of dimensions in the parameter list of the DECLARE statement; however, if you include the number, QuickBASIC will accept it.

You can also use DECLARE to define the names and calling conventions for mixed-language procedures stored in separately compiled modules or libraries. (See the entry for DECLARE (Non-BASIC procedures) in Chapter 20, "Mixed Language," for more information.)

Errors

If you call a procedure that has a variable of a type different from the one in the corresponding position in the parameter list of the DECLARE statement, QuickBASIC returns a "Parameter type mismatch" error message. If the number of parameters is greater than or less than the number of parameters listed in the DECLARE statement, QuickBASIC displays an "Argument-count mismatch" error message.

Compatibility

ANSI BASIC

ANSI BASIC uses the keyword DECLARE for declarations of numeric types and of data structures used for communications. ANSI BASIC does not support a statement that performs the same task as the DECLARE statement in QuickBASIC version 4.5.

Example

The following example contains two procedures—*BinDec&*, a function, and *DecBin*, a subprogram—that convert numbers between binary and decimal format. You can either insert them into your existing programs or you can compile them separately and store them in an external library. The DECLARE statements tell the compiler what kinds of procedures *BinDec&* and *DecBin* are and specify the number and type of arguments that they expect.

```
' declare procedures
DECLARE FUNCTION BinDec& (binry AS STRING)
DECLARE SUB DecBin (decimal AS LONG, bin AS STRING)

decimal& = 123456                  ' a decimal value
DecBin decimal&, bin$              ' convert from decimal to binary
PRINT "Binary  = "; bin$           ' display the result
PRINT "Decimal ="; BinDec&(bin$)   ' convert from binary to decimal
END

' converts a string of binary digits to its decimal equivalent
FUNCTION BinDec& (binary$) STATIC
    decimal& = 0: power% = 0
    binary$ = UCASE$(binary$)
    FOR i% = LEN(binary$) TO 1 STEP -1       ' convert from binary to decimal
        digit% = ASC(MID$(binary$, i%, 1)) - 48
        IF digit% < 0 OR digit% > 1 THEN decimal& = 0: EXIT FOR
        decimal& = decimal& + digit% * 2 ^ (power%)
        power% = power% + 1
    NEXT i%
    BinDec& = decimal&
END FUNCTION

' converts a decimal value to an equivalent string of binary digits
SUB DecBin (decimal&, bin$) STATIC
    bin$ = ""
    h$ = HEX$(decimal&)       ' convert from decimal to hexadecimal
    FOR i% = 1 TO LEN(h$)
        digit% = INSTR("0123456789ABCDEF", MID$(h$, i%, 1)) - 1
        IF digit% < 0 THEN bin$ = "": EXIT FOR
        j% = 8: k% = 4
        DO                    ' convert from hexadecimal to binary
            bin$ = bin$ + RIGHT$(STR$((digit% \ j%) MOD 2), 1)
            j% = j% - (j% \ 2): k% = k% - 1
            IF k% = 0 THEN EXIT DO
        LOOP WHILE j%
    NEXT i%
END SUB
```

DEF FN

See also: FUNCTION, STATIC, SUB

■ QB2	■ QB4.5	■ PowerBASIC
■ QB3	ANSI	✲ GW-BASIC
■ QB4	■ BASIC7	✲ MacQB

Purpose

DEF FN defines a function. QuickBasic provides this command so that programs that are written in versions that support only the DEF FN statement for user-defined functions can be easily ported to QuickBASIC. QuickBASIC extends the DEF FN statement by removing the restriction that confined such functions to a single program line.

Syntax

Single-line functions:

DEF FN*Name* [(*arg* [AS *type*] [, ...])] = *expr*

Multiple-line functions:

DEF FN*Name* [(*arg* [AS *type*] [, *arg* [AS *type*] ...])]
    [STATIC *var* [, *var* ...]]
    ⋮
    [EXIT DEF]
    ⋮
    FN*Name*[*type*] = *expr*
    ⋮
END DEF

Name is any legal QuickBASIC variable name; it must always be prefixed by the keyword FN, which indicates that it is a function. Because QuickBASIC regards *Name* as a variable, you should include a type-declaration character. If you don't, the value returned will be either the default single precision or the type defined in a DEF*type* statement.

arg is one or more optional arguments that are passed to the function. You should either include type-declaration characters or use the AS keyword with the keyword INTEGER, LONG, SINGLE, DOUBLE, or STRING to define the arguments as being of a particular type. You cannot pass arrays, fixed-length strings, or user-defined variable types as arguments to a DEF FN function.

Multiple-line DEF FN functions have two additional features. They can use variables other than those passed to them as arguments; however, these variables are visible to (and may be modified by) statements in the rest of the current module. To override this, use the STATIC keyword to explicitly declare the variables local to the function.

By using the EXIT DEF statement, you can allow a multiple-line function to terminate before the END DEF is encountered. If no value has been assigned to FN*Name* when the EXIT DEF executes, the function returns a 0 for numeric types and a null string ("") for string types.

Usage

```
DEF FNBitTest (number%, bit%) = -SGN(number% AND 2 ^ bit%)
```

A single-line DEF FN statement that tests a specified bit of the integer *number%*. It returns –1 (true) if *bit%* is set and 0 (false) if *bit%* is not set.

```
DEF FNMaximum! (a!, b!, c!)
    STATIC max!
    IF a! > b! THEN
        max! = a!
    ELSEIF c! > b! THEN
        max! = c!
    ELSE max! = b!
    END IF
    FNMaximum! = max!
END DEF
```

A multiple-line DEF FN statement that finds the maximum of three values. Note that the variable *max!* is declared in a STATIC statement to make it local to the function.

Description

DEF FN is traditionally used to add specialized functions to the built-in library used in BASIC. It lets you assign any expression to a variable whose name begins with the FN keyword; QuickBASIC then evaluates the expression every time the program references that DEF FN function. The following example demonstrates the procedure:

```
DEF FNBitSet(number%, bit%) = number% OR 2 ^ bit%
IF FNBitSet(attribute%, 7) THEN MakeBlink(character%)
```

DEF FN functions are similar to subroutines, but they are much more compact and efficient. However, unlike a subroutine, they return a value. You can use DEF FN functions as part of another expression or even call them from inside other functions or statements, as in the following example:

```
DEF FNBitReSet(number%, bit%) = number% AND (32767 - 2 ^ bit%)
PRINT CHR$(FNBitReSet(ASC("a"), 5))
```

In the above example, the ASC function (within the DEF FN) supplies *FNBitReSet* with a value of 97 (the ASCII value of "a"). Setting bit 5 of this number to 0 reduces it by 32 (to 65), and the CHR$ function converts the value 65 to "A".

Multiple-Line DEF FN statements

GW-BASIC and BASICA restrict the expression to be evaluated to a single executable statement. QuickBASIC relaxes this rule and lets you use as many statement lines as you need before assigning a value to the function. If you use multiple lines, however, you must also use the END DEF statement to mark the end of the function and return control to the line that called the function. If you use the EXIT DEF statement, you can force the function to terminate prematurely and return without making an assignment to the function.

You cannot call DEF FN functions from a separately compiled module.

The FUNCTION statement, introduced in QuickBASIC version 4.0, lets you write user-defined functions that can be called from other modules. Because these functions can also call themselves recursively, they are now the preferred method of creating new functions. You cannot use DEF FN functions recursively.

Errors

QuickBASIC attempts to convert the value returned by a DEF FN statement to the precision specified by the type of the function's name. If it cannot do so because, for example, the expression returns a numeric value and the function is defined as a string, QuickBASIC returns a "Type mismatch" error message.

DEF FN declarations must appear before any statements that reference them. If you call a function before it has been declared, QuickBASIC returns a "Function not defined" error message.

Compatibility

GW-BASIC and BASICA

DEF FN statements can appear anywhere in GW-BASIC and BASICA programs, provided that they are executed before the function is actually called. For example, programmers often place DEF FN definitions in a subroutine at the end of the program and use GOSUB to execute this routine shortly after the program starts. In QuickBASIC, the position of DEF FN statements is important—they must appear in the program code before any statements that call them.

GW-BASIC and BASICA also permit only single-line functions.

QuickBASIC for the Macintosh

QuickBASIC for the Macintosh supports only single-line DEF FN function declarations.

Programs that run in the QuickBASIC environment on the Macintosh differ in one important way from those that are separately compiled. In the environment, a DEF FN statement can appear anywhere in the program as long as it is executed before a call to the function that it defines. In stand-alone programs, DEF FN statements must appear in the code before any statements that call them.

Example

The following program uses a DEF FN statement to define a function that returns a string containing the day of the week for any date between 1901 and 2099. Notice that the variables *numDay!*, *numYear*, and *days$* are declared in a STATIC statement to make them local to the function. To use the function in your own programs, specify the parameters in the following ranges:

m% = month (1 - 12), d% = day (1 - 31), y% = year (1901 - 2099)

```
DEF FNWeekDay$ (m%, d%, y%)
    STATIC numDay!, numYear!, days$

    numYear! = y%
    IF numYear! < 1901 OR numYear! > 2099 THEN EXIT DEF

    days$ = "Friday   Saturday Sunday   Monday   Tuesday  WednesdayThursday "
    num! = VAL(MID$("000303060811131619212426", (m% - 1) * 2 + 1, 2))
    numDay! = numYear! * 365 + INT((y% - 1) \ 4) + (m% - 1) * 28
    numDay! = numDay! + num! - ((m% > 2) AND (y% MOD 4 = 0)) + d%

    FNWeekDay$ = MID$(days$, (numDay! - INT(numDay! \ 7) * 7) * 9 + 1, 9)
END DEF

CLS
PRINT "January 1, 2000, falls on a "; FNWeekDay$(1, 1, 2000)
```

FUNCTION

See also: DECLARE (BASIC procedures), DEF FN, EXIT, SHARED, STATIC, SUB

QB2	■ QB4.5	■ PowerBASIC
QB3	✲ ANSI	GW-BASIC
■ QB4	■ BASIC7	■ MacQB

Purpose

QuickBASIC includes many predefined functions that either perform mathematical calculations or return information about a variable. If, however, no standard function performs the programming task you require, QuickBASIC provides the FUNCTION statement so that you can define your own.

Syntax

FUNCTION *Name* [(*arg* [AS *type*][, *arg* [AS *type*]] ...)] [STATIC]
    [SHARED *var* [, *var* ...]]
    [STATIC *var* [, *var* ...]]
    ⋮
    [EXIT FUNCTION]
    ⋮
    Name = *expr*
    ⋮
END FUNCTION

Name is the name that you assign to the function. It must be a valid QuickBASIC variable name and include a type-declaration character, if necessary.

arg is the name of one or more variables that are passed to the function as arguments. They must include type-declaration characters or be declared with the AS clause with

INTEGER, LONG, SINGLE, DOUBLE, STRING, or a user-defined type. Arrays passed as arguments must include parentheses after the array name, although you do not need to specify the number of dimensions.

The SHARED statement specifies variables that are in the module-level code and that the function needs to use, but that are not specifically passed as arguments.

The STATIC statement specifies the local variables whose values are preserved between calls to the function. If you omit this statement, new local variables are created each time the function is called.

The EXIT FUNCTION statement returns control from the function before it reaches the normal exit point (the END FUNCTION statement).

Usage

```
FUNCTION Signed% (unSigned&) STATIC
    IF unSigned& > 32767 THEN
        Signed% = unsigned& - 65536
    ELSE
        Signed% = unsigned&
    END IF
END FUNCTION
```

This function converts an unsigned 4-byte long integer to its 2-byte signed integer equivalent. (This is useful for accessing memory addresses above location 32767.)

```
FUNCTION Attribute%(fore%, back%) STATIC
    temp% = (back% * 16) + fore%
    IF fore% > 15 THEN
        temp% = temp% + 112
    END IF
    Attribute% = temp%
END FUNCTION
```

This function calculates the BIOS screen attribute from the QuickBASIC foreground and background colors.

Description

A function is a separate set of statements that returns a value. The value returned by a function defined by a FUNCTION statement is usually assigned to another variable on return. However, you can also apply the value directly to another QuickBASIC statement or function. You can even use one function as the argument for another user-defined function or subprogram. The following statements are all valid applications of functions:

```
attrib% = Attribute%(foreGround%, backGround%)

PRINT PEEK(Signed%(65000))

CALL FastPrint(row%, column%, "HELLO WORLD!", Attribute%(0, 3))
```

Because a function always returns a value, QuickBASIC handles the function's name as a variable. The name, therefore, should include the appropriate type-declaration character for the value it returns. If you do not include a type-declaration character, QuickBASIC assumes that the value returned is single precision or of the type defined by a DEF*type* statement.

Functions usually take one or more variables as arguments. Define the types of these variables using either the appropriate type-declaration character or the AS clause with INTEGER, LONG, SINGLE, DOUBLE, STRING, or a user-defined type. When you pass an array variable to a function, include parentheses after the array name; however, you don't need to list the number of dimensions.

You may define any number of local variables within a user-defined function. By default these variables exist only while the function executes, and their contents are lost when control returns to the line that called the function. The STATIC keyword, however, instructs QuickBASIC to preserve the contents of all local variables between calls. This speeds program execution considerably because, after the first invocation, QuickBASIC doesn't need to spend time creating local variables each time the function is called.

Local variables, as their name implies, are available only to the specific function in which they are used; they cannot be accessed by other functions or by statements in the module-level code from which the function is called. Similarly, variables defined in the main program are normally invisible to a user-defined function unless they are specifically passed to it as arguments. The SHARED statement lets you override this default condition; use it to specify variables in the main module to which your function needs access. However, remember that any changes you make to the variables inside a function are returned to the main program when it regains control. You must declare shared variables at the start of the function code before any executable statements. If you've already defined a variable as shared in the main program, however, you do not need to define it again in the function in order to use it there.

To call a function from statements in another module, you must use a DECLARE statement in that module to define type-checking for the function and its arguments. If you use the QuickBASIC editor to write the function, QuickBASIC generates the DECLARE statement by default.

Errors

Although QuickBASIC regards the function name as a variable, you cannot define the type of the value that it returns with the AS type clause. The following statement, for example, causes QuickBASIC to return an "Expected: (or end-of-statement" error message:

```
FUNCTION HiByte AS INTEGER (number AS INTEGER) STATIC
```

You can, however, use the DEF*type* statement as an alternative method for defining a function type; for example,

```
DEFINT H
FUNCTION HiByte (number AS INTEGER) STATIC
```

correctly defines *HiByte* as an integer function.

Most users, though, prefer the economy of the standard method of assigning a variable type to a function:

```
FUNCTION HiByte% (number%) STATIC
```

Warnings

Whenever you use the STATIC keyword in a FUNCTION, remember that local variables retain the values assigned to them during prior calls to the function. Unless you initialize these variables each time you call the the function, the function might return an incorrect value. This is a common and hard-to-find source of programming errors.

Compatibility

ANSI BASIC

ANSI proposes a distinction between internal functions, which can be called only by statements in their module, and external functions, which can be used by other modules as well. QuickBASIC does not make this distinction. All functions (and subprograms) are regarded as external and may be called from anywhere in the program.

Example

Converting fractions to decimal numbers is easy: Merely divide the numerator by the denominator. It is not as easy, however, to convert decimals to fractions. The following QuickBASIC function performs this operation. The function makes the size of the denominator a variable so that fractions can be calculated to varying degrees of accuracy.

```
' converts a decimal number to a whole number and a fraction
FUNCTION ConDecFrac$ (number!) STATIC
    SHARED den%                              ' value of the denominator
    frac$ = ""
    whole& = INT(number!)                    ' get integer portion
    decimal! = number! - whole&              ' get decimal portion
    IF decimal! > 0 THEN
        num% = INT(den% * decimal!)          ' get numerator of fraction
        IF num% = 0 THEN num% = 1
        DO WHILE num% MOD 2 = 0 AND den% MOD 2 = 0
            num% = num% \ 2
            den% = den% \ 2
        LOOP                ' loop while numerator and denominator are both even
        frac$ = STR$(num%) + "/" + LTRIM$(STR$(den%))
    END IF
    ConDecFrac$ = LTRIM$(RTRIM$(STR$(whole&))) + frac$
END FUNCTION
```

GOSUB...RETURN

See also: CLEAR, GOTO, ON...GOSUB, SUB

■ QB2	■ QB4.5	■ PowerBASIC
■ QB3	✲ ANSI	■ GW-BASIC
■ QB4	■ BASIC7	■ MacQB

Purpose

The GOSUB statement directs a program to branch, unconditionally, to a subroutine elsewhere in the same module. RETURN marks an exit from the subroutine; this causes execution to resume either at the statement following the one that invoked the subroutine or at another section of the program. Because QuickBASIC now provides self-contained subprograms and functions as more structured alternatives to subroutines, programmers rarely use GOSUB statements. However, QuickBASIC retains the keyword to maintain compatibility with programs written in earlier versions of BASIC.

Syntax

GOSUB {*line* | *label*}
⋮
RETURN [{*line* | *label*}]

line or *label* specifies the destination in the current module of a GOSUB statement. Execution then proceeds until a RETURN statement is encountered. At this point, control returns either to the statement following the GOSUB statement or to the line number or label specified in the RETURN statement.

Usage

```
GOSUB 1000
```

Branches to the statement at line 1000 and executes the subroutine there.

```
GOSUB Update
```

Branches to the line labeled *Update*.

```
RETURN
```

Exits a subroutine and returns control to the statement following the original GOSUB statement.

```
RETURN Menu
```

Exits a subroutine and branches to the statement labeled *Menu*.

Description

GOSUB instructs QuickBASIC to make an unconditional branch to the line number or label specified; control transfers to the destination line, regardless of the result of previously executed statements. You can, however, make the GOSUB statement conditional by prefacing it with an IF statement.

```
IF x% < 0 OR x% > 639 THEN GOSUB OffScreen
```

The destination line must be in the same module as the GOSUB statement that names it. You cannot use GOSUB to transfer to a statement in a separately compiled module, nor can you use it to branch into or out of a subprogram or a user-defined function contained in the same module. You can, however, use a GOSUB statement to branch within a subprogram or function, provided that execution returns to a statement in the procedure.

When QuickBASIC executes a GOSUB, it pushes the address of the next statement in the program onto the program stack and then branches to the subroutine. When the subroutine completes (if no line number or label is specified in the RETURN statement) this address is retrieved from the stack, and the program resumes where it left off. Otherwise, RETURN discards the address from the stack and branches to the line number or label specified. The statement branched to must be in the same module as the original GOSUB statement.

GOSUB subroutines are part of the module-level code. All variables that they use are shared by other statements in the same module; any changes made to these variables are maintained when the subroutine exits. Subroutines can contain GOSUB statements that call other subroutines (nesting) or even call themselves (recursion); however, because the address of the statement to be returned to is stored on the stack, your program must allocate sufficient stack space to allow for the level of nesting used. The CLEAR statement lets you specify stack size. (See the CLEAR entry in Chapter 18, "DOS and Program Management," for more details.)

If you use RETURN with a line number or label to exit from a nested subroutine, the return address must be in the same subroutine that called it. If your subroutines are nested more than one level, you can return only to the level that called the subroutine.

Comments

GOSUB is not used much in current programming practice because its unrestricted branching can obscure a program's logic and make code difficult to understand or debug. Moreover, because QuickBASIC supports structured control statements, such as DO...LOOP and SELECT CASE, and also lets you call user-defined subprograms and functions, the need for GOSUB is greatly reduced. However, module-level subroutines are still required by the QuickBASIC event-trapping statements described under the various ON *event* GOSUB statements.

Tips

Although you can place subroutines anywhere in the module-level code, it is good programming practice to group them and place them outside the normal direction of program flow. This prevents control from accidently falling into a subroutine and triggering a "RETURN without GOSUB" error message.

Warnings

If you use RETURN with a line number or label, do so with caution; the statements following the target line must then allow for returns from subroutines that were called from any other line in the program.

Compatibility

ANSI BASIC

Although GOSUB is still listed in the ANSI standard, the ANSI committee is considering removing the statement because it encourages poor programming by letting you construct subroutines that have several entry points. The ANSI committee recommends that programmers refrain from using GOSUB, ON...GOSUB, and RETURN in new programs or when modifying existing programs.

Example

A subroutine might have more than one exit point, and the RETURN statement can branch control to any point in the program. The following program includes a subroutine that selectively branches to various destinations, depending on the user's response. The program draws designs on the screen until the user presses a key.

```
    CLEAR : SCREEN 1: COLOR 0, 1: RANDOMIZE TIMER
100
    VIEW
    LINE (0, 0)-(319, 199), 1, BF   ' draw a filled box the size of the screen
    VIEW (32, 4)-(287, 186), 0, 2   ' reduce the size of the graphics screen
    CLS
    xLimit% = 253: yLimit% = 180
    signA% = 0: version% = 1: x1% = 0: y1% = 0
    rate% = INT(RND * 3) + 2                       ' set the rate of change
    colors% = INT(RND * 3) + 1
110
    IF x1% <= 0 THEN x1% = 0: changeX% = signA%    ' set the direction of change
    IF y1% <= 0 THEN y1% = 0: changeY% = signA%
    IF x1% >= xLimit% THEN x1% = xLimit%: changeX% = -signA%
    IF y1% >= yLimit% THEN y1% = yLimit%: changeY% = -signA%
    IF signA% <= 1 THEN signA% = 1: signB% = 1
    IF signA% >= rate% THEN signA% = rate%: signB% = -1

    x2% = 255 - x1%: y2% = 181 - y1%
    IF version% = 1 THEN
        LINE (x1%, y1%)-(x2%, y2%), colors%, B      ' draw the outline of a box
        LINE (x1%, y1%)-(x2%, y2%), 0               ' draw a black diagonal line
        LINE (x1%, y2%)-(x2%, y1%), 0
        version% = 2
```

(continued)

continued

```
    ELSE
        LINE (x1%, y1%)-(x2%, y2%), 3, B            ' draw the outline of a box
        LINE (x1%, y1%)-(x2%, y2%), colors%         ' draw a diagonal line
        LINE (x2%, y1%)-(x1%, y2%), colors%
        version% = 1
        colors% = INT(RND * 3) + 1                  ' change color
    END IF
    x1% = x1% + changeX%
    y1% = y1% + changeY%
    signA% = signA% + signB%
    GOSUB 900: GOTO 110
120
    SCREEN 0, 0, 0: WIDTH 80: CLS
END

900
    IF INKEY$ <> "" THEN LOCATE 25, 1 ELSE RETURN
    PRINT "Q = Quit  R = Restart  C = Continue";
    key$ = UCASE$(INPUT$(1))
    SELECT CASE key$
        CASE "Q"
            RETURN 120
        CASE "R"
            RETURN 100
        CASE ELSE
            VIEW: LINE (0, 188)-(319, 199), 1, BF
            VIEW (32, 4)-(287, 186), , 2
    END SELECT
RETURN
```

SHARED

See also: COMMON, DIM, FUNCTION, SUB

✲ QB2	■ QB4.5	✲ PowerBASIC
✲ QB3	■ ANSI	GW-BASIC
■ QB4	■ BASIC7	■ MacQB

Purpose

Unless passed as arguments, variables used by subprograms and functions the user defines by SUB and FUNCTION statements are local to those procedures and cannot be accessed by statements in the module-level code. The SHARED statement lets you override the default and make specified variables available to both the procedure and the main program. This lets you return the results of operations within the procedure and lets functions, for example, return more than one value.

Syntax

SHARED *var* [AS *type*][, *var* [AS *type*]] ...

var is any valid QuickBASIC variable. A variable (other than the default single-precision type) must either include a type declaration character or be followed by the AS clause with INTEGER, LONG, SINGLE, DOUBLE, STRING (including a fixed-length string), or a user-defined type. If the variable is an array, it must be followed by parentheses, although you don't need to specify the number of dimensions.

SHARED statements must appear at the beginning of the procedure, before any executable statements.

Usage

```
SHARED cash
```

Allows the procedure to share the single-precision variable *cash* with the main program.

```
SHARED student%, grades!()
```

Makes the contents of an integer variable and a single-precision array available to the procedure in which the SHARED statement appears.

```
SHARED seconds AS LONG
```

Makes the contents of the long variable *seconds* available to the procedure in which the SHARED statement appears.

Description

SHARED statements may appear only in subprograms and user-defined functions; they specify the names of the variables in the main program that the subprogram or function needs to access. These variables are available to only those subprograms and functions in the program that include a SHARED statement. A procedure variable that is not shared can have the same name as a variable in the module-level code; because the variable is not in the scope of the module-level code, QuickBASIC considers the procedure variable different from the module variable.

Specifying variables in a SHARED statement saves you from having to pass them as explicit parameters. As with parameters, any changes made to a variable in the procedure that shares it are maintained when control returns to the main program.

The scope of SHARED statements extends only to the procedure and the main program code of the module that contains it. You cannot use SHARED to share variables with procedures in a Quick library or in a separately compiled module; use the COMMON statement for this. (See the entry for the COMMON statement for details.)

Tips

You can make specified variables available to all the functions and subprograms in a module by dimensioning them in a DIM statement with the SHARED keyword in the module-level code, as in the following example:

```
DIM SHARED volume!, radius!, diameter!
```

This eliminates the need for using separate SHARED statements in all the procedures that need to access those variables.

Compatibility

QuickBASIC 2.0 and QuickBASIC 3.0

Because QuickBASIC versions 2.0 and 3.0 do not support the FUNCTION statement, the SHARED statement can be used only in subprograms.

PowerBASIC

PowerBASIC includes a SHARED statement that works exactly like the QuickBASIC version. It also includes a LOCAL statement to let you explicitly name variables that are not shared with the main module. Because PowerBASIC procedure variables (like their QuickBASIC counterparts) are local by default, you need not always use LOCAL.

Example

In addition to the parameters passed to them and the values returned, you might want selected procedures to share certain standard variables that are defined in the module-level code. The following program uses a function to let the user select a filename. The function uses a SHARED statement to access variables that are defined in the main program.

```
DECLARE FUNCTION GetFile$ (pathName$)

CONST FALSE = 0, TRUE = NOT FALSE       ' constants are global

DIM SHARED abort AS INTEGER
cr$ = CHR$(13): esc$ = CHR$(27): bSpace$ = CHR$(8): cLeft$ = CHR$(29)

filename$ = GetFile$("*.*")
LOCATE 15, 1

IF abort THEN PRINT "Aborted!" ELSE PRINT " You chose "; filename$
END

FUNCTION GetFile$ (path$) STATIC
    SHARED cr$, esc$, bSpace$, cLeft$   ' shared with main program
    abort = FALSE                       ' shared with main program
    buffer$ = "": ptr% = 0
    CLS : FILES path$                   ' print the names of files
```

(continued)

continued

```
    PRINT "Enter the name of a file: ";
    DO
        key$ = UCASE$(INKEY$)
        SELECT CASE key$
            CASE esc$                       ' if Esc, exit loop
                abort = TRUE
                EXIT DO
            CASE bSpace$
                PRINT " "; cLeft$; cLeft$;
                ptr% = ptr% - 1
                buffer$ = LEFT$(buffer$, ptr%)
            CASE ""
            CASE ELSE
                PRINT key$;
                buffer$ = buffer$ + key$
                ptr% = ptr% + 1
            END SELECT
    LOOP UNTIL key$ = CHR$(13)              ' loop until user presses Enter
    GetFile$ = buffer$
END FUNCTION
```

STATIC

See also: COMMON, DIM, SHARED

✲ QB2	■ QB4.5	■ PowerBASIC
✲ QB3	ANSI	GW-BASIC
■ QB4	■ BASIC7	✲ MacQB

Purpose

By default, variables in a subprogram or function are dynamic. They are re-created each time the procedure is called. The STATIC statement preserves the contents of selected variables in the procedure, thereby allowing them to retain their values between calls. This lets you use the results of calculations in subsequent calls to the procedure.

Syntax

STATIC *var* [AS *type*][, *var* [AS *type*]] ...

var is any valid QuickBASIC variable. A variable (other than the default single-precision type) must either include a type-declaration character or be followed by the AS clause with INTEGER, LONG, SINGLE, DOUBLE, STRING, or a user-defined type. If the variable is an array, it must be followed by parentheses, although you don't need to specify the number of dimensions.

Usage

```
STATIC counter%, total
```

Makes an integer variable and a single-precision variable local to the procedure, and preserves their values after the procedure terminates.

```
STATIC files() AS STRING
```

Makes an array of strings local to the procedure and preserves its values after the procedure terminates.

Description

Unless you specify otherwise, all variables named in a function or a subprogram are dynamic. QuickBASIC creates them when the procedure is called (typically, to hold temporary values necessary to the procedure's task) and discards them and their contents when the procedure finishes executing. This type of variable is often called an *automatic* variable; it exists only while the function or subprogram is active and is destroyed on exit, thus freeing the memory assigned to it.

Sometimes, however, you might need to preserve the value of one or more variables between calls so that they can be used the next time the procedure is executed. To do so, use the STATIC statement, followed by a list of the variables whose values you want saved, at the beginning of the procedure, before any executable statements.

Alternatively, you can preserve all variables by using the keyword STATIC in the first line of the procedure definition, after the procedure name and argument list. This makes every local variable in the procedure static.

Static variables retain their contents even while the procedure is inactive. Because QuickBASIC does not have to create them each time you call the procedure, using static variables makes your program run slightly faster than it would otherwise, although less memory is available for other processing.

Dynamic variables are local to the subprogram or function that contains them because they do not exist when the procedure is not being executed. Static variables are also local. Even if a variable of the same name has been dimensioned in a DIM statement with SHARED or declared in a COMMON statement in the main program, QuickBASIC considers it to be a different variable. You cannot define a variable in both a SHARED and a STATIC statement in the same procedure.

Although the STATIC statement is most often used in subprograms and functions, you can also use it inside multiple-line DEF FN functions in the module-level code. This declares the variables local to the DEF FN function so that the variables can have the same name as variables in the rest of the program and yet not interfere with them.

Warnings

Do not confuse the STATIC statement with the $STATIC metacommand. The latter is an instruction to the compiler that allocates memory for arrays; it doesn't affect the existence or scope of variables after the program starts.

Compatibility

QuickBASIC 2.0, QuickBASIC 3.0, and QuickBASIC for the Macintosh

Because QuickBASIC versions 2.0 and 3.0 and QuickBASIC for the Macintosh do not support the FUNCTION statement, the STATIC statement can be used only in subprograms and functions defined by DEF FN statements.

Example

The following program demonstrates that the static variable *i%* retains its value between calls to the procedure *Counter* that contains it. Note that it is not affected by the variable of the same name in the module-level code. The variable *j%*, on the other hand, is a dynamic variable, so it is created with an initial value of 0 each time the procedure executes.

```
DECLARE SUB Counter (count AS INTEGER)

CLS
FOR i% = 0 TO 9
    j% = i%: PRINT
    Counter i%
NEXT i%
END

SUB Counter (count AS INTEGER)
    STATIC i%
    PRINT USING "   # "; count;
    FOR a% = 0 TO 9
        i% = i% + 1
        PRINT USING " ### "; i%;
    NEXT a%
    PRINT TAB(6);
    FOR a% = 0 TO 9
        j% = j% + 1
        PRINT USING " ### "; j%;
    NEXT a%
END SUB
```

SUB

See also: CALL (BASIC procedures), DECLARE, DEF FN, EXIT, FUNCTION, SHARED, STATIC

■ QB2	■ QB4.5	✲ PowerBASIC
■ QB3	■ ANSI	GW-BASIC
■ QB4	■ BASIC7	■ MacQB

Purpose

The SUB statement lets you define subprograms that can be called from anywhere in your program, even from separately compiled modules. This makes it easy for you to build a library of general-purpose routines that can be directly linked to new programs without having to be rewritten.

Syntax

SUB *Name* [(*arg* [AS *type*] [, *arg* [AS *type*] ...])] [STATIC]
    [SHARED *var* [, *var* ...]]
    [STATIC *var* [, *var* ...]]
    ⋮
    [EXIT SUB]
    ⋮
END SUB

Name is any valid QuickBASIC name, which you use to call the subprogram.

arg is the name of one or more variables that you can pass to the subprogram as arguments. You must indicate the types of these arguments, using either a type-declaration character or an AS clause with INTEGER, LONG, SINGLE, DOUBLE, STRING, or a user-defined type. Arrays passed as arguments must include parentheses after the array name, although you do not need to specify the number of dimensions.

The SHARED statement specifies in the module-level code variables that the subprogram needs to use but that are not specifically passed as arguments.

The STATIC statement specifies the local variables whose values are preserved between calls to the subprogram.

The EXIT SUB statement returns control from the subprogram before it reaches the normal exit point (the END SUB statement).

Usage

```
SUB CvtSign (unsign&, sign%)
    IF unsign& > 32767 THEN
        sign% = unsign& - 65536
    ELSE
        sign% = unsign&
    END IF
END SUB
```

Finds the signed, 2-byte, equivalent value of *unsign&* (an unsigned long integer) and assigns the value to the parameter *sign%*.

Description

Subprograms are self-contained procedures that you can add to QuickBASIC programs to perform a specific task. Like traditional subroutines, they can be called from anywhere in the current program but, unlike subroutines, they can also be called from a separately compiled module in the same program (if they are properly declared in that module)—for example,

```
DECLARE SUB QuickSort% (array%(), start%, finish%)
```

If you create a subprogram with the QuickBASIC editor, QuickBASIC immediately generates the appropriate DECLARE statement.

To execute a subprogram you must call it: Use the subprogram name as the object of the call, and substitute your own arguments for those named in the parameter list, as in the following example:

```
CALL QuickSort(scores%(), LBOUND(scores%), UBOUND(scores%))
```

Notice that arguments do not have to be actual variables. You can also use constants and expressions in the parameter list, provided that they evaluate to the type of argument that the subprogram expects.

If a DECLARE statement for the subprogram exists in the current module, you can omit the CALL keyword in a call to the subprogram. If you do so, however, you must also omit the parentheses around the parameter list:

```
QuickSort scores%(), LBOUND(scores%), UBOUND(scores%)
```

Other than arguments that are passed and variables that are specified in a SHARED statement, all variables are local to the subprogram. You can use any variable names without interfering with variables of the same name in the module-level code.

Unlike functions, subprograms do not return a value. However, because the arguments that they use are passed by reference, any changes the subprogram makes to the arguments are maintained when the subprogram completes.

Recursion

An important feature of subprograms (and functions) is that they can be recursive; that is, they can call themselves. Recursive procedures use a lot of stack space because each time a subprogram is called, QuickBASIC assigns a new set of local variables and stores them on the program stack. Because recursion requires the use of new local variables, do not use the STATIC keyword in recursive procedures.

Recursion is often the most efficient method for programming applications in which large blocks of data must be processed. The following subprogram, for example, uses recursion to sort an array.

```
SUB QuickSort (array%(), start%, finish%)
    top% = start%: bottom% = finish%
    compare% = array%((start% + finish%) \ 2)
    DO
        DO WHILE array%(top%) < compare% AND top% < finish%
            top% = top% + 1
        LOOP
        DO WHILE compare% < array%(bottom%) AND bottom% > start%
            bottom% = bottom% - 1
        LOOP
```

(continued)

continued

```
        IF bottom% > top% THEN
            SWAP array%(top%), array%(bottom%)
            top% = top% + 1: bottom% = bottom% - 1
        END IF
        IF bottom% = top% THEN top% = top% + 1
    LOOP UNTIL top% > bottom%
    IF start% < bottom% THEN QuickSort array%(), start%, bottom%   ' recursion
    IF top% < finish% THEN QuickSort array%(), top%, finish%       ' recursion
END SUB
```

This subprogram uses a quicksort algorithm to sort an integer array into ascending order. You supply it with the name of the array and the upper and lower bounds of the elements to be sorted. The subprogram works by dividing the elements into successively smaller partitions and calling itself recursively to sort each partition until the entire array has been ordered.

Warnings

QuickBASIC can sometimes mistake program labels for calls to subprograms that do not take parameters. This occurs only if the call is the first statement on the line and does not include the CALL keyword, as in the following example:

```
PrintScreen:
```

QuickBASIC is as likely to treat the statement as a line label as it is to treat it as a call to a subprogram. This mistake does not produce an error message. However, the subprogram never executes, and this might result in long hours of debugging time before you understand why.

To prevent this error, use an explicit CALL statement in such circumstances, even if the module includes a DECLARE statement for the subprogram.

Compatibility

PowerBASIC

The PowerBASIC implementation of the SUB statement is slightly different from the QuickBASIC version. Although the variables inside the subprogram are local by default, PowerBASIC provides a LOCAL keyword that explicitly declares them as such. You can still declare specified variables as being SHARED, but the STATIC statement differs because it applies to specific variables rather than to the procedure as a whole.

PowerBASIC also provides the SUB INLINE statement, which allows you to insert machine-code bytes directly into your program source code.

Example

Programmers often create subprograms that can be used in a wide range of programs. Tested and debugged subprograms can be stored, with other procedures, in a library and linked to any application that requires them. The following QuickBASIC program uses a subprogram to provide a standard menu handler. The calling program supplies the option list (as a string array) and the screen location where the menu is to be drawn. The subprogram draws the menu, handles user input, and returns with the option selected.

```
DECLARE SUB VerMenu (row%, col%, menu%)

CONST FALSE = 0, TRUE = NOT FALSE

DIM SHARED menu$(0 TO 9): menu% = 8
CLS : RESTORE

FOR i% = 1 TO menu%                         ' get menu options
    menu$(0) = menu$(0) + CHR$(i% + 64)
    READ menu$(i%)
    menu$(i%) = CHR$(i% + 64) + ". " + menu$(i%)
    menu$(i%) = LEFT$(menu$(i%) + SPACE$(24), 24)
NEXT i%

VerMenu 8, 28, menu%

LOCATE 20, 10, 1
IF abort% THEN
    PRINT "ABORTED!"
ELSE
    PRINT "Option"; choice%; "selected"
END IF
END

DATA "View current settings", "Read personal mail"
DATA "Read messages", "Send a message", "Download a file"
DATA "Upload a file", "Yell for Sysop", "Goodbye - log off"

SUB VerMenu (row%, col%, menu%) STATIC
    SHARED abort%, choice%

    abort% = FALSE: choice% = 1
    FOR i% = 1 TO menu%
        LOCATE row% + i%, col%, 0
        COLOR 15, 0: PRINT LEFT$(menu$(i%), 1);
        COLOR 7, 0: PRINT MID$(menu$(i%), 2);
    NEXT i%
```

(continued)

continued

```
    DO
        COLOR 14, 4
        hiLine% = row% + choice%
        LOCATE hiLine%, col%: PRINT menu$(choice%);
        DO
            key$ = INKEY$
        LOOP WHILE key$ = ""
        lastChoice% = choice%
        IF LEN(key$) < 2 THEN
            IF key$ = CHR$(13) THEN EXIT DO
            IF key$ = CHR$(27) THEN abort% = TRUE: EXIT DO
            key$ = UCASE$(key$)
            m% = INSTR(menu$(0), key$)
            IF m% > 0 THEN choice% = m%
        ELSE
            scanCode% = ASC(MID$(key$, 2, 1))
            IF scanCode% = 80 THEN choice% = choice% + 1
            IF scanCode% = 72 THEN choice% = choice% - 1
        END IF
        IF choice% > menu% THEN choice% = 1
        IF choice% < 1 THEN choice% = menu%
        IF choice% <> lastChoice% THEN
            LOCATE row% + lastChoice%, col%
            COLOR 15, 0: PRINT LEFT$(menu$(lastChoice%), 1);
            COLOR 7, 0: PRINT MID$(menu$(lastChoice%), 2);
        END IF
    LOOP WHILE 1
    COLOR 7, 0
END SUB
```

CHAPTER 5

Strings

Introduction

Although computers are often associated with "number crunching," much of the data they process involves characters in letters, reports, labels in a spreadsheet, names and addresses in a mailing list, and so on.

How QuickBASIC interprets the data in a byte or a group of bytes in memory depends on the type of the data that is represented. If your program manipulates numbers, you use numeric variables such as *total%* and *tax!*, in which the data in each byte of the variable is part of a binary number. The type of variable you define specifies how QuickBASIC groups the bytes in memory and how it interprets their values. For example, *total%* is a 2-byte integer, and *tax!* is a 4-byte, single-precision, floating-point integer. Thus if the value in a particular byte in memory is 65, the value of the variable that contains that byte depends on the type of the variable involved. If the variable is a 2-byte integer, the value of the variable depends on the value of 2 bytes.

On the other hand, if you define a string variable (for example, *firstName$*), each byte in the variable is treated either as an ASCII character with a value in the range 0 through 127 or as an IBM extended character in the range 128 through 255. Thus if a string variable contains the value 65 in a byte, the value is interpreted as an uppercase A

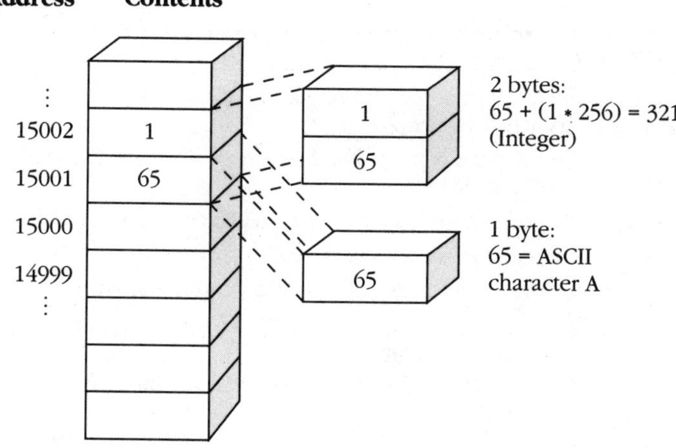

Figure 5-1.
Numeric versus character representation of a value.

rather than as part of a number. This is shown in Figure 5-1. The ASCII character set and the IBM extended character set contain 256 different characters, each of which corresponds to a specific numeric value. The ASCII set includes uppercase and lowercase letters, numerals, punctuation marks, mathematical symbols, and printer control characters (such as carriage return, linefeed, and formfeed). The IBM extended character set includes graphics characters, mathematical symbols, and characters for foreign languages.

You can use the QuickBASIC editor to enter nonkeyboard characters (such as a beep or a graphics character) directly into a string. To do this you first type the opening quote of the string, press Ctrl-P, and then hold down the Alt key while you enter the character's code on the numeric keypad (not the main keyboard). Release the Alt key, type the rest of the string, and then end the string with a closing quote.

For example, to make a PRINT statement sound a beep and display "Hello", type

PRINT "*<Ctrl-P><Alt>*7 Hello"

The disadvantage of using this method is that these characters appear in your listing as odd symbols such as diamonds and "happy faces"; the meanings of these symbols are unintelligible to a reader.

A *string* is simply a series of character values, such as "QuickBASIC" or CHR$(7) + CHR$(12). In the first example, the quotes enclose a string *literal,* the specific characters that make up the word "QuickBASIC." In the second example, the CHR$ function returns the character specified by the ASCII value. This string consists of ASCII character 7 (which sounds a beep) and ASCII character 12 (which either advances the print head to the next page or clears the screen). QuickBASIC offers many statements and functions that handle strings. Table 5-1 lists these functions and statements alphabetically.

Statement or function	**Purpose**
ASC	Returns the ASCII code (or IBM extended code) of a character or of the first character of a string
CHR$	Returns the character corresponding to the specified ASCII code (or IBM extended code)
INSTR	Returns the position in a string at which a given string begins
LCASE$	Returns a string in lowercase characters
LEFT$	Returns the specified number of characters, beginning at the left end of a string
LEN	Returns the length of a string
MID$ (Function)	Returns the specified number of characters, beginning at the specified position in the string

(continued)

Table 5-1.
QuickBASIC's string statements and functions.

Table 5-1. *(continued)*

Statement or function	Purpose
MID$ (Statement)	Replaces the characters in a string, beginning at the specified position, with the specified characters
RIGHT$	Returns the specified number of characters, beginning at the right end of a string
SPACE$	Returns a string consisting of the specified number of spaces (blanks)
STR$	Returns a string containing the string representation of the specified value
STRING$	Returns a string containing a character repeated the specified number of times
UCASE$	Returns a string in uppercase characters
VAL	Returns the numeric value that the numerals and other special characters in the specified string represent

Defining and Using Strings

Strings are versatile—you can define variables or constants that contain string values, store strings in an array, pass them to (or receive them from) functions or subprograms, and define your own string data types. Remember that strings are characters, not numbers. For example, QuickBASIC does not allow you to multiply one string by another string; however, you can add two strings together to form one long string. For example, after the statement

```
lang$ = "Quick" + "BASIC"
```

executes, the value of *lang$* is "QuickBASIC." Also, note that you can extract some of the characters from a string, but because a numeric value is stored in binary notation, you cannot extract some digits from a numeric value.

String Variables

To define a string variable, first select a name that describes its contents. For example, a variable that will hold the name of a city to be printed on a mailing label might be called *city$*. The dollar-sign ($) suffix indicates that the variable will hold string data. To assign a value to the string, use an equal sign (=) followed by a *string expression*. A string expression can contain a string (in quotes), a call to a string function, the name of another string variable, or a combination of these elements. Table 5-2 on the following page shows examples of valid assignments to string variables.

Assignment	Description
city$ = "Boston"	Assigns a string literal to the variable *city$*
box$ = CHR$(219)	Assigns IBM extended character 219 (a filled box) to *box$*
city$ = place$	Assigns the value of *place$* to *city$*
menuItem$ = item$ + box$	Assigns the value of *item$* plus the value of *box$* to *menuItem$*

Table 5-2.
Valid assignments to string variables.

You can also use the DEFSTR statement to specify that all variables whose names begin with a particular range of letters will be string variables by default. (You can override this specification by including one of the following suffixes with your numeric variables: %, &, !, or #.) For example, you might include the following statements in a program:

```
DEFSTR A-Z
city = "San Francisco"
```

In the above example, QuickBASIC treats *city* and *city$* as the same identifier; however, *city!* is still a single-precision numeric variable.

You can also define the type of a variable as string by using the DIM statement with the phrase AS STRING; for example,

```
DIM firstName AS STRING
```

defines *firstName* as a string variable.

Using DIM is a more complicated way to name a variable, but it enables you to declare the type of a variable before using it (as is required in most other languages).

String Constants

You can define a string constant with the CONST keyword. (This keyword is not available in earlier versions of BASIC.) The difference between a string constant and a regular string is that after you define a string constant you can't change its contents; for example, the statement

```
CONST DASHES$ = "---"
```

defines a string that prints three dashes. If you later create a statement that attempts to change the value of *DASHES$*, QuickBASIC displays the "Duplicate definition" error message.

You can also create numeric constants that contain the values of certain characters:

```
CONST FF = 12                ' ASCII value for form feed
CONST DOBEEP = 7             ' ASCII value for beep
```

Now you can write the string *CHR$(7) + CHR$(12)* as *CHR$(DOBEEP) + CHR$(FF)*. (You cannot use the name BEEP because BEEP is a reserved QuickBASIC keyword.) Because a constant cannot contain a function call as part of its value, you cannot define a string constant DOBEEP as follows:

```
CONST DOBEEP$ = CHR$(7)
```

QuickBASIC doesn't allow function calls in constant values because functions, like variables, can return different values each time they are used, and constants, by definition, can't change. (Of course, you could use a string variable instead: the statement *doBeep$ = CHR$(7)* is valid if *doBeep$* is a variable.) Use constants whenever you can, because QuickBASIC prevents you from inadvertently changing their values in your program.

String Arrays

Chapter 6, "Arrays and Data," describes arrays in detail and explains how to define them. To create a string array, simply use a string variable name in a DIM statement; for example,

```
DIM days$(7)
```

specifies an array named *days$* that contains seven strings. The following example uses this array:

```
DIM days$(7)
days$(1) = "Sunday": days$(2) = "Monday"
days$(3) = "Tuesday": days$(4) = "Wednesday"
days$(5) = "Thursday": days$(6) = "Friday"
days$(7) = "Saturday"

FOR day% = 1 TO 7
    PRINT days$(day%); " ";
NEXT day%
```

The program displays the days of the week.

Variable Length Strings and String Storage

Most versions of BASIC support only strings that can vary in length. Indeed, all the QuickBASIC string variables used thus far can contain as many as 32,767 characters. (Many early versions of BASIC do not allow strings of more than 255 characters.) QuickBASIC stores variable-length strings (along with static arrays, ordinary numeric variables, and the stack) in a 64-KB memory segment called DGROUP—the default data area. QuickBASIC creates a 4-byte string descriptor for each variable-length string: The first two bytes of the descriptor contain the address of the string within DGROUP, and the next 2 bytes contain the string's length. Figure 5-2 on the following page shows how QuickBASIC stores variable-length strings.

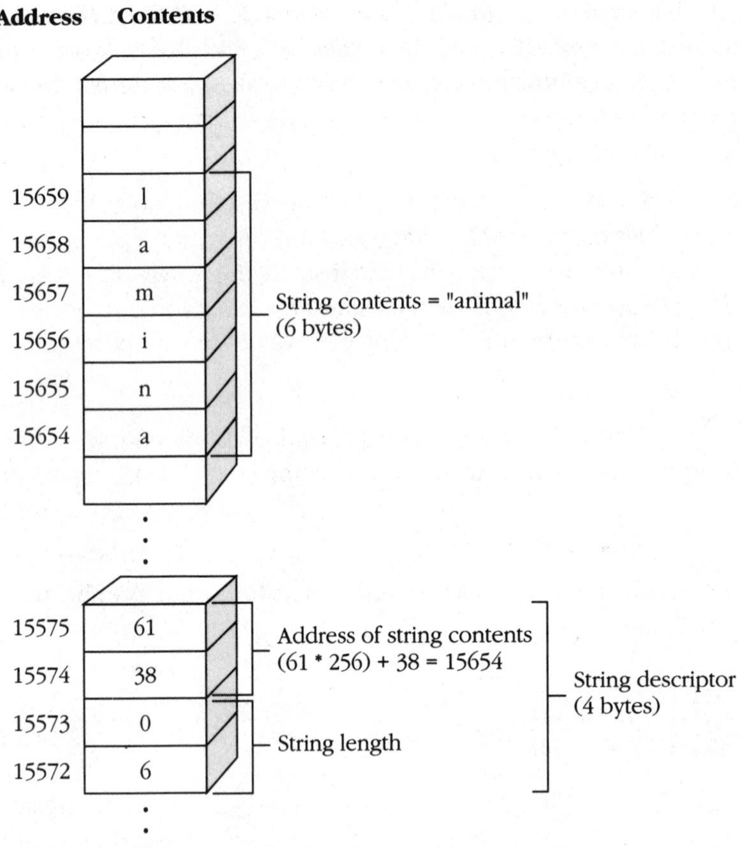

Figure 5-2.
Storage of variable-length strings.

Separating the descriptor from the contents lets QuickBASIC move strings in memory more efficiently: QuickBASIC updates the address in the descriptor only as necessary.

Understanding how QuickBASIC stores strings lets you manage available string memory in programs that use (and reuse) many strings or string arrays.

If you change the value of a string either by using an assignment statement or by calling one or more of the string functions described in this chapter, QuickBASIC allocates memory as necessary by changing the address in the descriptor and updating the length. Eventually, the memory taken by string values that are no longer being used is reclaimed through a process of "garbage collection." In earlier versions of BASIC, programs that use many strings slow down or pause at unpredictable times as BASIC's built-in garbage-collection routines reclaim the space taken by strings that are no longer in use. You can also force BASIC to perform garbage collection by using the *FRE("")* function call. Fortunately, QuickBASIC versions 4.0 and later perform continuous garbage collection; this frees the memory that holds obsolete strings as soon as a program changes the strings' contents.

Fixed-Length Strings

QuickBASIC 4.0 introduced a new kind of string that has a fixed length regardless of how many characters you actually assign to the string. To declare a fixed-length string, use a statement such as

```
DIM fixedStr AS STRING * 10
```

You can't use the $ suffix; the AS STRING qualifier establishes the variable type. Follow the asterisk (*) with the length of the string, in bytes (to a maximum of 32767). The number of bytes in a string is equal to the number of characters.

Because variable-length strings are not allowed in user-defined types, use fixed-length strings instead:

```
TYPE CustomerName
    firstName AS STRING * 15
    initial AS STRING * 1
    lastName AS STRING * 32
END TYPE
```

Here the type *CustomerName* contains three fixed-length strings, which give the entire record a fixed length of 48 characters.

The disadvantage of using fixed-length strings is that some space is usually wasted in each fixed-length string because the actual string value stored in the variable usually doesn't fill all the allotted space. Also, you cannot store a string longer than the length you specify.

The value you assign to a fixed-length string is left-justified, with spaces filling any unused character positions to the right; you don't have to use the LSET statement (which left-justifies a string) with fixed-length strings. You can use the RSET statement to assign to a variable a value that is right-justified in the string and that has leading spaces. (See Chapter 17, "Files," for more details about LSET and RSET.) For a fixed-length string, the LEN function returns the defined length, not the actual length.

String-manipulation Functions

String Comparison

You can test and compare strings much as you do numeric values. A string is "greater than" another string if the first differing character has a larger ASCII value. (The letter A, for example, has a smaller ASCII value than the letter Z, so Z is "greater than" A.) The following table contains some examples of string comparison:

Comparison	Result	Comparison	Result
a$ = "QuickBASIC"		a$ = "microsoft"	
b$ = "Programming"		b$ = "MICROSOFT"	
a$ > b$	True (–1)	a$ > b$	True (–1)
a$ < b$	False (0)		
		a$ = "Quick"	
DO WHILE LEN(a$)	True (–1)	b$ = "QuickBASIC"	
LOOP		b$ > a$	True (–1)
		b$ <> a$	True (–1)
a$ = ""			
LEN(a$)	False (0)		

These examples illustrate the following points:

- True comparisons of strings return a value of –1.
- False comparisons of strings return a value of 0.
- To test whether a string has a value (is not null), test the result of the LEN function. A null string has a length of 0, so the result of a test of a null string is false.
- Comparisons are case sensitive: Lowercase letters follow (are "greater than") uppercase letters.
- If all the characters in a shorter string match the corresponding characters in a longer string, the longer string is "greater than" the shorter one.

Extracting Parts of a String

For string comparison and formatting you often need to examine only part of a string. Use the LEFT$ function to retrieve a specified number of characters from the left side (or beginning) of a string. For example, if the variable *language$* equals "QuickBASIC," the statement

```
PRINT LEFT$(language$, 5)
```

displays "Quick". Note that all the functions that operate on strings return a modified copy of the string; the string itself is not affected.

Use the RIGHT$ function to examine characters beginning at the right end of the string. For example,

```
RIGHT$(language$,5)
```

returns the string "BASIC".

The RTRIM$ and LTRIM$ functions (discussed in detail in Chapter 17, "Files") remove trailing and leading blanks from a fixed-length string. Removing blanks prevents unintentional gaps in a printout and also prevents problems when you must compare a fixed-length string with a variable-length string. Consider the following example:

```
a$ = "Quick"              ' variable-length string
DIM b AS STRING * 10      ' fixed-length string
b = "Quick"               ' left-justified string
PRINT (b > a$)            ' compare the strings
```

Because *b* includes trailing blanks, *b* is "greater than" *a$* even though their meaningful contents are identical. However, if you use the statement

```
PRINT (RTRIM$(b) > a$)
```

in place of the fourth line in the above example, then *b* is not "greater than" a$.

You can use the MID$ function to extract one or more characters from any position in a string. When you call the MID$ function, specify the string, the position in the string at which extracting is to start, and the number of characters to be extracted. For example, if *a$* equals "Three blind mice", the call

```
MID$(a$,7,5)
```

returns "blind".

The MID$ function is perhaps most useful for "looping through" a string and examining each character in turn, as shown in the following statements:

```
a$ = "Three blind mice"
FOR char% = 1 TO LEN(a$)
    thisChar$ = MID$(a$, char%, 1)
    IF thisChar$ = " " THEN
        PRINT                  ' go to next line
    ELSE PRINT thisChar$;      ' print the character
    END IF
NEXT char%
```

The above example extracts each character with the MID$ function, using the position specified by the loop counter *char%*. If the character is a space, the output is moved to the next line; otherwise, the current character is printed in the next position on the line.

Finding Characters in a String

You will often need to check whether a character or a string is contained in another string. The INSTR function searches for one string within another. The function accepts two strings as parameters and returns the location of the second string within the first string. If the second string isn't contained within the first, INSTR returns 0, providing a value of false for any test—for example,

```
a$ = "QuickBASIC"
b$ = "BASIC"
c$ = "Q"
d$ = "Pascal"
PRINT INSTR(a$, b$)                                  ' displays 6
PRINT INSTR(a$, c$)                                  ' displays 1
IF INSTR(a$, d$) THEN PRINT "Pascal is in BASIC" ' doesn't display anything
```

In the first PRINT statement, the INSTR function returns the value 6 because "BASIC" begins at the sixth character in the string "QuickBASIC." In the second PRINT statement, INSTR returns the value 1 because position 1 in "QuickBASIC" is "Q." The THEN clause in the IF statement in the above example isn't executed because INSTR returns 0 (that is, the string "Pascal" isn't contained in the string "QuickBASIC"). Note that if there is a match anywhere in the string, the returned value is greater than 0. Because QuickBASIC considers any value other than 0 to be true, you can use INSTR with any statement that requires a condition (IF, WHILE, and so on); the condition is true only if the string is found.

INSTR can also take an optional first parameter that specifies the position in the first string at which INSTR will start looking for the second string. For example, the statement

```
INSTR(4,"one and one make two","one")
```

returns the value 9 because the search starts after the first "one" and returns the position of the second "one."

String Concatenation

QuickBASIC lets you add two strings together (by joining them with the + operator) and assign them to a string variable. This is called *concatenation* and is demonstrated in the following statement:

```
a$ = "Quick" + "BASIC"
```

Concatenation merely merges the strings. Because no white-space characters are added to the strings involved, you often have to add blanks to separate the strings. Because concatenation also doesn't delete any blanks in the strings, you might want to use the RTRIM$ function to remove the trailing blanks in any fixed-length string before adding another string. (For details, see the RTRIM$ entry in Chapter 17, "Files.")

Making "Filler" Strings

Two QuickBASIC functions, SPACE$ and STRING$, let you create "filler" strings that you can use to format and arrange your output. The SPACE$ function generates the requested number of blank spaces; for example,

```
filler$ = SPACE$(10)
```

assigns a value of 10 spaces to the string *filler$*.

STRING$ is a more general function that returns a string containing a character that is repeated the specified number of times—for example,

```
PRINT STRING$(10,"*")        ' displays **********
PRINT STRING$(10, " ")       ' same as SPACE$(10)
PRINT STRING$(20,CHR$(205))' displays ════════════════════
```

The third example uses the CHR$ function to return the IBM extended character 205, a double line, which is then replicated by the STRING$ function. Using this method, you can easily write subprograms that draw boxes.

Changing the Case of Letters

The UCASE$ function returns a copy of a string with all lowercase characters converted to uppercase; the LCASE$ function returns a copy of a string with all its uppercase characters converted to lowercase:

```
PRINT LCASE$("QuickBASIC")     ' prints quickbasic
PRINT UCASE$("QuickBASIC")     ' prints QUICKBASIC
```

Nonalphabetic characters, such as numerals and punctuation marks, are not affected by the UCASE$ and LCASE$ functions.

Changing Part of a String

You've already seen how the MID$ function locates the position of a particular character or characters in a string. QuickBASIC also includes the MID$ statement, which lets you substitute one character or group of characters for another in a string. For example, the following statement pairs display the strings "QuickBASIC", "QuickPascal", and "QuickC."

```
a$ = "QuickBASIC "
PRINT a$

MID$(a$, 6) = "Pascal"
PRINT a$

a$ = "QuickBASIC"  ' restore original value
MID$(a$, 6) = "C     "
PRINT a$
```

The characters in the assigned string replace their counterparts in the string that is specified in the first parameter to MID$, starting in the position given in the second parameter. Thus,

```
MID$(a$, 6) = "Pascal"
```

replaces characters in *a$* with the characters in the string "Pascal," starting with the sixth character (the "B" in "BASIC"). If you want to "blank out" parts of the string being replaced, simply include blanks in the replacement string. Because MID$ can't replace beyond the last character in the original string, you must include enough blanks in the original string to accommodate the longest anticipated replacement string. (You can also specify that only part of the replacement string be used; see the MID$ (Statement) entry for details.)

Note that unlike the string-manipulation functions that return modified copies of a string, the MID$ statement changes the original string.

Converting Numbers to Strings

Finally, this section reexamines string and numeric representations. To QuickBASIC, a binary number and a string of ASCII characters are completely different objects. Nevertheless, you often need to convert a string to a number and vice versa. In many applications you might want to get a number from the user in string form so that you can check its validity; that way you won't need to depend on the runtime error messages to inform the user that the wrong type of input was entered. You then probably want to convert the input to a number for further processing (calculations). Also, when you display numbers on the screen or in a printed report, you might want to convert the numbers back to strings so that you can easily format them.

Use the VAL function to return the numeric value of a string. Use the STR$ function to return the string that represents a numeric value—for example,

```
PRINT VAL("12.5")
PRINT VAL("9999999999999999")
PRINT STR$(12.5)
PRINT STR$(1.5D8)
```

results in the following output:

```
12.5
1D+16
12.5
150000000
```

The VAL function essentially interprets the string as though it was typed at the keyboard as a number. The result is usually a number with the same numerals as the string; however in some cases, as in the second example, QuickBASIC applies its rules for representing large numbers. The specified number was too large to be represented in decimal form, so QuickBASIC converted it to exponential (scientific) notation and rounded up to 10 to the 16th power. STR$ usually converts the numerals (and any sign or decimal point) to characters in a string. In the last example, however, because the number fits within the range that can be represented in decimal form, 1.5D8 is converted to 150000000.

Conclusion

You will find that the QuickBASIC string functions are among the tools that you find most useful and reach for most often. QuickBASIC contains other string functions, which are discussed in Chapter 8, "Simple I/O," Chapter 15, "Printer," and Chapter 17, "Files." Some string functions in those chapters perform the same task as those presented here. In many cases, you can do a job in more than one way; only experience can help you determine which works best.

Related Reading

Kernighan, Brian, and P. J. Plauger. *Software Tools.* Reading, Mass.: Addison-Wesley, 1976.

Prata, Stephen, and Mitchell Waite. *The Waite Group's Microsoft QuickBASIC Primer Plus.* Redmond, Wash.: Microsoft Press, 1990.

ASC

See also: CHR$, STRING$, VAL

■ QB2	■ QB4.5	■ PowerBASIC
■ QB3	ANSI	■ GW-BASIC
■ QB4	■ BASIC7	■ MacQB

Purpose

The ASC function returns the ASCII or IBM extended code value (in the range 0 through 255) for the first character in a string.

Syntax

ASC(*string*)

string can be any string variable, string constant, string literal, or string expression.

Usage

```
PRINT ASC("a")
```

Prints the value of the letter "a", which is 97.

```
PRINT ASC(" ")
```

Prints the value of the space character, which is 32.

```
PRINT ASC("Apple")
```

Prints the value of the letter "A", which is 65.

Description

The ASC function returns the ASCII character or IBM extended character value of the character specified in a string literal, string constant, or string variable. If a string of more than 1 character is used, ASC returns the value of only the first character.

The CHR$ function is the opposite of the ASC function: CHR$ returns the character whose ASCII value is specified.

Errors

If a null (length 0) string is given as the argument to the ASC function, QuickBASIC displays an "Illegal function call" error message. If the value supplied isn't a string, QuickBASIC returns a "Type mismatch" error message.

Example

The following program creates an encoded string by adding the ASCII value of each character in the message to the value of the corresponding character in the code key string. Most resulting characters are members of the IBM extended character set and look cryptic indeed! (As an exercise, write a program that decodes the strings encoded by this program.) Figure 5-3 shows an example of this program's output.

```
CLS
INPUT "Message text "; text$

DO
    INPUT "Code key "; key$
    IF LEN(key$) < LEN(text$) THEN
        PRINT "Key must be as least as long as message text."
    ELSE EXIT DO
    END IF
LOOP

FOR char% = 1 TO LEN(text$)
    textVal = ASC(MID$(text$, char%, 1))    ' character value for message
    codeVal = ASC(MID$(key$, char%, 1))     ' character value for key
    MID$(text$, char%, 1) = CHR$(codeVal + textVal) ' add values
NEXT char%

PRINT "Encoded text is: "; text$
```

```
Message text ? This is a secret message.
Code key ? This is the secret code for the secret message.
Encoded text is: ¿╨╥µ@╥µ@╒ê╪à╓╫╚µàßà╓Γ┼╠àö
```

Figure 5-3.
Output of ASC example program.

CHR$

See also: ASC, SPACE$, STRING$

■ QB2	■ QB4.5	✲ PowerBASIC
■ QB3	■ ANSI	■ GW-BASIC
■ QB4	■ BASIC7	■ MacQB

Purpose

The CHR$ function returns the ASCII or IBM extended character that corresponds to the specified ASCII code value. You can use this function to send special control characters to the printer or to draw objects using the IBM extended character set.

Syntax

CHR$(*val*)

val is the ASCII character or IBM extended character code of the character you want. It must be in the range 0 through 255.

Usage

```
LPRINT CHR$(12)
```

Sends a formfeed character to the printer.

```
PRINT CHR$(205)
```

Displays the ═ symbol.

```
a$ = "quoted"
PRINT CHR$(34)+a$+CHR$(34)
```

Displays "quoted" (including the quotation marks).

Description

There are many characters that you can't easily enter at your keyboard and put in a string, such as most control characters and the graphics characters (those characters with ASCII values of 128 and above). The CHR$ function lets you generate all 256 characters of the ASCII and IBM extended character sets. (See the tutorial to learn how to enter graphics and control characters directly from your keyboard instead of specifying them with CHR$.)

The ASC function is the opposite of CHR$: ASC returns the ASCII or IBM extended code value of the first character in the specified string.

Comments

If you want to generate spaces, the SPACE$ function is faster and easier than using a loop that repeatedly prints CHR$(32) or the string " ". If you want to generate a specific number of a particular character, use STRING$.

Errors

If the value specified with CHR$ isn't within the range 0 through 255, QuickBASIC returns an "Illegal function call" error message. If the value is a string variable or literal, QuickBASIC displays a "Type mismatch" error message. (If you specify a non-numeric character or string without quotation marks, the compiler generates no error message, and CHR$ merely returns the null character, or ASCII value 0.

Warnings

Be careful when sending special characters to the printer; some sequences of characters might be interpreted as printer control sequences.

Compatibility

PowerBASIC

PowerBASIC lets you specify more than one value in a call to the CHR$ function. CHR$ returns a string containing the ASCII or IBM extended characters that correspond to the specified values.

Example

The following example uses CHR$ to store three different filled-box characters in a string array. The user is asked to input the name and number sold of three items; the program then generates a bar chart that reflects those numbers. Figure 5-4 on the following page shows an example of this program's output.

```
DIM bar$(3)
bar$(1) = CHR$(176): bar$(2) = CHR$(177): bar$(3) = CHR$(178) ' three bars

maxItems = 3

TYPE ItemType                    ' data type for each item
    itemName AS STRING * 10
    sold AS INTEGER
END TYPE

DIM sales(3) AS ItemType         ' array to hold names and number sold

CLS
FOR item = 1 TO maxItems
    PRINT "Name of item #"; item;
    INPUT sales(item).itemName
    INPUT "How many were sold "; sold
    sales(item).sold = sold / 1000
NEXT item

'header for chart
PRINT : PRINT "          Number of Items Sold (in thousands)"
PRINT SPACE$(10); "         1         2         3"
PRINT SPACE$(10); "123456789012345678901234567890": PRINT

FOR item = 1 TO maxItems
    PRINT sales(item).itemName;
    FOR bar = 1 TO sales(item).sold
        PRINT bar$(item);
    NEXT bar
    PRINT : PRINT
NEXT item
```

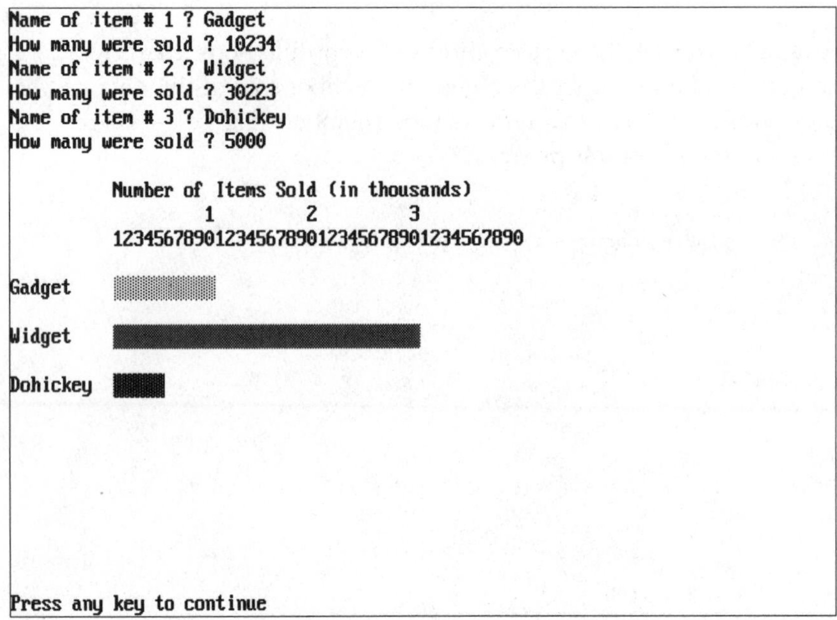

Figure 5-4.
Output of CHR$ example program.

INSTR

See also: LEFT$, MID$, RIGHT$

■ QB2	■ QB4.5	✲ PowerBASIC
■ QB3	✲ ANSI	■ GW-BASIC
■ QB4	■ BASIC7	■ MacQB

Purpose

The INSTR function returns the position of the first occurrence of a particular string in another string. This is useful for searching for text in database fields or for validating user input.

Syntax

INSTR ([*start*,] *string1*, *string2*)

start is an integer that specifies the position at which the search begins. If you don't specify *start*, the search begins at the first character.

string1 is the string that is searched; *string2* is the string that INSTR attempts to find. Both strings can be any string variable, string constant, string literal, or string expression.

Usage

```
PRINT INSTR("San Francisco", "San")
```

Displays the value 1 because "San" occurs at the first character in the string "San Francisco".

```
a$ = "San Francisco"
position% = INSTR(a$, "an")
```

Assigns the variable *position%* the value 2.

```
PRINT INSTR(5, "San Francisco", "an")
```

Displays the value 7 because "an" first occurs at position 7 when the search begins at position 5.

Description

The INSTR function returns the position of the first occurrence of one string in another string. If you merely want to test for the presence of the string, use a statement such as

```
IF INSTR(a$, b$) THEN
```

This condition is always true if *b$* is contained in *a$* because the value returned by INSTR will be a nonzero value. If you need to know the exact position at which the string was found, you can assign the position to a variable, as shown below:

```
found% = INSTR(a$, b$)
```

If INSTR does not find the string, the position returned is 0.

Optionally, you can precede the first string specified in the INSTR function call by a number that indicates the position at which the search starts. You can loop through a string and find all occurrences of the search string, as follows:

```
start% = 1
DO
    position% = INSTR(start%, a$, b$)
    IF position% <> 0 THEN PRINT position%
    start% = position% + 1
LOOP WHILE position% <> 0
```

Errors

If the optional starting position is 0 or less, QuickBASIC displays an "Illegal function call" error message. Specifying a starting position number greater than the length of the string to be searched doesn't result in an error: INSTR simply returns 0 (no match). If either the search string or the string for which you are searching isn't a string variable, string constant, or string literal, QuickBASIC returns a "Type mismatch" error message.

Compatibility

ANSI BASIC

ANSI BASIC does not support the INSTR function. Instead, it includes the POS function, which performs the same task as the QuickBASIC INSTR function.

PowerBASIC

PowerBASIC supports the use of the keyword ANY in the INSTR function. This lets you specify more than one string to be searched for in a call to INSTR. When one of the specified strings is found in the searched string, INSTR returns the position of that string.

Example

The following program prompts you to enter a string to be searched, a string for which to search in the first string, and a replacement string. The LEFT$ and RIGHT$ functions delete from the string any matching string found. The original string is reassembled with the replacement string substituted for the search string. The DO...LOOP statement repeats the search-and-replace until the INSTR function no longer finds an occurrence of the search string.

```
CLS
INPUT "Enter a string"; aStr$
INPUT "Search for:"; search$
INPUT "Replace with:"; replace$
newPos% = 1

DO WHILE newPos% > 0
    newPos% = INSTR(aStr$, search$)
    IF newPos% > 0 THEN
        temp1$ = LEFT$(aStr$, newPos% - 1)
        temp2$ = RIGHT$(aStr$, (LEN(aStr$) - newPos% - LEN(search$) + 1))
        aStr$ = temp1$ + replace$ + temp2$
    END IF
LOOP
PRINT aStr$
```

LCASE$

See also: CHR$, UCASE$

QB2	■ QB4.5	■ PowerBASIC
QB3	■ ANSI	GW-BASIC
■ QB4	■ BASIC7	MacQB

Purpose

The LCASE$ function returns a copy of a string in which all uppercase letters are converted to lowercase. You can use this function to make string comparisons case insensitive. You can also use it as the first step in normalizing text that was created entirely in uppercase letters (for example, on early personal computers or from some online services).

Syntax

LCASE$(*string*)

string can be any string variable, string constant, string literal, or string expression.

Usage

```
PRINT LCASE$("USING ALL CAPS IS LIKE SHOUTING")
```

Prints the string "using all caps is like shouting".

Description

The LCASE$ function returns a copy of the specified string variable, string constant, string literal, or string expression. In the copy, any letters that were uppercase in the original string are converted to lowercase. Nonalphabetic characters are not modified by LCASE$.

The UCASE$ function operates similarly except that it converts all lowercase letters to uppercase.

Errors

If the value supplied to the LCASE$ function is not a string, QuickBASIC displays a "Type mismatch" error message. Specifying a null string in a call to LCASE$ does not result in an error; the function merely returns a null string.

Example

The following program accepts a string and converts any uppercase characters to lowercase. Press Enter to exit the loop.

```
DO
    INPUT "Enter a string: "; aString$
    PRINT LCASE$(aString$)
LOOP UNTIL aString$ = ""
```

LEFT$

See also: INSTR, MID$ (Statement), RIGHT$

■ QB2	■ QB4.5	■ PowerBASIC
■ QB3	ANSI	✲ GW-BASIC
■ QB4	■ BASIC7	■ MacQB

Purpose

The LEFT$ function returns a copy of a string consisting of the specified number of characters from the left (beginning) of the string. You can combine LEFT$ with INSTR to extract the portion of a string either up to or including a specified substring.

Syntax

LEFT$(*string, num*)

string is a string variable, string constant, string literal, or string expression.

num can be any number in the range 0 through 32767.

Usage

```
a$ = "QuickBASIC Programmers' Association"
PRINT LEFT$(a$,10)
PRINT LEFT$(a$,99)
```

Displays "QuickBASIC" and "QuickBASIC Programmers' Association".

Description

The LEFT$ function returns a string that contains a copy of the number of characters you specify, starting at the beginning of the original string. If you specify a number of characters equal to or greater than the string's length, LEFT$ returns a copy of the entire string; for example,

```
LEFT$(a$, LEN(a$))
```

returns an exact copy of *a$*.

The following example shows how to use LEFT$ with INSTR to return selected portions of a string:

```
a$ = "QuickBASIC Programmers' Association"
b$ = "BASIC"
PRINT LEFT$(a$, INSTR(a$, b$) - 1)            ' display the characters to the substring
PRINT LEFT$(a$, INSTR(a$, b$) + LEN(b$) - 1) ' display the characters
                                              ' including the substring
```

The program displays the strings "Quick" and "QuickBASIC".

(See the "Example" section in the INSTR entry for a program that uses INSTR with LEFT$ and RIGHT$ to find and replace a portion of a string.)

Errors

If the first value in the call to LEFT$ isn't a string, QuickBASIC displays a "Type mismatch" error message. Specifying a null string or zero characters does not result in an error; LEFT$ merely returns a null string. If you specify fewer than zero characters, QuickBASIC returns an "Illegal function call" error message. If you specify more than 32767 characters, QuickBASIC displays an "Overflow" error message.

Compatibility

GW-BASIC and BASICA

Because GW-BASIC and BASICA limit their strings to 255 characters, the numeric arguments to LEFT$ must be in the range 0 through 255.

Example

The following program extracts the first name from a complete name and constructs the salutation of a letter:

```
INPUT "Enter first and last name together: "; name$
firstSpace% = INSTR(name$, " ")
firstName$ = LEFT$(name$, firstSpace% - 1)
PRINT "Dear "; firstName$; ","
```

LEN

See also: VARPTR, VARSEG

✲ QB2	■ QB4.5	✲ PowerBASIC
✲ QB3	✲ ANSI	✲ GW-BASIC
■ QB4	■ BASIC7	✲ MacQB

Purpose

The LEN function returns either the number of characters in a string or the number of bytes allocated to a numeric variable.

Syntax

LEN(*var*)

var can be any numeric variable (not a numeric literal) or any string variable, string constant, string literal, or string expression. If *var* is numeric, LEN returns the number of bytes needed to store the value of the variable. If *var* is a string, LEN returns the number of characters in the string. Note, however, that if *var* is a fixed-length string, LEN always returns the full length, regardless of the string's contents.

Usage

```
a$ = "QuickBASIC"
PRINT LEN(a$)
```

Prints the length of the string *a$*, which is 10.

```
total% = 10
PRINT LEN(total%)
```

Prints the number of bytes allocated to *total%*, which is 2.

Description

The LEN function returns the number of bytes used to store the value of a string variable, string constant, string literal, or string expression. For a string, the value returned by LEN is equal to the number of characters in the string. For a numeric variable or a variable of a user-defined data type, the value returned is the number of bytes used to store the value of the variable.

You use LEN most often to obtain the length of a string. A returned value of 0 indicates an empty (null) string. Thus you can force input of a non-null string value by using the following loop:

```
DO
    INPUT choice$
LOOP UNTIL LEN(choice$)
```

The loop repeats until the length of *choice$* is a nonzero value. Conversely, you can create a loop that exits when the user enters a null string (which the user can do by pressing Enter):

```
DO
    INPUT "Choice (or <Enter> to quit)"; choice$
    IF LEN(choice$) = 0 THEN EXIT DO
    ' process the choice
LOOP
```

You can also use the LEN function to obtain the length of a string for use in a loop that processes characters in the string one at a time. This is shown in the following FOR loop:

```
FOR char% = 1 TO LEN(a$)
    ch$ = MID$(a$,1,1)    ' get next character
    ' process the character in some way
NEXT char%
```

The use of LEN with numeric variables and user-defined data types was introduced in QuickBASIC version 4.0. The primary value of using LEN for numeric variables is that LEN determines the length of a user-defined type; this lets you estimate how many bytes each variable of that type will require. (Note that for an array, LEN returns the number of bytes per element.)

You can also use LEN to find the number of digits in a variable's value. First use the STR$ function to convert the number to a string, then call LEN to find the number of digits, as shown in the following example:

```
INPUT num#
var$ = STR$(num#)
PRINT LEN(var$)
```

The drawbacks of this operation are that STR$ adds a leading space character, that LEN counts any decimal point as one character in the length, and that STR$ might convert the number to exponential (scientific) notation.

Errors

If you supply a value to LEN that isn't a numeric variable or a string, QuickBASIC displays a "Variable required" error message.

Warnings

LEN works with string literals but not with numeric literals; that is, *LEN ("cat")* is a valid call to the function, but *LEN(1.24#)* returns a "Variable required" error message.

It is important to note that LEN returns only the number of bytes required to store the actual value of a variable, not the total amount of memory used by the variable. Each string, for example, also has a descriptor that uses an additional 4 bytes.

Compatibility

QuickBASIC 2.0, QuickBASIC 3.0, ANSI BASIC, PowerBASIC, GW-BASIC, BASICA, and QuickBASIC for the Macintosh

These versions of BASIC do not support using the LEN function to determine the number of bytes allocated to numeric variables. In these versions, LEN can be used only to return the length of a string.

Example

The following program underlines the string that was input by the user. The program uses the LEN function to provide the ending value for the FOR loop that generates the IBM extended character 196, which is used here as an underline character.

```
ul$ = CHR$(196)
INPUT "Type a string to be underlined: "; aString$
PRINT : PRINT aString$
FOR char% = 1 TO LEN(aString$)
    PRINT ul$;
NEXT char%
PRINT
```

MID$ (Function)

See also: LEFT$, LEN, RIGHT$

■ QB2	■ QB4.5	■ PowerBASIC
■ QB3	ANSI	✲ GW-BASIC
■ QB4	■ BASIC7	■ MacQB

Purpose

The MID$ function returns a copy of a string. The copy starts at a specified position and includes the given number of characters. You could, for example, use this function to extract the first name of a person from a string containing the full name.

Syntax

MID$(*string*, *start*[, *num*])

string is any string variable, string constant, string literal, or string expression.

start is the position of the first character to be extracted.

num is the number of characters to be extracted.

Usage

```
PRINT MID$("QuickBASIC Bible", 6 , 5)
```

Displays the string "BASIC".

```
PRINT MID$("QuickBASIC Bible", 6)
```

Displays the string "BASIC Bible".

Description

The MID$ function extracts a substring (a string within another string) from a string. When you call MID$, specify the string from which you want to extract a substring, the position of the first character you want to copy to the substring, and, optionally, the number of characters you want to include in the substring. (If you omit the number of characters, MID$ copies characters from the specified starting position to the end of the string.)

If you need to extract characters from either the beginning or the end of the string, use the more convenient LEFT$ and RIGHT$ functions. (See those entries for details.)

The starting position and number of characters specified as arguments to MID$ must be in the range 1 through 32767. If the starting position is greater than the length of the string, MID$ returns a null string. If the number of characters specified is greater than the number of characters from the starting position to the end of the string, the function returns all characters, beginning at the starting position. (Note that you can use the LEN function to obtain the length of a string.)

Errors

If the first item specified in the call to MID$ isn't a string variable, string literal, or string constant, QuickBASIC displays a "Type mismatch" error message. If the starting position or number of characters is less than 1, QuickBASIC returns an "Illegal function call" error message, and if the number is greater than 32767, QuickBASIC returns an "Overflow" error message.

Compatibility

GW-BASIC and BASICA

Because GW-BASIC and BASICA limit their strings to 255 characters, the numeric arguments to MID$ must be in the range 1 through 255.

Example

The following program examines each character in the string *aString$* to see whether it is a space. If the character is a space, a PRINT statement moves output to the next line; if it isn't, the program prints the character. The result is that each word in the string is printed on a separate line.

```
INPUT "Type a string: "; aString$

FOR char% = 1 TO LEN(aString$)
    thisChar$ = MID$(aString$, char%, 1)
    IF thisChar$ = " " THEN
        PRINT                   ' go to next line if character is a space
    ELSE PRINT thisChar$;       ' print the character
    END IF
NEXT char%
```

MID$ (Statement)

See also: LEFT$, MID$ (Function), RIGHT$

■ QB2	■ QB4.5	■ PowerBASIC
■ QB3	ANSI	✲ GW-BASIC
■ QB4	■ BASIC7	■ MacQB

Purpose

The MID$ statement replaces part of a string with another string. You could, for example, use this statement to replace a misspelled portion of a name with the correct spelling.

Syntax

MID$(*string*, *start*[, *num*]) = *replacement*

string is any string variable.

start is the position of the first character that is to be replaced.

num is the number of characters to use from the replacement string.

replacement is the replacement string variable, string constant, string literal, or string expression.

Usage

```
a$ = "Who put the cat out?"
MID$(a$, 13, 1) = "b"
PRINT a$
```

Prints the string "Who put the bat out?"

```
b$ = "QuickBASIC"
MID$(b$, 6) = "C    "
PRINT b$
```

Prints the string "QuickC".

Description

The MID$ statement, unlike the MID$ function and the LEFT$ and RIGHT$ functions, actually changes the specified string rather than returning a modified copy of it. When you call MID$, specify the string variable to be modified, the position of the first character to be replaced, and, optionally, the number of characters to be replaced. Follow the call with an equal sign and the replacement string, which can be any string expression (string constant, string variable, string literal, or combination.)

The starting position and number of characters to be replaced must be in the range 1 through 32767. The starting position cannot be greater than the length of the target string. If you specify more characters to be replaced than are available in the replacement string, only the available characters will be used. For example, in the statements

```
a$ = "brown rice"
MID$(a$,7,5) = "m"
```

the MID$ statement changes "brown rice" to "brown mice."

If the number of characters to be replaced would make the modified string longer than its original length, MID$ replaces characters only to the length of the original string. Thus in the example

```
a$ = "brown rice"
MID$(a$,6,14) = "ie points"
```

the variable *a$* has a value of "brownie po".

Errors

If you use a string literal instead of a string variable for the string you want to change, QuickBASIC displays an "Expected: variable" error message. If the variable you specify is not a string variable, QuickBASIC returns a "Type mismatch" error message. If the starting position or number of characters is less than 1, QuickBASIC displays an "Illegal function call" error message; if the number is greater than 32767, QuickBASIC returns an "Overflow" error message.

Warnings

Unlike many other string statements and functions, the target must be a string variable and cannot be a string literal; thus the following statement is illegal:

```
MID$("Who put the cat out?",13,3) = "hat"
```

Compatibility

GW-BASIC and BASICA

Because GW-BASIC and BASICA limit their strings to 255 characters, the numeric arguments to the MID$ statement must be in the range 1 through 255.

Example

The following program uses the MID$ function to check each character in a string to see whether it is a vowel. If it is a vowel, the program uses the MID$ statement to replace the character with an asterisk. You might use this program, for example, to develop a word-guessing game.

```
INPUT "Enter a string: "; aString$

FOR char% = 1 TO LEN(aString$)                ' check each character
    ch$ = MID$(aString$, char%, 1)            ' get next character
    IF INSTR("AEIOU", UCASE$(ch$)) THEN       ' is it a vowel?
        MID$(aString$, char%, 1) = "*"        ' replace vowel with *
    END IF
NEXT char%

PRINT aString$
```

RIGHT$

See also: INSTR, LEFT$, MID$ (Statement)

■ QB2	■ QB4.5	■ PowerBASIC
■ QB3	ANSI	✲ GW-BASIC
■ QB4	■ BASIC7	■ MacQB

Purpose

The RIGHT$ function returns a copy of a string. The copy consists of the specified number of characters from the right (end) of the string. You can use RIGHT$ to extract the last word in a string.

Syntax

RIGHT$(*string*, *num*)

string can be any string variable, string constant, string literal, or string expression.

num can be any number in the range 0 through 32767.

Usage

```
a$ = "the whole thing"
PRINT RIGHT$(a$,5)
PRINT RIGHT$(a$,99)
```

Prints the strings “thing” and “the whole thing”.

Description

The RIGHT$ function returns a string that contains a copy of the specified number of characters, beginning with the end of the original string. If the number of characters you specify is equal to or greater than the string's length, RIGHT$ returns a copy of the entire string; for example,

```
RIGHT$(a$, LEN(a$))
```

returns an exact copy of *a$*.

Errors

If the first value you use in the call to RIGHT$ isn't a string, QuickBASIC displays a "Type mismatch" error message. Specifying a null string or zero characters does not result in an error; RIGHT$ merely returns a null string. If you specify fewer than zero characters, QuickBASIC returns an "Illegal function call" error message. If you specify more than 32767 characters, QuickBASIC displays an "Overflow" error message.

Compatibility

GW-BASIC and BASICA

Because GW-BASIC and BASICA limit their strings to 255 characters, the numeric arguments to the RIGHT$ function must be in the range 0 through 255.

Example

The following program changes a string containing a name so that the last name is listed as the first word in the string. This program might be used to format a list of names as a prelude to sorting the names. The program uses the RIGHT$ function to extract the last name from the string.

```
INPUT "Enter a full name: "; name$

length% = LEN(name$)
FOR char% = length% TO 1 STEP -1                ' examine each character
    IF MID$(name$, char%, 1) = " " THEN         ' starting at end of name
        EXIT FOR                                ' found beginning of last name
    END IF
NEXT char%

IF char% <> 0 THEN
    lastName$ = RIGHT$(name$, LEN(name$) - char%)  'extract the last name
    restOfName$ = LEFT$(name$, char% - 1)
    PRINT lastName$; ", "; restOfName$
ELSE
    PRINT "You must enter an entire name"
END IF
```

SPACE$

See also: LSET, PRINT USING, RSET, SPC, TAB

■ QB2	■ QB4.5	■ PowerBASIC
■ QB3	ANSI	✲ GW-BASIC
■ QB4	■ BASIC7	■ MacQB

Purpose

The SPACE$ function returns a string that contains a specified number of spaces. This can be useful for indenting text.

Syntax

SPACE$(*num*)

num can be any number in the range 0 through 32767.

Usage

```
PRINT SPACE$(10); "Indented text"
```

Prints the string "Indented text" preceded by 10 spaces.

Description

The SPACE$ function returns a string consisting of the specified number of spaces (ASCII character 32). The number must be in the range 0 through 32767. If the number is not an integer, QuickBASIC rounds it to the nearest integer.

You can use the SPC and TAB statements to achieve similar effects in formatting output. See those entries, in Chapter 8, "Simple I/O and the Cursor," for details.

You do not need to use SPACE$ to pad fixed-length strings. By default, values assigned to fixed-length strings are left justified and padded on the right (if necessary) with spaces.

Errors

If the value you specify with SPACE$ isn't numeric, QuickBASIC displays a "Type mismatch" error message. If you use a numeric value that is less than 0, QuickBASIC returns an "Illegal function call" error message. For a numeric value greater than 32767, QuickBASIC displays an "Overflow" error message. Using a value of 0 does not produce an error; SPACE$ merely returns a null string.

Compatibility

GW-BASIC and BASICA

Because GW-BASIC and BASICA limit their strings to 255 characters, the numeric argument to the SPACE$ function must be in the range 0 through 255.

Example

The following program defines the function *Indent$*, which accepts an indention value and a string; the program also uses SPACE$ to indent the string when it is displayed. The program uses *Indent$* to format information on a page. Figure 5-5 shows the output of this program.

```
DECLARE FUNCTION Indent$ (spaces!, aString$)

CLS
PRINT Indent$(25, "Personal Information");
PRINT Indent$(15, "Page 1"): PRINT
PRINT Indent$(25, "Identification"): PRINT
PRINT Indent$(5, "Name  :"): PRINT
PRINT Indent$(5, "Street:"): PRINT
PRINT Indent$(5, "City  :");
PRINT Indent$(30, "State:");
PRINT Indent$(10, "Zip:")

FUNCTION Indent$ (spaces, aString$)
    Indent$ = SPACE$(spaces) + aString$  'returns an indented string
END FUNCTION
```

```
                         Personal Information               Page 1

                         Identification

     Name  :

     Street:

     City  :                              State:          Zip:














Press any key to continue
```

Figure 5-5.
Output of the SPACE$ example program.

STR$

See also: VAL

■ QB2	■ QB4.5	✲ PowerBASIC
■ QB3	✲ ANSI	■ GW-BASIC
■ QB4	■ BASIC7	■ MacQB

Purpose

The STR$ function returns a string representation of a number. This lets you manipulate a number as a string and apply the other string functions to it for validation and formatting.

Syntax

STR$(*num*)

num can be any numeric variable, numeric constant, numeric literal, or numeric expression.

Usage

```
PRINT STR$(99)
```

Prints the string "99".

```
num! = 3.1415
PRINT STR$(num!)
```

Prints the string "3.1415".

Description

The STR$ function accepts any valid numeric expression and returns the result as a string.

The VAL function converts in the opposite direction: It accepts a string and returns the number that its characters represent.

Errors

If the value you specify with STR$ is not numeric, QuickBASIC displays a "Type mismatch" error message. If you use a value that starts with numerals but contains characters that aren't valid in a number or expression (for example, a comma), QuickBASIC displays an "Expected:)" error message and highlights the invalid character.

Compatibility

ANSI BASIC

ANSI BASIC does not support the STR$ function. Instead, it includes the ORD$ function, which performs the same task as the QuickBASIC STR$ function.

PowerBASIC

PowerBASIC lets you specify in the STR$ function the number of digits that STR$ outputs. If the value to be output has more digits than the specified number of digits, STR$ rounds the value before returning its string representation. If the value has fewer digits than specified, STR$ pads the beginning of the string with spaces.

Example

The following example demonstrates how to print a number without leading or trailing spaces. When printing the amount on a check, for example, you should eliminate any leading or trailing spaces that might be used to alter the amount. The first PRINT statement, which displays a numeric variable, includes an unwanted leading space and a trailing space. The second PRINT statement doesn't display the unwanted spaces because the numeric amount has been converted to a string with the STR$ function and then stripped of the spaces with the LTRIM$ and RTRIM$ functions. (See Chapter 17, "Files," for details about LTRIM$ and RTRIM$.)

```
CLS
INPUT "How much money do you want"; num
PRINT "***"; num; "***"; " dollars"

num$ = STR$(num)                ' convert number to a string
num$ = LTRIM$(RTRIM$(num$))     ' strip trailing and leading blank space

PRINT "***"; num$; "***"; " dollars"
```

STRING$

See also: CHR$, SPACE$

■ QB2	■ QB4.5	■ PowerBASIC
■ QB3	✲ ANSI	✲ GW-BASIC
■ QB4	■ BASIC7	■ MacQB

Purpose

The STRING$ function returns a string containing a character that is repeated a specified number of times. You can use this function to create underlines, rows of asterisks, bordered windows, and so on.

Syntax

STRING$(*num*, *code*)

or

STRING$(*num*, *string*)

num is the number of characters (in the range 0 through 32767) in the resulting string.

code is the ASCII or IBM extended character code for the character you want in the returned string.

string is any string variable, string constant, string literal, or string expression. The string can have more than one letter, but STRING$ uses only the first letter to construct the resulting string.

Usage

```
PRINT STRING$(10, 42)
```

Prints the string "**********".

```
PRINT STRING$(10,"*")
```

Prints the string "**********".

```
a$ = STRING$(20,"BASIC")
```

Assigns the string "BBBBBBBBBBBBBBBBBBBB" to the variable *a$*.

Description

The STRING$ function is useful for creating a string consisting of repeated characters. The first argument in the STRING$ function specifies the number of characters in the string. The second argument is either a character code or a string variable, string constant, string literal, or string expression. The second argument specifies the character that STRING$ repeats. If the second argument is a string that has more than one character, only the first character is used in the generated string.

Use a string literal in the call to STRING$ if you can easily enter the character from the keyboard. For characters that aren't easy to enter, such as control characters or the IBM extended characters, use the character code instead.

If you use a character code with a value greater than 255, the value "wraps around" so that the value 256 produces the same character 0 produces, and so on. Negative codes also wrap around, so that the value –1 produces the same character 255 produces, and so on.

If you want to generate a string consisting only of spaces, the SPACE$ function is more convenient because you need only specify the number of spaces.

Comments

If you use the code value rather than a string literal, QuickBASIC generates faster and more compact executable code.

Errors

If the number you specify for the number of characters is negative, QuickBASIC displays an "Illegal function call" error message. If the number is greater than 32767, QuickBASIC displays an "Overflow" error message. Specifying zero characters results in a null string. If you specify a string as the first argument, QuickBASIC returns a "Type mismatch" error message. If you use a character code less than −32768 or greater than 32767 QuickBASIC displays an "Overflow" error message.

Compatibility

ANSI BASIC

ANSI BASIC does not support the STRING$ function. Instead, it includes the REPEAT$ function, which performs the same task as the QuickBASIC STRING$ function.

GW-BASIC and BASICA

Because GW-BASIC and BASICA limit their strings to 255 characters, the number of characters returned by the STRING$ function can be no greater than 255.

Example

The *BoxString* subprogram in the following program defines graphics character constants and then uses CHR$ (for single characters) and STRING$ (for multiple characters) to draw a box around a string. The subprogram checks the requested position of the box and prints a message if the entire box doesn't fit on the standard screen.

```
DECLARE SUB BoxString (row!, col!, aString$)

CLS
msg$ = "QuickBASIC 4.5"
BoxString 10, 30, msg$

SUB BoxString (row, col, aString$)    ' print a string in a box
    ' graphics characters
    CONST UPPERLEFT = 201
    CONST LOWERLEFT = 200
    CONST UPPERRIGHT = 187
    CONST LOWERRIGHT = 188
    CONST HORIZONTAL = 205
    CONST VERTICAL = 186

    CONST MAXLINE = 22            ' last line at which box can begin
    CONST MAXCOLS = 80            ' maximum number of screen columns
    IF row > MAXLINE THEN
        PRINT "Row must be 22 or fewer characters."
        EXIT SUB
    END IF

    farthestLeft = MAXCOLS - LEN(aString$) - 2

    IF col > farthestLeft THEN   ' too far to the left
        PRINT "Row for string "; aString$; " must be no greater than ";
        PRINT farthestLeft
        EXIT SUB
    END IF
```

(continued)

continued

```
    LOCATE row, col
    line$ = STRING$(LEN(aString$), HORIZONTAL)

    LOCATE row + 1, col
    PRINT CHR$(UPPERLEFT); line$; CHR$(UPPERRIGHT)    ' print top of box

    LOCATE row + 2, col
    PRINT CHR$(VERTICAL); aString$; CHR$(VERTICAL)    ' print sides of box

    LOCATE row + 3, col
    PRINT CHR$(LOWERLEFT); line$; CHR$(LOWERRIGHT);   ' print bottom of box
END SUB
```

UCASE$

See also: LCASE$

QB2	■ QB4.5	■ PowerBASIC
QB3	■ ANSI	GW-BASIC
■ QB4	■ BASIC7	■ MacQB

Purpose

The UCASE$ function returns a copy of a string in which all lowercase letters are converted to uppercase. Use this function for checking input that the user might enter in either uppercase or lowercase characters.

Syntax

UCASE$(*string*)

string can be any string variable, string constant, string literal, or string expression.

Usage

```
a$ = "QuickBASIC"
PRINT UCASE$(a$)
```

Prints the string "QUICKBASIC".

Description

The UCASE$ function returns a copy of the specified string variable, constant, literal, or expression in which every lowercase letter in the original string is converted to uppercase. Letters that are already uppercase and nonalphabetic characters are not modified by UCASE$.

The counterpart LCASE$ function returns a copy of a string in which all uppercase letters are converted to lowercase.

By using functions such as LEFT$ and RIGHT$ with the MID$ statement, you can use UCASE$ to selectively change characters in a string to uppercase. For example, the following program segment prints the string "Mary":

```
a$ = "mary"
MID$(a$, 1, 1) = UCASE$(LEFT$(a$, 1))
PRINT a$
```

Errors

If the value supplied to the UCASE$ function is not a string, QuickBASIC displays a "Type mismatch" error message. Sending UCASE$ a null string does not result in an error; the function merely returns a null string.

Example

The following program prompts the user to enter the letter A, B, C, D, or E. The UCASE$ function converts any lowercase input to uppercase so that the program needs to test only uppercase letters in the IF statements that work with the input. The program uses LEFT$ to strip all input characters after the first one; this allows users to enter full words (such as "copy").

```
CLS
PRINT "<Type E to exit program>"
DO
    INPUT "Type A, B, C, D, or E"; choice$
    choice$ = UCASE$(LEFT$(choice$, 1))
    IF INSTR("ABCDE", choice$) THEN
        PRINT "You chose: "; choice$
    END IF
    IF (choice$ = "E") THEN EXIT DO
LOOP
```

VAL

See also: STR$

■ QB2	■ QB4.5	■ PowerBASIC
■ QB3	■ ANSI	■ GW-BASIC
■ QB4	■ BASIC7	■ MacQB

Purpose

The VAL function returns the number represented by the digits (and other numeric symbols) in a string variable or expression. This function lets a program accept numeric input as a string, use the various string functions to validate the input, and then convert the input back to a number for use in calculations.

Syntax

VAL(*string*)

string can be any string variable, string constant, string literal, or string expression.

Usage

```
INPUT num$
value = VAL(num$)
```

Assigns the numeric value of the string entered to the variable *value*.

Description

The VAL function accepts the value of a string variable and scans it, beginning with the first character, until it encounters a character that cannot be part of a numeric literal (for example, a comma, letter, or dollar sign) or until it reaches the end of the string. The resulting string (which can include digits, a plus or minus sign, a decimal point, or the exponential D or E) is then converted into a valid QuickBASIC numeric value. The following strings are some examples:

Value of string	Result of call to VAL
500	500
4.4E7	44000000
123D-7	.0000123
99999999999999999	1D+17
4,000	4
xvi	0
2b or not 2b	2

Note that you can enter numbers using exponential notation (with D or E). VAL converts the numbers to regular decimal notation unless they have more than 16 digits, in which case they remain in exponential notation. VAL converts numbers with more than 16 digits that are entered in decimal notation to exponential notation.

VAL works with both variable-length and fixed-length string variables. It also works with string literals and string constants, although you will seldom find it useful to call VAL with string literals or string constants because you can more easily use numeric literals and constants.

The STR$ function performs the operation opposite to that of VAL: It returns a string containing the representation of a number.

Comments

VAL provides no error checking. To be robust, your program should check for strings input improperly such as “4,000”, “50%”, “1/2”, and so on, and respond appropriately.

Errors

If the expression you specify with VAL is not a string, QuickBASIC displays a "Type mismatch" error message.

Example

The following program accepts input into a string variable and uses VAL to convert the input to a number, which is stored in an array. Both your input and the converted value are displayed after each input. The program checks the length of the input string with the LEN function. If the length is 0 (that is, if only Enter was pressed), the program stops prompting for input.

```
DIM numbers(10)     ' array to hold input numbers
CLS
FOR i% = 1 TO 10
    INPUT "Enter number, press Enter to exit:", num$ ' input value as a string
    IF LEN(num$) = 0 THEN                ' user pressed Enter
        i% = i% - 1                      ' don't count this iteration
        EXIT FOR                         ' exit loop
    END IF

    value = VAL(num$)                    ' convert input to number
    PRINT "===> "; num$, value           ' display string, value
    numbers(i%) = value                  ' store number in the array
NEXT i%

total = 0
FOR j% = 1 TO i%
    total = total + numbers(j%)          ' add the values of the array
NEXT j%

IF i% = 0 THEN PRINT "No numbers entered": SYSTEM  'if no numbers entered, exit

average = total / i%                     ' find average
PRINT "*** Total: "; total; " *** Average: "; average
```

CHAPTER 6

Arrays and Data

Introduction

Arrays are efficient tools for storing and retrieving large quantities of data in memory, just as files are efficient tools for storing and retrieving data on disk. Some of the data your program uses is unique, such as a numeric variable to hold a month's sales total or a string variable to hold a user's name. In many cases, however, a program must manipulate many data items that have the same type and purpose. Suppose, for example, you need to process sales totals for 12 months and print 12 strings, each of which contains the name of a month. All the data items in these cases have the same type (single-precision and string) and purpose (sales total and month name).

Clearly, it would be tedious to have to create variables such as *janTotal*, *febTotal*, *marTotal*, and so on for the sales totals and *jan$*, *feb$*, *mar$*, and so on for the month names. Not only would you have to type all the different variable names into your program, but you would lack an easy way to refer to each total or name in turn. Suppose you want to add all the monthly totals to create a grand total. You have to write a statement such as *grandTotal = janTotal + febTotal + marTotal ... + decTotal*. Or suppose you are printing reports for the entire year and you want to print the name of the current month. You have to refer to the proper string variable for each month—for example, if the month is July, you must use the variable *july$*, and so on.

This section discusses how you use arrays as tools for organizing and processing data. An array lets you create an entire set of variables with a common name, such as *totals*. In effect, an array gives you a filing cabinet with many drawers, numbered from 0 (or sometimes 1) through any number you specify. You can retrieve the contents of a specific drawer (or store something there) merely by referring to the array name and the number of the drawer. If you want to systematically process all the drawers, use a simple loop (such as a FOR loop) to access each drawer, one at a time.

Table 6-1, on the following page, shows the array-related and data-related statements and functions in alphabetic order.

Statement or function	Purpose
DATA	Specifies a series of data values (usually to be read into arrays)
DIM	Dimensions (declares and allocates memory for) an array or specifies a variable's data type
ERASE	Reinitializes a static array or deallocates (frees) the memory used by a dynamic array
LBOUND	Returns the lowest valid subscript of a dimension of an array
OPTION BASE	Sets either 0 or 1 as the default lowest subscript
READ	Assigns the next item in a DATA statement to the specified variable
REDIM	Redefines subscript ranges for an array
RESTORE	Specifies the next DATA statement to be used for reading data
UBOUND	Returns the highest valid subscript of a dimension of an array

Table 6-1.
Array-related and data-related statements and functions.

Declaring and Using Arrays

The DIM (dimension) statement declares the name, size, and type of an array. In most cases you simply use the keyword DIM followed by the array name and its dimensions—for example,

```
DIM totals!(12)
DIM months$(12)
```

These statements declare two arrays. One, called *totals!*, can contain the sales total for each month; the other, called *months$*, can contain the name of each month. Note that array names can use the same type-declaration characters that specify the data types of ordinary variables. In this example, *totals!* is an array of single-precision numeric variables and *months$* is an array of strings. Or, you can use an AS clause to specify the data type:

```
DIM totals(12) AS SINGLE
DIM months(12) AS STRING
```

(Note that you can't use both the type suffixes and the AS clause—you must use one or the other.) You can also use a DEF*type* statement (such as DEFINT or DEFSTR) to apply a type to array names. Thus in the two statements

```
DEFSTR A-C
DIM a(5)
```

the array *a* is an array of strings because the DEFSTR statement makes the default type string for variables with names beginning with A, B, or C.

QuickBASIC also lets you implicitly dimension arrays with 10 or fewer elements without using a DIM statement. Thus if your program uses

```
grade(5) = 99
```

QuickBASIC acts as though the program contains the statement

```
DIM grade(10)
```

This practice is not recommended: It makes the code less readable, and future versions of QuickBASIC might not support it.

Dimensions and Subscripts

The number or numbers in parentheses following the array name in the DIM statement specify the number of individual variables (called "elements") in the array as well as the numbers (called "subscripts") that can be used to access the elements. QuickBASIC needs to know the number of elements in an array for two reasons. First, the number of elements multiplied by the size of each element specifies the amount of memory that the compiler allocates, or reserves, for the array. Second, QuickBASIC uses the specified values to check references to the array to prevent attempts to access nonexistent elements. After all, if you attempt to retrieve data from (or store data in) the 12th element of an array that has only 10 elements, you will be specifying a memory location outside the memory allocated to the array. This memory area might contain any type of information—such as the value of another variable or an undefined value. Figure 6-1 shows how the array *totals!*, defined above, is stored in memory.

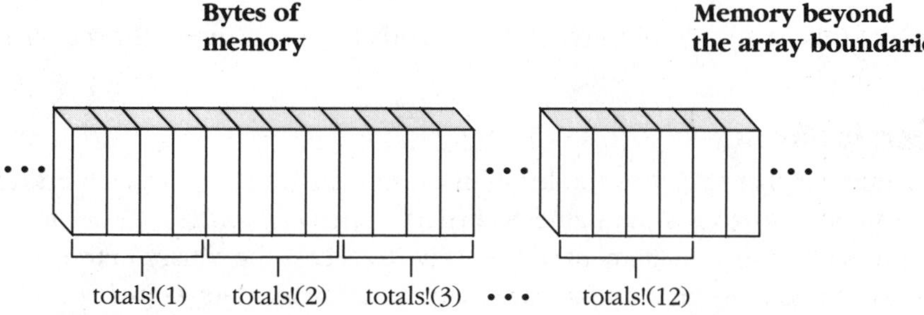

Figure 6-1.
How totals!, *a 12-element array of single-precision values, is stored in memory.*

In the previous example, both the *totals!* and *months$* arrays use the value 12 to specify that there are 12 elements in each array. By default, the subscript of the first element (the base) of every array is the number 0, so these arrays actually have 13 elements with subscripts ranging from 0 through 12. Because January is commonly considered the first—not the zeroth—month, it is more convenient to make 1 the base of the array. By using the statement

```
OPTION BASE 1
```

before you dimension any arrays, you can change the default so that the subscript of the first element of each array is the number 1.

Arrays with Multiple Dimensions

Sometimes it is useful to have more than one dimension in an array. For example, suppose you need an array that stores information about the status of a chessboard—such as what piece (if any) is on each square, the relative value of that square to the player, and so on. Because a chessboard is 8 squares long by 8 squares wide, it is logical to dimension the following array:

```
DIM board%(8, 8)
```

The *board%* array has two dimensions, each containing 8 elements; this assumes you have set the base of the array to 1 with an OPTION BASE statement. This array has 8 times 8, or 64, elements. In general, you can think of a two-dimensional array as being like a table or spreadsheet—having a certain number of rows and a certain number of columns.

QuickBASIC lets you specify many dimensions in an array; however, the most you will probably need for ordinary applications is three. Suppose you need a topographic map on which each point specifies an east-west coordinate, a north-south coordinate, and an altitude level. If the map measures 10 miles east to west, 10 miles north to south, and 30 thousand feet in altitude, you could declare the following array to represent the map:

```
DIM topo(10, 10, 30)
```

You might think of this as a stack of thirty 10-by-10 grids (or a big, three-dimensional chess set).

Specifying Subscript Ranges

A subscript is a number that specifies the location of an element along a given array dimension. For example, to access the name "February," specify *months$(2)* because "February" is stored in the second element of the array. To access the square in the second row of the fourth column on a chessboard, use the array element *board%(2, 4)*, which is shown in Figure 6-2. To access the region at 8 miles east, 7 miles north, and an altitude of 5000 feet from the reference point on the map, use the element *topo(8, 7, 5)*. These examples demonstrate that to access an array element you must provide its location along each dimension.

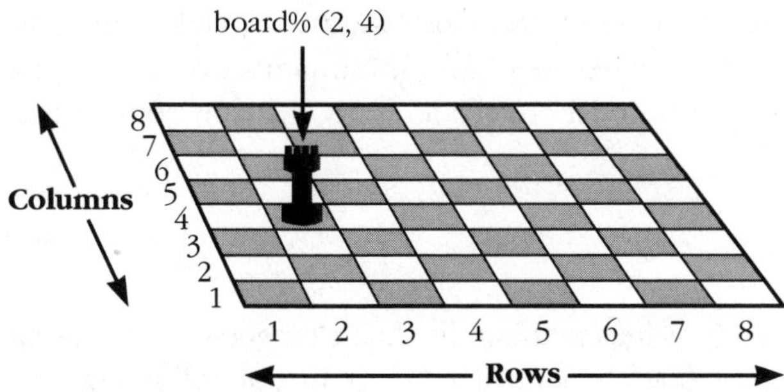

Figure 6-2.
Accessing an array element.

Thus far, our examples assume that every dimension begins at either 0 or 1 (depending on the base set with the OPTION BASE statement). Although this is appropriate in many cases, sometimes you might need to specify a base subscript other than 0 or 1. For example, the Cartesian coordinate system uses the point specified by the coordinates (0, 0) as its center (origin), places negative *x*-coordinates to the left of the *y*-axis, and places negative *y*-coordinates below the *x*-axis. The array that represents this coordinate system must allow negative subscripts; you can specify this by using the TO keyword when specifying the array's dimensions in a DIM statement, as in the following example:

```
DIM cartesian(-100 TO 100, -100 to 100)
```

The above DIM statement declares a two-dimensional array, called *cartesian,* whose subscripts are in the range –100 through 100. You can specify the point specified by (–50, –25) with *cartesian(–50, –25),* as shown in Figure 6-3.

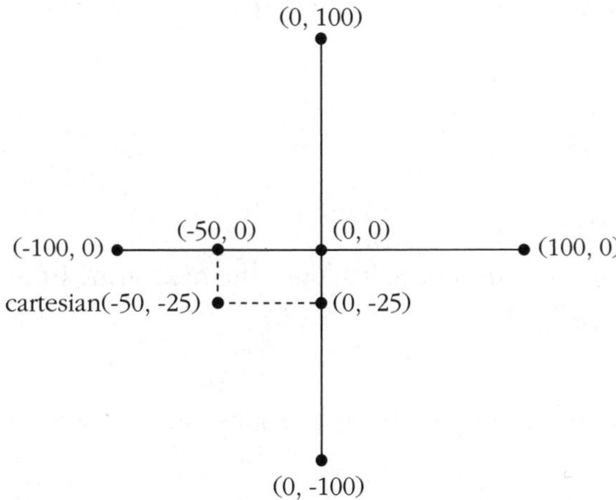

Figure 6-3.
Accessing a point in the Cartesian coordinate system.

You can use TO to specify any range of subscripts. Suppose you want to tally the number of students who receive each score on a test that had a minimum score of 40 and a maximum score of 100. The following statement creates an array that can contain this tally:

```
DIM totals%(40 TO 100)
```

Storing Data in an Array

After you create an array, you can assign values to the individual elements by specifying the array name and the subscript of the element, as shown in the following two statements:

```
totals!(1) = 244.45
totals!(2) = 389.90
```

The data for an array might also come from outside the program. If the data is in a file named SALES.DAT, you can transfer the data to the array one value at a time, as shown in the following program segment:

```
OPEN "SALES.DAT" FOR INPUT AS #1
FOR total% = 1 TO 12
    INPUT #1, totals!(total%)
NEXT total%
CLOSE #1
```

Accessing data from files is discussed in Chapter 17, "Files." Notice, however, that because arrays organize data sequentially, in order of the subscripts, a loop such as a FOR loop is all you need to fill the array with data.

You can also use a READ statement to assign data to the elements of an array. You usually use READ if the data items have fixed values that are the same whenever the program is run. Here is one way you can read the month names into the array *months$*:

```
FOR month% = 1 TO 12
    READ months$(month%)
NEXT month%

DATA January, February, March, April
DATA May, June, July, August
DATA September, October, November, December
```

In this example, each time the READ statement executes, it assigns the next string from the DATA statements to an element of *months$*.

Accessing Data in an Array

Recall that you access an element of an array by specifying the subscript along each dimension. Thus the statement

```
PRINT months$(4)
```

displays "April," and the statement

```
currentMonth! = totals!(8)
```

assigns the value stored in the eighth element of *totals!* to the *currentMonth!* variable. If an array has more than one dimension, you must specify a subscript for each dimension. Thus the statement

```
squareVal% = board%(3, 7)
```

references the seventh element in the third set (that is, in row 3 and column 7 on the chessboard) and assigns that element's value to the *squareVal%* variable.

To summarize: After you declare an array with a DIM statement, you can assign either a variable or constant to any element of the array, or you can assign an element's value to any variable that can accept that type of data. QuickBASIC treats each element of an array as a separate variable of whatever data type you have declared for the array.

Arrays of User-Defined Types

One drawback of using arrays is that each array can hold only one kind of data. You can't, for example, store both strings and integers in one array. One solution is to create one array for each kind of data. If, for example, you want to use arrays to store employee names, identification numbers, job titles, and salaries, you have to use one array for each of the four pieces of information. To reference the data for a particular employee, you might use a FOR loop:

```
FOR employee% = 1 TO totalEmployees%
    PRINT names$(employee%)
    PRINT id%(employee%)
    PRINT title$(employee%)
    PRINT salary(employee%)
NEXT employee%
```

Although this method works, it obscures the fact that you're actually dealing with a series of data records, each of which describes information about a particular employee. A better solution is to declare a *user-defined* type with a TYPE...END TYPE statement and then use an array of records of that type, as in the following example:

```
TYPE EmpRecord
    empName AS STRING
    id AS DOUBLE
    title AS STRING * 32
    salary AS SINGLE
END TYPE

DIM empInfo(1000) AS EmpRecord
```

```
FOR employee% = 1 TO totalEmployees
    PRINT empInfo(employee%).name
    PRINT empInfo(employee%).id
    PRINT empInfo(employee%).title
    PRINT empInfo(employee%).salary
NEXT employee%
```

In this example, creating an array of records enables you to assign the information about an employee to one element of the array. (See Chapter 1, "Types and Variables," for more information about user-defined types. Note that although you can have an array of record variables, a record variable cannot contain an array.)

Using Arrays in Subprograms and Functions

Usually you dimension an array in the module-level code unless the array is to be used only in a particular subprogram or function. There are several ways to make an array available to a subprogram or function. At the module level, the DIM statement can include the keyword SHARED, as shown in the following statement:

```
DIM SHARED globalData(100)
```

Using SHARED allows all subprograms and functions in the current module to access the array directly (rather than having it passed as a parameter). In other words, the array becomes global to the module.

Or, you can use a SHARED statement in a particular subprogram or function to enable the procedure to use an array declared at module level. Finally, you can pass an array as a parameter to a subprogram or function merely by including its name followed by an empty set of parentheses in the argument list, as shown in the following statement:

```
CrossTotal totals()
```

In this case, the subprogram *CrossTotal* would also have an array specified (with an empty set of parentheses) in its parameter list.

Which way is better? Modern program design stresses controlling access to data within your program to minimize errors. Passing the array as a parameter keeps the transaction "private" between the caller and the subprogram or function; it also invokes QuickBASIC's parameter-checking mechanism to help guard against the use of data that is not of the correct type. Using a SHARED statement within the subprogram or function provides similar privacy but less checking. Declaring the array to be shared at the module level lets any code in the module access it and is the least desirable method of making arrays available to subprograms and functions.

Dynamic and Huge Arrays

In early versions of BASIC, arrays were limited in flexibility and scope. All memory for arrays was allocated when the code was interpreted, not when the program ran, and the allocation couldn't be modified or deleted when the program no longer needed the array. Furthermore, all arrays were stored (along with all other variables) in a single, 64-KB segment of memory; indeed, in some implementations this segment had to contain the program's code as well as the program's data! However, QuickBASIC (beginning with version 2.0) permits dynamically allocated arrays, and version 4.0 introduces the capability for "huge" arrays consuming more than 64 KB of memory.

Static vs. Dynamic Arrays

If you declare an array using a literal or a constant as a dimension, as shown in the following statements, the array is static:

```
CONST ELEMENTS = 100
DIM n(ELEMENTS)
DIM p(10)
```

Both *n* and *p* are static arrays. QuickBASIC knows exactly what size they must be, and the compiler allocates the appropriate space in memory for each array when it encounters the array's DIM statement. There are two drawbacks to static arrays: First, you can't change their dimensions later in the program, and second, their size is limited by the amount of memory available in the 64-KB default data segment (called DGROUP). Implicitly dimensioned arrays (arrays that contain at most 10 elements and that are used without first being declared in a DIM statement) are also static.

On the other hand, if you either use a variable for the dimension or declare the array in a COMMON statement before you dimension it, the array is dynamic. This type of array has two advantages: First, the memory for the array is not allocated until runtime, and second, the memory is not limited to the 64 KB of the default data segment. QuickBASIC allocates memory for dynamic arrays from the "far heap" of memory (which is typically 200 to 300 KB or more). In the following example, the arrays *n* and *grid* are dynamic:

```
COMMON n()
DIM n(500)

rows% = 100
cols% = 50
DIM grid(rows%, cols%)
```

Furthermore, all arrays declared within a subprogram or function are dynamic unless you declare them in a STATIC statement. Because most subprograms or functions don't need to retain variable values between calls, using dynamic arrays ensures that the maximum amount of free memory is available at all times; this consideration is increasingly critical as programs get larger.

Declaring dynamic arrays also frees memory in the default data segment for variables that QuickBASIC stores there, such as simple variables and variable-length strings. (An ordinary string, such as *a$*, has variable length.) Although you can declare a dynamic array of variable-length strings, the strings are always stored in the default data segment. This is the only type of dynamic array that is not stored in the far heap. A fixed-length string, however, which you declare by using a statement such as *DIM lastName AS STRING * 30*, is stored in the far heap when you declare it as part of a dynamic array.

You can use the metacommands $STATIC and $DYNAMIC to set the default static or dynamic allocation for the various types of arrays. Following a $STATIC or $DYNAMIC metacommand, QuickBASIC allocates all arrays either statically or dynamically, as specified. (Variable-length strings are still stored in the default data segment, however, and implicitly dimensioned arrays, which are always static, are not affected.)

After you create a dynamic array, you can either use the ERASE statement to deallocate, or free, its memory for other uses or use the REDIM statement to change the array's subscript ranges (but not the number of dimensions). With a static array, ERASE reinitializes the array elements to 0 (or to the null string for string elements), but it does not free any memory. You cannot use the REDIM statement with static arrays.

Huge Arrays

Beginning with version 4.0, QuickBASIC not only lets you allocate dynamic arrays, it also lets you create huge arrays. Ordinarily, any one array (even a dynamic one) is limited to a maximum of 64 KB of memory space. By starting QuickBASIC with the /AH command-line switch (or by executing the command-line BASIC compiler with the /AH switch) you can create dynamic arrays that are limited only by the size of available memory.

There is one pitfall to avoid when you use huge arrays, however. QuickBASIC does not allow the memory allocated to an array element to cross the boundary between one 64-KB segment and another. If this is about to happen, QuickBASIC moves the element to the beginning of the next segment, thereby leaving a gap of unused memory. Only one such gap is allowed per array, so these arrays are limited to a maximum of 128 KB. You can avoid this problem by being sure that 64 KB (65,536 bytes) is evenly divisible by the size of an array element. Each standard type (integer, for example) evenly divides 64 KB, but user-defined types might not. If, for example, your program uses the following user-defined type, an array of that type could use only up to 128 KB of memory:

```
TYPE EmpRecord
    empName AS STRING * 40
    id AS DOUBLE
    title AS STRING * 30
    salary AS SINGLE
END TYPE
```

Suppose you want to create a huge array of this type. The problem is that the fields of the *EmpRecord* type total 82 bytes: 40 (for *empName*) plus 8 (for *id*) plus 30 (for *title*) plus 4 (for *salary*). This amount isn't evenly divisible into 64 KB; the next-higher amount that is evenly divisible is 128. The solution is to pad the type with a filler field 46 bytes long. The following program segment contains the complete declaration of the user-defined type and a huge dynamic array of this type:

```
' $DYNAMIC
TYPE EmpRecord
    empName AS STRING * 40
    id AS DOUBLE
    title AS STRING * 30
    salary AS SINGLE
    filler AS STRING * 46     ' brings element size to 128
END TYPE

DIM empInfo(1300) AS EmpRecord
```

Conclusion

Arrays are powerful tools for organizing and processing data. When combined with user-defined types, they allow related data of different types to be kept together and accessed using loop statements. QuickBASIC expands the utility of arrays by allowing them to be dynamically allocated; this enables them to use all available memory. If you are converting programs from an earlier version of BASIC to QuickBASIC, look for areas of your programs in which you can take advantage of these new capabilities.

Related Reading

Prata, Stephen with Harry Henderson. *The Waite Group's Microsoft QuickBASIC Primer Plus*. Redmond, Wash.: Microsoft Press, 1990.

DATA

See also: CONST, READ, RESTORE

■ QB2	■ QB4.5	■ PowerBASIC
■ QB3	■ ANSI	■ GW-BASIC
■ QB4	■ BASIC7	■ MacQB

Purpose

DATA statements store constant values that can be read into variables by the READ statement.

Syntax

DATA *val1* [,*val2*]...

val1 and *val2* are literal numeric or string values. Separate multiple values with commas. Enclose string literals in quotation marks only if the string contains commas, colons, or leading or trailing spaces.

Usage

```
DATA North, South, East, West
```

Stores four string constants that can be read only into string variables.

```
DATA 640, 320, 200, 16
```

Stores four numeric constants that can be read into either numeric or string variables.

Description

Each DATA statement contains a list of values separated by commas. If a program has a series of DATA statements, the values contained in all the data statements are treated as one list of data. The first READ statement executed by your program reads the first value from the data list into the specified variable, the second READ transfers the second value, and so on. QuickBASIC always marks its place with a pointer to keep track of the next value to be read. (You can reset this pointer or set it to point to the beginning of a labeled DATA statement by using the RESTORE statement.)

Each data value is interpreted according to the variable type specified in the READ statement. If the variable is numeric, the corresponding data value must consist only of legal numeric characters. If the variable is a string variable, the data value can be a value of any type. (To use a comma in a string data value or preserve leading or trailing spaces, you must enclose the string in quotation marks.) A value consisting of only a comma is treated as a null value; when a READ statement reads a null character, it sets numeric variables to 0 and string variables to the null (empty) string.

QuickBASIC allows DATA statements only in the module-level code; that is, you can't put them inside subprograms or functions. However, you can place READ statements anywhere in a program's code.

DATA statements are commonly used to hold a series of values that a loop reads into an array. (See the tutorial for an example.) However, DATA statements are not always appropriate. If your program uses only a few diverse values, using CONST statements makes the program more readable. Also, for large amounts of data, using many DATA statements makes the code unwieldy; therefore, the program probably should read the data from a file, although you must then ensure that the file always accompanies your program.

Errors

If a DATA value being read into a numeric variable has non-numeric characters, QuickBASIC displays a "Syntax error" message. If a READ statement attempts to read past the last DATA value (and a RESTORE statement hasn't reset the read pointer), QuickBASIC returns an "Out of DATA" error message. Having more data than you actually read is not an error; QuickBASIC simply ignores the extra values.

Example

The following program reads a variety of values from DATA statements. Note that all values are read into the string variable *item$*. The numeric value 3.14 is stored in *item$* as a string containing those characters. The quotation marks surrounding the "contains, a" value preserve the comma in the string. If the quotes were removed, the strings "contains" and "a" would be treated as separate data values. Notice that the null value, which is specified by a single comma, is printed as a blank line (because it is an empty string).

Although MAXVAL is the name of a constant, the READ statement treats it as the string "MAXVAL", not as the number 100. If this were read into a numeric value, it would generate a syntax error because MAXVAL cannot be treated as a number.

```
CLS
CONST MAXVAL = 100
FOR i% = 1 TO 5
    READ item$
    PRINT item$
NEXT i%

DATA Saturday, 3.14, "contains, a",, MAXVAL
```

DIM

See also: $DYNAMIC, ERASE, LBOUND, OPTION BASE, REDIM, SHARED, $STATIC, UBOUND

✲ QB2	■ QB4.5	✲ PowerBASIC
✲ QB3	✲ ANSI	✲ GW-BASIC
■ QB4	■ BASIC7	✲ MacQB

Purpose

The DIM statement declares arrays and allocates storage for them. You can also use DIM to specify the type of a variable.

Syntax

DIM [SHARED] *var* [(*subscripts*[,...])] [AS *type*]...

The optional keyword SHARED indicates that the item being declared will be accessible to subprograms or functions in the same program module.

var is the name of the variable or array.

subscripts indicates the maximum number of subscripts in the array. If the array has more than one dimension, the subscripts for the dimensions must be separated by commas.

AS followed by the name of a type specifies that *var* consists of elements of that data type or is a variable of that data type.

Usage

```
DIM totals%(10)
```

Declares a one-dimensional integer array.

```
maxX% = 640: maxY% = 480
DIM screen(maxX%, maxY%)
```

Declares a two-dimensional array with variables for subscripts. Because the subscripts are variables, the array is dynamic.

```
DIM SHARED flags(5)
```

Declares an array that subprograms and functions can access.

```
DIM ranking%(-10 TO 10)
```

Declares an array with subscripts in the range –10 through 10.

```
DIM names(100) AS STRING * 30
```

Declares an array of fixed-length strings.

```
DIM counter AS LONG
```

Declares a long-integer variable.

Description

The DIM statement is most commonly used to declare an array, which is a variable containing a series of values that are all of the same type. If you use DIM to declare more than one array, separate the declarations with commas.

There are several ways you can define the type of value that an array holds. One way is to include a type-declaration character (%, &, !, #, or $) at the end of the array's name in the DIM statement. Or, you can specify the type by using an AS clause in the DIM statement; this lets you specify either a user-defined type or a fixed-length string type. Finally, you can use a DEF*type* statement, which specifies that variables (including array variables) beginning with certain letters are of a default type.

The number or numbers in parentheses following the array name specify the number of individual variables (called elements) in the array as well as the numbers (called subscripts) that can be used to access the elements in the array. If you include only one number, QuickBASIC assumes that the number is the upper bound of the subscripts. The following DIM statement, for example, declares the array *players$* with subscripts ranging from 0 through 10:

```
DIM players$(10)
```

If you include an OPTION BASE statement to change the default lower bound (base) from 0 to 1, the subscripts in the above statements range from 1 through 10.

You can specify both the lower and upper bounds of the subscripts by using a TO clause in the parentheses following the array name. The following statement, for example, declares the array *ranking%* with subscripts ranging from –10 through 10:

```
DIM ranking%(-10 TO 10)
```

Sometimes it is useful to have more than one dimension in an array. To declare an array with more than one dimension, include the subscripts of each of the dimensions of the array in the parentheses following the array's name and separate the subscripts with commas. For example, the statement

```
DIM sheet(10, 20)
```

declares an array that contains 10 rows and 20 columns. Although QuickBASIC allows as many as 60 dimensions in an array, limit the number of dimensions in an array to 3 because an array that has more than 3 dimensions is difficult to conceptualize.

If you include the SHARED keyword in a DIM statement in module-level code, you can use the array in any subprogram or function in the module. Otherwise, you must either pass an array declared in module-level code as a parameter or specify the array in a SHARED statement within the subprogram or function.

Arrays you declare with literals or constant subscripts are static. The memory for a static array, which is allocated at compile time, cannot be changed during runtime and cannot exceed 64 KB.

On the other hand, arrays you declare with variable subscripts are dynamic. QuickBASIC allocates memory for a dynamic array at runtime; this enables your program to vary the amount of memory the array uses by calling the REDIM statement. The size of a dynamic array is limited only by the amount of memory available to the program; therefore, if you need to create a huge array, be sure to make the array dynamic.

You can also use the DIM statement to declare the type of a variable. This lets you declare variables without assigning them a value, making programs more readable and letting you check the types of the variables more readily. When you use DIM to declare a variable as a particular data type, you cannot include the type-declaration characters (%, !, #, &, and $).

The DIM statement initializes all elements of numeric arrays to 0 and all elements of string arrays to null strings. The fields of user-defined types (including fixed strings) are initialized to 0.

Comments

Static arrays are limited to the amount of memory available in the default data segment (DGROUP), which can hold 64 KB or less, depending on the number of other variables or strings in use. Dynamic arrays can use all available memory if you start the QuickBASIC environment or the BASIC compiler with the /AH command-line switch. Dynamic arrays can contain numeric types, fixed-length strings, or user-defined types containing these items. Variable-length strings are always stored in DGROUP, regardless of whether the array is dynamic or static.

QuickBASIC does not allow an array element to cross the boundary between two 64-KB segments. Therefore, if the size of an element does not evenly divide 64 KB, a gap in memory is left at the end of each segment. (This is not a problem with the standard numeric types; however, it can occur with arrays of fixed-length strings or user-defined data types.) QuickBASIC permits only 1 gap per array, so the maximum size for an array with such elements is 128 KB. To avoid this problem, pad your user-defined type so it evenly divides 64 KB. For example, if the data fields in the type total 58 bytes, include a field such as

```
pad AS STRING * 6
```

to bring the element size up to 64 bytes.

An array of fixed-length strings cannot be passed as a parameter to a subprogram or function. You can circumvent this limitation by using a COMMON SHARED statement to let the subprogram access the array. You can also include the fixed-length strings as fields within a user-defined data type and then use an array of that type.

If, in a program compiled in the QuickBASIC environment, you pass a static array to a subprogram located in a separately compiled source file (or Quick Library), you must use DIM to dimension the array in both the main source file and in the subprogram's source file. Or, you can compile the module containing the subprogram with the debug (/D) command-line switch.

Errors

If a program contains more than one DIM statement naming a particular array (without an intervening ERASE statement, in the case of a dynamic array) or if the program executes the same DIM statement more than once, QuickBASIC displays a "Duplicate definition" error message.

If the value of a subscript is not in the range –32768 through 32767, QuickBASIC returns an "Overflow" error message.

If a static array (or any array of variable-length strings) attempts to use more memory than is available in the default data segment (DGROUP), QuickBASIC displays an "Out of data space" or "Out of string space" error message. The "Out of data space" error also occurs if the far heap doesn't contain enough memory for a dynamic array. If the size of a static array is greater than 64 KB, QuickBASIC returns a "Subscript out of range" or "Array too large" error message.

If you use a subscript outside the range specified in the array's DIM or REDIM statement, QuickBASIC displays a "Subscript out of range" error message. This usually indicates an error in a loop statement.

Compatibility

QuickBASIC 2.0, QuickBASIC 3.0, ANSI BASIC, PowerBASIC, GW-BASIC, BASICA, and QuickBASIC for the Macintosh

Some versions of BASIC do not allow you to use the DIM statement to declare the type of a single variable. These versions, which include QuickBASIC versions 2.0 and 3.0, ANSI BASIC, PowerBASIC, GW-BASIC, BASICA, and QuickBASIC for the Macintosh, provide the DIM statement only for declaring arrays.

ANSI BASIC

In ANSI BASIC, the default lower bound for arrays is 1, not 0 as in QuickBASIC.

PowerBASIC

Unlike the extended capabilities of QuickBASIC's arrays, PowerBASIC limits arrays to 64 KB. PowerBASIC also requires a slightly different syntax to define a range of subscript values. You must substitute a colon (:) for the keyword TO. For example, the QuickBASIC statement

```
DIM applePie(5 TO 10)
```

must be written as follows in PowerBASIC:

```
DIM applePie(5:10)
```

PowerBASIC does not support the use of the keyword SHARED in the DIM statement. It does, however, support the keywords STATIC and DYNAMIC, which can be used to specify whether the defined array will be allocated at compile time or runtime.

GW-BASIC and BASICA

GW-BASIC and BASICA do not support the TO clause in the DIM statement. Therefore, you cannot create an array in these versions of BASIC that contains negative subscripts or that has a lower bound other than 0 or 1.

QuickBASIC for the Macintosh

The BASIC interpreter used in the environment of QuickBASIC for the Macintosh allows arrays with up to 255 dimensions. The QuickBASIC compiler for the Macintosh that you can use to create stand-alone executable files allows arrays with up to seven dimensions.

All arrays in the environment of QuickBASIC for the Macintosh are dynamic by default. To create a static array, include the keyword STATIC in the DIM statement.

Example

The following program uses DIM to declare two integer arrays—one to hold input values and one to hold the number of times each value occurs in the input. After the input is completed, the "mode" (the most commonly occurring value in the input) is calculated and displayed.

```
CONST TRUE = -1, FALSE = 0

CLS
INPUT "Minimum value: "; minVal%      ' get ranges of values to input
INPUT "Maximum value: "; maxVal%
INPUT "How many total values: "; maxInputs    ' get number of values to input

DIM vals%(maxInputs)                  ' array to hold input values
DIM freq%(minVal% TO maxVal%)         ' array to hold frequency of each value

FOR v% = 1 TO maxInputs
    DO                                ' get and validate an input value
        valid = TRUE
        PRINT "Enter integer value #"; v%; " ("; minVal%; "-"; maxVal%; "):";
        INPUT inputVal%
        IF INT(inputVal%) <> inputVal% THEN
            PRINT "Must be an integer"
            valid = FALSE
        END IF
        IF inputVal% < minVal% OR inputVal% > maxVal% THEN
            PRINT "Must be between "; minVal%; "  and "; maxVal%; ", inclusive"
            valid = FALSE
        END IF
    LOOP UNTIL valid = TRUE
    vals%(v%) = inputVal%
    freq%(inputVal%) = freq%(inputVal%) + 1    ' tally the input
NEXT v%
```

(continued)

continued

```
' find the mode
times% = 1
FOR v% = minVal% TO maxVal%
    IF freq%(v%) > times% THEN
        times% = freq%(v%)
        value% = v%
    END IF
NEXT v%

PRINT : PRINT "Mode values: ";
FOR v% = minVal% TO maxVal%                ' allow for more than one mode
    IF freq%(v%) = times% THEN PRINT v%; " ";
NEXT v%

PRINT : PRINT "occur "; times%; " times"
```

ERASE

See also: DIM, $DYNAMIC, REDIM, $STATIC

■ QB2	■ QB4.5	■ PowerBASIC
■ QB3	ANSI	■ GW-BASIC
■ QB4	■ BASIC7	✲ MacQB

Purpose

The ERASE statement either reinitializes the elements of a static array or releases the memory used by a dynamic array. Thus you can reuse an array (or the memory it uses) if you no longer need the contents of the array.

Syntax

ERASE *array* [,*array*]...

array is the name of the array to be erased.

Usage

```
sets% = 4
valsPerSet% = 100
DIM inputData(sets%, valsPerSet%)
:
ERASE inputData
```

Dimensions the dynamic array *inputData* and then releases the memory used by the array.

Description

With a static array, the ERASE statement merely resets all elements to their default value—0 if numeric, or null strings ("") if string. The dimensions of the static array defined in the DIM statement aren't changed, and no memory is released.

With a dynamic array, however, ERASE deallocates the memory used by the array, thereby freeing the memory for other dynamic arrays. Before you can reuse an erased array, you must dimension it again with DIM. (QuickBASIC offers the REDIM statement as an alternative to erasing and redimensioning a dynamic array. REDIM deallocates, redimensions, and reinitializes a dynamic array in one step.)

You can also erase an array of elements of a user-defined data type. All fields in each element, including fixed-length strings, are reinitialized.

Errors

After you erase a dynamic array, any reference to an element results in a "Subscript out of range" error message. You must first use a DIM or REDIM statement to redimension the array. If you specify the name of an array that does not exist, QuickBASIC returns an "Array not defined" error message.

Compatibility

QuickBASIC for the Macintosh

The QuickBASIC compiler for the Macintosh allows you to use the ERASE statement only to deallocate dynamic arrays. You cannot erase static arrays.

Example

The following program declares a dynamic array, erases it, and shows the amount of memory available for arrays before and after erasing the array. Notice that erasing the array frees all the memory used by the array.

```
DECLARE SUB ShowMem ()
CLS

PRINT "Before declaring array: ",
ShowMem

totalNums% = 2500
DIM dynArr$(totalNums%)    ' a dynamic array of 2500 strings

PRINT "After declaring array: ",
ShowMem

ERASE dynArr$              ' deallocate dynamic array
PRINT "After erasing array: ",
ShowMem
END

SUB ShowMem
    ' display amount of available memory
    PRINT "Total dynamic array space is "; FRE(-1)
END SUB
```

LBOUND

See also: UBOUND

■ QB2	■ QB4.5	■ PowerBASIC
■ QB3	■ ANSI	GW-BASIC
■ QB4	■ BASIC7	■ MacQB

Purpose

The LBOUND function returns the lower bound (lowest valid subscript value) of a dimension of an array. You can use LBOUND with the UBOUND statement to determine the size of an array.

Syntax

LBOUND (*array*[, *dim*])

array is the name of the array.

dim is the number of the array dimension whose lower bound is to be obtained. If you do not specify a dimension, LBOUND returns the lower bound of the first dimension.

Usage

```
DIM items(50,100)
low1% = LBOUND(items,1)
low2% = LBOUND(items,2)
```

Assigns the value 0 to *low1%* and *low2%*.

```
OPTION BASE 1
DIM n%(100)
low% = LBOUND(n)
```

Assigns the value 1 to *low%*.

```
DIM freq(500 TO 1000)
low% = LBOUND(freq)
```

Assigns the value 500 to *low%*.

Description

The LBOUND function returns the lowest legal subscript value of a dimension of the array you specify. If you do not specify a dimension, LBOUND returns the value of the lower bound of the first dimension. The lowest subscript of an array is 0 by default; however, the statement OPTION BASE 1 makes 1 the lowest value, and a TO clause can specify any lower bound when you dimension or redimension an array. (See the last example in the "Usage" section.)

You can calculate the size of an array by subtracting the value returned by LBOUND from the value returned by UBOUND.

Errors

If the variable you specify in the LBOUND statement isn't an array or if it is an array that has not been dimensioned, QuickBASIC displays an "Array not defined" error message. If you specify a dimension less than 0 or greater than the total number of dimensions in the array or if you specify a dynamic array that has been erased but not redimensioned, QuickBASIC returns a "Subscript out of range" error message. Specifying a dimension of 0 does not result in an error, but LBOUND returns a random value. Be sure you do not use 0 in a call to LBOUND.

Example

The following program passes an array to the subprogram *Total.* The latter uses the LBOUND and UBOUND functions in a FOR loop that accesses the elements of the array and totals their values. This is more concise than supplying the lowest and highest subscript values with the array name in the call to the subprogram.

```
DECLARE SUB Total (anArray%())
DIM values%(5 TO 10)

FOR num% = 5 TO 10
    values%(num%) = num%    ' assign values to the array
NEXT num%

Total values%()             ' get the sum of the elements of the array

SUB Total (anArray%())
    t = 0
    FOR n% = LBOUND(anArray%) TO UBOUND(anArray%)
        t = t + anArray%(n%)
    NEXT n%
    PRINT "Total of array values: "; t
END SUB
```

OPTION BASE

See also: DIM, LBOUND, UBOUND

■ QB2	■ QB4.5	✲ PowerBASIC
■ QB3	■ ANSI	■ GW-BASIC
■ QB4	■ BASIC7	■ MacQB

Purpose

The OPTION BASE statement specifies the default lowest subscript value for arrays; this can be 0 or 1.

Syntax

OPTION BASE [0 ¦ 1]

Usage

```
OPTION BASE 1
```

Sets the default lowest array subscript to 1.

Description

Use the OPTION BASE statement with a value of 0 or 1 to set the default lowest array subscript. By default, when you use an array that is not declared in a DIM statement or was not dimensioned with a TO clause, the default lowest subscript for each dimension is 0. By using the statement

```
OPTION BASE 1
```

you make 1 the first subscript in each dimension. Although many computer languages start array subscripts at 0, it is often more natural to label the first element of a list as number 1 and then to use the subscript 1 as the lower bound of the array that contains the list. Therefore, if you design code that never uses a 0 subscript, using the statement *OPTION BASE 1* offers two advantages: It guards you against inadvertently using the 0 subscript (by generating a "Subscript out of range" error message), and it saves memory by not allocating space for the element you don't use—the zeroth element.

When you include a TO clause for each dimension in a DIM statement, you can specify the lower and upper bounds of an array. Any bounds specified in a TO clause override the default lowest subscript.

Because the default lowest subscript is 0, the statement *OPTION BASE 0* is useful only to indicate to anyone reading the program that the lowest subscript is 0.

Errors

If you use a value other than 0 or 1 with the OPTION BASE statement, QuickBASIC displays an "Expected: 0 or 1" error message. If you attempt to use a second OPTION BASE statement in the same module, QuickBASIC returns an "Array already dimensioned" error message.

Warnings

You can use only one OPTION BASE statement in a program module. If your program contains more than one module, the default lowest subscript specified by an OPTION BASE statement in one module does not affect the default lowest subscript in any other module.

QuickBASIC ignores an OPTION BASE statement in a chained-to program if a dynamic array is passed to the program through a COMMON statement. In that case, the chained-to program inherits the default lowest subscript from the chained-from program.

Compatibility

PowerBASIC

PowerBASIC lets you specify any integer for the default lowest subscript value. In this version you can use the following statement, which sets the default lowest subscript to 10:

```
OPTION BASE 10
```

Example

The program below shows that the statement *OPTION BASE 1* changes the lowest array subscript to 1.

```
OPTION BASE 1          ' make default lowest subscript 1

DIM matrix(10, 10)
PRINT "First element in the two-dimensional array is matrix";
PRINT "("; LBOUND(matrix, 1); ","; LBOUND(matrix, 2); ")"
```

READ

See also: DATA, RESTORE

■ QB2	■ QB4.5	■ PowerBASIC
■ QB3	■ ANSI	■ GW-BASIC
■ QB4	■ BASIC7	■ MacQB

Purpose

The READ statement accesses values from one or more DATA statements and assigns the values to specified variables. A READ statement is commonly used inside loops to read values into an array.

Syntax

READ *var* [, *var*]...

var is any simple numeric or string variable type. Be sure to separate multiple variables with commas. (Arrays and user-defined types must be read one element or one field at a time.)

Usage

```
READ n$, a$, num
DATA Gary, Pittsburgh, 1
```

Reads the values "Gary," "Pittsburgh," and 1 into the variables *n$*, *a$*, and *num*.

Description

A READ statement retrieves the values in a DATA statement found in the same program module and stores the values in the specified variables. The READ statement always reads values in the order in which they appear in the DATA statements. (Note that you can use the RESTORE statement to reread values from the beginning of a DATA statement.)

When assigning values to variables, the READ statement converts values to the variable's data type as follows:

- Noninteger numeric values read into integer variables are rounded to the nearest integer.
- Numeric variables read into string variables are stored as a string of numerals.
- String values read into fixed-length string variables are truncated if they are too long. If a value is too short, it is left justified and padded on the right with blanks.

In early versions of BASIC, READ and DATA statements are used to establish the constant values needed by the program. The QuickBASIC CONST statement lets you name and specify the constants individually. Use the CONST statement instead of DATA and READ for a small number of constants because constants are more readable than the values in the DATA statement and are protected from inadvertent changes.

Errors

If you attempt to read more values than are available in DATA statements, QuickBASIC displays an "Out of DATA" error message. If you read fewer values than are available, the next READ statement (if one exists) begins reading at the first unread value. QuickBASIC does not check to ensure that all values specified in DATA statements are used. If you attempt to read a string value into a numeric variable, QuickBASIC returns a "Type mismatch" error message.

Warnings

You cannot read an entire user-defined data type (record) into a single variable. That is, if *custRec* is a variable of a user-defined type, you can't use the statement *READ custRec*. You must read the fields one at a time—for example,

```
READ custRec.name, custRec.street, custRec.city
```

Example

The following program uses a READ statement to read integers into an array. The values are then used to draw a star. Figure 6-4 shows the output of the program.

```
DIM points%(28)
FOR pt% = 1 TO 28
    READ points%(pt%)    ' read the data values into an array
NEXT pt%

' draw the star
SCREEN 1
PSET (points%(1), points%(2))
FOR pt% = 3 TO 28 STEP 2
    LINE -(points%(pt%), points%(pt% + 1))
NEXT pt%

DATA 100, 100, 150, 100, 175, 75, 200, 100
DATA 250, 100, 200, 125, 250, 150, 200, 150
DATA 175, 175, 150, 150, 125, 150, 100, 150
DATA 150, 125, 100, 100
```

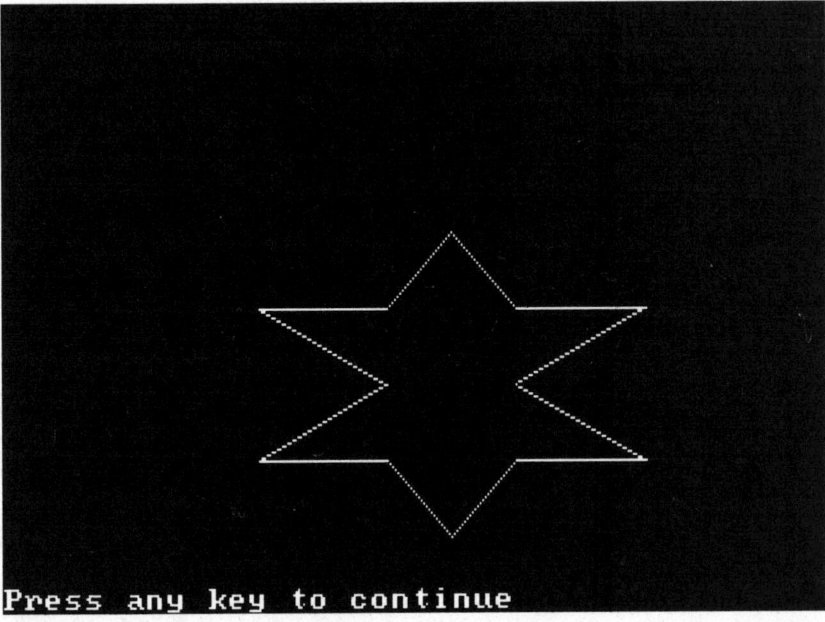

Figure 6-4.
Output of the READ example program.

REDIM

See also: DIM, ERASE

■ QB2	■ QB4.5	✲ PowerBASIC
■ QB3	ANSI	GW-BASIC
■ QB4	■ BASIC7	MacQB

Purpose

The REDIM statement deallocates, redimensions, and reinitializes a dynamic array. This lets a program use the same array for different sets of data during processing.

Syntax

REDIM [SHARED] *var* (*subscripts*[,...]) [AS *type*]...

The optional keyword SHARED indicates that the array being declared will be accessible to subprograms or functions in the same program module.

var is the name of the dynamic array variable to be redimensioned.

subscripts specifies the subscripts for each dimension of the array. If the array has more than one dimension, the subscripts for the dimensions must be separated by commas. The AS clause can specify the type of data the array will hold.

Usage

```
rows% = 10: cols% = 10
DIM matrix(rows%, cols%)
:
rows = 20: cols = 15
REDIM matrix(rows, cols)
```

Redimensions the array *matrix*.

Description

The REDIM statement can redimension only dynamic arrays (arrays that either use variables as subscripts in the DIM statement or have been made dynamic with the $DYNAMIC metacommand). QuickBASIC dimensions these arrays and allocates their memory at runtime rather than at compile time, as with static arrays. After you have used DIM or $DYNAMIC to establish a dynamic array, you can use REDIM anywhere in your program to reallocate memory and subscript ranges for that array.

The syntax for REDIM is the same as that for DIM. Follow REDIM with the keyword SHARED if you want the array to be accessible to all subprograms and procedures in the module. (Or, you can simply pass the array as a parameter to a subprogram or use a SHARED statement within a subprogram or function to make the array accessible to the subprogram or function.)

As with DIM, you can specify more than one array in the same REDIM statement; merely separate the declarations with commas.

Errors

If you attempt to change the number of dimensions in the redimensioned array, QuickBASIC displays a "Wrong number of dimensions" error message. If you changed the type of data stored in the array, QuickBASIC returns a "Duplicate definition" error message.

Warnings

You cannot use REDIM with a static array. You also cannot change the number of dimensions of the array or the type of data (integer, double, user-defined type, and so on) stored in the array.

To redimension an array so that it uses more than 64 KB of total storage, be sure to invoke QuickBASIC or the command-line compiler using the /AH switch.

Compatibility

PowerBASIC

PowerBASIC does not support the use of the keyword SHARED in the REDIM statement.

Example

The following program declares and fills an array and then uses the REDIM statement to redimension it; the program displays the contents of the array both before and after the redimensioning. The program also demonstrates how to pass an array to a subprogram and how to use LBOUND and UBOUND to access each element correctly.

```
DECLARE SUB FillMatrix (anArray%())
DECLARE SUB PrintMatrix (anArray%())

CLS
OPTION BASE 1                ' set lowest array subscript to 1
rows% = 5: cols% = 5
DIM matrix%(rows%, cols%)    ' declare a dynamic array
FillMatrix matrix%()         ' fill the array
PrintMatrix matrix%()        ' display the array

rows% = 6: cols% = 8
REDIM matrix%(rows%, cols%)  ' redimension the array
FillMatrix matrix%()         ' fill the array
PRINT : PRINT
PrintMatrix matrix%()        ' display the array

SUB FillMatrix (anArray%())
    ' fill a two-dimensional array
    FOR row% = LBOUND(anArray%, 1) TO UBOUND(anArray%, 1)
```

(continued)

continued

```
        FOR col% = LBOUND(anArray%, 2) TO UBOUND(anArray%, 2)
            anArray%(row%, col%) = col%
        NEXT col%
    NEXT row%
END SUB

SUB PrintMatrix (anArray%())
    ' print contents of any two-dimensional array
    FOR row% = LBOUND(anArray%, 1) TO UBOUND(anArray%, 1)
        FOR col% = LBOUND(anArray%, 2) TO UBOUND(anArray%, 2)
            PRINT anArray%(row%, col%); " ";
        NEXT col%
    PRINT
    NEXT row%
END SUB
```

RESTORE

See also: DATA, READ

■ QB2	■ QB4.5	■ PowerBASIC
■ QB3	■ ANSI	■ GW-BASIC
■ QB4	■ BASIC7	■ MacQB

Purpose

The RESTORE statement lets a READ statement either reuse all previously read DATA statements or reread DATA statements, beginning at a specified location. This allows your program to reread data from the beginning of the DATA statements or to read data selectively, based on a particular condition.

Syntax

RESTORE [*line* ¦ *label*]

line or *label* specifies the line that holds the DATA statement to be read next.

Usage

`RESTORE`

Rereads data from the beginning of the first DATA statement.

`RESTORE 500`

Rereads data from the DATA statement on line 500.

`RESTORE Monday`

Rereads data from the DATA statement on the line labeled "Monday".

Description

Normally, a READ statement reads data from the first item in the first DATA statement. Subsequent READ statements read data from DATA statements sequentially. The RESTORE statement lets you define a new starting point for reading data. If you use RESTORE without a line number or line label, the next READ statement accesses the data at the beginning of the first DATA statement. This is useful for reinitializing data before restarting a process.

If you use RESTORE with a line number or line label, the next READ statement reads the data at the beginning of the DATA statement on the line with the specified number or label. Note that RESTORE doesn't read anything; it merely specifies the DATA statement to be read by the next READ statement.

Errors

If you specify a nonexistent line label or number in a RESTORE statement, QuickBASIC displays a "Label not defined" error message.

Example

The following program labels three different DATA statements and reads the value of *wage!* from one of them, depending on the choice entered by the user. (In practice, you probably would define named constants—with the CONST statement—for the items in the DATA statements of this example. However, if you have several large sets of data items, use labeled DATA statements because they require much less memory.)

```
CLS
PRINT "Regular, Overtime, or Doubletime wage: "
INPUT "R, O, or D"; type$
SELECT CASE UCASE$(type$)
    CASE "R": RESTORE Regular
    CASE "O": RESTORE Overtime
    CASE "D": RESTORE Doubletime
END SELECT

READ wage!
PRINT "Your hourly wage is ";
PRINT USING "$##.##"; wage!

Regular:
DATA 5.00

Overtime:
DATA 7.50

Doubletime:
DATA 10.00
```

UBOUND

See also: LBOUND

■ QB2	■ QB4.5	■ PowerBASIC
■ QB3	■ ANSI	GW-BASIC
■ QB4	■ BASIC7	■ MacQB

Purpose

The UBOUND statement returns the upper bound (highest valid subscript value) of a dimension of an array. You can use UBOUND with the LBOUND statement to determine the size of an array.

Syntax

UBOUND (*array*[, *dim*])

array is the name of the array.

dim is the number of the array dimension whose upper bound is to be obtained. If you do not specify a dimension, UBOUND returns the upper bound of the first dimension.

Usage

```
DIM items(50,100)
high1% = UBOUND(items,1)
high2% = UBOUND(items,2)
```

Assigns the value 50 to *high1%* and the value 100 to *high2%*.

```
DIM freq(500 TO 1000)
high% = UBOUND(freq)
```

Assigns the value 1000 to *high%*.

Description

The UBOUND function returns the highest legal subscript value of a dimension of the specified array. If you do not specify a dimension, UBOUND returns the value of the upper bound of the first dimension.

You can calculate the size of an array by subtracting the value returned by the LBOUND function from the value returned by UBOUND. The UBOUND function is also useful for finding the upper limit of a loop that works with each element of an array.

Errors

If the variable you specify in the UBOUND statement isn't an array or if it is an array that has not been dimensioned, QuickBASIC displays an "Array not defined" error message. If you specify a dimension less than 0 or greater than the total number of dimensions in the array or if you specify a dynamic array that has been erased but not redimensioned, QuickBASIC returns a "Subscript out of range" error message. Specifying a dimension of 0 does not result in an error, but UBOUND returns a random value. Be sure you don't use 0 in a call to UBOUND.

Example

The following program uses the user-defined function *Sizeof* to determine the total number of bytes needed to store a specified integer array. When the program calls the function, it passes the array name and the number of dimensions in the array to the function.

For the array in this program, the program displays "The array uses 1890 bytes." Notice that because no lower bound is specified and no OPTION BASE 1 statement is used, the lower bound for each dimension is 0. Therefore the total number of array elements of type integer is 9 times 7 times 5 times 3; the function multiplies this value by 2 to find the total number of bytes occupied by the array.

```
DECLARE FUNCTION Sizeof (anArray%(), dimensions%)

DIM IntArray%(8, 6, 4, 2)
PRINT "The array uses"; Sizeof(IntArray%(), 4); "bytes."

FUNCTION Sizeof (anArray%(), dimensions%)
    ' return the size of an integer array
    size = 1                    ' holds product of dimensions
    FOR dimen% = 1 TO dimensions%
        subSize% = UBOUND(anArray%, dimen%) - LBOUND(anArray%, dimen%) + 1
        size = size * subSize%
    NEXT dimen%
    Sizeof = size * 2           ' 2 bytes per integer
END FUNCTION
```

CHAPTER 7

Math

Introduction

Most ordinary programming applications use only the standard arithmetic operations—addition, subtraction, multiplication, and division. In fact, you can write many useful programs without having any knowledge of mathematics beyond simple arithmetic.

Nevertheless, QuickBASIC's more advanced math functions are useful (and sometimes necessary) in many applications. You need to use trigonometric functions in surveying and in CAD (computer aided design) programs. Many games and simulations need a source of random numbers. Business applications require the ability to round numbers to a certain number of digits, and scientific applications often must determine the results of calculations to many places of precision. This tutorial explains the capabilities of QuickBASIC's math functions and offers suggestions for their use. Table 7-1 lists the math functions and statements in alphabetic order.

Statement or function	Purpose
ABS	Returns the absolute (positive) value of a number
ATN	Returns an angle, in radians, whose tangent is the given number
CDBL	Returns a number as a double-precision value
CINT	Returns a number rounded to the nearest integer
CLNG	Returns a number as a long-integer value
COS	Returns the cosine of an angle that is measured in radians
CSNG	Returns a number as a single-precision value
EXP	Returns *e* (the natural base, which equals 2.718282) to a specified power
FIX	Returns the integer part of a number
INT	Returns the next integer value less than or equal to a number
LOG	Returns the natural logarithm (base *e*) of a number
RANDOMIZE	Seeds the random-number generator (establishes a random-number sequence)
RND	Returns a value from a random-number sequence
SGN	Returns the sign value of number (–1, 0, or 1)
SIN	Returns the sine of an angle that is measured in radians
SQR	Returns the square root of a number
TAN	Returns the tangent of an angle that is measured in radians

Table 7-1.
QuickBASIC math functions and statements.

Trigonometric Functions and Square Roots

QuickBASIC includes four trigonometric functions: ATN (arctangent), COS (cosine), SIN (sine), and TAN (tangent). The results of these functions depend on relationships between an angle and the parts of a right triangle, as shown in Figure 7-1.

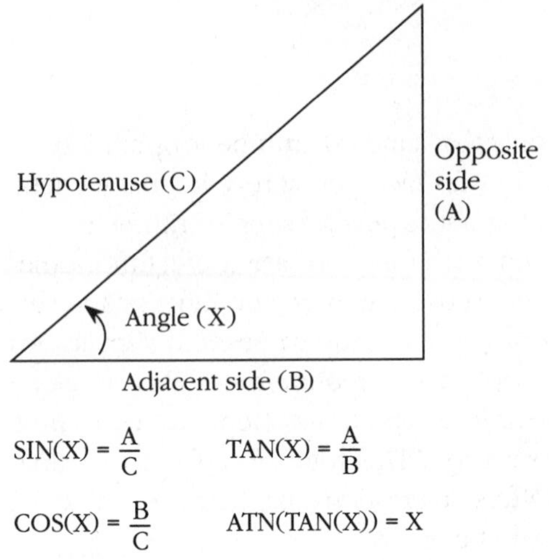

Figure 7-1.
Trigonometric functions.

The QuickBASIC functions SIN, COS, and TAN work with angles expressed in radians. (A radian is an angular measurement equal to the angle formed at the center of a circle by an arc equal to the circle's radius.) To convert from degrees to radians, multiply the number of degrees by the result of π divided by 180. To convert from radians to degrees, multiply the number of radians by the result of 180 divided by π, which is approximately 57.2958. You might want to declare the following constants in programs that perform conversion from degrees to radians:

```
CONST PI = 3.141593
CONST DEGREETORAD = PI / 180
```

(If you need more precision, define *PI* as a double-precision constant and add digits to the value.) Now, if you know how many degrees are in an angle, you can use the expression *angle * DEGREETORAD* to convert from degrees to radians, as shown in the following calculation:

```
result = SIN(angle * DEGREETORAD)
```

The above example expresses the values in single precision. The trigonometric functions return single-precision values by default; however, if you specify a double-precision value, the functions return a double-precision result.

Trigonometric functions are useful for calculating an unknown length or height when you know an angle and the length of one side of a right triangle. For example, by using Figure 7-1 as a guide, you can find the height of a tree without climbing it. Drive a stake at angle X into the ground a few feet away from the tree, and use a surveyor's transit to measure the angle to the top of the tree. Then stretch a line to measure side B (the distance to the base of the tree). Now QuickBASIC can calculate the height of the tree, as the following statements show:

```
INPUT "Angle in degrees: "; angleX      ' get angle
INPUT "Length of side B: "; lenB        ' get known side
radiansX = angleX * DEGREETORAD         ' convert angle to radians
tanX = TAN(radiansX)                    ' calculate tangent of angle X
height = tanX * lenB                    ' use algebra to calculate the height
```

The above example uses algebra to find the height of the tree. Because TAN(X) equals A divided by B, A (the height of the tree) equals TAN(X) times B.

You can derive many other trigonometric functions from the four that QuickBASIC provides. Table 7-2 shows some examples in which A is an angle in radians. The SQR function, used in some of the formulas in Table 7-2, returns the square root of any value that is greater than or equal to 0.

Function	Formula
Secant	SEC(A) = 1 / COS(A)
Cosecant	CSC(A) = 1 / SIN(A)
Cotangent	COT(A) = 1 / TAN(A)
Inverse sine	ARCSIN(A) = ATN(A / SQR(–A * A + 1))
Inverse cosine	ARCCOS(A) = PI/2 – ATN(A / SQR(–A * A + 1))
Inverse secant	ARCSEC(A) = ATN(SQR(A * A – 1)) + SGN(SGN(A) – 1) * PI
Inverse cosecant	ARCCSC(A) = ATN(1 / SQR(A * A – 1)) + SGN(SGN(A) – 1) * PI
Inverse cotangent	ARCCOT(A) = ATN(1 / A) – SGN(SGN(A) – 1) * PI
Hyperbolic sine	SINH(A) = (EXP(A) – EXP(–A)) / 2
Hyperbolic cosine	COSH(A) = (EXP(A) + EXP(–A)) / 2
Hyperbolic tangent	TANH(A) = (EXP(A) – EXP(–A)) / (EXP(A) + EXP(–A))
Hyperbolic secant	SECH(A) = 2 / (EXP(A) + EXP(–A))
Hyperbolic cosecant	CSCH(A) = 2 / (EXP(A) – EXP(–A))
Hyperbolic cotangent	COTH(A) = (EXP(A) + EXP(–A)) / (EXP(A) - EXP(–A))

Table 7-2.
Additional trigonometric functions.

Logarithms and Exponents

Two QuickBASIC functions perform operations with logarithms and exponents. The LOG function finds the natural logarithm of a specified number or expression. This is the power to which the base *e* (2.718282) must be raised to equal the specified value. The EXP function is the complement of LOG: It raises *e* to a specified value. To convert from natural logarithms to "common," or base 10, logarithms, divide the natural logarithm of the number by the natural logarithm of 10, as in the following function:

```
FUNCTION LOG10(number)
    LOG10 = LOG(number) / LOG(10)
END FUNCTION
```

Logarithms are often used in scientific models and simulations, such as simulations of population growth.

Numeric Conversion Functions

The next group of math functions convert numbers from one type to another, such as from single precision to double precision or from integer to long integer. This group of functions lets you convert a numeric value to the form expected by a function or subprogram. For example, if the function *Calc* expects two double-precision values as parameters, but you have been working with the single-precision variables *num1!* and *num2!*, you can call the function only by converting the variables, as the following statement shows:

```
result# = Calc(CDBL(num1!), CDBL(num2!))
```

To convert a number to double precision, use the CDBL function; to convert to single precision, use CSNG. To convert a number to an integer, use the CINT function; to convert to a long integer, use CLNG. Because precision increases with the number of significant (meaningful) digits, converting a number to a lower precision might reduce the number's accuracy. On the other hand, although converting a number to a higher precision adds more decimal places, it doesn't necessarily make the number more accurate.

Truncating and Rounding

Three functions let you round or truncate numbers. The INT and FIX functions truncate numbers by eliminating the digits following the decimal point and returning the integer; for example, *INT(3.445)* equals 3. INT and FIX differ only in the way they deal with negative numbers: INT returns the next-lower integer—for example, *INT(−3.52)* equals −4; FIX returns the next-higher integer—*FIX(−3.25)* equals −3. Truncation is useful when you want only the integer portion of a number.

The CINT ("convert integer") function rounds a value to the nearest integer. A positive decimal value greater than 0.5 is rounded to the next-higher integer. For example, *CINT(5.52)* equals 6 but *CINT(5.49)* equals 5; a negative decimal value greater than 0.5 is rounded to the next-lower integer: *CINT(−5.52)* equals −6, but *CINT(−5.49)* equals −5. (A fraction of exactly 0.5 is rounded to the nearest even integer.) Use the CINT function when you don't want to work with fractions but you do want to maintain a high degree of accuracy.

Random Numbers

The last two functions discussed in this section provide programmers with a means of generating "random" numbers. A random number is merely a number that has no inherent relationship to its predecessor (much as the result of one coin toss is not affected by the previous toss). Random numbers are useful for many games, in which they serve the same purpose as dice in the noncomputer world. Simulations also use them to model unpredictable behavior. The following program segment uses the RANDOMIZE statement and the RND function to print five random numbers:

```
RANDOMIZE 10

FOR randNum% = 1 TO 5
    PRINT RND
NEXT randNum%
```

The above program segment displays the following values:

```
.5749933
.2375866
.5295308
.2520258
.9770579
```

The RANDOMIZE statement "seeds" (initializes) the random-number generator with a value used in a formula that generates unpredictable results. However, each specific seed always generates the same sequence of random numbers. Although this type of "randomness" is useful for testing a simulation or game, a playable game requires that numbers be unpredictable as well as mathematically random. To generate a different sequence of random numbers every time you run a program, use the statement *RANDOMIZE TIMER*. The TIMER function returns the number of seconds counted by the system clock since the previous midnight, thus giving the RANDOMIZE statement a reasonably unpredictable seed value.

Related Reading

Graham, Ronald L., Donald E. Knuth, and Oren Patashnik. *Concrete Mathematics*. Reading, Mass: Addison-Wesley, 1989.

Hewitt, Paul G. *Conceptual Physics*. Boston, Mass: Little and Brown, 1985.

ABS

See also: SGN

■ QB2	■ QB4.5	■ PowerBASIC
■ QB3	■ ANSI	■ GW-BASIC
■ QB4	■ BASIC7	■ MacQB

Purpose

The ABS function returns the absolute value of a numeric constant, variable, or expression. The absolute value is the actual quantity of the number, regardless of its sign. For example, the absolute value of –1 is 1. All absolute values are positive numbers.

Syntax

ABS(*expr*)

expr is a numeric constant, numeric variable, or numeric expression that can be of any numeric type (integer, long integer, single precision, or double precision).

Usage

```
PRINT ABS(-45)
```

Displays 45, the absolute value of –45.

```
difference = ABS(guess1 - guess2)
```

Assigns to the variable *difference* the value of the absolute difference between the values of *guess1* and *guess2*.

Description

The ABS function returns the unsigned value of a numeric constant, variable, or expression. An expression can contain variables or constants of any numeric type. The precision of the value returned by ABS is the same as that used in the expression. For example, *ABS(–1)* returns 1 and *ABS(99.44555)* returns 99.44555.

The ABS function is often used in routines that use approximation to calculate values. For example, a program that calculates cube roots might compare the cube of the current calculated value to the original value. The program accepts the calculation when the absolute value of the difference between the two values is less than a specified tolerance, as demonstrated in the following DO...LOOP statement:

```
DO UNTIL ABS(target - result) < tolerance
    ' perform the calculation
LOOP
```

Such approximation has many other applications; for example, a program might read the current *x*- and *y*-coordinates of a ball on the screen and "bounce" the ball when the absolute value of the distance from a screen edge is small enough.

Errors

If you specify a non-numeric value with ABS, QuickBASIC displays a "Type mismatch" error message.

Example

The following program generates a random "target" on a 100-by-100-square grid and lets you guess the target's *x*- and *y*-coordinates. The program displays the difference between your guess and the target to indicate how close your guess was to the target. When the difference between your guess and the target is less than 5 (the "bulls-eye distance") for both the *x*- and *y*-coordinates, the target is "hit."

```
RANDOMIZE TIMER         ' get random-number sequence
DEFINT A-Z              ' define all variables as integers
targetX = RND * 100     ' random x-coordinate between 0 and 99
targetY = RND * 100     ' random y-coordinate between 0 and 99
bullseye = 5            ' distance within which "hit" occurs
xApproach = 100         ' x distance from target
yApproach = 100         ' y distance from target

CLS
PRINT "Try to hit a target in a 100-by-100-square grid": PRINT
DO UNTIL xApproach <= bullseye AND yApproach <= bullseye
    INPUT "X-coordinate of shot "; xShot
    INPUT "Y-coordinate of shot "; yShot
    xApproach = ABS(targetX - xShot)        ' get absolute distance
    yApproach = ABS(targetY - yShot)
    PRINT "x + y distance from the target is "; xApproach + yApproach: PRINT
LOOP

PRINT "You hit the target!"   ' x and y coordinates were in the bulls-eye
PRINT "Target was at x = "; targetX; "y = "; targetY
```

ATN

See also: COS, SIN, TAN

■ QB2	■ QB4.5	■ PowerBASIC
■ QB3	■ ANSI	■ GW-BASIC
■ QB4	■ BASIC7	■ MacQB

Purpose

The ATN function returns the arctangent of a numeric constant, numeric variable, or numeric expression. The arctangent is the angle (measured in radians) whose tangent is equal to the specified value.

Syntax

ATN(*expr*)

expr can be any combination of numbers or numeric variables (integer, long integer, single precision, or double precision). The result is expressed in radians, which can be converted to degrees by multiplying by 180 divided by pi, or approximately 57.2958.

Usage

`PRINT ATN(.8)`

Displays the arctangent of .8, which is .674741 radians.

`PRINT ATN(.8000001)`

Displays the arctangent of .8000001 in double precision, which is .6747410031991594 radians.

Description

The ATN function returns the size of the angle (in radians) whose tangent is the value of the specified expression. The function returns a single-precision floating-point value by default; however, if the given value is a double-precision value, the arctangent is also a double-precision value. The value returned by ATN will always be between $-\pi/2$ and $\pi/2$. (The value of π is approximately 3.141593.)

The ATN function (as with the other trigonometric functions) is useful for solving problems in geometry, trigonometry, or practical surveying. For example, if you know the lengths of the two sides of a right triangle, you can obtain the tangent of an angle by dividing the length of the opposite side by that of the adjacent side. As shown in the following statement, you can then find the size of the angle in radians by calculating the arctangent of the tangent, and you can convert the result to degrees:

```
angleInRadians = ATN(oppositeSide / adjacentSide)
angleInDegrees = angleInRadians * 57.2958
```

Errors

If you specify a non-numeric value with ATN, QuickBASIC returns a "Type mismatch" error message.

Example

The following program prompts the user to enter the known distance to an object and the known height of the object. The program then displays the angle in degrees between the user's position and the top of the object.

```
CONST RADTODEGREE = 57.2958    ' constant for conversion from radians to degrees

INPUT "Distance to object: "; distance
INPUT "Height of object: "; height
PRINT "Angle from observer to top of object in degrees is: ";

tangA = height / distance      ' tangent of observer angle
angleA = ATN(tangA)            ' find angle by using arctangent
PRINT angleA * RADTODEGREE     ' convert angle to degrees
```

CDBL

See also: CINT, CLNG, CSNG, FIX, INT

■ QB2	■ QB4.5	■ PowerBASIC
■ QB3	ANSI	■ GW-BASIC
■ QB4	■ BASIC7	■ MacQB

Purpose

The CDBL function converts a numeric constant, numeric variable, or numeric expression to a double-precision floating-point value.

Syntax

CDBL(*expr*)

expr is any combination of numbers or numeric variables (integer, long integer, single precision, or double precision).

Usage

```
a = 1.1
PRINT CDBL(a)
```

Displays the value of *a* converted to double precision, which is 1.100000023841858.

```
PRINT CDBL(3/7)
```

Displays the value .4285714285714285.

Description

The CDBL function converts a numeric constant, variable, or expression to double precision. Ordinarily, you use this function to force QuickBASIC to perform a calculation in double precision. For example, if a program uses two single-precision variables, *num1!* and *num2!*, the expression *CDBL(num1! / num2!)* returns the result of the division in double precision rather than in the default, single precision.

You can achieve the same effect by assigning the result of a calculation to a double-precision variable; for example, the statement

```
result# = num1! / num2!
```

yields a double-precision result and stores the value in *result#*.

Comments

The CDBL function cannot make an individual number more precise. Although the statement *PRINT CDBL(1.1)* displays the value 1.100000023841858, the extra digits are incorrect. However, the situation is different when determining the results of a calculation because a calculation (such as *3 / 7*) can be carried out to additional decimal places, thus making the result more precise.

In practical and scientific applications, the precision of a calculation depends on the precision of the components used in the calculation. Although you can divide two single-precision numbers to produce a double-precision result, the result is really no more accurate than the single-precision data used. The extra decimal places thus convey a false impression of accuracy. Do not use greater precision than is required by your data.

Errors

If you specify a non-numeric value with CDBL, QuickBASIC returns a "Type mismatch" error message.

Example

The following program demonstrates the methods of converting the result of a calculation to double precision. Notice that assigning the result of a calculation to a double-precision variable produces the same result as using the CDBL function does. Also notice that using CDBL separately with the numerator and denominator offers no advantage over using CDBL with the expression as a whole.

```
INPUT "Numerator: "; numerator
INPUT "Denominator: "; denominator

PRINT numerator / denominator, "(single-precision result)"

result# = numerator / denominator
PRINT result#;
PRINT "(result assigned to double-precision variable)"

PRINT CDBL(numerator / denominator); "(result converted with CDBL)"
PRINT CDBL(numerator) / CDBL(denominator);
PRINT "(result with values converted before dividing)"
```

CINT

See also: FIX, INT

■ QB2	✲ QB4.5	■ PowerBASIC
✲ QB3	ANSI	■ GW-BASIC
✲ QB4	✲ BASIC7	✲ MacQB

Purpose

The CINT function converts a numeric constant, numeric variable, or numeric expression to an integer value. For example, *CINT(99.7)* is 100.

Syntax

CINT(*expr*)

expr is any combination of numbers or numeric variables (integer, long integer, single precision, or double precision).

Usage

```
a = 100.43
PRINT CINT(a)
```

Displays the value 100.43 converted to an integer, which is 100.

```
PRINT CINT(-1.9)
```

Displays the value –1.9 converted to an integer, which is –2.

Description

Think of the name CINT as meaning "closest integer," because the function converts a numeric constant, variable, or expression to the nearest integer. For positive numbers, fractions greater than 0.5 are rounded to the next-higher integer, and fractions less than 0.5 are rounded to the next-lower integer. The opposite is true for negative numbers: Fractions greater than 0.5 are rounded to the next-lower integer, and fractions less than 0.5 are rounded to the next-higher integer.

You can use CINT with an expression of any numeric type; however, its value must be in the range –32768 through 32767, which is the range for signed integers.

Errors

If the value used with CINT is less than –32768 or greater than 32767, QuickBASIC displays the runtime error message "Overflow." If the value is non-numeric, QuickBASIC displays a "Type mismatch" error message. Using CINT with an integer or long integer value doesn't result in an error: The result is merely the same value as the value given.

Compatibility

QuickBASIC 3.0, QuickBASIC 4.0, QuickBASIC 4.5, and Microsoft BASIC 7.0

In these later versions of BASIC, CINT has one peculiarity: When the specified number contains a fractional part of exactly 0.5, CINT rounds the number to the nearest even integer. For example, *CINT(0.5)* equals 0, but *CINT(1.5)* equals 2. This behavior meets the IEEE (Institute of Electrical and Electronics Engineers) specification, and it applies to QuickBASIC versions 4.0, 4.5, and the 8087 version of QuickBASIC 3.0. It also applies to BASIC 7.0 when the program is compiled with the /FPi option. This procedure eliminates "rounding bias." If a fraction of 0.5 were always rounded up, the data would be skewed upward; rounding to the nearest even integer means that as many fractions ending in 0.5 are rounded up as are rounded down.

QuickBASIC for the Macintosh

QuickBASIC for the Macintosh is available in two versions, each of which supports a different internal storage format for floating-point numbers. (See Appendix D, "QuickBASIC for the Macintosh.") The binary version of QuickBASIC meets the IEEE standard specification. So, like QuickBASIC 4.5, CINT rounds a number that includes a fractional part of 0.5 to the nearest even number. The decimal version of QuickBASIC for the Macintosh, on the other hand, does not follow the IEEE standards. In this version, CINT always rounds a number ending in 0.5 to the next-higher integer.

Example

The following program prompts you to enter a number and then displays the number after converting it to an integer with the CINT function. Enter 0 (zero) to quit the program.

```
DO
    INPUT "Enter a number (enter 0 to quit): "; number
    PRINT "Closest integer is: "; CINT(number)
LOOP UNTIL number = 0   ' exit when 0 is entered
```

CLNG

See also: CINT, FIX, INT

QB2	✲ QB4.5	■ PowerBASIC
QB3	ANSI	GW-BASIC
✲ QB4	✲ BASIC7	✲ MacQB

Purpose

The CLNG function converts a numeric constant, numeric variable, or numeric expression to a long-integer value. Generally, you use this function to convert a value so that you can pass the value to a subprogram or function that is expecting a long integer. Fractions are rounded to the nearest integer.

Syntax

CLNG(*expr*)

expr is any combination of numbers or numeric variables (integer, long integer, single precision, or double precision).

Usage

```
PRINT CLNG(-32768.92)
```

Displays −32769.

```
PRINT CLNG(1483555.513)
```

Displays 1483556.

Description

The CLNG function can be used to convert a numeric variable or expression to a 4-byte long integer. Any fractional part is rounded to the nearest integer before conversion. For positive numbers, fractions greater than 0.5 are rounded to the next-higher integer, and fractions less than 0.5 are rounded to the next-lower integer. The opposite is true for negative numbers: fractions greater than 0.5 are rounded to the next-lower integer, and fractions less than 0.5 are rounded to the next-higher integer.

To pass an integer variable to a subprogram that expects a long integer, call it with a statement such as

```
LongSub& CLNG(value%)
```

The value used with CLNG cannot have a value of less than –2147483648 or greater than 2147483647 (the range for a long integer).

Errors

If the value used with CLNG is outside the range for a long integer, QuickBASIC displays the runtime "Overflow" error message. QuickBASIC returns a "Type mismatch" error message if the value is non-numeric.

Compatibility

QuickBASIC 4.0, QuickBASIC 4.5, and Microsoft BASIC 7.0

In these later versions of BASIC, CLNG has one peculiarity: When the specified number contains a fractional part of exactly 0.5, CLNG rounds the number to the nearest even integer. For example, *CLNG(0.5)* equals 0, but *CLNG(1.5)* equals 2. This behavior meets the IEEE (Institute of Electrical and Electronics Engineers) specification, and it applies to QuickBASIC versions 4.0 and 4.5. It also applies to BASIC 7.0 when the program is compiled with the /FPi option. This procedure eliminates "rounding bias." If a fraction of 0.5 were always rounded up, the data would be skewed upward; rounding to the nearest even integer means that as many fractions ending in 0.5 are rounded up as are rounded down.

QuickBASIC for the Macintosh

QuickBASIC for the Macintosh is available in two versions, each of which supports a different internal storage format for floating-point numbers. (See Appendix D, "QuickBASIC for the Macintosh.") The binary version of QuickBASIC supports the IEEE standard. So, like QuickBASIC 4.5, CLNG rounds a number with a fractional part of 0.5 to the nearest even number. The decimal version of QuickBASIC for the Macintosh, on the other hand, does not follow the IEEE standard. In this version, CLNG always rounds a number ending in 0.5 to the greater integer.

Example

The following program uses CLNG in preparing to call a subprogram that calculates population growth for each of three generations. Note that the value you enter, which is stored in *number%*, is of type integer. The subprogram *Populate* expects a long integer, *people&*. The CLNG function in the subprogram call converts the argument *number%* to a long integer before passing it to *Populate.*

```
DECLARE SUB Populate (people&)
DO
    INPUT "Enter number of people: ", number%
    IF number% = 0 THEN EXIT DO
    Populate CLNG(number%)
LOOP

SUB Populate (people&)
    ' show population after three generations (very simplistic)
    CONST KIDSPERCOUPLE = 1.8
    FOR generation% = 1 TO 3
        couples& = people& * .25    ' assume half the people have kids
        kids& = couples& * KIDSPERCOUPLE
        people& = people& + kids&
        PRINT "Population after generation "; generation%; ": "; people&
    NEXT generation%
END SUB
```

COS

See also: ATN, SIN, TAN

■ QB2	■ QB4.5	■ PowerBASIC
■ QB3	■ ANSI	■ GW-BASIC
■ QB4	■ BASIC7	■ MacQB

Purpose

The COS function returns the cosine of an angle.

Syntax

COS(*angle*)

angle is the angle measurement expressed in radians. You can convert degrees to radians by multiplying the number of degrees by the result of π divided by 180.

Usage

```
PRINT COS(57.2958)
```

Displays the cosine of 57.2958, which is .7336411.

```
PRINT COS(0)
```

Displays the cosine of 0, which is 1.

```
PRINT COS(3.1415)
```

Displays the cosine of 3.1415, which is –1.

Description

The COS function returns the cosine of an angle, which must be expressed in radians. To convert an angle from degrees to radians, use the formula *radians = degrees *pi / 180,* in which pi is 3.141593 in single precision or 3.141592653589793 in double precision.

By default, COS returns a single-precision value; however, if you supply a double-precision value, the return value will also be double precision.

Errors

If you specify a non-numeric value with the COS function, QuickBASIC returns a "Type mismatch" error message. If you don't convert a value in degrees to radians before passing it to the COS function, QuickBASIC does not display an error message; however, the result is wrong.

Example

The following program prints a table of the sines and cosines of 19 different angles. The table shows the relationship between the values and the repetition of the values of the sines and cosines. The program uses a PRINT USING statement to show all values carried to four decimal places.

```
CONST PI = 3.141593
CLS
PRINT : PRINT "Degrees   Radians   Sine     Cosine": PRINT
FOR angle% = 0 TO 360 STEP 20
    radians = angle% * PI / 180    ' convert angle to radians
    PRINT USING "###      "; angle%;
    PRINT USING "#.####    "; radians;
    PRINT USING "##.####   "; SIN(radians); COS(radians)
NEXT angle%
```

CSNG

See also: CDBL, CINT, CLNG, FIX, INT

■ QB2	■ QB4.5	■ PowerBASIC
■ QB3	ANSI	■ GW-BASIC
■ QB4	■ BASIC7	■ MacQB

Purpose

The CSNG function converts a numeric constant, numeric variable, or numeric expression to a single-precision floating-point value. This can be useful if you occasionally need to pass a variable that isn't single precision to a function or subprogram that expects a single-precision value.

Syntax

CSNG(*expr*)

expr is any combination of numbers or numeric variables (integer, long integer, single precision, or double precision).

Usage

```
doublePrec& = 1.23456789
PRINT CSNG(doublePrec&)
```

Displays the value of *doublePrec&* converted to single precision, which is 1.234568.

Description

The CSNG function converts a numeric constant, variable, or expression to a single-precision floating-point number. It rounds the value to the number of decimal places supported by single precision. Using this function has the same effect as assigning a value to a single-precision variable.

Errors

If you specify a non-numeric value with CSNG, QuickBASIC returns a "Type mismatch" error message.

Warnings

Remember that converting a number from a double-precision or long-integer number to a single-precision number might result in loss of accuracy.

Example

The following program stores in a double-precision variable the number the user inputs. The program first displays the value in double precision and then converts it to single precision and displays the new value.

```
DO
    INPUT "Enter value (enter 0 to exit): "; dbl#
    IF dbl# = 0 THEN EXIT DO
    PRINT "Value as double precision: "; dbl#
    PRINT "Value as single precision: "; CSNG(dbl#)
    PRINT
LOOP
```

EXP

See also: LOG

■ QB2	■ QB4.5	✲ PowerBASIC
■ QB3	■ ANSI	■ GW-BASIC
■ QB4	■ BASIC7	■ MacQB

Purpose

The EXP function raises the natural logarithmic base *e* to a specified power.

Syntax

EXP(*expr*)

expr is any combination of numbers or numeric variables (integer, long integer, single precision, or double precision).

Usage

```
PRINT EXP(-1)
```

Displays the value of *e* raised to the power −1, which is .3678795.

```
PRINT EXP(10)
```

Displays the value of *e* raised to the power 10, which is 22026.46.

Description

The natural logarithm of a number is the power to which the base *e* (a constant with an approximate value of 2.718282) must be raised to obtain the number. The EXP function is the inverse function of the natural log function. It returns the value of *e* to the specified power. (For more information about natural logarithms, see the entry for the LOG function.)

By default, the EXP function returns a single-precision value. However, if you supply a double-precision value, the returned value is also double precision. For example, EXP(1#) displays 2.718281828459045, which is the value of *e* in double precision.

Errors

If you specify a non-numeric value with EXP, QuickBASIC displays a "Type mismatch" error message.

Compatibility

PowerBASIC

In addition to the EXP function, PowerBASIC includes the EXP2 and EXP10 functions. EXP2 returns the value of 2 raised to a specified power, and EXP10 returns the value of 10 raised to a specified power.

Example

This program demonstrates the meaning of "exponential growth" by displaying the first 20 powers of *e*:

```
PRINT "Power                                    e to the power"
FOR power% = 1 TO 20
    PRINT USING "##"; power%;
    PRINT TAB(25);
    PRINT USING "##########.####"; EXP(power%)
NEXT power%
```

FIX

See also: CINT, INT

■ QB2	■ QB4.5	■ PowerBASIC
■ QB3	✲ ANSI	■ GW-BASIC
■ QB4	■ BASIC7	■ MacQB

Purpose

The FIX function truncates a number and returns the remaining integer. This allows a program to discard fractional parts of numbers so that it can perform faster integer arithmetic.

Syntax

FIX(*expr*)

expr is any combination of numbers or numeric variables (integer, long integer, single precision, or double precision).

Usage

```
PRINT FIX(1.5)
```

Displays the integer portion of 1.5, which is 1.

```
PRINT FIX(-1.25)
```

Displays the integer portion of –1.25, which is –1.

Description

The FIX function returns the integer, or whole, part of a specified numeric constant, literal, or expression. The fractional (decimal) part, if any, is simply truncated—no rounding occurs.

The FIX and INT functions perform the same operation with positive values. With negative values, however, FIX returns the next-higher integer, and INT returns the next-lower integer. Thus *FIX(–0.75)* returns 0, but *INT(–0.75)* returns –1.

Because no rounding is performed, using FIX can result in a considerable loss of accuracy.

Errors

If you specify a non-numeric value with FIX, QuickBASIC returns a "Type mismatch" error message.

Compatibility

ANSI BASIC

ANSI BASIC does not support the FIX function. Instead, it includes the IP (integer portion) function, which performs the same task as the QuickBASIC FIX function. ANSI BASIC also includes the FP function, which returns the fractional portion of a floating-point value.

Example

The following program lets you observe the behavior of the FIX function with values that you input:

```
DO
    INPUT "Enter a number (enter 0 to exit): "; number
    IF number = 0 THEN EXIT DO
    PRINT "Integer part of "; number; " is "; FIX(number)
LOOP
```

INT

See also: CINT, FIX

■ QB2 ■ QB4.5 ■ PowerBASIC
■ QB3 ■ ANSI ■ GW-BASIC
■ QB4 ■ BASIC7 ■ MacQB

Purpose

The INT function truncates the fractional part of a number and returns the remaining integer. This allows a program to trade accuracy for speed by discarding fractions so that QuickBASIC can use integer arithmetic, which is faster than floating-point arithmetic.

Syntax

INT(*expr*)

expr is any combination of numbers or numeric variables (integer, long integer, single precision, or double precision).

Usage

```
PRINT INT(3.33)
```

Displays the integer portion of 3.33, which is 3.

```
PRINT INT(-1.89)
```

Displays the next-lower integer, which is –2.

Description

The INT function returns the integer, or whole, part of a specified numeric constant, literal, or expression. The fractional (decimal) part, if any, is simply truncated—no rounding occurs.

The FIX and INT functions perform the same operation with positive values. With negative values, however, FIX returns the next-higher integer and INT returns the next-lower integer. Thus *FIX(–0.75)* returns 0, but *INT(–0.75)* returns –1.

Because no rounding is performed, using INT can result in a considerable loss of accuracy.

Errors

If you specify a non-numeric expression with INT, QuickBASIC displays a "Type mismatch" error message.

Example

The following program demonstrates how much more quickly QuickBASIC performs math operations when you convert numbers to integers by using INT. Of course, you must determine whether the loss of accuracy is acceptable in your application.

```
' perform floating-point math
floatA = 1.8975: floatB = 2.113
time1 = TIMER

CLS : PRINT "Seconds elapsed for floating-point math: ";
FOR time% = 1 TO 5000
    temp = floatA * floatB
NEXT time%
time2 = TIMER
PRINT time2 - time1

' perform integer math
intA% = INT(floatA): intB% = INT(floatB)
time1 = TIMER

PRINT "Seconds elapsed for integer math: ";
FOR time% = 1 TO 5000
    temp% = intA% * intB%
NEXT time%
time2 = TIMER
PRINT time2 - time1
```

LOG

See also: EXP

■ QB2	■ QB4.5	✲ PowerBASIC
■ QB3	✲ ANSI	■ GW-BASIC
■ QB4	■ BASIC7	■ MacQB

Purpose

The LOG function returns the natural logarithm of a number. (Natural logarithms should not be confused with common logarithms, which are based on 10 rather than on *e*, which is approximately 2.718282.)

Syntax

LOG(*expr*)

expr is any combination of numbers or numeric variables (integer, long integer, single precision, or double precision). However, each value must be greater than 0.

Usage

```
PRINT LOG(1)
```

Displays the natural logarithm of 1, which is 0.

```
PRINT LOG(2.718282)
```

Displays the natural logarithm of *e*, which is 1.

```
PRINT LOG(100)
```

Displays the natural logarithm of 100, which is 4.60517.

Description

The natural logarithm function finds the power to which the constant *e* (2.718282 in single precision) must be raised to obtain a given number. Because *e* to the third power is 20.08554, for example, the natural logarithm of 20.08554 is 3. You can find the natural logarithm of a number by using the LOG function.

The LOG function by default returns the natural logarithm of a number in single precision. However, if the given value is double precision, the function returns a double-precision value.

Errors

If you specify a non-numeric value with EXP, QuickBASIC displays a "Type mismatch" error message. If you use a numeric value that is less than or equal to 0, QuickBASIC returns an "Illegal function call" error message.

Compatibility

ANSI BASIC and PowerBASIC

In addition to the LOG function, ANSI BASIC and PowerBASIC include the LOG2 and LOG10 functions. LOG2 returns the power to which the value 2 must be raised to obtain a specified power, and LOG10 returns the power to which the value 10 must be raised to obtain a specified number.

Example

The following program displays the base 10 logarithmic curve. The program uses the function *Log10!* to convert the natural logarithm to a base 10 logarithm, which is multiplied by a scaling factor of 100 so that the progression is large enough to show clearly on the screen.

```
DECLARE FUNCTION Log10! (number%)
SCREEN 9            ' EGA or VGA adapter
CONST XMAX = 640

FOR x% = 1 TO XMAX
    PSET (x%, Log10!(x%) * 100)
NEXT x%

FUNCTION Log10! (number%)
    Log10! = LOG(number%) / LOG(10!)
END FUNCTION
```

RANDOMIZE

See also: RND, TIMER

■ QB2	■ QB4.5	■ PowerBASIC
■ QB3	■ ANSI	■ GW-BASIC
■ QB4	■ BASIC7	■ MacQB

Purpose

Use the RANDOMIZE statement to specify a particular initial value or "seed value" for the random-number generator, thus specifying the random-number series to be used when the program calls the RND function.

If you use the value returned by the TIMER function as the seed, RANDOMIZE generates the unpredictable random numbers that are necessary for applications such as games and simulations. (The TIMER function returns the number of seconds that have elapsed since midnight. For more information, see the TIMER function in Chapter 10, "Time.")

Syntax

RANDOMIZE [*expr*]

expr is any combination of numbers or numeric variables (integer, long integer, single precision, or double precision).

If no value is specified, RANDOMIZE prompts the user for a seed value.

Usage

```
RANDOMIZE 10
```

Specifies the value 10 as the seed for the random-number generator.

```
RANDOMIZE TIMER
```

Generates a different set of random numbers each time the user runs the program.

Description

The RANDOMIZE statement specifies a seed for the random-number generator. (You can then use the RND function to return random values from the set of values generated.)

You can use any type of numeric expression with RANDOMIZE. If you don't specify a value in the statement, QuickBASIC prompts the user for a value in the range –32768 through 32767. If a program doesn't include a RANDOMIZE statement, all calls to the RND function return the values generated by using the seed 0.

Note that additional RANDOMIZE statements in the same program reseed the random-number generator; however, they do not generate the entire random-number sequence from the beginning. If the program generates three random numbers before calling RANDOMIZE with a new seed, the fourth random number is the fourth value in the sequence of the new seed.

For games, the most convenient way to ensure that each run uses a different series of random numbers is to use the statement *RANDOMIZE TIMER*. (The TIMER function returns the number of seconds that have elapsed on the system clock since midnight.)

Errors

If you specify a non-numeric value with RANDOMIZE, QuickBASIC returns a "Type mismatch" error message.

Example

The following program uses RANDOMIZE to initialize the random-number generator and then "flips" the requested number of "coins." The program takes into account the small chance of a coin landing on its edge.

```
RANDOMIZE               ' prompts user for seed
CLS : INPUT "Enter number of coins to flip: ", numFlips%
heads% = 0: tails% = 0
edgies% = 0             ' coins that landed on their edge

FOR flip% = 1 TO numFlips%
    randVal = RND(1)
    IF randVal > .5005 THEN
        heads% = heads% + 1
    ELSEIF randVal < .4995 THEN
        tails% = tails% + 1
    ELSE edgies% = edgies% + 1
    END IF
NEXT flip%

PRINT "Total flips: "; numFlips%
PRINT "Heads = "; heads%
PRINT "Tails: "; tails%
PRINT edgies%; " coins landed on their edge."
```

RND

See also: RANDOMIZE, TIMER

■ QB2	■ QB4.5	■ PowerBASIC
■ QB3	■ ANSI	■ GW-BASIC
■ QB4	■ BASIC7	■ MacQB

Purpose

The RND function returns a random single-precision floating-point number between 0 and 1. The same sequence of random numbers is generated each time the program runs unless you use the RANDOMIZE statement to specify a different sequence.

Syntax

RND[(*expr*)]

expr, an optional parameter, is any combination of numbers or numeric variables (integer, long integer, single precision, or double precision). The value of *expr* dictates the value returned by RND, as described in the "Description" section below.

Usage

```
PRINT RND
```

Displays a random value.

```
PRINT RND(0)
```

Displays the value of the last random number.

```
PRINT RND(-23)
```

Displays the random value associated with the number –23.

Description

The RND function returns what is called a "pseudo-random" number. This kind of number is generated from a stored value (called a seed) using a formula designed to produce numbers that have no pattern or order and thus appear to be random. Each seed, however, creates a fixed sequence of numbers: For example, if the program contains no previous RANDOMIZE statement, the first three values returned by RND are always .7055475, .533424, and .5795186.

The RANDOMIZE statement changes the seed and thus the sequence generated. You can use RANDOMIZE with a random seed returned by the TIMER function to generate thoroughly random numbers.

The value specified in a call to RND dictates the value RND returns. If the value is greater than 0 or is not specified, RND returns the next random value in the sequence. If the value specified is equal to 0, RND returns the random value that was last returned. Finally, if the value is less than 0, RND returns the random number associated with that value.

Many applications (such as simulations and games) require random integers that fall within a specified range. To create a random integer within the range *lower* through *upper*, use the expression

```
INT((upper - lower + 1) * RND + lower)
```

Errors

If you specify a non-numeric value with RND, QuickBASIC returns a "Type mismatch" error message.

Example

The following program defines a function called *RandInt%* that returns a value returned by RND as an integer in a specified range. The program uses this function to set random *x*- and *y*-coordinates, radius, and color, and uses that information to draw circles of varying position, size, and color on the screen.

The DO...LOOP in the main module continues to draw circles until the user presses any key.

```
DECLARE FUNCTION RandInt% (lowest!, highest!)

SCREEN 9         ' use 9 for EGA, 1 for CGA, and 12 for VGA
maxX = 640       ' use 640 for EGA or VGA, and 320 for CGA
maxY = 350       ' use 350 for EGA, 200 for CGA, and 480 for VGA
colors = 15      ' use 15 for EGA or VGA, 3 for CGA

DO
    x% = RandInt(-maxX, maxX)                ' random x-coordinate
    y% = RandInt(-maxY, maxY)                ' random y-coordinate
    radius = RandInt(5, 50)                  ' random radius
    circleColor% = RandInt(0, colors)        ' random color
    CIRCLE (x%, y%), radius, (circleColor%)  ' draw circle
    PAINT (x%, y%), circleColor%             ' fill in circle
LOOP WHILE INKEY$ = ""                       ' continue until user presses a key

FUNCTION RandInt% (lowest, highest)
    ' return a random number between lowest and highest
    RandInt = INT((highest - lowest + 1) * RND + lowest)
END FUNCTION
```

SGN

See also: ABS

■ QB2	■ QB4.5	■ PowerBASIC
■ QB3	■ ANSI	■ GW-BASIC
■ QB4	■ BASIC7	■ MacQB

Purpose

The SGN function returns the value of the sign (negative, positive, or 0) of a number or numeric expression. You might use this function to quickly determine the direction in which an object on the screen is moving or whether a temperature is either above or below 0 degrees.

Syntax

SGN(*expr*)

expr is any combination of numbers or numeric variables (integer, long integer, single precision, or double precision).

Usage

```
PRINT SGN(-145)
```

Displays the sign of –145, which is –1.

```
PRINT SGN(0)
```

Displays the sign of 0, which is 0.

```
PRINT SGN(12645.33)
```

Displays the sign of 12645.33, which is 1.

Description

The SGN function tests whether a value is negative, positive, or 0. For example, the following two tests are equivalent:

```
number < 0
SGN(number) = -1
```

Remember that SGN(0) returns 0, which might not be appropriate if you are treating 0 as a positive value.

Errors

If you specify a non-numeric value with SGN, QuickBASIC returns a "Type mismatch" error message.

Example

The following program generates random numbers centered at 0; approximately half the random numbers are positive and half are negative. The program then uses SGN to detect a number's sign, and a SOUND statement plays a low "A" note for negative numbers and a higher "A" note for positive ones. (Durations of the tones are random.)

```
CONST LOW = 220        ' the note "A"
CONST HIGH = 440       ' the note "A" one octave higher

DO
    rndVal = RND(1) - .5           ' distribute random value around 0
    duration = ABS(rndVal * 50)    ' specify the tones duration
    IF SGN(rndVal) = -1 THEN
        SOUND LOW, duration
    ELSE
        SOUND HIGH, duration
    END IF
    SOUND 32767, 9.1               ' about half a second of silence
LOOP WHILE INKEY$ = ""
```

SIN

See also: ATN, COS, TAN

■ **QB2** ■ **QB4.5** ■ **PowerBASIC**
■ **QB3** ■ **ANSI** ■ **GW-BASIC**
■ **QB4** ■ **BASIC7** ■ **MacQB**

Purpose

The SIN function returns the sine of an angle.

Syntax

SIN(*angle*)

angle is the angle measurement expressed in radians. You can convert degrees to radians by multiplying the number of degrees by the result of π divided by 180.

Usage

```
PRINT SIN(.1)
```

Displays the sine of .1, which is 9.983342E-02.

```
PRINT SIN(1.570796)
```

Displays the sine of 1.570796, which is 1.

Description

The SIN function returns the sine of an angle, which must be expressed in radians. To convert an angle from degrees to radians, use the formula *radians = degrees * pi / 180*, in which pi is 3.141593 in single precision or 3.141592653589793 in double precision.

By default, SIN returns a single-precision value. However, if you specify a double-precision value, the return value will also be double precision.

Errors

If you specify a non-numeric value with SIN, QuickBASIC displays a "Type mismatch" error message. If you use degrees rather than radians, no error is generated; however, the result is wrong.

Example

Imagine that you are a mountaineer who has thrown a grappling hook with a line attached so that the hook is stuck high on a rock. You know the length of the line, and you measure the angle defined by the line and the ground. The following program determines the height of the hook from the ground.

```
CONST PI = 3.141593
CONST DEGREETORAD = PI / 180
CLS

DO
    INPUT "Number of feet of line paid out (enter 0 to quit): ", length
    IF length = 0 THEN EXIT DO
    INPUT "Angle of line to ground (in degrees): ", angle
    radians = angle * DEGREETORAD
    height = length * SIN(radians)
    PRINT "Height of hook is "; height; " feet."
LOOP
```

SQR

■ QB2	■ QB4.5	■ PowerBASIC
■ QB3	■ ANSI	■ GW-BASIC
■ QB4	■ BASIC7	■ MacQB

Purpose

The SQR function returns the square root of a numeric constant, numeric variable, or numeric expression.

Syntax

SQR(*expr*)

expr is any combination of numbers or numeric variables (integer, long integer, single precision, or double precision), but it must be a positive value (0 or greater).

Usage

```
PRINT SQR(16)
```

Displays the square root of 16, which is 4.

```
PRINT SQR(1000)
```

Displays the square root of 1000, which is 31.62278.

Description

The SQR function returns the square root of a positive numeric value (0 or greater). The value returned is single precision by default. However, if you specify a double-precision value, the return value is also double precision.

There is no function that squares a number in QuickBASIC; instead, use the exponentiation operator for this purpose. Thus, the square of the variable *number* can be calculated by

```
number ^ 2
```

Errors

If you specify a non-numeric value for SQR, QuickBASIC displays a "Type mismatch" error message. If the value is numeric but is less than 0, QuickBASIC returns an "Illegal function call" error message.

Example

The following program uses the Pythagorean theorem ($c^2 = a^2 + b^2$, where *a* is the length of the adjacent side, *b* is the length of the opposite side, and *c* is the length of the hypotenuse) to calculate the length of the hypotenuse of a right triangle.

```
CLS
DO
    INPUT "Length of adjacent side (enter 0 to quit): "; adjacent
    IF adjacent = 0 THEN EXIT DO
    INPUT "Length of opposite side: "; opposite
    hypot = SQR(adjacent ^ 2 + opposite ^ 2)
    PRINT "Length of hypotenuse is: "; hypot: PRINT
LOOP
```

TAN

See also: ATN, COS, SIN

■ QB2	■ QB4.5	■ PowerBASIC
■ QB3	■ ANSI	■ GW-BASIC
■ QB4	■ BASIC7	■ MacQB

Purpose

The TAN function returns the tangent of an angle.

Syntax

TAN(*angle*)

angle is the angle measurement expressed in radians. You can convert degrees to radians by multiplying the number of degrees by the result of π divided by 180.

Usage

```
PRINT TAN(.75)
```

Displays the tangent of .75, which is .9315965.

```
PRINT TAN(3.1415)
```

Displays the tangent of 3.1415, which is –9.265741E-05.

Description

The TAN function returns the tangent of an angle, which must be expressed in radians. To convert an angle from degrees to radians, use the formula *radians = degrees * pi / 180,* in which pi is either 3.141593 in single precision or 3.141592653589793 in double precision.

By default, TAN returns a single-precision value. However, if you specify a double-precision value, the return value is also double precision.

Errors

If you specify a non-numeric value with TAN, QuickBASIC displays a "Type mismatch" error message.

Warnings

Avoid using the tangent of 90 degrees, which is equal to infinity. QuickBASIC does not return an "Overflow" error in this case; it merely returns a very large number.

Example

The following program prints a table of angles and their tangents.

```
CONST PI = 3.141592653589793#          ' pi in double precision
CONST DEGREETORAD = PI / 180

PRINT "Angle in Degrees         Tan(Angle)"

FOR angle% = 0 TO 85 STEP 5
    PRINT USING "##"; angle%; TAB(26);
    PRINT USING "###.######"; TAN(angle% * DEGREETORAD)
NEXT angle%
```

CHAPTER 8

Simple I/O

Introduction

This chapter discusses the interface between QuickBASIC programs and users. It includes the statements and functions that enable your programs to

- Generate prompts and accept data from the keyboard
- Check for keypresses without interrupting program execution
- Respond to input from the function keys, the arrow keys, and nonprinting key combinations
- Display text at any location on the screen
- Display text and numeric values in a variety of formats
- Change the number of rows and columns of text that can be displayed on the screen
- Define the size of the viewport in which text is displayed
- Clear the display or the specified viewport
- Control the size of the cursor

Table 8-1 lists the QuickBASIC input/output statements and functions alphabetically.

Statement or function	Description
CLS	Clears the display or specified viewport
CSRLIN	Returns the current cursor row
INKEY$	Reads a character from the keyboard
INPUT	Prompts for and reads input from the keyboard
INPUT$	Reads a specified number of characters from a file or device; if no file is specified, INPUT$ reads input from the keyboard
LINE INPUT	Prompts for and reads a string of characters from the keyboard
LOCATE	Positions the text cursor at the specified row and column and specifies the size of the cursor
POS	Returns the current cursor column
PRINT	Displays text and data on the screen at the current cursor position
PRINT USING	Displays numeric and string data in a specified format

Table 8-1.
Input/output statements and functions.

(continued)

Table 8-1. *(continued)*

Statement or function	Description
SPC	Advances the cursor or print head by a specified number of columns relative to the last character printed
TAB	Advances the cursor or print head to the specified column position
VIEW PRINT	Defines the area of the screen to which QuickBASIC must direct all text output
WIDTH	Defines the number of rows and columns on the screen or other device or sets the width of a file
WRITE	Outputs data (including delimiters) to the screen or a file

Keyboard Input

QuickBASIC provides three methods for retrieving keyboard input. The standard method, using the INPUT statement, pauses the program while the user types characters; execution does not resume until the user presses the Enter key to indicate that input is complete. This method is available in all versions of BASIC.

QuickBASIC offers two versions of the INPUT statement. One version of INPUT lets the user enter both numeric and character data and then assigns the data to one or more variables of the appropriate type. Another version, LINE INPUT, accepts data entered at the keyboard as one string of characters and then assigns all the characters to a single string variable. The advantage of the second method is that it prevents the user from inputting numeric data if the program requires characters.

Both the INPUT and LINE INPUT statements can display a prompt, which lets you describe the kind of input you want the user to enter. They also let the user edit or make corrections to the data before entering it. Table 8-3 in the INPUT entry lists the key combinations that can be used to edit input.

Another method for retrieving keyboard input, using the INKEY$ function, does not interrupt the program. INKEY$ merely checks to see whether a key has been pressed: If so, it immediately returns the character; if not, it returns a null (or empty) string. This method also lets your program respond to keys that do not produce printable characters, such as the arrow keys, Pg Up, Pg Dn, and the function keys. Table 8-2 in the INKEY$ entry lists the nonprinting keys that INKEY$ can trap.

The third method for retrieving keyboard input, using the INPUT$ function, reads a specified number of characters from an input device, which is usually a file that has been opened for input. However, if you do not specify a file, INPUT$ reads from the keyboard after the user types the requisite number of characters. Using INPUT$ with the keyboard is not recommended because it doesn't let the user edit input, it doesn't echo the input on the screen, and it doesn't accept nonprinting characters. Furthermore, the user must enter the exact number of characters specified because INPUT$ does not recognize the Enter key as a signal of input termination.

Input Redirection

INPUT, LINE INPUT, and INPUT$ (but not INKEY$) actually read data from the standard input device, which is the keyboard by default. Programs that are run outside the QuickBASIC environment, from the DOS command line, can accept input from another device, such as a file or a serial port, instead of from the keyboard. To change the standard input device, you must use a DOS redirection symbol when you start the program. For example, the command

```
YOURPROG < SCRIPT.TXT
```

runs the program YOURPROG and directs the program to receive its input from the file SCRIPT.TXT. Any INPUT, LINE INPUT, or INPUT$ statement in YOURPROG reads characters from the file and ignores the keyboard completely. However, if there is a call to INKEY$ in the program, INKEY$ still reads input from the keyboard.

Text Output

The QuickBASIC PRINT statement displays text and numeric values on the screen. You can use this statement to display literal text and the contents of numeric or string variables. PRINT displays output beginning at the current cursor position and continues until it has displayed all specified characters or variables.

The WRITE statement, which is similar to PRINT, outputs data to the screen in teletype fashion. It updates the cursor position after displaying each character and scrolls the display when output reaches the bottom line of the screen. Unlike PRINT, however, WRITE encloses the strings it displays with quotation marks and separates all items in the list with commas.

Use WRITE primarily to output data to a file; even when you use WRITE to output to the screen, the statement formats the data as if it were writing it to a sequential file.

Formatted Printing

The PRINT statement does not format output. However, another version of the statement does: PRINT USING lets you specify a template string containing the fields in which the statement displays the output. You can then use this template to print a column of figures, for example, in which all decimal points are aligned. PRINT USING is particularly useful for designing reports or lists that must be presented in a readable way.

Two other QuickBASIC functions can also help you format lines of text. The SPC function inserts a specified number of blank spaces into a line that was output by PRINT or LPRINT; this lets you separate printed items and produce a neat display. TAB performs a similar function except that it moves the cursor to a specified position on the line; this lets you easily indent and align the columns of a report.

Output Redirection

Recall that you can redirect input so that INPUT, LINE INPUT, and INPUT$ read data from a device other than the keyboard. You can also redirect output so that PRINT, PRINT USING, and WRITE send output to a device other than the screen. Possible output devices include a parallel printer, a serial port, and a file. Once again, you must use a DOS redirection symbol when you execute the program from the command line; for example,

```
YOURPROG > PRN
```

runs the program YOURPROG and sends all output to the printer rather than to the screen. (Be sure your printer is on and loaded with paper before you try this; if it is not, DOS returns an error message when the program tries to access the unavailable device.)

You cannot use output redirection with programs you run in the QuickBASIC environment.

The Text Cursor

As previously mentioned, the PRINT, PRINT USING, and WRITE statements output text to the screen at the current cursor position. You can use the LOCATE statement to move the cursor to any position on the screen so that subsequent printing proceeds from that position. The TAB and SPC functions also move the cursor, but only within the current screen row.

LOCATE lets you move the cursor to a specified row and column. It also lets you change the size of the cursor—from invisible to the usual underline to a full block.

QuickBASIC also provides two functions that report the current position of the cursor. POS returns the cursor column, and CSRLIN returns the cursor row.

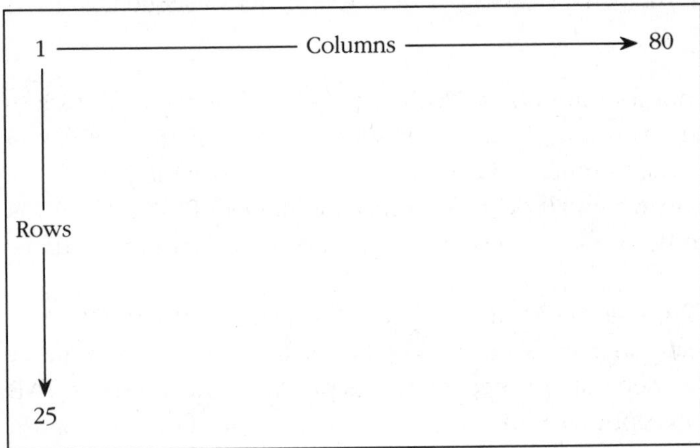

Figure 8-1.
Rows and columns on the standard text screen.

Screen Dimensions

The standard text screen, which is displayed when QuickBASIC runs a program, can contain up to 2000 characters in a grid of 25 rows by 80 columns. (Figure 8-1 illustrates the organization of the standard text screen.) QuickBASIC lets you change this format, however, by using the WIDTH (Screen) statement, which, despite its name, can also change the height of the screen.

QuickBASIC offers only two widths—80 columns (the default) and 40 columns. The latter displays broader characters. You cannot change the screen height (the number of rows displayed) unless your computer has an EGA, VGA, or MCGA adapter: the default of 25 rows can be increased to 43 with an EGA and to either 43 or 50 with a VGA. The VGA and MCGA adapters can also display text formats of 80 by 30 and 80 by 60 characters, but only in the graphics screen modes 11 and 12. (See the SCREEN (Statement) entry in Chapter 11, "Graphics.")

The WIDTH statement affects the appearance of the output of a program, not the appearance of the QuickBASIC environment. Although 80 columns by 25 rows is the standard mode, you can change the default of the environment by starting QuickBASIC with the /H switch. For example,

```
QB /H
```

instructs QuickBASIC to display the QuickBASIC environment in the highest resolution your video adapter permits, producing a text format of 80 by 43 characters with an EGA and 80 by 50 characters with a VGA.

The Text Viewport

QuickBASIC also lets you restrict text output to only part of the entire screen. This can be advantageous when you combine text and graphics on the same screen because it prevents text from overwriting the graphics display.

The VIEW PRINT statement lets you define a specified number of screen rows as the text viewport. After calling the statement, the actions of all PRINT, PRINT USING, and WRITE statements are confined to the text viewport and do not spill into the surrounding areas of the screen. Figure 8-2 on the following page shows as a shaded rectangle the viewport created by the following statement, which limits text output to screen rows 20 through 23:

```
VIEW PRINT 20 TO 23
```

You cannot move the text cursor outside the text viewport after you initialize it; therefore, the LOCATE statement works only with row numbers inside the viewport area.

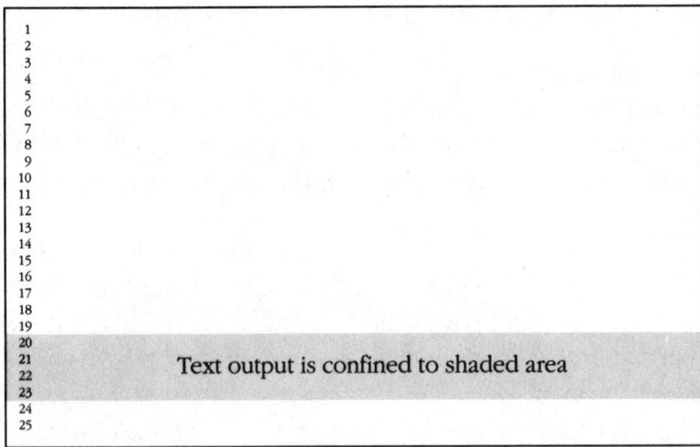

Figure 8-2.
A text viewport defined by VIEW PRINT.

Clearing the Display

In addition to the statements that position text on the screen, QuickBASIC provides one statement that lets you erase that text when you no longer need it. By default, CLS clears the entire screen. You can, however, restrict the action of CLS so that it clears only the text viewport, leaving any graphics on the screen intact. Or, if you have also defined a graphics viewport (discussed in the VIEW entry in Chapter 11, "Graphics"), you can direct CLS to clear only the contents of the graphics viewport.

Related Reading

Davies, Russ. *Mapping the IBM PC and PCjr.* Greensboro, N.C.: Compute! Books, 1985.

Wilton, Richard. *Programmer's Guide to PC and PS/2 Video Systems.* Redmond, Wash.: Microsoft Press, 1987.

CLS

See also: VIEW, VIEW PRINT, WIDTH (Screen)

■ QB2	■ QB4.5	✲ PowerBASIC
■ QB3	✲ ANSI	✲ GW-BASIC
■ QB4	■ BASIC7	✲ MacQB

Purpose

The CLS statement clears the viewport and returns the cursor to the upper left corner of the viewport. All versions of BASIC provide this statement; however, QuickBASIC extends the statement's range by letting you clear from the screen only graphics, only text, or both.

Syntax

CLS [{0 ¦ 1 ¦ 2}]

Usage

```
CLS
```

Clears the currently active viewport. If neither a graphics viewport nor a text viewport is defined, the statement clears the entire screen.

```
CLS 0
```

Clears the entire screen, regardless of the currently active viewport.

```
CLS 1
```

Clears only the current graphics viewport (defined by the last VIEW statement). If no graphics viewport is open, the statement clears the entire screen.

```
CLS 2
```

Clears only the current text viewport (defined by the last VIEW PRINT statement). If no text viewport is open, the statement clears the entire screen.

Description

CLS called without an argument does not clear the QuickBASIC screen; it clears the currently active viewport. Often the active viewport is the full screen. However, you can also divide the screen into separate viewports for text (discussed in the VIEW PRINT entry) and graphics (discussed in the VIEW entry); if you do this, CLS clears only the one in use.

QuickBASIC also lets you specify the viewport to be cleared by including an argument with the CLS statement. The statement *CLS 1* clears the graphics viewport, *CLS 2* clears the text viewport, and *CLS 0* clears the entire display.

When you clear the text viewport, QuickBASIC fills it with blank spaces in the current background color and returns the cursor to the upper left corner of the viewport. If no text viewport has been defined, QuickBASIC clears the entire screen and returns the cursor to row 1, column 1 (the home position). Note that when CLS clears a text viewport it does not clear the bottom line of the screen, which is called the function key display.

To clear the text viewport and set a new background color, use CLS with the COLOR statement. For example, the statements

```
COLOR , 1
CLS 2
```

clear the text viewport and create a blue background. All subsequent text is printed on a blue background until you use COLOR again to change it.

When CLS clears the graphics viewport, it resets all pixels to the background color and resets the graphics cursor to its default position, the center of the viewport. If the next graphics statement uses relative addressing (by using the STEP keyword), QuickBASIC calculates the location of the specified point from the center point of the viewport.

Compatibility

ANSI BASIC

The ANSI equivalent of CLS is the CLEAR statement. CLEAR erases the entire display of text and graphics or, if the current output device is a printer, advances the paper to a new page. Do not confuse the ANSI CLEAR statement with the QuickBASIC CLEAR statement, which reinitializes variables and reserves memory for the stack.

PowerBASIC and BASICA

PowerBASIC and BASICA support CLS only without parameters. In these versions of BASIC, CLS does, however, clear only the active viewport. By default, CLS clears the entire screen.

QuickBASIC for the Macintosh

In QuickBASIC for the Macintosh, CLS clears only the current output window. CLS does not support parameters and does not affect edit fields or "radio buttons" in the window.

Example

Although you can use VIEW to define any rectangular portion of the screen as a graphics viewport, VIEW PRINT defines only a text viewport, which contains complete screen rows. Therefore, you cannot use CLS to clear an area of text narrower than the width of the screen.

The ROM BIOS, however, includes routines that let you define the row coordinates and column coordinates of an area on the text screen and then clear that rectangle and gives it any valid background color.

The following program uses the CALL INTERRUPT statement to implement selective screen scrolling and give you additional control over the video display. To use the program, you must invoke QuickBASIC with the command line QB/L QB.QLB.

```
' $INCLUDE: 'QB.BI'          ' prototype for CALL INTERRUPT

DECLARE SUB Scroll (y1%, x1%, y2%, x2%, rows%, clr%, direction%)
DIM SHARED inRegs AS RegType, outRegs AS RegType

CLS 0                        ' clear the entire screen
LOCATE , , 0: clr% = 1: delay% = 1
DO
    IF delay% MOD 2 = 1 THEN
        Scroll 1, 21, 5, 60, 1, clr%, 0
        Scroll 6, 6, 20, 20, 1, clr%, 0
        Scroll 6, 61, 20, 75, 1, clr%, 1
        Scroll 21, 21, 25, 60, 1, clr%, 1
        IF delay% = 1 THEN
            COLOR clr%, 0
            LOCATE 18, 25: PRINT "SCROLLING UP";
            Scroll 8, 23, 18, 38, 1, 0, 0
            LOCATE 8, 44: PRINT "SCROLLING DOWN";
            Scroll 8, 43, 18, 58, 1, 0, 1
        END IF
    END IF
    clr% = clr% + 1: IF clr% = 8 THEN clr% = 1
    delay% = delay% + 1: IF delay% = 14 THEN delay% = 1
LOOP UNTIL INKEY$ = CHR$(27)
COLOR 7, 0
END

SUB Scroll (y1%, x1%, y2%, x2%, rows%, clr%, direction%) STATIC
    ' uses an external function to clear a portion of the screen
    IF direction% = 0 THEN ah% = 6 ELSE ah% = 7
    inRegs.ax = ah% * 256 + rows%             ' set values of parameters
    inRegs.bx = ((16 * clr%) + 15) * 256
    inRegs.cx = ((y1% - 1) * 256) + x1% - 1
    inRegs.dx = ((y2% - 1) * 256) + x2% - 1
    CALL INTERRUPT(&H10, inRegs, outRegs)     ' call the external function
END SUB
```

CSRLIN

See also: LOCATE, POINT, POS, WIDTH (Screen)

■ **QB2**	■ **QB4.5**	■ **PowerBASIC**
■ **QB3**	✲ **ANSI**	■ **GW-BASIC**
■ **QB4**	■ **BASIC7**	■ **MacQB**

Purpose

The CSRLIN function returns the row number (vertical coordinate) of the text cursor. (Use the POS function to return the cursor's column number.)

Syntax

CSRLIN

Usage

```
yPosition% = CSRLIN
```

Assigns the screen row in which the cursor is located to the variable *yPosition%*.

Description

QuickBASIC includes two functions that report the current position of the cursor. The CSRLIN (cursor line) function returns the number of the current cursor row. Usually this number is an integer in the range 1 through 25; however, it might extend to 43 for systems using EGA adapters or to 60 for VGA and MCGA adapters. The POS function returns the column number of the cursor. (See the POS entry.)

For example, your program might need to know the cursor position to prevent text from being written to the bottom row, which causes the screen to scroll upward. Or, a program might need to halt a print operation temporarily and display a message to the operator, perhaps in response to a keypress. In such a case, you use CSRLIN and POS to store the current cursor position values in variables; then, when the interruption ends, use those values in a LOCATE statement to reposition the cursor at the correct location.

Compatibility

ANSI BASIC

ANSI BASIC does not include the CSRLIN function. This version does, however, propose a general-purpose function, ASK, which returns information about the status of I/O devices, including the display. This information can include the row position of the cursor.

Example

Programs that branch to subroutines whenever an event-trapping statement is triggered need to preserve the current cursor position so that the position can be restored when the subroutine returns. The following program uses the TIMER statement and the CSRLIN function to display the time continuously while the program outputs other information to the screen. Updating the clock does not interfere with the output to the screen.

```
CLS : TIMER ON
ON TIMER(1) GOSUB Tick
DO
    LOCATE 2, 1: clr% = clr% + 1
    IF clr% > 7 THEN clr% = 1
    COLOR , clr%
```

(continued)

continued

```
    DO                              ' color the screen one line at a time
        PRINT " ";
        IF INKEY$ <> "" THEN        ' see whether user pressed a key
            xCursor% = POS(0): yCursor% = CSRLIN     ' find position of cursor
            COLOR 14, 4: LOCATE 24, 1: PRINT SPACE$(80);
            LOCATE 24, 34, 1: PRINT "Quit (Y/N)? ";
            response$ = UCASE$(INPUT$(1))
            COLOR 7, 0: LOCATE 24, 1: PRINT SPACE$(80);
            COLOR , clr%
            IF response$ = "Y" THEN
                done% = -1
            ELSE
                LOCATE yCursor%, xCursor%, 0
            END IF
        END IF
    LOOP UNTIL CSRLIN > 22
LOOP UNTIL done%
COLOR 7, 0
END

' this subroutine is executed once per second
Tick:
    xStop% = POS(0): yStop% = CSRLIN          ' save the position of the cursor
    COLOR 11, 0: LOCATE 1, 36: PRINT TIME$;
    COLOR , clr%: LOCATE yStop%, xStop%       ' reset the cursor
RETURN
```

INKEY$

See also: INPUT, INPUT$, LINE INPUT, ON KEY(*n*) GOSUB

■ QB2	■ QB4.5	■ PowerBASIC
■ QB3	✲ ANSI	■ GW-BASIC
■ QB4	■ BASIC7	✲ MacQB

Purpose

INKEY$ reads a character from the keyboard. QuickBASIC offers several functions and statements that allow a program to accept data from the keyboard. In most cases, however, those statements force the program to stop and wait until the user enters information. INKEY$ is an exception; it reads a character from the keyboard and returns immediately, whether a character is available or not. INKEY$ also enables your programs to respond to special keys, such as the function keys or the arrow keys.

Syntax

INKEY$

Usage

```
keyPress$ = INKEY$
```

Checks the keyboard and, if a key has been pressed, assigns the key character to the string variable *keyPress$*. If no key has been pressed, INKEY$ returns a null string.

```
response$ = UCASE$(INKEY$)
```

Converts a character from the keyboard to uppercase and then assigns it to *response$*.

```
asciiCode% = ASC(INKEY$)
```

Converts a character from the keyboard to its ASCII value and then assigns the result to the integer variable *asciiCode%*. (Note that *asciiCode%* has a value of 0 if no key was pressed or if the key was a function key.)

Description

When you press a key on the keyboard, your computer stores the character in a buffer until the program is ready to process it. The standard buffer can contain as many as 15 characters. INKEY$ checks the buffer to see whether any keys have already been pressed. If the buffer contains characters, INKEY$ reads the first character and returns it to the program; otherwise, INKEY$ returns a null string. INKEY$ never waits for a keypress, so it never interrupts program execution. (For a sample program that displays the contents of the keyboard buffer, see the "Example" section in the INPUT$ entry.)

INKEY$ returns the 1-byte or 2-byte string representing the key that was pressed. For ASCII characters and IBM extended characters, INKEY$ returns a 1-byte string; for function keys, INKEY$ returns a 2-byte string.

ASCII and IBM extended characters include the alphanumeric characters 0 through 9 and A through Z (in both uppercase and lowercase) as well as punctuation characters and arithmetic symbols, such as + and =. They also include graphics characters, characters with accents, and some special keys, such as Enter and Esc. If an ASCII key is pressed or an IBM extended key is entered, INKEY$ returns a string containing the character itself. (For a list of ASCII characters and IBM extended characters, see Appendix H, "ASCII Characters.")

The set of function keys includes the arrow keys, Pg Up, Pg Dn, Home, End and keys F1 through F10 (F1 through F12 if you have an extended keyboard). The set of function keys also includes the alphanumeric keys combined with the Alt key. When a function key is pressed, INKEY$ returns a 2-byte string consisting of a 0 byte (a character whose ASCII value is 0) followed by the key's scan code.

Every key on the keyboard has a different scan code, even the ASCII keys. However, INKEY$ reads only the scan codes of function keys. The following statements assign to the variable *scan%* the scan code of any function key that has been pressed:

```
ky$ = INKEY$
IF LEN(ky$) > 1 THEN scan% = ASC(MID$(ky$, 2, 1)
```

INKEY$ cannot trap all keystrokes. For example, it cannot detect the Ctrl, Alt, and Shift keys unless they are used with other keys. The following key combinations trigger special actions by the system hardware so that INKEY$ cannot retrieve them:

Ctrl-Break	Halts program execution; does not work with stand-alone executable programs that were compiled without the /D switch
Ctrl-Alt-Delete	Reboots the system
Ctrl-Num Lock (or Pause)	Suspends program execution until the spacebar is pressed
Prt Scrn	Copies the screen contents to the printer.

Table 8-2 lists the scan codes of all the function keys that INKEY$ can trap. The list includes only those keys that return a scan code to the QuickBASIC INKEY$ function.

Function keys F11 and F12 are available only with the 101-key and 102-key extended keyboards.

Alt-– and Alt-+ can be trapped only on the main keyboard; the – and + keys on the numeric keypad do not return a scan code when used with Alt.

Tips

If your programs include function-key trapping, always remember that the keys you select might clash with the "hot keys" used by installed TSR (terminate-and-stay-resident) programs. Borland International's Sidekick, for example, moves itself to the foreground in response to Ctrl-Alt and therefore prevents this key combination from ever reaching your program. In such circumstances, let the user select alternate hot keys, perhaps during the configuration routine of your program.

Compatibility

ANSI BASIC

ANSI BASIC does not propose a direct equivalent to INKEY$. In ANSI BASIC, however, the INPUT statement can include a TIMEOUT parameter, which lets you specify the number of seconds it should wait for a response before returning control to the program.

QuickBASIC for the Macintosh

Because the Macintosh keyboard is different from the PC keyboard, the QuickBASIC INKEY$ function for the Macintosh returns only a single character (or a null string if no character is buffered), even for function keys. In addition, INKEY$ can read a character from the keyboard only when the current program displays an active output window; otherwise, INKEY$ ignores all keyboard activity.

Example

The program following Table 8-2 monitors the keyboard and reports the ASCII values and scan codes of each key pressed. It also displays the character returned if doing so does not disturb the display.

KEYBOARD SCAN CODES

Key	Scan code	Key	Scan code	Key	Scan code
Alt-A	30	Alt-0	129	Ctrl-F9	102
Alt-B	48	Alt-–	130	Ctrl-F10	103
Alt-C	46	Alt-=	131	Ctrl-F11	137
Alt-D	32	F1	59	Ctrl-F12	138
Alt-E	18	F2	60	Alt-F1	104
Alt-F	33	F3	61	Alt-F2	105
Alt-G	34	F4	62	Alt-F3	106
Alt-H	35	F5	63	Alt-F4	107
Alt-I	23	F6	64	Alt-F5	108
Alt-J	36	F7	65	Alt-F6	109
Alt-K	37	F8	66	Alt-F7	110
Alt-L	38	F9	67	Alt-F8	111
Alt-M	50	F10	68	Alt-F9	112
Alt-N	49	F11	133	Alt-F10	113
Alt-O	24	F12	134	Alt-F11	139
Alt-P	25	Shift-F1	84	Alt-F12	140
Alt-Q	16	Shift-F2	85	Home	71
Alt-R	19	Shift-F3	86	Up arrow	72
Alt-S	31	Shift-F4	87	Pg Up	73
Alt-T	20	Shift-F5	88	Left arrow	75
Alt-U	22	Shift-F6	89	Right arrow	77
Alt-V	47	Shift-F7	90	End	79
Alt-W	17	Shift-F8	91	Down arrow	80
Alt-X	45	Shift-F9	92	Pg Dn	81
Alt-Y	21	Shift-F10	93	Ins	82
Alt-Z	44	Shift-F11	135	Del	83
Alt-1	120	Shift-F12	136	Ctrl-PrintScrn	114
Alt-2	121	Ctrl-F1	94	Ctrl-Left arrow	115
Alt-3	122	Ctrl-F2	95	Ctrl-Right arrow	116
Alt-4	123	Ctrl-F3	96	Ctrl-End	117
Alt-5	124	Ctrl-F4	97	Ctrl-Pg Dn	118
Alt-6	125	Ctrl-F5	98	Ctrl-Home	119
Alt-7	126	Ctrl-F6	99	Ctrl-Pg Up	132
Alt-8	127	Ctrl-F7	100		
Alt-9	128	Ctrl-F8	101		

Table 8-2.
Scan codes trapped by INKEY$.

```
CLS : LOCATE 10, 1, 0
PRINT "ASCII Code :     Character :    Scan Code :";
DO
    DO
        response$ = INKEY$
    LOOP WHILE response$ = ""          ' wait for keypress
    asciiCode% = ASC(response$)        ' find ASCII code
    LOCATE 10, 14: PRINT USING "###"; asciiCode%;     ' display ASCII code
    LOCATE 10, 30
    IF asciiCode% > 31 THEN            ' display printable characters
        PRINT CHR$(asciiCode%);
    ELSE
        PRINT " ";                     ' erase previous character
    END IF
    LOCATE 10, 45
    IF LEN(response$) > 1 THEN         ' display scan code of function keys
        scanCode% = ASC(MID$(response$, 2, 1))
        PRINT USING "###"; scanCode%;
    ELSE
        PRINT "   ";                   ' erase previous character
    END IF
LOOP UNTIL asciiCode% = 27             ' exit loop if user presses Esc
END
```

INPUT

See also: INKEY$, INPUT$, LINE INPUT

■ QB2	■ QB4.5	✲ PowerBASIC
■ QB3	✲ ANSI	■ GW-BASIC
■ QB4	■ BASIC7	■ MacQB

Purpose

The INPUT statement retrieves data from the keyboard. Although INPUT is included in all versions of BASIC, QuickBASIC expands the statement by adding to it a full set of editing keys.

Syntax

INPUT [;] ["*prompt*"{; | ,}] *var* [, *var*] ...

A semicolon immediately after the keyword INPUT keeps the cursor on the same line after the user presses Enter.

prompt is an optional string of text that is displayed immediately before the entry field. A semicolon immediately after the prompt directs INPUT to display a question mark before the entry field. A comma immediately after the prompt suppresses the question mark. If no prompt is used, INPUT displays only a question mark.

var is the QuickBASIC variable to which input is assigned. A variable can be of any type or precision. It can also be an element of either an array or a user-defined type. To use more than one variable, separate the variable names with commas.

Usage

```
INPUT response$
```

Pauses program execution and displays a question mark until the user enters a string of characters. The string is then assigned to the variable *response$*.

```
INPUT a%, b!, c&(d%), e$
```

Waits for the user to enter three numbers and a string and then assigns them to variables of the appropriate type.

```
TYPE PartType
    name AS STRING * 30
    number AS LONG
    level AS INTEGER
END TYPE

DIM part AS PartType
INPUT "Enter Stock Name, Number"; part.name, part.number
```

Prompts the user to enter two items and assigns them to elements of the user-defined variable *part.*

Description

The INPUT statement lets a program accept characters from the keyboard until input is terminated when the user presses Enter. However, the data items that are entered must match—in type and number—the variables to which they are assigned.

You can add a prompt to the INPUT statement to tell the user what kind of data the program expects. If a semicolon follows the prompt string, INPUT prints a question mark after the prompt. If a comma follows the prompt string, INPUT suppresses the question mark.

INPUT echoes to the screen all printable characters that are entered. It accepts characters until the user presses the Enter key. This carriage return is not considered part of the entered data even though it usually causes the cursor to move to the beginning of the next line. Using a semicolon immediately after the INPUT statement suppresses the carriage return and leaves the cursor on the same line, immediately to the right of the last character entered.

If INPUT requires more than one item, the user must insert a comma between input items. The INPUT statement assumes that a new item starts with the first character after a comma that is not a white-space character (space, tab, linefeed, or carriage return). The user can enclose strings of characters in quote marks if the string must contain leading spaces, colons, or commas.

The INPUT statement lets the user edit the characters in the entry field before entering them, and it provides a set of editing keys for this purpose. Table 8-3 lists the key combinations that move the cursor and insert and delete characters within the entry field.

Key combination	**Description**
Left arrow or Ctrl-]	Moves cursor 1 character to the left
Ctrl-Left arrow or Ctrl-B	Moves cursor 1 word to the left
Right arrow or Ctrl-\	Moves cursor 1 character to the right
Ctrl-Right arrow or Ctrl-F	Moves cursor 1 word to the right
Home or Ctrl-K	Moves cursor to the beginning of the entry field
End or Ctrl-N	Moves cursor to the end of the entry field
Ins or Ctrl-R	Toggles insert mode. When insert mode is on (indicated by a block cursor) and characters are inserted, any characters that follow the cursor are shifted to the right
Tab or Ctrl-I	Tabs cursor to the right
Delete	Deletes the character at the cursor
Ctrl-End or Ctrl-E	Deletes characters from the cursor position through the end of the entry field
Esc or Ctrl-U	Erases the entire entry field
Backspace or Ctrl-H	Deletes the character to the left of the cursor and moves the cursor to the left. If the cursor is in the first position of the entry field, the character at the cursor is deleted
Ctrl-T	Toggles the function-key label display on the status line
Enter or Ctrl-M	Terminates input and stores the data from the input field
Ctrl-Break or Ctrl-C	Aborts input and terminates the program

Table 8-3.
INPUT editing key combinations.

Errors

Entering too few items or data of the wrong type does not generate an error. Instead, QuickBASIC displays the "Redo from start" error message. If this occurs, the user must retype all of the items in the input field. INPUT does not assign any data items to variables until all are entered correctly.

You can't prevent the user from entering improper data, but you can reduce the number of input errors by using a prompt message that tells the user exactly what kind of information the program expects. Another technique is to let INPUT accept all the items as a single string within a set of quotation marks. You must then write a procedure that extracts the items from the string, using the STR$ function (discussed in Chapter 5, "Strings") to convert them to numeric values where necessary. If one of the items is incorrect, the program can prompt the user for another.

Compatibility

ANSI BASIC

The INPUT statement in ANSI BASIC includes a TIMEOUT clause that cancels the statement if INPUT doesn't receive a response within a specified number of seconds. You can also include an ELAPSED clause in the statement, which returns the number of seconds taken to obtain the response.

PowerBASIC

When entering data with the PowerBASIC version of INPUT, you can separate items with blank spaces as well as with commas.

Example

INPUT is most useful when a program needs to accept several data items of different types at the same time. The following program, for example, asks the user to type a name and a complete birthdate. It then uses the information to calculate the number of days remaining until the user's birthday.

```
DECLARE FUNCTION Date2days& (month%, day%, year&)

month1% = VAL(LEFT$(DATE$, 2)):       ' extract current month
day1% = VAL(MID$(DATE$, 4, 2)):       ' extract day of the month
year1& = VAL(RIGHT$(DATE$, 4)):       ' extract current year

CLS : PRINT
PRINT "Enter your name and date of birth"
INPUT "(Name, Month, Day, Year) > ", name$, month2%, day2%, year2&

diff& = Date2days&(month1%, day1%, year1&) - Date2days&(month2%, day2%, year1&)
PRINT : PRINT
IF diff& > 0 THEN
    PRINT diff&; "days since your birthday,"; name$
    PRINT " What presents did you get?"
ELSEIF diff& < 0 THEN
    PRINT ABS(diff&); "days to your birthday,"; name$
    PRINT " What are you expecting?"
ELSE
    PRINT "It's your birthday TODAY, "; name$
    PRINT " - How nice!"
END IF
END

FUNCTION Date2days& (month%, day%, year&) STATIC
    ' convert date to a numeric value
    temp& = year& * 356 + INT((year& - 1) \ 4) + (month% - 1) * 28
    temp2& = VAL(MID$("000303060811131619212426", (month% - 1) * 2 + 1, 2))
    Date2days& = temp& + temp2& - ((month% > 2) AND (year& MOD 4 = 0)) + day%
END FUNCTION
```

INPUT$ (Keyboard)

See also: INKEY$, INPUT, LINE INPUT

■ QB2	■ QB4.5	■ PowerBASIC
■ QB3	ANSI	■ GW-BASIC
■ QB4	■ BASIC7	■ MacQB

Purpose

The INPUT$ (Keyboard) function reads a specified number of characters from a logical device. Usually the device to be read from is a file (discussed in the INPUT$ (File I/O) entry in Chapter 17, "Files"); however, if no file number is specified, INPUT$ reads input from the standard input device, which, by default, is the keyboard.

Syntax

INPUT$(*chars*)

chars is the number of characters to be read and must be in the range 0 through 32767.

Usage

```
buffer$ = INPUT$(5)
```

Reads five characters from the keyboard and assigns them to the string variable *buffer$*.

Description

INPUT$, like INKEY$, does not echo received characters to the display. Unlike INKEY$, however, INPUT$ can read more than one keypress and halts program execution until the requisite number of bytes have been read. INPUT$ cannot read function keys or the arrow keys, or allow the user to edit the input field, as INPUT and LINE INPUT do.

INPUT$ handles control characters (such as tab and carriage return) as printable characters that are passed to the program without affecting the screen display. The function halts program execution either until it reads the specified number of characters or until the user interrupts it by pressing Ctrl-Break.

In its simplest form, INPUT$ is useful for pausing program execution until the user is ready to continue, as the following example shows:

```
PRINT "Press any key to continue";
temp$ = INPUT$(1)
```

INPUT$ is also useful whenever the user must enter an exact number of characters.

Example

Your computer stores information about keystrokes in a buffer until the program is ready to process it. This enables users to enter responses before prompts. The following program displays the contents of the buffer, continuously updating it as keystrokes are entered. The program uses INPUT$ to empty the buffer when it becomes full and when the program finishes. Figure 8-3 shows the output of this program.

```
' output display template
COLOR 15, 0: CLS
READ items%
FOR i% = 1 TO items%
    READ row%, col%, display$
    LOCATE row%, col%, 0: PRINT display$;
NEXT i%
LOCATE 11, 68: COLOR 11

' set BIOS segment and display addresses of buffer
DEF SEG = &H40
start% = &H400 + PEEK(&H80): finish% = &H400 + PEEK(&H82)
PRINT RIGHT$("0000" + HEX$(start%), 4); " ";
PRINT RIGHT$("0000" + HEX$(finish%), 4);

DO

    ' display positions of beginning of buffer (head) and next key (tail)
    LOCATE 11, 4: COLOR 11
    head% = &H400 + PEEK(&H1A): tail% = &H400 + PEEK(&H1C)
    PRINT RIGHT$("0000" + HEX$(head%), 4); " ";   ' display location of head
    PRINT RIGHT$("0000" + HEX$(tail%), 4);        ' display location of tail
    COLOR 13: LOCATE 9, 17: PRINT SPACE$(48);
    LOCATE 9, 17 + ((head% - &H41E) \ 2) * 3: PRINT CHR$(25);  ' point to head
    COLOR 12: LOCATE 13, 17: PRINT SPACE$(48);
    LOCATE 13, 17 + ((tail% - &H41E) \ 2) * 3: PRINT CHR$(24); ' point to tail

    ' read and display characters in the buffer
    FOR i% = 0 TO 15
        character% = PEEK(&H1E + (i% * 2))
        scanCode% = PEEK(&H1E + (i% * 2) + 1)
        IF character% < 32 THEN key$ = "  " ELSE key$ = CHR$(character%) + " "
        LOCATE 11, 17 + (i% * 3): COLOR 14: PRINT key$;  ' display character
        LOCATE 14, 17 + (i% * 3): COLOR 9
        PRINT RIGHT$("0" + HEX$(character%), 2);        ' display ASCII code
        LOCATE 15, 17 + (i% * 3): COLOR 10
        PRINT RIGHT$("0" + HEX$(scanCode%), 2);         ' display scan code
    NEXT i%

    ' display the number of characters in the buffer
    IF head% >= tail% THEN
        numkeys% = 16 - ((head% - tail%) \ 2)
    ELSE
        numkeys% = (tail% - head%) \ 2
    END IF
    LOCATE 14, 76: IF numkeys% = 16 THEN numkeys% = 0
    PRINT RIGHT$(" " + LTRIM$(RTRIM$(STR$(numkeys%))), 2);

    ' if buffer is full, use INPUT$ to clear it
    IF numkeys% = 15 THEN
        LOCATE 15, 67: COLOR 28: PRINT "BUFFER FULL";
```

(continued)

continued

```
        dummy$ = INPUT$(16)
        LOCATE , 67: PRINT SPACE$(11);
    END IF
LOOP UNTIL PEEK((tail% - &H400) - 2) = 27          ' quit when user presses Esc

' restore segment and empty the buffer
DEF SEG : COLOR 7, 0: LOCATE 20, 1, 1
dummy$ = INPUT$(numkeys%)
END

' data for display template
DATA 20, 6, 4, "Head Tail", 6, 33, "Keyboard Buffer"
DATA 6, 67, "Buffer Area", 8, 4, "041A 041C"
DATA 8, 17, "1E 20 22 24 26 28 2A 2C 2E 30 32 34 36 38 3A 3C"
DATA 8, 68, "0480 0482", 10, 3,"-----¦-----"
DATA 10, 16, "¦--¦--¦--¦--¦--¦--¦--¦--¦--¦--¦--¦--¦--¦--¦--¦--¦"
DATA 10, 67, "-----¦-----",11, 3,"           ", 11, 16, " "
DATA 11, 64, " ", 11, 67, "           ", 12, 3, "-----¦-----"
DATA 12, 16, "¦--¦--¦--¦--¦--¦--¦--¦--¦--¦--¦--¦--¦--¦--¦--¦--¦"
DATA 12, 67, "-----¦-----", 14, 3, "ASCII Codes"
DATA 14, 67, "Waiting", 15, 3, "Scan Codes"
DATA 24, 30, "Press Esc to quit"
```

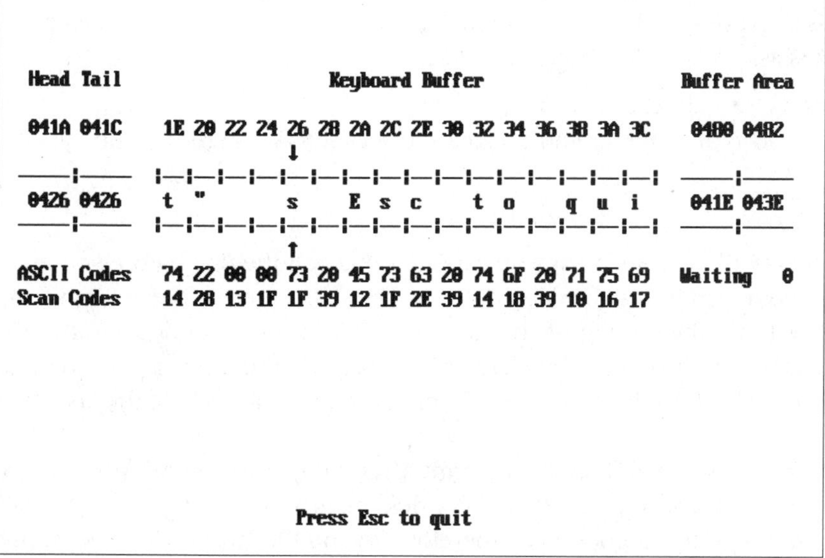

Figure 8-3.
Output of the INPUT$ example program.

LINE INPUT

See also: INKEY$, INPUT, INPUT$, LINE INPUT #

■ QB2	■ QB4.5	■ PowerBASIC
■ QB3	✲ ANSI	■ GW-BASIC
■ QB4	■ BASIC7	■ MacQB

Purpose

The LINE INPUT statement accepts all data entered as ASCII text and assigns it to a single string variable. This statement lets the user enter any characters—even commas and quotation marks—that are regarded as delimiters by the INPUT statement.

Syntax

LINE INPUT [;] ["*prompt*";] *var*

A semicolon after the keyword INPUT keeps the cursor on the same line after the user presses Enter.

prompt is an optional string of text, displayed immediately before the entry field, that can prompt the user for the required data.

var is a QuickBASIC string variable to which input is assigned.

Usage

```
LINE INPUT; entry$
```

Pauses program execution until the user enters a line of text at the keyboard. No prompt string is displayed, and the cursor remains on the same line after the data is entered. The data is assigned to the string variable *entry$*.

```
LINE INPUT "What is your name? "; name$
```

Prompts the user to type a name and assigns the characters entered to the variable *name$*.

Description

LINE INPUT accepts all printable characters and lets you edit the line before you press Enter. The carriage return is not considered part of the data entered; it ends input and moves the cursor to the beginning of the next line. If you use a semicolon after the LINE INPUT statement, however, QuickBASIC suppresses the carriage return and leaves the cursor on the same line, positioned immediately to the right of the last character entered.

Unlike INPUT, LINE INPUT does not print a question mark unless you include one as part of the prompt string. The data entry field begins immediately after the last character in the prompt. It is a good idea, therefore, to end the string with at least one blank space so that the prompt and input are clearly separated on the screen.

The variable to which LINE INPUT assigns input can be an ordinary string variable, an element of a string array, or a fixed-length string. If you assign input to a fixed-length string, LINE INPUT discards any characters that exceed the string length. If you enter only a carriage return in response to a LINE INPUT statement, the statement assigns a null string to the variable.

LINE INPUT provides the same editing key combinations as INPUT does. Table 8-3, in the INPUT entry, lists the available key combinations.

Comments

LINE INPUT always accepts up to 255 characters. You cannot limit the number of accepted characters. This makes LINE INPUT unsuitable for accepting formatted input in which the user must enter a fixed number of characters (a Social Security number, for example).

Compatibility

ANSI BASIC

The LINE INPUT statement in ANSI BASIC includes a TIMEOUT clause, which cancels the statement if LINE INPUT doesn't receive a response within a specified number of seconds. You can also include an ELAPSED clause in the statement, which returns the number of seconds taken to obtain the response.

Example

LINE INPUT accepts data from the standard input device. Usually the input device is the keyboard, but you can also use redirection symbols to direct a program to receive input from a file. For example, the following statement used at the DOS prompt directs DOS to run the program LINEINP and use the file OUTFILE.DAT as input:

```
LINEINP < OUTFILE.DAT
```

Type the following text into a file named OUTFILE.DAT:

> The LINE INPUT statement accepts input one line at a time and stores the entry in one variable.

Blank lines in the output file must have at least one blank space character in them except for the last line, which has only a single element, a carriage return.

Then create the following program to display the text on the screen by using input redirection. Compile the program as a stand-alone program so that you can run it from the command line and use input redirection.

```
PRINT : PRINT

DO
    LINE INPUT " : "; a$   ' get a line of input
    PRINT "<"; a$; ">"     ' print the line
LOOP UNTIL a$ = ""
END
```

LOCATE

See also: CSRLIN, POS, WIDTH

■ QB2	■ QB4.5	■ PowerBASIC
■ QB3	✲ ANSI	■ GW-BASIC
■ QB4	■ BASIC7	✲ MacQB

Purpose

The LOCATE statement positions the cursor on the screen, thus marking the point at which text will subsequently be printed. LOCATE can also control the appearance of the cursor, making it visible or invisible and setting its size within the character cell.

Syntax

LOCATE [*row*][, [*column*][, [*visible*][, [*start*][, *stop*]]]]

row is the number of the row at which the cursor is positioned. Usually this number is an integer in the range 1 through 25, but it can extend to 43 for computers with an EGA adapter or to 50 with a VGA adapter. *row* can be in the range 1 through 60, with VGA and MCGA adapters in screen modes 11 and 12.

column is the number of the column at which the cursor is positioned. It ranges from 1 to 40 or from 1 to 80 depending on the current screen width.

visible determines whether the cursor is displayed or hidden. A value of 1 displays the cursor; 0 hides it.

start and *stop* are the CRT scan lines at which the cursor begins and ends. Values must be in the range 0 through 31.

All arguments are optional and can be numeric constants, variables, or expressions. If you omit any arguments, QuickBASIC uses the previous values of those arguments. If you omit an argument from the middle of the statement, you must insert a comma to hold its place. You do not need to insert commas for arguments missing from the end of the statement.

Usage

```
LOCATE 10, 1
```

Positions the cursor at the first column of row 10.

```
LOCATE , 30
```

Positions the cursor at column 30 of the current screen row.

```
LOCATE , , 1, 0, 7
```

Makes the cursor visible and sets it to the size of a full character cell without changing its position.

```
LOCATE topRow% + 5, leftSide%
```

Moves the cursor to five rows below the row number in the variable *topRow%* and to the column number in the variable *leftSide%.*

Description

You can use the LOCATE statement simply to position the text cursor on the screen. You can also use the statement to change the appearance of the cursor.

Every video adapter creates characters on the screen by filling certain locations in a character cell. A Color Graphics Adapter (CGA), for example, uses an 8-by-8 grid for each character cell in which the adapter can draw a character. Other adapters (including MDA, MCGA, EGA, and VGA) use character cells with an 8-by-14, 9-by-14, 8-by-16, or 9-by-16 grid. If an adapter uses a character cell with many locations, it can create high-resolution characters.

The LOCATE statement always uses an 8-by-8 grid to form the cursor. If the adapter you are using has a character cell with higher resolution, LOCATE maps the values for the start and stop scan lines of the cursor to the values appropriate to the installed graphics adapter. Figure 8-4 shows the cursor under the letter A in a character cell of a VGA adapter and in a character cell of a CGA adapter.

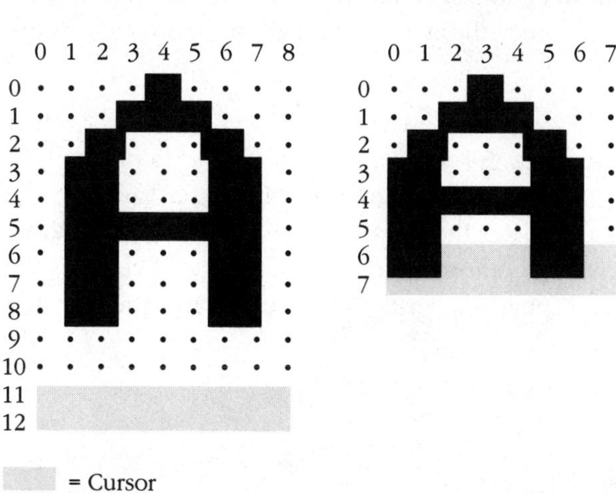

Figure 8-4.
Cursors and character cells.

Although LOCATE accepts values in the range 0 through 31, use only values in the range 0 through 7 because the statement maps these values directly to the 8-by-8 grid. Any value greater than 7 is converted to a value in the range 0 through 7.

If the value of the stop scan line is less than the value of the start scan line and you are using an adapter other than VGA (Video Graphics Array), LOCATE splits the cursor into two parts. If you are using a VGA adapter, setting the start scan line greater than the stop scan line produces a cursor that fills the character cell.

Warnings

LOCATE does not move the cursor to the bottom line of the display if the "soft key" display has been activated with KEY ON. (See the KEY entry in Chapter 14, "Keyboard".)

Options for setting the size and visibility of the cursor are effective only in SCREEN 0, the text mode. In graphics modes, LOCATE doesn't display the cursor.

Compatibility

ANSI BASIC

In ANSI BASIC, LOCATE is a statement that finds the coordinates of a point on the graphics screen. ANSI does not have a statement that positions the cursor, although TAB can be used to advance the cursor position along the current line.

QuickBASIC for the Macintosh

QuickBASIC for the Macintosh supports only the row and column arguments for LOCATE. Row and column numbers are relative to the upper left corner of the current output window, which is not necessarily the same as the screen.

LOCATE assumes that all characters have the same width, the width of the character 0. However, because many Macintosh character fonts are proportionally spaced, the column number might not accurately reflect the actual number of characters on the current line.

Example

You will find the LOCATE statement most useful when you want to place a prompt at a certain location on the screen. The following program uses LOCATE to move the prompt to the middle of the screen and to set the cursor to full height. The program uses INPUT four times to prompt for strings of text. Before each prompt, it changes the shape of the cursor. The program then repeats the strings at the corners of the screen.

```
CLS
LOCATE 10, 1, 1, 0, 7                           ' full-height cursor
INPUT "Enter first string of text : ", entry1$
LOCATE , , 1, 3, 7                              ' half-height cursor
INPUT "Enter second string of text : ", entry2$
LOCATE , , 1, 5, 7                              ' quarter-height cursor
INPUT "Enter third string of text : ", entry3$
LOCATE , , 1, 7, 7                              ' single-line cursor
INPUT "Enter fourth string of text : ", entry4$
```

(continued)

continued

```
' display the strings in the corners of the screen
LOCATE 1, 1, 0                                    ' invisible cursor
PRINT entry1$
LOCATE 1, 80 - LEN(entry2$)
PRINT entry2$
LOCATE 22, 1
PRINT entry3$
LOCATE 22, 80 - LEN(entry4$)
PRINT entry4$
END
```

POS

See also: CSRLIN, LOCATE, LPOS, POINT, WIDTH (Screen)

■ QB2	■ QB4.5	■ PowerBASIC
■ QB3	✲ ANSI	■ GW-BASIC
■ QB4	■ BASIC7	✲ MacQB

Purpose

The POS function returns the column (horizontal coordinate) number of the current text cursor. (Use the CSRLIN function to return the cursor's row number.)

Syntax

POS(*n*)

n is a dummy argument; although it is not used by the function, its presence is always required. It's easiest to use 0 as the dummy argument.

Usage

```
xPosition% = POS(0)
```

Returns the column number at which the cursor is located and assigns the value to the variable *xPosition%*.

Description

The POS function returns the column position of the character that will be output to the display by the next PRINT statement. The value can be in the range 1 through 40 or 1 through 80 depending on the current screen width. The leftmost column is always position number 1. POS is commonly used with the CSRLIN function to preserve the cursor position before a program displays a special message (such as "Press a key to continue") so that the program can resume the task at the position at which it was interrupted.

Tips

POS is useful if you want to clear a line from the cursor position. You can do this with the following statement:

```
PRINT SPACE$((80 - POS(0)) + 1);
```

Also, if you do not want the initial cursor position to change, you can save the position in a variable, clear the line, and then restore the cursor, as follows:

```
p% = POS(0)
PRINT SPACE$((80 - p%) + 1);
LOCATE , p%
```

Similarly, you can also use POS to clear from the beginning of the line to the cursor:

```
p% = POS(0)
LOCATE , 1
PRINT SPACE$(p% - 1);
```

(See the sample program in the CALL INTERRUPT entry in Chapter 20, "Mixed Language," for a procedure that uses POS and CSRLIN to clear from the cursor position to the end of the screen.)

Compatibility

ANSI BASIC

The POS function in ANSI BASIC returns the position of one string within another. It is the equivalent of the INSTR function in QuickBASIC. ANSI does not include a function that returns the column position of the cursor. However, ANSI proposes a general-purpose function, ASK, which returns information about the status of I/O devices, including the display. This information can include the current column position of the cursor.

QuickBASIC for the Macintosh

The column position returned by POS in QuickBASIC for the Macintosh assumes that all characters have the same width, the width of the character 0. However, because many Macintosh character fonts are proportionally spaced, the value might not accurately reflect the actual number of characters on the current line.

Example

A word processor can wrap incomplete words at the end of a line to the next line. The following text-entry program emulates this feature by testing for the end of the line after the user enters each character. If the program encounters the end of the line while a word is still being entered, that word is removed from the current line and transferred to the beginning of the next one.

```
CLS
LOCATE , , 1: PRINT TAB(33); "WORDWRAPPING"
PRINT STRING$(80, "_")
VIEW PRINT 4 TO 22
DO
    DO
        keyStroke$ = INKEY$
    LOOP WHILE keyStroke$ = ""          ' wait for a keypress
    keyCode% = ASC(keyStroke$)          ' get ASCII value
    IF keyCode% > 31 THEN               ' printable characters
        buffer$ = buffer$ + keyStroke$
        PRINT keyStroke$;
        IF POS(0) > 79 THEN             ' check for end of line
            ptr% = POS(0)               ' find beginning of word
            DO
                ptr% = ptr% - 1
                IF MID$(buffer$, ptr%, 1) = " " THEN EXIT DO
            LOOP UNTIL ptr% = 1
            IF ptr% = 1 THEN            ' don't wrap unbroken lines
                buffer$ = "": PRINT
            ELSE                        ' wrap word to the next line
                temp$ = MID$(buffer$, ptr% + 1)
                LOCATE , 1: PRINT LEFT$(buffer$, ptr%);
                PRINT SPACE$((80 - POS(0)) + 1)
                buffer$ = temp$: PRINT buffer$;
            END IF
        END IF
    ELSEIF keyCode% = 13 THEN           ' if user pressed Enter, start a new line
        buffer$ = "": PRINT
    END IF
LOOP UNTIL keyCode% = 27                ' quit when user presses Esc
END
```

PRINT

See also: LOCATE, PRINT #, PRINT USING, TAB, WRITE

■ QB2	■ QB4.5	■ PowerBASIC
■ QB3	■ ANSI	■ GW-BASIC
■ QB4	■ BASIC7	■ MacQB

Purpose

PRINT outputs data to the standard output device, which, by default, is the display. Use PRINT to display any message or data.

Syntax

PRINT [*data*] [{;¦,}] ...

data is any numeric or string constant, variable, or expression. If you specify more than one item, separate the items with commas or semicolons.

If you use a semicolon between data items, the next item is displayed immediately after the previous one. If you use a comma between data items, the next item is displayed in the next print zone. (Each print zone is 14 characters in length.) A semicolon or comma at the end of a PRINT statement keeps the cursor on the same line for the next PRINT statement.

Usage

```
PRINT
```

Moves the text cursor to the beginning of the next line.

```
PRINT "Press a key.";
```

Displays the message in quotes and positions the cursor immediately after the last character printed.

```
PRINT  x, x^2, x^3
```

Displays the value of the variable, *x*, *x* squared, and *x* cubed. The text cursor moves to the next print zone after each value is printed.

Description

When you create program lines, you can abbreviate the keyword PRINT as a question mark (?). If you are using the QuickBASIC environment editor, the question mark is translated into PRINT as soon as you enter the line.

PRINT outputs the supplied data to the screen, starting at the current cursor position. If a data item is too long for the part of the line remaining after the cursor, PRINT issues a linefeed before sending the data to the screen. The following PRINT statement, for example, moves the cursor to the beginning of line 11 before printing 60 equal signs:

```
LOCATE 10, 40
PRINT STRING$(60, "=")
```

If the output contains more characters than can fit on one line, PRINT fills the line and continues displaying the output on the following line.

If you use PRINT without supplying any data, QuickBASIC outputs a linefeed character, which moves the cursor to the next line. The contents of the line on which the cursor was positioned are unaffected.

Numeric values displayed by PRINT are always followed by a blank space. If the number is positive, PRINT precedes it with a space; otherwise, it precedes the number with the minus sign (–).

QuickBASIC displays numeric values in fixed-point format if it can. If a single-precision number can be represented with 7 digits or less, it is displayed in fixed-point format. Numbers of more than 7 digits are displayed in scientific notation. For example,

```
a! = 1234567: PRINT a!
```

displays 1234567, but

```
b! = 12345678: PRINT b!
```

displays 1.234568E+07. This also applies to double-precision numbers except that they are displayed in scientific notation only when the number has more than 16 digits.

Tips

For programs executed at the command line, you can also direct output to a device other than the screen. This can be useful for recording the output of a program that is run from a batch file. To do this, use the DOS output redirection symbol (>) when you start the program. For example,

```
YOURPROG > PRN
```

executes YOURPROG and sends the output from any PRINT, WRITE, or PRINT USING statement to the line printer.

Example

PRINT can also display graphics characters from the IBM extended character set. In fact, before the advent of high-resolution graphics support, PRINT was the only statement available for drawing pictures on the screen. The program below uses PRINT to produce kaleidoscopic patterns on the text screen.

The program builds patterns from only five characters:

Character	Code
█	219
▄	220
▌	221
▐	222
▀	223

The program uses a combination of the LOCATE statement and PRINT to display the characters in diagonal lines across the text screen, in six different high-intensity colors. Because the patterns are generated randomly, you see a different sequence each time you press any key except Esc, which stops the program.

```
LOCATE , , 0: RANDOMIZE TIMER
leftEdge% = 1: rightEdge% = 80: top% = 1: bottom% = 25
DO
    COLOR RND * 7 + 8
    character% = RND * 5 + 218
    CLS
```

(continued)

continued

```
    changeX% = RND * 3 + 1: changeY% = SGN((RND * 2) - 2)
    x% = RND * (rightEdge% - leftEdge%) + leftEdge%
    y% = RND * (bottom% - top%) + top%
    DO
        IF x% + changeX% >= rightEdge% OR x% + changeX% <= leftEdge% THEN
            changeX% = -changeX%
        END IF
        IF y% + changeY% >= bottom% OR y% + changeY% <= top% THEN
            changeY% = -changeY%
        END IF
        x% = x% + changeX%: y% = y% + changeY%
        LOCATE y%, x%
        IF SCREEN(y%, x%) = character% THEN
            character% = character% + 1                    ' change character
            IF character% > 223 THEN character% = 219
            clr% = clr% + 1: IF clr% > 15 THEN clr% = 9     ' change color
            COLOR clr%
        END IF
        PRINT CHR$(character%);                             ' print character
        LOCATE y%, rightEdge% - x%: PRINT CHR$(character%);
        LOCATE bottom% - y%, rightEdge% - x%: PRINT CHR$(character%);
        LOCATE bottom% - y%, x%: PRINT CHR$(character%);
        keyStroke$ = INKEY$
    LOOP WHILE keyStroke$ = ""
LOOP UNTIL keyStroke$ = CHR$(27)
END
```

PRINT USING

See also: PRINT, PRINT # USING

■ QB2	■ QB4.5	■ PowerBASIC
■ QB3	✲ ANSI	■ GW-BASIC
■ QB4	■ BASIC7	■ MacQB

Purpose

PRINT USING defines a template that specifies the length and format of each item to be displayed and then displays the result on the screen. Use PRINT USING to format data for a screen display or for a preprinted form in which each variable must fit into a particular field.

Syntax

PRINT USING *templateString*; *var*[; *var* ...][{,|;}]

templateString is either a string constant (enclosed in quotation marks) or a variable. It can contain literal text, which is printed unchanged, and one or more special formatting characters that determine how the variables or expressions following the template string are to be printed.

A comma at the end of the statement causes the cursor to remain on the current line and move to the next print zone. A semicolon causes the cursor to remain positioned directly after the last character displayed.

Usage

```
price! = 79.95
PRINT USING "ONLY $$##.##"; price!
```

Prints the contents of the single-precision variable *price!*, preceding it with a message and a leading dollar sign.

```
cost! = 37.485
PRINT USING "Cost is ##.#% of price"; cost! / price! * 100
```

Evaluates the expression following the template and rounds the result. This produces the line *Cost is 46.9% of price.*

```
payment$ = "**$#####,.##"
checkAmount! = 2449.73
PRINT USING payment$; checkAmount!
```

Displays a payment amount with a comma inserted between every third character to the left of the decimal point. The display is also padded on the left with asterisks to produce a field of 12 characters. The displayed line reads: ****$2,449.73*.

```
surName$ = "Sutcliffe"
PRINT USING "Sortname: \   \"; UCASE$(surName$)
```

Converts surName$ to uppercase and then displays the first 5 characters of the result along with the label *Sortname:*. (Five characters are printed because there are three blank spaces between the backslash characters, which represent character positions.)

```
fullName$ = "John Sutcliffe"
PRINT USING "!.&"; fullName$; surName$
```

Prints John Sutcliffe's first-name initial and full surname—J. Sutcliffe. The exclamation mark (!) extracts the first character from *fullName$*; the ampersand (&) displays *surName$* without any formatting. Note that because the period (.) is not part of a numeric field, it is interpreted as a literal character, not a decimal point.

Description

PRINT USING accepts any variables and fits them into the fields of a template string. This template controls the length of each variable, its position in the output line, and the way it is formatted. You can use the template to format both numeric and string data.

Each field in the template is indicated by one or more special formatting characters; usually, the number of formatting characters in a field controls how many characters or digits of the variable are to be printed. See Table 8-4 for a list of formatting characters for strings; see Table 8-5 for a list of formatting characters for numbers.

Character	Description
!	Displays only the first character of the specified string.
&	Displays the entire string regardless of its length.
\ \	Displays as many characters from the beginning of the source string as are in the field deliminated by the backslashes. The backslashes are considered part of the field; therefore the number of characters output will be equal to the number of blank spaces between the backslashes plus 2. If the source string doesn't contain enough characters to fill the field, the string is padded on the right with blank spaces.
_	Indicates that the next character is to be interpreted as a literal character. Use the underscore to include formatting characters in the actual text. For example, "_!" prints an exclamation mark, not the first character of a string.

Table 8-4.
PRINT USING formatting characters for strings.

Character	Description
#	Displays a single numeric digit. Use multiple number symbols to indicate the maximum number of digits to be displayed. Numbers having fewer digits are right-justified within the field and padded with leading spaces.
$$	Appends a single dollar sign immediately to the left of the number in a numeric field. If the number to be displayed is negative, a minus sign is displayed immediately to the left of the dollar sign.
**	Fills any leading spaces in the numeric field with asterisks. Two asterisks must be included, each of which represents a digit position in the field.
**$	Combines the effects of $$ and ** by displaying a dollar sign to the left of the number and filling with asterisks any leading spaces before the dollar sign.
+	Displays the sign of both positive and negative numbers. If the plus character appears at the beginning of the field, the sign is displayed immediately to the left of the number; if it appears at the end, the sign is displayed immediately to the right of the number.
,	Displays a comma in front of every third digit before the decimal. To use this character, place a comma immediately to the left of the decimal point in the print field.
-	Displays negative numbers with a trailing minus sign. Append the hyphen to the field.
.	Marks the position of the decimal point in a numeric field. If any digits to the left of the decimal are specified and the number to be displayed is less than 1, a single leading 0 is displayed. The decimal part of the number is rounded to fit into the number of digits to the right of the decimal point.

Table 8-5. *(continued)*
PRINT USING formatting characters for numbers.

Table 8-5. *(continued)*

Character	Description
^^^^[^]	Prints the number in exponential format. Four carets (^) display a 2-digit exponent (E+*nn*); five carets display a 3-digit exponent (E+*nnn*). Use number symbols (#) in front of the caret symbols to indicate the length of the significant digit field. You can use any numeric formatting character except the comma in an exponential field.

If you send more arguments to PRINT USING than there are fields in the template, QuickBASIC does not ignore the excess. Instead, after the contents of the last assigned field have been printed, it will start again at the beginning of the template, inserting the extra variables into the same set of fields. In the following example, the variables *a%*, *c%*, and *e%* are formatted with the first field, the variables *b$*, *d$*, and *f$* are formatted with the second field:

```
PRINT USING "### \   \"; a%; b$; c%; d$; e%; f$
```

Notice in this example how important it is that you don't position string variables so that they are fitted into numeric fields, and vice versa.

If a numeric variable contains more digits than will fit into the field of the template assigned to it, the displayed value overflows the template, and a percent sign (%) is inserted in front of the value. PRINT USING does not truncate numeric variables if their fields will not contain them.

Errors

If you specify a numeric value for a string field or a string value for a numeric field, QuickBASIC returns a "Type mismatch" error message. If the number of digits of a field specified in the template of a PRINT USING statement exceeds 24 characters, QuickBASIC returns an "Illegal function call" error message.

Compatibility

ANSI BASIC

ANSI BASIC has a similar PRINT USING statement; however, its formatting characters in the template string are different. A new feature of ANSI is PRINT USING *image_line*, in which *image_line* is a separate program line that contains the template image—for example,

```
100 IMAGE :##### ##### ##.##
900 PRINT USING 100: "ONE", 2, 3
```

produces

```
ONE       2  3.00
```

Notice that in ANSI the number symbol (#) can format text characters as well as numeric digits; however, text is left-justified in the field and numbers are centered. You can change the default justification in ANSI BASIC by including a less-than (<) sign for left justification or a greater-than (>) sign for right justification.

ANSI also proposes a USING$ function to return the formatted representation of a variable without displaying it.

Example

PRINT USING is often used to format data so that it fits neatly on the screen display. The following program reads elements of a customer's transactions from DATA statements and then writes them to the screen in the form of an account statement. Note that although the data in this example is read from DATA statements, an accounting application would receive the data from a file or the keyboard.

```
CLS
dateTemp$ = " \\_/\\_/\\"        ' date template
moneyTemp$ = " $$###,.##"       ' money template
tranTemp$ = " ######  \         \  \" + SPACE$(18) + "\"    ' transaction template

READ accountNo&, fullName$, surName$
PRINT TAB(32); "SINGULAR  SOFTWARE": PRINT
PRINT TAB(31); "STATEMENT OF ACCOUNT"
PRINT USING dateTemp$; LEFT$(DATE$, 2); MID$(DATE$, 4, 2); RIGHT$(DATE$, 2);
PRINT TAB(39 - (LEN(surName$) \ 2));
PRINT USING "!.&"; fullName$; surName$;
PRINT TAB(72); USING "########"; accountNo&
PRINT STRING$(80, "-")
PRINT "   Item    Date    Description";
PRINT TAB(59); "Credit"; TAB(75); "Debit"
PRINT STRING$(80, "-")
total! = 0: length% = 9
DO
    READ item&
    IF item& < 0 THEN EXIT DO
    READ dte$, desc$, debit!, credit!
    PRINT USING tranTemp$; item&; dte$; desc$;
    IF debit! > 0 THEN
        PRINT TAB(70); USING moneyTemp$; debit!
        total! = total! + debit!
    ELSEIF credit! > 0 THEN
        PRINT TAB(55); USING moneyTemp$; credit!
        total! = total! - credit!
    END IF
    length% = length% + 1       ' add one to length of list
LOOP WHILE 1
FOR i% = 1 TO 22 - length%
    PRINT
NEXT i%
PRINT STRING$(80, "-")
PRINT TAB(63); USING "Total: $$####,.##"; total!
END
```

(continued)

continued

```
' account data
DATA 460755, "Jim Bates", "BATES"
DATA 3850, "08/01/89", "b/f", 2862.30, 0
DATA 3863, "08/03/89", "System", 1795, 0
DATA 3864, "08/03/89", "Monitor", 379, 0
DATA 3879, "08/10/89", "BASIC", 60, 0
DATA 3888, "08/18/89", "Diskettes", 19.95, 0
DATA 3925, "08/22/89", "Hard drive", 529, 0
DATA 3926, "08/22/89", "Check", 0, 5000
DATA 3933, "08/23/89", "Graphical interface", 116.95, 0
DATA 3976, "08/28/89", "Backup program", 139.95, 0
DATA -1
```

SPC

See also: SPACE$, TAB, WIDTH (Screen)

■ QB2	■ QB4.5	■ PowerBASIC
■ QB3	✲ ANSI	✲ GW-BASIC
■ QB4	■ BASIC7	■ MacQB

Purpose

The SPC function moves the cursor or print head forward the specified number of spaces. You can use SPC in PRINT, LPRINT, and PRINT # statements. Use SPC to format output so that you can read it easily.

Syntax

SPC(*col*)

col is the number of character positions the cursor or print head will be advanced. It can be a constant, variable, or expression, but it must evaluate to a positive integer in the range 0 through 32767.

Usage

```
LPRINT "CODE"; SPC(16); "DESCRIPTION"; SPC(19); "LOCATION"
```

Prints the heading of a report. The string "CODE" is separated from "DESCRIPTION" by 16 blank spaces. "DESCRIPTION" is, in turn, separated from "LOCATION" by another 19 spaces.

Description

The SPC function advances the text cursor or print head a specified number of columns (from the column in which the last character is printed) and fills the intervening columns with blank spaces. Use SPC to insert a specific number of spaces between items regardless of the position of the items.

SPC works as though it has a trailing semicolon. If you use SPC at the end of a line of data, it suppresses the normal carriage return and linefeed, leaving the cursor or print head positioned immediately to the right of the last space character printed.

If the width of a data item following a call to SPC is greater than the number of columns remaining on the line, QuickBASIC displays the entire data item on the next line. If the specified number of columns is greater than the width of the current output device, SPC uses the number of columns modulo (MOD) the width as the number of spaces to output.

Errors

If you use a value greater than 32767 with the SPC function, QuickBASIC returns an "Overflow" error message. A negative value does not produce an error; QuickBASIC merely ignores the function.

Warnings

BC.EXE, the command-line BASIC compiler for QuickBASIC 4.5, has a bug. The SPC function (when used with a PRINT, LPRINT, or PRINT # statement) affects the pointer system to numeric arrays; this causes QuickBASIC to return incorrect array contents. The following program, for example, illustrates how the use of SPC interferes with the array pointers.

```
DEFINT A-Z
DIM array(1 TO 4)

FOR j = 1 TO 4
    array(j) = j
NEXT j
FOR j = 1 TO 4
    PRINT array(j)
    PRINT SPC(10); array(j)
NEXT j
END
```

The program displays the following results after being compiled with BC.EXE:

```
1
          4765
2
          3504
3
          112
4
          821
```

Although the above example uses a static array, the bug is also present with dynamic arrays, in which the erroneous values are all 0. Only numeric arrays are affected. The bug occurs even if you copy the array contents to a simple variable before you use SPC. Therefore, using SPC and a numeric array in the same module might generate unreliable results. The following list presents several ways to avoid this bug:

- Use the /D (debug) or /AH (huge arrays) switch on the compile command line.
- For screen display using PRINT, use LOCATE rather than TAB.
- For printer or file output, substitute the PRINT USING statement for TAB.
- For LPRINT, write a subprogram that uses LPOS to emulate the action of TAB by finding the current print head position and then printing the appropriate number of spaces.

Note that in QuickBASIC 4.5 the bug occurs only with BC.EXE. QuickBASIC 4.0 and BASIC 7.0 do not have the bug.

Compatibility

ANSI BASIC

ANSI BASIC does not include the SPC function, nor does it include a SPACE$ function to return a string of blank spaces. The nearest ANSI equivalent is the REPEAT$ function, which returns a specified number of copies of any ASCII character.

GW-BASIC and BASICA

GW-BASIC and BASICA limit the range that can be used with the SPC function to 0 through 255. Any value greater than 255 results in an error.

Example

You can use SPC with the PRINT # statement to format data sent to a file. Doing this saves you from having to format the data again when you print the file. The following program writes a simple geometric pattern to a disk file and then displays the contents of the file. Figure 8-5 shows the output of this program.

```
CLS
OPEN "DIAGONAL" FOR OUTPUT AS #1
FOR i% = 1 TO 24
    PRINT #1, STRING$(15, CHR$(219)); SPC(i%);
    PRINT #1, STRING$(25, CHR$(219)); SPC(25 - i%);
    PRINT #1, STRING$(15, CHR$(219));
NEXT i%
CLOSE
SHELL "TYPE DIAGONAL"
END
```

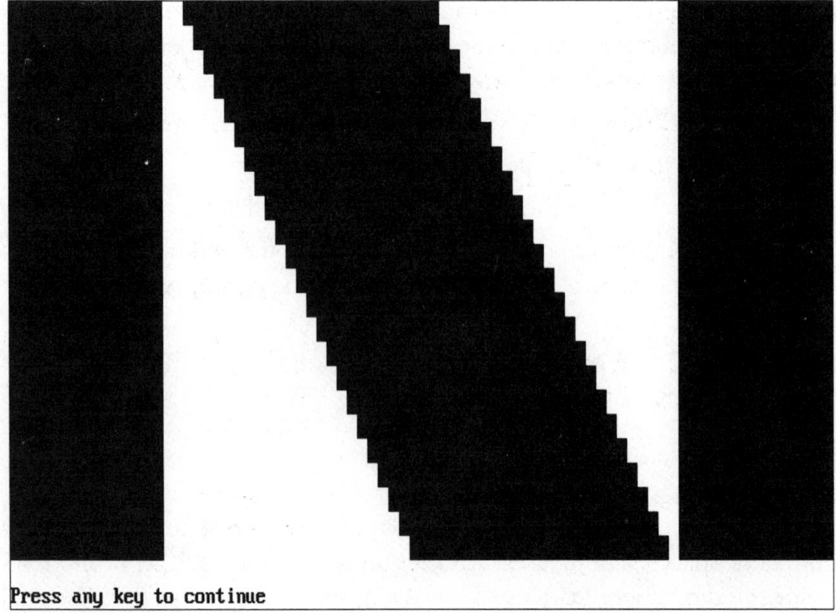

Figure 8-5.
Output of the SPC example program.

TAB

See also: SPC, WIDTH (Screen)

■ QB2	■ QB4.5	■ PowerBASIC
■ QB3	■ ANSI	✲ GW-BASIC
■ QB4	■ BASIC7	■ MacQB

Purpose

TAB sets the column position of the next character to be displayed on the current line. You can use TAB with the PRINT, LPRINT, and PRINT # statements. Use TAB when an item must appear in a particular column on the line.

Syntax

TAB(*col*)

col is any numeric constant, variable, or expression. It indicates the column number to which the print head or cursor will be moved. The number must evaluate to a positive integer in the range 0 through 32767.

Usage

```
PRINT TAB(10)
```

Moves the cursor to column 10 in the current line but does not display anything.

```
LPRINT TAB(indent%) "->";
```

Moves the print head to the column specified by the variable *indent%* and prints the characters surrounded by the quotes. The trailing semicolon suppresses a linefeed and keeps the print head positioned after the last character printed.

```
PRINT #1, TAB(16) "PRICE:   " TAB(36 - (LEN(price$))) price$
```

Outputs to a sequential file a line of data that contains 36 characters. The line begins with 16 blank spaces, continues with the quoted string, and ends with the contents of the variable *price$* right-justified in the 36-character field.

Description

Use TAB to advance the text cursor or print head to a specific column along a line.

You cannot use TAB to move to a column number greater than the width of the device being printed to. The maximum number of columns per line is usually 80 for both printer and screen. If the specified column number is greater than the current output width, TAB does not return an error; instead, it advances to the position that equals the value of the column modulo (MOD) the width. If TAB receives a negative value, it sets the column number to 1.

TAB works as though it has a trailing semicolon; it suppresses the normal carriage return and linefeed usually added to the end of a PRINT statement. This ensures that the print position is held at the specified column.

Errors

If you use a value greater than 32767 with the TAB function, QuickBASIC returns an "Overflow" error message. A negative value does not produce an error; TAB merely moves the text cursor or print head to the first column of the row.

Warnings

BC.EXE, the command-line BASIC compiler for QuickBASIC 4.5, has a bug because TAB (when used with a PRINT, LPRINT, or PRINT # statement) affects the pointer system to numeric arrays, causing QuickBASIC to return incorrect array contents. For example, the following program illustrates how the use of TAB interferes with the array pointers.

```
DEFINT A-Z
DIM array(1 TO 4)
FOR j = 1 TO 4
    array(j) = j
NEXT j
FOR j = 1 TO 4
    PRINT array(j)
    PRINT TAB(10); array(j)
NEXT j
END
```

The program displays the following results after being compiled with BC.EXE:

```
1
        4765
2
        3504
3
        112
4
        821
```

Although the above example uses a static array, the bug is also present with dynamic arrays. In this case the erroneous values are all 0. Only numeric arrays are affected. The bug occurs even if you copy the array contents to a simple variable before you use TAB. Therefore, using TAB and a numeric array in the same module might generate unreliable results.

The following list presents several ways to avoid this bug:

- Use the /D (debug) or /AH (huge arrays) switch on the compile command line.
- For screen display using PRINT, use LOCATE rather than TAB.
- For printer or file output, substitute the PRINT USING statement for TAB.
- For LPRINT, write a subprogram that uses LPOS to emulate the action of TAB by finding the current print head position and then printing the appropriate number of spaces.

Note that in QuickBASIC 4.5 this problem occurs only with BC.EXE. QuickBASIC 4.0 and BASIC 7.0 do not have this bug.

Compatibility

GW-BASIC and BASICA

GW-BASIC and BASICA limit the range that can be used with the TAB function to 0 through 255. Any value greater than 255 results in an error.

Example

When you use TAB to format text, TAB ensures that the line contains the proper number of characters by filling intervening columns with blank spaces. The following program displays a formatted page of text that has a border. Figure 8-6 shows the output of the program.

```
PRINT CHR$(201); STRING$(77, CHR$(205)); CHR$(187)
FOR i% = 1 TO 5
    PRINT CHR$(186); TAB(79); CHR$(186)
NEXT
message$ = "QuickBASIC BIBLE"
PRINT CHR$(186); TAB(40 - (LEN(message$) \ 2)); message$; TAB(79); CHR$(186)
FOR i% = 1 TO 4
    PRINT CHR$(186); TAB(79); CHR$(186)
NEXT
message$ = "The Ultimate Reference"
PRINT CHR$(186); TAB(40 - (LEN(message$) \ 2)); message$; TAB(79); CHR$(186)
message$ = "for"
PRINT CHR$(186); TAB(40 - (LEN(message$) \ 2)); message$; TAB(79); CHR$(186)
message$ = "QuickBASIC Programmers"
PRINT CHR$(186); TAB(40 - (LEN(message$) \ 2)); message$; TAB(79); CHR$(186)
FOR i% = 1 TO 8
    PRINT CHR$(186); TAB(79); CHR$(186)
NEXT
PRINT CHR$(200); STRING$(77, CHR$(205)); CHR$(188)
END
```

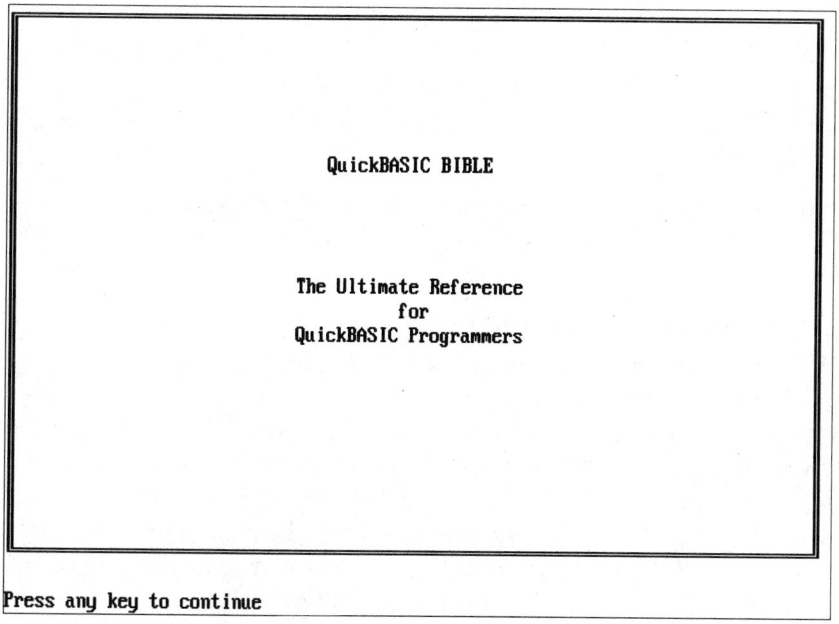

```
QuickBASIC BIBLE


The Ultimate Reference
for
QuickBASIC Programmers


Press any key to continue
```

Figure 8-6.
Output of the TAB example program.

VIEW PRINT

See also: CLS, LOCATE, PRINT, SCREEN (Function), VIEW (Graphics), WIDTH (Screen)

■ QB2	■ QB4.5	PowerBASIC
■ QB3	ANSI	■ GW-BASIC
■ QB4	■ BASIC7	MacQB

Purpose

The VIEW PRINT statement defines a rectangular area of the screen and confines all text output to within its borders. This area is known as the *text viewport*. If your program uses both text and graphics, you can create a text viewport to keep the two types of output separate, preventing text from overwriting any pictures that are drawn.

Syntax

VIEW PRINT [*top* TO *bottom*]

top is the number of the row that marks the upper boundary of the viewport; *bottom* is the number of the row that marks the lower boundary. Both parameters have a range of 1 through the maximum number of rows available with the installed video adapter (by default, 25). The value of *bottom* must be greater than that of *top*.

Usage

```
VIEW PRINT 10 TO 24
```

Defines the 15 rows from line 10 through 24 as the area for text output.

```
VIEW PRINT
```

Disables the currently active text viewport and sets the text viewport to the entire screen.

Description

Use the VIEW PRINT statement to specify the part of the screen in which text output will appear. VIEW PRINT does not affect the output of graphics statements.

After you define a text viewport with VIEW PRINT, the output from any PRINT statement is confined to the viewport. Note that a PRINT statement executed on the bottom row of the viewport scrolls the viewport up one line exactly as if it were the actual bottom row of the screen.

If the function key display is active, you cannot specify the bottom row of the display as a parameter for VIEW PRINT. See the KEY statement in Chapter 14, "Keyboard," for details about enabling and disabling the function key display.

The number of rows available for the viewport depends on the number of rows your video adapter can display. The number is usually 25; however, if your system has an EGA adapter, you can extend this to 43 (50 rows with a VGA adapter, and 60 rows with a VGA or MCGA adapter in screen modes 11 and 12). See the WIDTH (Screen) entry for details about setting the number of rows on the display.

Errors

After you define a text viewport, you cannot move the text cursor outside the area. For example, if you use the statements

```
VIEW PRINT 1 TO 12
LOCATE 16, 1
```

QuickBASIC returns an "Illegal function call" error message. QuickBASIC returns an "Illegal function call" error message if you use a negative number in the call to VIEW PRINT, if the value of the top row is greater than the value of the bottom row, or if the value of the bottom row exceeds the number of rows available.

Tips

VIEW PRINT creates a viewport of complete rows. You cannot define a rectangle of partial rows and confine output to the range of columns within those lines. See the CLS entry, however, for a sample program that lets you specify a rectangle on the screen that does not contain complete rows and clear it to any color or scroll it upward and downward as many lines as you want.

Example

VIEW PRINT is commonly used in applications that mix text and graphics on the same display. Defining separate viewports for text and graphics lets you isolate the two forms of output, preventing them from interfering with each other. The following program constructs a pie chart in the graphics viewport from data entered in the text viewport.

```
CONST PI = 3.14159

' dimension arrays for data and pie-chart labels
DIM items(1 TO 7) AS SINGLE, label(1 TO 6) AS STRING

' set up the screen and text viewport
SCREEN 9: LINE (0, 0)-(639, 349), 1, BF
VIEW PRINT 20 TO 25
CLS 2: PRINT "Enter up to six values for the pie chart ";
PRINT "(0 = last item, -1 = quit)": PRINT STRING$(80, "_")
DO

    ' collect pie-chart data in the text viewport (maximum six items)
    VIEW PRINT 22 TO 25
    CLS 2                          ' clear text viewport
    total! = 0
    INPUT "Title for chart :", title$
    title$ = LEFT$(title$, 60)
    FOR itemNum% = 1 TO 6
        PRINT "Item #"; itemNum%; : INPUT ; items(itemNum%)
        total! = total! + items(itemNum%)
        IF items(itemNum%) <= 0 THEN EXIT FOR
        PRINT TAB(41); "Label"; : INPUT label(itemNum%)
```

(continued)

continued

```
        NEXT itemNum%
        itemNum% = itemNum% - 1
        IF items(itemNum% + 1) < 0 THEN EXIT DO

        VIEW PRINT                  ' disable text viewport
        ' initialize graphics viewport
        VIEW (10, 5)-(629, 245), 0, 15
        CLS 1                       ' clear graphics viewport
        start! = .0001: units! = 2 * PI / total!
        row% = 2: column% = 12

        ' draw pie chart
        FOR i% = 1 TO itemNum%
            finish! = items(i%) * units! + start!
            IF finish! > 2 * PI THEN finish! = 2 * PI
            CIRCLE (310, 120), 80, i%, -start!, -finish!
            midPoint! = finish! - ((finish! - start!) / 2)
            x = 310 + 40 * COS(midPoint!)
            y = 120 - 40 * SIN(midPoint!)
            PAINT (x, y), i%, i%
            CIRCLE (310, 120), 80, 0, -start!, -finish!

            ' draw key and print labels
            start! = finish!
            LINE (10, column%)-(20, column% + 5), i%, BF
            LOCATE row%, 10: PRINT LEFT$(label(i%), 20)
            row% = row% + 1: column% = column% + 14
        NEXT i%
        LOCATE 17, 40 - (LEN(title$) \ 2): PRINT title$;
    LOOP WHILE 1
    END
```

WIDTH (Screen)

See also: SCREEN (Statement), WIDTH (File), WIDTH LPRINT

✲ QB2	■ QB4.5	✲ PowerBASIC
■ QB3	ANSI	✲ GW-BASIC
■ QB4	■ BASIC7	✲ MacQB

Purpose

The WIDTH statement resets the number of columns on the screen. If your computer has a high-resolution video adapter, you can also use WIDTH to increase the number of rows available on the screen.

Syntax

WIDTH [*cols*][,*rows*]

cols is the number of characters in a screen line, either 40 or 80 (the default). *rows* is the number of screen lines; possible settings include 25 (the default), 43, 30, 50, and 60.

Usage

```
WIDTH 40
```

Sets the number of columns to 40.

```
WIDTH ,43
```

Sets the number of rows to 43 without changing the number of columns.

Description

Use WIDTH to select the number of columns and rows of text that can be displayed. Changing the display size also clears the screen.

Possible values for the number of rows depend on the current screen mode and the capabilities of the installed video adapter. The number of columns is always either 40 or 80. Table 8-6 lists the text display sizes available in each screen mode.

Screen mode	Width values	Video adaptor
0	80 by 25	MDA, Hercules, CGA, EGA, MCGA, VGA
	80 by 43	EGA, VGA
	80 by 50	VGA
	40 by 25	CGA, EGA, MCGA, VGA
	40 by 43	EGA, VGA
	40 by 50	VGA
1	40 by 25	CGA, EGA, MCGA, VGA
2	80 by 25	CGA, EGA, MCGA, VGA
3	80 by 25	Hercules
7	40 by 25	EGA, VGA
8	80 by 25	EGA, VGA
9	80 by 25	EGA, VGA
	80 by 43	EGA, VGA
10	80 by 25	EGA, VGA
	80 by 43	EGA, VGA
11	80 by 30	MCGA, VGA
	80 by 60	MCGA, VGA
12	80 by 30	VGA
	80 by 60	VGA
13	40 by 25	MCGA, VGA

Table 8-6.
Valid WIDTH row and column values for QuickBASIC screen modes.

WIDTH is particularly useful in screen modes 9 through 13 (discussed in the SCREEN (Statement) entry in Chapter 11, "Graphics"), in which you can use it to control the height of labels for graphs and charts. Be sure that you use WIDTH to set the character size before you begin drawing; otherwise, it will clear any existing graphics from the screen. Remember also that screen modes 9 through 13 do not allow fewer than 80 columns.

Errors

Trying to set the number of columns to a value other than 40 or 80 or the number of rows to a value that is not supported by your video adapter causes QuickBASIC to stop your program and return an "Illegal function call" error message.

Tips

To avoid errors caused by attempting to set an illegal display size, your program should always test for the video hardware of the current system. See the CALL ABSOLUTE entry in Chapter 20, "Mixed Language," for a procedure that can detect the type of video adapter installed.

Compatibility

QuickBASIC 2.0, PowerBASIC, GW-BASIC, and BASICA

Some versions of BASIC, including QuickBASIC version 2.0, PowerBASIC, GW-BASIC, and BASICA, do not support changing the number of rows with the WIDTH statement. You can use WIDTH only for changing the number of columns.

QuickBASIC for the Macintosh

In QuickBASIC for the Macintosh, the WIDTH statement does not let you specify the number of rows. It does, however, have an additional option that lets you set the print-zone size. Print zones are equivalent to tab stops; they specify the number of columns the cursor will advance when you use a comma between elements in a PRINT, LPRINT, or PRINT # statement.

Example

The following program demonstrates the difference in character size when you change the width of the screen. The program uses WIDTH to change the number of columns in a line from 80 to 40.

```
CONST MESSAGE$ = "QuickBASIC Bible"
CLS
WIDTH 80, 25
PRINT MESSAGE$
LOCATE 23, 1
PRINT "Press any key to change the screen width to 40 columns"

DO
LOOP WHILE INKEY$ = ""

WIDTH 40, 25
PRINT MESSAGE$
```

WRITE

See also: PRINT, WRITE #

■ QB2	■ QB4.5	■ PowerBASIC
■ QB3	ANSI	■ GW-BASIC
■ QB4	■ BASIC7	■ MacQB

Purpose

The WRITE statement displays data on the screen. WRITE separates each item with a comma and encloses each string item in quotation marks.

Syntax

WRITE [*expr*]

expr is a list of one or more items of data, separated by commas. These items can be numeric or string variables, constants, or expressions. If you don't specify an expression list, only a carriage return and linefeed are written.

Usage

```
WRITE
```

Advances the cursor to the next line of the display.

```
a% = 6: price = 9.95: tax = 1.15
WRITE a%, "Blender", price * tax
```

Displays three items of data on the screen, beginning at the current cursor position. WRITE displays commas to separate the output items and deletes all blank spaces.

Description

Use WRITE to output data to the screen in teletype fashion, starting at the current cursor position and advancing the cursor to a new line after the data has been written. QuickBASIC evaluates numeric expressions in the data list, and WRITE displays the resulting value without leading or trailing spaces. WRITE encloses character strings in quotation marks and separates the items in the list with commas. The commas in the expression list do not move the cursor to the next print zone, as the commas in PRINT do. In fact, WRITE requires that commas be used as the separator between data items.

Control characters written to the screen with WRITE have the same effect as they would have if you wrote them to the screen with a PRINT statement. The statement *WRITE CHR$(7)*, for example, sounds the computer's bell and *WRITE CHR$(12)* clears the screen. However, after writing character 12, the cursor is positioned at line 2 because WRITE appends a carriage return and linefeed at the end of the expression list. You cannot suppress the linefeed by adding a semicolon, as you can in a PRINT statement.

Example

The following program compares WRITE and PRINT by using the two statements to output the same data in a variety of ways.

```
CLS
DIM wrd(1 TO 9) AS STRING

FOR i% = 1 TO 9
    READ wrd(i%)              ' read a data item
    PRINT i%, wrd(i%),        ' display item with PRINT
    WRITE i%, wrd(i%)         ' display item with WRITE
NEXT i%
PRINT


' display the data on the screen with PRINT
PRINT wrd(1); wrd(2); wrd(3); wrd(4); wrd(5); wrd(6); wrd(7); wrd(8); wrd(9)


' display the data on the screen with WRITE
WRITE wrd(1), wrd(2), wrd(3), wrd(4), wrd(5), wrd(6), wrd(7), wrd(8), wrd(9)
END

DATA "The ", "moving ", "finger ", "writes ", "and, ", "having "
DATA "writ, ", "moves ", "on."
```

CHAPTER 9

Trapping and Errors

Introduction

Errors in programs can be divided into two main categories—compiler errors and runtime errors. Compiler errors include syntax errors (for example, a misspelled QuickBASIC keyword) and references to array variables that use an index outside the array's range. QuickBASIC immediately warns you about such errors when you either compile a program or try to run it in the QuickBASIC environment. Indeed, if you write your programs in the environment, QuickBASIC warns you of syntax errors in a line immediately after you enter it.

Runtime errors are more difficult to find. By definition, they occur only when you run the program, after a successful compilation. Furthermore, a particular error might not occur every time you run the program; it might appear only when a certain combination of circumstances occurs.

A runtime error might not even be your fault: If a user forgets to turn the printer on before the program attempts to print a report, a runtime error can occur. This is the type of error your program must be able to handle; the program must either trap the error or end safely so that the user doesn't lose any data.

This chapter discusses how QuickBASIC lets you trap and handle runtime errors as well as user-defined events. Table 9-1 is an alphabetic list of QuickBASIC's error-handling and event-trapping statements and functions.

Statement or function	**Description**
ERDEV	Returns the DOS error code set by the critical error handler and information concerning the device in which an error occurred
ERDEV$	Returns the name of the device that generated an error
ERL	Returns the line number of the statement that caused an error
ERR	Returns the QuickBASIC code of the most recent error
ERROR	Simulates an error
ON ERROR GOTO	Establishes error trapping and specifies an error-handling routine
ON UEVENT GOSUB	Establishes user-event trapping and specifies an event-handling routine

Table 9-1. *(continued)*
QuickBASIC error-handling and event-trapping statements and functions.

Table 9-1. *(continued)*

Statement or function	Description
RESUME	Specifies the return from an error-handling routine
UEVENT ON/OFF/STOP	Enables, disables, or suspends user-event trapping

Error Trapping

Many runtime errors are first detected by the computer hardware. If your program instructs the CPU to divide a number by 0, for example, the CPU sends DOS an interrupt. (See Chapter 20, "Mixed Language," for details about interrupts.) Similarly, if your program tries to read a disk when the drive door is open, DOS generates the critical error interrupt, which produces the familiar message

```
Abort, Retry, Fail?
```

QuickBASIC, however, intercepts the interrupts generated by errors and passes the interrupts to its internal error-handling routines. It also collects information about the circumstances that caused the error. QuickBASIC passes this information to the program, either as a message in a dialog box (if the program is running in the environment) or as an error code (displayed by a stand-alone application). The stand-alone program displays the error code in the following format:

Error *nn* in module *progname* at address *ssss:oooo*

In this format, *progname* is the name of the program, *ssss:oooo* is the segment and offset address of the statement QuickBASIC was executing when the error occurred, and *nn* is a 1-digit or 2-digit code that QuickBASIC uses to describe the error. (See Appendix F, "Error Messages & Error Codes," for a complete list of QuickBASIC error codes.) If you compile the program using the /D, /E, or /W switch, the stand-alone program also prints the line number (if any) of the statement.

This information can help you understand how to modify your program to prevent the error from occurring in the future. However, the error message cannot prevent the error from stopping the program. To enable your program to handle all errors, use an ON ERROR GOTO statement. This statement activates error trapping and specifies the line number or label that marks the beginning of the error-handling routine in your program.

If you use an ON ERROR GOTO statement, an error will no longer halt your program. Instead, execution will branch to the specified routine, which contains statements to handle errors.

Error Handlers

If your program traps errors, you must write an error-handling routine, called an error handler, that specifies what your program will do if a particular error occurs. QuickBASIC provides functions that return information about the nature of each error. Use these functions in your error handler so that it responds properly to each error. The ERR function returns QuickBASIC's code for the error. The ERDEV function returns the DOS code for the error and information concerning the device in which a hardware error occurred, and the ERDEV$ function returns the name of that device. If your program uses line numbers, the ERL function returns the number of the line in which the error occurred.

After an error occurs, QuickBASIC disables further error trapping until the handling routine finishes. This prevents any other errors from causing the error handler to be entered recursively. However, if an error occurs while the handling routine is executing, the error will not be trapped; this causes the program to terminate and display an error message.

Your program can encounter two types of errors—"recoverable" errors and "fatal" errors. If a recoverable error occurs, your error-handling routine can take the necessary steps to correct it (for example, by instructing the user to turn the printer on). After offering a solution to the problem, the program can use the RESUME statement to try again to execute the statement that triggered the error. Or, the program can ignore the error by using RESUME NEXT to execute the statement following the one that caused the error. However, if the error is fatal and cannot be rectified or ignored, the program should call the RESUME statement with a specified line number or label to direct control to the line number or label of an exit routine that safely terminates execution.

If an error that your routine cannot handle occurs, you can pass control to QuickBASIC by using the following statement within the error-handling routine:

```
ON ERROR GOTO 0
```

The above statement causes QuickBASIC to terminate the program and print its own error message. Using this statement outside an error-handling routine disables error trapping without terminating the program.

QuickBASIC also provides a statement that lets you test error-handling routines in programs you are developing. The ERROR statement simulates a specified error, so you do not have to wait for it to occur naturally. When you call the ERROR statement, your program executes the error-handling routine specified by the last ON ERROR GOTO statement exactly as if a real error had occurred.

Scope of Errors

Errors can be trapped across program modules. If an error occurs in a module that does not include an ON ERROR GOTO statement, the program responds to an ON ERROR GOTO statement in the module that invoked the current module. If that module does not include an ON ERROR GOTO statement, the program moves to the previous module in the line of execution. If the program uses an error handler that is not found in the module in which the error occurred, execution resumes in the module containing the error handler. The program cannot move back to the module that contained the error.

To use one error-handling routine for all modules and return to the module that caused the error, define the error-handling routine in a subprogram. You can then call the subprogram from error handlers in each module. This is demonstrated in the skeleton of a program shown in Figure 9-1.

If you use an ON ERROR GOTO statement in a subprogram or function, the line number or label that the statement specifies must be in the module-level code, not in the subprogram or function.

Note that the functions ERR, ERDEV, and ERDEV$ return values about an error and can be called from any module of the program, regardless of the location of the statement that caused the error.

Error Trapping In Stand-alone Programs

Programs that include error trapping require you to specify special switches when you compile them using BC.EXE, the command-line compiler. If your program uses an ON ERROR GOTO statement to set error trapping and a RESUME statement that specifies a line number or label to return from an error handler, you must use the /E switch when compiling it. If your program uses a RESUME or RESUME NEXT statement, you must specify the /X and /E switches. You do not need to use these switches with programs run in the QuickBASIC environment.

Using RESUME or RESUME NEXT greatly increases the size of the executable file that the compiler produces. When you compile using the /X switch, BC.EXE assigns a 2-byte pointer to each statement. These pointers let the program return to the appropriate statement after an error has been trapped; however, it also adds overhead that increases the size of the executable file.

Main Module

```
DECLARE SUB ErrorTrap
DECLARE SUB DoThis (that%)
COMMON SHARED /Errors/quit%

ON ERROR GOTO Trap

'main program code

DoThis(now%)
IF quit% THEN GOTO Egress

Trap:
    ErrorTrap
    IF NOT quit% THEN RESUME NEXT
    RESUME Egress

Egress:
    END
```

Support Module 1

```
COMMON SHARED/Errors/quit%

SUB ErrorTrap () STATIC

    'error-handling code

END SUB
```

Support Module 2

```
DECLARE SUB ErrorTrap
COMMON SHARED /Errors/quit%

SUB DoThis (that%)
    ON ERROR GOTO Handler
    IF quit% THEN EXIT SUB
END SUB

    Handler:
    ErrorTrap
    RESUME NEXT
```

Figure 9-1.
Program that traps errors across modules by using a subprogram.

User Events

In addition to its error-trapping capabilities, QuickBASIC lets you trap for other events that might occur when your program is running. Many of these events are predefined and already have statements dedicated to them. For example, ON COM GOSUB transfers execution to a special routine whenever the program receives data from the serial port; ON TIMER GOSUB lets you create a subroutine that is executed whenever a specified number of seconds has elapsed on the system clock.

QuickBASIC 4.5 introduces UEVENT (user event) statements, which let you trap events that you define. A "user event" is usually a signal from a special hardware device that is installed in your computer (for example, a data-acquisition device, such as a scanner).

QuickBASIC can detect the signal only if you link your program with a specially written routine that handles the interrupt generated by the device. The interrupt routine must, in turn, set QuickBASIC's event flag so that the main program knows when to execute its event handler, which is specified by the ON UEVENT GOSUB statement. (Note that the UEVENT entry includes a sample interrupt-handler routine.) You can enable, disable, or suspend trapping of user events with the statements UEVENT ON, UEVENT OFF, and UEVENT STOP.

Related Reading

Duncan, Ray, et al. *The MS-DOS Encyclopedia*. Redmond, Wash.: Microsoft Press, 1988.

The Waite Group. *MS-DOS Papers*. Indianapolis, Ind.: Howard W. Sams & Co., 1988.

ERDEV

See also: ERDEV$, ERR, IOCTL, IOCTL$, ON ERROR GOTO

■ QB2	■ QB4.5	■ PowerBASIC
■ QB3	ANSI	■ GW-BASIC
■ QB4	■ BASIC7	MacQB

Purpose

The ERDEV function returns an integer describing the device that produced an error and the error itself. Call this function to determine what kind of error has occurred. Your program can then take the appropriate measures to either rectify the problem or shut down safely.

Syntax

ERDEV

Usage

```
errorCode% = ERDEV
```

Assigns the error code to the integer variable *errorCode%* (after a hardware fault has occurred).

Description

The integer value returned by ERDEV contains two separate pieces of information. The lower, or least significant, byte (LSB) contains the MS-DOS error code that reveals the nature of the error. The upper, or most significant, byte (MSB) contains selected information from the "device attribute word," a 2-byte collection of flags that is part of the device-driver program in memory. To separate the two components of the information returned by ERDEV, use the following statements:

```
deviceID% = VAL("&H" + LEFT$(HEX$(ERDEV), 2))
errorCode% = VAL("&H" + RIGHT$(HEX$(ERDEV), 2))
```

(Note that the translation to and from hexadecimal format masks the sign bit; this prevents *deviceID%* and *errorCode%* from becoming negative numbers.)

For an interpretation of the information in *deviceID%* (the MSB of the value returned by ERDEV), see Table 9-2. The possible values for *errorCode%* (the LSB of the value returned by ERDEV) are listed in Table 9-3.

Bit	Meaning if bit equals 1
0	Device is the standard input device
1	Device is the standard output device
2	Device is the NUL device
3	Device is a clock device
4	Not used (always 0)
5	Device is a non-IBM-type disk driver
6	Device supports I/O control
7	Device is a character device

Table 9-2.
Meaning of the bits in the MSB returned by ERDEV.

Error code	Description
0	Write-protect error
1	Unknown unit
2	Drive not ready
3	Unknown command request
4	Data error (CRC)
5	Bad request structure length
6	Seek error
7	Unknown media type
8	Sector not found
9	Printer out of paper
10	Write fault
11	Read fault
12	General failure
13	Not used
14	Not used
15	Invalid disk change (MS-DOS 3.x only)

Table 9-3.
Error codes in the LSB returned by ERDEV.

Warnings

QuickBASIC retains the information set by the last device error even after you call the ERDEV function. This lets you call ERDEV more than once for the same error. Be sure, however, that your program does not read an old value and respond to a nonexistent error. If an error was caused by something other than a device, ERDEV continues to return information about the device that last caused an error. You might find it safer to rely on the ERR function, which always returns the code of the current error.

Example

ERDEV is most useful in programs that must communicate with user-installed devices. However, you can use it to gather information about standard devices, such as disk drives and printers. The following program uses ERDEV in an error handler to report the meaning of the error code. When you run this program, leave the door of the A drive open so that the OPEN statement produces an error that can be trapped.

```
ON ERROR GOTO Handler

OPEN "A:\ERDEV.DAT" FOR OUTPUT AS #1
END

Handler:
    code% = VAL("&H" + RIGHT$(HEX$(ERDEV), 2))
    SELECT CASE code%
    CASE 0
        PRINT "Write-protect error"
    CASE 1
        PRINT "Unknown unit"
    CASE 2
        PRINT "Drive not ready"
    CASE 3
        PRINT "Unknown command request"
    CASE 4
        PRINT "Data error"
    CASE 5
        PRINT "Bad request structure length"
    CASE 6
        PRINT "Seek error"
    CASE 7
        PRINT "Unknown media type"
    CASE 8
        PRINT "Sector not found"
    CASE 9
        PRINT "Printer out of paper"
    CASE 10
        PRINT "Write fault"
    CASE 11
        PRINT "Read fault"
    CASE 12
        PRINT "General failure"
    END SELECT
    RESUME NEXT
```

ERDEV$

See also: ERDEV, ERR, IOCTL, IOCTL$, ON ERROR GOTO

■ QB2	■ QB4.5	■ PowerBASIC
■ QB3	ANSI	■ GW-BASIC
■ QB4	■ BASIC7	MacQB

Purpose

The ERDEV$ function returns the name of the device that generated an error. Call the function to let the program gain information that enables it to either rectify the problem or end without destroying data.

Syntax

ERDEV$

Usage

```
device$ = ERDEV$
```

Assigns to the variable *device$* the name of the device in which an error has occurred.

```
IF ERDEV$ = "LPT1    " THEN PRINT "Error produced by the printer"
```

Prints a message if the printer connected to the parallel port produces an error.

Description

The ERDEV$ function returns the name of the device that caused the error. It returns a 2-character string if a block device, such as a disk drive (A: or B:), produced the error. Otherwise, it returns an 8-character string that contains the name of a character device, such as a printer port or a serial port (for example, LPT1 or COM1). Occasionally, one of the devices listed in your CONFIG.SYS file causes an error; in that case, ERDEV$ returns the name of the device.

Warnings

QuickBASIC retains the information set by the last device error even after you call the ERDEV$ function. This lets you call ERDEV$ more than once for the same error. Be sure, however, that your program does not read an old value and respond to a non-existent error. If the error was caused by something other than a device, ERDEV$ continues to return the name of the device that last caused an error.

Example

ERDEV$ is most useful in programs that must interface with user-installed devices. See the example in the ON ERROR GOTO entry for an error-handling routine that uses ERDEV$ to help the user decide how to correct a recoverable error.

ERL

See also: ERDEV, ERDEV$, ERR, ERROR, ON ERROR GOTO, RESUME

■ QB2	■ QB4.5	■ PowerBASIC
■ QB3	✲ ANSI	■ GW-BASIC
■ QB4	■ BASIC7	■ MacQB

Purpose

The ERL function returns the line number of the statement that caused an error or the number of the preceding line that contains a line number. You use ERL primarily as a debugging aid to fix runtime errors that occur in your program.

Syntax

ERL

Usage

```
PRINT ERL
```

Displays the line number of the statement that caused an error.

```
errorLine& = ERL
```

Assigns to the variable *errorLine&* the line number at which the most recent error occurred.

Description

ERL is useful only if your program uses line numbers. It does not work with line labels, nor does it return the number of the source-code line containing an error. If the line that incurred the error does not contain a line number, ERL returns the number of a line before it that does contain a line number. The value ERL returns is a number from 0 through 65529, depending on the range of line numbers in your program. QuickBASIC treats any line numbers that are greater than 65529 as line labels, so ERL will not return a value greater than 65529. Because programs written specifically for QuickBASIC tend to use labels rather than line numbers, you might only use this function for programs that have been ported from GW-BASIC or BASICA.

Compatibility

ANSI BASIC

ANSI BASIC refers to errors as "exceptions." Therefore, the ANSI equivalent of the ERL function is the EXLINE function.

Example

Because the user of a program usually has no access to the source code, the ERL function is typically a debugging tool—used during program development and deleted from the finished application. The following debugging routine, intended for inclusion in the test version of a program, reports the type of error that occurred and the line number at which it occurred. (Note that this program returns an error line number of 100—the preceding line number nearest to the statement that causes the error.)

```
1 ON ERROR GOTO Debug

10        ' program code starts here

100

ERROR 73  ' test error handler by generating an error

9999 END

Debug:
     PRINT : PRINT : PRINT
     PRINT "A type"; STR$(ERR); " error has just occurred ";
     PRINT "in line"; STR$(ERL): BEEP: PRINT
     ERROR ERR
```

ERR

See also: ERDEV, ERDEV$, ERL, ERROR, ON ERROR GOTO, RESUME

■ QB2	■ QB4.5	■ PowerBASIC
■ QB3	✲ ANSI	■ GW-BASIC
■ QB4	■ BASIC7	■ MacQB

Purpose

The ERR function returns the code for the most recent error. You can use this code in an error-handling routine to help identify the problem and determine whether the program can recover from the error.

Syntax

ERR

Usage

```
PRINT ERR
```

Displays the QuickBASIC error code of the most recent error.

```
errCode% = ERR
```

Assigns the value of the most recent error to the integer variable *errCode%*.

```
ERROR ERR
```

Repeats the most recent error that occurred. (Used inside an error handler, this statement halts the program and prints the default message for the error.)

Description

The ERR function returns a value in the range 1 through 255; this number is the QuickBASIC error code of the most recent error. (See Appendix F, "Error Messages & Error Codes," for a complete list of QuickBASIC error codes and their meanings.) If no error has occurred, ERR returns 0.

QuickBASIC uses only the numbers 1 through 76 to specify various errors. Not all the numbers in this range are used, and each version of QuickBASIC adds new codes to accommodate new features of the language. If the error is not in a predefined category, QuickBASIC returns error code 21 and uses the message "Unprintable error" to report it.

If you simulate an error with the ERROR statement, ERR returns the code that corresponds to the simulated error. ERR can be called from anywhere in the program, even if the actual error occurred in another module. However, ERR cannot be called by any mixed-language procedures that are linked to the program.

Microsoft uses the same error codes in all BASIC dialects, including QuickBASIC for the Macintosh. This standardization helps make programs more portable and has, in fact, been adopted by other vendors of the language. PowerBASIC, for example, also uses the Microsoft error codes.

Compatibility

ANSI BASIC

ANSI BASIC refers to errors as "exceptions." Therefore, the ANSI equivalent of the ERR function is the EXTYPE function. The range of error codes is much wider in ANSI BASIC than in QuickBASIC, and it can vary with implementations of the language for different computer systems.

Example

You can use the ERR function to test an error to see whether it can be corrected by the user. The following error-handling routine identifies four recoverable errors and gives the user appropriate instructions.

```
DIM eMessage(0 TO 4) AS STRING

eMessage(0) = "027061068071"                    ' error code values
eMessage(1) = " Printer out of paper, please reload"
eMessage(2) = " Disk full, please insert a new disk"
eMessage(3) = " Device is off line, please switch it on"
eMessage(4) = " Drive not ready, please close drive door"

CLS
ON ERROR GOTO Trap
```

(continued)

continued

```
ERROR 61   ' simulate disk-full error to test whether routine works

Finish:
    COLOR 7, 0
END

Trap:
    xPos% = POS(0): yPos% = CSRLIN: COLOR 14, 4
    LOCATE 23, 1: PRINT SPACE$(160);
    errCode$ = RIGHT$("00" + LTRIM$(RTRIM$(STR$(ERR))), 3)
    recoverable% = INSTR(eMessage(0), errCode$)
    LOCATE 23, 6

    IF recoverable% THEN
        recoverable% = recoverable% \ 3 + 1
        PRINT LTRIM$(RTRIM$(ERDEV$));
        PRINT eMessage(recoverable%); " and try again.": BEEP
        PRINT "     Press a key when ready, Esc to abort. > ";
        LOCATE , , 1
        r$ = INPUT$(1)
        IF r$ = CHR$(27) THEN RESUME Finish   ' abort if user presses Esc
        COLOR 7, 0: LOCATE 23, 1: PRINT SPACE$(160);
        LOCATE yPos%, xPos%, 0: RESUME
    ELSE
        PRINT "A type"; STR$(ERR); " error has just occurred!"
        BEEP: PRINT "     "; : ERROR ERR
    END IF
```

ERROR

See also: ERDEV, ERDEV$, ERL, ERR, ON ERROR GOTO, RESUME

■ QB2	■ QB4.5	■ PowerBASIC
■ QB3	✲ ANSI	■ GW-BASIC
■ QB4	■ BASIC7	■ MacQB

Purpose

The ERROR statement simulates the occurrence of a specified error. ERROR is especially useful for debugging error-handling routines. Instead of waiting for a specific error to occur, you can simulate the error to see whether the handler responds to it properly. You can also use ERROR to define your own codes for errors not specified in QuickBASIC's predefined codes.

Syntax

ERROR *errorcode*

errorcode is the number of the error you want to simulate; it must be in the range 1 through 255.

Usage

```
ERROR 10
```

Generates a "Duplicate definition" error.

```
ERROR 251
```

Generates a user-specified error. (QuickBASIC does not define the error code 251.)

```
ERROR ERR
```

Repeats the last error that occurred. (If used inside an error handler, this statement halts the program and prints the default message for this error.)

Description

The ERROR statement causes the program to behave exactly as if a real error had occurred: If error trapping is enabled, the program branches to the line indicated by the last ON ERROR GOTO statement; otherwise, QuickBASIC halts execution and prints the error message that corresponds to the specified error code.

If the specified value corresponds to a number used by QuickBASIC and error trapping is not enabled, the program stops and generates the appropriate error message; otherwise, it stops and displays an "Unprintable error" error message. You can, however, replace this catchall message with one of your own by writing an error-handling routine that traps the error.

You can use the ERROR statement to define your own errors so that you can check your trapping of circumstances or exceptions that you want to prevent but that are not easily caused. To use this technique, be sure the error code you choose is one not already reserved by QuickBASIC. Then check for that error code in the error-handling routine.

Errors

If you specify in an ERROR statement a value that is greater than 255 or less than 1, QuickBASIC returns an "Illegal function call" error message.

Compatibility

ANSI BASIC

ANSI BASIC refers to errors as "exceptions." Therefore, the ANSI equivalent of the ERROR statement is the CAUSE EXCEPTION statement.

Example

Most programs impose constraints on the kinds of entries the user can make; for example, a program might refuse to accept inappropriate data even if the data is within the limits of the variable and would not normally cause an input error. The following game program responds to a player's mistakes by using ERROR to define and set a program-defined error.

```
RANDOMIZE TIMER
CLS
PRINT "The object of this game is to keep the man from falling off the"
PRINT "table. Use the left and right arrow keys to help him stay put."
PRINT "< Press any key to continue >"
DO WHILE INKEY$ = ""
LOOP

CLS : LOCATE 12, 25, 0: PRINT STRING$(30, CHR$(223))
x% = 40: counter% = 0: score% = 0: lives% = 5
leftArrow$ = CHR$(0) + CHR$(75)
rightArrow$ = CHR$(0) + CHR$(77)
escape$ = CHR$(27)
ON ERROR GOTO Trap
DO
    LOCATE 1, 38: PRINT USING "#####"; score%
    LOCATE 11, x%: PRINT " ";
    IF counter% > 20 THEN
        x% = x% + SGN(RND - .5) * (difficulty% / 200 + 1)
        score% = score% + 1
        difficulty% = difficulty% + 1     ' make task more difficult
        counter% = 0
    END IF
    keyStroke$ = INKEY$
    IF keyStroke$ = leftArrow$ THEN x% = x% - 1
    IF keyStroke$ = rightArrow$ THEN x% = x% + 1
    IF keyStroke$ = escape$ THEN EXIT DO
    LOCATE 11, x%: PRINT CHR$(2);
    IF x% < 25 THEN ERROR 251      ' error for falling off left side
    IF x% > 55 THEN ERROR 252      ' error for falling off right side
    counter% = counter% + 1
LOOP WHILE lives%
LOCATE 24, 35: PRINT "You lose";
END

Trap:
    LOCATE 11, x%: PRINT " "; : difficulty% = 0: x% = 40
    SELECT CASE ERR
    CASE 251      ' program-defined error for falling off of left side
        LOCATE 24, 25: PRINT "You fell off of the left side!";
        BEEP: LOCATE 24, 25: PRINT SPACE$(28);
```

(continued)

continued

```
        lives% = lives% - 1
        RESUME NEXT
    CASE 252     ' program-defined error for falling off of right side
        LOCATE 24, 25: PRINT "You fell off of the right side!";
        BEEP: LOCATE 24, 25: PRINT SPACE$(28);
        lives% = lives% - 1
        RESUME NEXT
    CASE ELSE
        LOCATE 24, 26: ERROR ERR
    END SELECT
```

ON ERROR GOTO

See also: ERDEV, ERDEV$, ERL, ERR, ERROR, RESUME

■ QB2	■ QB4.5	■ PowerBASIC
■ QB3	✲ ANSI	■ GW-BASIC
■ QB4	■ BASIC7	■ MacQB

Purpose

The ON ERROR GOTO statement enables error handling and specifies the location of the error handler. It lets your program trap runtime errors that usually halt execution so that your program executes an error handler that reports the error and helps the user recover from it.

Syntax

ON ERROR GOTO {*line* ¦ *label*}

line or *label* is the line number or label that indicates the first program line of the error handler.

Usage

```
ON ERROR GOTO Trap
```

Enables error trapping and specifies *Trap* as the label of the error-handling routine.

```
ON ERROR GOTO 0
```

Turns off error handling.

Description

Your program must execute an ON ERROR GOTO statement before the program can trap errors. You can use as many ON ERROR GOTO statements as you have routines to handle them. Whenever the program executes a new ON ERROR GOTO statement, it replaces the information from the previous ON ERROR GOTO statement with new information. The section of code that an ON ERROR GOTO statement specifies is called an error handler or an error-handling routine.

After the program executes an ON ERROR GOTO statement, the occurrence of any subsequent error causes the program to branch to the specified line number or label. The program then executes an error-handling routine until it encounters a RESUME statement, which either returns control to the interrupted task or branches to another part of the program.

If you specify line number 0 in an ON ERROR GOTO statement, ON ERROR GOTO turns off error handling. If the program is already in an error handler, the program halts and prints the appropriate error message.

Comments

A program that includes error trapping requires you to specify special switches when you compile it using BC.EXE, the command-line compiler. If your program uses an ON ERROR GOTO statement to set error trapping and a RESUME statement that specifies a line number or label to return from an error handler, compile the program using the /E switch. If your program uses a RESUME or RESUME NEXT statement, compile the program using both the /E and /X switches. (You do not need to use these switches with programs run in the QuickBASIC environment.)

Errors

If you specify, in an ON ERROR GOTO statement, a line number or label that does not exist in your program, QuickBASIC returns a "Label not defined" error message.

Compatibility

ANSI BASIC

ANSI BASIC refers to errors as "exceptions." It uses the statement WHEN EXCEPTION IN...USE...END WHEN to define an error-handling routine. ANSI executes the error-handling routine defined in the statements that follow the USE keyword only if the error occurs in the statements of the block of code delimited by WHEN EXCEPTION IN and END WHEN.

Example

Many runtime errors can be corrected without terminating the program if the program instructs the user how to fix the problem. The following program uses an ON ERROR GOTO statement so that control branches to an error-handling routine that recognizes two recoverable errors and lets the user correct the problems.

```
CONST FALSE = 0, TRUE = NOT FALSE

ON ERROR GOTO Trap    ' begin error trapping and specify error handler

CLS
ERROR 27   ' simulate printer-out-of-paper error to test whether routine works

Egress:
    COLOR 7, 0: LOCATE 20, 1, 1: RESET
END

Trap:
    device$ = ERDEV$  ' get name of device that caused the error
    recoverable% = FALSE
    COLOR 14, 4

    SELECT CASE ERR
    CASE 27
        message1$ = "PRINTER " + device$ + " IS OUT OF PAPER"
        message2$ = "Load paper and press any key."
        recoverable% = TRUE
    CASE 71
        message1$ = "DISK IN DRIVE " + device$ + "IS NOT READY"
        message2$ = "Check that drive door is closed and press any key."
        recoverable% = TRUE
    CASE ELSE
        message1$ = "A type" + STR$(ERR) + " error has just occurred."
    END SELECT

    IF NOT recoverable% THEN
        LOCATE 24, 1: PRINT SPACE$(80);
        message1$ = message1$ + ", aborting program. Press any key."
        LOCATE 24, 6: PRINT message1$; : BEEP
        r$ = INPUT$(1)
        RESUME Egress
    ELSE
        col% = POS(0): row% = CSRLIN
        LOCATE 23, 1: PRINT SPACE$(160);
        LOCATE 23, 40 - (LEN(message1$) \ 2): PRINT message1$;
        message2$ = message2$ + " Press Esc to quit program."
        LOCATE 24, 40 - (LEN(message2$) \ 2): PRINT message2$;
        r$ = INPUT$(1)
        IF r$ = CHR$(27) THEN RESUME Egress
        COLOR 7, 0: LOCATE 23, 1: PRINT SPACE$(160);
        LOCATE row%, col%
        RESUME
    END IF
```

ON UEVENT GOSUB

See also: ON COM GOSUB, ON KEY(n) GOSUB, ON PEN GOSUB, ON PLAY GOSUB, ON STRIG GOSUB, ON TIMER GOSUB, UEVENT ON/OFF/STOP

QB2	■ QB4.5	PowerBASIC
QB3	ANSI	GW-BASIC
QB4	■ BASIC7	MacQB

Purpose

The ON UEVENT GOSUB statement specifies the first line of the subroutine to which execution branches whenever a user-defined event occurs. You might, for example, control the movements of a robot arm by using the ON UEVENT GOTO statement to transfer control to a certain routine every time the arm moves beyond a certain point.

Syntax

ON UEVENT GOSUB {*line* ¦ *label*}

line or *label* indicates the first program line of the event-trapping subroutine.

Usage

```
ON UEVENT GOSUB 9000
```

Defines line 9000 as the first line of the subroutine that executes when a user-defined event occurs.

```
ON UEVENT GOSUB Handler
```

Defines the subroutine following the label *Handler* as the subroutine for a user-defined event.

Description

QuickBASIC 4.5 allows you to set and respond to a special global variable, or flag, that records the occurrence of a user event. A program cannot directly access this event flag; however, when event trapping is enabled, QuickBASIC checks the flag after each statement executes to see whether it has been set. If the event flag is set, QuickBASIC suspends the current task, and execution branches to the subroutine defined by the last ON UEVENT GOSUB statement. The program executes the subroutine until it encounters a RETURN statement, at which point control returns to the statement following the one that was executed before the event occurred. Returning from the subroutine always clears the event flag so that it is ready for the next event.

You determine the specific event that triggers execution of the subroutine; however, the event must set the event flag in order to be recognized. To set the flag, call the built-in QuickBASIC procedure *SetUEvent* by entering the following statement:

```
CALL SetUEvent
```

As with other procedures, you can omit the CALL keyword if you have previously defined the procedure with a DECLARE statement:

```
DECLARE SUB SetUEvent ()
SetUEvent
```

Notice that *SetUEvent* takes no parameters; it merely sets the event flag. Be aware that this procedure is available only if you started the QuickBASIC environment with the /L switch, which loads the Quick library QB.QLB. Although *SetUEvent* is part of QuickBASIC, you must use the /L switch to make it available to your program.

If you use the command-line compiler, BC.EXE, to compile a program that calls *SetUEvent*, you must use either the /V or the /W switch. These switches enable trapping and force the program to check the event flag, either between statements (/V) or between program lines (/W).

Although it can be called from QuickBASIC, *SetUEvent* is intended for use by a mixed-language procedure that is either linked to your executable file or stored in a Quick library. The mixed-language procedure is usually an interrupt handler that redirects one of the interrupt vectors to point to itself. See the tutorial in Chapter 20, "Mixed Language," for a description of mixed-language programming. Then, when the specified interrupt occurs, the handler calls *SetUEvent*, which sets the event flag so that QuickBASIC can respond to it after the current statement (or line) has been executed.

Typically, the interrupt being handled is generated by a hardware device as a signal that an event that requires the program's attention has occurred. Because interrupt processing is a background task that continues while your program executes other statements, QuickBASIC does not have to poll the device to see whether the event has occurred. When the event occurs, QuickBASIC is informed.

Although ON UEVENT GOSUB defines the subroutine that is executed when the event flag is set, you must enable trapping before QuickBASIC can respond to the event and execute the subroutine. (See the UEVENT ON/OFF/STOP entry for details.)

Tips

During program development, call *SetUEvent* from QuickBASIC to test whether an event-trapping subroutine works properly; doing this prevents you from having to install the interrupt handler. This is one of the few uses of *SetUEvent* in a QuickBASIC program.

Warnings

If you use your own interrupt-handling routine, remember to disable it and restore the original interrupt vectors before your program ends. If you don't, the next time the interrupt occurs the program will try to execute a routine that no longer exists.

Example

Although ON UEVENT GOSUB is intended primarily for use with specially written hardware device drivers, you can use it with any device that generates its own interrupts, such as the keyboard. The following program installs a replacement keyboard interrupt handler contained in the assembly-language source file USERVENT.ASM and then reports to the user whenever the user presses a specific "hotkey." (You could, of course, substitute ON KEY(*n*) GOSUB, QuickBASIC's built-in keyboard event-trapping statement, for this routine.)

To create the stand-alone executable version of the program, use the following commands:

```
BC /O/V ONUEVENT;
LINK ONUEVENT USERVENT;
```

To use the program in the environment, first build a Quick library and then start QuickBASIC by using the following commands:

```
LINK /QU USERVENT,,,BQLB45.LIB;
QB ONUEVENT.BAS /L USERVENT.QLB
```

```
' specify the location of the interrupt handler
DECLARE SUB IntEnable (BYVAL switch AS INTEGER)

' give instructions to the user
CLS
LOCATE 24, 1: COLOR 15, 1: PRINT SPACE$(80);
LOCATE 24, 9: PRINT "Hotkey is Alt-F10, press Esc to quit.";
LOCATE 10, 1: COLOR , 0

ON UEVENT GOSUB Report              ' define event handler
UEVENT ON                           ' enable event trapping
IntEnable 1                         ' enable interrupt handler

DO                                  ' do-nothing loop
LOOP UNTIL INKEY$ = CHR$(27)
UEVENT OFF                          ' disable event trapping
IntEnable 0                         ' disable interrupt handler
END

' event-handling routine
Report:
    PRINT "YOU PRESSED THE HOTKEY!"   ' Alt-F10 was pressed
    PRINT
    RETURN
```

The program listing below is the assembly-language source code for the interrupt handler. Create an object file by using the following command to assemble the program with MASM 5.x:

```
MASM /V/W2/Z USERVENT;
```

Then either place the object file in a Quick library or link it directly to the executable program. Do not convert the object file into data statements and load them into a QuickBASIC variable because the routine redirects the BIOS keyboard interrupt to point to itself. If QuickBASIC moves the variable while the handler is active, the system crashes. This interrupt handler monitors INT 9H, the keyboard interrupt, checking whether the user pressed Alt-F10. When Alt-F10 is pressed, the interrupt handler calls *SetUEvent* to enable the QuickBASIC event-trapping function.

```
        public NewKey, IntEnable
        extrn SetUEvent: far

; hotkey definition data, change to suit your own preference
scanCode    equ     68                      ; scan code for F10
keyMask     equ     8                       ; bit mask for Alt

            .model   medium
            .code

; local data stored in the code segment
enabled     db     0                        ; handler-enabled flag
oldKey      dd     ?                        ; address of previous keyboard handler

; replacement for keyboard interrupt handler at INT 9 (Hex)
NewKey      proc  far
            push  es                        ; save working registers
            push ax
            in     al,60h                   ; read scan code
            pushf                           ; adjust stack
            cli                             ; disable interrupts
            call  cs:oldKey                 ; call previous handler
            sti                             ; enable interrupts
            cmp   al,scanCode               ; check whether user pressed F10
            jne   KeyEnd                    ; ignore keys other than F10
            mov   ax,40h                    ; move to BIOS data area
            mov   es, ax
            mov   al,es:[17h]               ; get shift-key status
            test  al,keyMask                ; check whether the Alt key is down
            jz    KeyEnd                    ; ignore keys other than Alt
            call  SetUEvent                 ; set event flag
```

(continued)

continued

```
KeyEnd:
        pop   ax                       ; restore the stack
        pop es
        iret
NewKey endp

; install or disable replacement keyboard interrupt handler
; if argument equals 1, enable; if argument equals 0, disable
IntEnable   proc  far
        push  bp                       ; save base pointer
        mov   bp,sp                    ; establish stack frame
        push  ds                       ; save working registers
        push es
        push si
        mov   ax,[bp+6]                ; get argument to IntEnable
        push  cs                       ; point DS to
        pop   ds                       ; local code
        cmp   ax,1                     ; check whether argument equals 1
        jne   DisAble                  ; disable handler if argument equals 0
        cmp   enabled,1                ; check whether handler already enabled
        je     Egress                  ; don't enable handler
        mov   ax,3509h                 ; DOS Service 53
        int   21h                      ; -- get interrupt vector
        mov   word ptr oldKey[0],bx    ; save offset
        mov   word ptr oldKey[2],es    ; save segment
        mov   dx,offset NewKey         ; offset of new handler
        mov   ax,2509h                 ; DOS Service 37
        int   21h                      ; -- set interrupt vector
        mov   enabled,1                ; set enabled flag
        jmp   short Egress             ; complete process
disable:
        cmp   enabled,1                ; check whether handler enabled
        jne   Egress                   ; don't enable again
        lds   dx,oldKey                ; get old vector
        mov   ax,2509h                 ; DOS Service 37
        int   21h                      ; -- set interrupt vector
        mov   cs:enabled,0             ; reset enabled flag
Egress:
        pop   si                       ; restore the stack
        pop es
        pop ds
        pop bp
        ret   2                        ; return to QuickBASIC
IntEnable endp

        end
```

RESUME

See also: ON ERROR GOTO

■ QB2	■ QB4.5	■ PowerBASIC
■ QB3	✲ ANSI	■ GW-BASIC
■ QB4	■ BASIC7	■ MacQB

Purpose

The RESUME statement redirects program execution from an error-trapping handler. If a runtime error is recoverable, the error-handling routine that traps it must let program execution continue after the error has been corrected.

Syntax

RESUME [*line* ¦ *label*]
RESUME NEXT

line or *label* is the line number or label that indicates the line at which execution continues.

Usage

```
RESUME
```

Retries the statement that caused an error.

```
RESUME NEXT
```

Skips the statement that caused an error and resumes execution with the next statement.

```
RESUME Egress
```

Resumes execution, after an error, with the statement following the label *Egress.*

Description

The RESUME statement transfers control back to the statement that caused the error, allowing the program to try to proceed. RESUME NEXT skips the statement that caused the error and continues the program at the next statement. The RESUME statement with a line number or label specified branches execution to the specified line.

You can use a RESUME statement only in an error-handling routine that has already been enabled by an ON ERROR GOTO statement. When a runtime error triggers a branch to the handling routine, QuickBASIC disables the trapping of subsequent errors so that new errors do not cause the handler to be entered recursively. RESUME enables error trapping again so that the error handler specified in the previous ON ERROR GOTO statement will be used in the event of an error.

All error-handling routines must contain at least one RESUME statement to direct control back to the main program. You cannot end the program inside the handler.

RESUME is useful when the error that occurred is recoverable—for example, when the program tries to read from a floppy-disk drive when the drive door is open. If your error handler is sophisticated enough to recognize this error, it can first instruct the user to close the drive door and then execute a RESUME statement to try the operation again.

If the operation cannot be tried again but the error was not sufficiently serious to warrant terminating the program, your handler can execute a RESUME NEXT statement to ignore the line containing the error and continue processing with the statement that follows.

Avoid using RESUME statements that specify a line number or label. The code at the target line must be capable of handling returns from errors throughout the program. Specifying a line has two main uses: It handles returns from special-purpose error traps built around a particularly vulnerable section of code, and it directs control to a routine that safely terminates the program when all else fails. The target line must be in the same module and at the same level as the error-handling routine. You cannot use RESUME to branch to another module or into a subprogram or function.

Errors

If an error-handling routine does not include a RESUME statement, QuickBASIC returns a "No RESUME" error message. If you use RESUME with a line number or label that does not exist, QuickBASIC returns a "Label not defined" error message.

Compatibility

ANSI BASIC

ANSI BASIC does not use RESUME to exit an error handler. Instead, it uses either RETRY (to retry the operation that caused the error) or CONTINUE (to ignore the error and continue processing).

Example

A program can run under several types of computer configurations by first determining the host system's capabilities at runtime and then modifying its behavior accordingly. The simplest way to do this is to use a hardware-specific feature and see whether an error occurs. The following routine uses this technique to see whether the system supports a 43-line display. If the system supports only 25 lines, the program uses a RESUME NEXT statement to continue the program.

```
screenLines% = 43           ' assume 43-line display
ON ERROR GOTO VideoTrap     ' enable error trapping
WIDTH , 43                  ' try to set 43 lines
ON ERROR GOTO 0             ' turn off error trapping
```

(continued)

continued

```
Egress:
    IF screenLines% = 43 THEN WIDTH , 25    ' reset standard screen
END

VideoTrap:
    screenLines% = 25       ' change to 25 lines
    IF ERR = 5 THEN         ' check whether error was illegal function call
       RESUME NEXT          ' continue execution
    ELSE                    ' terminate program if it was any other error
       RESUME Egress
    END IF
```

UEVENT ON/OFF/STOP

See also: ON UEVENT GOSUB

QB2	■ QB4.5	PowerBASIC
QB3	ANSI	GW-BASIC
QB4	■ BASIC7	MacQB

Purpose

The three UEVENT statements enable, disable, and suspend event trapping in programs. Use them with ON UEVENT GOSUB to trap user-defined events.

Syntax

UEVENT ON
UEVENT OFF
UEVENT STOP

Usage

`UEVENT ON`

Enables user-defined event trapping.

`UEVENT OFF`

Disables user-defined event trapping.

`UEVENT STOP`

Suspends user-defined event trapping.

Description

A user event is a signal. It is usually produced by a mixed-language procedure that is an interrupt handler. The interrupt handler sets a flag in QuickBASIC whenever a particular hardware device requires attention. If event trapping is enabled, QuickBASIC checks this flag after each statement is executed; if the flag is set, execution branches to a subroutine designed to handle the situation.

UEVENT ON enables the trapping of user-generated events. Before you use this statement, you must define the subroutine that will be executed when the event occurs. The ON UEVENT GOSUB statement specifies the location of this routine.

UEVENT OFF disables UEVENT trapping. After your program executes this statement, subsequent events are ignored because QuickBASIC stops checking the event flag between statements.

UEVENT STOP suspends event trapping. QuickBASIC continues to check the event flag after every statement, but execution does not branch to the handler routine if the flag is set. However, if the flag has been set and trapping is reinstated by another UEVENT ON statement, execution immediately branches to the handling routine.

QuickBASIC executes an implicit UEVENT STOP whenever it enters an event-handling subroutine. This ensures that another occurrence of the event does not cause the handler to be entered recursively. When the program encounters a RETURN statement and returns to the main program, the program reinstates event trapping and clears the event flag so that it is ready for the next event.

Warnings

If your program uses its own interrupt handler, you cannot merely disable event trapping (with UEVENT OFF) when the program ends. You must also disable the interrupt handler itself and then restore the original interrupt vectors that it replaced. If you do not do this, the next time the interrupt occurs the program will try to execute a routine that no longer exists.

Example

See the ON UEVENT GOSUB entry for an extended example of user-defined event trapping. The example includes the source code for an interrupt handler that you can link to a QuickBASIC program.

CHAPTER 10

Time (Timing, Date, and Time)

Introduction

QuickBASIC offers several statements and functions that work with the date and time. These statements and functions enable your programs to provide users with information about when or for how long a certain event took place. The most basic of these tasks include displaying the date and time. Other QuickBASIC features let your program time an activity or perform tasks at regular intervals.

In most computers time is clocked by a microchip. On the IBM PC, the timer chip (the Intel 8253-5) interrupts the computer 18.2 times per second. Each interruption is called a clock tick. During each interruption, the ROM BIOS of the computer notes that one more tick has occurred. When you ask for the time, DOS calculates the time by counting the number of ticks that have passed since midnight.

This tutorial summarizes QuickBASIC's timing capabilities and offers some suggestions for their use. Table 10-1 lists QuickBASIC's timing statements and functions alphabetically.

Statement or function	**Description**
DATE$ (Statement and function)	Sets or returns the current date
ON TIMER GOSUB	Specifies the location of a timer event-handling routine and the number of seconds between executions of the routine
SLEEP	Pauses the program
TIME$ (Statement and function)	Sets or returns the current time
TIMER	Returns the number of seconds since midnight
TIMER ON/OFF/STOP	Enables, disables, or temporarily suspends the timer event trap specified by the ON TIMER statement

Table 10-1.
QuickBASIC timing statements and functions.

Setting and Getting the Current Date

When you start your computer, DOS might ask you to specify the date and time; however, most computers now include clocks that don't stop when you turn off your computer. These clocks maintain the current date and time. DOS uses the date and time to time stamp your files on disk. You see this time stamp whenever you use the DIR command to produce a directory listing of your files. You can use the DATE$ statement in QuickBASIC to change the date that DOS uses. Be careful when you use the DATE$ statement because any files you create or update will have an incorrect time stamp if you change the date.

To access the current date in QuickBASIC, use DATE$ as a function. DATE$ returns the current date; however, if you've used the DATE$ statement to change the date, the DATE$ function returns the new date.

Setting and Getting the Current Time

In addition to the date, DOS includes the current time on the time stamp of a file when the file is created or updated. The TIME$ statement lets you change the time that DOS uses. When you use TIME$, DOS keeps track of time beginning at the moment you specify. If you change the time with the TIME$ statement, any files you create or update will be stamped with a time that depends on the time you specified.

To access the current time, use TIME$ as a function. TIME$ returns the current time; however, if you've used the TIME$ statement to change the time, the TIME$ function returns the new time. Computers aren't perfect timekeepers, and their internal clocks are likely to be slightly inaccurate. Because the IBM PC timer ticks 18.2 times a second, the time of day is accurate to approximately 54/1000 of a second.

If you need to time the length of a specific operation, you can use the QuickBASIC TIMER function. The TIMER function returns the number of seconds past midnight. To use it, call TIMER, perform the operation, and then call TIMER again. The difference between the two results is the number of seconds the operation took to complete.

A program that uses TIMER has a potential problem if a user runs it late at night. Because the TIMER function returns the number of seconds that have elapsed since midnight, TIMER returns the value 0 at midnight. Therefore, if a program is running at 11:59 P.M. and stops at 12:01 A.M., you must adjust the results, as shown in the following program segment:

```
startTime& = TIMER
⋮
endTime& = TIMER

IF endTime& < startTime& THEN          ' check was executing at midnight
    endTime& = endTime& + 86400        ' adjust time
END IF

PRINT endTime& - startTime&; "seconds elapsed"
```

Pausing the Program

If you want to give the user a chance to read a screen or perform a task, use QuickBASIC's SLEEP statement. SLEEP pauses the program for the length of time you specify. However, users who finish reading the screen or complete their task before the specified time can simply press a key to interrupt the SLEEP statement.

Setting Up and Managing the Timer Event Trap

QuickBASIC also provides a set of statements that set a timer event trap. This event trap lets the program branch to a subroutine that executes every time a specified number of seconds has passed. You might use a timer event trap to update the time on the screen every minute or to save the user's file on disk periodically.

QuickBASIC's event-trapping statements for the timer are ON TIMER GOSUB, TIMER ON, TIMER OFF, and TIMER STOP. You must initialize all timer event trapping with the ON TIMER GOSUB statement and then enable trapping using TIMER ON. Forgetting to enable trapping is a common mistake.

The following lines initialize an event trap and enable the program to execute the subroutine at the label *ShowClock* every 60 seconds:

```
ON TIMER(60) GOSUB ShowClock     ' initialize event trap
TIMER ON                         ' enable it
```

Because event trapping slows your program considerably, you might want to turn off event trapping during critical operations in your program, such as serial I/O communications. You turn off timer event trapping with the TIMER OFF statement. While timer event trapping is disabled, your program executes as though the timer event trap didn't exist. You can also turn off the timer event trap with the TIMER STOP statement. When you use the TIMER STOP statement, the program notes whether the specified number of seconds passes, but it doesn't immediately execute the event trap. However, when you execute another TIMER ON statement, the program executes the subroutine.

Related Reading

Norton, Peter, and Richard Wilton. *The* New *Peter Norton Programmer's Guide to the IBM PC & PS/2.* Redmond, Wash.: Microsoft Press, 1988.

Prata, Stephen, with Harry Henderson. *The Waite Group's Microsoft QuickBASIC Primer Plus.* Redmond, Wash.: Microsoft Press, 1990.

DATE$ (Statement and function)

■ QB2	■ QB4.5	■ PowerBASIC
■ QB3	✲ ANSI	■ GW-BASIC
■ QB4	■ BASIC7	■ MacQB

See also: TIME$ (Statement and function)

Purpose

The DATE$ statement sets the date kept by the computer to a new date. The DATE$ function returns the current date kept by the computer. You can use DATE$ to print a specified date on report headings.

Syntax

Statement:

DATE$ = *expr*

Function:

DATE$

expr is a string expression that must be in one of the following forms: *mm-dd-yy*, *mm-dd-yyyy*, *mm/dd/yy*, or *mm/dd/yyyy*. *mm* represents the month number, *dd* the day number, *yy* the year within the twentieth century, and *yyyy* the year including the century. Note that QuickBASIC doesn't require a leading zero in front of single-digit month or day values.

Usage

```
PRINT "Today is "; DATE$
```

Displays the current date.

```
todaysDate$ = DATE$
```

Assigns the current date to the string variable *todaysDate$*.

```
DATE$ = "01-21-1992"
```

Sets the date to January 21, 1992.

```
DATE$ = todaysDate$
```

Sets the date to the date contained in the variable *todaysDate$*.

Description

You can use DATE$ as both a statement and a function. When you use it as a statement, QuickBASIC changes the date; when you use it as a function, QuickBASIC returns the current date.

DATE$ as a Statement

Use the DATE$ statement to set the system's date, the date used by both QuickBASIC and DOS. The DATE$ statement requires a syntax different from that of most QuickBASIC statements. You must use DATE$ in an assignment statement whose left side is the DATE$ keyword and whose right side is a string that specifies the new date.

DATE$ as a Function

Use the DATE$ function to retrieve the current date. The DATE$ function returns the date in the form *mm-dd-yyyy*: two digits for the month (1 through 12), a dash, two digits for the day (1 through 31), a dash, and four digits for the year. Notice that any single-digit number includes a leading zero.

Errors

If you use an invalid date (such as "June 31" or "1979") with the DATE$ statement, QuickBASIC returns an "Illegal function call" error message. If you use an expression other than a string expression in the DATE$ statement, QuickBASIC returns a "Type mismatch" error message.

Warnings

You cannot set or retrieve a date that is earlier than January 1, 1980, or later than December 31, 2099.

Compatibility

ANSI BASIC

ANSI BASIC supports only the DATE$ function. You cannot use DATE$ as a statement to set the current date. The DATE$ function in ANSI BASIC returns the date in the form *yyyymmdd*, so that the year is followed by the month and then the day.

Example

The following program uses DATE$ to change the date to the user's birthday and then display the date.

```
DEFINT A-Z

DIM months(12) AS STRING, numMonth AS INTEGER
DIM day AS INTEGER, year AS INTEGER, suffix AS STRING

FOR i% = 1 TO 12                    ' get month names from DATA statements
    READ months(i%)
NEXT

INPUT "What is your birthday <day-month>"; birthday$
oldDate$ = DATE$                    ' save the current date
DATE$ = birthday$ + "-1990"         ' change the date
```

(continued)

continued

```
numMonth = VAL(LEFT$(DATE$, 2))   ' get month from mm-dd-yyyy
day = VAL(MID$(DATE$, 4, 2))      ' get day from mm-dd-yyyy
year = VAL(RIGHT$(DATE$, 4))      ' get year from mm-dd-yyyy

SELECT CASE day
    CASE 1, 21, 31                ' ordinals that end in "st"
        suffix = "st"

    CASE 2, 22                    ' ordinals that end in "nd"
        suffix = "nd"

    CASE 3, 23                    ' ordinals that end in "rd"
        suffix = "rd"

    CASE ELSE                     ' ordinals that end in "th"
        suffix = "th"
END SELECT

PRINT USING "Your birthday is & ##&, ####"; months(numMonth); day; suffix; year
DATE$ = oldDate$                  ' reset the date to the current date

DATA "January", "February", "March", "April", "May", "June", "July"
DATA "August", "September", "October", "November", "December"
```

ON TIMER GOSUB

See also: TIMER ON/OFF/STOP

■ QB2	■ QB4.5	■ PowerBASIC
■ QB3	ANSI	■ GW-BASIC
■ QB4	■ BASIC7	■ MacQB

Purpose

QuickBASIC's ON TIMER GOSUB statement specifies the subprogram that a program branches to every time a specified number of seconds has passed. You can use the ON TIMER GOSUB statement to specify the subroutine that displays and updates the time at regular intervals.

Syntax

ON TIMER(*time*) GOSUB {*line* | *label*}

time is an integer in the range 1 through 86400 that specifies the number of seconds that must pass before control branches to a subroutine.

line or *label* is the line number or label that specifies the first line of a subroutine.

Usage

```
ON TIMER(60) GOSUB UpdateClock TIMER ON
```

Specifies that the subroutine starting at label *UpdateClock* will be executed every 60 seconds.

Description

The ON TIMER GOSUB statement specifies the location of a timer event-handling routine and the number of seconds between executions of the routine. An event-handling routine is a subroutine that is executed when a specified event occurs. The ON TIMER GOSUB statement specifies the details of a timer event trap, which executes a subroutine after the number of seconds specified in the ON TIMER GOSUB statement. Note that you cannot specify a subroutine that is contained in another subprogram.

When the timer event-handling subroutine begins executing, QuickBASIC implicitly executes a TIMER STOP statement so that the event-handling subroutine is not entered recursively. However, because QuickBASIC uses TIMER STOP, if another timer event occurs while the subroutine executes, QuickBASIC keeps track of the event and executes the subroutine at the next TIMER ON statement. When the subroutine encounters a RETURN statement, QuickBASIC executes a TIMER ON statement unless the subroutine executed a TIMER OFF statement.

The event-trapping subroutine can end with a RETURN statement that specifies a line number or label. The statement causes execution to branch to a specified line in your program. This version of the RETURN statement can cause serious problems because the event trap can occur at any point in your program. Also, the RETURN statement that specifies a line or label cannot return control to a subprogram or function. (See the GOSUB...RETURN entry in Chapter 4, "Procedures," for details.)

Errors

If you specify in an ON TIMER GOSUB statement a line number or label that does not exist or that is either in a different module or in a procedure, QuickBASIC returns a "Label not defined" error message. If you specify more than 86400 seconds (the number of seconds in 24 hours) or less than 1 second, QuickBASIC returns an "Illegal function call" error message. If you specify a non-numeric expression as the number of seconds, QuickBASIC returns a "Type mismatch" error message.

Tips

Using event trapping increases the size of your executable programs and slows them considerably. Try to avoid using event trapping in routines in which speed is a critical factor.

Example

The following program uses the ON TIMER GOSUB statement to specify the location of the subroutine that updates a time display every 60 seconds.

```
CLS
GOSUB UpdateClock                  ' display the initial time

ON TIMER(60) GOSUB UpdateClock     ' specify location and timing of event trap
TIMER ON                           ' enable timer event trapping

LOCATE 5, 1: PRINT "Press any key to quit"
DO UNTIL INKEY$ <> ""              ' loop until user presses a key
LOOP
END

UpdateClock:
    LOCATE 1, 1
    PRINT DATE$, LEFT$(TIME$, 5)  ' display the hours and minutes
    RETURN
```

SLEEP

See also: ON COM GOSUB, ON KEY(n) GOSUB, ON PEN GOSUB, ON PLAY GOSUB, ON STRIG GOSUB, ON TIMER GOSUB, ON UEVENT GOSUB, TIMER

QB2	■ QB4.5	PowerBASIC
QB3	ANSI	GW-BASIC
QB4	■ BASIC7	MacQB

Purpose

The SLEEP statement pauses the program until a specified number of seconds has passed, a key is pressed, or an event occurs. You can use the SLEEP statement to pause a program so that the user has time to read an output screen.

Syntax

SLEEP [*time*]

time is an integer expression that specifies the number of seconds the program will pause.

Usage

```
SLEEP
```

Pauses the program until the user presses a key or an event occurs.

```
SLEEP 5
```

Pauses the program for 5 seconds or until the user presses a key or an event occurs.

Description

The SLEEP statement lets you insert pauses in a program. SLEEP suspends execution until one of the following occurs:

- The specified number of seconds pass
- The user presses a key
- QuickBASIC encounters a trapped event. (See ON COM GOSUB, ON KEY(n) GOSUB, ON PEN GOSUB, ON PLAY GOSUB, ON STRIG GOSUB, ON TIMER GOSUB, or ON UEVENT GOSUB)

The number of seconds specified must be an integer expression; if it is less than 1 (or not specified), the program pauses until either the second or third condition occurs.

The SLEEP statement responds only to keystrokes and events that occur *after* the SLEEP statement executes. Therefore, all keystrokes in the keyboard buffer are ignored.

Trapped events can interrupt the SLEEP statement only if they have been enabled by the appropriate ON statement and have not been turned off or suspended by the corresponding OFF or STOP statement.

Comments

The specified number of seconds is an integer expression, and therefore its accuracy is limited to whole seconds. If you need to pause for increments of less than a second, use the TIMER function in a loop statement.

Errors

If you specify a non-numeric expression in a SLEEP statement, QuickBASIC returns a "Type mismatch" error message.

Warnings

You can press any key to interrupt a SLEEP statement, including the Shift, Ctrl, Alt, Caps Lock, Num Lock, and Scroll Lock keys. Therefore, the user cannot press the Shift-PrtSc key combination to produce a screen dump during a pause created by the SLEEP statement.

Example

The following program uses the SLEEP statement to pause the display so that the user has time to read the screen.

```
CLS
PRINT "You have"; FRE(-1); "bytes of free space for arrays."
PRINT "You have"; FRE(-2); "bytes of free stack space."

PRINT
PRINT "Copy this information and then press any key to continue."
PRINT
PRINT "This screen will self-destruct in 10 seconds..."
SLEEP 10
CLS
```

TIME$ (Statement and function)

■ QB2	■ QB4.5	■ PowerBASIC
■ QB3	✲ ANSI	■ GW-BASIC
■ QB4	■ BASIC7	■ MacQB

See also: DATE$ (Statement and function), TIMER ON/OFF/STOP

Purpose

The TIME$ statement sets the time kept by the computer to a new time. The TIME$ function returns the current time kept by the computer. For example, you can use TIME$ to print a specific time on report headings.

Syntax

Statement:

TIME$ = *expr*

Function:

TIME$

expr is a string expression that must appear in one of the following forms:

hh	Sets the hour; minutes and seconds default to 0
hh:mm	Sets the hour and minutes; seconds default to 0
hh:mm:ss	Sets the hour, minutes, and seconds

hh represents the hour (0 through 23), *mm* the minutes (0 through 59), and *ss* the seconds (0 through 59). Note that QuickBASIC doesn't require leading zeros in front of single-digit hour, minute, or second values.

Usage

```
PRINT "It is now "; TIME$
```

Displays the current time.

```
now$ = TIME$
```

Assigns the current time to the string variable *now$*.

```
TIME$ = "10:35:30"
```

Sets the time to 35½ minutes after 10 A.M.

```
TIME$ = "10"
```

Sets the time to 10 A.M.

```
TIME$ = now$
```

Sets the time to that contained in the variable *now$*.

Description

You can use TIME$ as both a statement and a function. When you use it as a statement, QuickBASIC sets the current time; when you use it as a function, QuickBASIC returns the current time.

TIME$ as a Statement

Use the TIME$ statement to set the current time of the system's internal clock; the clock will begin counting at the time you specify. The TIME$ statement requires a syntax different from those of most QuickBASIC statements. You must use TIME$ in an assignment statement whose left side is the TIME$ keyword and whose right side is a string that specifies the new time.

TIME$ as a Function

Use the TIME$ function to retrieve the current time. The TIME$ function returns the current time in the form *hh:mm:ss*: two digits for the hour (0 through 23), a colon, two digits for the minutes (0 through 59), a colon, and two digits for the seconds (0 through 59). Notice that single-digit numbers include leading zeros.

Errors

If you use an invalid time (such as "26:65:00") with the TIME$ statement, QuickBASIC returns an "Illegal function call" error message. If you use an expression other than a string expression in the TIME$ statement, QuickBASIC returns a "Type mismatch" error message.

Compatibility

ANSI BASIC

ANSI BASIC supports only the TIME$ function. You cannot use TIME$ as a statement to set the current time. The TIME$ function in ANSI BASIC returns the time in the form *hh:mm:ss*, exactly as it does in QuickBASIC.

Example

The following program uses TIME$ to change the system time to 3:30 A.M. and then display the time.

```
DEFINT A-Z

DIM hour AS INTEGER, minute AS INTEGER, suffix AS STRING

oldTime$ = TIME$                    ' save the current system time
TIME$ = "3:30"                      ' set the time to 3:30 A.M.

hour = VAL(LEFT$(TIME$, 2))         ' get the hour from hh:mm:ss
minute = VAL(MID$(TIME$, 4, 2))     ' get the minute from hh:mm:ss
```

(continued)

continued

```
IF hour = 0 THEN                    ' show midnight as 12 A.M.
    hour = 12
    suffix = "A.M."
ELSEIF hour < 12 THEN
    suffix = "A.M."
ELSE
    hour = hour - 12
    suffix = "P.M."
END IF

PRINT USING "The time is now ##:## &"; hour; minute; suffix

TIME$ = oldTime$                    ' reset time
END
```

TIMER

See also: ON TIMER GOSUB, TIMER ON/OFF/STOP

■ QB2	■ QB4.5	■ PowerBASIC
■ QB3	✲ ANSI	■ GW-BASIC
■ QB4	■ BASIC7	■ MacQB

Purpose

The TIMER function returns the number of seconds that have elapsed since midnight. Use the TIMER function to time the length of specific operations.

Syntax

TIMER

Usage

`startTime& = TIMER`

Assigns the current number of seconds past midnight to the long integer named *startTime&*.

Description

The TIMER function returns values in the range 1 to 86400. Sometimes you need to know how much time certain operations require. The TIMER function provides an easy way to time operations: Merely subtract the TIMER value at the beginning of the operation from the TIMER value at the end; the result is the duration (in seconds) of the operation.

Comments

Because the value TIMER returns is always changing, programmers often use this function as the argument in the RANDOMIZE statement. (See the RANDOMIZE entry in Chapter 7, "Math," for details.)

Warnings

Because the TIMER function returns the number of seconds that have elapsed since midnight, the timer returns the value 0 at midnight. Therefore, if a program that uses TIMER will be run at midnight, be sure to adjust the results properly.

Compatibility

ANSI BASIC

ANSI BASIC provides the TIME function, which performs the same task as the TIMER function does in QuickBASIC.

Example

The following program uses the TIMER function to calculate the time it takes to generate and display 2000 random numbers. The TIMER function is also used in the RANDOMIZE statement to reseed the random-number generator.

```
CLS
startTime& = TIMER

FOR i% = 1 TO 2000
    RANDOMIZE TIMER
    PRINT RND * 1000,
NEXT

endTime& = TIMER
PRINT
PRINT endTime& - startTime&; "seconds elapsed"
```

TIMER ON/OFF/STOP

See also: ON TIMER GOSUB

■ QB2	■ QB4.5	■ PowerBASIC
■ QB3	ANSI	■ GW-BASIC
■ QB4	■ BASIC7	■ MacQB

Purpose

The TIMER statements enable, disable, or suspend timer event trapping. Use a TIMER ON statement, for example, to enable event trapping that updates a clock displayed on the screen.

Syntax

TIMER ON
TIMER OFF
TIMER STOP

Usage

```
ON TIMER(60) GOSUB EveryMinute
TIMER ON
```

Turns on event trapping so that the program executes the subroutine beginning at the label *EveryMinute* every 60 seconds.

```
TIMER OFF
```

Disables event trapping.

Description

After you call the ON TIMER GOSUB statement to specify the details of a timer event trap, you must enable the event trapping by using the TIMER ON statement. Then, after every statement, QuickBASIC checks to see whether the time specified in the ON TIMER statement has elapsed. If it has, QuickBASIC executes the routine specified in the ON TIMER GOSUB statement. (See the ON TIMER GOSUB entry in this chapter for details.)

The TIMER OFF statement disables timer event trapping. No event trapping occurs until the program executes another TIMER ON statement.

The TIMER STOP statement suspends timer event trapping. No event trapping occurs until the program executes another TIMER ON statement. However, if an event occurs after the TIMER STOP statement, the program sets a flag so that it "remembers" the event. When the program encounters another TIMER ON statement, the event is trapped.

QuickBASIC executes an implicit TIMER STOP whenever it enters a timer event-handling routine. This ensures that another occurrence of the event does not cause the handler to be entered recursively. When the program encounters a RETURN statement and returns to the main program, it reinstates the timer event trap by executing a TIMER ON statement.

If you use the command-line compiler, BC.EXE, to compile a program that uses timer event trapping, you must use either the /V or the /W switch. These switches enable trapping and force the program to check the time, either between statements (/V) or between program lines (/W).

Tips

Event-trapping statements increase the size of your executable programs and slow them considerably. Try to avoid using event-trapping statements in routines in which speed is a critical factor.

Example

See the example in the ON TIMER GOSUB entry in this chapter.

SECTION

II

MULTIMEDIA

CHAPTER 11

Graphics

Introduction

One of the strengths of QuickBASIC is its built-in set of graphics commands. QuickBASIC includes support for the additional colors and high-resolution video modes of the new generation of EGA and VGA graphics adapters.

Table 11-1 is an alphabetic list of QuickBASIC's graphics statements and functions.

Statement or function	Description
CIRCLE	Draws a circle or ellipse at a given location on the screen. You can specify the radius, color, and aspect ratio of the circle and also draw arcs and segments.
COLOR	Sets the default foreground and background colors for the current screen. In some video modes, it can also set the color of the screen border.
DRAW	Executes a string of instructions that define the size, shape, angle, and color of a graphics figure.
GET (Graphics)	Copies a graphics image from the screen into an array in memory.
LINE	Draws a line connecting two sets of coordinates, or draws a rectangle with the two sets of coordinates specifying its opposite corners.
PAINT	Fills an outlined area of the display with a specified color or pattern.
PALETTE, PALETTE USING	Assigns color values to the display attributes in EGA, VGA, and MCGA systems.
PCOPY	Copies the contents of one screen page to another.
PMAP	Translates between logical and physical pixel coordinates.
POINT	Returns the color of the specified pixel or the coordinates of the graphics cursor.
PRESET	Resets a pixel on the screen to the background color or to a specified color.
PSET	Sets a pixel on the screen to the foreground color or to a specified color.
PUT (Graphics)	Copies a graphics image from an array in memory to a specified location on the screen.
SCREEN (Function)	Returns the character or color attribute for the character at the specified row and column.

Table 11-1. *(continued)*
QuickBASIC graphics statements and functions.

Table 11-1. *continued*

Statement or function	Description
SCREEN (Statement)	Sets the current display mode and screen page.
VIEW	Defines the physical coordinates of the current graphics viewport.
WINDOW	Defines a logical coordinate system on which graphics images are plotted.

Display Adapters

Table 11-2 lists the types of display adapters supported by QuickBASIC.

Name	Abbreviation
Monochrome Display and Printer Adapter	MDPA
Color Graphics Adapter	CGA
Hercules Graphics Card	HGC
Enhanced Graphics Adapter	EGA
Multi-Color Graphics Array	MCGA
Video Graphics Array	VGA

Table 11-2.
Display adapters supported by QuickBASIC.

The MDPA and CGA were the original display adapters used in the IBM PC. The MDPA adapter can display 25 rows of 80-column text on a monochrome display, but it has no graphics capabilities. This 80-by-25-character format is the default text mode for all display adapters.

The CGA supports graphics in addition to text. The CGA is usually paired with an RGB color monitor; however, it can also be used with a monochrome display, a composite monitor, or even a television set. When used with a color monitor, it can display 25 rows of 80-column text in 16 foreground and 8 background colors. Two graphics modes are available: medium resolution (320-by-200-pixel with 4 colors) and high resolution (640-by-200-pixel with 2 colors).

In addition to 80-by-25-character text, the Hercules Graphics Card (HGC) can display graphics in high resolution (720-by-348-pixel) on a monochrome monitor. Only QuickBASIC version 4.5 supports the HGC. To use an HGC adapter to produce graphics in the QuickBASIC environment, you must first install a resident driver program (MS-HERC.COM) in memory. Microsoft includes MS-HERC.COM in the QuickBASIC package.

New display adapters introduced higher resolution and more colors yet preserved compatibility with previous standards. The EGA, which is now the standard display adapter for PCs, supports the MDPA text mode and the CGA graphics modes and adds further graphics modes. The highest resolution possible with an EGA adapter is 640 by 350 pixels with 16 colors.

The IBM PS/2-series computers introduced two new video adapters. The MCGA is similar to the CGA, but it adds two extra graphics modes: a medium-resolution mode (320-by-200-pixel with 256 colors) and a very high-resolution mode (640-by-480-pixel with 2 colors). The MCGA does not support the EGA graphics modes. The successor to the EGA is the VGA, which can display all the modes of the MDPA, CGA, EGA, and MCGA, as well as its own 640-by-480-pixel 16-color mode. Additional colors for the MCGA and VGA adapters are created through the use of analog monitors, which blend colors on the screen to produce a vast range of shades and textures.

Pixels and Resolution

The previous section referred to the capabilities of the adapters in graphics modes by using pixels to indicate their degree of resolution. A pixel is one picture element—the smallest point that can be individually set or reset on the screen. The more pixels available, the higher (or finer) the resolution of the pictures that can be drawn. For example, a medium-resolution display can display 320 by 200 (64,000) pixels; higher resolutions can display 640 by 480 (307,200) pixels.

Another factor that distinguishes adapters is color. Not all adapters can display color; the HGC adapter, for example, can display pixels on the screen in only two ways—either on or off. The CGA and EGA adapters have resolutions that can display pixels in 2, 4, or 16 colors, and the VGA and MCGA adapters can blend colors, thus displaying as many as 256 different shades in a medium-resolution graphics mode.

Table 11-3 lists display resolutions, the number of colors available at each resolution, and the mode and adapters required to produce them.

Resolution	Colors	Mode	Adapters required
320-by-200-pixel	4	1	CGA, MCGA, EGA, VGA
	16	7	EGA, VGA
	256	13	MCGA, VGA
640-by-200-pixel	2	2	CGA, MCGA, EGA, VGA
	16	8	EGA, VGA

Table 11-3. (continued)
Graphics resolution and colors and the mode and adapters required to produce them.

Table 11-3. *continued*

Resolution	Colors	Mode	Adapters required
640 by 350	4	10	EGA, VGA
	16	9	EGA, VGA
720 by 348	2	3	HGC
640 by 480	2	11	MCGA, VGA
	16	12	VGA

Screen Modes

The QuickBASIC SCREEN statement lets you select from your adapter's available display modes. To switch to a 640-by-350-pixel 16-color EGA mode, for example, you execute the statement *SCREEN 9.*

The screen mode you use defines the graphics resolution and the number of available colors. QuickBASIC offers 10 modes for graphics and 1 mode for text. The "Mode" column in Table 11-3 lists the numbers that you use with the SCREEN statement to access different graphics screen modes. Specify the text mode by using the statement *SCREEN 0.*

Notice that the table does not include modes 4, 5, and 6. These CGA modes are used by the BASICA and GW-BASIC interpreters of the PCjr and Tandy 1000, and they are not available in QuickBASIC.

Screen Coordinates

The pixels on a graphics screen are numbered in rows and columns. Columns are numbered from the left of the screen to the right, and rows are numbered from the top to the bottom. The number of rows and columns available depends on the screen resolution: screen mode 2, for example, has 640 columns by 200 rows.

You locate an individual pixel by using a pair of coordinates that specifies the pixel's row and column. The first coordinate, usually referred to as the horizontal (or x) coordinate, is the column number, and the second, the vertical (or y) coordinate, is the row. Figure 11-1 shows the range of pixel coordinates available in screen mode 9. Because coordinate values begin at 0, the pixel at the upper left corner of the screen is specified by the coordinate pair (0, 0) in any graphics mode. In a 640-by-350-resolution screen (screen mode 9), the pixel in the center of the screen is at the point specified by the coordinates (319, 174).

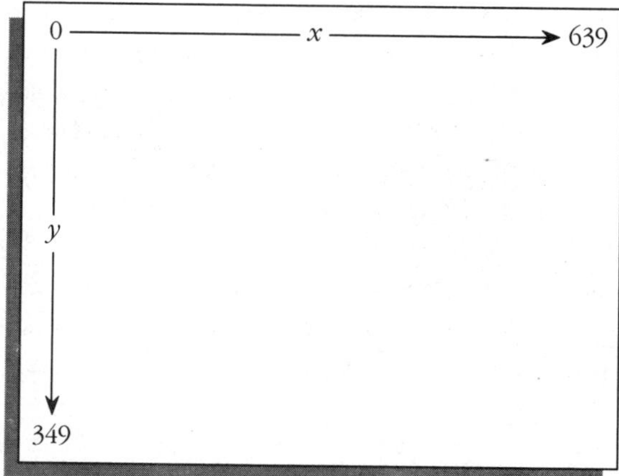

Figure 11-1.
Pixel coordinates in screen mode 9.

Drawing on the Screen

QuickBASIC provides two statements that can draw individual pixels. The PSET statement draws a pixel of the given color. If you don't specify a color, PSET draws the pixel in the current foreground color. The PRESET statement also draws a pixel of the given color. But if you don't specify a color, PRESET draws the pixel in the background color. Use PRESET to erase pixels. The POINT function returns information about a pixel. If you specify a particular location, POINT returns the current color of the pixel. You can also use POINT to find the current *x*- or *y*-coordinate.

Other QuickBASIC graphics statements use coordinates to plot more elaborate figures. The CIRCLE statement draws a circle or ellipse whose center is at the specified coordinate and whose radius is the specified length. You can also specify the color of the circle and draw arcs and segments instead of a complete circle. To draw a circle with the center at the location (50, 50), a radius of 30, and a green outline, use the following statement:

```
CIRCLE (50, 50), 30, 2
```

The LINE statement draws either a straight line between two coordinate pairs or a rectangle whose opposite corners are located at the specified coordinates.

After you have drawn the outline of an object, you can use the PAINT statement to fill the object with a specified color or pattern. PAINT requires you to provide the coordinates of only one point that is within the outline of the shape you want filled. To color the circle drawn earlier in green, for example, use the statement

```
PAINT (50, 50), 2
```

Instead of using specific, or absolute coordinates, you can use relative coordinates. With relative addressing, the *x*- and *y*-coordinates specified in a statement do not refer to actual row and column coordinates on the screen but to the horizontal and vertical distance of the current pixel from the graphics-cursor position. The graphics-cursor position is usually the location of the most recent point drawn by the previous graphics statement; however, if no statement has been executed, the cursor position defaults to the center of the screen.

Relative addressing is useful for constructing elaborate displays because by changing the original location you can move an entire figure to a different part of the screen. To use relative addressing, you need only add the STEP keyword before the coordinates in a graphics statement.

Colors

All the drawing statements accept arguments that let you specify the color of the figure being drawn. However, QuickBASIC also provides two statements that let you control the default colors of the current screen mode.

The COLOR statement specifies the default foreground and background colors for the display. In some screen modes, you can also select the color of the screen border or choose the palette of colors that will be used. The PALETTE and PALETTE USING statements let you change any or all of the colors that can be displayed. This feature is available only for computers using EGA, VGA, or MCGA adapters.

Viewports and Windows

Although the entire screen is available for graphics, you can restrict output to a smaller section, thus leaving the rest of the screen for text output. The area to which graphics output is restricted is called the graphics "viewport." Use the VIEW statement to specify the coordinates that define this rectangular viewport. All subsequent graphics statements must refer to locations within the viewport; any coordinates that fall outside this area are not drawn.

After you define a viewport, the *x*- and *y*-coordinates are measured from the upper left corner of the viewport, not the screen. QuickBASIC programs can define more than one viewport during the course of execution, but only one viewport at a time can be active.

Coordinates on the vertical (*y*) axis are measured downward (from the top of the screen). However, because objects in the real word are often measured from the bottom up, you might prefer to use the Cartesian coordinate system, in which *y*-coordinates are measured from the bottom of the screen. Moreover, the range of pixels on either axis rarely corresponds exactly to the range of values you need to use to plot values from everyday applications.

To avoid these problems, QuickBASIC provides the WINDOW statement. This statement lets you define a set of logical, or view, coordinates that match the scale of the figure to be drawn. WINDOW maps these coordinates to the physical viewport, which is the viewport whose coordinates correspond to actual pixel locations. After WINDOW has been called, graphics statements such as LINE, CIRCLE, and PAINT accept arguments from your set of logical coordinates, and QuickBASIC translates the arguments into the physical coordinates that correspond to pixels on the screen.

The logical window shown in Figure 11-2, for example, can be defined by using the statement

```
WINDOW (0, 0)-(1000, 1000)
```

to map a logical coordinate system that uses *x* and *y* values in the range 0 through 1000 onto a 640-by-350-pixel viewport. Vertical coordinates in this logical window are plotted from the bottom of the display.

To plot the point (70, 820) in the logical window, use the PSET statement as you would with absolute coordinates, but use logical coordinates instead:

```
PSET (70, 820)
```

QuickBASIC translates the logical coordinates into physical coordinates, thus setting the pixel at the physical location (45, 63).

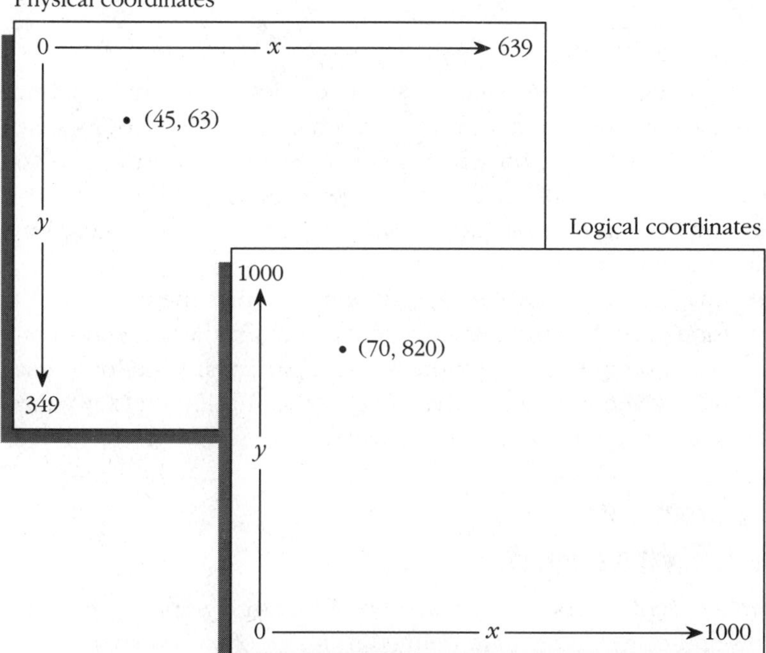

Figure 11-2.
Mapping logical coordinates to physical coordinates.

Because the conversion of logical into physical coordinates is automatic when you use WINDOW, you rarely need to know the actual address of a pixel. However, if you do need to know, the PMAP function returns the physical location of any logical coordinate.

The WINDOW statement lets you easily produce graphs and charts from your data. It also has many advanced uses. You can, for example, define a logical window that uses a smaller range of coordinates than those defining the physical dimensions of the screen. Any graphics images you then plot are "magnified" when compared to the same images plotted using physical coordinates. Furthermore, by expanding, contracting, or displacing the window's coordinates, you can create the effect of panning or zooming the display.

Animation

Any image that is drawn on the screen can be captured and stored in memory by the GET statement, which copies the contents of a specified screen area into an array in memory. To restore the captured image at a different screen location, use the PUT statement. PUT copies the contents of an array onto the screen, starting at a specified location. By copying the image to the screen many times and in many different locations, you can produce a variety of animation effects.

Screen Pages

If your adapter provides enough memory, some video modes let you maintain several screens of information; each is stored in a separate "screen page." The SCREEN statement lets you select the "active" page, on which graphics statements draw, and the "visible" page, which the program displays. The two pages need not be the same. You can produce animation by changing visible pages containing an image that occupies a slightly different position on each page.

QuickBASIC also provides the PCOPY statement, which copies the contents of a source page to a destination page. You use this statement to transfer the contents of one screen page to another. For example, if you routinely use a particular page for animation and you want to save a given instance of that page, you can call the PCOPY procedure to copy the image to a page the program won't alter.

Displaying Graphics by Using the DRAW Statement

The graphics statements described above use a system of "vector" graphics, in which the end points of lines and curves drawn are defined in terms of screen coordinates. The DRAW statement provides another method of drawing on the screen: It lets you define a line in terms of direction and length.

The DRAW statement lets you control the movement of the graphics cursor by using various commands to produce a figure of a specified size, shape, color, and orientation. QuickBASIC provides a wide range of DRAW commands—enough so that the DRAW statement is a versatile graphics language in its own right.

Related Reading

McGregor, Jim, and Alan Watt. *The Art of Graphics for the IBM PC.* Menlo Park, Calif.: Addison-Wesley, 1986.

Wilton, Richard. *Programmer's Guide to PC and PS/2 Video Systems.* Redmond, Wash.: Microsoft Press, 1987.

CIRCLE

See also: COLOR, PAINT, SCREEN (Statement), WINDOW

■ QB2	■ QB4.5	■ PowerBASIC
■ QB3	ANSI	■ GW-BASIC
■ QB4	■ BASIC7	■ MacQB

Purpose

The CIRCLE statement draws a circle of the specified size. Although the default of the statement is the circle, you can use it to draw ellipses, arcs, and segments.

Syntax

CIRCLE [STEP] (*x*, *y*), *radius* [, [*color*] [, [*start*] [, [*stop*] [, *aspect*]]]]

x and *y* are the screen coordinates of the center of the circle. If the STEP keyword is used, these coordinates are relative to the coordinates of the graphics-cursor position; otherwise, they are absolute references.

radius is the distance from the center of the circle to its circumference; it is measured in the current coordinate system.

color is the color assigned to the circle; if no color is specified, the current foreground color is used.

start and *stop* are angles (in radians) that specify the beginning and end points of an arc or a segment.

aspect is the aspect ratio, which is the ratio of the vertical radius of the ellipse to the horizontal one. The default value of *aspect* is the value that produces a perfect circle in the current screen mode.

Arguments to CIRCLE can be numeric constants, numeric variables, or numeric expressions. Only *x*, *y*, and *radius* are required. The *color*, *start*, *stop*, and *aspect* parameters are optional and, if omitted, are replaced by the default values. If you omit arguments from the middle of a CIRCLE statement, you must include commas to hold their position; however, you do not need to include commas in place of arguments omitted from the end of the statement.

Usage

```
CIRCLE (160, 100), 40
```

Draws a circle with a radius of 40 pixels at the center of the screen mode 1 display. Because no color is specified, QuickBASIC draws the circle in the current foreground color.

```
CIRCLE (xPos%, yPos%), 100, clr% MOD 4, , , .5
```

Draws an ellipse with an aspect ratio of .5, so that the ellipse is twice as wide as it is high. Note that commas hold the place of the *start* and *stop* parameters.

```
CONST PI = 3.14159
CIRCLE STEP (50, -40), 60, 2, -PI, -PI * 2
```

Draws in green an arc with its center 50 pixels to the right and 40 pixels above the graphics-cursor position. The values of the *start* and *stop* parameters are negative; therefore, the resulting arc is joined to the center by radii, producing a half circle.

Description

CIRCLE not only draws circles; it can also be used to produce ellipses, arcs, and segments. By default, however, QuickBASIC adjusts the shape of the figure to produce the closest approximation to a perfect circle in the current graphics mode; hence the name CIRCLE.

To draw a circle, you must specify its location and size. You define its location by using a pair of coordinates to measure the horizontal (*x*) and vertical (*y*) distance of the center of the circle from the upper left corner of the display. These distances are measured in the current coordinate system (as they are with all graphic statements), and the range of possible values is determined by the graphics mode set by the previous SCREEN statement. For example, to position a circle at the center of the screen in screen mode 1 (medium-resolution graphics), you specify *x*- and *y*-coordinates of 160 and 100, but in VGA screen modes 11 and 12 you would use coordinates of 320 and 240.

Another way to position a circle is to use the keyword STEP to specify that the *x*- and *y*-coordinates are offset from the graphics-cursor position, which is the most recent position of the figure drawn by the previous graphics statement. STEP causes CIRCLE to perform "relative addressing", which has many useful applications. By merely changing the coordinates of the original starting point, a program can completely relocate a large and complex figure.

You define the size of a circle by specifying its radius, which is the distance from the center to the perimeter, drawn along the major (longest) axis of the figure. Measurement is, once again, in the current coordinate system. Circles can be of any size, although any portion of the circle located beyond the screen boundaries is not drawn.

Aspect Ratio

To create the appearance of a circle, QuickBASIC actually draws an ellipse, or oval. This would not be necessary if the pixels on your screen were equal in height and width; however, because pixels are taller than they are wide, a radius of 50 pixels is shorter horizontally than vertically. Thus a "true" circle would appear taller than it is wide.

Because the size of a pixel on screen depends on the current screen mode, QuickBASIC calculates a different default aspect ratio for each screen mode in order to produce "round" circles. It does this by using the following formula, in which *xPixels* and *yPixels* are the maximum number of pixels in the *x* and *y* axes:

aspect = (*yPixels* / *xPixels*) * 4 / 3

In a medium-resolution screen mode (320-by-200-pixel), the default aspect is 0.83333 (5/6). In high-resolution mode (640-by-200-pixel), it is half of this, or 0.41667 (5/12). Thus to draw an ellipse that appears longer horizontally than vertically, you must specify an aspect ratio that is less than the default for the current screen mode. To draw a tall ellipse, you must specify an aspect value greater than the default. (See Figure 11-3.) If the specified aspect is less than the default, the radius is measured along the horizontal axis; if the aspect is greater than the default, the radius is measured vertically. So the specified radius is always the value of the longer axis of the ellipse.

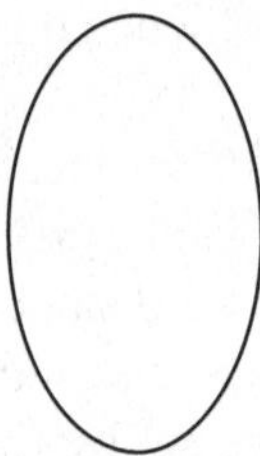

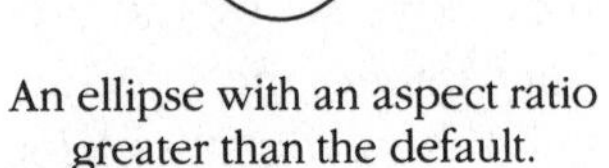

An ellipse with an aspect ratio greater than the default.

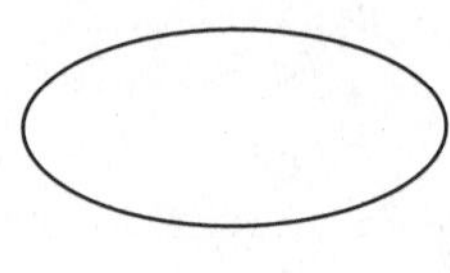

An ellipse with an aspect ratio less than the default.

Figure 11-3.
Effects of specifying an aspect ratio.

Users of QuickBASIC for the Macintosh do not have these aspect ratio problems—the Macintosh screen has an aspect ratio of 1 to 1, which produces square pixels. Because of this, a "round" circle has an aspect of 1.0. Therefore, calculating values for ellipses becomes an elementary procedure.

Arcs and Segments

To draw an arc, you must define a beginning point and an end point. These points are defined by angles (in radians) measured from the three o'clock position on the perimeter of the circle of which the arc is a part. The number of radians increases in a counterclockwise direction, from 0 at the origin to 6.2832 (or 2 * pi), which is the number of radians that form an entire circle. This is shown in Figure 11-4, on the following page.

If the start and stop values are negative, the angles they represent are still treated as positive, but the CIRCLE statement draws a radius connecting the start or stop point on the arc to the center of the circle, thus producing a segment. Figure 11-5, on the following page, shows three examples of the CIRCLE statement.

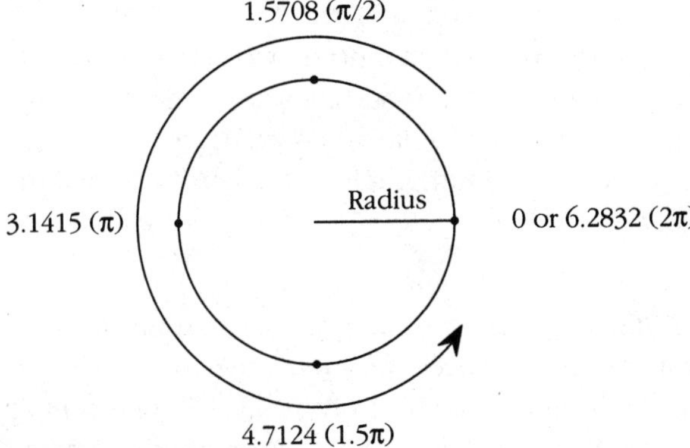

Figure 11-4.
CIRCLE start *and* stop *coordinates.*

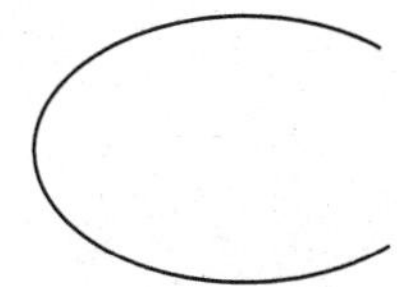

Arc
CIRCLE (30, 30), 25, 3, 1.2, 5.2

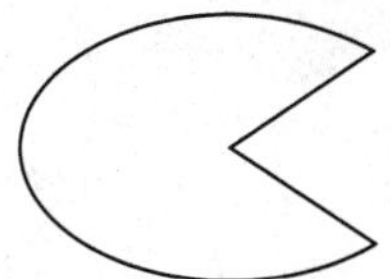

Segment
CIRCLE (30, 30), 25, 3, -1.2, -5.2

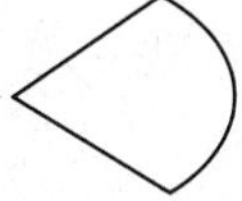

Segment
CIRCLE (30, 30), 25, 3, -5.2, -1.2

Figure 11-5.
Creating arcs and segments with the CIRCLE statement.

Tips

You can always use CIRCLE with the STEP keyword, even if no previous graphics statement was executed. When QuickBASIC changes screen modes, it sets the graphics cursor to the center of the display and plots subsequent relative coordinates from there. With a little planning, you can use this feature to build graphics displays that have the same layout (but a different scale) in any resolution.

Example

One of the most useful features of CIRCLE and of most other graphics statements is the STEP keyword, which plots the coordinates of the current figure relative to the position of the graphics cursor. The following program uses STEP in the CIRCLE statement to draw a picture of an extraterrestrial being. You can change the location of this complex graphics image simply by changing the value of the initial coordinates. The output of the program is shown in Figure 11-6.

```
DEFINT A-Z

x = 160: y = 120                          ' initial coordinates
clr0 = 0: clr1 = 1: clr2 = 2: clr3 = 3    ' values for setting color

SCREEN 1
LINE (0, 0)-(319, 199), clr3, BF          ' paint entire screen

' draw the creature
CIRCLE (x, y), 35, clr0: PAINT STEP(0, 0), clr0, clr0
CIRCLE STEP(-30, -40), 20, clr0: PAINT STEP(0, 0), clr0, clr0
CIRCLE STEP(0, 0), 15, clr2, , , .5: PAINT STEP(0, 0), clr1, clr2
CIRCLE STEP(0, 0), 5, clr3, , , 6: PAINT STEP(0, 0), clr2, clr3
CIRCLE STEP(60, 0), 20, clr0: PAINT STEP(0, 0), clr0, clr0
CIRCLE STEP(0, 0), 20, clr0: CIRCLE STEP(0, 0), 15, clr2
PAINT STEP(0, 0), clr1, clr2: CIRCLE STEP(0, 0), 5, clr3, , , 6
PAINT STEP(0, 0), clr2, clr3
CIRCLE STEP(-15, 10), 11, clr0, 2.1, 3.3
CIRCLE STEP(0, 0), 6, clr0, 2, 3.3: PAINT STEP(-8, -4), clr0, clr0
CIRCLE STEP(-22, 4), 11, clr0, .01, 1.3
CIRCLE STEP(0, 0), 6, clr0, 6.1, 1.3: PAINT STEP(8, -4), clr0, clr0
CIRCLE (x, y + 10), 30, clr2, , , .5: PAINT STEP(0, 0), clr1, clr2

FOR i! = .001 TO .5 STEP .07       ' draw details of creature's mouth
    CIRCLE STEP(0, 0), 25, clr0, , , i!
NEXT i!
END
```

Figure 11-6.
Output of CIRCLE example program.

COLOR

See also: PALETTE, SCREEN (Statement)

■ QB2	■ QB4.5	■ PowerBASIC
■ QB3	✲ ANSI	■ GW-BASIC
■ QB4	■ BASIC7	MacQB

Purpose

The COLOR statement selects the display attributes of objects on the screen. If your computer has a color monitor, these attributes are translated into actual display colors. On monochrome monitors display attributes control the intensity of the displayed objects. COLOR can also be used to set the display attributes in text mode.

Syntax

COLOR [*foreground*][, [*background*][, *border*]] (Screen mode 0)
COLOR [*foreground*][, *palette*] (Screen mode 1)
COLOR [*foreground*][, *background*] (Screen modes 7-10)
COLOR [*foreground*] (Screen modes 12-13)

foreground is an integer value that specifies the color of the text and graphics displayed on the screen.

background is an integer value that specifies the color of the background of the screen.

palette is an integer value used in screen mode 1 that specifies which of two sets of colors to use in graphics display.

Usage

```
SCREEN 1
COLOR 9, 1
```

Sets the background color to light blue and the palette to palette number 1, which contains the colors cyan, magenta, and white.

```
SCREEN 8
COLOR 1, 14
```

Sets the foreground color to blue and the background color to light yellow.

Description

The number and purpose of the arguments supplied to COLOR vary with the selected screen mode. (See the SCREEN (Statement) entry.) However, all arguments that specify an attribute represent one of the colors listed in Table 11-4.

Attribute number	Color	Attribute number	Color
0	Black	8	Dark gray
1	Blue	9	Light blue
2	Green	10	Light green
3	Cyan	11	Light cyan
4	Red	12	Light red
5	Magenta	13	Light magenta
6	Brown	14	Yellow
7	White	15	Bright white

Table 11-4.
COLOR attribute numbers.

Note that the colors corresponding to attributes 8 through 15 are the same as those corresponding to 0 through 7 except that an added intensity makes them appear brighter. On some color monitors, the color 6 (brown) appears as dark yellow and is useful as a flesh color for graphics.

The COLOR statement performs different tasks; the screen mode in use determines the task.

COLOR with screen mode 0

Screen mode 0 is the text screen mode. In this mode, COLOR controls the appearance of characters printed on the display and the color of the background. Numbers for the foreground color can be in the range 0 through 31. Numbers 0 through 15 are the attribute numbers for the colors; these are listed in Table 11-4. Numbers 16 through 31 are the same colors in the same order, but blinking. Numbers for the background color range from 0 through 7 and represent the first eight colors; these are listed in Table 11-4. For background colors, you cannot specify colors with higher intensity or colors that blink.

Issuing a COLOR statement in text mode has no effect on characters that are already displayed; however, all subsequent output has the specified foreground and background colors. Use the CLS statement to clear the screen to the new background color.

Colors, of course, are not produced on monochrome monitors. Text displayed with foreground numbers in the range 8 through 15 appear brighter than characters in the range 0 through 7. If you have an MDPA or an HGC adapter, a foreground number of 1 displays underlined text.

Background numbers 0 through 6 have no effect on monochrome monitors, but number 7 used with a foreground number of 0 changes the display to inverse video.

On computers that use a Color Graphics Adapter (CGA), you can also use COLOR to set the color of the screen border to any color in the range 0 through 15.

COLOR with screen mode 1

Screen mode 1 is the medium-resolution (320-by-200-pixel) graphics mode. Note that the COLOR statement in this mode cannot set the foreground color. It can, however, set the screen background to a color from the full range listed in Table 11-4. Calling the COLOR statement immediately changes the color of the display.

Graphics statements, such as LINE, CIRCLE, and PAINT, that are used in screen mode 1 can be drawn using one of four (0 through 3) color attributes. The colors assigned to these attributes depend on the color set, or palette, specified in the COLOR statement. Two palettes are available. They are described in Table 11-5:

Attribute number	Palette 0	Palette 1
0	Current background color	Current background color
1	Green	Cyan
2	Red	Magenta
3	Brown	White

Table 11-5.
COLOR attribute numbers for each palette.

If you do not assign an explicit color argument to graphics statements, QuickBASIC draws the graphics statements in the color corresponding to attribute 3. For example,

```
LINE (50, 35)-(216, 60)
```

is plotted in brown if palette 0 is active and in white if palette 1 is active.

When you first select screen mode 1, the default COLOR setting is a black background and palette 1 (cyan, magenta, and white).

COLOR with screen modes 7 through 10

In screen modes 7 through 10, foreground and background colors are by default bright white on black. Screen modes 7, 8, and 9 let you select from 16 attributes (numbers 0 through 15) that specify the colors of the foreground and background.

Modes 7, 8, and 9 can be used only if your EGA or VGA adapter has a color monitor, which lets you display up to 16 different colors at once. In modes 7 and 8, these colors are selected from the 16 color attributes listed in Table 11-4. In mode 9 you can select from an extended palette of 64 color attributes (numbered 0-63), provided that your adapter has more than 64 KB of memory and that your monitor can display 64 colors. Screen mode 10, the monochrome EGA and VGA mode, supports 4 attributes for the foreground pseudocolor. Table 11-6 lists the four available attributes.

Attribute number	Description of pseudocolor
0	Sets no pixels
1	Sets normal intensity
2	Sets blink on
3	Sets high intensity

Table 11-6.
Available attribute numbers for foreground of screen mode 10.

Screen mode 10 supports nine color numbers for the background pseudocolors. Table 11-7 lists these pseudocolors.

Color number	Description of pseudocolor
0	Sets no pixels
1	Blinks between off and normal intensity
2	Blinks between off and high intensity
3	Blinks between normal intensity and off
4	Sets normal intensity, no blink
5	Blinks between normal intensity and high intensity
6	Blinks between high intensity and off
7	Blinks between high intensity and normal intensity
8	Sets high intensity, no blink

Table 11-7.
Available color numbers for background of screen mode 10.

COLOR with screen modes 12 through 13

You can select only foreground attributes in screen modes 12 and 13. To change the default background color from black, use the PALETTE statement to assign the color of your choice to attribute 0. Screen mode 12 supports 16 foreground attributes, and screen mode 13 supports 256 foreground attributes. Each attribute can be assigned to one of 262,144 colors by using the PALETTE or PALETTE USING statement.

Errors

The COLOR statement is not valid in screen modes 2, 3, and 11. If you use it in these modes, QuickBASIC returns an "Illegal function call" error message. QuickBASIC also returns an "Illegal function call" error message if any of the parameters you set are not in the range specified by the screen mode.

Tips

If your computer has a Color Graphics Adapter (CGA), you can generate a third color palette in screen mode 1. This palette consists of the colors cyan, red, and white on the background selected by the most recent COLOR statement. To enable the third palette, issue the following statement:

```
OUT &H3D8, PEEK(&H465) OR 4
```

The colors produced are the same, regardless of whether your previous palette setting was 0 (green, red, and brown) or 1 (cyan, magenta, and white). To disable the effect and restore the previous palette, use the following statement:

```
OUT &H3D8, PEEK(&H465) AND 251
```

This trick does not work on computers that use EGA or VGA video adapters (even if screen mode 1 is selected); however, the statements do not cause errors if you use them.

On systems with CGA adapters, the COLOR statement accepts a number for the border color only in screen mode 0. However, if your computer has an EGA or VGA adapter, you can call a BIOS interrupt to select the border color. The following example uses the CALL INTERRUPT statement to select a blue border for the display. (See the CALL INTERRUPT entry in Chapter 20, "Mixed Language.")

```
' $INCLUDE: 'QB.BI'

DIM inRegs AS RegType, outRegs AS RegType

clr% = 1                              ' select a blue border
inRegs.ax = &H1001                    ' specify function set border color
inRegs.bx = clr% * 256                ' set BH equal to the color number
CALL INTERRUPT(&H10, InRegs, OutRegs) ' call BIOS system service
```

To work, the header file QB.BI, which is supplied with QuickBASIC, must be included, and the Quick library QB.QLB must be loaded into the environment. (Link QB.LIB to produce an executable version.) Color numbers are in the range 0 through 15 and represent the same border colors as they do in the COLOR statement. An advantage of using this method is that it works with graphics modes and the text mode (SCREEN 0).

Compatibility

ANSI BASIC

The COLOR statement is more specific in ANSI BASIC than in QuickBASIC. In ANSI BASIC, for example, you can use the AREA COLOR, LINE COLOR, POINT COLOR, and TEXT COLOR clauses to set the colors of an image.

Example

The COLOR statement varies depending on the adapter your system uses and the mode the program sets with the SCREEN statement. If you write a program that must be portable between systems, be sure you take the different types of adapters into consideration. The following program contains the COLOR statement in three different formats; the format used depends on the value the user enters.

```
ON ERROR GOTO WrongMode

PRINT "What type of video adapter are you using?"
INPUT "<Enter 1 for CGA, 2 for EGA, and 3 for VGA or MCGA>: ", adapt%

ShowColors:
SELECT CASE adapt%
CASE 1                  ' show background colors of mode 1 for CGA
    SCREEN 1
    PRINT "You can use one of 15 background colors."
    PRINT "Press any key to see them."
    DO WHILE INKEY$ = "": LOOP
    CLS
    FOR i% = 0 TO 14
        COLOR i%
        LOCATE 10, 10: PRINT "Color:"; i%
        SLEEP 1
    NEXT i%
CASE 2                  ' show background and foreground colors for EGA
    SCREEN 7
    PRINT "You can use one of 15 background and"
    PRINT "one of 15 foreground colors."
    PRINT "Press any key to see them."
    DO WHILE INKEY$ = "": LOOP
    FOR i% = 0 TO 14
        COLOR , i%
        CLS
        FOR j% = 0 TO 14
            COLOR j%
            PRINT "Foreground:"; j%; "Background:"; i%
```

(continued)

continued

```
        NEXT j%
        SLEEP 1
    NEXT i%
CASE 3                  ' show foreground colors of VGA or MCGA
    SCREEN 13
    PRINT "You can use one of 256 foreground colors."
    PRINT "Press any key to see them."
    DO WHILE INKEY$ = "": LOOP
    CLS
    FOR i% = 0 TO 255:
        COLOR i%
        PRINT "Color:"; i%
    NEXT i%
END SELECT
END

WrongMode:
IF ERR = 5 THEN
    PRINT "Your system does not support screen modes for that adapter."
    INPUT "Enter a different number: ", adapt%
    RESUME ShowColors
ELSE
    ON ERROR GOTO 0
END IF
```

DRAW

See also: VARPTR$, WINDOW

QB2	■ QB4.5	■ PowerBASIC
QB3	ANSI	✲ GW-BASIC
■ QB4	■ BASIC7	MacQB

Purpose

The DRAW statement draws the figure specified in a string expression. DRAW uses a "macro language" that lets you describe lines in relative terms, by specifying the distance and direction of graphics-cursor movement.

Syntax

DRAW *commandString*

commandString is a string literal, string variable, or string expression that contains a sequence of drawing commands. Enclose literal strings in quotes. You can enter commands in either uppercase or lowercase, and you can separate them with blank spaces or semicolons; doing this, however, merely makes the string more readable and is not a syntax requirement.

Usage

```
DRAW "C4 U45 R75 D45 L75"
```

Draws a rectangle 45 units high by 75 units wide in color number 4 (red, by default).

```
DRAW box$
```

Draws the figure specified by the commands in the string variable *box$*.

```
DRAW "C=" + VARPTR$(clr%)
```

Sets the color for subsequent DRAW statements to the color specified by the value of the integer variable *clr%*.

Description

The DRAW command accepts a string that contains a list of macro commands. The commands specify graphics-cursor movement, scaling, rotation, and color. The following sections group the macro commands by function.

Cursor Movement

The **M*x*,*y*** command is the only DRAW command that specifies coordinates. The M command moves the graphics cursor to the screen location specified by coordinates *x* and *y*. If *x* is preceded by a sign operator, plus (+) or minus (–), cursor movement is relative to the current position of the graphics cursor; otherwise, QuickBASIC assumes *x* and *y* are the absolute coordinates of a location on screen. In both cases, a line is drawn between the graphics-cursor position and the new location, and this location becomes the new graphics-cursor position. For example, the statement

```
DRAW "M10,25"
```

draws a line from the graphics-cursor position to location (10, 25) on the screen. However, the statement

```
DRAW "M-10,-25"
```

draws a line from the position of the graphics cursor to a point 10 pixels to the left and 25 pixels above the current location.

The **B** command indicates the movement command that follows moves the graphics cursor but does not draw a line. By default, all cursor movements result in a line being drawn from the previous point to the new location. Prefixing a movement command with the B command, however, produces a "blank" move, in which the cursor position is updated but no points are drawn between it and the previous location.

The **N** command indicates the movement command that follows does not update the graphics-cursor position. When the N command prefixes a movement command, the DRAW statement draws the line but then returns the graphics cursor to its original position.

Table 11-8 lists commands that move the graphics cursor in various directions. You control how far the cursor moves in the chosen direction by specifying the length of the resulting line in "units". By default, a unit is equal to one pixel, but you can adjust this by modifying the current scale factor with the S command. (See the next section, "Scaling.") If you do not specify a length, DRAW moves the cursor one unit in the direction specified.

Command	Description
U*n*	Move *n* units upward
D*n*	Move *n* units downward
R*n*	Move *n* units to the right
L*n*	Move *n* units to the left
E*n*	Move *n* units diagonally upward and to the right
F*n*	Move *n* units diagonally downward and to the right
G*n*	Move *n* units diagonally downward and to the left
H*n*	Move *n* units diagonally upward and to the left

Table 11-8.
Commands that move the graphics cursor.

Scaling

Sn, the scale command, specifies a number (in the range 1 through 255) that is divided by four to determine the number of pixels moved for each unit of distance given in a movement command. The default scale value is 4, which makes one unit of movement equal to a single pixel.

The S command is very useful when you want to draw multiple copies of the same figure, but in different sizes. The following program, for example, draws four copies of the same triangle, each with a scale factor twice the size of the last.

```
SCREEN 9
triangle$ = "E10 F10 L20"
x% = 10: y% = 174

FOR i% = 1 TO 4
    move$ = "BM" + STR$(x%) + "," + STR$(y%)
    scale$ = "S" + STR$(i% * 4)
    DRAW move$ + scale$ + triangle$
    x% = x% + 150
NEXT i%
END
```

Rotation

DRAW lets you rotate the vertical and horizontal axes of a figure a full 360 degrees. By default, the U (up) command moves the graphics cursor upward at an angle of 0 degrees. However, if the axes are rotated 45 degrees, a U command draws a diagonal line upward and to the left. The other direction commands are affected similarly. The DRAW statement includes two rotation commands. These commands affect only the commands following them; they do not rotate any lines that have already been drawn.

The **A*n*** command rotates the axes in 90-degree steps. The value of *n* can be a number between 0 and 3. DRAW multiplies the value by 90 to calculate the number of degrees to rotate. Angles are measured in a counterclockwise direction, 12:00 being 0 degrees.

The **TA*n*** command rotates the axes *n* degrees, where *n* is a number in the range –360 through 360. Positive values of *n* rotate the axes in a counterclockwise direction; negative values rotate the axes clockwise.

Shifts in the axes remain in effect for subsequent commands. The following program segment produces a pattern of nested diamonds by drawing a single diamond and then drawing it at every 12 degrees of a circle:

```
SCREEN 2
FOR angle% = 0 TO 360 STEP 12
    DRAW "TA=" + VARPTR$(angle%)
    DRAW "U50 E50 D50 G50"
NEXT angle%
```

Color

DRAW includes a command that allows you to specify the color of the line drawn. The possible range of colors is determined by the current screen mode. (See the COLOR entry for details about the colors available in various screen modes.) If you do not specify a color, the DRAW statement defaults to the current foreground color.

The **C*n*** command sets the color of the lines drawn by direction and movement commands to the color associated with the value *n*.

The **P*c*,*b*** command performs the same task as the PAINT statement does; it fills the interior of the figure enclosing the current graphics-cursor position with the color specified by *c*. Specify the border color of the figure with *b*.

If you have just drawn the figure to be painted, you must move the graphics cursor off the border and into the interior of the figure; otherwise, painting will not take place. The best way to do this is to execute a blank move, as in the following example:

```
DRAW "C2 R50 D30 L50 U30"         ' draw a green rectangle
DRAW "BF10"                       ' move cursor inside the figure
DRAW "P3,2"                       ' fill it with cyan
```

Substrings

The **X** ("execute") command lets you specify substrings for DRAW to execute from the current command string. This is an extremely powerful feature of the DRAW macrolanguage. To use the X command, you must use the VARPTR$ function to supply DRAW with the address of the substring to be executed. (VARPTR$ returns in string format a pointer to the variable; see Chapter 20, "Mixed Language," for details.) For example, when DRAW encounters the statement

```
"X" + VARPTR$(boat$)
```

in a larger string, DRAW executes the commands specified in the string variable *boat$* before completing the original string. The variable *boat$* can contain its own X commands, thus executing further substrings that might also contain X commands, and so on.

Variables

You can use numeric variables in the DRAW statement in two ways. First, you can use the STR$ function to convert their values to string form before using them in a DRAW statement, as shown in the following statements:

```
move$ = "BM" + STR$(x%) + "," + STR$(y%)
DRAW move$
```

You can also use the VARPTR$ function to supply a numeric variable argument within the DRAW statement. If you do this, the command must have an equal sign (=) between it and the VARPTR$ expression. For example,

```
DRAW "G=" + VARPTR$(pixels%)
```

draws a diagonal line down and left. The length of the line (in units) is specified by the value of the integer variable *pixels%*.

Compatibility

GW-BASIC and BASICA

Although GW-BASIC and BASICA support the VARPTR$ method of using numeric variables in DRAW commands, those versions also let you use the variables directly. The following statements, which are illegal in QuickBASIC, are valid in GW-BASIC and BASICA:

```
DRAW "Xboat$"
DRAW "G = pixels%"
```

Example

The DRAW command is well suited for drawing patterns using fractals, or figures constructed from smaller versions of the same figure. The following program lets you experiment with fractals: By changing the parameters that govern the line length and the number of sides in the subprogram *Flake*, you can draw many intricate and beautiful patterns. Figure 11-7 on page 419 shows the output of this program.

```
DECLARE SUB Fractal (n AS INTEGER)
DECLARE SUB Flake (n AS INTEGER, sides AS INTEGER)
DECLARE SUB IncAngle (increment AS INTEGER)

DIM SHARED angle AS INTEGER
SCREEN 9
Flake 120, 9
END

SUB Flake (n AS INTEGER, sides AS INTEGER) STATIC
    move$ = "BM+" + STR$(n \ 2) + ",+" + STR$(n \ 2)
    DRAW move$                          ' move graphics cursor
    turn% = 360 \ sides
    FOR i% = 1 TO sides
        Fractal n                       ' draw a portion of the fractal
        IncAngle turn%
        DRAW "TA=" + VARPTR$(angle)     ' rotate axes
    NEXT i%
END SUB

SUB Fractal (n AS INTEGER)
    IF n < 4 THEN
        DRAW "U=" + VARPTR$(n)           ' draw a portion of the fractal
    ELSE
        Fractal n / 3                    ' recursively call Fractal subprogram
        IncAngle -60
        DRAW "TA=" + VARPTR$(angle)
        Fractal n / 3
        IncAngle 120
        DRAW "TA=" + VARPTR$(angle)
        Fractal n / 3
        IncAngle -60
        DRAW "TA=" + VARPTR$(angle)
        Fractal n / 3
    END IF
END SUB

SUB IncAngle (increment AS INTEGER) STATIC
    angle = angle + increment
    IF angle > 360 THEN
        angle = angle - 360
    ELSEIF angle < 0 THEN
        angle = angle + 360
    END IF
END SUB
```

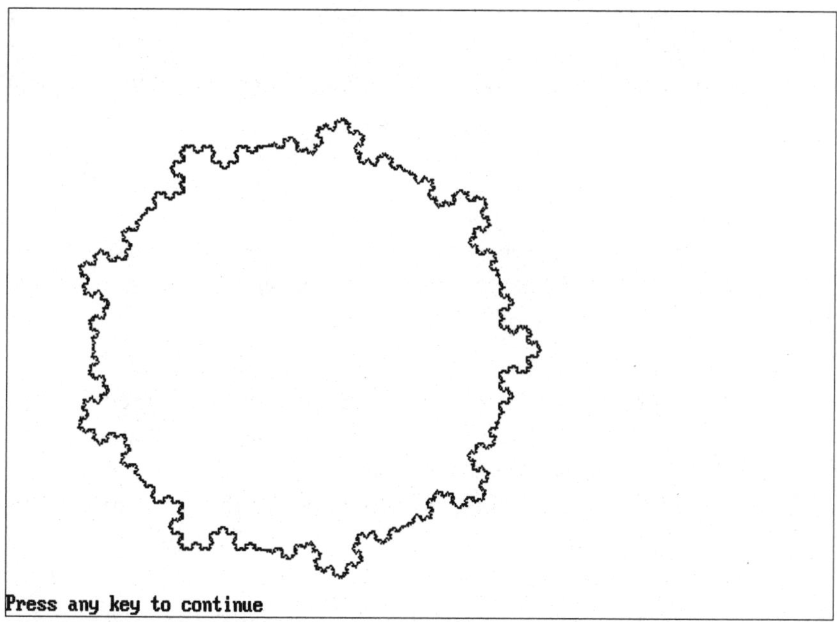

Figure 11-7.
Output of the DRAW example program.

GET (Graphics)

See also: PUT, SCREEN (Statement), VIEW, WINDOW

✲ QB2	■ QB4.5	■ PowerBASIC
✲ QB3	ANSI	■ GW-BASIC
■ QB4	■ BASIC7	✲ MacQB

Purpose

The GET statement copies a rectangular area of the screen into an array. Its counterpart, the PUT statement, copies the contents of the array back onto the screen at any position that you specify. Together, the statements let you move an image from one part of the display to another without having to draw it again.

Syntax

GET [STEP](*x1*, *y1*)-[STEP](*x2*, *y2*), *array*[(*subscript*)]

x1, *y1*, *x2*, and *y2* are screen coordinates that specify the opposite corners of the rectangular area to be copied. The STEP keyword indicates that the location to which the coordinates refer is relative to the position of the graphics cursor.

array is the name of the numeric array that will hold the image data. You can specify the array element in which storage of the image starts by including *subscript* in parentheses. If you omit the subscript, GET begins storing the image in the first element of the array.

Usage

```
GET (0, 0)-(19, 14), sprite%
```

Copies the contents of a rectangle (20 pixels wide by 15 pixels high) into the integer array *sprite%*. If no VIEW or WINDOW statements have been executed, the rectangle begins at the upper left corner of the screen.

```
GET STEP(20, -5)-STEP(xInc, yInc), image&(0, 5)
```

Defines a rectangle whose upper left corner is 20 pixels to the right of the graphics cursor and 5 pixels above it. The bottom right corner of the rectangle is offset from the new location of the graphics cursor by *xInc* horizontal pixels and *yInc* vertical pixels. The contents of this rectangle are then copied into column 5 of the two-dimensional array *image&*.

Description

Do not confuse this statement with the file I/O version of GET, which is used to read data from a random access file. The GET statement for graphics reads data from the screen and then copies it into an array in memory; usually the data is in the form of a figure that has been plotted by one or more of the other graphics statements.

The coordinates of the source rectangle, from which the picture is copied, are specified in the same way they are for the LINE statement. You can use actual pixel numbers measured from the upper left corner of the current viewport. (See the VIEW entry for an explanation of viewport coordinates.) If a WINDOW statement has been executed, you can use the logical coordinate system defined by that statement.

Because GET copies every pixel from the source rectangle into the target array, you must be sure the array is large enough to hold them all. Use the following formula to calculate the size of the array required:

bytes = 4 + INT(((*width*) * *bits_per_pixel*/*bit_planes*) + 7) /8 * *bit_planes* * *height*

width is the horizontal extent of the source rectangle. To extract this information from the *x*-coordinates, use the following formula:

width = (*x2* - *x1*) + 1

Similarly, you can obtain the value of *height*, the vertical extent of the source rectangle, by using the following formula:

height = (*y2* - *y1*) + 1

bits_per_pixel is based on the number of colors available on the display. Table 11-9 lists the *bits_per_pixel* value for each screen mode.

bit_planes is the number of different areas in memory used to store the color of a pixel. Table 11-9 lists the *bit_planes* value for each screen mode.

Screen mode	Bits per pixel	Bit planes
1	2	1
2	1	1
3	1	1
7	4	4
8	4	4
9	2	2 (if EGA adapter has 64 KB)
	4	4 (if EGA adapter has more than 64 KB)
10	2	2
11	1	1
12	4	4
13	8	1

Table 11-9.
Bits per pixel and bit planes for each screen mode.

In screen modes 7, 8, 9, and 12, the adapter divides the four bits for the color of each pixel among four separate rows of bits called bit planes; screen mode 10 divides the two bits for the color of each pixel between two bit planes. The values listed in Table 11-9 take this division into account.

The above formula returns the size of the array, in bytes. The actual number of elements required in the array depends on the type of array you use. Table 11-10 lists the element size (in bytes) for different array types.

Array type	Bytes per element
Integer	2
Long integer	4
Single precision	4
Double precision	8

Table 11-10.
Element size for different types of numeric arrays.

To copy the source rectangle defined by the coordinates (50, 20) and (69, 34) in screen 9, for example, you would need to dimension an integer array of 92 elements, as determined by the following calculation:

(4 + INT(((20) * (4 / 4) + 7) / 8) * 4 * 15) / 2 = 92

After you make the above calculation, you can execute the following statements to copy the source rectangle to *array*:

```
DIM array(0 TO 91) AS INTEGER
GET (50, 20)-(69, 34), array
```

Compatibility

QuickBASIC 2.0, QuickBASIC 3.0, and QuickBASIC for the Macintosh

QuickBASIC versions 2.0 and 3.0 and QuickBASIC for the Macintosh support the GET statement with only a few differences from QuickBASIC version 4.5. In these versions, you cannot use the STEP keyword in GET, so the coordinates you specify are always absolute coordinates. Also, QuickBASIC versions 2.0 and 3.0 do not allow you to specify the subscript of the element in which the storage of the image starts.

Example

See the PUT entry for an extended example that uses both GET and PUT.

LINE

See also: PALETTE, SCREEN (Statement)

■ QB2	■ QB4.5	■ PowerBASIC
■ QB3	✲ ANSI	■ GW-BASIC
■ QB4	■ BASIC7	✲ MacQB

Purpose

The LINE statement uses a straight line of a specified color and style to join two points on the graphics screen. The specified coordinates can also mark the corners of a rectangle, which can be filled with a color.

Syntax

LINE [[STEP](*x1*, *y1*)]-[STEP](*x2*, *y2*)[, [*color*][, [B[F]][, *style*]]]

x1, *y1*, *x2*, and *y2* are screen coordinates that specify the two ends of the line to be drawn. The optional STEP keyword indicates that the locations to which the coordinates refer are relative to the position of the graphics cursor.

color is the attribute number corresponding to the color in which the line is drawn.

The letter B directs LINE to draw a rectangle using the specified coordinates as the upper left and lower right corners. Adding an F creates a rectangle and fills it with the selected color.

style is a 16-bit value that specifies the style of the line drawn.

You must define the start and end points in the LINE statement by using either absolute or relative coordinates; all other arguments are optional. If you omit any argument that is not the last argument in the parameter list, you must insert a comma to mark its position.

Usage

```
LINE (120, 100)-(30, 15)
```

Draws a line (using the current foreground color) from location (30, 15) to (120, 100).

```
LINE (0, 0)-(639, 349), 9, BF
```

Draws a 640-by-350-pixel rectangle and fills the rectangle with light blue.

```
LINE -(100, 50), , B
```

Draws in the current foreground color a rectangle that has one corner at the graphics-cursor position and the opposite corner at the absolute coordinate (100, 50).

```
LINE -STEP(-60, -10), 14
```

Draws a bright yellow line from the graphics cursor position to a position 10 pixels above it and 60 pixels to its right.

```
LINE(x%, y%)-(x% + 20, y% + 12), c%, BF
```

Draws a box 12 pixels high and 20 pixels wide with the upper left corner specified by the integer variables *x%* and *y%*. The box is filled with the color specified by the value contained in *c%*.

```
LINE (100, 60)-(50, 30), 6, B, &H5555
```

Draws a rectangle with corners at the locations (100, 60) and (50, 30). The box is drawn with a brown dotted line.

Description

The range of coordinates allowed for the locations specified depends upon the dimensions of the current screen mode. (See the SCREEN (Statement) entry.) If you use the B or BF parameter, QuickBASIC draws a rectangle whose diagonally opposite corners are the specified points. Otherwise, LINE draws a straight line between the two points. If either of the coordinates refers to a point outside the current viewport, QuickBASIC does not report an error but merely draws the part of the line that is within the viewport.

The order of the two specified locations makes no difference. In fact, the following two statements produce the same line:

```
LINE (35, 18)-(178, 86)
LINE (178, 86)-(35, 18)
```

The number of available colors also depends on the current screen mode. The numbers for the colors correspond to the attribute numbers used by the COLOR statement. (See Table 11-4 in the COLOR entry.) However, if your computer has an EGA, VGA, or MCGA adapter, you can remap the attribute numbers to other colors by using the PALETTE statement.

By default, the lines and the outlines of the rectangles are solid and unbroken. You can, however, draw broken or dotted lines in a variety of styles. You can specify an integer argument whose bits are read (from left to right) as a mask that determines whether a particular pixel on the line is set. You usually specify the argument as a hexadecimal number. For example, &H5555 (21845 decimal) produces a dotted line with alternate pixels set, and &H0707 produces a dashed line, as shown in Figure 11-8.

Hexadecimal	Binary	Line drawn
&H5555	0101010101010101	▪▪▪▪▪▪▪▪
&H0707	0111011101110111	▬ ▬ ▬ ▬

Figure 11-8.
Examples of line styles.

You can define the pattern for both single lines and the sides of rectangles. The pattern does not affect the way that LINE fills the boxes; even if the lines that compose the sides of the rectangle are broken, the paint does not "leak" past the box boundaries.

Compatibility

ANSI BASIC

ANSI BASIC uses the GRAPH statement to draw geometrical figures. In ANSI BASIC you draw a line by using the GRAPH LINES statement followed by the coordinates of the two end points. To draw a rectangle, you use GRAPH LINES followed by coordinates specifying the four corners of the rectangle.

QuickBASIC for the Macintosh

The LINE statement in QuickBASIC for the Macintosh does not support the style parameter. Otherwise, this statement is identical to the LINE statement in QuickBASIC version 4.5.

Example

A powerful feature of the LINE statement is the STEP clause—it lets you draw complex figures without having to calculate the absolute coordinates of each point referenced. The following example uses LINE to draw a three-dimensional bar chart; plotting the coordinates of each bar with STEP makes the program much simpler because each bar is identical in shape and differs only in height. Figure 11-9 shows the output of this program.

```
SCREEN 9
LINE (0, 0)-(639, 349), 9, BF          ' paint entire screen blue
VIEW (32, 4)-(607, 345), 0, 15         ' define a viewport
WINDOW SCREEN (0, 0)-(255, 191)        ' define logical coordinate system

READ numItems%
DIM item!(numItems%)

xInt% = 240 \ numItems%                ' initialize interval for x
xWidth% = xInt% - 10
zWidth% = xWidth% * 2
```

(continued)

continued

```
FOR i% = 1 TO numItems%
    READ item!(i%)
    IF item!(i%) > max! THEN max! = item!(i%)
NEXT i%

yInt! = 160 / max!: i% = 1: clr% = 1

FOR x% = 15 TO 239 STEP xInt%          ' draw bars of the chart
    yLen% = item!(i%) * yInt!
    LINE (x%, 180)-(x% + xWidth%, 180 - yLen%), clr%, BF
    LINE -STEP(5, -3), clr%: LINE -STEP(-xWidth%, -0), clr%
    LINE -STEP(-5, 3), clr%: LINE -STEP(xWidth%, 0), clr%
    LINE -STEP(5, -3), clr%: LINE -STEP(0, yLen%), clr%
    LINE -STEP(-5, 3), clr%: i% = i% + 1: clr% = clr% + 1
    IF clr% = 7 THEN clr% = 9
NEXT x%
r$ = INPUT$(1)
END

DATA 12
DATA 356.21, 216.53, 99.9, 25.8, 176, 282.75
DATA 303.4, 111.11, 168.3, 271.9, 333.3, 88
```

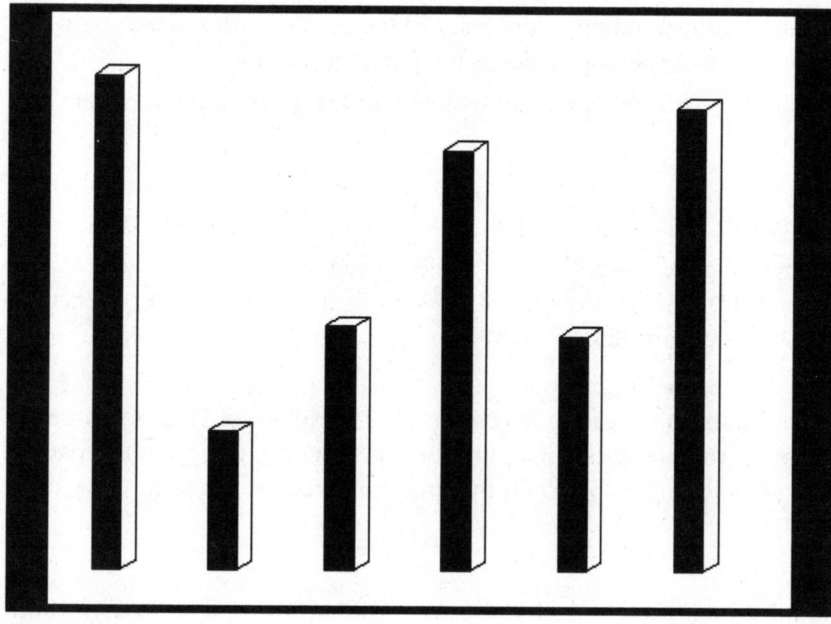

Figure 11-9.
Output of the LINE example program.

PAINT

See also: COLOR, PALETTE, SCREEN (Statement)

✲ QB2	■ QB4.5	■ PowerBASIC
✲ QB3	✲ ANSI	■ GW-BASIC
■ QB4	■ BASIC7	MacQB

Purpose

The PAINT statement fills an enclosed figure with a specified color. You can specify either a solid color or a mixture of colors that produces pixel patterns in a variety of colors.

Syntax

PAINT [STEP](*x*, *y*)[, [*color*][, [*border*][, *background*]]]

x and *y* are the coordinates of the point at which painting starts. The optional STEP keyword indicates that the coordinates are relative to the position of the graphics cursor.

color can be either a numeric expression or a string expression. A numeric expression specifies the attribute number corresponding to the color that will fill the area. A string expression defines a new paint pattern. If you omit *color*, PAINT fills the area with the current foreground color.

border is the number corresponding to the color of the area's border. If you omit this parameter, PAINT defaults to the same color as the parameter *color*.

background is a single-character string expression defining a background pattern that can be painted over.

Usage

```
PAINT (319, 174), 14, 4
```

Moves the graphics cursor to the center of a screen mode 9 display and fills the area with yellow (attribute 14) paint. Painting continues until either a red border is encountered or the entire viewport is filled.

```
PAINT STEP(xinc, yinc), pattern$, c$)
```

Moves the graphics cursor to a location *xinc* pixels to the right and *yinc* pixels below the current position of the graphics cursor and begins painting, using the tile pattern supplied in *pattern$*. Painting stops when the area bordered by a line in color *c$* is filled.

Description

To call PAINT to fill a figure, you must first specify the coordinates of a location within the figure at which painting is to start. The range of possible values of the coordinates is determined by the current graphics mode. For example, you can use the coordinates

(159, 99) to position the cursor at the center of the screen in screen mode 1 (medium-resolution graphics); for screen modes 11 and 12, however, you specify the screen center at coordinates (319, 239).

If you use the WINDOW statement to define your own logical coordinate system, QuickBASIC translates the logical coordinates sent to PAINT into physical pixel locations and plots them correctly. (See the WINDOW entry.)

PAINT assumes the border of the figure has already been drawn. It uses a "flood-fill" algorithm to set all the pixels within the border to the specified color attribute. If you do not specify a fill color, PAINT uses the current foreground color. If you do not specify the border color, PAINT fills the space defined by a border with the same color that it uses for painting. Be sure the area to be painted is totally enclosed by the border; if it is not, the paint "leaks" and fills the rest of the display (unless the figure is enclosed by another figure).

PAINT uses the program stack to record the location of pixels that are already set, so if the edges of the figure are particularly jagged, your program might report an "Out of stack space" error message. If this happens, use the CLEAR statement to increase the stack size. (See the CLEAR entry in Chapter 18, "DOS and Program Management.")

Paint Tiling

You can use a number to specify the solid color with which PAINT fills the enclosed figure. The values you can use are limited to the range of colors available in the current screen mode. By using a string value, however, you can specify a mixture of colors to produce a great variety of shades, textures, and patterns. This process of mixing paint colors is known as "tiling."

To understand how tiling works, you must first know how QuickBASIC produces solid colors in the screen mode you are using. In the 4-color graphics mode (screen mode 1), each pixel is represented by 2 bits of screen memory that specify one of the four colors. In the 2-color graphics mode (screen mode 2), each pixel is represented by 1 bit. In 16-color graphics modes (screen modes 7, 8, 9, and 12), each pixel is represented by four bits of screen memory, each of which defines an attribute of color. The four bits define a mixture of blue, red, green, and color intensity. The setting of each bit combines with the other bit settings to determine the color of the pixel. For example, a pixel set with bit values of 1010 is displayed in color 10, which is light green. Note that the value of the binary number 1010 is 10 in decimal. As Table 11-11 shows, the numbers of the 16 available colors specify the bit setting that creates the color.

If you want to create your own pattern for PAINT, you must design a tile, which is a rectangular grid of pixels that defines the pattern. The grid must always be eight bits across and can be up to 64 bits high. When you use PAINT with the tile, PAINT draws the tile repeatedly in order to fill an area.

Bit settings	Decimal value	Color
0000	0	Black
0001	1	Blue
0010	2	Green
0011	3	Cyan
0100	4	Red
0101	5	Magenta
0110	6	Brown
0111	7	White
1000	8	Gray
1001	9	Light blue
1010	10	Light green
1011	11	Light cyan
1100	12	Light red
1101	13	Light magenta
1110	14	Yellow
1111	15	Bright white

Table 11-11.
Bit settings for colors.

For screen mode 1, each row of the grid must contain the representation of 4 pixels to fill 8 bits. For screen mode 2, each row of the grid must contain the representation of 8 pixels. In screen modes 7, 8, 9, and 12, the four bits that represent each pixel are stored in four different areas of video memory, which are called "bit planes." Each byte of video memory (or row in the grid), therefore, contains one bit from eight different pixels.

For example, to produce an intermediate shade of green, you can design a tile in which adjacent pixels are two different intensities of green, as shown in Figure 11-10.

To specify the tile in the PAINT statement, you supply a string in which each byte contains the bits of each bit plane. For example, to produce the tile of eight pixels defined by the grid in Figure 11-10, you must specify a 4-character string in which the value of each character is the summation of the bits in one of the bit planes:

```
tile$ = CHR$(0) + CHR$(255) + CHR$(0) + CHR$(85)
```

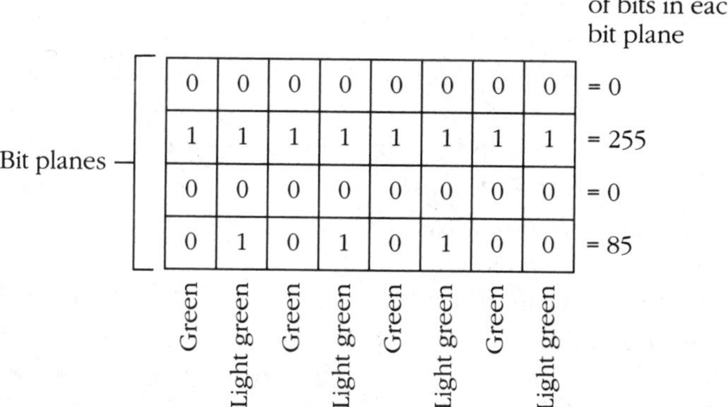

Figure 11-10.
A tile pattern of an intermediate shade of green for PAINT.

The following program paints three circles, using this tile pattern to paint one of them in a shade of green that is between the two intensities provided by QuickBASIC.

```
tile$ = CHR$(0) + CHR$(255) + CHR$(0) + CHR$(85)

SCREEN 9
FOR x% = 100 TO 500 STEP 200
    CIRCLE (x%, 174), 80, 4
NEXT x%

PAINT (100, 174), 2, 4
PAINT (300, 174), tile$, 4
PAINT (500, 174), 10, 4
END
```

You can, of course, blend different colors in the tile pattern, not merely different shades of the same color. This lets you produce many more interesting shades and textures.

PAINT also lets you create pattern strings as long as 64 characters, with each set of 4 characters defining the pattern for successive rows of eight pixels. Designing tile patterns can be tedious; however, it is worth the effort because you can use the same patterns in many different programs. You can even build your own library of patterns.

Compatibility

QuickBASIC 2.0 and QuickBASIC 3.0

QuickBASIC versions 2.0 and 3.0 do not support the STEP clause in the PAINT statement. The coordinates specified must be absolute.

ANSI BASIC

There is no PAINT statement in ANSI BASIC. To produce a filled-in area, use the GRAPH AREA statement.

Example

Paint tiling lets you obtain many more colors and shades than are normally available from the screen mode in use. It lets you create much more interesting and realistic effects than solid colors. The following program draws a mountain landscape and adds just enough color and texture to create "atmosphere."

One problem with paint tiling is blending the outline color with the interior texture of the figure being painted. This program solves the problem by retracing the border (using the LINE statement) with a style option that matches the bit pattern of the tile. This can produce some striking effects, especially if the figure has a complex outline.

```
SCREEN 8
DIM tile$(1 TO 8)
lnStyl% = &H55AA                       ' line style for the fourth pattern
PAINT (319, 99), 15
VIEW (14, 6)-(624, 123), 15, 0

FOR i% = 1 TO 21
    READ x1%, y1%, x2%, y2%, clr%      ' read line coordinates
    LINE (x1%, y1%)-(x2%, y2%), 0      ' draw landscape outline
NEXT i%

FOR i% = 1 TO 8
    READ j%                            ' read number of bytes in tile
    FOR k% = 1 TO j%
        READ byte%                     ' read pixel data
        tile$(i%) = tile$(i%) + CHR$(byte%)  ' build paint tile
    NEXT k%
NEXT i%

FOR i% = 1 TO 8
    READ x%, y%                        ' read coordinate for PAINT
    PAINT (x%, y%), tile$(i%), 0       ' paint enclosed area
NEXT i%

RESTORE                                         ' reset data pointer
FOR i% = 1 TO 21
    READ x1%, y1%, x2%, y2%, clr%               ' read line coordinates and color
    LINE (x1%, y1%)-(x2%, y2%), clr%            ' erase outline
NEXT i%

LINE (400, 90)-(430, 87), 4, , lnStyl%          ' touch up edge of fourth pattern 4
LINE -(520, 84), 4, , lnStyl%
LINE -(610, 82), 4, , lnStyl%
END
```

(continued)

continued

```
' screen coordinates and colors for lines
DATA 0, 75, 130, 66, 5, 130, 66, 150, 65, 9, 150, 65, 215, 60
DATA 9, 215, 60, 305, 65, 9, 305, 65, 380, 55, 9, 380, 55, 395
DATA 50, 9, 395, 50, 415, 55, 9, 415, 55, 460, 62, 9, 460, 62
DATA 520, 68, 9, 520, 68, 610, 75, 9, 0, 58, 130, 66, 9, 305
DATA 65, 610, 80, 5, 615, 98, 305, 98, 1, 305, 98, 380, 93, 1
DATA 380, 93, 400, 90, 1, 400, 90, 430, 87, 2, 430, 87, 520, 84
DATA 2, 520, 84, 610, 82, 2, 0, 90, 400, 90, 1, 0, 98, 610, 112
DATA 2, 615, 104, 285, 104, 14

' values for pattern tiles
DATA 4, 255, 0, 0, 255, 4, 255, 0, 0, 0
DATA 8, 0, 255, 170, 0, 0, 255, 85, 0
DATA 8, 0, 170, 85, 0, 0, 85, 170, 0
DATA 8, 85, 170, 255, 170, 170, 85, 255, 85
DATA 4, 255, 0, 255, 0, 4, 255, 0, 255, 170
DATA 4, 0, 255, 255, 255

' coordinates of areas for painting
DATA 10, 10, 10, 95, 305, 113, 600, 95, 305, 85
DATA 380, 60, 10, 63, 605, 110
```

PALETTE, PALETTE USING

■ QB2	■ QB4.5	■ PowerBASIC
■ QB3	ANSI	✲ GW-BASIC
■ QB4	■ BASIC7	■ MacQB

See also: COLOR, SCREEN (Statement)

Purpose

The PALETTE statement changes one color in the available palette to another; PALETTE USING changes every color in the palette. You can use the PALETTE USING statement to produce stunning graphics effects. For example, you might draw a complex screen image with every color set to the background attribute; the construction of the figure would proceed invisibly until, with one statement, you reset the palette and flashed the picture into view.

Syntax

PALETTE [*color, display*]
PALETTE USING *array*(*subscript*)

color is the attribute number of the color to be changed; *display* is the number of the new color to which the attribute is mapped.

array is the name of an array containing values of the colors to be mapped to the current palette; *subscript* identifies the element of the *array* at which remapping begins.

Usage

```
PALETTE 6, 14
```

Changes the color associated with attribute 6 from brown to yellow.

```
PALETTE USING clrs&(9)
```

Changes every attribute in the palette to the color value of an element in the array *clrs&*. The remapping begins at the element whose subscript is 9, so attribute 0 is assigned the color value contained in *clrs&* (9).

```
PALETTE
```

Sets every pixel on the display to its default color.

Description

The collection of display colors available in a specific screen mode is known as its *palette.* Depending on the current screen mode, a palette might contain 2, 4, 16, or even 256 colors. Each of these colors is assigned its own attribute number, which indicates that color's position in the palette. In computers with an EGA, VGA, or MCGA adapter, however, you can remap these attribute numbers to other colors so that, for example, a figure that was originally drawn in red can be changed to blue.

When a screen mode is selected for the first time, QuickBASIC assigns a default color number to each attribute in the palette for that mode. In screen modes with 16 colors (screen modes 7, 8, 9, and 12) the default palette is configured as shown in Table 11-12.

Attribute number	Color number	Color
0	0	Black
1	1	Blue
2	2	Green
3	3	Cyan
4	4	Red
5	5	Magenta
6	6	Brown
7	7	White
8	8	Gray
9	9	Light blue
10	10	Light green
11	11	Light cyan
12	12	Light red
13	13	Light magenta
14	14	Yellow
15	15	Bright white

Table 11-12.
Attribute and color numbers for 16-color screen modes.

PALETTE lets you change the color number assigned to any single attribute in the palette. Doing this causes every pixel on the screen with that attribute to be displayed in the new color. This change also affects subsequent graphics output to the screen: any graphics statements in which you can specify an attribute (LINE, CIRCLE, or PAINT, for example) will draw using the color assigned to the attribute.

All changes remain in effect until you either change the screen mode or cancel the changes by using another PALETTE statement. Using PALETTE without arguments restores the attribute of every pixel on the screen to its default color for that screen mode.

PALETTE USING lets you use a single statement to change the colors assigned to all the attributes in the palette. To use this statement, you must first dimension an array that contains at least the same number of elements as there are colors in the current palette. The elements of the array must be the correct type to hold the color values. In EGA modes, an integer array is sufficient; because of the way VGA and MCGA modes create colors, however, these modes require long integers. To specify the color values of the new palette, assign values to the elements of the array. If you do not want to change an attribute, assign a value of –1 instead of a color number to the element. For example, if you fill an array with the values specified in Table 11-13, you can use the array in a PALETTE USING statement to change the palette.

Subscript	Number	Color
0	–1	Retain current value (black by default)
1	9	Change to light blue
2	–1	Retain current value (green by default)
3	1	Change to blue
4	6	Change to brown
5	12	Change to light red
6	14	Change to yellow
7	15	Change to bright white
8	0	Change to black
9	–1	Retain current value (light blue by default)
10	2	Change to green
11	–1	Retain current value (light cyan by default)
12	4	Change to red
13	4	Change to red
14	–1	Retain current value (yellow by default)
15	–1	Retain current value (bright white by default)

Table 11-13.
Example of values in an array used in PALETTE USING.

To put these new colors into effect, you need only call the statement

```
PALETTE USING array
```

In this statement, *array* is the name of the array containing the color numbers listed in Table 11-13.

Although the previous examples use color numbers only in the range 0 through 15, you can assign as many as 64 different colors in EGA modes and 262,144 colors in VGA and MCGA modes.

The color numbers for the EGA modes range from 0 through 63. Although there are 262,144 different colors available in the VGA and MCGA modes, their numbers do not range from 0 through 262,143. Instead, you must calculate the value for each color. Each color in these modes is a specific mixture of intensities of the colors blue, green, and red. The color intensity can range from 0 through 63. To calculate a color's value, use the following formula, in which *blue*, *green*, and *red* are values specifying the intensity:

value = (65536 * *blue*) + (256 * *green*) + *red*

If you want to create a pure, bright blue, for example, use in the calculation an intensity of 63 for *blue* and an intensity of 0 for *green* and for *red*. The result of the calculation is the value 4128768.

Tips

You can use the PALETTE USING statement to conceal from the user the construction of a complex graphics display. To do this, first define an array large enough to hold the palette of colors for the current screen mode. The following is an example for screen mode 9:

```
DIM clrs%(0 TO 15) AS INTEGER
PALETTE USING clrs%
```

When the array is first defined, every element is assigned a value of 0; therefore, the PALETTE USING statement remaps every screen color to 0, which is the background color. Now when you draw the display it remains invisible to the user until you execute the PALETTE statement without any parameters.

Using this statement without any parameters restores the default colors and flashes the completed design onto the screen in an instant.

Compatibility

GW-BASIC and BASICA

BASICA does not support the PALETTE and PALETTE USING statements. GW-BASIC supports these statements only when the computer has an EGA adapter.

Example

Because the PALETTE USING statement changes screen colors without redrawing the figures displayed, it is often used to produce animation effects. The following program cycles through a regular succession of color changes to create the illusion of movement through a tunnel.

```
SCREEN 9
DIM array(0 TO 32) AS INTEGER
PALETTE USING array(0)              ' set every color to the background color
FOR i% = 1 TO 32: array(i%) = (i% MOD 15) + 1: NEXT  ' fill array for palette
LINE (0, 0)-(639, 399), 1, BF
clr% = 0                            ' change foreground color to the background
FOR i% = 440 TO 10 STEP -10         ' paint screen with concentric circles
    clr% = clr% + 1
    IF clr% > 15 THEN clr% = 1      ' give each circle a different color
    IF clr% = 8 THEN clr% = 9
    CIRCLE (320, 200), i%, 0
    PAINT (320, 200), clr%, 0
NEXT i%
PALETTE                             ' restore the default colors
DO
    FOR i% = 15 TO 1 STEP -1
        a1% = array(i%): array(i%) = 0  ' set first color of new palette to 0
        PALETTE USING array(i%)         ' change palettes
        array(i%) = a1%
        IF INKEY$ = CHR$(27) THEN EXIT FOR
    NEXT i%
LOOP UNTIL i%
END
```

PCOPY

See also: SCREEN (Statement)

■ QB2	■ QB4.5	PowerBASIC
■ QB3	ANSI	✲ GW-BASIC
■ QB4	■ BASIC7	MacQB

Purpose

The PCOPY statement copies one screen page to another. Computers with graphics adapters can switch between as many as eight different screen pages; the current screen mode and the amount of available video memory determine the number of screen pages available.

Syntax

PCOPY *source, destination*

source is an integer that specifies the number of the screen page to be copied; *destination* is an integer that specifies the number of the screen page to which the source page is copied.

Usage

```
PCOPY 3, 0
```

Copies the contents of display page 3 to page 0, the first screen page.

```
PCOPY page%, page% + 1
```

Copies the contents of the display page specified by *page%* to the display page that follows it.

Description

To use PCOPY, your computer must have a display adapter that supports multiple screen pages. Systems with EGA and VGA adapters permit as many as eight screen pages in screen modes 0, 7, 8, 9, and 10; CGA and MCGA systems can display as many as eight pages in screen mode 0. Computers with monochrome display adapters are limited to a single screen page and do not support PCOPY. (See the SCREEN (Statement) entry for a complete list of the number of pages available in different graphics modes.)

Errors

If you issue a PCOPY statement in a screen mode that does not support multiple screen pages, QuickBASIC returns an "Illegal function call" error message. Attempting to use PCOPY to copy either to or from a page number that is outside of the range available to the current screen mode also results in an "Illegal function call" error message.

Tips

PCOPY works only in text screen mode 0 and in graphics screen modes 7 and higher, so owners of computers equipped with CGA cannot use PCOPY in graphics mode. However, the entry for the SADD statement (discussed in Chapter 20, "Mixed Language") includes a sample routine that copies the contents of the screen to and from a string variable. You can use this routine to simulate the action of PCOPY in screen modes 1 and 2.

Compatibility

GW-BASIC and BASICA

GW-BASIC supports PCOPY; BASICA does not.

Example

When used with the SCREEN statement, PCOPY can store graphics and text on a screen page; you can then copy the screen page to the active display whenever you need it. The following program includes an offline help screen. The user can display Help with a single keypress and then restore the original display with another keypress.

```
' this program will not run on monochrome systems
SCREEN 0, , 1, 0       ' sets active page to page 1, displayed page to page 0

' draw Help screen on the active page
COLOR , 1: CLS : COLOR , 0
FOR row% = 11 TO 16
    LOCATE row%, 29: PRINT SPACE$(24):
NEXT row%
COLOR 0, 3

' draw box
LOCATE 10, 28: PRINT CHR$(201); STRING$(22, 205); CHR$(187);
FOR row% = 11 TO 14
    LOCATE row%, 28: PRINT CHR$(186); SPACE$(22); CHR$(186);
NEXT row%
LOCATE row%, 28: PRINT CHR$(200); STRING$(22, 205);
PRINT CHR$(188): : LOCATE 12, 34

' display the message
FOR i% = 1 TO 11: READ a%: PRINT CHR$(a%); : NEXT
LOCATE 13, 30
FOR i% = 1 TO 20: READ a%: PRINT CHR$(a%); : NEXT


SCREEN , , 0, 0        ' change active page to page 0, the displayed page
COLOR 14, 2: CLS
LOCATE 3, 28: PRINT " PCOPY  DEMONSTRATION ";
LOCATE 5, 1: PRINT STRING$(80, "-"); : COLOR 14, 4
LOCATE 24, 1: PRINT SPACE$(80);
PCOPY 0, 2             ' copy displayed page to page 2
LOCATE 24, 26: PRINT "Press any key for help."

r$ = INPUT$(1)
PCOPY 1, 0             ' copy Help screen to displayed page
LOCATE 24, 1: PRINT SPACE$(80):
LOCATE 24, 29: PRINT "Press any key to resume."

r$ = INPUT$(1)
PCOPY 2, 0             ' restore original page
COLOR 7, 0
END

DATA  73, 84, 39, 83, 32, 65, 76, 76, 32, 73, 78
DATA  84, 72, 69, 32, 81, 117, 105, 99, 107, 66, 65
DATA  83, 73, 67, 32, 66, 73, 66, 76, 69
```

PMAP

See also: VIEW, WINDOW

■ QB2	■ QB4.5	■ PowerBASIC
■ QB3	ANSI	■ GW-BASIC
■ QB4	■ BASIC7	MacQB

Purpose

The PMAP function maps a physical coordinate to a logical coordinate or vice versa. If your display contains a mixture of logical and physical coordinates, you can use the PMAP function to convert coordinates from one system to the other.

Syntax

PMAP(*coordinate, action*)

coordinate is a single-precision value that represents one of the coordinates of the pixel to be mapped.

action is an integer value that indicates whether *coordinate* is an *x*- or a *y*-coordinate and whether the coordinate value should be translated from the logical to the physical system or vice versa. *action* can have the following values:

Value	Description
0	Converts the coordinate from a logical coordinate to a physical *x*-coordinate
1	Converts the coordinate from a logical coordinate to a physical *y*-coordinate
2	Converts the coordinate from a physical coordinate to a logical *x*-coordinate
3	Converts the coordinate from a physical coordinate to a logical *y*-coordinate

Usage

```
myY! = PMAP(180, 1)
```

Translates physical coordinate 180 on the *y*-axis to a logical value; the logical value is determined by the coordinate system defined in the most recent WINDOW statement. The logical *y*-coordinate returned is assigned to the single-precision variable *myY!*.

```
CIRCLE (PMAP(160, 2), PMAP(100, 3)), 50, 3
```

Draws a circle using physical coordinates for the location of the center. This ensures that the circle is always centered on a 320-by-200-pixel viewport, regardless of the current logical coordinate system.

Description

PMAP does not directly affect pixels on the screen. It merely translates pixel coordinates from one coordinate system for use in graphics statements.

The physical coordinate system is determined by the number of pixels available in the current screen mode and by the limits of the current graphics viewport defined by the most recent VIEW statement. (See the VIEW entry.) If no VIEW statement has been executed, the viewport is the size of the screen.

You can use the WINDOW statement to define your own logical coordinate system and to map it onto the viewport. (See the WINDOW entry.) This lets you use logical coordinates in graphics statements, such as LINE, CIRCLE, PAINT, GET, PUT, PSET, and PRESET.

The value returned by PMAP when translating from logical to physical coordinates will most often be a single-precision variable because the act of translating physical coordinates into logical coordinates rarely produces an integer value.

The following program segment maps a logical coordinate system that has values for *x* and *y* that range from -1000 through 1000 onto a 640-by-200-pixel physical coordinate system:

```
SCREEN 2
WINDOW (-1000, -1000)-(1000, 1000)
```

Figure 11-11 illustrates the mapping of the logical coordinate system onto the physical coordinate system. Notice that the origin of the logical coordinate system, the location specified by (0, 0), is the center of the screen and that the greatest value of *y* is at the

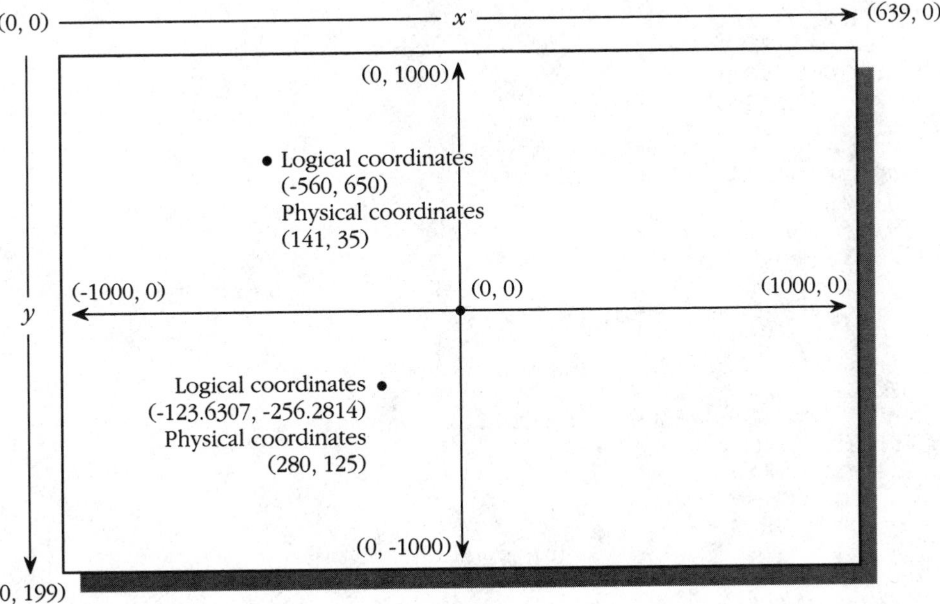

Figure 11-11.
PMAP translates between logical and physical coordinate systems.

top of the screen. In the physical coordinate system, the origin is at the upper left corner of the screen, and the greatest *y* value is at the bottom of the screen.

Example

The WINDOW statement is particularly useful because it lets you specify a logical coordinate system that is smaller than the physical dimensions of the current viewport. Only those points whose coordinates are within the logical frame of the window can be plotted, thus displaying a small section of what might be a much larger picture. Furthermore, by changing the window's range of logical coordinates you can bring other parts of the display into view, as though you were panning a video camera.

Usually, however, when the camera pans, it focuses on an object that is moving against a stationary background. You can achieve the same effect in QuickBASIC by keeping the object stationary and moving the background instead. To do this, use PMAP to plot the foreground image using physical coordinates, so that the image appears at the same position in the viewport regardless of which part of the logical display is visible in the background. The following program uses the PMAP function to translate physical coordinates to logical coordinates, so that each of five windows has the foreground image as its focus. Figure 11-12 shows the output of this program.

```
DECLARE SUB DrawWorld ()

SCREEN 9: LINE (0, 0)-(639, 349), 9, BF
x1 = 100: x2 = 256: y1 = 10: y2 = 70          ' define coordinates for window
x% = 10: y% = 10                              ' define coordinates for viewport
xChange = -100: numIter% = 1
DO
    VIEW (x%, y%)-(x% + 300, y% + 155), 0, 15     ' define a viewport
    WINDOW SCREEN (x1, y1)-(x2, y2)               ' define a window
    DrawWorld                                     ' draw background image
    numIter% = numIter% + 1
    xPhys = PMAP(150, 2): yPhys = PMAP(75, 3)
    IF y1 > 10 THEN                               ' draw foreground image
        CIRCLE (xPhys, yPhys), 10, 13, -.8, -5.78
    ELSE
        CIRCLE (xPhys, yPhys), 10, 13, -3.9, -2.2
    END IF
    PAINT (PMAP(150, 2), PMAP(68, 3)), 13, 13
    CIRCLE (PMAP(150, 2), PMAP(68, 3)), 1, 1, , , 3
    x% = x% + 320
    IF numIter% = 3 THEN
        x% = 10: y% = 175
        x1 = x1 - 100: x2 = x2 - 100: xChange = -xChange
        y1 = y1 + 22: y2 = y2 + 22
    END IF
    x1 = x1 + xChange: x2 = x2 + xChange
    r$ = INPUT$(1)
LOOP UNTIL numIter% = 5
```

(continued)

continued

```
VIEW (160, 97)-(460, 252), 0, 15
WINDOW SCREEN (0, 0)-(256, 120): DrawWorld        ' draw entire background
CIRCLE (138, 84), 10, 13, -3.9, -2.2              ' draw foreground image
PAINT (138, 86), 13, 13
CIRCLE (138, 81), 1, 1, , , 3
END

SUB DrawWorld STATIC
    LINE (0, 0)-(256, 27), 14, BF: LINE (0, 28)-(256, 118), 4, B
    LINE (4, 30)-(252, 116), 4, B: LINE (30, 50)-(251, 52), 4, B
    PAINT (128, 51), 4, 4: LINE (3, 72)-(226, 74), 4, B
    PAINT (128, 73), 4, 4: LINE (30, 94)-(251, 96), 4, B
    PAINT (128, 95), 4, 4: PAINT (128, 29), 4, 4
    PAINT (2, 80), 4, 4: PAINT (254, 70), 4, 4
    LINE (208, 27)-(251, 30), 14, BF
    CIRCLE (118, 84), 10, 6: PAINT (118, 84), 6, 6
    CIRCLE (114, 82), 4, 0: CIRCLE (122, 82), 4, 0
    PAINT (114, 82), 15, 0: PAINT (122, 82), 15, 0
    CIRCLE (117, 82), 2, 1: CIRCLE (119, 82), 2, 1
    CIRCLE (118, 86), 2, 0: PAINT (118, 86), 0, 0
END SUB
```

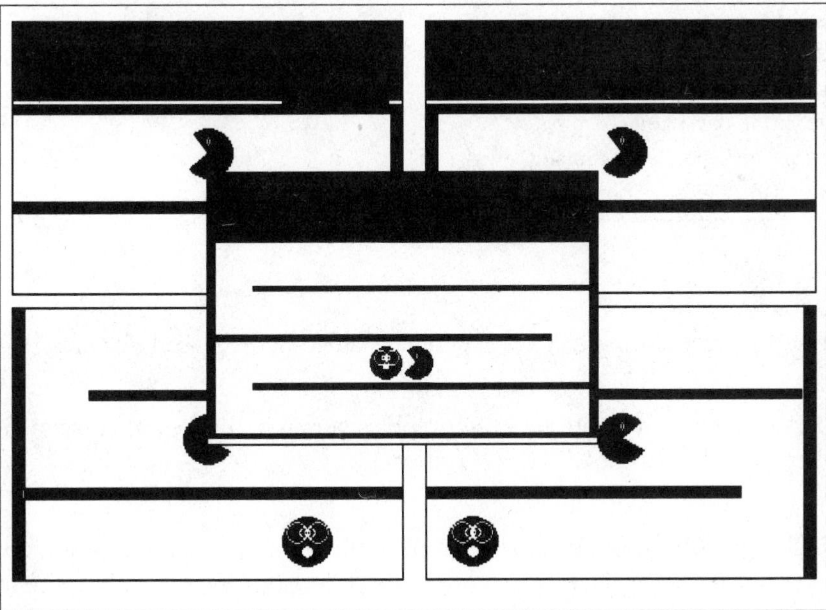

Figure 11-12.
Output of the PMAP example.

POINT

See also: PALETTE, PMAP, PSET, WINDOW

■ QB2	■ QB4.5	■ PowerBASIC
■ QB3	ANSI	■ GW-BASIC
■ QB4	■ BASIC7	✲ MacQB

Purpose

The POINT function returns either the color of a pixel or one of its coordinates. If the function is called with a pair of coordinates, it returns the color attribute number of the pixel at the specified location. If called with a single argument, it returns the *x*- or *y*-coordinate of the graphics cursor as either a logical or a physical coordinate.

Syntax

POINT(*x*, *y*)

or

POINT(*switch*)

x and *y* are the horizontal and vertical coordinates of the pixel to be examined.

switch is an integer value in the range 0 through 3 that specifies the graphics cursor coordinate to be returned. *switch* can have the following values:

Value	Description
0	Returns the physical *x*-coordinate
1	Returns the physical *y*-coordinate
2	Returns the logical *x*-coordinate
3	Returns the logical *y*-coordinate

Usage

```
PRINT POINT(319, 174)
```

Prints the attribute number of the pixel at the center of a 640-by-350-pixel display.

```
lastY! = POINT(3)
```

Assigns to *lastY!* the horizontal position of the graphics cursor in the logical coordinate system defined by the most recent WINDOW statement.

Description

The POINT function can be used to return the attribute number of a specified pixel. Note that the number of the displayed color might be different if the colors have been remapped by the PALETTE statement. If the given coordinates specify a point outside the current viewport, POINT returns a value of –1.

If you call POINT with a single argument, the function returns one of the coordinates of the graphics cursor. The coordinate can be the *x*- or the *y*-coordinate in either the physical or the logical coordinate system.

If no WINDOW statement is in effect, POINT returns the physical *x*- and *y*-coordinates of the graphics cursor even if the argument specifies logical coordinates.

The graphics cursor is not a physical object, as the text cursor is. It is merely a term that refers to the most recent point referenced on the graphics screen. Therefore, if you draw a line between two points by calling the statement

```
LINE (10, 10)-(110, 60), 3
```

the graphics cursor is at the endpoint of the line, which is the location (110, 60). The next LINE statement, however, would change the cursor position again. If you select a new screen mode or use CLS to clear the display, the graphics cursor moves to its default location at the center of the current viewport.

It is possible for the graphics cursor to be outside the boundaries of the current coordinate system. Although QuickBASIC doesn't draw the parts of lines or circles that are outside the viewport, it still plots their endpoints so the objects can be clipped correctly. In such cases, the graphics cursor position that POINT returns can be greater than the maximum or less than the minimum value defined by the current coordinate system.

Compatibility

QUICKBASIC for the Macintosh

The POINT function in QuickBASIC for the Macintosh does not return the position of the graphics cursor. It merely examines the pixel at the specified *x*- and *y*-coordinates and returns a value of 33 if the pixel is set (nonwhite) or 30 if it is not set (white).

Example

Programs that draw patterns often use POINT to test the color of a pixel before changing it to a different color. The following example uses this procedure when drawing diagonal lines to set the color of only those pixels that are currently turned off; the pixels that are turned on are set to the background color. The result is an intricate and everchanging pattern.

```
SCREEN 1: COLOR 0, 1: DEFINT A-Z: RANDOMIZE TIMER

DO
    CLS
    xMin = 0: xMax = 319: yMin = 0: yMax = 199      ' define boundaries
    clr = INT(RND * 3) + 1
    xChange = SGN((RND * 2) - 1.5): yChange = SGN((RND * 2) - 1.5)
    xStart = INT(RND * (xMax - xMin)) + xMin
    yStart = INT(RND * (yMax - yMin)) + yMin
```

(continued)

continued

```
    DO
        IF xStart + xChange > xMax OR xStart + xChange < xMin THEN
            xChange = -xChange
        END IF
        IF yStart + yChange > yMax OR yStart + yChange < yMin THEN
            yChange = -yChange
        END IF
        xStart = xStart + xChange: yStart = yStart + yChange
        x = xStart: y = yStart

        IF POINT(x, y) = 0 THEN                         ' check color of pixel
            LINE (x, y)-(x + 2, y + 3), clr, BF
            x = xMax - xStart: LINE (x, y)-(x + 2, y + 3), clr, BF
            y = yMax - yStart: LINE (x, y)-(x + 2, y + 3), clr, BF
            x = xStart: LINE (x, y)-(x + 2, y + 3), clr, BF
        ELSE
            LINE (x, y)-(x + 2, y + 3), 0, BF
            x = xMax - xStart: LINE (x, y)-(x + 2, y + 3), 0, BF
            y = yMax - yStart: LINE (x, y)-(x + 2, y + 3), 0, BF
            x = xStart: LINE (x, y)-(x + 2, y + 3), 0, BF
        END IF
        r$ = INKEY$
        clr = clr + 1: IF clr > 3 THEN clr = 1
    LOOP WHILE r$ = ""
LOOP UNTIL r$ = CHR$(27)
SCREEN 0: WIDTH 80: COLOR 15, 0: CLS
END
```

PRESET, PSET

See also: COLOR, SCREEN (Statement)

■ QB2	■ QB4.5	■ PowerBASIC
■ QB3	ANSI	■ GW-BASIC
■ QB4	■ BASIC7	■ MacQB

Purpose

PRESET and PSET statements set or reset a single point, or pixel, on the graphics screen. Typically these statements are used within a program's loop structure for plotting graphs and geometric figures.

Syntax

PRESET [STEP](*x*, *y*) [, *attribute*]
PSET [STEP](*x*, *y*) [, *attribute*]

x and *y* are the horizontal and vertical coordinates of the pixel to be set.

attribute is the pixel's display attribute, which defines the color to which the pixel will be set.

The STEP keyword indicates that the location to which the coordinates refer is relative to the position of the graphics cursor.

Usage

```
PRESET (xPos%, yPos%)
```

Moves the graphics cursor to the coordinate specified by the variables *xPos%* and *yPos%* and sets the pixel to the current background color.

```
PSET (160, 100), 3
```

Sets the pixel at the location specified by the coordinates 160 and 100 to the color assigned to attribute 3 in the current palette.

```
PSET STEP(20, -10)
```

Moves to the location 20 pixels to the right and 10 pixels up from the position of the graphics cursor and sets that pixel to the current foreground color.

Description

The only difference between PRESET and PSET is that if the attribute parameter is omitted, PRESET sets a pixel with the current background color, whereas PSET sets the pixel with the foreground color. The numbers of the color attribute you can use depend on the current screen mode.

QuickBASIC does not report an error if the specified coordinates are outside the current viewport; however, in this case, no pixel on the screen is either set or reset.

Example

Programs rarely need to set only a single pixel. Sometimes, however, the shape of the figure to be drawn is determined by calculations made while the program is executing and is too complex for the usual LINE or CIRCLE statements. The following program accepts data that is entered and uses it to plot a geometric figure.

The program uses the number of degrees the user specifies to plot a series of points that form a spiral. The user also must choose between points and lines. If lines are specified, the program uses PSET to connect the points of the spiral. After drawing the spiral, the progam uses PRESET to erase it. Figure 11-13 shows the output of this program.

```
CLS
INPUT "Enter angle between points, in degrees: ", degrees
PRINT : INPUT "<P>oints or <L>ines"; s$
s$ = UCASE$(LEFT$(s$, 1))

xMax = 319: yMax = 199: SCREEN 1        ' screen limits
CLS
x1 = xMax / 2: y1 = yMax / 2            ' set x1 and y1 to half screen limits
PRINT degrees; "Degrees"
radians = degrees / 57.29578            ' convert degrees to radians
IF s$ = "P" THEN PRINT "Points" ELSE PRINT "Lines"

FOR black% = 0 TO 1                     ' first draw points, then erase them
    FOR angle = 0 TO yMax / 2 STEP radians
        x = angle * COS(angle) + (xMax / 2)
        y = angle * SIN(angle) + (yMax / 2)
        IF x < 0 OR x > xMax OR y < 0 OR y > yMax THEN
            EXIT FOR
        END IF
        r$ = INKEY$: IF r$ = CHR$(27) THEN EXIT FOR
        IF s$ = "P" THEN
            IF black% THEN
                PRESET (x, y)           ' erase points
            ELSE
                PSET (x, y)             ' draw points
            END IF
        ELSE                            ' draw (or erase) lines
            IF x = x1 THEN
                IF y1 < y THEN change = 1 ELSE change = -1
                FOR z = y1 TO y STEP change
                    IF black% THEN
                        PRESET (x1, z)          ' erase lines
                    ELSE
                        PSET (x1, z)            ' draw lines
                    END IF
                NEXT z
            ELSE
                slope = (y - y1) / (x - x1)
                IF ABS(slope) > 1 THEN change = ABS(1 / slope) ELSE change = 1
                IF x1 > x THEN change = -change
                FOR z = x1 TO x STEP change
                    IF black% THEN
                        PRESET (z, slope * (z - x1) + y1)     ' erase lines
                    ELSE
                        PSET (z, slope * (z - x1) + y1)       ' draw lines
                    END IF
                NEXT z
                x1 = x: y1 = y
            END IF
        END IF
    NEXT angle
NEXT black%
END
```

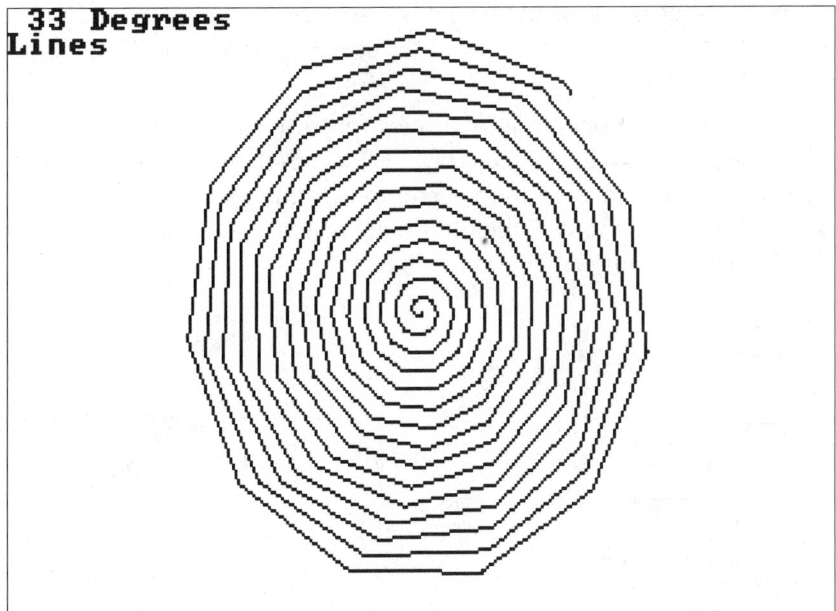

Figure 11-13.
Output of the PRESET, PSET example program.

PUT (Graphics)

See also: GET (Graphics), PSET, WINDOW

✲ QB2	■ QB4.5	■ PowerBASIC
✲ QB3	ANSI	■ GW-BASIC
■ QB4	■ BASIC7	✲ MacQB

Purpose

The PUT statement copies a graphics image from the array in which it has been stored into a specified screen location. Its counterpart, the GET statement, copies an area of the screen into an array. This lets you move an image from one part of the display to another.

Syntax

PUT [STEP](*x*, *y*), *array*[(*subscript*)] [, *action*]

x and *y* are the screen coordinates of the upper left corner of the rectangle into which the image is copied. The STEP keyword specifies that the location to which these coordinates refer is relative to the position of the graphics cursor.

array is the name of the numeric array that holds the image data. You can specify the array element from which copying starts by including *subscript* in parentheses. If you omit *subscript*, the image is copied starting with the first element in the array.

action is a constant that specifies how the image is displayed on the screen if another image already exists. If no constant is provided, PUT uses XOR by default. The following list describes the constants.

- AND Performs a logical AND operation with each pixel in the target rectangle and the corresponding pixel in the source array. PUT writes the resulting value to the screen. If corresponding bits of the source and destination pixels are the same, the resulting bit is unchanged. If the bits do not match, the resulting bit is 0, as shown in the following example:

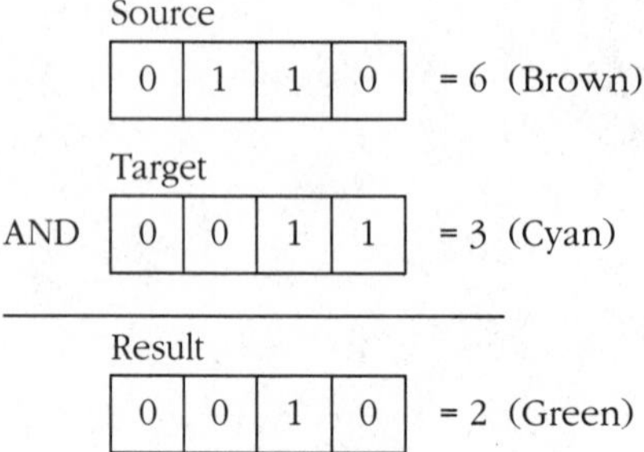

- OR Performs a logical OR operation with each pixel in the target rectangle and the equivalent pixel in the source array. PUT writes the resulting value to the screen. If either of the corresponding bits in the pixel is 1, the resulting bit is 1, as shown in the following example:

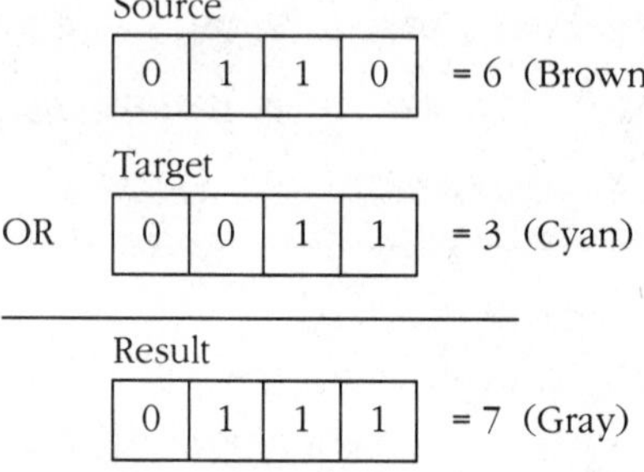

- PRESET Overwrites the target rectangle with the image stored in the source array and logically inverts the image as it is transferred, as shown in the following example:

Source

0	1	1	0	= 6 (Brown)

Result

1	0	0	1	= 9 (Light blue)

- PSET Overwrites the target rectangle with the image stored in the source array.
- XOR Performs a logical XOR (exclusive or) operation with each pixel in the source array and the corresponding target pixel. PUT writes the resulting value to the screen. XOR inverts the screen image. If either but not both of the corresponding bits in the pixel is 1, the resulting bit is 1, as shown in the following example:

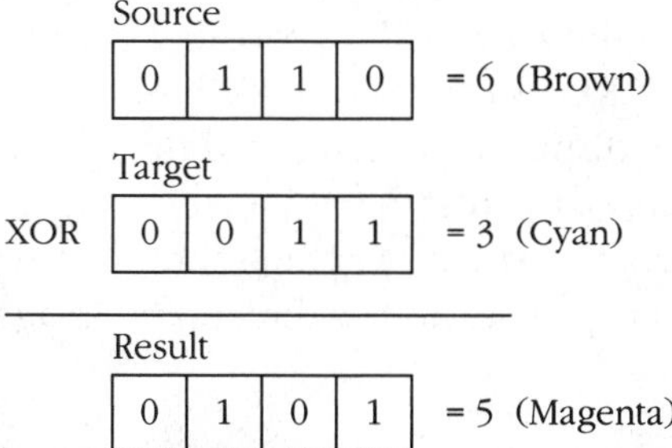

Note that using PUT twice in succession with XOR restores the original contents of the target rectangle. This is a useful technique for generating animation effects in which the movement of an image must not destroy its background.

Usage

```
PUT (160, 100), image%
```

Copies the image stored in the integer array *image%* into a screen rectangle whose upper left corner is at position (160, 100). PUT performs logical XOR operations with the image and the existing display.

```
PUT STEP(xInc, yInc), image(0, 5), PSET
```

Defines a rectangular area of the screen whose upper left corner is offset *xInc* pixels on the *x*-axis and *yInc* pixels on the *y*-axis from the graphics-cursor position. PUT copies the image stored in the fifth column of the two-dimensional array *image* into this area, thus overwriting any previous contents.

Description

The GET statement lets you copy the pixels from a rectangular area of the screen into a numeric array. PUT lets you copy these pixels back onto the screen at any location.

QuickBASIC lets you specify a logical operator with the PUT statement so that you can either combine the stored image with graphics already on the screen or overwrite the current contents of the display. You can, for example, reverse the original image (PRESET), superimpose it onto the existing pixels (OR), or invert each screen pixel that matches a pixel in the source array (XOR).

XOR is particularly useful for animation effects, because using PUT twice with the same image at the same location draws and then erases the image, thus restoring that area of the screen to its original state. You can, therefore, make an image appear to move against a constant background by using PUT with XOR twice and then repeating the process again at the next location in the sequence. (Be careful to specify a long enough interval between the two PUT statements; too short a gap causes the image to flicker unpleasantly.)

Warnings

Usually, the *x*- and *y*-coordinates you pass to the PUT statement define the upper left corner of the rectangle into which the contents of the array will be copied. However, if you use the WINDOW statement without the SCREEN keyword to define your own logical coordinate system, the vertical axis of the display is reversed and the specified *x*- and *y*-coordinates indicate the lower left corner of the rectangle. The following program illustrates this by copying an image to an array and then switching coordinate systems. When the program uses PUT to copy the image back to the screen, the image is inverted horizontally.

```
DIM array(100) AS INTEGER

SCREEN 1
LINE (150, 40)-(170, 60), 3
GET (150, 40)-(170, 60), array
WINDOW (0, 0)-(320, 200)
PUT (150, 100), array, PSET
END
```

Compatibility

QuickBASIC 2.0, QuickBASIC 3.0, and QuickBASIC for the Macintosh

QuickBASIC versions 2.0 and 3.0 and QuickBASIC for the Macintosh support the PUT statement with only a few differences from QuickBASIC version 4.5. You cannot use the STEP keyword in PUT. The coordinates you specify must be absolute coordinates. Also, QuickBASIC versions 2.0 and 3.0 do not allow you to specify the subscript of the array element at which the copying of the image begins.

QuickBASIC for the Macintosh lets you change the shape or size of the image by including coordinates for the lower right corner of the destination rectangle.

Example

You can use PUT to copy graphics images that have been stored by the GET statement to successive areas of the screen; this produces the effect of animation. The following program implements this technique and lets you use the arrow keys to "walk" a pair of footprints around the screen. It also illustrates how images can be stored in and copied from multidimensional arrays.

The first part of the program builds a collection of images from one basic image. Notice how the DRAW statement rotates the original figure to produce images pointing in four directions (corresponding to the four arrow keys).

The program uses the loop in the second part of the program to control the animation sequence. Two PUT statements that use XOR are made to each location, one to draw the image and one to erase it. This ensures that the background is restored before the program moves the image to a new location.

```
DIM ftUp%(25), ftDown%(25), ftLeft%(25), ftRight%(25)
DIM feet%(50, 3, 1)
DIM xInc%(3), yInc%(3)         ' arrays for incrementing position
DIM forward%(8)                ' array to figure which foot will be forward

FOR i% = 0 TO 3: READ xInc%(i%), yInc%(i%): NEXT

upArrow$ = CHR$(0) + CHR$(72): downArrow$ = CHR$(0) + CHR$(80)
leftArrow$ = CHR$(0) + CHR$(75): rightArrow$ = CHR$(0) + CHR$(77)
foot$ = "C2 S4 R2 D2 L2 U2 BM+1,+1P2,2BM-1,+3R2 D1 L2 U1 BM+1,+1P2,2"

SCREEN 1: x% = 50: y% = 50

' draw a foot for each direction and get the image
DRAW "BM52,51" + foot$
GET (x% + 2, y% + 1)-(x% + 4, y% + 6), ftUp%
DRAW "BM104,56 TA180" + foot$
GET (x% + 52, y% + 1)-(x% + 54, y% + 6), ftDown%
DRAW "BM152,54 TA90" + foot$
GET (x% + 102, y% + 2)-(x% + 109, y% + 4), ftLeft%
DRAW "BM208,52 TA270" + foot$
GET (x% + 152, y% + 2)-(x% + 159, y% + 4), ftRight%

' display the second foot for each direction
' and the pairs with the opposite foot forward
FOR i% = 1 TO 3
    READ xChange%, yChange%
    PUT (x% + xChange%, y% + yChange%), ftUp%, PSET
    READ xChange%, yChange%
    PUT (x% + xChange%, y% + yChange%), ftDown%, PSET
    READ xChange%, yChange%
    PUT (x% + xChange%, y% + yChange%), ftLeft%, PSET
    READ xChange%, yChange%
    PUT (x% + xChange%, y% + yChange%), ftRight%, PSET
NEXT i%

' get the image for each of the eight pairs of feet
GET (52, 50)-(59, 59), feet%(0, 0, 0)        ' up, left foot front
GET (102, 50)-(109, 59), feet%(0, 1, 0)      ' down, left foot front
GET (151, 51)-(162, 57), feet%(0, 2, 0)      ' left, right foot front
GET (201, 51)-(212, 57), feet%(0, 3, 0)      ' right, right foot front
GET (52, 100)-(59, 109), feet%(0, 0, 1)      ' up, right foot front
GET (102, 100)-(109, 109), feet%(0, 1, 1)    ' down, right foot front
GET (151, 101)-(162, 107), feet%(0, 2, 1)    ' left, left foot front
GET (201, 101)-(212, 107), feet%(0, 3, 1)    ' right, left foot front
```

(continued)

continued

```
' perform animation
CLS : x% = 160: y% = 100
arrow$ = upArrow$ + downArrow$ + leftArrow$ + rightArrow$
PUT (x%, y%), feet%(0, 0, 0), XOR
DO
    DO
        keyStroke$ = INKEY$
    LOOP WHILE keyStroke$ = ""
    move% = INSTR(arrow$, keyStroke$)
    IF move% THEN
        move% = ((move% + 1) \ 2) - 1         ' figure direction to move
        newX% = x% + xInc%(move%): newY% = y% + yInc%(move%)
        IF newX% < 10 OR newX% > 300 OR newY% < 10 OR newY% > 180 THEN
            PLAY "T255 L16 O1 G#"             ' a foot hit the border
        ELSE

            ' erase previous image
            PUT (x%, y%), feet%(0, lastMove%, forward%(lastMove%)), XOR
            thisMove% = move%
            IF thisMove% = lastMove% THEN    ' change which foot will be forward
                IF forward%(thisMove%) = 0 THEN
                    forward%(thisMove%) = 1
                ELSE
                    forward%(thisMove%) = 0
                END IF
            END IF

            ' draw new image
            PUT (newX%, newY%), feet%(0, thisMove%, forward%(thisMove%)), XOR
            lastMove% = thisMove%
            x% = newX%: y% = newY%
        END IF
    END IF
LOOP UNTIL keyStroke$ = CHR$(27)
END

DATA  0, -5, 0, 5, -5, 0, 5, 0
DATA  6, 3, 56, 3, 105, 5, 155, 5, 2, 53, 52, 53, 105, 52, 155
DATA  52, 6, 51, 56, 51, 102, 55, 152, 55
```

SCREEN (Function)

See also: COLOR, LOCATE, SCREEN (Statement)

■ QB2	■ QB4.5	■ PowerBASIC
■ QB3	ANSI	■ GW-BASIC
■ QB4	■ BASIC7	MacQB

Purpose

The SCREEN function returns information about a specified location. By default, the function returns the ASCII code of the character at the position (row and column) specified; in text mode it can also return the color attribute number of that character.

Syntax

SCREEN(*row*, *column* [, *color*])

row and *column* are integers that specify the position of the character. *color* is an optional integer: If you omit it, the SCREEN function returns the ASCII code of the character at that position; if you include a nonzero value for *color*, SCREEN returns the attribute number of the character's color.

Usage

```
PRINT SCREEN(5, 10)
```

Prints the ASCII code of the character currently displayed on the screen at row 5, column 10.

```
clr% = SCREEN(row%, col%, 1)
```

Assigns the attribute number of the character's color at the position specified by *row%* and *col%* to the integer variable *clr%*.

Description

The SCREEN function is the text mode version of the graphics POINT function. The SCREEN function returns information about the character at a specified location on the screen. It returns either the ASCII code of the character displayed there or the attribute number of the character's color.

In monochrome systems, the attribute number controls the intensity of the character and whether it is displayed as reverse video, blinking, or underlined.

The SCREEN function also returns ASCII values in graphics modes. It returns attribute numbers only in screen mode 0, the text mode. (See the SCREEN (Statement) entry for a description of the different screen modes.)

Errors

If you use the VIEW PRINT statement to define a text viewport, the SCREEN function operates only within this viewport. If you attempt to read a character on a line outside the viewport, QuickBASIC returns an "Illegal function call" error message.

Example

The SCREEN function is useful for reading data that was output to the screen by DOS or by another program. The following example uses the function with the SHELL command to determine the volume label of the disk in a specified drive.

```
CLS : LOCATE 10, 1
INPUT "Volume label for which drive"; drive$
IF drive$ <> "" THEN
    drive$ = " " + LEFT$(drive$, 1) + ":"
END IF
VIEW PRINT 20 TO 21
label$ = ""
SHELL "VOL" + drive$        ' call the DOS function VOL
FOR i% = 23 TO 33
    label$ = label$ + CHR$(SCREEN(21, i%))          ' read the label
NEXT i%
VIEW PRINT: LOCATE 22, 1
PRINT "The VOL function returned the label "; label$  ' display the label
END
```

SCREEN (Statement)

See also: COLOR, PALETTE, PCOPY, VIEW, WIDTH (Screen), WINDOW

✲ QB2	■ QB4.5	✲ PowerBASIC
✲ QB3	ANSI	■ GW-BASIC
■ QB4	■ BASIC7	MacQB

Purpose

The SCREEN statement defines various screen characteristics. If your computer has anything other than a Monochrome Display and Printer Adapter (MDPA) installed, it is capable of displaying graphics as well as text. The SCREEN statement lets you select different video modes, each of which controls the number of pixels, colors, and screen pages available for display.

Syntax

SCREEN [*mode*][, [*color*][, [*active*][, *visible*]]]

mode is a number in the range 0 through 13 that specifies the display mode. QuickBASIC does not support modes 4, 5, and 6.

color is a numeric expression that when true (nonzero) disables color display on computers connected to a composite monitor or a color television. *color* is ignored in all modes except 0 and 1.

active is an integer that specifies the screen page to which screen output is written, and *visible* is an integer that specifies the screen page that is currently displayed. The two integers need not be the same.

Usage

```
SCREEN 1, 1
```

Selects screen mode 1, the medium-resolution (320-by-200-pixel), four-color mode, and disables color on composite monitors or color televisions.

```
SCREEN 9, , 1, 0
```

Selects the high-resolution (640-by-350-pixel), 16-color mode available on EGA and VGA adapters. All subsequent graphics statements draw on screen page 0; page 1 becomes the displayed screen page. Notice that although the color argument is not valid in this mode, its place in the parameter list of the statement must be held by a comma.

```
SCREEN , , , 1
```

Switches the displayed screen page to page 1 without changing the screen mode or active page.

```
SCREEN 0
```

Disables graphics output and returns to screen mode 0, the text mode.

Description

The screen modes available to your computer are determined by the type of display adapter you have installed. QuickBASIC supports all adapters commonly used with the IBM PC, XT, AT, PS/2, and compatibles. Table 11-14 lists these adapters and the screen modes that they display:

Adapter		Available screen modes
MDPA	(Monochrome Display and Printer Adapter)	0
CGA	(Color Graphics Adapter)	0, 1, 2
MCGA	(Multi-Color Graphics Array)	0, 1, 2, 11, 13
HGC	(Hercules Graphics Card)	0, 3
EGA	(Enhanced Graphics Adapter)	0, 1, 2, 7, 8, 9, 10*
VGA	(Video Graphics Array)	0, 1, 2, 7, 8, 9, 10*, 11, 12, 13

* Screen 10 is available only for EGA and VGA adapters that are connected to high-resolution monochrome monitors.

Table 11-14.
Video adapters and the available screen modes.

Note that, with the exception of the MCGA and HGC adapters, the latest video adapters are downwardly compatible with their predecessors and support all previous screen modes.

Some video adapters can store more than one page of screen information at a time in memory. These pages are called screen pages. Screen pages are numbered from 0 through the maximum number available. Not only can you use SCREEN to select the active and visible pages, you can also copy the screen contents from one page to another with the PCOPY statement. Table 11-15 lists the maximum number of screen pages available in each screen mode for different types of video adapters.

Screen	MDPA	CGA	MCGA	HGC	EGA	VGA	Remarks
0	1	4	8	2	8	8	80 by 25 text
	-	8	8	-	8	8	40 by 25 text
	-	-	-	-	8	8	40 by 43 text
	-	-	-	-	-	4	40 by 50 text
	-	-	-	-	4	4	80 by 43 text
	-	-	-	-	-	4	80 by 50 text
1	-	1	1	-	1	1	
2	-	1	1	-	1	1	
3	-	-	-	2	-	-	Hercules only
7*	-	-	-	-	8	8	
8*	-	-	-	-	4	4	
9*	-	-	-	-	2	2	
10*	-	-	-	-	4	4	
11	-	-	1	-	-	1	
12	-	-	-	-	-	1	
13	-	-	1	-	-	1	

* Values for screen modes 7, 8, 9, and 10 assume an EGA or VGA adapter with 256 KB of dedicated memory.

Table 11-15.
Number of screen pages available in each screen mode.

Screen mode 0

Screen mode 0 is the text screen mode and is the default mode of all video adapters. If you have an MDPA, HGC, or an EGA or VGA with a monochrome adapter, the only display size available is 25 rows by 80 columns. Other text formats are available with different adapters and color monitors, as shown in Table 11-16.

Use the WIDTH (Screen) statement to modify the number of rows and columns. (See the WIDTH (Screen) entry in Chapter 8, "Simple I/O.")

Text can be displayed in any combination of 16 foreground and 8 background attributes. On monochrome monitors, the attribute numbers control underlining and two degrees of character intensity; on color monitors, they determine text and background color. Both types of monitors support blinking characters. (See the COLOR entry for more details.) Computers with an EGA, VGA, or MCGA adapter and a color monitor can remap color attributes to different display colors using the PALETTE statement.

None of the QuickBASIC graphics statements are supported in this mode. However, you can produce text mode graphics by using the PRINT statement with IBM extended characters 176 through 223. (See the PRINT entry in Chapter 8, "Simple I/O," for an example.)

Columns and rows	Adapters
80 by 25	MDPA, HGC, CGA, MCGA, EGA, VGA
40 by 25	CGA, MCGA, EGA, VGA
40 by 43	EGA, VGA
40 by 50	VGA
80 by 43	EGA, VGA
80 by 50	VGA

Table 11-16.
Text formats and corresponding adapters.

By default, computers connected to a television or composite monitor do not display text in color in screen mode 0. To enable color, call the color SCREEN statement with the third argument set to any nonzero value.

Screen mode 1

Screen mode 1 is a medium-resolution (320-by-200-pixel) graphics mode with a text format of 25 rows by 40 columns. Because televisions and composite monitors can display both graphics and text in this mode, color is enabled by default. To disable color, call the SCREEN statement with the third argument set to a nonzero value.

Four colors are available in screen mode 1. The background color can be any of the 16 standard attributes listed in Table 11-4. You can choose between the two color palettes listed in Table 11-5 to specify the three available foreground colors.

As in other screen modes, you can use the PALETTE statement to remap these attributes to display different colors on computers with an EGA, VGA, or MCGA adapter.

Screen mode 2

Screen mode 2 is a high-resolution (640-by-200-pixel) graphics mode with a text format of 25 rows by 80 columns. This mode supports only two colors. Normally these are white (foreground) and black (background), but you can use the PALETTE statement with EGA, VGA, and MCGA systems to map the two colors to any of the 16 standard colors.

Screen mode 3

Screen mode 3 is a high-resolution (720-by-348-pixel) graphics mode with a text format of 25 rows by 80 columns. Screen mode 3 is available only on computers using the Hercules Graphics Card (HGC) adapter. To enable the adapter, you must run the program MS-HERC.COM before using QuickBASIC. (The MS-HERC.COM program is included with the QuickBASIC 4.5 and BASIC 7 compilers.)

SCREEN 3 supports monochrome graphics only; you cannot remap the foreground and background colors with the PALETTE statement.

Screen mode 7

Screen mode 7 is available only on computers that use an EGA or VGA adapter and is similar to screen mode 1 except that 16 colors are available instead of 4. The colors can be remapped with the PALETTE statement. Screen mode 7 has a resolution of 320 by 200 pixels and a text format of 25 rows by 40 columns. As many as eight screen pages are available in this mode, depending on the amount of video memory in your adapter.

Screen mode 8

Screen mode 8 is an enhanced version of screen mode 2 for computers that use an EGA or VGA adapter. Screen mode 8 has a resolution of 640 by 200 pixels and a text format of 25 rows by 80 columns. This mode supports 16 colors, which can be remapped with the PALETTE statement. Four screen pages are available in this mode to adapters that have 256 KB of display memory.

Screen mode 9

Screen mode 9 is the standard graphics mode for computers with an EGA adapter, although systems with a VGA adapter can also use it. Screen mode 9 has a resolution of 640 by 350 pixels and a text format of either 80 rows by 25 columns or 80 rows by 43 columns.

The number of colors and screen pages available is determined by the amount of video memory that is available in the adapter. Early versions of the EGA include only 64 KB of memory, which supports only one screen page and 4 colors out of a palette of 16. VGA and EGA adapters with 256 KB or more of memory can switch between two pages and display 16 colors from a palette of 64 colors.

Screen mode 10

Screen mode 10 is available only to computers with an EGA and VGA adapter that is connected to a high-resolution monochrome monitor. Screen mode 10 has a resolution of 640 by 350 pixels and a text format of either 80 rows by 25 columns or 80 rows by 43 columns. Four display pages are available to adapters with 256 KB of video memory.

This mode supports four attributes. Each attribute can support one of 9 pseudo-colors, which control such characteristics as intensity and blink. (See the COLOR entry.)

Screen mode 11

Screen mode 11 is available only to computers using a VGA or MCGA adapter. Screen mode 11 has a resolution of 640 by 480 pixels and a text format of either 80 rows by 30 columns or 80 rows by 60 columns. 80-row-by-25-column text is not available.

Only two display attributes are available (one for foreground and one for background), but each can be assigned one of 262,144 colors with the PALETTE statement.

Screen mode 12

Screen mode 12 is available only to computers using a VGA adapter. Like screen mode 11 it has a graphics resolution of 640 by 480 pixels and either an 80-row-by-30-column or 80-row-by-60-column text format. Unlike screen mode 11, however, it supports 16 attributes from a palette of 262,144 colors.

Screen mode 13

Screen mode 13 is a medium-resolution (320-by-200-pixel) mode with a 40-row-by-25-column text format and is available to both VGA and MCGA adapters. In this mode, graphics can be drawn with any of 256 attributes from a palette of 262,144 colors.

Tips

When QuickBASIC changes screen modes, it clears the display of all graphics and text. Usually, this is a necessary precaution: graphics in screen mode 9, for example, cannot be displayed properly in screen mode 1. However, occasionally you might want to switch modes without clearing the display, perhaps to generate some special effect, such as an explosion in a game.

You can change modes without clearing the screen only by bypassing the SCREEN statement and using BIOS services to select the video mode you want. The CALL INTERRUPT statement provides a way to do this. Interrupt 16 (10 hexadecimal) includes a function that lets you select the current mode by calling it with a 0 in the AH register and the mode number in AL. In addition, if you set the top bit of AL (by adding 128 to the mode number), the display buffer is not cleared when the mode changes. (See the CALL INTERRUPT entry in Chapter 20, "Mixed Language," for details.)

This technique is complicated by the fact that video mode numbers used by the BIOS differ from the QuickBASIC screen mode numbers. Table 11-17 lists the corresponding modes.

QuickBASIC screen mode	BIOS video mode	Adapter required	Description
1	4	CGA	320 by 200 2-color
	5	CGA	320 by 200 monochrome
2	6	CGA	640 by 200 2-color
	8	CGA	160 by 200 16-color*
	9	CGA	320 by 200 16-color*
	10	CGA	640 by 200 4-color*
7	13	EGA	320 by 200 16-color
8	14	EGA	640 by 200 16-color
9	16	EGA	640 by 350 16-color
10	15	EGA	640 by 350 monochrome
11	17	VGA	640 by 480 monochrome
12	18	VGA	640 by 480 16-color
13	19	VGA	320 by 200 256-color

* BIOS video modes 8, 9, and 10 are available only on systems using an enhanced CGA, such as the one used by the PCjr and the Tandy 1000. QuickBASIC does not support these modes.

Table 11-17.
QuickBASIC and BIOS screen modes.

Be sure you select only those screen modes that your display adapter can support. The BIOS does not provide any error trapping, so requesting BIOS mode 15 (screen mode 10, or the monochrome EGA mode) when you are using a color monitor, for example, will cause your computer to lock up and force you to reboot.

Notes

In graphics modes, changing the number of character columns on the screen by using the WIDTH (Screen) statement has the same effect as changing the screen mode number. Executing the statement WIDTH 40 in mode 2, for example, immediately switches the display to screen mode 1.

If you select a screen mode other than the current one, QuickBASIC clears the display, exactly as if you had also executed a CLS statement. However, if you use the SCREEN statement to select another page, but you don't change screen modes, QuickBASIC does not clear graphics or text from the screen page. Note, however, that the graphics or text might no longer be visible because the page might no longer be the visible screen page.

Compatibility

QuickBASIC 2.0 and QuickBASIC 3.0

QuickBASIC versions 2.0 and 3.0 support only screen modes 0 through 10. They do not offer the screen modes designed for VGA or MCGA adapters.

PowerBASIC

PowerBASIC supports EGA screen modes 7, 8, 9, and 10 and VGA modes 11 and 12 but not VGA and MCGA screen mode 13, the 256-color medium-resolution mode.

Example

See the example in the COLOR entry for a program that demonstrates the SCREEN statement.

VIEW

See also: PMAP, SCREEN (Statement), VIEW PRINT, WINDOW

■ QB2	■ QB4.5	■ PowerBASIC
■ QB3	ANSI	■ GW-BASIC
■ QB4	■ BASIC7	MacQB

Purpose

The VIEW statement defines a rectangular area of the screen and confines all subsequent graphics output within its borders. This area is known as the *graphics viewport.* The VIEW PRINT statement does the same for text. (See the VIEW PRINT entry in Chapter 8, "Simple I/O.") If your program uses both text and graphics, you can create a graphics viewport to keep the two types of output separate, thus preventing your graphics figures from overwriting any text on the screen.

Syntax

VIEW [[SCREEN] (*x1, y1*)-(*x2, y2*) [,[*attribute*] [,*border*]]]

The SCREEN keyword controls coordinates that can be used in subsequent graphics statements. If you use the SCREEN keyword, all subsequent graphics statements continue to use the upper left corner of the physical screen as the origin. If you omit the SCREEN keyword, all subsequent graphics statements use the upper left corner of the viewport as the origin, which is specified by (0, 0).

x1, y1, x2, y2 are integer values that indicate the physical screen coordinates of opposite corners of the viewport being defined. *x1* and *x2* can range from 0 to the maximum horizontal resolution, and *y1* and *y2* can range from 0 to the maximum vertical resolution of the current screen mode.

attribute is an integer expression that specifies the background color. Using this parameter clears the viewport and sets it to the specified color. If you omit *attribute*, the viewport is not cleared, and any existing graphics or text within the viewport continue to be displayed.

border is an integer expression that when true (nonzero) draws a line in the specified color around the viewport. (If you use *border* but do not specify an attribute, you must include the first comma to hold the *attribute* position in the argument list.)

Using the VIEW statement without arguments cancels any previous VIEW statements and defines the entire screen as the current graphics viewport. However, VIEW does not clear the screen or change the display.

Usage

```
VIEW SCREEN (50, 20)-(150, 100)
```

Defines the specified physical coordinates as the new limits of the graphics viewport. Because the SCREEN keyword has been specified, subsequent graphics output uses absolute coordinates whose origin is located at the upper left corner of the physical screen.

```
SCREEN 9
VIEW (159, 74)-(479, 274), , 14
```

Selects a 640-by-350-pixel screen and defines a 320-by-200-pixel viewport centered inside it. VIEW draws the border of the viewport in bright yellow, but because an attribute number is omitted, the viewport's interior is not cleared. All subsequent graphics statements are plotted relative to the upper left corner of the viewport. Note that if your program uses graphics written for a medium-resolution (screen mode 1) display, this example lets you run the program in high-resolution mode without your having to rewrite the coordinates of any graphics statements. The colors, however, will be different in high-resolution mode.

Description

The VIEW statement lets you define the area of the screen in which graphics will appear. You can also use VIEW to remap the display coordinate system. Graphics locations are, by default, mapped in physical coordinates from an origin at the upper left corner of the screen—horizontally from left to right (*x*-axis) and vertically from top to bottom (*y*-axis). VIEW, when used with the SCREEN keyword, retains the physical coordinate system. Without the SCREEN keyword, VIEW changes the position of the origin to the upper left corner of the viewport.

VIEW does not display any graphics outside the viewport you specify, although any portion of a figure within the viewport is displayed. A figure that is not completely enclosed in a viewport is called a "clipped" figure.

The following program segment selects screen mode 9 (a 640-by-350-pixel resolution display), draws one circle after calling VIEW with the SCREEN keyword and then draws another after calling VIEW without the SCREEN keyword. Figure 11-14 shows the output of this program segment. Because the origin of the coordinates used to draw the first circle is at the upper left corner of the screen, the circle is clipped. The circle drawn in the viewport that has its origin at the upper left corner of the viewport is not clipped.

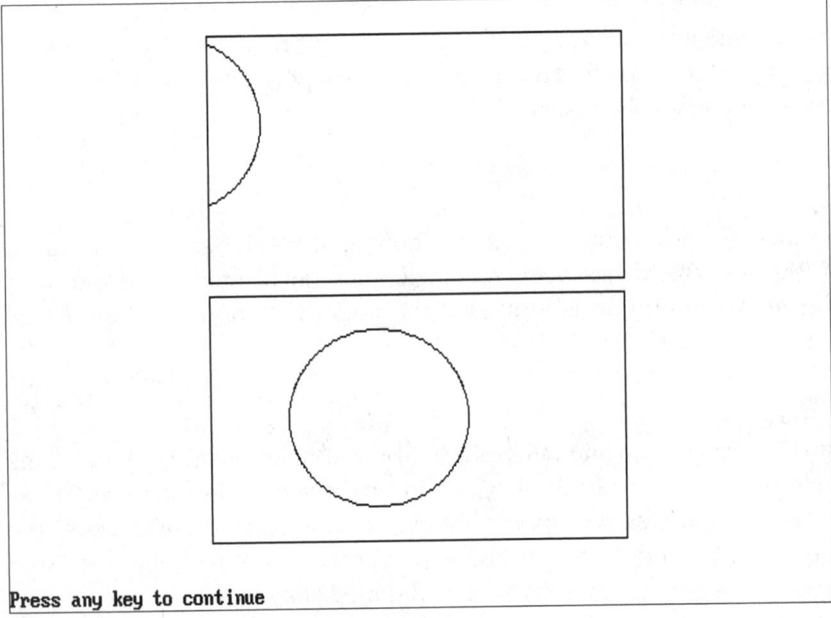

Figure 11-14.
The VIEW statement used with and without the SCREEN keyword.

```
SCREEN 9
VIEW SCREEN (160, 20)-(480, 160), 0, 15
CIRCLE (130, 70), 70, 15

VIEW (160, 170)-(480, 310), 0, 15
CIRCLE (130, 70), 70, 15
```

You can use many VIEW statements in a program; however, graphics appear only in the currently active viewport, which is the area defined by the most recent VIEW statement. Because the coordinates specified in the VIEW statement are always interpreted as physical screen coordinates, you do not need to keep the new coordinates within the current viewport.

If you use VIEW to initialize a graphics viewport, the CLS statement clears only the contents of that viewport. However, if the program subsequently executes a VIEW PRINT statement, the defined text viewport becomes the active area, and a call to CLS clears only the text viewport. (See the CLS entry in Chapter 8, "Simple I/O," for details.)

Example

The following program graphs a profit-and-loss statement for an imaginary company. The program uses VIEW to create one viewport for the labels of the graph and another viewport for the contents of the graph.

```
SCREEN 9: LINE (0, 20)-(639, 349), 1, BF

VIEW (120, 180)-(510, 330), 0, 15  ' define viewport for labels of graph
WINDOW (0, -20000)-(12, 20000)
LOCATE 14, 33: PRINT "The Big Picture"
LOCATE 14, 18: PRINT "20000"
LOCATE 19, 16: PRINT "  0": LOCATE 23, 17: PRINT "-20000"
LINE (1, 0)-(12, 0), 15: LINE (1, -14000)-(1, 16000)

VIEW (153, 180)-(510, 330)         ' define viewport for the contents of graph
WINDOW (1, -20000)-(12, 20000)
PSET (0, 0)
RESTORE
FOR i% = 1 TO 12
    READ gainLoss!: LINE -(i%, gainLoss!), 15      ' get data for the graph
NEXT i%

PAINT (3, 2000), 14, 15: PAINT (10, -3000), 12, 15  ' draw the graph
PAINT (12, 800), 14, 15: VIEW: WINDOW
LOCATE 23, 30: PRINT "Profit"
LINE (300, 310)-(320, 320), 14, BF
LOCATE 23, 47: PRINT "Loss"
LINE (420, 310)-(440, 320), 12, BF
END

DATA 4013.28, 7269.88, 11152.75, 9327.08, 4148.20, 828.74
DATA -159.15, -788.61, -2693.80, -5164.02, -1176.53, 1297.63
```

WINDOW

See also: PMAP, VIEW

■ QB2	■ QB4.5	■ PowerBASIC
■ QB3	ANSI	■ GW-BASIC
■ QB4	■ BASIC7	✲ MacQB

Purpose

The WINDOW statement defines a logical coordinate system for the current viewport. (The VIEW statement lets you define the screen boundaries of the viewport in which graphics will appear.) Use WINDOW to remap these physical coordinates into a logical coordinate system of your choice. You can also use the statement to reverse the normal, top-down orientation of the graphics display and use the Cartesian plotting system (with the origin at the bottom left corner of the viewport).

Syntax

WINDOW [[SCREEN] (*x1*, *y1*)-(*x2*, *y2*)]

x1, *y1*, *x2*, and *y2* are single-precision values in the range –3.37E+38 through 3.37E+38. They define the logical dimensions of the current viewport. The lesser of the two *x*-coordinates is the left boundary, and the greater *x*-coordinate is the right boundary. By default, the lesser *y*-coordinate specifies the bottom edge of the viewport and the greater *y*-coordinate specifies the top. If you use the SCREEN keyword, however, the lesser *y*-coordinate is the top of the viewport.

If you use WINDOW without any arguments, the graphics statement no longer uses logical coordinates but instead uses the default, physical coordinates of the viewport.

Usage

```
WINDOW (88.09, 1.5E+6)-(89.09, 2.5E+6)
```

Defines the logical coordinates for a viewport that displays a graph created from large numbers. Note that you can use both decimal and floating-point numbers as the logical coordinates.

```
WINDOW SCREEN (-xVal!, -yVal!)-(xVal!, yVal!)
```

Defines the logical coordinates for a viewport by using single-precision variables to indicate the dimensions. In this example, point (0, 0) is at the center of the viewport, and increasing values of *y* are plotted downward from the upper boundary.

```
WINDOW
```

Disables the logical coordinate system. QuickBASIC uses physical coordinates to plot subsequent graphics statements.

Description

The WINDOW statement lets you translate real-world data into graphics coordinates without having to scale each value so that it fits into the boundaries of the physical screen. If your program calls WINDOW, the size and shape of the graphics drawn by your program appear approximately the same in screen mode 1 as in screen mode 9. (See the SCREEN (Statement) entry for a list of available screen modes). The only differences between modes when the WINDOW statement is used are that the colors differ and that lines and curves in screen modes with lower resolution are noticeably more jagged.

In the Cartesian coordinate system, the height of an object is measured from bottom to top, not from top to bottom as in the physical graphics coordinate system. WINDOW uses the Cartesian coordinate system by default, although you can override it by using the SCREEN option in the WINDOW statement.

After you define a logical coordinate system, subsequent graphics statements, such as LINE, CIRCLE, PAINT, PSET, PRESET, GET, and PUT use the values of this system as coordinates. QuickBASIC translates these logical coordinates into physical screen locations when drawing an image. The DRAW statement is an exception because it accepts only physical screen coordinates.

If your program refers to points outside the logical dimensions of the viewport, QuickBASIC plots them but does not display them on the screen. (This is called "clipping.") Plotting the points ensures that any lines or curves that pass through the points are correctly drawn to their intersection with the screen boundaries. Figures 11-15 and 11-16 illustrate the difference between lines drawn to an off-screen coordinate in a language that doesn't perform clipping and in QuickBASIC, which does perform clipping.

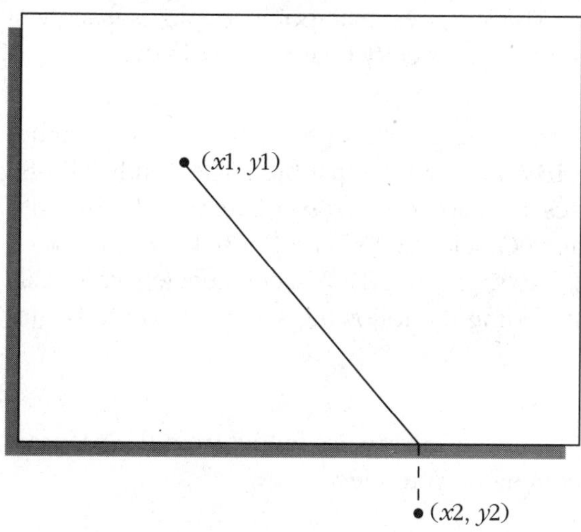

Figure 11-15.
Clipping is not performed.

Note that in Figure 11-15 the line is drawn to the point on the viewport boundary that is closest to the out-of-bounds coordinate.

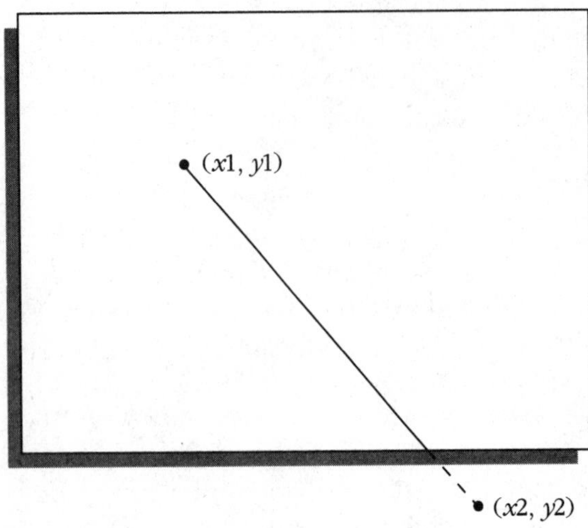

Figure 11-16.
Clipping is performed.

In Figure 11-16, the QuickBASIC LINE statement calculates where a straight line drawn to the out-of-bounds coordinate would intersect with the viewport boundary. The program then plots the line to that position.

If a graphics statement draws a figure so that the last point plotted is outside the viewport boundary, the position of the graphics cursor remains at that point even though it is outside the viewport. QuickBASIC uses that point to plot subsequent graphics statements that use the STEP keyword to specify relative coordinates.

Tips

The WINDOW statement is useful for translating graphics programs written for other computers so that they can be used on IBM PCs and compatibles. The Tandy TRS-80 Color Computer (CoCo), for example, uses a version of Microsoft Extended BASIC with graphics statements that are very similar to QuickBASIC's. The CoCo, however, uses a standard screen resolution of 256 by 192 pixels. The WINDOW statement lets you easily port a CoCo program to QuickBASIC by adding the following statement to the beginning of the program:

```
WINDOW SCREEN (0, 0)-(255, 191)
```

After you use this statement, QuickBASIC scales the graphics output from the program to fit the PC screen, regardless of the screen mode you select.

Compatibility

QuickBASIC for the Macintosh

The WINDOW statement in QuickBASIC for the Macintosh serves a different purpose from the one in QuickBASIC 4.5. It is used to open, close, or direct output to one of the windows on the screen. Windows on the Macintosh are defined using physical screen coordinates and cannot be remapped to a different logical coordinate system.

Example

You can use WINDOW to "zoom away" from a picture by drawing it within successively larger coordinate systems. The converse is also true: Defining smaller values for the logical dimensions of successive viewports magnifies the images in them. The following program uses this technique. It draws a figure six times, each time using smaller dimensions for the logical coordinates, which magnify the figure. Figure 11-17 shows the output of this program.

```
DECLARE SUB DrawPicture ()

SCREEN 9
LINE (0, 0)-(639, 349), 11, BF
x1 = 0: x2 = 1020: y1 = 0: y2 = 764
xPos% = 10: yPos% = 10: i% = 1

DO
    VIEW (xPos%, yPos%)-(xPos% + 200, yPos% + 155), 0, 15  ' define viewport
    WINDOW SCREEN (x1, y1)-(x2 / i%, y2 / i%)  ' define logical coordinates
    DrawPicture
    i% = i% + 1
    xPos% = xPos% + 210
    IF i% = 4 THEN xPos% = 10: yPos% = 175
LOOP UNTIL i% = 7
END

DATA  68, 4, 200, 76, 52, 12, 112, 44, 128, 52, 172, 76, 128, 52
DATA  68, 84, 112, 44, 84, 60, 128, 68, 100, 84, 68, 36, 96, 52
DATA  128, 68, 154, 84, 128, 68, 128, 116, 130, 54, 130, 68, 68
DATA  4, 52, 12, 172, 76, 142, 90, 142, 76, 142, 108, 142, 108
DATA  200, 76, 200, 76, 200, 92, 200, 92, 68, 164, 128, 116, 84
DATA  140, 52, 12, 52, 154, 52, 154, 68, 164, 68, 164, 68, 100
DATA  68, 36, 68, 84, 84, 45, 84, 76, 84, 109, 84, 140, 68, 100
DATA  96, 116, 84, 124, 112, 108, 68, 84, 128, 116, 85, 75, 113
DATA  91, 112, 77, 112, 108, 84, 119, 92, 115, 142, 86, 150, 82
DATA  180, 66, 186, 62, 186, 62, 236, 90, 236, 90, 68, 184, 68
DATA  184, 16, 154, 16, 154, 52, 133, 16, 154, 16, 160, 16, 160
DATA  68, 190, 68, 190, 68, 184, 68, 190, 236, 96, 236, 96, 236
DATA  90
```

(continued)

continued

```
SUB DrawPicture STATIC
    RESTORE
    FOR i% = 1 TO 40        ' read coordinates
        READ x1%, y1%, x2%, y2%: LINE (x1%, y1%)-(x2%, y2%), 1  ' draw outline
    NEXT i%

    ' paint figure
    PAINT (56, 20), 1, 1: PAINT (136, 64), 1, 1
    PAINT (120, 80), 1, 1: PAINT (152, 110), 14, 1
    PAINT (76, 48), 14, 1: PAINT (124, 60), 14, 1
    PAINT (68, 12), 2, 1: PAINT (80, 84), 2, 1
    PAINT (92, 128), 2, 1: PAINT (36, 150), 12, 1
    PAINT (150, 125), 12, 1: PAINT (80, 120), 14, 1
    PAINT (36, 168), 1, 1: PAINT (150, 142), 14, 1
    PAINT (88, 118), 12, 1: PAINT (144, 86), 12, 1
    PAINT (100, 120), 2, 1: PAINT (165, 90), 2, 1
END SUB
```

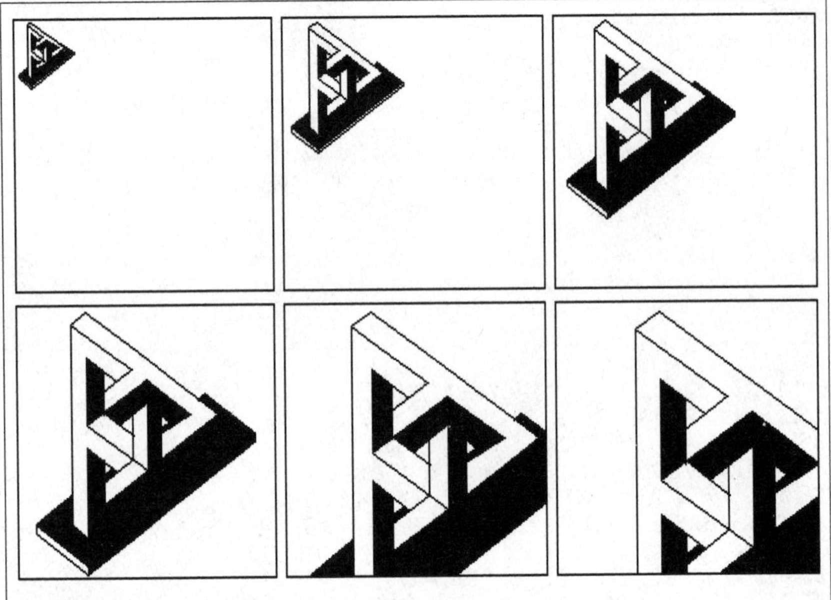

Figure 11-17.
Output of the WINDOW example program.

CHAPTER 12

Sound

Introduction

Imagine that you've just written a flashy, new QuickBASIC program: It has colorful graphics, windows, and a friendly interface. But something seems to be missing. Is your program so quiet it's deafening? Music and sound effects can make games, educational programs, and other applications more interesting to the user. You can add a simple melody to the opening screen, a beep as a warning, or a pleasing tone for positive reinforcement. The statements and functions described in this chapter let your programs make sounds.

Table 12-1 lists QuickBASIC's sound-related statements and functions.

Statement or function	Description
BEEP	Sounds a beep on the computer's speaker
ON PLAY GOSUB	Specifies the subroutine that adds notes to the music buffer; the notes are played in the background
PLAY (Function)	Returns the number of notes remaining in the music buffer
PLAY (Statement)	Plays the specified melody; executes commands for the octave, pitch, duration, tempo, and foreground or background
PLAY ON/OFF/STOP	Enables, disables, or suspends the play event trapping that occurs when the music buffer has fewer than the specified number of notes remaining
SOUND	Generates a tone of the specified frequency for the specified duration

Table 12-1.
QuickBASIC sound-related statements and functions.

Using Music in Your Program

Before you decide what music to play in your program, first consider the purpose of the program: How will music help you entertain or communicate with the user? Aside from forming the core of programs whose explicit purpose is to teach or demonstrate music, music usually serves two purposes in programs.

The first—often used in games—is to provide atmosphere by playing music in the background while the program executes other statements. (A melody might also entertain the user while the program is not generating any visual output.)

The second purpose of music is to get the user's attention—to issue a cue, a warning, or a reward. In an educational program, for example, a triumphant "bugle call" might mean the student correctly answered a difficult question; or a melody might mean "Wrong—please try again." The program could also play a brief tune that lets the student know it's time to answer a question or enter some information; this would be helpful in programs for young children or for visually impaired persons.

In most cases you should use music sparingly. Most PCs have small speakers that can't generate very low or very high frequencies, and they don't have the kind of built-in sound system that is found in other types of machines. (The Macintosh, for example, has a more sophisticated sound system that includes four customizable voices, stereo sound, and the ability to easily store digitized sounds.)

Translating a Musical Score into PLAY Statements

You probably won't be using QuickBASIC to compose your own music—although the various statements for playing music aren't hard to use, they aren't as easily read as a musical score. More likely, you will transcribe music written in standard notation. Figure 12-1 shows the melody of the tune "Red River Valley" written on a musical staff. Below the staff are the commands you use with the QuickBASIC PLAY statement to generate the notes.

The PLAY statement executes the tasks that are specified in a string of commands indicating the pitch (for example, A, C-sharp, or E), duration, tempo, and other characteristics of the music. You don't have to use spaces to separate the commands in the string, but doing so makes the string easier to read. The following program uses one PLAY statement for each measure of music in "Red River Valley" to improve readability. When translating a note into PLAY commands, you must specify both the pitch and the duration of each note.

```
' Red River Valley
PLAY "O3" ' set octave 3, middle C
PLAY "L2 NO < L4 G > C"
PLAY "L2 E L4 E D"
PLAY "L2 C L4 D C"
PLAY "< L2 A > L1 C L4 < G > C"
PLAY "L2 E L4 E E"
PLAY "L2 G L4 F E"
PLAY "L1 D. < L4 G > C"
PLAY "L2 E L4 E D"
PLAY "L2 C L4 D E"
PLAY "L2 G L1 F < L4 A A"
PLAY "L2 G L4 > C D"
PLAY "L2 E L4 D D"
PLAY "L1 C. L2 NO"
```

Red River Valley

Figure 12-1.
"Red River Valley" in standard musical notation and in QuickBASIC notation.

Specifying Pitch and Duration

Examine the listing of the program that plays "Red River Valley." The first statement (*PLAY "O3"*) sets the octave. (Note that the command begins with the letter O, not the number 0.) You can play music in any of seven octaves numbered from 0 through 6, with 0 corresponding to the lowest octave, 3 corresponding to the octave containing middle C, and 6 corresponding to the highest octave.

The commands in the string of the second PLAY statement specify the following actions:

L2 N0	Play a rest (note 0) for 2 beats (the length of a half note)
<	Shift subsequent notes down one octave
L4 G	Play the pitch G for 1 beat (the length of a quarter note)
>	Shift subsequent notes up one octave
C	Play the pitch C for 1 beat (the length of a quarter note)

Usually it is most convenient to specify the pitch of notes by using the standard letters—A through G; however, you can also use the N command to specify the absolute note number—N0 through N84. N30, for example, plays the 30th note in the 7-octave range. Table 12-2 lists the pitches and their corresponding numbers. N0 specifies a period of silence (a rest). You can also specify a rest by using the P command followed by a number that specifies the duration of the rest. For example, P4 specifies a quarter-note rest.

Although the "Red River Valley" example doesn't use sharps or flats to raise or lower pitches, QuickBASIC lets you do so by following the note's letter name with a plus sign (+) or a number sign (#) for a sharp and a minus sign (–) for a flat. You cannot use the plus sign, number sign, or minus sign with a note specified by the N command and a number because every number corresponds to a different pitch. The command N38, for example, specifies the note C♯ in the third octave, as you can see in Table 12-2.

Octave	Pitch	Number	Octave	Pitch	Number
0	C	1	0	G♯/A♭	9
0	C♯/D♭	2	0	A	10
0	D	3	0	A♯/B♭	11
0	D♯/E♭	4	0	B	12
0	E	5	1	C	13
0	F	6	1	C♯/D♭	14
0	F♯/G♭	7	1	D	15
0	G	8	1	D♯/E♭	16

Table 12-2.
Pitches and their corresponding number.

(continued)

Table 12-2. *continued*

Octave	Pitch	Number
1	E	17
1	F	18
1	F♯/G♭	19
1	G	20
1	G♯/A♭	21
1	A	22
1	A♯/B♭	23
1	B	24
2	C	25
2	C♯/D♭	26
2	D	27
2	D♯/E♭	28
2	E	29
2	F	30
2	F♯/G♭	31
2	G	32
2	G♯/A♭	33
2	A	34
2	A♯/B♭	35
2	B	36
3	C	37
3	C♯/D♭	38
3	D	39
3	D♯/E♭	40
3	E	41
3	F	42
3	F♯/G♭	43
3	G	44
3	G♯/A♭	45
3	A	46
3	A♯/B♭	47
3	B	48
4	C	49
4	C♯/D♭	50
4	D	51
4	D♯/E♭	52
4	E	53
4	F	54
4	F♯/G♭	55
4	G	56
4	G♯/A♭	57
4	A	58
4	A♯/B♭	59
4	B	60
5	C	61
5	C♯/D♭	62
5	D	63
5	D♯/E♭	64
5	E	65
5	F	66
5	F♯/G♭	67
5	G	68
5	G♯/A♭	69
5	A	70
5	A♯/B♭	71
5	B	72
6	C	73
6	C♯/D♭	74
6	D	75
6	D♯/E♭	76
6	E	77
6	F	78
6	F♯/G♭	79
6	G	80
6	G♯/A♭	81
6	A	82
6	A♯/B♭	83
6	B	84

You specify the length (duration) of a note with the L command followed by a number; for example, L2 N0 plays a half-note rest. The duration is specified as a fraction of a whole note: L1 specifies a whole note (4 beats), L2 a half note (2 beats), L4 a quarter note (1 beat), and so on to L64, a sixty-fourth note (1/8 of a beat). The L command sets the length of all subsequent notes until a new L command is given. Or, you can specify a particular note's length (without affecting subsequent notes) by inserting only the length number after the note; for example, C8 plays the pitch C as an eighth note.

You can also make a note last half again as long as the specified length by following the note letter with a period. For example, L1 D. specifies a D whole note that is held for an additional half note, for a total duration of 1½ whole notes (6 beats). You can use this notation to transcribe any note in a musical score that has a dot after it.

Because notes in many songs range through several octaves, QuickBASIC includes a convenient way to shift octaves: the greater-than sign (>) shifts the subsequent notes up one octave, and the less-than sign (<) shifts the subsequent notes down one octave. A shift remains in effect until a new shift is specified or until the O command specifies a particular octave. In "Red River Valley," the notes are in octaves 2 and 3.

Tempo and Other Modifiers

QuickBASIC lets you control the speed, or tempo, of the music you compose. The T command in the PLAY statement specifies the tempo in terms of how many quarter notes will be played per minute, ranging from 32 through 255; the default is 120. Note that at a fast tempo (for example, T200) short notes such as sixty-fourth notes might not sound because the interval is shorter than the tick of the computer's clock, which QuickBASIC uses for timing. (See Chapter 10, "Time.")

You can alter the length of notes by using the following commands:

ML (music legato)	Each note plays for full length
MN (music normal)	Each note plays for 7/8 length
MS (music staccato)	Each note plays for 3/4 length

This lets you create effects that correspond to the spirit of the music.

Playing Commands from a String Variable

You can assign a series of PLAY commands to a string variable and then execute its contents by inserting it into a PLAY statement. For example, the following statements cause a scale to play:

```
scale$ = "CDEFGAB"
PLAY "X" + VARPTR$(scale$)
```

To use a string variable in a PLAY statement, you must first place an X in the PLAY command string, followed with a set of closing quotation marks, and then add a call to the VARPTR$ function. (This function returns the address of the string variable so that PLAY can find the commands in the string.)

Playing Music in the Background

The MB (music background) command for PLAY specifies that the music will play in the background while your program continues execution.

When music is to be played in the background, notes generated by the PLAY statements aren't played immediately—they are stored in an internal buffer. After the program executes a statement, it checks the music buffer to see whether there are any notes to play. If there are, zero or more notes are played. The number of notes played is determined by the durations of the notes and whether any time has elapsed since the most recent note sounded.

The buffer can hold only 32 notes, so if you want to play more than a brief melody in the background, you must execute more PLAY statements to refill the buffer.

If you want to play background music continuously, you must set up a play event trap that refills the music buffer every time the number of notes in the buffer drops below a specified value. To do this, first create a subroutine containing the PLAY statements that will refill the buffer. (To be sure the music will be played in the background, include in your program a PLAY statement that contains the MB command.) Then specify that subroutine in an ON PLAY GOSUB statement. For example, the statement

```
ON PLAY(5) GOSUB MoreMusic
```

specifies that when fewer than five notes remain in the music buffer, the program will execute the subroutine *MoreMusic*. You might have to experiment with the number of notes you specify: If the number is too low, the buffer might empty before QuickBASIC can check it; if the number is too high, the program might refill the buffer so frequently that program execution slows.

After you set up your music subroutine with an ON PLAY GOSUB statement, use the PLAY ON statement to turn on the play event-trapping mechanism. Then you must fill the buffer initially by calling the subroutine with a GOSUB statement. The program outline looks like the following listing:

```
ON PLAY(5) GOSUB MusicSub ' set up music subroutine
PLAY ON                   ' turn on trapping
PLAY "MB"                 ' specify music in background
GOSUB MusicSub            ' begin the music
' other statements execute while music plays
' buffer is regularly refilled by MusicSub
END

MusicSub:
    ' PLAY statements
    RETURN
```

QuickBASIC provides two other statements for use with PLAY. The PLAY OFF statement stops play event trapping. It prevents the program from executing the music subroutine so that the background music stops after all notes in the buffer have been played. The

PLAY STOP statement also prevents the music subroutine from being executed; however, the program remembers whether the number of notes in the music buffer goes below the specified threshold, and when the next PLAY ON statement is executed, the music subroutine executes and refills the buffer. Thus you can use PLAY STOP to temporarily disable the music subroutine (so that a critical part of the program won't be slowed down, for example) and then use PLAY ON to restore the background music.

If you would like to perform a task only when the music buffer has a certain number of notes in it, use the PLAY function to check the number of notes remaining in the buffer.

Other Sound-producing Statements

The BEEP statement sounds a beep on the computer's built-in speaker, exactly as if you had executed the statement *PRINT CHR$(7)*.

The SOUND statement produces a sound of a specified frequency and duration and can be used for various sound effects. (The example program in the SOUND entry creates the sound of a police siren.) Follow the keyword SOUND with the frequency in cycles per second, or hertz, (a value in the range 37 through 32767), a comma, and the duration in clock ticks. (The PC clock "ticks" 18.2 times per second.) Thus the statement

```
SOUND 440, 18.2
```

generates a 440-cycle tone (which is the pitch A) for 1 second. The SOUND statement is more versatile than PLAY because it is not limited to the recognized musical notes; on the other hand, the sounds produced by SOUND cannot be played in the background.

Related Reading

Enders, Bernd, and Bob Peterson. The Waite Group. *BASIC Primer for the IBM PC & XT.* New York, N.Y.: New American Library, 1984.

BEEP

See also: PLAY (Statement), SOUND

■ QB2	■ QB4.5	✲ PowerBASIC
■ QB3	ANSI	■ GW-BASIC
■ QB4	■ BASIC7	■ MacQB

Purpose

The BEEP statement sounds a beep on the computer's speaker. A beep is often used to call attention to an error or to warn the user of the consequences of an action such as deleting a file.

Syntax

BEEP

Usage

```
BEEP
```

Sounds a beep on the speaker.

```
FOR n% = 1 TO 3
    BEEP
NEXT n%
```

Sounds three consecutive beeps on the speaker.

Description

The BEEP statement sounds a beep on the speaker for about half a second. You can achieve the same effect with the statement *PRINT CHR$(7)*, which "displays" the nonprinting Ctrl-G character. (This character is sometimes referred to as the "bell" character because on older terminals it sounded a bell.)

You can't control the duration of a single beep, but you can make the beep seem longer by repeating the BEEP statement in a loop. You also can't control the pitch of the beep: To generate another sound or a musical note, you must use the SOUND statement or the PLAY statement.

Compatibility

PowerBASIC

PowerBASIC supports an optional argument for use with the BEEP statement. You can specify the number of times BEEP sounds the computer's speaker by following the keyword BEEP with an integer value.

Example

The following program uses a loop to request input of one of the following characters: A, B, C, or D (either lowercase or uppercase). If the user enters an invalid character, the program sounds a beep by calling BEEP and prompts the user to try again.

```
CLS
DO
    PRINT "Type A, B, C, or D."
    INPUT char$
    choice$ = UCASE$(char$)
    IF INSTR("ABCD", choice$) THEN
        PRINT "Very good!"
        EXIT DO
    ELSE
        BEEP
        PRINT "Please try again."
    END IF
LOOP
```

ON PLAY GOSUB

See also: PLAY (Function), PLAY (Statement), PLAY ON/OFF/STOP

■ QB2	■ QB4.5	■ PowerBASIC
■ QB3	ANSI	■ GW-BASIC
■ QB4	■ BASIC7	MacQB

Purpose

The ON PLAY GOSUB statement specifies the start of the subroutine that is executed whenever the number of notes left in the music buffer goes below a specified value. You can use this statement to specify the subroutine that fills the music buffer with notes to be played in the background while your program continues execution.

Syntax

ON PLAY(*notes*) GOSUB {*label* ¦ *line*}

notes is the number that specifies the fewest number of notes that can be in the music buffer before the program executes the subroutine. It must be an integer in the range 1 through 32.

label or *line* is the label or line number of the subroutine to be executed when fewer notes than specified by *notes* remain to be played in the buffer.

Usage

```
ON PLAY(3) GOSUB MoreMusic
```

Specifies that the subroutine *MoreMusic* will be executed when there are fewer than three notes left to be played in the music buffer.

Description

The ON PLAY GOSUB statement sets up play event trapping for filling the music buffer. It specifies the subroutine to which the program branches when the number of notes stored in the music buffer changes to one less than the specified value. Play event trapping keeps the music buffer full so that music can be played in the background until event trapping is disabled or paused. After you call the ON PLAY GOSUB statement, you must call PLAY ON to begin the event trapping.

Errors

If you specify a number of queued notes outside the range 1 through 32, QuickBASIC returns an "Illegal function call" error message.

Example

See the example program in the PLAY ON/OFF/STOP entry for an illustration of the usage of the ON PLAY GOSUB statement.

PLAY (Function)

See also: ON PLAY GOSUB, PLAY (Statement), PLAY ON/OFF/STOP

■ QB2	■ QB4.5	■ PowerBASIC
■ QB3	ANSI	■ GW-BASIC
■ QB4	■ BASIC7	MacQB

Purpose

The PLAY function returns the number of notes that remain to be played in the music buffer. You can use this function to check the status of the buffer; if the buffer is almost empty, you can execute a PLAY statement to fill it.

Syntax

PLAY(*n*)

n is a dummy value that is used to distinguish the PLAY function from the PLAY statement. It can have any numeric value.

Usage

```
IF PLAY(1) < 10 THEN PLAY "C D E F G A B"
```

Puts the notes of a scale in the music buffer if fewer than 10 notes remain to be played.

Description

The PLAY function returns the number of notes remaining to be played in the music buffer. The music buffer holds notes only when music is being played in the background. By having your program check this value periodically, you can execute PLAY statements to refill the buffer and enable the background music to continue playing. The PLAY statement used with the MB command specifies that music is to be played in the background.

If music is being played in the foreground (the default for the PLAY statement when the MB command isn't specified), the PLAY function returns 0.

Comments

If your program is long or has considerable variation in its path of execution, the PLAY function might not be executed often enough to prevent the music buffer from being emptied (thus causing the music to stop playing). In these cases, use the ON PLAY GOSUB statement to make the program branch to a subroutine that refills the buffer when the buffer is nearly empty.

Example

The following program repeatedly plays a scale in the background. It calls the PLAY function each time through a loop and reports the number of notes in the music buffer. When the buffer contains fewer than three notes, the program refills it by calling the PLAY statement.

```
PLAY "MB"                       ' set background music mode
CLS

DO
    LOCATE 5, 1
    PRINT "Number of notes left to play: ";
    IF PLAY(1) < 3 THEN         ' refill music buffer if fewer than 3 notes remain
        PLAY "< C D E F G A B > C"
    END IF
    PRINT PLAY(1)
LOOP UNTIL INKEY$ <> ""         ' loop until user presses a key
END
```

PLAY (Statement)

See also: ON PLAY GOSUB, PLAY ON/OFF/STOP

■ QB2	■ QB4.5	■ PowerBASIC
■ QB3	ANSI	✲ GW-BASIC
■ QB4	■ BASIC7	MacQB

Purpose

The PLAY statement plays specified musical notes. You can control the pitch and duration of each note and include pauses (rests). You can play the music in the foreground or in the background (while other statements of the program are being executed).

Syntax

PLAY *string*

string is a string literal, string variable, or string expression that contains a series of music commands. Enclose literal strings in sets of quotation marks. You can enter commands in uppercase or lowercase, and you can separate them with blank spaces or semicolons, although this merely makes the string more readable and is not a syntax requirement.

Usage

```
PLAY "C D E F G A B"
```

Plays a scale.

```
PLAY "O6 C"
```

Plays the pitch C in the highest possible octave.

```
PLAY "T80"
```

Sets the tempo to 80 quarter notes per minute.

```
PLAY "X" + VARPTR$(cmd$)
```

Plays the commands in the string variable *cmd$*.

Description

The PLAY statement uses a "macro language" that enables your program to play melodies. The string in quotes (or in a string variable) following the PLAY keyword consists of a series of macro commands that specify the pitch and duration of notes, the overall tempo, and whether the music is to be played in the foreground or background.

Pitch

You can play notes in as many as seven octaves. Use the O command with a number in the range 0 through 6 to specify the octave of subsequent notes. (The fourth octave, or O3, contains middle C.) You can also use a greater-than sign (>) to specify the next-higher octave or a less-than sign (<) to specify the next-lower one. (Specifications above octave 6 or below octave 0 are ignored.)

You can use either of two methods to specify the pitch to be played: Use the N command followed by the note number (0 through 84), or merely specify the musical letter (A through G). (Remember, when you use note letters, QuickBASIC plays that particular note within the last octave specified.) The command N0 indicates a rest (a period of silence). With the letter notation, a plus sign (+) or number sign (#) indicates a sharp, and a minus sign (–) indicates a flat. Sharps and flats affect only the current note.

You can also specify a pause by using the P command followed by the fraction of a whole note (in the range 1 through 64) that specifies the length of time to pause. See the "Duration" section for an explanation of the length.

Duration

Duration is the relative length of time for which a note sounds. Use the L command followed by the length of subsequent notes: 1 is a whole note, 2 a half note, 4 a quarter note, 8 an eighth note, 16 a sixteenth note, and 32 a thirty-second note. The shortest note value is 64 (a sixty-fourth note). After you specify a length with the L command, all subsequent notes use that length until you change it. If you want to change the length of only one note, specify a number after that note. For example, the command *PLAY "L4 C G A"* plays C, G, and A as quarter notes. If the next command were *PLAY "F8 B C"*,

F would be an eighth note, and B and C would be played as quarter notes (the most recently specified length).

In accordance with musical notation, you can also follow a note with a dot to make its length 1½ times the last specified length. To do this, put a period after the note. For example, the command *PLAY "L8 G A."* plays G as an eighth note and then plays A as 1½ eighth notes (a "dotted eighth note").

The length of all notes being played can also be modified by the following commands:

ML (music legato)	Each note plays for full length
MN (music normal)	Each note plays for ⅞ length
MS (music staccato)	Each note plays for ¾ length

Any of these three commands remains in effect until you specify another one.

The length of a note is its relative duration—that is, how long the note plays in relation to a whole note. The actual amount of time (in seconds) that a note plays is determined by tempo, the rate at which the music is played. In PLAY, tempo is expressed in quarter notes per minute and is specified by T followed by a number in the range of 32 through 255. The default is T120, which means 120 quarter notes can be played per minute.

Note that the interrupt rate of the system clock limits how short and fast individual notes can be. For example, if the tempo is set to 255, your program won't be able to play sixty-fourth notes (T255 L64) because the system cannot check the clock for the timing and produce the note in such a short interval.

Foreground and background music

The PLAY statement includes two commands that specify the mode in which the program plays the specified notes. By default, music plays in the foreground (specified by MF). This means that a QuickBASIC program executes PLAY statements and sounds the specified notes without executing any other statements until all the music has been played.

If you use the MB (music background) command, however, the notes specified in PLAY statements are put into a buffer and played in the background. Execution of the program continues while the music plays. After each statement in your program is executed, QuickBASIC checks the buffer and plays zero or more notes. (The number of notes played is determined by the durations of the notes and whether any notes are still being played; that is, QuickBASIC tries to maintain the tempo you have set.) The buffer can hold a maximum of 32 notes; therefore, you must continually refill the buffer before it runs out of notes if you want the music to be played continuously. (See the tutorial and the ON PLAY GOSUB entry for details.)

Playing commands in a string variable

For convenience, you can assign a series of PLAY commands to a string variable and then use the variable in a PLAY statement. For example, the statement *cmd$ = "C D E"* assigns three PLAY commands to the variable *cmd$*. When you include this variable as a substring within a PLAY command string, QuickBASIC executes the commands in the substring. To use the substring, type an X at the end of your PLAY command and add a call to the VARPTR$ function, as in the following statement:

```
PLAY "03 A B- X" + VARPTR$(cmd$)
```

If you want to use an integer variable in the PLAY statement to specify the value following a command, you must follow the letter designating the command with an equal sign and a set of closing quotation marks. Then add the variable in a call to VARPTR$ to the command string. For example, if the variable *octave%* contains the number of the octave for a particular melody, you could set the octave with the following statement:

```
PLAY "O=" + VARPTR$(octave%)
```

Comments

You cannot play two or more notes at a time (multiple voices, or chords) using QuickBASIC. The standard sound system in the IBM PC lacks the appropriate hardware to generate simultaneous notes.

Errors

If you specify an integer that is out of range for a particular PLAY command, QuickBASIC returns an "Illegal function call" error message. QuickBASIC returns the same message if you use a letter in the command string that isn't a command.

Compatibility

GW-BASIC and BASICA

In GW-BASIC and BASICA, you can play the commands in a string simply by naming the string in your PLAY command—for example, *PLAY "O3 Xcmd$"*.

Example

The following program uses PLAY statements to play the song "Here Comes the Sun" by the Beatles (1969 Harrisongs, Ltd).

```
PLAY "T255"    ' set tempo to 255 quarter notes per minute
PLAY "03"
PLAY "< < L2 A > > > L4 C# < A B > L2 C#."
PLAY "L2 N0 L4 C# < L2 B A F#"
PLAY "A B A F# L1 E."
PLAY "< < L2 A > > > L4 C# < A B > L2 C#."
PLAY "L2 N0 L4 C# < L2 B A L2 F#."
PLAY "> L4 C# < L2 B A L1 B B L1 N0"
```

(continued)

continued

```
PLAY "< < L2 A > > > L4 C# < L2 B > L2 C# < L2 A."
PLAY "> L4 C# < A B > L2 C#."
PLAY "< < L2 A > > > L4 C# < L2 B > C# < L2 A."
PLAY "L4 NO A L2 B A"
PLAY "L2 NO > L2 C# < B A NO"
PLAY "L4 F# A B E A B D A B A G# F# E"
```

PLAY ON/OFF/STOP

See also: PLAY (Function), PLAY (Statement)

■ QB2	■ QB4.5	■ PowerBASIC
■ QB3	ANSI	■ GW-BASIC
■ QB4	■ BASIC7	MacQB

Purpose

The PLAY statements enable, disable, or suspend play event trapping. This statement lets you refill the music buffer continuously while music is being played in the background. Thus background music can continue while your program executes other statements.

Syntax

PLAY ON
PLAY OFF
PLAY STOP

Usage

```
ON PLAY(3) GOSUB Refill
PLAY ON
```

Refills the music buffer as specified in the ON PLAY GOSUB statement.

```
PLAY OFF
```

Stops the play event trapping that refills the music buffer.

```
PLAY STOP
```

Disables the play event trapping that refills the music buffer but remembers if the buffer needs filling so that a subsequent PLAY ON will refill the buffer.

Description

When you specify that music be played in the background (with the MB command in a PLAY statement), the notes are stored in an internal buffer rather than played immediately. After a PLAY ON statement is executed, QuickBASIC checks the buffer after each subsequent statement is executed and plays as many notes as possible. When the number of notes remaining to be played falls below the number specified in the ON PLAY GOSUB statement, the subroutine specified in that statement is executed. (Usually this subroutine executes PLAY statements or calls subroutines that execute PLAY subroutines, thus refilling the buffer with notes.)

To completely disable background music, use the PLAY OFF statement. Executing PLAY OFF prevents the ON PLAY GOSUB subroutine from being executed. Thus the buffer soon runs out of notes and the background music stops playing.

To temporarily suspend the background music (for example, while your program is executing instructions that might be affected by the repeated interruptions to refill the music buffer), use the PLAY STOP statement. The remaining notes in the buffer will be played, and then the background music will stop playing. To restart the background music, merely execute another PLAY ON statement. If the number of notes falls below the number specified in the ON PLAY GOSUB statement after PLAY STOP has been called, QuickBASIC sets an internal flag indicating that the buffer needs refilling so that the program will execute the subroutine when PLAY ON is called.

If you use the command-line compiler, BC.EXE, to compile a program using play event trapping, you must use either the /V or the /W switch. These switches enable trapping and force the program to check the music buffer, either between statements (/V) or between program lines (/W).

Example

The following program uses a PLAY ON statement to turn on play event trapping and uses an ON PLAY GOSUB statement to send control to the *Replay* subroutine when the music buffer needs to be refilled. Note that the *PLAY "MB T255"* statement specifies that music be played in the background and sets a speedy tempo. The song played in this program is "Here Comes the Sun" by the Beatles.

The main FOR loop in the program draws progressively larger circles in changing colors to represent the sun. The outer DO loop executes the program until the user presses Esc.

The IF statements control the flag variable *music*. The first time a key (other than Esc) is pressed, *music* is set to 0 and a PLAY STOP statement is executed. This suspends event trapping and stops the music. The next time the user presses a key, *music* is set to 1, and a PLAY ON statement immediately refills the music buffer (because QuickBASIC "remembers" the last event—the nearly empty buffer), and the music resumes. If you replace the PLAY STOP statement with PLAY OFF, the music does not resume.

The *Replay* subroutine contains the PLAY statements that fill the music buffer.

```
SCREEN 9        ' for EGA; use 1 for CGA, 12 for VGA
maxX% = 640     ' for EGA; use 320 for CGA
maxY% = 350     ' for EGA; use 200 for CGA, 480 for VGA

x = maxX% / 2
y = maxY% / 2               ' starting position for circle
maxColors% = 9
startRad = maxY% / 16       ' starting radius of circle

DIM colors(maxColors%)

FOR clr% = 1 TO 9           ' read the foreground color values
   READ colors(clr%)
NEXT clr%

' set up sound
ON PLAY(3) GOSUB Replay      ' refill buffer when three or fewer notes
GOSUB Replay                 ' fill music buffer initially
PLAY ON                      ' turn on music event trapping
music = 1                    ' flag indicating whether music is played

DO                           ' main loop shows graphic
    FOR clr% = 1 TO maxColors%                  ' FOR loop steps through values
        circleColor = colors(clr%)
        rad = startRad * clr%
        CIRCLE (x, y), rad, (circleColor)       ' draw circle
        PAINT (x, y), circleColor               ' fill in the circle
    NEXT clr%
    inky$ = INKEY$
    IF inky$ = CHR$(27) THEN EXIT DO            ' exit loop if user presses Esc
    FOR n = 1 TO 500: NEXT n
    PAINT (x, y), 0          ' erase circle
    IF inky$ <> "" THEN      ' toggle PLAY status
        IF music THEN
            PLAY STOP        ' pause event trapping
            music = 0
        ELSE
            PLAY ON          ' enable event trapping
            music = 1
        END IF
    END IF
LOOP UNTIL inky$ = CHR$(27)                     ' exit loop if user presses Esc
PLAY OFF
END
```

(continued)

continued

```
' subroutine to fill music buffer
Replay:
    PLAY "MB T255"
    PLAY "O3"
    PLAY "< < L2 A > > > L4 C# < A B > L2 C#."
    PLAY "L2 NO L4 C# < L2 B A F#"
    PLAY "A B A F# L1 E."
    PLAY "< < L2 A > > > L4 C# < A B > L2 C#."
    PLAY "L2 NO L4 C# < L2 B A L2 F#."
    PLAY "> L4 C# < L2 B A L1 B B L1 NO"

    PLAY "< < L2 A > > > L4 C# < L2 B > L2 C# < L2 A."
    PLAY "> L4 C# < A B > L2 C#."
    PLAY "< < L2 A > > > L4 C# < L2 B > C# < L2 A."
    PLAY "L4 NO A L2 B A"
    PLAY "L2 NO > L2 C# < B A NO"
    PLAY "L4 F# A B E A B D A B A G# F# E"
    RETURN

' foreground colors of the circles
DATA 4, 12, 5, 13, 5, 12, 14, 12, 14
```

SOUND

See also: BEEP, PLAY (Statement)

■ QB2	■ QB4.5	■ PowerBASIC
■ QB3	ANSI	■ GW-BASIC
■ QB4	■ BASIC7	✲ MacQB

Purpose

The SOUND statement generates a tone of a specified frequency and duration on the computer's speaker. You can use this statement to create sound effects other than the standard musical notes generated by the PLAY statement.

Syntax

SOUND *frequency*, *duration*

frequency is an integer expression from 37 through 32767; it represents the sound's frequency in cycles per second (hertz).

duration is an integer expression from 0 through 65535; it represents the length of the sound in clock ticks. (The PC clock ticks 18.2 times per second.)

Usage

```
SOUND 440, 18.2
```

Sounds a 440-cycle tone (musical A) for 1 second (18.2 clock ticks).

```
SOUND 500, 0
```

Terminates the current sound. Any 0 duration turns off the sound currently being generated.

Description

The SOUND statement generates a sound of the specified number of cycles per second (hertz) for the specified number of clock ticks. The human ear can hear approximately 20 through 20,000 hertz, so be sure to limit the sounds to this range. A duration of 0 ticks in a SOUND statement turns off any SOUND statement currently running.

The PC's speaker isn't designed to reproduce sounds higher than a few thousand hertz. Unlike the PLAY statement, the SOUND statement can't run in the background. However, the current sound continues for its full duration while QuickBASIC executes subsequent statements.

Errors

If you use a string value with SOUND, QuickBASIC displays a "Type mismatch" error message. Any numeric value that is out of range results in an "Illegal function call" error message.

Compatibility

QuickBASIC for the Macintosh

The SOUND statement supported by QuickBASIC for the Macintosh is more complex than the one in QuickBASIC 4.5. Although the duration of a note can range only from 0 through 77 clock ticks, the statement also includes two optional arguments—one for volume and the other for voice. The value for volume can be in the range 0 through 255. The voice argument controls the number of the voice (voices 0 through 3). The SOUND statement can be used with the WAVE statement to produce harmonies, or chords.

Example

The following program plays a rising and falling glissando, which produces a "police siren" sound effect. To create the glissando, the program calls the SOUND statement in a FOR loop that modifies the note played by 4 hertz each iteration.

```
CLS
PRINT "PULL OVER!"
PRINT "<Press any key to stop>"
DO
    FOR i% = 440 TO 880 STEP 4
        SOUND i%, i% / 880
        IF INKEY$ <> "" THEN EXIT DO
    NEXT
    FOR i% = 880 TO 440 STEP -4
        SOUND i%, i% / 880
        IF INKEY$ <> "" THEN EXIT DO
    NEXT
LOOP UNTIL INKEY$ <> ""
```

CHAPTER 13

Light Pen and Joystick

Introduction

This chapter discusses two auxiliary input devices that can be connected to personal computers—the light pen and the joystick. Like the mouse, trackball, and touch pad, the light pen and the joystick are pointing devices. Whether users must deal with invading aliens or cell ranges in a spreadsheet, nowadays they expect to be able to point at what they want to work with on the screen and directly manipulate it.

For "point-and-click" business applications (and an increasing number of games), the preferred pointing device today is the mouse, which fits the hand, rolls on the desktop, and provides easy, precise cursor movement on the screen. Because QuickBASIC does not include specific statements or functions for the mouse, mouse programming is not covered in this book. However, several third-party libraries contain complete sets of mouse routines you can call from QuickBASIC, and many principles of light pen and joystick programming also apply to the mouse. The "official" and most complete book on mouse programming is the *Microsoft Mouse Programmer's Reference* (Microsoft Press, 1989).

The basic concepts you use to program the light pen are virtually identical to those you use for the joystick; therefore, this tutorial introduces these devices separately but discusses programming for them together. Table 13-1 lists the QuickBASIC light pen and joystick statements and functions in alphabetic order.

Statement or function	Description
ON PEN GOSUB	Specifies the subroutine to be executed when the light pen is activated and light-pen event trapping is enabled
ON STRIG GOSUB	Specifies the subroutine to be executed when a specified joystick button is pushed and joystick event trapping is enabled
PEN	Returns the *x* or *y* (column or row) position of the light pen
PEN ON/OFF/STOP	Enables, disables, or suspends event trapping for the light pen
STICK	Returns the *x* or *y* (column or row) position of the joystick
STRIG	Determines whether a specified joystick button has been (or is being) pressed
STRIG ON/OFF/STOP	Enables, disables, or suspends event trapping of a specified joystick button

Table 13-1.
Light pen and joystick statements and functions.

Light Pens

A light pen is a pen-shaped pointer that you use to interact directly with the monitor's screen. Figure 13-1 shows two types of light pens. You activate the push-tip type by pressing the tip against an appropriate area of the screen (such as a menu selection). You activate the touch-ring type by holding it slightly above the appropriate area of the screen and pressing on the cliplike touch ring.

Light pens are used primarily in point-of-sale operations and computer-aided design, and occasionally in educational software. The advantage of using the light pen is that you merely point at what you want in order to choose it. Unlike the mouse, the program doesn't need to convert mechanical motion (on the desk) to cursor motion (on the screen). Although using the pen is perhaps more intuitive than using the mouse, when using the pen you must reach to the screen to issue a command. In addition, the push-tip type can scratch or smear the screen surface.

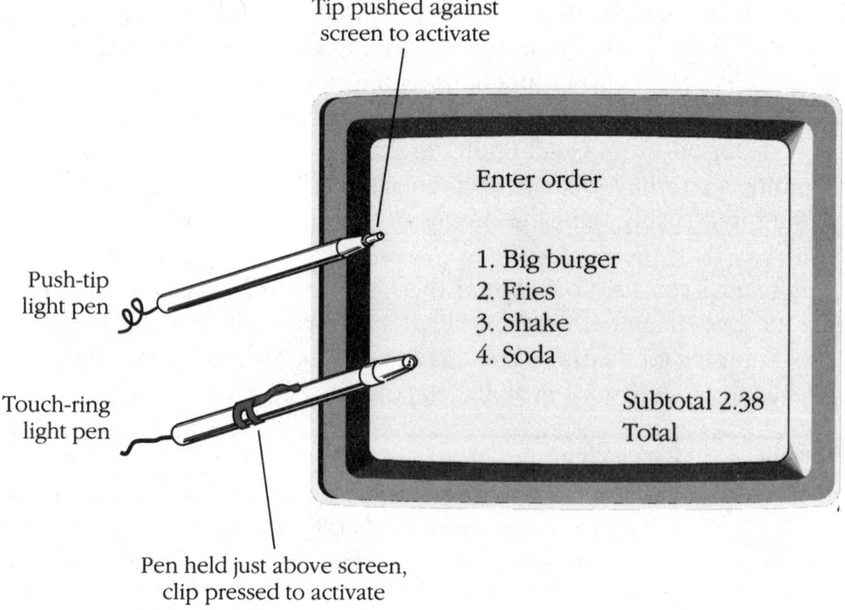

Figure 13-1.
How light pens are used.

Joysticks

Joysticks are used more often than light pens; in fact, anyone who has watched children play computer games has probably seen joysticks in action. You can use either one or two joysticks with a PC. Although a few educational applications accept input from joysticks, joysticks are used mainly in games and simulations. In addition to their uses in flight simulators and arcade shoot-'em-up games, joysticks can also be used to move pieces in strategic games. (An increasing number of games also support the mouse because it is now widely used with business-oriented personal computers.) Joysticks vary in the number of buttons they provide and in their layout; Figure 13-2 shows a typical configuration. You might have to experiment to determine how your joystick buttons correspond to the "upper" and "lower" buttons recognized by QuickBASIC.

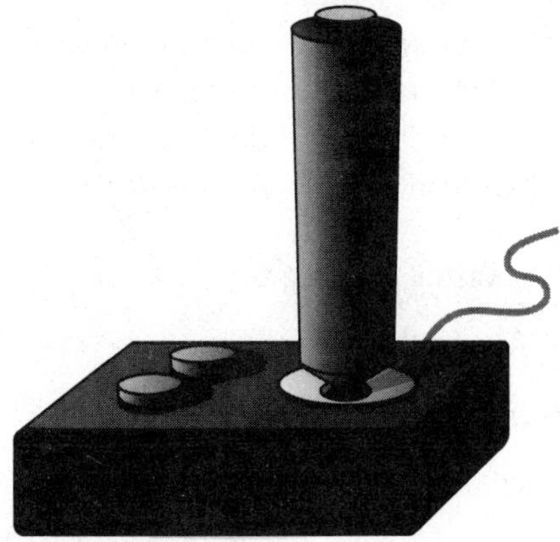

Figure 13-2.
A typical joystick.

Setting Up Event Trapping

The programming concept you need to master to use the light pen or joystick in your programs is event trapping. A program performs event trapping by checking for input from the light pen or joystick and then executing the correct subroutine when that input occurs.

First you set up event trapping by specifying the names of the subroutines to which you want execution to branch when the light pen or joystick is activated. To set up event trapping for the light pen, use the ON PEN GOSUB statement. For the joystick, use the ON STRIG GOSUB statement. In addition to specifying the subroutine in the ON STRIG GOSUB statement, you include a number that specifies the joystick button to which the event trapping will respond. Table 13-2 on the following page lists the numbers and their corresponding button.

Number	Button
0	Lower button on the first joystick
2	Lower button on the second joystick
4	Upper button on the first joystick
6	Upper button on the second joystick

Table 13-2.
Numbers used with ON STRIG GOSUB and the button to which each corresponds.

Next you enable the event trapping by calling PEN ON for light pens and STRIG ON for joysticks. You must specify the joystick button that will be trapped by including in the STRIG ON statement the appropriate number listed in Table 13-2. Note that even if you don't use light-pen event trapping, you must use the PEN ON statement before calling any statements (other than ON PEN GOSUB) that work with the light pen.

Now you must write the necessary subroutines. Unfortunately, the light pen and joystick event-trapping statements are part of the BASIC heritage and don't support the new procedures recommended for programming in QuickBASIC. You have to use subroutines.

To summarize, the following program skeleton outlines a program that uses the light pen:

```
ON PEN GOSUB DoChoice    ' specify subroutine for light-pen event trapping
PEN ON                   ' enable light-pen event trapping
⋮
END      ' stop execution before it moves to the subroutines

DoChoice:
    ' statements executed when user activates light pen
    ⋮
    RETURN
```

The following program skeleton outlines a program that uses a single joystick:

```
ON STRIG(0) GOSUB DoChoice1    ' subroutine for lower button, joystick 1
ON STRIG(4) GOSUB DoChoice2    ' subroutine for upper button, joystick 1
STRIG(0) ON                    ' enable trapping for lower button
STRIG(4) ON                    ' enable trapping for upper button
⋮
END       ' stop execution before it moves to the subroutines

DoChoice1:
    ' statements executed when user presses lower button
    ⋮
    RETURN

DoChoice2:
    ' statements executed when user presses upper button
    ⋮
    RETURN
```

Because the button configuration and the number of each joystick can vary from joystick to joystick, a program that uses the joystick should direct the user to press each button to define which is the upper button and which is the lower. If you want the program to respond to either joystick, simply trap both of them—use one subroutine for both lower buttons and another subroutine for both upper buttons.

If you want to disable light-pen or joystick event trapping during part of your program, you can turn off trapping by using the PEN OFF or STRIG OFF statement. Program execution will speed up because the program will no longer monitor the light pen or joystick. If you want to suspend event trapping but direct the program to remember whether the light pen or joystick was used during the time trapping was suspended, use PEN STOP or STRIG STOP. When the program executes the next PEN ON or STRIG ON statement, the program will branch to the correct subroutine if the light pen or joystick was activated.

You can use this technique to prevent your program from being interrupted during a time-critical operation (such as reading a serial port) but still allow timely response to user requests.

Reading Position Values

Of course, your program must be able to determine the location at which the light pen or joystick is positioned when it triggers an event trap. When the program knows the location, it can perform the appropriate task, such as activating a menu choice or moving a game piece.

For the light pen, use the PEN function with a number that specifies the information PEN returns. (See the PEN entry for the list of numbers.) Note that the PEN function can return the coordinates of a location in either character format (character-cell location) or graphics format (pixel location). PEN can return either the position at which the light pen was activated or the position at which it was last aimed. (The two are not necessarily the same.) PEN can read the position of the light pen even when the light pen is not activated. Thus a drawing program can let the user activate the light pen at the starting point and then draw a line of points as the pen moves. This action is demonstrated in the following program segment:

```
SCREEN 1
PEN ON

DO
    IF PEN(0) = -1 THEN PSET (PEN(4), PEN(5))
LOOP UNTIL INKEY$ = CHR$(27)
```

For the joystick, use the STICK function with a number that specifies the *x*- or *y*-coordinate that STICK will return. (See the STICK entry for the list of numbers.) The joystick uses a coordinate system that is independent of the coordinate system used in the current screen mode. Different joysticks vary in the values they return. Some return coordinates in the range 1 through 80; others can use coordinates even higher than 200. The STICK function returns values only in the range 1 through 200. If you assume that the variables *maxX%* and *maxY%* contain the greatest *x*- and *y*-coordinates in the present graphics mode and that *maxXJoy%* and *maxYJoy%* contain the greatest joystick return values, you can calculate the scale factor for converting from joystick coordinates to screen coordinates by using the following statements:

```
xScale% = maxX% / maxXJoy%
yScale% = maxY% / maxYJoy%
```

Then, to convert a joystick coordinate to a screen coordinate, multiply the joystick coordinate by the scale factor. For example, to assign the position of joystick number 1 to the variables *xPos%* and *yPos%*, use the following statements:

```
xPos% = STICK(0)
yPos% = STICK(1)
```

Then, if you want to use the PUT statement to display an image at the position specified by the joystick, use the following statement:

```
PUT (xPos% * xScale%, yPos% * yScale%), graphArray%, PSET
```

Because of the variations in joystick design and configuration, your program should let the user calibrate the joystick by aiming it at specific points on the screen. During calibration, the program can use the values returned by STICK to perform the scaling.

The STRIG function returns information about the joystick buttons. You include a number in the call to STRIG to specify which button STRIG examines. This function is especially useful if the program contains a subroutine to which execution branches when any button is pressed. By using STRIG, the subroutine can determine which button was pressed.

Using the Mouse as a Light Pen

If you don't have a light pen attached to your computer but you do have a mouse with a driver installed, you can use the mouse somewhat like a light pen. Although you can't point the mouse at the screen, the PEN function will return the character row and column at which the mouse cursor is positioned if both buttons on the mouse are pressed. Using the mouse as a light pen is useful for testing statements such as *PRINT PEN(4), PEN(5)* which are in programs you expect will be used with a light pen. However, if you are writing a program that uses the mouse, create routines that access the mouse directly.

Disabling Light-Pen Emulation

Because the mouse emulates the light pen, QuickBASIC does not respond to the light pen if a mouse driver is also installed in your system. If you want to use both a mouse and a light pen, you must disable the mouse's light-pen emulation.

You can disable the emulation in your program by calling DOS Interrupt 33H with Function 14. The following program segment shows how to disable light-pen emulation in QuickBASIC. Be sure to start QuickBASIC with the command line

```
QB /L QB.QLB
```

so that the program can call the *InterruptX* subprogram, which is found in the QB.QLB Quick library.

```
TYPE RegTypeX
    ax AS INTEGER
    bx AS INTEGER
    cx AS INTEGER
    dx AS INTEGER
    bp AS INTEGER
    si AS INTEGER
    di AS INTEGER
    flags AS INTEGER
    ds AS INTEGER
    es AS INTEGER
END TYPE

DECLARE SUB InterruptX (intnum%, iRegX AS RegTypeX, oRexX AS RegTypeX)

DIM iRegX AS RegTypeX
DIM oRegX AS RegTypeX

iRegX.ax = 14
InterruptX &H33, iRegX, oRegX
```

Related Reading

Microsoft Press and the Hardware Division of Microsoft Corporation. *Microsoft Mouse Programmer's Reference.* Redmond, Wash.: Microsoft Press, 1989.

Prata, Stephen, with Harry Henderson. *The Waite Group's Microsoft QuickBASIC Primer Plus.* Redmond, Wash.: Microsoft Press, 1990.

Schneider, David L. *Handbook of BASIC.* 3d ed. Boston, Mass.: Brady, 1988.

ON PEN GOSUB

See also: PEN, PEN ON/OFF/STOP

■ QB2	■ QB4.5	■ PowerBASIC
■ QB3	ANSI	■ GW-BASIC
■ QB4	■ BASIC7	MacQB

Purpose

The ON PEN GOSUB statement specifies the subroutine to which execution branches when a light pen is activated. Use this statement when you want the program to respond to the light pen by performing light-pen event trapping that executes a certain task.

Syntax

ON PEN GOSUB {*line* ¦ *label*}

line or *label* specifies the line or label number that begins the subroutine to which execution branches.

Usage

```
ON PEN GOSUB HandlePen
```

Specifies that the *HandlePen* subroutine will be executed when the light pen is activated.

Description

You can use light-pen event trapping in your program to execute a specified subroutine when the program detects that a light pen has been activated. First call the ON PEN GOSUB statement to specify the subroutine to be executed. Then use a PEN ON statement to enable trapping (detection) of the light pen.

Errors

If the light pen is not connected or is not properly calibrated, QuickBASIC displays an "Illegal function call" error message.

Warnings

QuickBASIC will not respond to the light pen if a mouse driver is also installed in your system. See the "Disabling Light-Pen Emulation" section in this chapter's tutorial for instructions on how to use both a light pen and a mouse in the same program.

Or, you can use the mouse to emulate a light pen. See the tutorial for a discussion about how the light-pen statements and functions work with a mouse.

Example

The following program demonstrates light-pen event trapping. It specifies in an ON PEN GOSUB statement that the subroutine *Active* will be executed when the pen is activated. The subroutine merely sounds a beep, prints a message, and exits the program. If you have a 2-button mouse, you can press both mouse buttons simultaneously to trigger the subroutine.

```
CLS
ON PEN GOSUB Active    ' specify subroutine for light-pen event trapping
PEN ON                 ' enable light-pen event trapping

DO
    LOCATE 1, 1
    PRINT "Activate the light pen."
LOOP UNTIL INKEY$ = CHR$(27)      ' exit loop when user presses Esc
END

Active:                ' light pen has been activated
    BEEP
    PRINT "The light pen has been activated."
    SYSTEM             ' quit program
    RETURN
```

ON STRIG GOSUB

See also: STRIG, STRIG ON/OFF/STOP

■ QB2	■ QB4.5	■ PowerBASIC
■ QB3	ANSI	■ GW-BASIC
■ QB4	■ BASIC7	MacQB

Purpose

The ON STRIG GOSUB statement specifies a subroutine to which execution branches when a particular joystick button is pressed. Use this statement when you want the program to respond to a joystick button press by performing joystick event trapping that executes a certain task.

Syntax

ON STRIG GOSUB(*button*) {*line* | *label*}

button is either 0, 2, 4, or 6. 0 specifies the lower button of joystick 1, 2 specifies the lower button of joystick 2, 4 specifies the upper button of joystick 1, and 6 specifies the upper button of joystick 2.

line or *label* specifies the line number or label that begins the subroutine to which execution branches.

Usage

```
ON STRIG(4) GOSUB Fire
```

Specifies that the *Fire* subroutine will be executed when the upper button on the first joystick is pressed.

```
ON STRIG(0) GOSUB Warp
```

Specifies that the *Warp* subroutine will be executed when the lower button on the first joystick is pressed.

Description

You can use joystick event trapping in your program to execute a subroutine when the program detects that a certain joystick button has been pressed. (QuickBASIC supports either one or two joysticks with one or two buttons on each.) The ON STRIG GOSUB statement specifies which of the four buttons to respond to and the subroutine that will be executed. The button numbers 0 and 4 refer to the lower and upper buttons on the first joystick; 2 and 6 refer to the lower and upper buttons on the second joystick. Some joysticks have one or two buttons on the base and a button on top of the stick. The latter is usually called an upper button. See your joystick documentation for details about button designations.

After calling ON STRIG GOSUB, you must use the STRIG ON statement to enable trapping (detection) of the specified joystick button.

Example

The following program traps both the lower and upper buttons of the first joystick. When a button is pressed, the program executes the subroutine specified by ON STRIG GOSUB. Each subroutine sounds a beep and displays a message. The subroutine for the upper button also exits the program by calling the SYSTEM statement.

```
CLS
ON STRIG(0) GOSUB Lower     ' specify subroutine for lower button, first joystick
ON STRIG(4) GOSUB Upper     ' specify subroutine for upper button, first joystick

STRIG(0) ON                 ' enable trapping for lower button
STRIG(4) ON                 ' enable trapping for upper button

PRINT "Press either joystick button."
PRINT "Pressing the upper button causes the program to end."
```

(continued)

continued

```
LOCATE 4, 1
PRINT "Press either joystick button."
DO
LOOP UNTIL INKEY$ = CHR$(27)
END

Lower:                        ' subroutine for lower button
    BEEP
    LOCATE 6, 1
    PRINT "You pressed the lower button."
    RETURN

Upper:                        ' subroutine for upper button
    BEEP
    LOCATE 6, 1
    PRINT "You pressed the upper button."
    SYSTEM
```

PEN

See also: ON PEN GOSUB, PEN ON/OFF/STOP

■ QB2	■ QB4.5	■ PowerBASIC
■ QB3	ANSI	■ GW-BASIC
■ QB4	■ BASIC7	MacQB

Purpose

The PEN function returns the current status of the light pen. Use this function to determine the location of the light pen on the screen.

Syntax

PEN(*number*)

number is an integer in the range 0 through 9.

Usage

```
IF PEN(3) GOSUB PenDown
```

Executes the *PenDown* subroutine if the light pen is being activated.

```
lastX% = PEN(1)
lastY% = PEN(2)
```

Assigns the pixel coordinates of the location at which the light pen was last activated to the variables *lastX%* and *lastY%*.

```
lastRow% = PEN(6)
lastCol% = PEN(7)
```

Assigns the row and column of the location at which the light pen was last activated to the variables *lastRow%* and *lastCol%*.

Description

Use the PEN function to determine whether the light pen has been activated or is currently being activated; you can also use this function to find the graphics or text coordinates at which the pen was last activated or pointed. Before you can use the PEN statement, you must enable light-pen trapping by using a PEN ON statement.

Follow the keyword PEN with a number from 0 through 9 that is surrounded by parentheses. The number specifies the information that PEN will return. Table 13-3 describes the value that PEN returns for each number.

Number	Value returned
0	−1 if the light pen has been activated since the most recent call to PEN; 0 if not
1	*x*-coordinate of the pixel at which the light pen was most recently activated
2	*y*-coordinate of the pixel at which the light pen was most recently activated
3	−1 if the light pen is currently activated; 0 if not
4	*x*-coordinate of the pixel at which the light pen was most recently pointed
5	*y*-coordinate of the pixel at which the light pen was most recently pointed
6	character row in which the light pen was most recently activated
7	character column in which the light pen was most recently activated
8	character row in which the light pen was most recently pointed
9	character column in which the light pen was most recently pointed

Table 13-3.
Values returned by the PEN function.

The difference between the PEN(0) and PEN(3) functions is that PEN(0) returns a value of true (−1) if the pen has been activated since the most recent call to the PEN function, but the PEN(3) function returns true only if the pen is active at the time PEN(3) is called.

The PEN function can be used in either graphics or text mode. In graphics mode, use the PEN(1) and PEN(2) functions to determine the approximate *x*- and *y*-coordinates of the pixel at which the light pen was last activated, and use PEN(4) and PEN(5) to determine the coordinates at which the light pen is currently aimed. The location coordinates are approximate because most light pens do not have as fine a resolution as the graphics screen. For example, the light pen might be able to access only the *x*-coordinates 0, 8, 16, 24,...320 and the *y*-coordinates 0, 2, 4, 6,...200. A light pen aimed at the point (238, 149) might return the coordinates 240 and 150.

In text mode, use the PEN(6) and PEN(7) functions to determine the text row and column in which the light pen was most recently activated, and use PEN(8) and PEN(9) to determine the row and column at which the light pen was most recently pointed.

Warnings

QuickBASIC does not respond to the light pen if a mouse driver is also installed in your system. See the "Disabling Light-Pen Emulation" section in the tutorial for instructions about how to use both a light pen and a mouse in the same program.

Or you can use the mouse to emulate a light pen. See the tutorial for a discussion about how the light-pen statements and functions work with a mouse.

Example

The following program displays all the information provided by the PEN function. It also displays a small box and ends when the light pen is pressed against the box (or aimed at the box if the light pen is a touch-ring type).

```
PEN ON
CLS
LOCATE 10, 35
PRINT "Press the box to exit the program. "; CHR$(219)    ' box character
DO
    LOCATE 20, 1
    PRINT "Light pen has ";
    IF PEN(0) THEN                          ' check activation of light pen
        PRINT "been     activated";
    ELSE PRINT "not been activated";
    END IF

    LOCATE 20, 40
    PRINT "Switch currently ";
    IF PEN(3) THEN                          ' check whether light pen is active
        PRINT "    down";
    ELSE PRINT "not down";
    END IF

    LOCATE 21, 1
    PRINT "Last activated at X: "; PEN(1);
    LOCATE 21, 40
    PRINT "Last activated at Y: "; PEN(2);

    LOCATE 22, 1
    PRINT "Now at X: "; PEN(4);
    LOCATE 22, 40
    PRINT "Now at Y: "; PEN(5);

    LOCATE 23, 1
    PRINT "Activated at row: "; PEN(6);
    LOCATE 23, 40
    PRINT "Activated at col: "; PEN(7);
```

(continued)

continued

```
    LOCATE 24, 1
    PRINT "Now at row.: "; PEN(8);
    LOCATE 24, 40
    PRINT "Now at col: "; PEN(9);

    ' check whether light pen activated at the box
    IF (PEN(6) = 10) AND (PEN(7) = 70) THEN SYSTEM
LOOP
```

PEN ON/OFF/STOP

See also: ON PEN GOSUB, PEN

■ QB2	■ QB4.5	■ PowerBASIC
■ QB3	ANSI	■ GW-BASIC
■ QB4	■ BASIC7	MacQB

Purpose

The three PEN statements enable, disable, or suspend the trapping of light-pen events. The PEN ON statement also enables the PEN function, which you can use to obtain information about the light pen's status.

Syntax

PEN ON
PEN OFF
PEN STOP

Usage

`PEN ON`

Enables both light-pen event trapping and the PEN function.

`PEN OFF`

Disables light-pen event trapping.

`PEN STOP`

Suspends light-pen event trapping, but notes whether the light pen has been activated; if it has, a subsequent PEN ON statement branches execution to the appropriate subroutine.

Description

Use the PEN ON statement to begin tracking the movements and status (activated or not activated) of the light pen. If the light pen is activated and an ON PEN GOSUB statement has been called, the program branches to the subroutine specified in the ON PEN

GOSUB statement. (Use the PEN function to gain information about the light pen's position and status.)

The PEN OFF statement disables light-pen event trapping. This means that the program will not branch to the subroutine when the light pen is activated. Also note that no information about the light pen is returned by the PEN function after the program calls PEN OFF. When you restore light-pen event trapping, the program does not remember events that occurred while trapping was off.

The PEN STOP statement suspends light-pen event trapping. The program continues to note light-pen activity but does not execute the subroutine specified in the ON PEN GOSUB statement. The next time a PEN ON statement is executed, the subroutine will be executed if the light pen was activated while event trapping was suspended.

The program executes an implicit PEN STOP whenever it enters the subroutine specified by ON PEN GOSUB. This ensures that another occurrence of the event does not cause the subroutine to be entered recursively. When the program encounters a RETURN statement and returns to the main program, it reinstates play event trapping by executing an implicit PEN ON statement.

If you use the command-line compiler, BC.EXE, to compile a program that performs light-pen event trapping, you must use either the /V or the /W switch. These switches enable trapping and force the program to check the event flag, either between statements (/V) or between program lines (/W).

Tips

Light-pen event trapping slows program execution slightly; you might want to turn off event trapping when you don't expect user input from the light pen.

QuickBASIC will not respond to the light pen if a mouse driver is also installed in your system. See the "Disabling Light-Pen Emulation" section in this chapter's tutorial for instructions about how to use both a light pen and a mouse in the same program.

Or you can use the mouse to emulate a light pen. See the tutorial for a discussion about how the light-pen statements and functions work with a mouse.

Example

The following example uses the PEN ON statement to enable light-pen event trapping. The program executes the *Active* subroutine when the light pen is first activated. The subroutine assigns 1 to the variable *trapped%*, which causes the program to execute the PEN STOP statement found in the main loop. Light-pen event trapping is enabled again when you exit the loop by pressing a key. The program, however, remembers whether you activated the pen after the PEN STOP, and it executes *Active* again if you did. Note that a call to PEN STOP is not effective if it is within the subroutine because the program always calls PEN ON when it exits the subroutine.

```
CLS
ON PEN GOSUB Active
PEN ON                       ' turn on event trapping for light pen
trapped% = 0                 ' flag signaling whether event occurred

DO
    LOCATE 1, 1
    PRINT "Activate the light pen."
    IF trapped% = 1 THEN PEN STOP
LOOP UNTIL INKEY$ <> ""      ' exit if user presses any key

PEN ON       ' executes the Active subroutine if light pen has been activated
END

Active:      ' light pen has been activated
    BEEP
    PRINT "The Active subroutine will be executed one more time"
    PRINT "if you activate the light pen and then press any key."
    trapped% = 1
    RETURN
```

STICK

See also: ON STRIG GOSUB, STRIG, STRIG ON/OFF/STOP

■ QB2	■ QB4.5	■ PowerBASIC
■ QB3	ANSI	■ GW-BASIC
■ QB4	■ BASIC7	MacQB

Purpose

The STICK function returns the *x*- and *y*-coordinates pointed to by a joystick.

Syntax

STICK (*number*)

number is an integer in the range 0 through 3.

Usage

```
stick1X% = STICK(0)
```

Assigns the *x*-coordinate of the first joystick to the variable *stick1X%*.

```
stick1Y% = STICK(1)
```

Assigns the *y*-coordinate of the first joystick to the variable *stick1Y%*.

Description

The STICK function returns information about the *x*- and *y*-coordinates pointed to by a joystick. The coordinate returned depends on the specified number. Table 13-4 lists each number and the corresponding value that STICK returns.

Number	Value returned
0	*x*-coordinate of the first joystick
1	*y*-coordinate of the first joystick
2	*x*-coordinate of the second joystick
3	*y*-coordinate of the second joystick

Table 13-4.
Values returned by the STICK function.

Different joysticks vary in the values they return. Some return coordinates in the range 1 through 80; others can use coordinates as high as 200 or more. The *x*- and *y*-coordinates returned by STICK are always in the range 1 through 200, regardless of the screen mode. If you want to draw (or redraw) a cursor to be moved by the joystick (as the sample program does, below), you must scale the joystick coordinates to the actual screen coordinates. For example, if you are using a 640-by-480-pixel graphics screen and a joystick whose coordinates range from 1 through 200, the *x* value returned by the STICK function must be multiplied by 640/200, or 3.2, and the *y* value must be multiplied by 480/200, or 2.4.

Use the STRIG function to determine whether a joystick button has been pressed.

Comments

The 1-through-200 coordinate range limits the resolution of joystick coordinates and therefore, the accuracy of the joystick. However, the result is still adequate for letting users make menu selections and for tracking motion in simple arcade-style games.

Unlike the PEN function, which can return information about the mouse instead of the light pen (if a mouse driver is installed), the STICK function does not allow the use of a mouse in place of the joystick. On the other hand, the installation of a mouse driver doesn't interfere with the values returned by the joystick functions, as it does with the light pen.

If no joystick is connected to your system, any call to the STICK function returns the value 0 and does not produce an error message.

Example

The following program draws a "gunsight" that you can move on the screen by using the joystick. When you press the lower joystick button, the program uses the STICK function to display the current joystick coordinates at the bottom right corner of the screen. When you press the upper button, the program ends. You might have to change the values of the scaling variables *xScale* and *yScale* if your joystick can return coordinates outside the range 1 through 80.

```
CLS
PRINT "Move gunsight with joystick number 1."
PRINT "Press lower button to see the coordinates."
PRINT "Press upper button to exit the program."
PRINT "< Press any key to begin. >"
DO
LOOP UNTIL INKEY$ <> ""

ON STRIG(0) GOSUB ShowCoords   ' show current coordinates
ON STRIG(4) GOSUB ExitProg     ' exit the program

STRIG(0) ON        ' trap lower button of first joystick
STRIG(4) ON        ' trap upper button of first joystick

' global variables
oldX = 0           ' x-coordinate of last gunsight drawn
oldY = 0           ' y-coordinate of last gunsight drawn
newX = 0           ' x-coordinate of new gunsight
newY = 0           ' y-coordinate of new gunsight

' the scale factors assume the joystick goes to 80 in each direction
xScale = 4         ' scaling factor for x in CGA
yScale = 2.5       ' scaling factor for y in CGA


SCREEN 1           ' CGA screen mode

DO                 ' loop until upper button pushed
   GOSUB Gunsight ' call subprogram to draw gunsight
LOOP

ShowCoords:        ' show coordinates when lower button pushed
    LOCATE 24, 20
    PRINT "X = "; STICK(0);
    LOCATE 24, 30
    PRINT "Y = "; STICK(1);
    RETURN

Gunsight:          ' draw gunsight
    newX = STICK(0) * xScale
    newY = STICK(1) * yScale

    ' erase old gunsight
    LINE (oldX, oldY)-(oldX + 5, oldY), 0
    LINE (oldX, oldY)-(oldX - 5, oldY), 0
    LINE (oldX, oldY)-(oldX, oldY + 3), 0
    LINE (oldX, oldY)-(oldX, oldY - 3), 0
```

(continued)

continued

```
    ' draw new gunsight
    LINE (newX, newY)-(newX + 5, newY), 1
    LINE (newX, newY)-(newX - 5, newY), 1
    LINE (newX, newY)-(newX, newY + 3), 1
    LINE (newX, newY)-(newX, newY - 3), 1

    oldX = newX
    oldY = newY
    RETURN

ExitProg:
    SYSTEM
    RETURN
```

STRIG

See also: ON STRIG GOSUB, STRIG ON/OFF/STOP

✲ QB2	■ QB4.5	✲ PowerBASIC
✲ QB3	ANSI	✲ GW-BASIC
■ QB4	■ BASIC7	MacQB

Purpose

The STRIG function returns the status of a joystick button. You can use this information to process a user menu selection or to execute a "fire" command for a game.

Syntax

STRIG (*number*)

number is an integer in the range 0 through 7.

Usage

```
IF STRIG(0) GOSUB FireA
```

If the user presses the lower button of joystick 1, the program executes the subroutine *FireA*.

Description

Use the STRIG function with a number from 0 through 7 to determine whether a particular joystick button either has been pressed since the most recent call to STRIG with the same number or is currently being pressed. This is shown in Table 13-5. In each case, QuickBASIC returns a value of –1 (true) if the button is being pressed, and 0 (false) if the button is not being pressed. QuickBASIC supports two joysticks with two buttons each.

Number	Value returned
0	−1 if the lower button of joystick 1 has been pressed since the most recent STRIG(0) call; 0 if not
1	−1 if the lower button of joystick 1 is currently being pressed; 0 if not
2	−1 if the lower button of joystick 2 has been pressed since the most recent STRIG(2) call; 0 if not
3	−1 if the lower button of joystick 2 is currently being pressed; 0 if not
4	−1 if the upper button of joystick 1 has been pressed since the most recent STRIG(4) call; 0 if not
5	−1 if the upper button of joystick 1 is currently being pressed; 0 if not
6	−1 if the upper button of joystick 2 has been pressed since the most recent STRIG(6) call; 0 if not
7	−1 if the upper button of joystick 2 is currently being pressed; 0 if not

Table 13-5.
Values returned by the STRIG function.

As an alternative to using an IF or other conditional statement to test the value of a STRIG call, you can use the ON STRIG GOSUB statement to set up joystick event trapping that executes a specific subroutine when the user presses a particular button.

If the joystick referred to in a STRIG function call isn't installed, the call returns the value 0 (false). QuickBASIC does not display an error message.

Many joysticks have one or two buttons built into their base and a button at the top of the stick. It isn't always obvious which of these buttons is the lower button and which is the upper. Your program should always tell the user what action each button performs in the program. Your program might also prompt the user to press the button preferred for performing a certain task. By using the STRIG function, the program can determine which button was pressed and then use that button in subsequent program statements.

Compatibility

QuickBASIC 2.0, QuickBASIC 3.0, PowerBASIC, GW-BASIC, and BASICA

Several versions of BASIC require that you call the STRIG ON statement before calling the STRIG function. If the program subsequently calls the STRIG OFF statement, it cannot use the STRIG function again until STRIG ON is called. These versions of BASIC include QuickBASIC versions 2.0 and 3.0, PowerBASIC, GW-BASIC, and BASICA.

Example

The following program tells you which button you have pressed on the first joystick and sounds the computer's built-in speaker.

```
STRIG(0) ON                  ' lower button, joystick 1
STRIG(4) ON                  ' upper button, joystick 1

DO
    IF STRIG(0) THEN PRINT "Lower button pressed "; CHR$(7)
    IF STRIG(4) THEN PRINT "Upper button pressed "; CHR$(7)
LOOP UNTIL INKEY$ <> ""     ' exit loop when user presses a key
```

STRIG ON/OFF/STOP

See also: ON STRIG GOSUB, STICK, STRIG

■ QB2	■ QB4.5	■ PowerBASIC
■ QB3	ANSI	■ GW-BASIC
■ QB4	■ BASIC7	MacQB

Purpose

The three STRIG statements enable, disable, or suspend the trapping of joystick button presses.

Syntax

STRIG(*button*) ON
STRIG(*button*) OFF
STRIG(*button*) STOP

button is either 0, 2, 4, or 6. 0 specifies the lower button of joystick 1, 2 specifies the lower button of joystick 2, 4 specifies the upper button of joystick 1, and 6 specifies the upper button of joystick 2.

Usage

`STRIG(0) ON`

Enables trapping for the lower button of joystick 1.

`STRIG(2) OFF`

Disables trapping for the lower button of joystick 2.

`STRIG(4) STOP`

Suspends trapping for the upper button of joystick 1; however, if this button is pressed while trapping is disabled, the next STRIG ON statement causes execution to branch to the appropriate subroutine.

Description

Use the STRIG ON statement to begin tracking the status (pressed or not pressed) of the joystick button specified by the given number. See Table 13-6 for a list of the numbers and the buttons to which they correspond.

Number	Button
0	Lower button of joystick 1
2	Lower button of joystick 2
4	Upper button of joystick 1
6	Upper button of joystick 2

Table 13-6.
The joystick numbers and the button to which each corresponds.

If a button is pressed, the program executes the subroutine specified in the ON STRIG GOSUB statement for that button. (Use the STICK function to return information about the joystick position; use the STRIG function to check whether the joystick is pressed.

The STRIG OFF statement disables event trapping of the specified joystick button. To resume trapping a joystick button, you must execute a STRIG ON statement for that button. Any button presses that occurred while trapping was off will not be remembered by the program.

The STRIG STOP statement suspends joystick trapping. The program continues to note joystick activity but does not execute the subroutine specified by the corresponding ON STRIG GOSUB statement. The next time a STRIG ON statement for the button is executed, the subroutine will be executed if the button was pressed while event trapping was suspended.

The program executes an implicit STRIG STOP whenever it enters the subroutine specified by ON STRIG GOSUB. This ensures that another occurrence of the event does not cause the subroutine to be entered recursively. When the program encounters a RETURN statement and returns to the main program, the program reinstates joystick event trapping by executing an implicit STRIG ON statement.

If you use the command-line compiler, BC.EXE, to compile a program that performs joystick event trapping, you must use either the /V or the /W switch. These switches enable trapping and force the program to check the event flag, either between statements (/V) or between program lines (/W).

Tips

Joystick event trapping slows program execution slightly; you might want to turn off event trapping when you don't expect user input from the joystick.

Example

The following program demonstrates joystick event trapping. The trapping is set so that if the lower or upper button is pushed, the program will execute the *Lower* or *Upper* subroutine. If you press the lower button, *Lower* uses a STRIG OFF statement to turn off trapping for the lower button, so this subroutine won't be executed for subsequent presses of the lower button. If you then press the upper button, *Upper* uses a STRIG(0)

ON statement to re-enable trapping of the lower button, so the program will again respond to the lower button (and then turn it off again).

```
CLS

ON STRIG(0) GOSUB Lower   ' set up trapping for lower button, joystick 1
ON STRIG(4) GOSUB Upper   ' set up trapping for upper button, joystick 1

STRIG(0) ON               ' enable trapping for lower button
STRIG(4) ON               ' enable trapping for upper button

LOCATE 1, 1
PRINT "Either press a joystick button or press any key to quit."
PRINT STRING$(56, "_")

VIEW PRINT 3 TO 7         ' set text viewport to rows 3 through 7
DO
LOOP UNTIL INKEY$ <> ""   ' loop until user presses any key
END

Lower:                    ' subroutine for lower button
    BEEP
    PRINT "You pressed the lower button."
    PRINT "The lower button will not be trapped again"
    PRINT "until you press the upper button."
    PRINT STRING$(55, "_")
    STRIG(0) OFF          ' disable trapping for lower button
    RETURN

Upper:                    ' subroutine for upper button
    BEEP
    STRIG(0) ON           ' re-enable trapping for lower button
    PRINT "You pressed the upper button."
    PRINT STRING$(55, "_")
RETURN
```

SECTION III

DEVICES

CHAPTER 14

Keyboard

Introduction

The QuickBASIC statements that manage keyboard input provide an essential link between the user and the program. Most IBM PCs and compatible computers have keyboards that include 10 or 12 function keys; the keyboard statements let you offer shortcuts to users by assigning long key sequences to each of these keys. The keyboard event-trapping statements let you set up a routine that is called whenever the user presses a specific key. Many programs, for example, use an event trap to display a Help screen whenever the user presses the F1 function key.

This tutorial summarizes QuickBASIC's keyboard-management statements and offers some suggestions for their use. Table 14-1 lists the keyboard-management statements.

Statement	Description
KEY	Sets up soft (shortcut) keys
KEY(*n*) ON/OFF/STOP	Enables, disables, or suspends keyboard event trapping set up by the ON KEY(*n*) GOSUB statement
ON KEY(*n*) GOSUB	Sets up keyboard event trapping

Table 14-1.
QuickBASIC keyboard statements.

Soft Keys

If you have used GW-BASIC or BASICA you are probably familiar with the list specifying function keys and corresponding abbreviated statements that is displayed on the bottom line of the screen. These keys are called soft keys, or shortcut keys, and they let you use the function keys to enter common statements with a single keypress. You can create soft keys for your programs by using the QuickBASIC KEY statement.

By using the following statement, for example, you can make the F1 function key a soft key that is an abbreviation for the string "HELP":

```
KEY 1, "HELP"
```

Now, whenever the user presses the F1 function key while the program executes, any keyboard input function or statement (including INKEY$, INPUT, and LINE INPUT) accepts the word "HELP" as input.

Use the KEY LIST statement to display the current soft-key settings, which appear one per line on the screen. The KEY ON statement displays your soft-key settings on the bottom line of the screen, and the KEY OFF statement erases this display. The soft keys can be used even if they are not displayed.

Note that although they appear similar to the KEY(*n*) ON and KEY(*n*) OFF event-trapping statements, the KEY ON and KEY OFF statements apply only to the soft-key display.

Keyboard Event Trapping

QuickBASIC provides a set of statements that enable and manage keyboard event trapping. You can trap a certain key so that the program executes a subroutine every time the user presses the key. For example, you might use the keyboard event trap to display context-sensitive help whenever the user presses the F1 function key. QuickBASIC lets you trap function keys, arrow keys, and user-defined key combinations.

You set up event trapping by first calling the ON KEY(*n*) GOSUB statement that specifies the name of the subroutine to which you want execution to branch when the user presses the specified key. Next you enable event trapping by calling the KEY(*n*) ON statement.

The following lines set up an event trap and enable it to execute the subroutine that begins at the label *ShowHelp* whenever the user presses the F1 key:

```
ON KEY(1) GOSUB ShowHelp
KEY(1) ON
```

Related Reading

Norton, Peter, and Richard Wilton. *The* New *Peter Norton Programmer's Guide to the IBM PC & PS/2.* Redmond, Wash.: Microsoft Press, 1988.

Prata, Stephen, with Harry Henderson. *The Waite Group's Microsoft QuickBASIC Primer Plus.* Redmond, Wash.: Microsoft Press, 1990.

KEY

See also: KEY(*n*) ON/OFF/STOP, ON KEY(*n*) GOSUB

✲ QB2	■ QB4.5	■ PowerBASIC
✲ QB3	ANSI	✲ GW-BASIC
■ QB4	■ BASIC7	MacQB

Purpose

The KEY statement lets you initialize a soft key (that is, assign a string to a function key). You also use the KEY statement to display the soft keys. You can use the KEY statement to give the user a method of generating a long sequence of keypresses by pressing one key.

Syntax

KEY *num*, *string*
KEY LIST
KEY ON
KEY OFF

num is the number of a function key; valid numbers are 1 through 10, 30 (F11), and 31 (F12).

string is a string expression of 1 through 15 characters; a null string disables the corresponding soft key.

Usage

```
KEY 1, "EXIT" + CHR$(13)
```

Sets the F1 function key as a soft key that generates the word EXIT and a carriage return.

```
KEY LIST
```

Displays the string assignments for all soft keys.

Description

The KEY statement manages soft keys, which are function keys that you press to produce strings. To create or change soft keys, follow the keyword KEY with a function key number and a string. The function key number specifies the soft key: Use 1 through 10 for function keys F1 through F10 and 30 and 31 for function keys F11 and F12 on 101-key keyboards. The string parameter to KEY must be a string expression of no more than 15 characters; KEY ignores any characters following the first 15. After you use the KEY statement to make an assignment, pressing that function key generates the corresponding string, exactly as if the user had typed it at the keyboard.

You can display all the current soft-key settings by using the KEY LIST statement. This 12-line list (one line for each function key) displays all 15 characters of each setting.

The KEY ON statement displays the first six characters of the first 10 soft-key settings on the bottom line of the screen. The soft-key settings for function keys 11 and 12 are not displayed. The KEY OFF statement disables the display at the bottom of the screen but does not prevent the soft keys from producing their corresponding strings.

Comments

The string parameter to KEY can include control characters such as CHR$(13), the Enter key. You can use a variant of the KEY statement to define a key combination for use with keyboard event trapping. See the KEY(*n*) ON/OFF/STOP entry for more details.

Errors

In a KEY statement that specifies a number and a string, if the number parameter is not 1 through 10 or either 30 or 31, QuickBASIC returns an "Illegal function call" error message.

Compatibility

QuickBASIC 2.0, QuickBASIC 3.0, GW-BASIC, and BASICA

QuickBASIC versions 2.0 and 3.0, GW-BASIC, and BASICA can handle only function keys F1 through F10. GW-BASIC and BASICA also have a default setting for each soft key. These are shown in Table 14-2.

Function key	Function
F1	LIST
F2	RUN [Enter]
F3	LOAD "
F4	SAVE "
F5	CONT [Enter]
F6	, "LPT1:" [Enter]
F7	TRON [Enter]
F8	TROFF [Enter]
F9	KEY
F10	SCREEN 0,0,0 [Enter]

Table 14-2.
Default settings for function keys in GW-BASIC and BASICA.

Example

The following program uses the KEY statement to provide users with shortcut keys. The program displays a menu of options that can be chosen by pressing a function key or typing a word.

```
' set up soft keys
KEY 1, "Add" + CHR$(13)        ' F1-add records
KEY 2, "Change" + CHR$(13)     ' F2-change record
KEY 3, "Quit" + CHR$(13)       ' F3-quit program

MainMenu:
    CLS
    PRINT : PRINT : PRINT
    PRINT "<Add>......Add records......[F1]"
    PRINT "<Change>...Change records...[F2]"
    PRINT "<Quit>.....Quit program.....[F3]"
    PRINT
    PRINT "Type a word and press Enter or press a function key: ";
    LINE INPUT selection$

    SELECT CASE UCASE$(selection$)
        CASE "ADD"
            PRINT : PRINT : PRINT
            PRINT "Add records."

        CASE "CHANGE"
            PRINT : PRINT : PRINT
            PRINT "Change records."

        CASE "QUIT"
            PRINT : PRINT : PRINT
            PRINT "Quit the program."

        CASE ELSE
            PRINT : PRINT : PRINT
            PRINT "Invalid selection--try again."
            BEEP
            SLEEP 1
            GOTO MainMenu
    END SELECT
```

KEY(*n*) ON/OFF/STOP

See also: KEY, ON KEY(*n*) GOSUB

✲ QB2	■ QB4.5	■ PowerBASIC
✲ QB3	ANSI	✲ GW-BASIC
■ QB4	■ BASIC7	MacQB

Purpose

The KEY(*n*) statements enable, disable, or suspend event trapping for specific keys. Use keyboard event trapping to direct your program to execute a subroutine when the user presses a specified key.

Syntax

KEY(*n*) ON
KEY(*n*) OFF
KEY(*n*) STOP

n is a number that corresponds to a function key, an arrow key, or a user-defined key; valid numbers are 1 through 25, 30, and 31.

Usage

```
ON KEY(1) GOSUB GetHelp
KEY(1) ON
```

Enables event trapping for the function key F1 so that execution will branch to *GetHelp* when the user presses F1.

```
KEY(1) STOP
```

Suspends event trapping for the function key F1.

Description

Use the KEY(*n*) ON statement to enable event trapping of a particular key. After executing a KEY(*n*) ON statement, the program checks after every statement to see whether the specified key was pressed. If it was, the program executes the routine specified in the ON KEY(*n*) GOSUB statement.

Table 14-3 lists the numbers corresponding to keys that can be trapped.

Key numbers	Keyboard keys
1 through 10	Function keys F1 through F10
11	Up arrow key
12	Left arrow key
13	Right arrow key
14	Down arrow key
15 through 25	User-defined keys
30 and 31	Function keys F11 and F12

Table 14-3.
Valid key numbers.

User-defined keys (key numbers 15 through 25) can be defined by using the following variant of the KEY statement:

KEY *num*, CHR$(*shift*) + CHR$(*scan*)

num indicates a user-defined key for keyboard event trapping and must be in the range 15 through 25.

shift is a combination of any of the hexadecimal values listed in Table 14-4. These values indicate the state of the various "shift" keys on the keyboard. You can add these values together to indicate that several shift keys must be held down at the same time before the user-defined key can be trapped. For example, a *shift* parameter of *&H04 + &H08* would indicate that both the Ctrl and Alt keys must be held down. QuickBASIC does not make a distinction between left and right Shift keys; therefore, codes *&H01*, *&H02*, and *&H03* are handled identically.

Value	Shift key
&H00	None
&H01 through &H03	Either or both Shift keys
&H04	Ctrl
&H08	Alt
&H20	Num Lock
&H40	Caps Lock
&H80	Extended keys on the 101-key keyboard

Table 14-4.
The hexadecimal values for shift states.

scan is a scan code of one of the standard 83 keys of the keyboard. See Table 14-5 on the following pages for a complete list of IBM PC scan codes.

The KEY(*n*) ON statement enables event trapping for the key specified in the statement.

The KEY(*n*) OFF statement disables event trapping for the specified key. No event trapping of the key occurs until the program executes another KEY(*n*) ON statement. No events that occurred while trapping was off are remembered by the program.

The KEY(*n*) STOP statement suspends event trapping for the specified key. No event trapping occurs until the program executes another KEY(*n*) ON statement. However, if an event occurs while trapping is suspended, the program remembers the event and, the next time a KEY(*n*) ON statement is executed, the program branches to the appropriate subroutine.

The program executes an implicit KEY(*n*) STOP whenever it enters the subroutine specified by ON KEY(*n*) GOSUB. This ensures that another occurrence of the event does not cause the subroutine to be entered recursively. When the program encounters a RETURN statement and returns to the main program, it reinstates keyboard event trapping by executing an implicit KEY(*n*) ON statement.

If you use the command-line compiler, BC.EXE, to compile a program that performs keyboard event trapping, you must use either the /V or the /W switch. These switches enable trapping and force the program to check the event flag, either between statements (/V) or between program lines (/W).

Key	Scan code
ESC	&H01
! or 1	&H02
@ or 2	&H03
# or 3	&H04
$ or 4	&H05
% or 5	&H06
^ or 6	&H07
& or 7	&H08
* or 8	&H09
(or 9	&H0A
) or 0	&H0B
– or _	&H0C
+ or =	&H0D
Left	&H0E
Tab	&H0F
Q	&H10
W	&H11
E	&H12
R	&H13
T	&H14
Y	&H15
U	&H16
I	&H17
O	&H18
P	&H19
{ or [	&H1A
} or]	&H1B
Enter	&H1C
Ctrl	&H1D
A	&H1E
S	&H1F
D	&H20
F	&H21
G	&H22
H	&H23
J	&H24
K	&H25
L	&H26
: or ;	&H27
" or '	&H28
~ or `	&H29
Left Shift	&H2A
¦ or \	&H2B
Z	&H2C
X	&H2D
C	&H2E
V	&H2F
B	&H30
N	&H31
M	&H32
< or ,	&H33
> or .	&H34
? or /	&H35
Right Shift	&H36
PrtSc or *	&H37
Alt	&H38
Spacebar	&H39
Caps Lock	&H3A
F1	&H3B
F2	&H3C
F3	&H3D
F4	&H3E
F5	&H3F
F6	&H40
F7	&H41
F8	&H42
F9	&H43
F10	&H44
Num Lock	&H45
Scroll Lock	&H46
Home or 7	&H47
Up or 8	&H48

(continued)

Table 14-5.
Scan codes for the IBM PC keyboard.

Table 14-5. *(continued)*

Key	Scan code	Key	Scan code
PgUp or 9	&H49	End or 1	&H4F
– (keypad)	&H4A	Down or 2	&H50
Left or 4	&H4B	PgDn or 3	&H51
5	&H4C	Ins or 0	&H52
Right or 6	&H4D	Del or .	&H53
+ (keypad)	&H4E		

Errors

If the value of the specified key number is not in the range 1 through 25 or either 30 or 31, QuickBASIC returns an "Illegal function call" error message.

Tips

Using event-trapping statements increases the size of your executable programs and makes them run more slowly. Try to avoid using event-trapping statements that are not essential.

Compatibility

QuickBASIC 2.0, QuickBASIC 3.0, GW-BASIC, and BASICA

The only function keys that QuickBASIC versions 2.0 and 3.0, GW-BASIC, and BASICA can handle are F1 through F10; these versions don't support trapping of the F11 and F12 function keys (numbers 30 and 31). These versions also support the arrow keys and user-defined keys.

Example

See the sample program in the ON KEY(*n*) GOSUB entry.

ON KEY(*n*) GOSUB

See also: KEY, KEY(*n*) ON/OFF/STOP

✲ QB2	■ QB4.5	■ PowerBASIC
✲ QB3	ANSI	✲ GW-BASIC
■ QB4	■ BASIC7	MacQB

Purpose

The ON KEY(*n*) GOSUB statement specifies a subroutine that is executed whenever the user presses a certain key. You can use the ON KEY(*n*) GOSUB statement to set up keyboard event trapping so that the program prints a help message when the user presses the F1 key.

Syntax

ON KEY(*n*) GOSUB {*line* ¦ *label*}

n is a number that corresponds to a function key, an arrow key, or a user-defined key; valid numbers are 1 through 25, 30, and 31.

line or *label* indicates the first program line of the event-trapping subroutine.

Usage

```
ON KEY(1) GOSUB ShowHelp
```

Specifies that the *ShowHelp* subroutine will be executed when the user presses the F1 function key.

Description

Use the ON KEY(*n*) GOSUB statement to set up an event trap that executes a subroutine when a specified key is pressed. Only function keys, arrow keys, and user-defined keys can be specified in the statement. When the specified key is pressed, the program executes the subroutine.

When the subroutine begins, the program executes an implicit KEY(*n*) STOP so that another event trap doesn't cause the subroutine to be entered recursively. However, if another timer event occurs while the subroutine is executing, the program remembers it. When the subroutine finishes, the program executes a KEY(*n*) ON statement (unless the subroutine explicitly executed a KEY(*n*) OFF statement) and immediately executes the suspended event.

The specified subroutine can end with a RETURN statement that branches to a specified line in the program. However, this version of the RETURN statement can cause serious problems because the event-trapping subroutine might have interrupted a critical operation. Also, you cannot use the RETURN statement with a specified line number or label to branch to a subprogram, function, or DEF FN function. (See the GOSUB...RETURN entry in Chapter 4, "Procedures," for details.)

QuickBASIC performs keyboard event trapping in the following order:

1. The line printer echo-toggle key (Ctrl-PrtSc); redefining this key as a user-defined key has no effect.
2. Function keys and arrow keys; redefining these keys does not affect QuickBASIC key trapping because they are predefined.
3. User-defined keys.

The ON KEY(*n*) GOSUB statement can trap any key combination, including Ctrl-Break and Ctrl-Alt-Delete. You could, therefore, use it to prevent a user from breaking out of your program or even to perform a "warm" reboot of the computer. After you trap a key, you cannot use an INPUT or INKEY$ statement to retrieve the value of the key that caused the event.

Errors

If the value of the specified key number is not in the range 1 through 25 or either 30 or 31, QuickBASIC returns an "Illegal function call" error message.

Tips

Using event-trapping statements increases the size of your executable programs and makes them run more slowly. Try to avoid using event-trapping statements that aren't essential.

Compatibility

QuickBASIC 2.0, QuickBASIC 3.0, GW-BASIC, and BASICA

BASICA and GW-BASIC handle only user-defined keys and the function keys F1 through F10; they don't support trapping of the F11 and F12 function keys (that is, numbers 30 and 31).

Example

The following program uses keyboard event trapping to display helpful information when the user presses the F1 key. The program also traps the PrtSc (print screen) key as well as the PrtSc key pressed with a Shift key, the Num Lock key, or both. When any of these key combinations is pressed, the program executes the *NoPrintScreen* subroutine.

```
CLS
LOCATE , , 1

ON KEY(1) GOSUB ShowHelp              ' F1 function key
KEY(1) ON

KEY 15, CHR$(&H80) + CHR$(&H37)       ' PrtSc key
ON KEY(15) GOSUB NoPrintScreen
KEY(15) ON

KEY 16, CHR$(&H83) + CHR$(&H37)       ' Shift-PrtSc key combination
ON KEY(16) GOSUB NoPrintScreen
KEY(16) ON

KEY 17, CHR$(&HA0) + CHR$(&H37)       ' PrtSc with Num Lock on
ON KEY(17) GOSUB NoPrintScreen
KEY(17) ON

KEY 18, CHR$(&HA3) + CHR$(&H37)       ' Shift-PrtSc with Num Lock on
ON KEY(18) GOSUB NoPrintScreen
KEY(18) ON
```

(continued)

continued

```
PRINT "Enter a new patient's name: "
name$ = ""
DO
    keybd$ = INKEY$
    IF keybd$ = CHR$(8) THEN        ' check for Backspace key
        LOCATE CSRLIN, POS(0) - 1
        PRINT " ";
        LOCATE CSRLIN, POS(0) - 1
        name$ = LEFT$(name$, LEN(name$) - 1)
    ELSE
        PRINT keybd$;
        name$ = name$ + keybd$
    END IF
LOOP UNTIL keybd$ = CHR$(13)        ' exit loop when user presses Enter
PRINT "You entered the name: "; name$
END

ShowHelp:
    LOCATE 5, 1
    PRINT "Enter the name of a new patient in the following form:"
    PRINT
    PRINT "     last name, first name"
    LOCATE 2, 1
    RETURN

NoPrintScreen:
    LOCATE 5, 1
    PRINT "Sorry, but you can't print this screen!"
    BEEP
    LOCATE 2, 1
    RETURN
```

CHAPTER 15

Printer

Introduction

QuickBASIC provides a group of statements that offer a convenient way to print and to manage printed output. You can, of course, open the printer as a file and use a PRINT statement, as in the following example:

```
OPEN "LPT1:" AS #1
PRINT #1, "The quick brown fox"
```

But using the LPRINT statement is more intuitive and convenient, as shown in the statement

```
LPRINT "The quick brown fox"
```

(Note that opening a printer file and then using the LPRINT and LPRINT USING statements produces unpredictable output.)

Table 15-1 lists QuickBASIC's printer-related statements and functions in alphabetic order.

Statement or function	Description
LPOS	Returns the current position of the output column within the printer buffer.
LPRINT	Prints output on the LPT1: printer.
LPRINT USING	Prints a formatted string or other value on the printer. A special string specifies the format.
WIDTH LPRINT	Sets the column width of the printer output.

Table 15-1.
QuickBASIC printer statements and functions.

Printing Text

The operation of the LPRINT and LPRINT USING statements, which direct output to the printer, is the same as that of PRINT and PRINT USING, which direct output to the screen. Therefore, you can find further discussion and related examples in the PRINT and PRINT USING entries in Chapter 8, "Simple I/O." This tutorial addresses matters involving only the printer.

Using LPRINT with no parameters directs the printer to skip a line. When you use LPRINT with a numeric or string variable or with a constant string, such as "The quick brown fox," the printer prints the value and then prints a carriage return and a linefeed (CR/LF), which moves the print head to the beginning of a new line. If you don't want the print head to move to a new line after printing, use a semicolon at the end of the LPRINT statement. For example, the statement

```
LPRINT "No new line yet.";
```

suppresses the CR/LF so that subsequent output is printed on the same line. QuickBASIC doesn't insert spaces between items; if you want blank spaces, you must include them. For example, the statement

```
LPRINT firstName$; " "; lastName$
```

inserts a space between the first and last names. You can space items at regular intervals by using a comma after each item in the LPRINT statement. Each new item is printed at the start of the next 14-space print zone. Thus the statement

```
LPRINT "Widely", "Spaced", "Text"
```

results in the output

```
Widely        Spaced        Text
```

A comma at the end of an LPRINT statement moves the print head to the next print zone and suppresses the CR/LF.

The LPRINT USING statement specifies a format string and the item or items to be printed. For example, the following statement prints ******$29.99*:

```
LPRINT USING "**$#####.##", 29.99
```

(Format strings are described in the PRINT USING entry in Chapter 8, "Simple I/O.")

Printer Control

The LPRINT statement is also useful for sending to the printer special control sequences that make it possible for a QuickBASIC program to access your printer's special features.

QuickBASIC assumes the printer is a line printer. On all printers (including page printers such as laser printers), the statement *LPRINT CHR$(12)* prints a formfeed character, thus advancing the print head to the top of the next page. On most printers, the default length of one page is 66 lines.

Note that the LPRINT statement appends a carriage return (ASCII character 13) and a linefeed (ASCII character 10) to a line of output. If you use LPRINT with a printer that is set up to insert its own linefeeds, the output will contain extra blank lines. You can correct this by using the DOS printer device in binary mode—for example,

```
OPEN "LPT1" FOR BINARY AS #1
```

Then, to send the output to the printer, use the PUT statement as shown in the following program segment:

```
words$ = "The quick brown fox"
PUT #1, words$
```

The PUT statement does not append a carriage return or a linefeed to the output.

The commands used to access the features of many printers begin with an Esc character (ASCII character 27). Thus, if the command Esc + C sets the page length on your printer (as it does on IBM and Epson printers), you can set the page length to 14 inches by using the statement:

```
LPRINT CHR$(27); "C"; CHR$(14)
```

To send instructions from your program to any printer, all you need to know are the printer's control commands. The example program in the LPRINT entry sets up an HP LaserJet II to print program listings in "landscape mode" (which rotates the page 90 degrees) and uses compressed print.

The QuickBASIC WIDTH LPRINT statement sets a width for the printer. When output reaches the specified width, the printer prints a CR/LF.

If you need more exact control over the position of the print head, use the LPOS function to determine the location of the print head in the current line. Your program can then decide whether it needs to begin a new line. You can also use LPOS to format output on the page by calling LPOS and then moving the print head a specific number of spaces, which depends on the value the function returns.

If a program will be used with several different printers, begin by defining null string variables for printer commands, as shown in the following statements:

```
escapeChar$ = ""
compressed$ = ""
elite$ = ""
setForm$ = ""
```

The program can then prompt the user to enter the type of printer that will be used. After the user enters a printer type, the program can open a file, input the appropriate command string into each variable, and then use those variables to access the printer's features. For example, if the program needs to set printing to a compressed mode, it uses the statement

```
LPRINT escapeChar$; compressed$
```

Further Exploration

Read your printer manual and note the features that are available. Laser printers, in particular, have many sophisticated features. For practice, you might want to write a program that presents a menu and sets fonts, pitch, line spacing, margins, and so on.

Several commercial, shareware, and public domain BASIC routine libraries also include extensive text-formatting routines that can help you prepare text for printing.

Related Reading

Schneider, David L. *Handbook of BASIC.* 3d ed. New York, N.Y.: Brady, 1988.

LPOS

See also: POS

■ QB2	■ QB4.5	■ PowerBASIC
■ QB3	ANSI	■ GW-BASIC
■ QB4	■ BASIC7	■ MacQB

Purpose

The LPOS function returns the position of the current output column for the printer at the specified port. Your program can use this information to determine when to start a new line of output, "wrap" words, and so on.

Syntax

LPOS(*port*)

port must be the number 1, 2, or 3, which refers to port LPT1: (or PRN:), LPT2:, or LPT3:.

Usage

```
LPRINT name$
col = LPOS(1)
```

Sends the string in *name$* to the printer and then stores the current output column of LPT1: in the variable *col*.

Description

In most cases, characters sent to the printer are not immediately printed. Rather, they are stored in the printer's buffer until an entire line or a linefeed is received from the computer. (The LPRINT and PRINT statements send a carriage return and a linefeed to the printer unless the statement ends in a comma or a semicolon.) Immediately after a linefeed, a call to LPOS returns a 1 to indicate that the printer is beginning a new line of output. Some printers have a larger buffer, which stores a page or more of text.

The LPOS function does not actually return the print head position; instead, it returns the number of characters that have been output on the current line. LPOS cannot make adjustments to determine the correct print head position if you are using proportional fonts.

Warnings

The LPOS function counts a tab character as only one character; however, the printer normally expands a tab to consist of several spaces. Thus the value returned by LPOS does not correspond to the actual print head position after a tab is printed.

Turning the printer off resets the print head position to the left margin and clears any characters in the print buffer. When you turn the printer on again, QuickBASIC is unaware that the buffer has been cleared, and the value of LPOS is the same as it was before the printer was turned off.

Example

The following program prompts you to specify the column numbers of the left and right margins and to type words at the keyboard. The program prints the entered line of text, one word at a time, using the specified margins. Before a word is printed, the program checks its length against the difference between the right margin position and the value of LPOS; if the word requires space beyond the margin, the program instead prints it at the beginning of a new line.

The *NextWord* subprogram parses each line of input into words, one word at a time, and returns the word (*word$*) and the remaining portion of the string. Notice that this subprogram is defined with the keyword STATIC because it must maintain the values of its variables between calls.

```
DECLARE SUB NextWord (aString$, sep$, word$)

sep$ = " "                       ' use a space to separate words
INPUT "Left margin column "; leftMargin
INPUT "Right margin column "; rightMargin
PRINT "Type text a line at a time."
PRINT "Press <Enter> by itself to exit the program."
GOSUB NewLine                    ' start printing on a new line
DO
    LINE INPUT line$
    IF LEN(line$) = 0 THEN
        LPRINT                   ' LPRINT to flush buffer
        LPRINT CHR$(12)
        SYSTEM
    END IF
    GOSUB Justify
LOOP
END

Justify:
    DO
        CALL NextWord(line$, sep$, word$)       ' get next word
        IF (LEN(word$) > (rightMargin - LPOS(1))) THEN
            GOSUB NewLine    ' move to next line if word hits right margin
        END IF
        LPRINT word$; " ";
    LOOP UNTIL LEN(word$) = 0
    RETURN

NewLine:
    LPRINT                       ' move to next line
    FOR space% = 1 TO leftMargin
        LPRINT " ";     ' print spaces to the left margin
    NEXT space%
    RETURN
```

(continued)

continued

```
SUB NextWord (aString$, sep$, word$) STATIC
    word$ = ""
    strlen% = LEN(aString$)
    IF aString$ = "" THEN
        EXIT SUB
    END IF

    FOR char1% = 1 TO strlen%
        IF INSTR(sep$, MID$(aString$, char1%, 1)) = 0 THEN
            EXIT FOR
        END IF
    NEXT char1%

    FOR char2% = char1% TO strlen%
        IF INSTR(sep$, MID$(aString$, char2%, 1)) THEN
            EXIT FOR
        END IF
    NEXT char2%

    FOR char3% = char2% TO strlen%
        IF INSTR(sep$, MID$(aString$, char3%, 1)) = 0 THEN
            EXIT FOR
        END IF
    NEXT char3%

    IF char1% > strlen% THEN
        aString$ = ""
        EXIT SUB
    END IF

    IF char2% > strlen% THEN
        word$ = MID$(aString$, char1%)
        aString$ = ""
        EXIT SUB
    END IF

    word$ = MID$(aString$, char1%, char2% - char1%)

    IF char3% > strlen% THEN
        aString$ = ""
    ELSE
        aString$ = MID$(aString$, char3%)
    END IF
END SUB
```

LPRINT

See also: LPRINT USING, PRINT, PRINT USING

■ QB2 ■ QB4.5 ■ PowerBASIC
■ QB3 ANSI ■ GW-BASIC
■ QB4 ■ BASIC7 ✲ MacQB

Purpose

The LPRINT statement prints the contents of numeric or string variables or literals on the printer. QuickBASIC assumes the printer is connected to the first parallel port (LPT1: or PRN:). You can also use LPRINT to send control codes to the printer.

Syntax

LPRINT *expr* [{,¦;}]...

expr can be any numeric or string constant, expression, or variable. If you specify more than one item, separate them with commas or semicolons. If you use a semicolon between two items, the second item will be printed immediately after the first one. If you use a comma between items, the second item will be printed in the next print zone. (Each print zone is 14 characters long.) A semicolon or comma at the end of an LPRINT statement keeps the print head from moving to the next line after printing.

Usage

```
LPRINT "Hello";
```

Prints the word "Hello" but does not move the print head to a new line.

```
LPRINT num1, num2, num3
```

Prints the values of the variables *num1*, *num2*, and *num3*; each value is printed at the beginning of a print zone.

```
LPRINT subtotal + tax
```

Prints the sum of the variables *subtotal* and *tax*.

```
LPRINT CHR$(12)
```

Sends a formfeed character to the printer.

Description

The LPRINT statement works in exactly the same way as the PRINT statement does except that its output is sent to the parallel printer instead of the screen. (This printer is often referred to as the line printer, even though laser printers print an entire page at a time.) LPRINT can also use the CHR$ function to send any character (including nonprinting characters) to the printer. This lets your program send control commands to the printer in order to access the printer's special features. For an HP LaserJet, for example, you can use the following statement to double-space printed output:

```
LPRINT CHR$(27); "&l3D"
```

Each kind of printer has a different set of control commands. See your printer manual for details.

Errors

If the printer is not connected or is not online, QuickBASIC displays a "Device timeout" error message.

Tips

QuickBASIC has no statement equal to LPRINT for printing directly to a serial printer. However, if you use the DOS command

```
MODE LPT1=COM1
```

to redirect parallel printer output to a serial printer connected to port COM1:, the output of LPRINT and LPRINT USING is sent to the serial printer. Or you can open the device COM1:, assign it a file number, and then print to it by using the PRINT statement.

Compatibility

QuickBASIC for the Macintosh

The LPRINT statement does not work with non-character printers such as the LaserWriter or printers connected by AppleTalk. Be sure that the printer attached to the system supports LPRINT before you use the statement.

Example

The following program uses LPRINT to set up an HP LaserJet printer to print a disk file in landscape (sideways) orientation and with a compressed typeface. This format might be useful for printing program listings on which you will be making extensive notes. Figure 15-1 shows one page of the program's output, as printed on the HP LaserJet.

```
DECLARE SUB DoHeader ()
CONST linesPerPage% = 20           ' lines per page, including header
CONST TRUE = 1
CONST FALSE = NOT TRUE
firstTime% = TRUE                  ' flag used to avoid formfeed before first page

' set up printer
LPRINT CHR$(27); "&l1O";           ' set landscape orientation
LPRINT CHR$(27); "(s0T";           ' set line printer typeface
LPRINT CHR$(27); "&k2S";           ' set compressed size
LPRINT CHR$(27); "&l3d";           ' set double spacing
LPRINT CHR$(27); "&l2E";           ' set 2-line top margin

INPUT "Name of file to print: "; file$  ' specify a file to be printed
ON ERROR GOTO BadFile
```

(continued)

continued

```
OPEN file$ FOR INPUT AS #1      ' open specified file

DoHeader                        ' print header for first page
firstTime% = FALSE              ' turn off flag so formfeeds are printed

DO                              ' print a page
    LINE INPUT #1, line$        ' get next line from file
    LPRINT line$                ' print the line
    currentLine% = currentLine% + 1      ' count the lines printed
    IF currentLine% = linesPerPage% THEN DoHeader
LOOP WHILE NOT EOF(1)

CLOSE #1                        ' close input file
LPRINT CHR$(27); "E";           ' reset printer for next job
END

BadFile:                        ' error-handling routine
    errnum% = ERR
    SELECT CASE errnum%
    CASE 29
        PRINT "Write fault."
    CASE 30
        PRINT "Read fault."
    CASE 52
        PRINT "Bad filename."
    CASE 53
        PRINT "File not found."
    CASE 68
        PRINT "Device not available. Be sure printer is ";
        PRINT "connected and turned on."
    END SELECT
    SYSTEM                      ' exit to operating system on error

SUB DoHeader STATIC
    SHARED firstTime%, currentLine%
    IF firstTime% = FALSE THEN
        LPRINT CHR$(12)                  ' formfeed
    ELSE
        pageNum% = 1
    END IF
    LPRINT UCASE$(file$); SPC(10);       ' print filename
    LPRINT DATE$; SPC(10);               ' print current date
    LPRINT TIME$; SPC(5);                ' print current time
    LPRINT SPC(5);
    LPRINT "Page "; pageNum%             ' print page number
    pageNum% = pageNum% + 1              ' increment page number
    currentLine% = 1                     ' set current line
END SUB
```

```
        04-03-1990          09:05:15          Page  1

DECLARE SUB DoHeader ()

CONST linesPerPage% = 20        ' lines per page, including header

CONST TRUE = 1

CONST FALSE = NOT TRUE

firstTime% = TRUE               ' flag used to avoid formfeed before first page


' set up printer

LPRINT CHR$(27); "&l1O";        ' set landscape orientation

LPRINT CHR$(27); "(s0T";        ' set line printer typeface

LPRINT CHR$(27); "&k2S";        ' set compressed size

LPRINT CHR$(27); "&l3d";        ' set double spacing

LPRINT CHR$(27); "&l2E";        ' set 2-line top margin


INPUT "Name of file to print: "; file$  ' specify a file to be printed

ON ERROR GOTO BadFile


OPEN file$ FOR INPUT AS #1      ' open specified file


DoHeader                        ' print header for first page
```

Figure 15-1.
Output from the LPRINT example program.

LPRINT USING

See also: LPRINT, PRINT USING

■ QB2 ■ QB4.5 ■ PowerBASIC
■ QB3 ANSI ■ GW-BASIC
■ QB4 ■ BASIC7 ✲ MacQB

Purpose

The LPRINT USING statement prints formatted numbers or strings on the printer and specifies the length and format of each item printed.

Syntax

LPRINT USING *template*; *var* [; *var*...][{, | ;}]

template is a string constant or a string variable that can contain literal text and one or more special formatting characters that determine how the variables are to be printed.

var is a numeric or string expression that will be printed in the format specified by *template.*

A comma at the end of a statement causes the print head to remain on the current line and to move to the next print zone. A semicolon causes the print head to remain on the space immediately after the last character printed.

Usage

```
LPRINT USING "##.#"; 24.99
```

Prints *25.0*. Each number sign holds a place for a numeric digit. Because *template* specifies only three digits, LPRINT USING rounds off the number.

```
LPRINT USING "$##.##"; 24.99;
```

Prints *$24.99* and keeps the print head on the current line.

```
LPRINT USING "##.###^^^^"; 10500
```

Prints *1.050D+04*. The period indicates placement of the decimal point, and the caret symbols (^) specify scientific notation.

```
LPRINT USING "&"; "QuickBASIC"
```

Prints *QuickBASIC.*

Description

The LPRINT USING statement requires a special formatting string that is either in a string variable or enclosed in quotation marks. The formatting string provides great versatility in formatting numbers and strings. You can use it to print numbers rounded off to a specified number of decimal places, preceded by dollar signs or other special characters, or printed in scientific notation. You can also use it to print strings in various formats, such as truncated or justified. (See the PRINT USING entry in Chapter 8, "Simple I/O," for a complete discussion of formats.)

As with PRINT, ending the expression to be printed with a semicolon suppresses the carriage return and linefeed, and ending it with a comma causes the next LPRINT statement to begin printing in the next 14-character print zone.

Errors

If the printer is not connected or is not on line, QuickBASIC displays a "Device timeout" error message.

Compatibility

QuickBASIC for the Macintosh

The LPRINT statement does not work with non-character printers such as the LaserWriter or printers connected by AppleTalk. Be sure the printer attached to the system supports LPRINT before you use the statement.

Example

The following program lets the user enter numbers and formatting strings to see the effect. You can use this program to practice using the print formats. To use the program with string rather than numeric values, simply change the variable *num#* to a string variable (for example, *aString$*).

```
CLS
DO
    INPUT "Number to be printed (0 to quit) "; num#
    IF num# = 0 THEN EXIT DO
    INPUT "Format to use "; format$
    IF format$ = "" THEN
        LPRINT "You must enter a formatting string."
    ELSE
        LPRINT USING format$; num#
    END IF
LOOP
```

WIDTH LPRINT

See also: LPOS, POS, WIDTH (Screen)

■ QB2	■ QB4.5	✲ PowerBASIC
■ QB3	ANSI	✲ GW-BASIC
■ QB4	■ BASIC7	✲ MacQB

Purpose

The WIDTH LPRINT statement specifies the width of a printed line. QuickBASIC begins a new line whenever the print head reaches the end of a line.

Syntax

WIDTH LPRINT *col*

col is an integer in the range 1 through 255 that specifies the maximum number of columns in each printed line.

Usage

```
WIDTH LPRINT 40
```

Prints all output in no more than 40 columns per line.

Description

The WIDTH LPRINT statement specifies the column at which the printer will issue a carriage return and linefeed (CR/LF). Any additional CR/LF sent by an LPRINT statement sends the print head to the next line. After you call WIDTH LPRINT, a line cannot exceed the specified width.

If the width you set is greater than the width of the paper in the printer, the printer truncates the characters specified in the LPRINT or LPRINT USING statement that fall between the edge of the paper and the specified width before printing a CR/LF. Specifying a width of 255 columns suppresses the CR/LF. Even if the output of an LPRINT or LPRINT USING statement extends past 255 columns, the print head does not move to the next line. It moves to the next line only when the program calls another LPRINT or LPRINT USING statement.

Compatibility

PowerBASIC, GW-BASIC, and BASICA

PowerBASIC, GW-BASIC, and BASICA do not support the WIDTH LPRINT statement. To specify the width of a printed line, you must use the WIDTH (FILE I/O) statement, specifying the output device LPT1: as the first parameter to the statement and the number of columns as the second parameter.

QuickBASIC for the Macintosh

In addition to setting the width of a printed line, the WIDTH LPRINT statement offered by QuickBASIC for the Macintosh can reset the width of the print zones (which are by default 14 characters wide). When two data items in an LPRINT or LPRINT USING statement are separated by a comma, the print head moves to the next print zone.

Example

The following program prompts the user to set a column width for the printer and to type lines of text that the program sends to the printer.

```
INPUT "Enter the line width of the printer: "; column%
WIDTH LPRINT column%
PRINT "Type one line at a time. Press Enter to quit."

DO
    LINE INPUT line$      ' get a line
    IF LEN(line$) = 0 THEN EXIT DO
    LPRINT line$;         ' don't force a linefeed
LOOP
LPRINT CHR$(12)           ' print a formfeed character
```

CHAPTER 16

Communications Port

Introduction

PC communications involve the transfer of data between a PC and another computer system. The data might be program (binary) files, spreadsheet and database records, text documents, electronic mail, messages from bulletin boards, graphics images, or any other information that can be encoded in a digital format. The other computer might be a PC or a giant mainframe thousands of miles away. It might be running DOS, OS/2, UNIX, or some other operating system. The data might be transmitted through a cable directly connected to the other computer, or it might be sent through the phone lines by way of a modem.

As a QuickBASIC programmer, you don't need to know many details about the transmitting and receiving systems themselves; all you need to know is that PC communications lets you transfer data to and from a serial communications port, which is a physical connection to the PC and its associated memory buffer. As far as QuickBASIC is concerned, you communicate with the serial port, not with another computer or operating system.

This chapter shows you how to use the QuickBASIC statements that open the serial port connection, establish a temporary memory buffer to hold data, signal when data has been received, and close the connection when it is no longer needed. Table 16-1 lists QuickBASIC's communications statements.

Statement	Description
COM ON/OFF/STOP	Enables, disables, or suspends communications event trapping.
ON COM GOSUB	Specifies the subroutine to which control branches when a specified communications port receives data.
OPEN COM	Opens a serial port connection and assigns a buffer and file number to it. The statement also lets you specify characteristics of communication, such as baud rate, parity, number of data bits, number of stop bits, and modem control.

Table 16-1.
QuickBASIC communications statements.

Ports and Buffers

A port in a PC consists of three elements: a physical (electronic) connection, a particular location in memory for status information about the connection, and a memory buffer for the temporary storage of incoming or outgoing data. QuickBASIC can transmit or receive data by way of the PC's standard serial ports. (The term "serial" means that data is transmitted as a series of individual bits, one bit at a time.) QuickBASIC supports only the COM1: and COM2: serial ports.

Each port has a specific memory address assigned to it. (In hexadecimal, the address for COM1: is 03F8H, and for COM2: it is 02F8H.) Each of these addresses (and the seven bytes that follow it) is dedicated to either setting or indicating the status of the connection, as you will see later.

QuickBASIC assigns another memory area, called a buffer, to each port. This temporary storage area is necessary because usually a program must do other work while it transfers characters to and from a communications port. If the program had to stop whatever it was doing every time a character arrived at the port, execution would slow to a crawl—and at higher transmission speeds, characters would be lost before they could be used in the program. To make the data more manageable, the input buffer accumulates characters until it is full (or nearly full); then the program transfers the contents of the buffer to the screen, a file, or a string array, depending on the application. Similarly, outgoing characters are accumulated in the output buffer and then sent when the buffer is full.

Establishing the Connection

When you send information from QuickBASIC, the first step is to call the OPEN COM statement to specify both the serial port you want to use and the status of the connection. For example, the statement

```
OPEN "COM1:1200,N,8,1" FOR RANDOM AS #1
```

specifies that the port COM1: will be used and that the speed of character transmission will be 1200 baud (1200 bits per second). The transmission speed and other characteristics of the connection must be the same for both sender and receiver. That is, if you want your QuickBASIC program to connect to a system that allows 300-baud, 1200-baud, or 2400-baud connections, you can pick one of these speeds but not, for example, 9600 baud.

The above statement uses the arguments N, 8, and 1 to indicate that there will be no parity bit, 8 data bits per character, and 1 stop bit. "Parity checking" is a method of detecting transmission errors by ensuring that the number of bits in a character with a value of 1 (or 0, depending on the type of parity checking) is even (or odd); you perform parity checking by setting a "parity bit." The value of the parity bit indicates whether the number of bits should be even or odd. If the character arrives at the destination without the appropriate even or odd number of bits, the receiver requests that it be sent again. The "data bits" are bits that actually contain the data being transmitted (such as ASCII characters). Note that 7 bits are enough to transmit the 128 ASCII characters but that 8 bits are needed for numeric data or for the characters in the IBM extended character set. "Stop bits" indicate the end of one set of data bits. You will most often use only 1 stop bit; use 2 bits only for the slowest transmission speeds (110 baud or less). Use the 1.5-bit setting only when you specify 5 data bits.

Use the FOR clause in the OPEN COM statement to specify how the program will use the data sent to and received from the port. FOR RANDOM, the default in QuickBASIC, means the data will be treated like records in a random-access file. You can specify the record length by using a LEN clause. Random-access mode is convenient for sending fixed-length blocks of data—for example, when implementing error-correcting protocols such as XMODEM, which protect against transmission errors. You can also specify FOR INPUT in the OPEN COM statement so that the program receives only sequential input, and FOR OUTPUT so that it sends only sequential output.

The AS clause is the final part of the example OPEN COM statement. AS #1 specifies that the COM1: port can be accessed as file #1. It is important to note that QuickBASIC treats the communications port as a file. Thus you can open it and then either receive input from or send output to its buffer. QuickBASIC uses separate transmit (TB) and receive (RB) buffers; the default size of each buffer in QuickBASIC is 512 bytes.

Additional Communications Settings and Modem Control

The OPEN COM statement also lets you change other communications settings: It can specify whether data is treated as ASCII characters or binary values, the size of the receive and transmit buffers, the printing of linefeeds on a serial printer, and how long the modem control signal is monitored before a time-out occurs. A "time-out" is the termination of communication that occurs when the time allowed for establishing the connection or performing an operation has been exceeded. Without time-outs, the program would simply "hang" if it encountered a problem with the connection. If you don't specify time-outs, QuickBASIC uses default time-outs of 1 second. The above options are discussed in detail in the OPEN COM entry. If you have trouble with time-outs caused by poor connections or by differences between the sending and receiving hardware, try increasing the time-out values.

You can set the size of the receive buffer by using the /C compiler switch. (In QuickBASIC versions 4.0 and later, you can also set the transmit buffer in this way.) For example, starting QuickBASIC version 4.0 by using the command line *QB /C:1024* sets both the transmit and receive buffers to 1024 bytes and then runs QuickBASIC.

Accessing the Serial Port Directly

The above information is probably all you need for communications with many applications. However, you can directly access and change the data stored at the COM1: and COM2: port addresses by using the INP (in port) and OUT (out port) statements. (The memory specified by an address that is associated with a port is called a "register.") Some applications require you to test individual bits in a register. For example, a program might check the value of the first and second bits in the Line Status Register to determine the number of data bits being used. Usually you do this is by converting the desired bit value to a hexadecimal number and then using a conditional statement to determine whether a bit has been set or whether a status bit contains the desired value. (A set bit indicates that a particular event has occurred.)

For example, the following program segment loops until the modem data carrier is detected:

```
port = &H3F8            ' base address for COM1:
DO
    LOCATE 1, 1
    PRINT "Waiting for carrier..."
LOOP WHILE (INP(port + 6) < &H80)
```

Using the variable *port* and an offset lets the program accommodate either serial port. Here the loop compares the value in the Modem Status Register with the value &H80. When a carrier is detected, the bit that is set makes the test false, and the program exits the loop.

Accessing registers directly can be tricky, but it can improve speed as well as accommodate communications devices that do not follow the standard scheme used by QuickBASIC. Table 16-2 lists the contents of the standard addresses of the registers for the COM1: and COM2: ports.

Register	**COM1:**	**COM2:**
Base Port Address	&H3F8	&H2F8
Interrupt Enable (IER)	&H3F9	&H2F9
Interrupt Identifier (IIR)	&H3FA	&H2FA
Line Control (LCR)	&H3FB	&H2FB
Modem Control (MCR)	&H3FC	&H2FC
Line Status (LSR)	&H3FD	&H2FD
Modem Status (MSR)	&H3FE	&H2FE

Table 16-2.
Port registers and their addresses.

If you are using QuickBASIC with OS/2, note that OS/2 makes direct access to device ports difficult and often impossible. In most cases you must call the appropriate OS/2 system functions, instead.

Retrieving and Sending Characters

To retrieve characters from the input buffer, first use the EOF function to determine whether there are any characters to process. (Because QuickBASIC treats the communications device as a file, the "end-of-file" status means there are no more characters to retrieve.) Next, use the INPUT$ function with the LOC function to retrieve all the characters in the buffer. Do not use the INPUT or LINE INPUT statements because they might not retrieve all the characters: INPUT stops at a comma, new line, and sometimes at a space or pair of double quotation marks; LINE INPUT stops at a new line. Do not use the GET statement because it waits for the buffer to fill, and the buffer might overflow before the characters can be transferred.

The following loop shows the recommended technique for retrieving characters. The loop waits until there are characters at the COM1: port (assuming the port has been opened properly) and displays them on the screen:

```
DO
    IF NOT EOF(1) THEN                  ' port was opened as file #1
        PRINT INPUT$(LOC(1), #1)
    END IF
LOOP
```

To send characters to the serial port (and thus to the connected system), you can use any appropriate PRINT or PUT statement. If you assign each line of input to a string called *line$*, the statement

```
PRINT #1, line$
```

will store the characters in *line$* in the transmit buffer. QuickBASIC sends the contents of the buffer to the port.

Because a communications session uses files for serial input and output, use a CLOSE statement at the end of your program to close the files.

Managing Communications with Event Trapping

In many cases, you do not want your program to begin waiting for data from the communications buffer until communication occurs. QuickBASIC includes a set of statements that branch control to a designated subroutine when data is received. Executing a subroutine when an event occurs is called event trapping.

The ON COM GOSUB statement specifies the subroutine to which execution branches when characters are available for processing in the communications buffer.

Your program must also execute a COM ON statement to activate communications event trapping. The COM STOP statement suspends communications event trapping; characters continue to arrive at the buffer, but control does not branch to the subroutine. You might use this statement to turn off communications event trapping while your program performs a time-critical function, but be sure that you enable trapping again before the buffer overflows. A buffer overflow causes data to be lost and can halt the program. When you use another COM ON statement to resume event trapping, QuickBASIC remembers any events that occurred while communications event trapping was off and executes the subroutine. This lets your program catch up with communications activity. The COM OFF statement simply turns off communications event trapping and does not remember any communications events.

In each communications event-trapping statement, the keyword COM is followed by the number of the communications port (either 1 or 2) in parentheses. (This number refers to either the COM1: or COM2: port. Do not confuse it with the file number you assign in the OPEN COM statement.)

A program that includes communications event trapping uses the following schematic form: (The example below uses the COM1: port)

```
OPEN "COM1:1200,N,8,1" FOR RANDOM AS #1     ' open the connection
ON COM(1) GOSUB DoCom              ' specify subroutine
COM(1) ON                          ' begin event trapping

DO                                 ' program's main processing loop
    :
    COM(1) STOP                    ' begin time-critical activity
    :
    COM(1) ON                      ' restore event trapping
LOOP
CLOSE
END

DoCom:                             ' event-handler subroutine
    :
    RETURN
```

Further Explorations

To see a simple working communications program, examine the TERMINAL.BAS program that QuickBASIC provides. For more examples, look at the source code of some communications programs provided on bulletin boards.

You don't need two modems (or even one modem) to perform serial communications. If you have two DOS computers, you can connect their serial ports with a null modem cable (available at most electronics or computer stores) and run QuickBASIC programs simultaneously on the two machines; this lets you test output from one and input to the other. You can test your connection by using the sample programs provided in the "Example" section of the ON COM GOSUB entry.

Sophisticated communications programs can be difficult to develop because they have to deal with matters of timing, file-transmission protocols, terminal emulation, and so on. See the books in the following bibliography to further your understanding of this subject.

Related Reading

Barkakati, Nabajyoti. "Programming the Serial Port with C," in *MS-DOS Papers*, by The Waite Group. Indianapolis, Ind.: Howard W. Sams & Co., 1988.

The Waite Group. *MS-DOS Developer's Guide.* 2d ed. Indianapolis, Ind.: Howard W. Sams & Co., 1989.

Willen, David C., and Jeffrey I. Krantz. *8088 Assembler Language Programming: The IBM PC.* 2d ed. Indianapolis, Ind.: Howard W. Sams & Co., 1984.

COM ON/OFF/STOP

See also: ON COM GOSUB, OPEN COM

■ QB2	■ QB4.5	■ PowerBASIC
■ QB3	ANSI	■ GW-BASIC
■ QB4	■ BASIC7	MacQB

Purpose

The COM ON/OFF/STOP statements enable, disable, or suspend communications event trapping. Use communications event trapping if you want the program to execute a subroutine whenever the specified communications port receives characters.

Syntax

COM(*port*) ON
COM(*port*) OFF
COM(*port*) STOP

port must be either 1 or 2. It specifies the communications port (either COM1: or COM2:) that will be used.

Usage

```
COM(1) ON
```

Enables communications event trapping at the COM1: port.

```
COM(1) OFF
```

Disables communications event trapping at the COM1: port.

```
COM(1) STOP
```

Suspends event trapping at COM1:, but notes whether characters have arrived so that a subsequent COM ON statement branches execution to the appropriate subroutine.

Description

QuickBASIC lets you trap the arrival of characters at the communications (serial) port. Use the COM ON statement to enable trapping so that when a character arrives, control transfers to the subroutine designed to handle the communications input. (The subroutine is specified by an ON COM GOSUB statement.)

Note that you must open the serial port you want with an OPEN COM statement before a communications event will be available for trapping.

If your program is performing some other time-critical activity (such as working with another device), you might need to use the COM OFF statement to turn off event trapping at a specified port. Incoming characters will continue to be placed in the receive buffer, but if the buffer overflows, data will be lost and a fatal error might halt the program.

Use the COM STOP statement to suspend the trapping of events from the specified communications port. Until you execute a subsequent COM ON statement, incoming data continues to arrive at the input buffer for the specified port; however, the subroutine specified in an ON COM GOSUB statement is not executed. QuickBASIC sets a flag recording that an event occurred so that the trap is triggered after the next COM ON statement is executed.

The program executes an implicit COM STOP whenever it enters the subroutine specified by ON COM GOSUB. This ensures that another occurrence of the event does not cause the subroutine to be entered recursively. When the program encounters a RETURN statement and returns to the main program, it reinstates communications event trapping by executing an implicit COM ON statement.

Warnings

If you use the command-line compiler, BC.EXE, to compile a program that performs communications event trapping, you must use either the /V or the /W switch. These switches enable trapping and force the program to check the event flag, either between statements (/V) or between program lines (/W).

When you write communications programs and subprograms, use the ON ERROR GOTO statement to trap any errors that occur. Always test your communications programs under a variety of conditions (different speeds, different degrees of line noise, and so on) to ensure dependable performance.

Be sure your buffer is large enough to hold all characters that might arrive while trapping is suspended or off. Note that you might have to increase the buffer size at higher communications speeds (2400 baud and higher). You can set the communications buffer size either by using the /C compiler switch or by using the TB and RB parameters in the OPEN COM statement.

Example

The following program uses the COM ON statement to enable communications event trapping and the COM STOP statement to suspend communications event trapping until a key is pressed. The program begins by executing the subroutine *Event* every time characters arrive at the COM1: port. If you press a key, however, trapping is suspended, and the program will stop displaying the message "Trapped an event at the COM1: port.". When you press another key, trapping resumes. Press Esc to exit the loop.

```
COM(1) ON                        ' enable trapping for port COM1:

ON COM(1) GOSUB Event            ' specify subroutine for event trapping
OPEN "COM1:1200,N,8,1" FOR INPUT AS 2    ' open port

toggle = -2                      ' start with toggle off
```

(continued)

continued

```
DO
    PRINT "Waiting for something to happen..."
    inky$ = INKEY$
    IF inky$ <> "" AND inky$ <> CHR$(27) THEN
        toggle = NOT toggle    ' reverse toggle setting
    END IF
    IF toggle THEN
        PRINT "Suspending event trapping."
        COM(1) STOP
    END IF
    IF NOT toggle THEN
        COM(1) ON
        PRINT "Event trapping resumed."
    END IF
LOOP UNTIL inky$ = CHR$(27)    ' exit loop if user presses Esc
END

Event:
    PRINT "Trapped an event at the COM1: port. "
    RETURN
```

ON COM GOSUB

See also: COM ON/OFF/STOP, OPEN COM

■ QB2	■ QB4.5	■ PowerBASIC
■ QB3	ANSI	■ GW-BASIC
■ QB4	■ BASIC7	MacQB

Purpose

The ON COM GOSUB statement specifies the subroutine to which execution branches whenever data is received at the specified communications port. This feature lets your program perform other tasks without having to check constantly for communications activity.

Syntax

ON COM(*port*) GOSUB {*line* ¦ *label*}

port must be either 1 or 2. It specifies the communications port (either COM1: or COM2:) that will be used.

line or *label* specifies the line that begins the subroutine to which execution branches.

Usage

```
ON COM(1) GOSUB DoComm
```

Specifies that the *DoComm* subroutine will be executed when data arrives at the COM1: port.

Description

The ON COM GOSUB statement specifies the event-handling subroutine for a serial communications port. Event handling is the ability of the program to respond automatically to signals from the hardware—in this case, the signals indicate that data was received at a serial communications port.

To set up communications event handling, you must perform the following steps:

- Open a communications port by using the OPEN COM statement.
- Specify the open port and the subroutine that will handle communications events by using an ON COM GOSUB statement.
- Activate event handling, or event trapping, with a COM ON statement that specifies the open port.
- Define the subroutine that will process the communications.

The programs in the "Example" section demonstrate how these steps can be used with the COM1: serial port. Note that the QuickBASIC communications statements support only two serial ports—1 refers to COM1: and 2 refers to the COM2: serial port.

Example

This section contains two programs. The first one opens the COM1: port for output and sends the string "This is a test..." to that port until you press a key. The second program opens the COM1: port to receive input, specifies that the subroutine *HandleComm* be executed whenever data arrives at the port, and activates communications event trapping. The subroutine uses the INPUT$ function to retrieve any waiting characters. (The LOC function returns the number of characters in the buffer.) If you have two computers, you can connect a null modem cable (which is available at most electronics or computer stores) to their serial ports and run the first program on one and the second on the other. (This is easiest if you compile both programs as standalone executable files.) If you have two computers connected by modem, you can have one dial the other to establish the connection. After you have opened the communications port as file #1, for example, the statement

```
PRINT #1, "ATDT1234567"
```

instructs a Hayes-compatible modem at that port to dial the number 123-4567.

In the OPEN COM statements used in these programs, the parameters *CD0*, *CS0*, *DS0*, *OP0*, and *RS* prevent time-outs and waiting for the Request to Send lines. If you don't use these parameters (or you don't specify larger time-out values), one of the programs would probably issue a time-out while waiting for the other to send or receive characters.

```
' open the port
OPEN "COM1:1200,N,8,1,CD0,CS0,DS0,OP0,RS" FOR OUTPUT AS #1

DO
    PRINT #1, "This is a test..."
LOOP WHILE INKEY$ = ""
CLOSE     ' close the port
END
```

```
' open the port
OPEN "COM1:1200,N,8,1,CD0,CS0,DS0,OP0,RS" FOR INPUT AS #1

ON COM(1) GOSUB HandleComm          ' specify event-handling subroutine
COM(1) ON                           ' activate trapping

CLS
DO
    LOCATE 1, 1
    PRINT "Waiting for data at the COM1: port. "
    PRINT "Press any key to quit."
    IF INKEY$ <> "" THEN SYSTEM
LOOP
CLOSE     ' close the port
END

HandleComm:
    DO WHILE NOT EOF(1)
        PRINT INPUT$(LOC(1), #1);     ' display the data
    LOOP
    RETURN
```

OPEN COM

See also: COM ON/OFF/STOP, ON COM GOSUB

✲ QB2	■ QB4.5	✲ PowerBASIC
✲ QB3	ANSI	✲ GW-BASIC
■ QB4	■ BASIC7	MacQB

Purpose

The OPEN COM statement establishes a serial communications connection to a QuickBASIC program. You can set many characteristics of the connection, including baud rate (transmission speed), parity, number of data and stop bits, buffer sizes, and time-out values for modem lines.

Syntax

OPEN "COM*port*:*params1 params2*" [FOR *mode*] AS [#]*file* [LEN=*length*]

port must be either 1 or 2. This number specifies the communications port (either COM1: or COM2:) that will be opened.

params1 is a list of the four parameters described in Table 16-3 on the following page. You must use a comma as a placeholder for any parameter you do not use.

params2 is a list of the parameters described in Table 16-4 also on the following page. You can specify these parameters in any order, provided you separate them by using commas.

mode is the keyword RANDOM, INPUT, or OUTPUT.

file is the number of the file from which you access the communications port.

length is an integer that specifies the record size used with the port. You can use *length* if the value of *mode* is RANDOM.

Usage

```
OPEN "COM1:1200,N,8,1" FOR RANDOM AS #1
```

Establishes a simple serial port connection so that COM1: has a transmission speed of 1200 baud, does not perform parity checking, and uses 8 data bits and 1 stop bit. The port is opened as a random file that can be accessed by #1.

```
OPEN "COM2:2400,E,7,1,BIN,CD0,CS0,DS0,OP0" FOR RANDOM AS #2
```

Opens a serial port connection and supplies data-communication specifications. COM2: is opened so that it has a transmission speed of 2400 baud, performs even parity checking, and uses 7 data bits and 1 stop bit. The port does not expand tabs or force carriage returns. The port does not use any time-outs, so it will wait for transmission and reception. The port is opened as a random file that can be accessed by #2.

Description

You must use the OPEN COM statement before your program can access a serial communications port. (See the tutorial for a discussion about ports, their memory addresses, and methods of access.) The syntax of the statement requires you to follow the keyword OPEN with a quote, the port number to be used (either COM1: or COM2:), and the parameters you want, which are separated by commas. You can specify any parameters listed in Tables 16-3 and 16-4.

Table 16-3 lists the first four parameters of the parameter list. They must appear in the order shown; if you skip a parameter, you must insert a comma as a placeholder. Use the parameters listed in Table 16-4 after setting those in Table 16-3; you can enter these parameters in any order.

Parameter	Meaning	Comments
Speed	Baud rate (bits per second).	Use the value 75, 110, 150, 300, 600, 1200, 1800, 2400, or 9600. Most dial-up connections are 1200 or 2400 baud. The modem you use must support the speed you specify.
Parity	Type of parity checking used for error detection.	Use the letter N (none), E (even), O (odd), S (space), or M (mark). If you do not know which letter to use, try N first.
Data bits	Number of bits in each group that represent actual data.	Use the value 5, 6, 7, or 8. Use 8 only if parity checking is not performed; use 7 if it is.
Stop bits	Number of bits used to mark the end of each word.	Use 1, 1.5, or 2. The appropriate choice is usually 1. Use 2 for slow transmission rates, and use 1.5 only if the number of data bits is 5.

Table 16-3.
The first four parameters for the OPEN COM statement.

Parameter	Meaning	Comments
ASC	Specifies characters as ASCII, expands tabs, forces a carriage return at the end of each line, and treats Ctrl-Z as the EOF marker.	Usually the best setting for sending and receiving ASCII text files.
BIN	Performs none of the actions specified for ASC.	This is the default. Use either ASC or BIN but not both.
CD*ms*	Specifies the number of milliseconds to wait for the time-out on Data Carrier Detect (DCD) line.	*ms* must be a number in the range 0 through 65535; 0 disables the time-out. The default is 0.
CS*ms*	Specifies the number of milliseconds to wait for the time-out on Clear to Send (CTS) line.	*ms* must be a number in the range 0 through 65535. The default is 1000 (1 second).
DS*ms*	Specifies the number of milliseconds to wait for the time-out on Data Set Ready (DSR) line.	*ms* must be a number in the range 0 through 65535. The default is 1000 (1 second).
LF	Adds a linefeed character to every carriage return.	Use for printing on serial printers.
OP*ms*	Specifies the number of milliseconds to wait for OPEN to be successful.	*ms* must be a number in the range 0 through 65535. The default is 10000 (10 seconds).
RB*bytes*	Allocates a number of bytes to the receive data buffer.	*bytes* must be in the range 0 through 32767. The default is 512.
RS	Suppresses detection of the Request to Send (RTS) signal.	
TB*bytes*	Allocates a number of bytes to the transmit data buffer.	*bytes* must be a number in the range 0 through 32767. The default is 512.

Table 16-4.
The remaining parameters for the OPEN COM statement.

Following the parameter list, use the keyword FOR and one of the following keywords:

RANDOM	For random file I/O
INPUT	For sequential input
OUTPUT	For sequential output

RANDOM is the most commonly used option, and QuickBASIC uses it as the default if you don't specify another mode. If you use RANDOM, you can follow it with the keyword LEN and the record size (in bytes) that will be used. The default record size is 128 bytes.

Comments

See Appendix A, "Microsoft KnowledgeBase," for a list of articles that can help you use the serial port and learn the quirks of various versions of QuickBASIC.

Timing problems can be difficult to handle. Start by using the most relaxed conditions your application can tolerate. Specify the time-out parameters as 0 so there will be no time-outs, set generous buffers, and start with a low speed (such as 1200 baud rather than 2400 or higher). The most commonly used setting specifies no parity, 8 data bits, and 1 stop bit. When you feel more comfortable using communications, begin varying the OPEN COM statement to meet the needs of your program.

Errors

A "Bad file name" error message displayed during the compilation of an OPEN COM statement usually indicates a syntax error of some sort. In addition, many other errors can occur during communications. DOS errors referring to "read fault" or "write fault" on device COM1: or COM2: usually indicate that the port was not opened. A "Device time-out" runtime error message indicates that a required signal took too long to arrive at the port. A "Fatal error" message might indicate a buffer overflow (usually the receive buffer); you might have to increase the buffer size to avoid this problem.

Warnings

Note that the ASC (ASCII text) parameter in the OPEN COM statement does not support XON/XOFF handshaking. The Ctrl-S and Ctrl-Q characters are treated as ordinary characters rather than as signals to start or stop data transmission.

In QuickBASIC versions 1.0 through 3.0, if a program leaves open any of the communications port lines when it quits, subsequent programs might not be able to open that port. QuickBASIC version 3.0 leaves the DTR (Data Terminal Ready) and RTS (Request to Send) lines open after a time-out; later versions clear these lines after a time-out.

In QuickBASIC version 4.0 and BASIC versions 6.0 and 7.0, using Ctrl-Break to interrupt a program sets to zero the internal pointer to the port address. Subsequent attempts to open the port return a "Device unavailable" error message. To detect this situation at the COM1: port, use the statement

```
DEF SEG = &H40
```

and then test the contents of the segment by using the following expression:

```
PEEK(0)=0 AND PEEK(1)=0
```

If the expression is true, reset COM1: by using the following statements:

```
POKE 0, &HF8
POKE 1, 3
```

Similarly, for COM2:, test the contents of the segment by using the expression

```
PEEK(2) = 0 AND PEEK(3) = 0
```

If the expression is true, reset the address with the following statements:

```
POKE 2, &HF8
POKE 3, 2
```

If a program is chained to another and compiled with the BRUN runtime module, the /C command-line option does not change the size of the communications buffer for the second program. Recompile the first (chaining) program with the buffer size of the second program.

Compatibility

QuickBASIC 2.0 and QuickBASIC 3.0

QuickBASIC versions 2.0 and 3.0 do not support the OP*ms*, RB*bytes*, TB*bytes*, and RANDOM parameters of OPEN.

PowerBASIC, GW-BASIC, and BASICA

PowerBASIC, GW-BASIC, and BASICA do not support the FOR clause in the OPEN statement. These versions of BASIC also do not support the ASC, BIN, OP*ms*, RB*bytes*, and TB*bytes* parameters. They do, however, support the PE parameter, which enables parity checking.

Example

The following program prompts the user to enter the port number, baud rate, data bits, and stop bits values and then performs an OPEN COM statement with those values.

```
CONST TRUE = 1, FALSE = NOT TRUE
CLS

DO
valid% = TRUE
PRINT "Which port do you want to use"
INPUT "1) COM1:   2) COM2:   3) Quit program "; choice%
SELECT CASE choice%
    CASE 1
        port$ = "COM1:"
    CASE 2
        port$ = "COM2:"
    CASE 3
        SYSTEM
```

(continued)

continued

```
    CASE ELSE
        PRINT "Choose 1, 2, or 3."
        valid% = FALSE
END SELECT
LOOP UNTIL valid% = TRUE

PRINT
DO
valid% = TRUE
PRINT "What transmission speed"
INPUT "1) 300 baud   2) 1200 baud    3) 2400 baud    4) 9600 baud "; choice%
SELECT CASE choice%
    CASE 1
        speed$ = "300"
    CASE 2
        speed$ = "1200"
    CASE 3
        speed$ = "2400"
    CASE 4
        speed$ = "9600"
    CASE ELSE
        PRINT "Choose 1, 2, 3, or 4."
        valid% = FALSE
END SELECT
LOOP UNTIL valid% = TRUE

PRINT
DO
valid% = TRUE
PRINT "What parity should be used"
INPUT "1) Even   2) Odd   3) None "; choice%
SELECT CASE choice%
    CASE 1
        parity$ = "E"
    CASE 2
        parity$ = "O"
    CASE 3
        parity$ = "N"
    CASE ELSE
        PRINT "Choose 1, 2, or 3."
        valid% = FALSE
END SELECT
LOOP UNTIL valid% = TRUE

PRINT
DO
valid% = TRUE
PRINT "How many data bits per byte"
INPUT "1) 5   2) 6   3) 7   4) 8 "; choice%
```

(continued)

continued

```
SELECT CASE choice%
    CASE 1
        dataBits$ = "5"
    CASE 2
        dataBits$ = "6"
    CASE 3
        dataBits$ = "7"
    CASE 4
        dataBits$ = "8"
        IF parity$ <> "N" THEN
            PRINT "Must use 'no parity' with 8 data bits."
            PRINT "Setting parity to none (N)."
            parity$ = "N"
        END IF
    CASE ELSE
        PRINT "Choose 5, 6, 7, or 8."
        valid% = FALSE
END SELECT
LOOP UNTIL valid% = TRUE

PRINT
DO
valid% = TRUE
PRINT "How many stop bits"
INPUT "1) 1   2) 1.5   3) 2 "; choice%
SELECT CASE choice%
    CASE 1
        stopBits$ = "1"
    CASE 2
        stopBits$ = "1.5"
    CASE 3
        stopBits$ = "2"
    CASE ELSE
        PRINT "Choose 1, 2, or 3."
        valid% = FALSE
END SELECT
LOOP UNTIL valid% = TRUE

portSpec$ = port$ + speed$ + "," + parity$ + "," + dataBits$ + "," + stopBits$
PRINT "Your communications settings are: "; portSpec$

' open the communications port
OPEN portSpec$ FOR RANDOM AS #2
```

CHAPTER 17

Files

Introduction

The QuickBASIC statements that manage file input and output provide an essential link between your program and the outside world. Most applications programs are useful because data that the user enters can be saved; after it is initially entered, the data is always available on file. By storing a form letter, a payroll, or an inventory list, you can instantly access information that took days or weeks to produce.

QuickBASIC includes a complete set of file-management statements. Files can be stored on a floppy disk, a hard disk, a RAM disk, a network disk in a remote computer, or even a CD-ROM disk. QuickBASIC generally lets you handle all of these devices the same way—you don't need to write hardware-specific programs.

A file, stored in any manner, is merely a collection of bytes. The way those bytes are interpreted gives them meaning, as a patient history file, a record of sales transactions, or the like. Usually, programmers group information by using the following structures:

- *Fields.* A field is an individual piece of information, analogous to a simple variable. A field might contain a name, a birthdate, an inventory number, and so on. (The "field length" is the length of the field; it is usually measured in bytes.)
- *Records.* A record is a collection of fields that constitute a set of related information, analogous to a record variable defined by TYPE...END TYPE in QuickBASIC version 4.0 and later. A record might include a name, an address, and employment information. (The "record length" is the length of a single record; it is usually measured in bytes.)
- *Files.* A file is a set of records, analogous to an array of record variables in QuickBASIC version 4.0 and later. A file might comprise records for all of the employees of a company. (The "file length" is the combined length of all the records in the file; it is usually measured in bytes.)

Sequential Files

A "sequential file" is a continuous stream of characters that has no fields or records. A sequential file is line oriented rather than record oriented. This means that the exact location of information in a sequential file is unpredictable—to find line number 100, for example, you must first look through lines numbered 1 through 99. Sequential files are a lot like cassette tapes: To find a song in the middle of the tape, you must fast-forward through all the previous songs.

Sequential files can contain only ASCII characters. Each number in a sequential file is represented by 1 byte per digit.

Random-Access Files

A "random-access file" fully supports record structures. In fact, a random-access file contains a sequence of records, and a program can read only records from it or write only records to it. All records in a random-access file are the same length, so QuickBASIC can calculate the exact location of any record in the file. Accessing a record is as easy as accessing the last song on a compact disk; because you know where every record (song) begins and ends, you can merely skip to the appropriate location.

Binary Files

A "binary file" is a variation of both random-access and sequential files. A binary file *can* support fields and records, but it can also do without them. If you want to ignore the field and record structures that are normally present in a random-access file, you can open the file as a binary file instead. QuickBASIC treats a binary file as a sequence of bytes (not characters, as in a sequential file), so you can use a binary file to hold any type of information.

QuickBASIC provides statements and functions to efficiently manage the different file types and their structures. This tutorial summarizes QuickBASIC's file I/O abilities and offers some suggestions for their use. Table 17-1 lists QuickBASIC's file I/O statements and functions in alphabetic order.

Statement or function	**Description**
CLOSE	Closes an open file or device
CVD	Converts an 8-byte string (created by MKD$) to a double-precision value
CVDMBF	Converts an 8-byte string containing a double-precision value (created by MKDMBF$) from Microsoft Binary format to IEEE format
CVI	Converts a 2-byte string (created by MKI$) to an integer value
CVL	Converts a 4-byte string (created by MKL$) to a long-integer value
CVS	Converts a 4-byte string (created by MKS$) to a single-precision value
CVSMBF	Converts a 4-byte string containing a single-precision value (created by MKSMBF$) from Microsoft Binary format to IEEE format
EOF	Returns −1 (true) when the file pointer is at the end of a file
FIELD	Defines a buffer for a random-access file
FILEATTR	Returns information about a file

Table 17-1.
QuickBASIC file I/O statements and functions.

(continued)

Table 17-1. *continued*

Statement or function	Description
FILES	Displays the filename of each file in the current or specified directory
FREEFILE	Returns the next available file number
GET (File I/O)	Reads data from a random-access or binary file
INPUT #	Reads data from a sequential file
INPUT$	Reads the specified number of bytes from the keyboard or from a file
LINE INPUT #	Reads data from a sequential file
LOC	Returns the current location in a file
LOCK	Prevents other programs from accessing a file
LOF	Returns the length of a file in bytes
LSET	Puts data in a random-access file buffer
LTRIM$	Removes blank spaces from the left end of a string
MKD$	Converts a double-precision value to an 8-byte string for output to a random-access file
MKDMBF$	Converts a double-precision value stored in IEEE format to an 8-byte string containing the value in Microsoft Binary format for output to a random-access file
MKI$	Converts an integer value to a 2-byte string for output to a random-access file
MKL$	Converts a long-integer value to a 4-byte string for output to a random-access file
MKS$	Converts a single-precision value to a 4-byte string for output to a random-access file
MKSMBF$	Converts a single-precision value stored in IEEE format to a 4-byte string containing the value in Microsoft Binary format for output to a random-access file
NAME	Renames a file or directory
OPEN	Opens a file
PRINT #	Writes data to a sequential file
PRINT # USING	Writes formatted data to a sequential file
PUT (File I/O)	Writes data to a random-access or binary file
RESET	Closes all files
RSET	Puts data in a random-access file buffer
RTRIM$	Removes blank spaces from the right end of a string
SEEK (Function)	Returns the current location in a file
SEEK (Statement)	Moves to a specified location in a file
UNLOCK	Unlocks a file so other programs can access it
WIDTH (File I/O)	Sets the maximum width of a sequential file
WRITE #	Writes data to a sequential file

Opening a File or Device

QuickBASIC references files by means of a file number. The OPEN statement associates a file with a file number so you can later access the file by specifying that number. If you are not certain which number to use, call the FREEFILE function, which returns the next free file number. The OPEN statement also performs several other functions—it creates a file if the specified file does not exist, sets access modes, manages the file buffer, and manages file access in a multiuser environment.

The access mode specified in an OPEN statement determines the way your program can use the file. Use one of the following keywords to specify the access mode: INPUT, OUTPUT, APPEND, RANDOM, or BINARY.

The keywords INPUT, OUTPUT, and APPEND open a file as a sequential file containing a sequence of characters. Your program can retrieve data from a sequential file only by opening it with INPUT and can write data to a sequential file only by opening it with OUTPUT or APPEND. The OUTPUT keyword specifies that a new sequential file will be created; the APPEND keyword specifies that an existing file will be opened and that data will be added to the end of it.

Using the RANDOM keyword in an OPEN statement opens a file in random-access mode. If you do not specify an access mode, OPEN uses random access by default. Using the BINARY keyword opens a file in binary mode.

A buffer is an area of memory in which a program places data that will be written to the file and data that is read from the file. Because reading information from a disk is a mechanical (and therefore slow) process, QuickBASIC uses the buffer to hold data while the program continues execution. In order to further speed up program execution, each time a program accesses a disk file by using a read operation, it fills the buffer with data. When the program executes another read operation, the program does not need to access the disk; instead it gets the data from the buffer.

Programs that run on a network can either share files or restrict access to files. The lock clause in the OPEN statement lets you specify the kind of access other programs can have to an open file. Table 17-2 lists QuickBASIC's lock specifications.

Lock clause	Description
(Default)	No other process can open the file.
SHARED	Any process can open the file in any mode.
LOCK READ	No other process can open the file by using an ACCESS READ clause; no other process can already have ACCESS READ privileges.
LOCK WRITE	No other process can open the file by using an ACCESS WRITE clause; no other process can already have ACCESS WRITE privileges.
LOCK READ WRITE	No other process can open the file by using an ACCESS READ WRITE clause; no other process can already have ACCESS READ WRITE privileges.

Table 17-2.
Network-access lock definitions.

In a networking environment, you can specify the kind of access you want by including an ACCESS clause in the OPEN statement. You can choose from ACCESS READ, ACCESS WRITE, and ACCESS READ WRITE for input only, output only, and both input and output access. If another program uses an OPEN statement with a lock clause to open a file, and if your program tries to open the same file by using an OPEN statement with an ACCESS clause specifying the same access as the one specified in the lock clause, your program cannot open the file.

Closing a File or Device

The OPEN statement lets you access a file; the CLOSE statement ends communication with a file and clears all data from the associated buffer space. If the data in the buffer is output from the program, CLOSE writes the data to the file. The CLOSE statement either closes specific files or closes all files at once. The RESET statement, however, always closes all files and clears the file buffers.

Managing Random-Access Files

A random-access file contains a sequence of records that are broken into fields. QuickBASIC 4.0 introduced the TYPE...END TYPE statement, which lets you create a user-defined type that specifies a number of fields and then declare record variables of that type. (See the TYPE...END TYPE entry in Chapter 1, "Types and Variables," for details.) Random-access files can contain records defined in this manner.

Early versions of BASIC do not support the TYPE...END TYPE statement. With these versions of BASIC you must use the FIELD statement to specify the fields of the records in a random-access file. The fields of these records must be strings. Because the FIELD statement allocates space for each field in the buffer that is associated with the file, you must use the LSET and RSET statements to assign values to the fields.

The "L" in LSET stands for left-justify, and the "R" in RSET stands for right-justify. LSET places a value at the left end of a string field and adds spaces to fill the right side of the field. RSET places a value at the right end and adds spaces to the left side of the field.

Because the FIELD statement can define only string fields, BASIC provides several functions that convert numbers to strings; corresponding functions convert the strings back into numbers. QuickBASIC supports these functions to maintain compatibility with other versions of BASIC. Table 17-3 summarizes the string-conversion and number-conversion functions.

The conversion functions MKSMBF$ and MKDMBF$ convert numbers in IEEE format to strings containing numbers in Microsoft Binary format. The functions CVSMBF and CVDMBF convert strings containing numbers in Microsoft Binary format to numbers in IEEE format. These functions let you access files created by earlier versions of BASIC that support only the Microsoft Binary format.

Numeric type	From number to string	From string to number
Integer	MKI$	CVI
Long integer	MKL$	CVL
Single precision	MKS$	CVS
MBF* single precision	MKSMBF$	CVSMBF
Double precision	MKD$	CVD
MBF* double precision	MKDMBF$	CVDMBF

*MBF stands for Microsoft Binary format, the numeric format used in GW-BASIC, BASICA, and QuickBASIC versions 3.0 and earlier; subsequent versions of QuickBASIC use IEEE numeric format.

Table 17-3.
QuickBASIC string-conversion and number-conversion functions.

For example, if your program includes a field named *pastDueAmount$* that was defined in a FIELD statement, you might use the following statements to write a numeric value to the disk file:

```
LSET pastDueAmount$ = MKD$(169.85)
PUT #1
```

The MKD$ function converts the number 169.85 into a string, and LSET places the string in the *pastDueAmount$* field, which can then be written to the file. The PUT statement writes the current record to the disk file.

To read the value of this field from the file, you might use the following statements:

```
GET #1
pastDueAmt# = CVD(pastDueAmount$)
```

The GET statement retrieves a record from the disk. *pastDueAmt#* is a double-precision variable, and the CVD function converts *pastDueAmount$* from a string back into a double-precision value.

Reading Data from Random-Access or Binary Files

You use the GET statement to read records from random-access and binary files. You specify in the GET statement both the record number (the byte number in a binary file) and the variable to be read. For example, to read the first record of a random-access file whose file number is 3 and assign it to the record variable *info*, you use the statement

```
GET #3, 1, info
```

Reading data from a binary file is just as simple. The following statement begins reading at byte number 129 in a binary file whose file number is 2 and assigns the value it reads to a variable named *invoices*:

```
GET #2, 129, invoices
```

When you read from a random-access file a record defined by a FIELD statement, you cannot specify a record variable in the GET statement that will be assigned the values. When no record variable is specified, GET retrieves a record and places it in the file buffer. You must then use an INPUT #, LINE INPUT #, or PRINT # statement after the GET statement to read the values from the file buffer. Using record variables is much more convenient than working with the FIELD statement. If your version of BASIC supports the TYPE...END TYPE statement, be sure to use it when you work with random-access files.

You can also use the INPUT$ function to read values from a random-access or binary file. The INPUT$ function reads the specified number of characters in a file. The maximum number of characters is the length of a record in a random-access file or 32,767 bytes in a binary file.

Writing Data to Random-Access or Binary Files

You use the PUT statement to write records to random-access and binary files. You specify in the PUT statement both the record number (the byte number in a binary file) and the variable to be written. For example, to write the values contained in the record variable *info* to record 31 of the random-access file whose file number is 1, you use the statement

```
PUT #1, 31, info
```

Writing to a binary file is also a simple operation. The following statement writes the contents of the variable *inventory* to a binary file whose file number is 12, beginning at byte number 1537:

```
PUT #12, 1537, inventory
```

When you write a record defined by a FIELD statement, you do not specify a variable in the PUT statement. If no variable is specified, the PUT statement writes to the file any values placed in the file buffer by LSET or RSET statements.

Reading Data from Sequential Files

You can use one of two statements or a function to read sequential files—INPUT #, LINE INPUT #, and INPUT$. Generally, you use the INPUT # statement to read numbers from a sequential file and the LINE INPUT # statement to read an entire line of text. The INPUT$ function reads the specified number of characters from a sequential file.

The INPUT # statement reads data from a sequential file until it reaches a "delimiter"—a space, comma, carriage return, or linefeed. (See the INPUT # entry for an explanation of the usage of delimiters in this statement.) The following statement, for example, uses the INPUT # statement to read a string variable and an integer variable from the file whose file number is 3:

```
INPUT #3, studentName$, grade%
```

The LINE INPUT # statement is more flexible because it recognizes only one delimiter—the carriage return and linefeed pair. Therefore, LINE INPUT # can read an entire line into a variable and include any delimiters in that line. A single LINE INPUT # statement, however, cannot read multiple lines. Also, LINE INPUT # can assign the data from the file only to a string variable, not to a numeric one. (See the LINE INPUT # entry for a description of the usage of delimiters in this statement.) The following statement illustrates how you might use the LINE INPUT # statement. It reads a line from the file whose file number is 5 and assigns it to the variable *code$*:

```
LINE INPUT #5, code$
```

The INPUT$ function reads a specified number of characters from a sequential file. Note that you cannot specify more than 32767 characters. You also must be sure not to specify more characters than are in the file. The INPUT$ function, unlike INPUT # and LINE INPUT #, recognizes no delimiters; you can read *any* character by using INPUT$. The following statement demonstrates the use of the INPUT$ function. It reads one character from the file whose file number is 3 and assigns the character to the variable *character$*:

```
character$ = INPUT$(1, #3)
```

Writing Data to Sequential Files

The PRINT # statement is the most commonly used statement for writing sequential output. It works much like the PRINT statement, which displays output on the screen. (See Figures 17-7 and 17-8 in the PRINT # entry for examples of the output of this statement.) For example, the following statement writes the number 123.15 to the file whose file number is 1:

```
PRINT #1, 123.15
```

The WRITE # statement is similar to the PRINT # statement, but it places a comma between expressions in the file and includes sets of quotation marks around string variables. The punctuation enables the INPUT # statement to read the file more easily. (See the INPUT # entry.) For example, the statement

```
WRITE #1, "DOE, JOHN", 012170, 150.25
```

writes to the file corresponding to file number 1 the following output (including all punctuation):

```
"DOE, JOHN",12170,150.25
```

Removing Blank Spaces from Strings

If a string includes spaces on either end (as happens when you use the LSET or RSET statement for random-access files), you can use the LTRIM$ or RTRIM$ function to remove them. For example, if you use one variable for a person's first name and another for his or her last name, and if you are creating forms in which the first and last names appear together, remove the extra spaces from the right end of the string that contains the person's first name. To do so, you might use the following statement:

```
PRINT #checks, "Pay to the order of "; RTRIM$(firstName$); " "; lastName$
```

If you want to remove the spaces from both ends of a string, you can use both the LTRIM$ and RTRIM$ functions, as shown in the following statement:

```
patient$ = LTRIM$(RTRIM$(patient$))
```

Moving Within a File

For every open file, QuickBASIC maintains a pointer that indicates a location in the file. Any input or output that the program performs begins at this location unless another location is specified in the input or output statement. You can move the file pointer to any location in the file by calling the SEEK statement. If you use SEEK for a random-access file, you specify the number of the record to which you want to move the pointer. On the other hand, if you use SEEK for a sequential or binary file, you specify the number of the byte to which you want the pointer to move. For example, to position the pointer at record 256 of a random-access file whose file number is 17, you would use the following statement:

```
SEEK #17, 256
```

Determining File Characteristics

Although QuickBASIC shields you from having to know the low-level details about files, it does let you access some of that information. The FILEATTR function, for example, returns the mode (INPUT, OUTPUT, APPEND, RANDOM, or BINARY) in which a file was opened; it can also be used to return the DOS file handle for that file. DOS uses the DOS file handle number to access the file, just as QuickBASIC uses the file number; you probably need to know the file handle number only if you are using routines written in assembly language or C in your QuickBASIC programs.

The EOF function tests to see whether the file pointer is positioned at the end of a file. You can use this function in a loop that reads the entire contents of a file, as shown in the following example.

```
DEFINT A-Z

fileNum = FREEFILE
OPEN "REPORT.RPT" FOR INPUT AS #fileNum

DO UNTIL EOF(fileNum)
    LINE INPUT #fileNum, text$
    LPRINT text$
LOOP

CLOSE
```

The LOF function returns the size of a file, in bytes. You can use LOF to calculate the number of records in a specified random-access file by using the following formula:

numRecords = LOF(*file*) \ *recordLength*

QuickBASIC also provides the LOC and SEEK functions. The LOC function returns the number of the record that was most recently written or read, for a random-access file; the current byte number divided by 128, for a sequential file; or the byte position of the last byte read or written, for a binary file. The SEEK function, however, returns the position of the *next* record that will be written or read, for a random access file, or the byte position of the next byte to be written or read, for a sequential or binary file.

Managing Files on Disk

QuickBASIC includes several statements that help you manage files. Chapter 18, "DOS and Program Management," discusses additional statements that manage files and directories.

The QuickBASIC FILES statement displays a listing of the current or specified directory. It is similar to the DOS DIR /W command, which displays filenames in several columns across the screen. You can use the FILES statement to let the user see which data files are available.

The NAME statement changes the name of an existing file, much as the DOS command RENAME does. The NAME statement is more powerful than REN, however, because it can also be used to move files between directories on a disk. For example, the following statement moves a file to the REPORTS directory and changes its name to REPORT01.RPT.

```
NAME "C:\ACCT\REPORT.RPT" AS "C:\REPORTS\REPORT01.RPT"
```

Locking and Unlocking Files

When programs are used on a local area network, conflicts can arise if several programs try to access the same file. DOS versions 3.1 and later support file locking and record locking. If you lock a file or record, only your program can access the file or record. If another program wants access to a locked file or record, it must wait until your program unlocks the file or record.

QuickBASIC provides the LOCK and UNLOCK statements to manage locking. The LOCK statement can lock an entire file or merely a portion of it. The UNLOCK statement complements the LOCK statement and must be used to release the lock.

Please note that Microsoft guarantees support for QuickBASIC only on the IBM PC Network, MS-Network systems, and compatible systems. Although limited success has been reported using some other networks, such as Novell and 3Com, problems can occur. If much of your programming is for networks other than those supported by Microsoft, consider using a third-party file manager that supports them.

Setting the Maximum Width for Sequential Files

If you are creating sequential files to be printed on a printer that uses narrow paper, you must limit the width of each line in the file so that it will fit within the paper's margins. You can do this by using the WIDTH (File I/O) statement. When used with a file number, WIDTH limits lines to a specified width. Long lines are wrapped to the next line of the file when they exceed the specified width. This saves you the work of calculating maximum widths yourself.

Related Reading

Dettmann, Terry. *DOS Programmer's Reference.* Indianapolis, Ind.: Que, 1988.

Duncan, Ray, et al. *The MS-DOS Encyclopedia.* Redmond, Wash.: Microsoft Press, 1988.

Norton, Peter. *The Peter Norton Programmer's Guide to the IBM PC.* Redmond, Wash.: Microsoft Press, 1985.

The Waite Group. *MS-DOS Developer's Guide,* 2d ed. Indianapolis, Ind.: Howard Sams & Co., 1989.

Prata, Stephen, with Harry Henderson. *The Waite Group's QuickBASIC Primer Plus.* Redmond, Wash.: Microsoft Press, 1990.

The Waite Group. *Using PC DOS.* Indianapolis, Ind.: Howard Sams & Co., 1989.

CLOSE

See also: OPEN

■ QB2	■ QB4.5	■ PowerBASIC
■ QB3	■ ANSI	✲ GW-BASIC
■ QB4	■ BASIC7	■ MacQB

Purpose

The CLOSE statement closes an open file or device. Use CLOSE after you conclude all input and output operations with a file or device.

Syntax

CLOSE [[#]*filenum*[, [#]*filenum*]...]

filenum is the file number associated with an open file.

Usage

```
CLOSE
```

Closes all open files and devices.

```
CLOSE #1
```

Closes the file or device that was opened as file number 1 by an OPEN statement.

```
CLOSE 5, #15
```

Closes the files or devices that were opened as file numbers 5 and 15. Note that the number sign is optional.

Description

The CLOSE statement lets you close a file you previously opened with an OPEN statement. The OPEN statement allocates buffer space for the records in a file. The CLOSE statement writes any data remaining in the buffer space to the appropriate file or device and then releases the memory space reserved for the buffer. Using a CLOSE statement with no parameters closes all open files and devices.

After you close a file, you cannot reference it with another I/O statement until you specify the file in another OPEN statement. When you close a file, you can use the file number associated with that file when you reopen it or open any other file. That is, any closed file can be reopened under any unused file number.

When a program executes its last statement or executes a CLEAR, END, RESET, RUN, or SYSTEM statement, QuickBASIC closes all open files and devices. Still, good programming practice dictates that you issue a CLOSE statement for every OPEN statement in your program.

Comments

Closing a file that has not been opened will not cause an error.

Warnings

All fields defined by a FIELD statement are set to null strings after you close a file. If you want to save the contents of the fields, you must assign them to variables.

Compatibility

GW-BASIC and BASICA

In GW-BASIC and BASICA, a variable defined by a FIELD statement retains its value after you use a CLOSE statement to close the file associated with the FIELD statement.

Example

The following program opens a sequential file and the printer device, writes the date and time to both, and then closes them.

```
OPEN "REPORT.TXT" FOR OUTPUT AS #5        ' open a sequential file for output
OPEN "LPT1:" FOR OUTPUT AS #6             ' open the printer device

PRINT #5, "Today's date is "; DATE$       ' write the date to the file
PRINT #5, "and the time is "; TIME$       ' write the time to the file

PRINT #6, "Today's date is "; DATE$       ' write the date to the printer
PRINT #6, "and the time is "; TIME$       ' write the time to the printer
PRINT #6, CHR$(12)                        ' write a formfeed to the printer

CLOSE #5, #6                              ' close the file and the device
```

CVD

See also: CVDMBF, DOUBLE, FIELD, MKD$, MKDMBF$

✲ QB2	■ QB4.5	■ PowerBASIC
■ QB3	ANSI	✲ GW-BASIC
■ QB4	■ BASIC7	■ MacQB

Purpose

The CVD function converts an 8-byte string returned by the MKD$ function to its double-precision numeric value. You use the CVD function after reading the string representation of a double-precision number in a random-access file that contains records defined by the FIELD statement.

Syntax

CVD(*string*)

string is an 8-byte string variable created by the MKD$ function.

Usage

```
past# = CVD(pastDue$)
```

Assigns the double-precision value contained in the string variable *pastDue$* to the variable *past#*.

Description

Many versions of BASIC do not let you store numeric values in random-access files; you must convert numbers to strings before storing them and then convert them back to numbers when you read the file. (QuickBASIC 4.0 introduced the TYPE...END TYPE statement, which enables you to store numeric values.) The CVD function converts an 8-byte string to its double-precision numeric value.

The string that CVD converts must be contained in a string variable that was created by the MKD$ function, as in the following example:

```
string$ = MKD$(100.25)
```

Comments

If you specify the command-line switch /MBF, QuickBASIC assumes that the string parameter to the CVD function is a number in Microsoft Binary format. (See the CVDMBF entry for details.) Otherwise, QuickBASIC assumes that the string parameter in the CVD function contains a double-precision number in IEEE format.

Compatibility

QuickBASIC 2.0, GW-BASIC, and BASICA

QuickBASIC version 2.0, GW-BASIC, and BASICA do not support the IEEE formatting of floating-point values. Because these versions use only Microsoft Binary format, the value contained in the string parameter of the CVD function is in Microsoft Binary format.

Example

The following program converts values into strings, writes the strings to the random-access file SOL.DAT, and then converts each string stored in the file to a numeric value. The file contains information about the solar system, including the planet name, its diameter, its perihelion and aphelion, its highest and lowest temperatures, and the year in which it was discovered. (The perihelion of an orbit is the closest distance from the planet to the sun. The aphelion is the farthest distance from the planet to the sun.)

The program first lets you choose the number of the record that you want the program to read from the file. The program uses the functions CVL, CVD, CVDMBF, CVS, CVSMBF, and CVI to display the values of the record's fields. The program then uses the functions MKL$, MKD$, MKDMBF$, MKS$, MKSMBF$, and MKI$ to prepare new field values to write to the file.

```
OPEN "SOL.DAT" FOR RANDOM AS #1 LEN = 45
FIELD #1, 15 AS name$, 4 AS diameter$, 8 AS perihelion$, 8 AS aphelion$
FIELD #1, 35 AS dummy$, 4 AS highTemp$, 4 AS lowTemp$, 2 AS yearDiscovered$


CLS
INPUT "Information about which planet"; planetNum%
GET #1, planetNum%

PRINT "The diameter of planet "; RTRIM$(name$); " is";
PRINT CVL(diameter$); "kilometers"
PRINT "The perihelion of planet "; RTRIM$(name$); " is";
PRINT CVD(perihelion$); "kilometers"
PRINT "The aphelion of planet "; RTRIM$(name$); " is";
PRINT CVDMBF(aphelion$); "kilometers"
PRINT "The highest temperature of planet "; RTRIM$(name$); " is";
PRINT CVS(highTemp$); "degrees"
PRINT "The lowest temperature of planet "; RTRIM$(name$); " is";
PRINT CVSMBF(lowTemp$); "degrees"
PRINT "The planet was discovered in"; CVI(yearDiscovered$)
PRINT


INPUT "Do you want to change the record [Y/N] ", response$
IF UCASE$(response$) = "Y" THEN
    INPUT "Name: ", newName$
    INPUT "Diameter: ", newDiameter&
    INPUT "Perihelion: ", newPerihelion#
    INPUT "Aphelion: ", newAphelion#
    INPUT "Highest temperature: ", newHighTemp!
    INPUT "Lowest temperature: ", newLowTemp!
    INPUT "Year of discovery: ", newYear%

    LSET name$ = newName$
    LSET diameter$ = MKL$(newDiameter&)
    LSET perihelion$ = MKD$(newPerihelion#)
    LSET aphelion$ = MKDMBF$(newAphelion#)
    LSET highTemp$ = MKS$(newHighTemp!)
    LSET lowTemp$ = MKSMBF$(newLowTemp!)
    LSET yearDiscovered$ = MKI$(newYear%)
    PUT #1, planetNum%
END IF

CLOSE #1
```

CVDMBF

See also: CVD, DOUBLE, FIELD, MKD$, MKDMBF$

QB2	■ QB4.5	✲ PowerBASIC
■ QB3	ANSI	GW-BASIC
■ QB4	■ BASIC7	MacQB

Purpose

The CVDMBF function converts an 8-byte string containing a value in Microsoft Binary format to its double-precision numeric value in IEEE format. You use the CVDMBF function after reading the string representation of a double-precision number in a random-access file that contains strings in Microsoft Binary format; the file must contain records defined by the FIELD statement.

Syntax

CVDMBF(*string*)

string is an 8-byte string variable created by the MKDMBF$ function or by the MKD$ function in a version of BASIC that supports only the Microsoft Binary format.

Usage

```
past# = CVDMBF(pastDue$)
```

Assigns the double-precision value contained in the string variable of *pastDue$* to the variable *past#*.

Description

Many versions of BASIC do not let you store numeric values in random-access files; you must convert numbers to strings before storing them and then convert them back to numbers when you read the file. (QuickBASIC 4.0 introduced the TYPE...END TYPE statement, which enables you to store numeric values.) The CVDMBF function converts an 8-byte string to its double-precision numeric value in IEEE format.

The string that CVDMBF converts must be contained in a string variable that was created either by the MKD$ function in a version of BASIC that supports only the Microsoft Binary format or by the MKDMBF$ function, as in the following example:

```
aString$ = MKDMBF$(100.25)
```

Comments

QuickBASIC assumes that the string parameter in the CVDMBF function is a number in Microsoft Binary format.

Compatibility

PowerBASIC

PowerBASIC supports the CVMD function, which performs the same task that the CVDMBF statement does in QuickBASIC 4.5.

Example

See the "Example" section in the CVD entry.

CVI

See also: FIELD, INTEGER, MKI$

■ QB2	■ QB4.5	■ PowerBASIC
■ QB3	ANSI	■ GW-BASIC
■ QB4	■ BASIC7	■ MacQB

Purpose

The CVI function converts a 2-byte string returned by the MKI$ function to its integer numeric value. You use the CVI function after reading the string representation of an integer in a random-access file that contains records defined by the FIELD statement.

Syntax

CVI(*string*)

string is a 2-byte string variable created by the MKI$ function.

Usage

```
acct% = CVI(acctNum$)
```

Assigns the integer value contained in the string variable *acctNum$* to the variable *acct%*.

Description

Many versions of BASIC do not let you store numeric values in random-access files; you must convert numbers to strings before storing them and then convert them back to numbers when you read the file. (QuickBASIC 4.0 introduced the TYPE...END TYPE statement, which enables you to store numeric values.) The CVI function converts a 2-byte string to its integer value.

The string that CVI converts must be contained in a string variable or expression that was created by the MKI$ function, as in the following example:

```
aString$ = MKI$(256)
```

Comments

Because the CVI and MKI$ functions operate on integer values and not floating-point values, the /MBF command-line option has no effect on them.

Example

See the "Example" section in the CVD entry.

CVL

See also: FIELD, LONG, MKL$

QB2	■ QB4.5	■ PowerBASIC
QB3	ANSI	GW-BASIC
■ QB4	■ BASIC7	■ MacQB

Purpose

The CVL function converts a 4-byte string returned by the MKL$ function to its long-integer numeric value. You use the CVL function after reading the string representation of a long-integer number in a random-access file that contains records defined by the FIELD statement.

Syntax

CVL(*string*)

string is a 4-byte string variable created by the MKL$ function.

Usage

```
serial& =CVL(serialNum$)
```

Assigns the long-integer value contained in the string variable *serialNum$* to the variable *serial&*.

Description

Many versions of BASIC do not let you store numeric values in random-access files; you must convert numbers to strings before storing them and then convert them back to numbers when you read the file. (QuickBASIC 4.0 introduced the TYPE...END TYPE statement, which enables you to store numeric values.) The CVL function converts a 4-byte string to its long-integer value.

The string that CVL converts must be a string variable that was created by the MKL$ function, as in the following example:

```
aString$ = MKL$(16777216)
```

Comments

Because the CVL and MKL$ functions operate on integer values and not floating-point values, the /MBF command-line option has no effect on them.

Example

See the "Example" section in the CVD entry.

CVS

See also: CVSMBF, FIELD, MKS$, MKSMBF$

✲ QB2	■ QB4.5	■ PowerBASIC
■ QB3	ANSI	✲ GW-BASIC
■ QB4	■ BASIC7	■ MacQB

Purpose

The CVS function converts a 4-byte string returned by the MKS$ function to its single-precision numeric value. You use the CVS function after reading the string representation of a single-precision number in a random-access file that contains records defined by the FIELD statement.

Syntax

CVS(*string*)

string is a 4-byte string variable created by the MKS$ function.

Usage

```
past! = CVS(pastDue$)
```

Assigns the single-precision value contained in the string variable *pastDue$* to the variable *past!*.

Description

Many versions of BASIC do not let you store numeric values in random-access files; you had to convert numbers to strings before storing them and then convert them back to numbers when you read the file. (QuickBASIC 4.0 introduced the TYPE...END TYPE statement, which enables you to store numeric values.) The CVS function converts a 4-byte string to its single-precision numeric value.

The string that CVS converts must be contained in a string variable that was created by the MKS$ function, as in the following example:

```
aString$ = MKS$(100.25)
```

Comments

If you specify the command-line option /MBF, QuickBASIC assumes that the string parameter to the CVS function is a number in Microsoft Binary format. (See the CVSMBF entry for details.) Otherwise, QuickBASIC assumes that the string parameter in the CVS function contains a single-precision number in IEEE format.

Compatibility

QuickBASIC 2.0, GW-BASIC, and BASICA

QuickBASIC version 2.0, GW-BASIC, and BASICA do not support the IEEE formatting of floating-point values. Because these versions of BASIC use only Microsoft Binary format, the value contained in the string parameter of the CVD function is in Microsoft Binary format.

Example

See the "Example" section in the CVD entry.

CVSMBF

See also: CVS, FIELD, MKS$, MKSMBF$, SINGLE

QB2	■ QB4.5	✲ PowerBASIC
■ QB3	ANSI	GW-BASIC
■ QB4	■ BASIC7	MacQB

Purpose

The CVSMBF function converts a 4-byte string containing a value in Microsoft Binary format to its single-precision numeric value in IEEE format. You use the CVSMBF function after reading the string representation of a single-precision number in a random-access file that contains strings in Microsoft Binary format; the file must contain records defined by the FIELD statement.

Syntax

CVSMBF(*string*)

string is a 4-byte string variable created by the MKSMBF$ function or by the MKS$ function in a version of BASIC that supports only the Microsoft Binary format.

Usage

```
past! = CVSMBF(pastDue$)
```

Assigns the single-precision value contained in the string variable *pastDue$* to the variable *past!*.

Description

Many versions of BASIC do not let you store numeric values in random-access files; you must convert numbers to strings before storing them and then convert them back to numbers when you read the file. (QuickBASIC 4.0 introduced the TYPE...END TYPE statement, which enables you to store numeric values.) The CVSMBF function converts a 4-byte string to its single-precision numeric value in IEEE format.

The string that CVSMBF converts must be contained in a string variable that was created either by the MKS$ function in a version of BASIC that supports only the Microsoft Binary format or by the MKSMBF$ function, as in the following example:

```
aString$ = MKSMBF$(100.25)
```

Comments

QuickBASIC assumes that the string parameter in the CVSMBF function is a number in Microsoft Binary format.

Compatibility

PowerBASIC

PowerBASIC supports the CVMS function, which performs the same task that the CVSMBF statement does in QuickBASIC 4.5.

Example

See the "Example" section in the CVD entry.

EOF

See also: LOC, LOF, SEEK

■ QB2	■ QB4.5	■ PowerBASIC
■ QB3	■ ANSI	■ GW-BASIC
■ QB4	■ BASIC7	■ MacQB

Purpose

The EOF function returns –1 (true) if the file pointer is positioned at the end of a file; it returns 0 (false) if the file contains information past the location of the file pointer. You use EOF to decide whether to continue processing a file.

Syntax

EOF(*filenum*)

filenum is the file number associated with an open file.

Usage

```
IF EOF(1) THEN GOTO EndOfJob
```

Branches execution to the line labeled *EndOfJob* if the file pointer is at the end of the file associated with file number 1.

```
DO UNTIL EOF(1)
    LINE INPUT #1, info$
    LPRINT info$
LOOP
```

Accesses the contents of the file associated with file number 1, using the LINE INPUT # statement to retrieve the information and the LPRINT statement to print it.

Description

When processing the contents of a file, you need to know when to stop processing because the program has reached the end of the file. For sequential files, EOF returns –1 (true) when the most recent input statement reaches the end of the file. For random-access and binary files, the EOF function returns –1 (true) only if the most recent GET statement couldn't read an entire record. If GET cannot read an entire record, you specified in the GET statement a record number that was beyond the end of the file.

The QuickBASIC devices SCRN:, KYBD:, CONS:, and LPT*n*: have no logical end of file. Although there might be no data available for these devices to read, QuickBASIC cannot detect whether the flow of data has been terminated.

EOF performs differently if the specified file number is the file associated with a communications device (COM1: or COM2:) and if the COM*n*: device was opened in ASCII or binary mode. When you use COM1: or COM2: in ASCII communications mode, the EOF function returns –1 (true) only after it reads a Ctrl-Z character (ASCII code 26). EOF then continues to return –1 until the file is closed. In binary communications mode, the EOF function returns –1 when the input queue is empty; otherwise, it returns 0 (false). (See the LOC entry for details about communication input queues.)

Errors

Unlike most QuickBASIC file I/O statements, EOF does not accept a number sign (#) with the file number. If you precede the number with #, QuickBASIC returns an "Expected: expression" error message.

If you use EOF with a file number that has not been specified by an OPEN statement, QuickBASIC returns a "Bad file name or number" error message.

Example

The following program uses EOF to merge the lines of two sequential files into a third file. The resulting file contains (in order) the first line from file #1, the first line from file #2, the second line from file #1, and so on.

```
OPEN "FIRST" FOR INPUT AS #1      ' open the first source file
OPEN "SECOND" FOR INPUT AS #2     ' open the second source file
OPEN "THIRD" FOR OUTPUT AS #3     ' open the destination file

DO
    IF NOT EOF(1) THEN            ' check whether at the end of the file
        LINE INPUT #1, first$     ' get a line of text
        PRINT #3, first$          ' write the line to the destination file
    END IF

    IF NOT EOF(2) THEN            ' check whether at the end of the file
        LINE INPUT #2, second$    ' get a line of text
        PRINT #3, second$         ' write the line to the destination file
    END IF
LOOP UNTIL EOF(1) AND EOF(2)      ' repeat until both files have been read

CLOSE 1, 2, 3
```

FIELD

See also: CLOSE, GET, LSET, OPEN, PUT, RSET

■ QB2	■ QB4.5	✲ PowerBASIC
■ QB3	ANSI	✲ GW-BASIC
■ QB4	■ BASIC7	■ MacQB

Purpose

The FIELD statement defines the structure of records to be used in a random-access file. FIELD is compatible with earlier versions of BASIC, such as QuickBASIC 3.0 and GW-BASIC. If possible, however, use the TYPE...END TYPE structure, introduced in QuickBASIC 4.0, to define the structure of records in a random-access file.

Syntax

FIELD [#]*filenum*, *width* AS *var*[, ...]

filenum is the file number assigned to a file in an OPEN statement. It can be preceded by a number sign (#).

width is the size, in bytes, of *var*.

var is a field that will contain a string to be written to or read from the file.

Usage

```
OPEN "CUSTOMER.DAT" FOR RANDOM AS #1 LEN = 200
FIELD #1, 32 AS custName$, 32 AS custAddress$, 32 AS custCityStZip$
```

Opens a file named CUSTOMER.DAT and defines a record that contains three fields, each of which contains a 32-character string.

Description

Each record in a random-access file can consist of many different fields. A field is a location in a record that can be accessed by a field name. The records defined by the FIELD statement are analogous to the structures defined by the TYPE...END TYPE statement.

You can specify a single file number in multiple FIELD statements. This lets different variables share the same data in a record at the same time. Because a FIELD statement defines the record structure for a file, using more than one FIELD statement lets you define a record whose FIELD statement would be too long for a single line. Consider the following example:

```
FIELD #1, 10 AS firstName$, 20 AS lastName$
FIELD #1, 30 AS dummy$, 6 AS birthDate$
FIELD #1, 36 AS dummy$, 32 AS address$
```

When the above statements specify *dummy$* as a field, they assign to the variable the number of bytes used in the previous FIELD statements. These FIELD statements perform the same task as the following single statement:

```
FIELD #1, 10 AS firstName$, 20 AS lastName$, 6 AS birthDate$, 32 AS address$
```

When you define fields in a FIELD statement, QuickBASIC positions them within the file buffer's memory space. Because fields are not regular QuickBASIC variables, you must use them with caution. QuickBASIC frees a file's buffer space when you close the file, so fields defined in FIELD statements become undefined after the file is closed. Also, fields defined in FIELD statements cannot be used in the INPUT, LINE INPUT, or variable-assignment (*field* = *value*) statements because these statements relocate the field's pointer into normal string space, so that the field becomes a regular variable. You can, however, safely reference variables defined in FIELD statements in an arithmetic or logical expression.

Comments

The FIELD statement can define only fields that are variable-length strings; to use numeric variables, you must perform extra steps to convert the numbers to their string equivalents and then back to numbers again. The functions MKD$, MKDMBF$, MKI$, MKL$, MKS$, and MKSMBF$ convert numbers to strings, and the functions CVD, CVDMBF, CVI, CVL, CVS, and CVSMBF convert these strings back to numbers. Using the TYPE...END TYPE statement to define a record eliminates the need to perform this complicated procedure.

Errors

The sum of sizes of the fields defined in a FIELD statement must not exceed the record length specified in the LEN clause when you opened the file. If it does, QuickBASIC returns a "Field overflow" error message.

Compatibility

PowerBASIC

PowerBASIC supports the QuickBASIC syntax for the FIELD statement as well as the following syntax:

FIELD [#]*filenum*, FROM *start* TO *stop* AS *var* [, ...]

filenum is the file number assigned to the file to be used.

start and *stop* specify the position of the field *var* in the file buffer.

PowerBASIC also lets you specify the record structure for a random-access file by using the MAP statement. You can use only flex strings and flex string arrays as the fields of a record defined by MAP. The flex string is a data type, unique to PowerBASIC, that is similar to an array of variable-length strings. You can not only change the length of a flex string at runtime; you can also map smaller flex strings onto a larger one to create a data structure.

GW-BASIC and BASICA

GW-BASIC and BASICA handle file buffers differently from the way QuickBASIC does. After you close a file, GW-BASIC and BASICA retain the values of the fields defined in FIELD statements.

Example

The following program uses two random-access files that include records defined by FIELD statements. It copies data from an old file into a new file that uses a different record structure.

```
OPEN "PATIENTS.OLD" FOR RANDOM AS #1 LEN = 128
FIELD #1, 25 AS oldPatientName$, 25 AS oldInsuredsName$

OPEN "PATIENTS.NEW" FOR RANDOM AS #2 LEN = 256
FIELD #2, 32 AS newPatientName$, 32 AS newInsuredsName$

IF LOF(1) > 0 THEN
    FOR recNum% = 1 TO LOF(1) \ 128
        GET #1, recNum%
        LSET newPatientName$ = oldPatientName$    ' assign information from
        LSET newInsuredsName$ = oldInsuredsName$  ' the old file to the new one
        PUT #2, recNum%
    NEXT

    PRINT "Conversion complete."
ELSE
    PRINT "You have no records in PATIENTS.OLD to convert."
END IF

CLOSE
```

FILEATTR

See also: OPEN

QB2	■ QB4.5	■ PowerBASIC
QB3	ANSI	GW-BASIC
■ QB4	■ BASIC7	MacQB

Purpose

The FILEATTR function returns either the file mode or the DOS file handle of an open file. You can use FILEATTR, for example, to determine whether a file is read only so that if it is, your program doesn't attempt to write to it.

Syntax

FILEATTR(*filenum*, *attribute*)

filenum is the file number assigned to a file in an OPEN statement.

attribute can be 1 or 2. If it is 1, FILEATTR returns information about the mode in which the file was opened; if it is 2, FILEATTR returns the file's DOS file handle.

Usage

```
OPEN "INFO.TXT" FOR INPUT AS #1
PRINT "The file mode of INFO.TXT is"; FILEATTR(1, 1)
```

Displays the number 1, which indicates that the file was opened in input mode.

```
OPEN "INFO.TXT" FOR INPUT AS #1
PRINT "The file handle of INFO.TXT is"; FILEATTR(1, 2)
```

Displays the DOS file handle under which the file INFO.TXT was opened.

Description

The file number you use to open a file in QuickBASIC is not directly related to the DOS file-accessing number—the file handle. However, some assembly-language subroutines require you to supply the file handle, and FILEATTR lets you obtain this information. FILEATTR can also provide information for programs that need the mode of the file to determine what type of I/O they can perform.

To obtain the mode in which the file was opened, use the number 1 as the second parameter to FILEATTR. For example,

```
fileMode% = FILEATTR(4, 1)
```

returns the value that indicates the mode for the file opened as file number 4. The value that FILEATTR returns will be one of those listed in Table 17-4. For example, if *fileMode%* was assigned the value 32 in the above statement, the file was originally opened as a binary file.

Returned value	File mode
1	Input
2	Output
4	Random
8	Append
32	Binary

Table 17-4.
Values returned by FILEATTR.

To obtain the DOS file handle, use the number 2 as the second parameter to FILEATTR. For example,

```
fileHandle% = FILEATTR(4, 2)
```

returns the DOS file handle for the file opened as file number 4. Although QuickBASIC does not use this file handle, some machine language subroutines might require you to specify it.

Errors

Unlike most QuickBASIC file I/O statements, FILEATTR does not accept a number sign (#) with the file number. If you precede the number with a number sign, QuickBASIC returns an "Expected: expression" error message.

If you use FILEATTR with a file number that has not been specified by an OPEN statement, QuickBASIC returns a "Bad file name or number" error message.

Example

The following program uses FILEATTR to determine a file's DOS file handle and file mode.

```
CLS
OPEN "GARFIELD.DAT" FOR APPEND AS #7

fileMode% = FILEATTR(7, 1)
fileHandle% = FILEATTR(7, 2)

PRINT "GARFIELD.DAT has DOS file handle"; fileHandle%; "and was opened as a ";

SELECT CASE fileMode%
    CASE 1
        PRINT "sequential file for input.";
    CASE 2
        PRINT "sequential file for output.";
    CASE 4
        PRINT "random-access file for input or output.";
    CASE 8
        PRINT "sequential file for appending.";
    CASE 32
         PRINT "binary file for input or output.";
END SELECT

CLOSE
```

FILES

See also: CHDIR

■ QB2	■ QB4.5	■ PowerBASIC
■ QB3	ANSI	■ GW-BASIC
■ QB4	■ BASIC7	■ MacQB

Purpose

The FILES statement displays names of files that match a given file specification. You use FILES to display all or some of the files in the current directory or in a specified directory.

Syntax

FILES [*filespec*]

filespec is a string expression that specifies the files you want to display. *filespec* can contain a drive name, pathname, and filename; the filename can include the wildcard characters, ? and *.

Usage

```
FILES
```

Displays the filenames of all files in the current directory (on the current drive).

```
FILES "*.DAT"
```

Displays the filenames of all files in the current directory that have the extension DAT.

```
FILES "C:\BIN\*.*"
```

Displays the filenames of all files in the directory BIN on drive C.

Description

The FILES statement is similar to the DOS command DIR /W. It displays in a columnar format the names of either all files in the current directory or the specified files. For example, the statement FILES "C:\QB45*.*" displays the following:

```
C:\
        .   <DIR>           ..  <DIR> DEMO01   .BAS       DEMO02   .BAS
DEMO3   .BAS       QB      .BI        QCARDS   .BAS       QCARDS   .DAT
REMLINE .BAS       SORTDEMO.BAS       TORUS    .BAS       EXAMPLES     <DIR>
QB      .EXE       QB      .INI       QB45QCK  .HLP       BC       .EXE
BRUN45  .EXE       LIB     .EXE       LINK     .EXE       BQLB45   .LIB
BRUN45  .LIB       QB      .LIB       QB       .QLB       BCOM45   .LIB
MOUSE   .COM       NOEM    .OBJ       QB       .PIF       SMALLERR.OBJ
QB45ENER.HLP       QB45ADVR.HLP       ADVR_EX      <DIR>
 102288 Bytes free
```

The file-specification parameter is an optional string expression that specifies the files you want to display. It can contain a drive name, pathname, and filename; the filename can contain the wildcard characters, ? and *. In DOS, filenames can have no more than eight characters for a name, a period, and three characters for an extension. The wildcard character ? matches any character in the same position in the filename, and the wildcard character * matches one or more characters beginning in the same position in the filename.

If you omit the drive name from the file specification, FILES uses the current drive. If you omit the pathname, FILES uses the current directory. If you omit the file specification altogether, FILES displays all files in the current directory on the current drive.

Unlike the DOS DIR /W command, the FILES statement displays a 1-line header that contains the current directory even if you specify another pathname in the FILES statement. After FILES lists all filenames that match the specification, it displays a line containing the number of free bytes that remain on the specified drive.

Comments

You can use wildcards only in the filename of the file specification. QuickBASIC doesn't recognize wildcards in the drive name or pathname.

If a listing contains more than a single screen of filenames, the FILES statement scrolls the first names off the top of the screen.

Errors

If the file specification matches no files, QuickBASIC displays a "File not found" error message. If you specify the letter of an external drive that does not contain a disk, QuickBASIC displays a "Disk not ready" error message. If you specify a disk drive that does not exist, QuickBASIC returns a "Device unavailable" error message.

Example

The following program uses the FILES statement to display a listing of the directory and drive the user specifies. It also performs error trapping so that if a user enters a file specification incorrectly the program does not end.

```
ON ERROR GOTO CheckError

DO
    PRINT "Enter a drive name, pathname, and file specification"
    PRINT "(file specification may include wildcards)"
    PRINT
    LINE INPUT fileSpec$

    IF fileSpec$ = "" THEN EXIT DO

    PRINT
    FILES fileSpec$
    PRINT
LOOP UNTIL fileSpec$ = ""
END

' perform error handling of user input
CheckError:
    numError% = ERR
    SELECT CASE numError%
        CASE 53
             PRINT "The file does not exist."
             RESUME NEXT
        CASE 64
             PRINT "The filename is in the wrong format."
             RESUME NEXT
```

(continued)

continued

```
        CASE 68
            PRINT "The device is unavailable."
            RESUME NEXT
        CASE 71
            PRINT "The drive does not have a disk in it."
            RESUME NEXT
        CASE ELSE
            ON ERROR GOTO 0      ' disable error handling for any other errors
    END SELECT
```

FREEFILE

See also: OPEN

QB2	■ QB4.5	■ PowerBASIC
QB3	ANSI	GW-BASIC
■ QB4	■ BASIC7	MacQB

Purpose

The FREEFILE function returns the lowest file number that is not associated with an open file. You use FREEFILE when you need to open a file and you don't know which file numbers are available.

Syntax

FREEFILE

Usage

```
filenum% = FREEFILE
OPEN "CONFIG.DAT" FOR RANDOM AS #filenum%
```

Opens a file and assigns the next available file number to it.

Description

You must access a QuickBASIC file by using a file number in the range 1 through 255; however, you cannot specify a file number that has already been assigned a file in an OPEN statement. FREEFILE solves this problem by returning the lowest available file number (in the range 1 through 255). Simply assign the value FREEFILE returns to a numeric variable, and use that variable in subsequent OPEN, CLOSE, and other I/O statements.

Warnings

QuickBASIC 4.5 allows no more than 15 files to be open at once. If you try to open a 16th file, QuickBASIC returns a "Path/file access" error message.

Example

The following program uses the FREEFILE function to assign file numbers to five data files.

```
OPEN "BUFF1.DAT" FOR OUTPUT AS #1

FOR i% = 1 TO 5
    fileNum% = FREEFILE
    fileName$ = "BUFF" + MID$(STR$(fileNum%), 2) + ".DAT"
    OPEN fileName$ FOR OUTPUT AS #fileNum%
    PRINT fileName$
NEXT i%
CLOSE
```

GET (File I/O)

See also: FIELD, INPUT #, LINE INPUT #, OPEN, PUT (File I/O), TYPE...END TYPE

✲ QB2	■ QB4.5	✲ PowerBASIC
✲ QB3	✲ ANSI	✲ GW-BASIC
■ QB4	■ BASIC7	✲ MacQB

Purpose

The GET statement reads information from a random-access or binary file into the fields defined by a FIELD statement or into a record variable defined by a TYPE...END TYPE statement.

Syntax

GET [#]*filenum*[, [*position*][, *variable*]]

filenum is the file number assigned to a file in an OPEN statement.

position is the number of the record (in random-access files) or byte (in binary files) at which the program begins reading data. The number is in the range 1 through 2147483647.

variable is the variable that receives the data from the file.

Usage

`GET #1, 1`

Retrieves the first record in a random-access file that contains records defined by a FIELD statement.

`GET #1, , info`

Retrieves the next record (if one exists) in a random-access file and assigns it to the record variable *info*.

```
OPEN "CONFIG.DAT" FOR BINARY AS #1
GET #1, 100, config%
```

Opens a binary file, retrieves from the 100th byte position an integer and assigns it to the variable *config%*.

Description

With sequential files, you can use the INPUT # and LINE INPUT # statements to read data from the file, a line at a time. With random-access and binary files, however, you must use the GET statement to read from the file.

When you use GET with a random-access file, you can specify the number of the record to be read. Each record consists of as many bytes as the record length that was specified in the LEN clause of the OPEN statement for that file. The first record number in a file is record number 1. If you do not specify a record number, GET reads the record that follows the record used in the most recent GET or PUT operation or that was specified in the most recent SEEK statement.

When you use GET with a binary file, you can specify the number of the byte at which reading begins. (Note that binary files are unstructured and contain no records.) The first byte in a file is byte number 1. If you do not specify a byte number, GET reads the byte that follows those used in the most recent GET or PUT operation or that was specified in the most recent SEEK statement.

When you use GET with a random-access file containing records defined by a TYPE...END TYPE statement, you can specify any variable whose size in bytes is no larger than the record length specified when the file was opened. The GET statement reads the data into this variable. For example, if the variable is a long integer, the GET statement reads 4 bytes from the file into the variable. You will most often specify a record variable whose structure matches the structure of the file's records.

You cannot use a variable in a GET statement if the records in the file were defined by a FIELD statement. QuickBASIC returns a "FIELD statement active" error message if you specify a variable. If you do not specify a variable, GET assumes that the records contained in the file were defined by a FIELD statement. After calling GET, you can access the values that were read by using the field names in an output statement or by reading the values into other variables with an INPUT # or LINE INPUT # statement.

When you use GET with a binary file, you can specify a variable of any type and length. As long as there are enough bytes in the file, GET reads as many bytes as necessary to fill the variable.

When you specify a variable-length string variable in a GET statement, GET reads only the number of characters already in the variable. For example, if you use a string variable that has 5 characters, GET reads 5 characters into the variable, overwriting the original characters.

The largest possible string or record-variable size is 32,767 bytes. Therefore, 32,767 bytes is also the largest possible size for each record in a file and for the variable that QuickBASIC accepts for the GET statement from a random-access or binary file.

Tips

If you specify a record or byte number beyond the end of the file, QuickBASIC does not return an error message as it would with other file I/O statements, such as INPUT # and LINE INPUT #. If you specify a record or byte that is beyond the end of a random-access or binary file, GET either fills the specified variable with blank spaces or sets it to 0. You must use EOF or LOF to explicitly test whether the program has reached the end of the file.

Warning

Although GET and the PUT statement allow fixed-length access from a file opened as a communications device, a communications failure causes GET to wait indefinitely for characters. Instead, use the INPUT # statement or the INPUT$ function to read data from a communications device.

Compatibility

QuickBASIC 2.0, QuickBASIC 3.0, ANSI BASIC, GW-BASIC, BASICA, and QuickBASIC for the Macintosh

QuickBASIC versions 2.0 and 3.0, ANSI BASIC, GW-BASIC, BASICA, and QuickBASIC for the Macintosh do not support the TYPE...END TYPE statement. Because of this, you cannot specify a record variable in a GET statement. In these versions of BASIC, the GET statement works only with files containing records defined by the FIELD statement.

PowerBASIC

PowerBASIC does not support the TYPE...END TYPE statement. Because of this, you cannot specify a record variable in the GET statement. In PowerBASIC, the GET statement works with random-access files containing records defined either by the FIELD statement or by the MAP statement. To read binary files in PowerBASIC, you must use the PowerBASIC GET$ statement.

Example

The following program creates a record variable that stores the color choices used in a program. This example uses PUT to store and GET to retrieve the variable from a configuration file.

```
CLS
TYPE ConfigType
    normal AS INTEGER                  ' color of box internal area
    highlight AS INTEGER               ' color of letter highlight
    inverseHighlight AS INTEGER        ' color of the inverse of letter highlight
    inverse AS INTEGER                 ' color of highlight bar
    help AS INTEGER                    ' color of help line
    cursorNormal AS INTEGER            ' cursor size when overstriking
    cursorInsert AS INTEGER            ' cursor size when inserting
END TYPE
DIM config AS ConfigType               ' define the record variable config

OPEN "CONFIG.DAT" FOR BINARY AS #1     ' open the file
    IF LOF(1) = 0 THEN                 ' set default colors if file is empty
        config.normal = 7
        config.highlight = 15
        config.inverseHighlight = 126
        config.inverse = 112
        config.help = 1
        config.cursorNormal = 7
        config.cursorInsert = 15
        PUT #1, 1, config              ' write the defaults to the file
    ELSE
        GET #1, 1, config              ' read current configuration information
    END IF
CLOSE #1

' display current configuration information
PRINT "Normal color = "; config.normal
PRINT "Highlight color = "; config.highlight
PRINT "Inverse highlight color = "; config.inverseHighlight
PRINT "Inverse color = "; config.inverse
PRINT "Help color = "; config.help
PRINT "Overstrike cursor size = "; config.cursorNormal
PRINT "Insert cursor size = "; config.cursorInsert

END
```

INPUT

See also: INKEY$, INPUT, INPUT$, LINE INPUT, LINE INPUT #

■ QB2	■ QB4.5	■ PowerBASIC
■ QB3	■ ANSI	■ GW-BASIC
■ QB4	■ BASIC7	■ MacQB

Purpose

The INPUT # statement reads data values from a sequential file or device into variables. You can use INPUT # to read either formatted data from an ASCII file or ASCII data from a device.

Syntax

INPUT #*filenum*, *var*[, *var*...]

filenum is the file number with which the file was opened for sequential input.

var is the numeric or string variable that receives the data from the file.

Usage

```
INPUT #1, title$
```

Reads a value into the string variable *title$* from the sequential file associated with file number 1.

```
INPUT #10, x%, y%, z%
```

Reads values into the integer variables *x%*, *y%*, and *z%* from the sequential file associated with file number 10.

```
FOR i% = 1 TO 5
    INPUT #5, x%(i%)
NEXT i%
```

Reads five integer values into the array *x%* from the sequential file associated with file number 5.

Description

The INPUT # statement is useful for reading numeric variables from sequential ASCII files. INPUT # ignores leading spaces, carriage returns, and linefeeds when it reads data into the specified variables. INPUT # stops reading a number if it encounters a space, carriage return, linefeed, comma, or the end of the file. INPUT # stops reading a string when it encounters quotation marks, a carriage return, a linefeed, a comma, or the end of the file.

You can specify a variable that is a simple variable, an array element, or a record-variable element. You can specify several variables in one statement by separating them with a comma.

The INPUT # statement reads data in ASCII format as if you had entered the data from the keyboard in response to an INPUT statement.

Figure 17-1 illustrates the contents of a sequential file.

1	2		8		T	h	i	s	,	t	h	a	t	EOF

Figure 17-1.
A sequential file.

After QuickBASIC executes the following INPUT # statements, in which file number 1 specifies the file shown in Figure 17-1, *x%* and *y%* contain the values 12 and 8. The variable *a$* contains the string "This", and *b$* contains "that".

```
INPUT #1, x%, y%
INPUT #1, a$
INPUT #1, b$
```

Figure 17-2 shows the position of the file pointer after each of the above statements is executed.

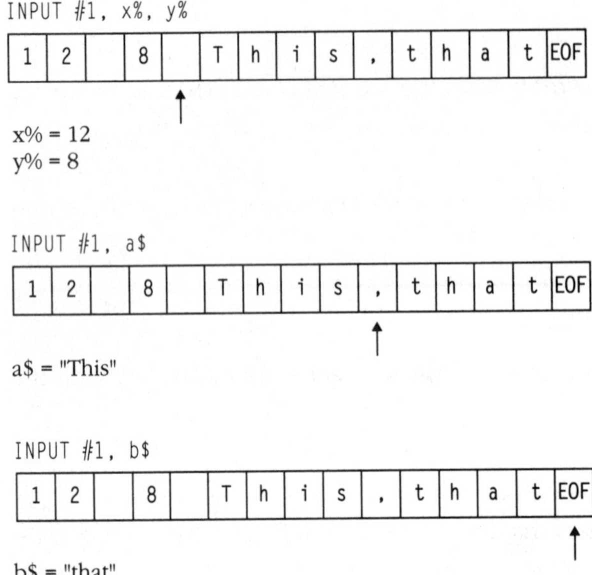

Figure 17-2.
Using INPUT # to read a sequential file.

Comments

If INPUT # reads a floating-point number (containing a decimal) from a sequential file into an integer or long-integer variable, INPUT # rounds off the floating-point number to fit the integer.

Using INPUT # to read an alphabetic character into a numeric variable does not cause an error. However, QuickBASIC sets that numeric variable to 0.

Warnings

Because INPUT # uses commas to separate data items in a file, a string cannot contain embedded commas unless the entire string is enclosed in sets of quotation marks. For example, *Goodbye, all.* is read as two strings: *Goodbye* and *all.* However, INPUT # reads *"Goodbye, all."* as one string.

Example

The following program writes to a file a line of text and the values of 2 raised to the exponents 1 through 25. It then uses the INPUT # statement to read the contents of the file.

```
CLS
OPEN "2EXP.DAT" FOR OUTPUT AS #1

WRITE #1, "2EXP.DAT contains the value of 2 raised to the powers 1 through 25."
FOR i% = 1 TO 25
    result& = 1
    FOR j% = 1 TO i%
        result& = result& * 2
    NEXT j%
    WRITE #1, result&
NEXT i%
CLOSE #1

OPEN "2EXP.DAT" FOR INPUT AS #1

INPUT #1, description$
PRINT description$

PRINT "Press any key to continue."
DO: LOOP UNTIL INKEY$ <> ""

FOR i% = 1 TO 25
    INPUT #1, value&
    PRINT value&
NEXT i%
CLOSE #1
```

INPUT$ (File I/O)

See also: INPUT, LINE INPUT

■ QB2 ■ QB4.5 ■ PowerBASIC
■ QB3 ANSI ■ GW-BASIC
■ QB4 ■ BASIC7 ■ MacQB

Purpose

The INPUT$ function reads a specified number of bytes from the keyboard, a file, or a device. You can use INPUT$ to strictly control the amount of input.

Syntax

INPUT$(*num* [, [#]*filenum*])

num is the number of characters to be read. (The largest string that INPUT$ can read is 32,767 bytes.)

filenum is the file number you can associate with the file from which characters will be read.

Usage

```
PRINT "Press any key to continue: "; INPUT$(1);
```

Prompts the user to press a key and then uses INPUT$ to read the keystroke.

```
DO UNTIL EOF(1)
    PRINT INPUT$ (1, #1)
LOOP
```

Displays the contents of the file opened for sequential input as file number 1, using the INPUT$ function to read the file character by character.

Description

The INPUT$ statement is useful when a program needs to retrieve a specified number of characters rather than process strings (as INPUT # and LINE INPUT # do). Note, however, that INPUT$ isn't a reasonable choice if you do not know the number of characters you need to read.

If you specify a file number, INPUT$ retrieves characters from the associated file or device. If you omit a file number, INPUT$ reads characters from the keyboard. If the file was opened as a random-access file, the number of characters that INPUT$ reads can be no more than the number of characters in each record that is specified in the OPEN statement for that file (in the LEN clause). If the file was opened as a binary or sequential file, INPUT$ can read no more than 32,767 characters.

INPUT$ does not display any characters it reads from the keyboard, file, or device. Your program can, of course, use the PRINT statement to echo the characters. The program in the "Example" section, however, demonstrates the advantages of not echoing characters. Note that INPUT$ reads all characters except the Ctrl-Break combination, which interrupts the program.

Comments

INPUT$ reads data from the DOS standard input device if no file number is specified. Although this is usually the keyboard, you can change it by using the DOS redirection operator <. This lets your compiled program use input from a file or a device when the input must otherwise be entered by the user.

Errors

If you specify the file number of an unopened file, QuickBASIC returns a "Bad file name or number" error message. Note that the number of characters must be available from the specified file. If the file doesn't contain enough characters, QuickBASIC returns an "Input past end of file" error message. If the number of characters specified for a random-access file is greater than the record length, QuickBASIC returns a "Field overflow" error message. If the number of characters specified for a sequential or binary file is greater than 32767, QuickBASIC returns an "Overflow" error message.

Tips

The INPUT$ function is the preferred method for communication device I/O because it lets you specify the number of characters to retrieve. When used with the LOC function, INPUT$ can always keep up with incoming communications.

Warnings

If you omit a file number, the number of characters specified must be entered at the keyboard—Enter does not indicate the end of input, as it does with the INPUT and LINE INPUT statements.

Example

The following program uses INPUT$ to retrieve an 8-character password from a file and then to accept an 8-character password from the keyboard. If the two passwords do not match, the program displays the message "Access denied."

```
OPEN "PASSWORD.DAT" FOR INPUT AS #1

password$ = INPUT$(8, #1)      ' read a password from the file

PRINT "Enter password:";
userPassword$ = INPUT$(8)      ' read a password from the keyboard

IF password$ = userPassword$ THEN
    PRINT "Access granted."
ELSE
    PRINT "Access denied."
    STOP
END IF
CLOSE
```

LINE INPUT

See also: INPUT, INPUT #, INPUT$, LINE INPUT

■ QB2	■ QB4.5	■ PowerBASIC
■ QB3	ANSI	✲ GW-BASIC
■ QB4	■ BASIC7	✲ MacQB

Purpose

The LINE INPUT # statement reads data from a sequential file or device into a string variable. Unlike the INPUT # statement, which reads strings separated by delimiters, LINE INPUT # reads the contents of a sequential file line by line. For example, you can use LINE INPUT # to read instructions from an ASCII file.

Syntax

LINE INPUT #*filenum*, *var*

filenum is the file number with which the file was opened for sequential input.

var is the string variable that receives the data read from the file.

Usage

```
LINE INPUT # 1, title$
```

Reads a line of the file associated with file number 1 and assigns it to the string variable *title$*.

Description

Usually, you use the LINE INPUT # statement to read a line of text from a sequential file or a device. LINE INPUT # reads all the characters on a line. LINE INPUT # cannot read more than 32767 characters because that is the maximum number of characters that can be assigned to a string variable. The INPUT # statement ignores leading spaces and stops reading if it encounters a comma or a carriage-return/linefeed pair. However, LINE INPUT # doesn't ignore leading spaces and reads all characters—including commas—to the carriage return/linefeed pair, which indicates the end of the line.

The LINE INPUT # statement is often used for reading a text file from a word processor or database. If you can read the characters in a file when you use the DOS TYPE command, you can use the LINE INPUT # statement to read the file.

Figure 17-3 illustrates the contents of a sequential file. The initials CR and LF in the figure represent the carriage return and linefeed characters.

1	2		8		CR	LF	T	h	i	s	,	t	h	a	t	EOF

Figure 17-3.
A sequential file.

After executing the following statements, in which file number 1 specifies the file shown in Figure 17-3, the variable *x$* contains the string "12 8" and the variable *a$* contains the string "This,that".

```
LINE INPUT #1, x$
LINE INPUT #1, a$
```

Figure 17-4 shows the position of the file pointer after each of the above statements is executed.

```
LINE INPUT #1, x$
```

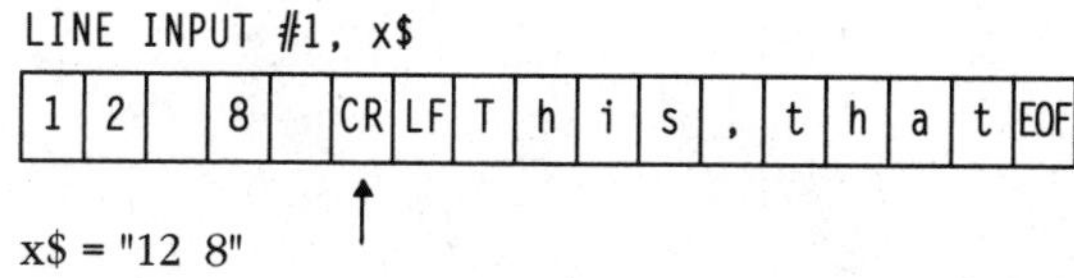

x$ = "12 8"

```
LINE INPUT #1, a$
```

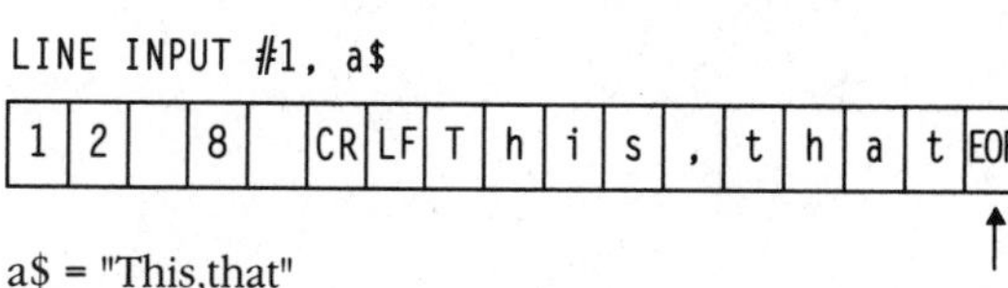

a$ = "This,that"

Figure 17-4.
Using LINE INPUT # to read a sequential file.

Comments

The only way you can delimit text in a file that will be read by LINE INPUT # is to place data on separate lines. LINE INPUT # reads commas in the middle of strings as characters, not delimiters.

Tips

Because string variables can contain any characters, including numeric digits, reading a number from a file doesn't cause an error; LINE INPUT # simply reads the numeric digits into the string variable. You can use VAL to convert the digits into numeric variables. (See the VAL entry in Chapter 5, "Strings," for details.)

Compatibility

GW-BASIC and BASICA

Because strings in GW-BASIC and BASICA are limited to 255 characters, LINE INPUT # can read only 255 characters into a string.

QuickBASIC for the Macintosh

In QuickBASIC for the Macintosh, LINE INPUT # can read only 1023 characters into a string.

Example

The following program shows some of the differences between using INPUT # and LINE INPUT # with text. Note that LINE INPUT # returns the file line by line, exactly as the file appears when displayed with the TYPE command in DOS.

```
OPEN "TEXT.DAT" FOR INPUT AS #1

PRINT "INPUT # sample:"
PRINT
number = 0
DO
    number = number + 1
    INPUT #1, text$
    PRINT number; text$
LOOP UNTIL EOF(1)

PRINT
PRINT "LINE INPUT # sample:"
PRINT

number = 0
SEEK #1, 1        ' move to beginning of the file
DO
    number = number + 1
    LINE INPUT #1, text$
    PRINT number; text$
LOOP UNTIL EOF(1)

CLOSE
```

Suppose, for example, that TEXT.DAT contains the following data:

```
FIRST NAME, LAST NAME, ADDRESS
"FIRST NAME, LAST NAME, ADDRESS"
100.00
```

Then the above program displays the following output:

```
INPUT # sample:

 1 FIRST NAME
 2 LAST NAME
 3 ADDRESS
 4 FIRST NAME, LAST NAME, ADDRESS
 5 100.00

LINE INPUT # sample:

 1 FIRST NAME, LAST NAME, ADDRESS
 2 "FIRST NAME, LAST NAME, ADDRESS"
 3 100.00
```

LOC

See also: GET (File I/O), OPEN, PUT (File I/O)

■ QB2	■ QB4.5	■ PowerBASIC
■ QB3	ANSI	✲ GW-BASIC
■ QB4	■ BASIC7	✲ MacQB

Purpose

For every open file, QuickBASIC maintains a pointer that shows where the next read or write operation will take place. The LOC function returns the current position of this pointer in an open file. You can use LOC to determine whether you are at the proper location in the file before executing a PUT or GET statement.

Syntax

LOC(*filenum*)

filenum is the file number with which the file was opened.

Usage

```
PRINT "Current position in file 1 is"; LOC(1)
```

Displays the location in the file that will be accessed by the next file I/O statement.

Description

The GET and PUT statements for file I/O (which differ from the GET and PUT statements for graphics) let you input from or output to the current file position. You can use the LOC function to check the current position so that you don't retrieve the wrong record or write over another record.

The values that LOC returns depend on the mode in which the file was opened and whether the file is a communications device. If the file was opened for random access, LOC returns the number of the record last read from or written to the file.

If the file was opened for sequential input or output access, LOC returns the current byte position divided by 128 and rounded to an integer. Because a QuickBASIC buffer is 128 bytes long, this operation returns the current position in the buffer.

If the file was opened for binary access, LOC returns the number of the byte most recently read from or written to the file. For example, if your program reads from a binary file a string variable 100 bytes long named *title$*, LOC returns 100. The next byte position is 101.

If the file is a communications device (COM1: or COM2:) opened in binary mode, LOC returns the number of characters remaining in that device's input buffer. If the file is a communications device opened in any other mode, LOC returns the number of characters remaining in that device's input buffer up to but not including the Ctrl-Z end-of-file character. (This information is important because if you try to input characters beyond the end-of-file marker, QuickBASIC returns an "Input past end of file" error message.)

Comments

Before you read from or write to a file, the LOC function returns 0 because no I/O has taken place. Avoid using the LOC function until you have read or written data.

The maximum value that LOC can return is 2147483647.

Warnings

The LOC function returns 0 when used with the QuickBASIC SCRN:, KYBD:, CONS:, or LPT*n*: device. The LOC function returns meaningful values only when used with files and a COM*n*: device.

Compatibility

GW-BASIC and BASICA

In GW-BASIC and BASICA, the LOC function returns the value of the record or byte position modulo 32767, because GW-BASIC and BASICA don't support integers larger than 32767.

QuickBASIC for the Macintosh

QuickBASIC for the Macintosh supports the use of the LOC function with the KYBD: device; QuickBASIC used in DOS does not. In QuickBASIC for the Macintosh, the LOC function returns 1 if any characters are waiting to be read in the keyboard buffer, and it returns 0 if none are waiting. Also, in QuickBASIC for the Macintosh, the LOC function returns 1 before you perform any sequential I/O; QuickBASIC in DOS returns 0.

Example

The following program uses the LOC function to determine the number of bytes used in each output operation to a binary file.

```
CLS

OPEN "EX-LOC.DAT" FOR BINARY AS #1

FOR size% = 1 TO 23
    currentPosition& = LOC(1) + 1            ' find current position in the file

    stringVariable$ = STRING$(size%, "*")    ' assign asterisks to the variable
    PUT #1, , stringVariable$                ' write the variable to the file

    newPosition& = LOC(1)                    ' find the next position in the file
    PRINT "Adding asterisks to the file from position ";
    PRINT USING "### to position ###."; currentPosition&; newPosition&
NEXT

CLOSE
```

LOCK

See also: OPEN, UNLOCK

■ QB2	■ QB4.5	PowerBASIC
■ QB3	ANSI	✲ GW-BASIC
■ QB4	■ BASIC7	MacQB

Purpose

The LOCK statement prevents other processes on a network from accessing all or part of a shared file. A shared file is one that different processes or users on a multitasking, multiuser, or networking system can access. You can use the LOCK statement to prevent access to a record after your program alters that record.

Syntax

LOCK [#]*filenum*[, {*record* ¦ [*start*] TO *end*}]

filenum is the file number of an open file.

record is the number of the record or byte to be locked.

start and *end* are integers that specify a range of records or bytes to be locked.

Usage

```
LOCK #1
```

Locks the entire file opened as file number 1. No other process can access this file until the program unlocks the file with the UNLOCK statement.

```
OPEN "VENDORS.DAT" FOR RANDOM AS #4
LOCK #4, 10
```

Locks record 10 of the random-access file opened as file number 4.

```
OPEN "TRANS.DAT" FOR BINARY AS #2
LOCK #2, TO 512
```

Locks bytes 1 through 512 of the binary file opened as file number 2.

Description

In a networked environment in which several users or processes share the same files, you must prevent different processes from updating the same record simultaneously. If you don't, only one process's update take effect; changes made by other processes are overwritten. The LOCK statement prevents this by allowing one process to have exclusive rights to a file or a record in a file and denying other processes access to that record or file while the process is using it. A LOCK statement must always be followed by a matching UNLOCK statement. (See the UNLOCK entry for details.)

In a binary file, you specify the bytes to be locked. The first byte in the file is byte number 1. In a file opened for random access, you specify the records. The first record in the file is record number 1.

If you include only one record or byte number, only that record or byte is locked for exclusive use by your program. If you include the TO keyword, the records or bytes in the range specified by the numbers surrounding TO are locked for exclusive use by your program. If you omit a number for the beginning of the range, LOCK uses record or byte 1 as the default starting position. If you don't specify any records or bytes, the LOCK statement locks the entire file for exclusive use by your program.

You can lock individual records or bytes only in random-access and binary files. With sequential files, you can lock only the entire file.

LOCK functions at runtime only if the program is running under DOS version 3.1 or later with the SHARE.EXE program activated. SHARE.EXE is a program supplied with DOS that supports file sharing and locking for Microsoft networks. If you use LOCK with an earlier version of DOS, QuickBASIC returns an "Advanced feature unavailable" error message.

Errors

Locked portions of files can be accessed only by the program that performed the LOCK statement. If another QuickBASIC program tries to read from or write to the locked portion of that file, QuickBASIC returns a "Permission denied" error message.

Tips

If you must use QuickBASIC with networks other than the IBM-PC Network or MS-Network, consider using a third-party file manager that supports other popular networks. See Appendix C, "Third-Party Add-Ons," for information about third-party file manager products.

Warnings

Microsoft supports QuickBASIC only on IBM-PC Network, MS-Network, and compatible systems. Although limited success has been reported using other networks, such as Novell and 3Com, problems can occur.

If you lock a file and then either lose power or reboot your computer before you execute the matching UNLOCK statement, data in the locked file might be lost. To minimize the danger of losing data, use LOCK to lock records only as long as necessary.

Compatibility

GW-BASIC and BASICA

GW-BASIC supports the LOCK and UNLOCK statements. BASICA does not.

Example

The following example uses the LOC and LOCK statements to protect portions of a binary file while the program updates them.

```
CLS

OPEN "EX-LOCK.DAT" FOR BINARY AS #1

FOR size% = 1 TO 23
    currentPosition& = LOC(1) + 1             ' find current position in file
    newPosition& = currentPosition& + size%   ' find next position in file

    LOCK #1, currentPosition& TO newPosition&     ' lock a portion of the file
    stringVariable$ = STRING$(size%, "*")
    PUT #1, , stringVariable$                     ' output the variable
    UNLOCK #1, currentPosition& TO newPosition&   ' unlock the portion

    PRINT "Adding asterisks to the file from position ";
    PRINT USING "##### to position #####."; currentPosition&; newPosition&
NEXT

CLOSE
```

LOF

See also: LOC, OPEN

✲ QB2	■ QB4.5	✲ PowerBASIC
✲ QB3	ANSI	✲ GW-BASIC
■ QB4	■ BASIC7	✲ MacQB

Purpose

The LOF function returns the number of bytes in an open file. You use the LOF function when you need to know the length of a file before you begin processing it.

Syntax

LOF(*filenum*)

filenum is the file number with which the file was opened.

Usage

```
PRINT "The file is"; LOF(1); "bytes long."
```

Displays a message that gives the length of the file opened as file number 1.

Description

Use LOF to determine the current size of an open file. LOF returns the size, in bytes, of a file that has been opened in any mode. The maximum value that LOF can return is 2147483647.

If the open file is a communication device (COM1: or COM2:), LOF returns the number of characters available in that device's output buffer. You cannot use LOF with a number associated with the QuickBASIC SCRN:, KYBD:, CONS:, LPT1:, or LPT2: device.

Compatibility

QuickBASIC 2.0, QuickBASIC 3.0, PowerBASIC, GW-BASIC, BASICA, and QuickBASIC for the Macintosh

In these versions of BASIC, when you use LOF with a communications device (COM*n*:), the LOF function returns the number of characters that are available in that device's input buffer (not the output buffer, as in QuickBASIC versions 4.0 and 4.5).

Example

The following program uses the LOF function to monitor the size of a file.

```
CLS

OPEN "EX-LOF.DAT" FOR OUTPUT AS #1

FOR size% = 1 TO 23
    PRINT "Current file size is"; LOF(1); "bytes."

    stringVariable$ = STRING$(size%, "*")  ' assign asterisks to the variable
    PRINT #1, stringVariable$              ' write the variable to the file
NEXT

CLOSE #1
```

LSET

See also: FIELD, MKD$, MKDMBF$, MKI$, MKL$, MKS$, MKSMBF$, PUT (File I/O), RSET

✲ QB2	■ QB4.5	✲ PowerBASIC
✲ QB3	ANSI	✲ GW-BASIC
■ QB4	■ BASIC7	✲ MacQB

Purpose

The LSET statement puts the value of an expression or a variable into a specified field of a random-access file's buffer. LSET also left-justifies this expression or variable. LSET can also be used to left-justify any string variable or to assign one record variable to another.

Syntax

LSET *var* = *expr*

var and *expr* must both be strings if LSET is being used for left-justification or for placing a value into a field. They must both be record variables if LSET is being used to assign one record variable to another.

Usage

```
LSET address$ = "123 PARK ST."
```

Left-justifies the string constant "123 PARK ST." and places it into the *address$* field if *address$* is the name of a field defined by a FIELD statement. If *address$* is a string variable, LSET only left-justifies it within the current length of *address$*.

```
LSET amtDue$ = MKD$(total#)
```

Places the string representation of the contents of *total#* into *amtDue$*, which can be either the name of a field defined by a FIELD statement or a string variable.

Description

The FIELD statement allocates a special storage buffer when it defines the record for a random-access file. Because of this special allocation, you cannot use the equal sign (=) or the LET statement to assign values to the fields defined by the FIELD statement. Instead, you must use the LSET or RSET statement to make the assignment. Note that you can also use LSET with string variables and record variables.

Using LSET with fields

When you specify a field name as the first parameter in an LSET statement, the LSET statement copies the value of the second parameter (which must be a string) into the location in a random-access buffer allocated for the specified field.

If the length of the field is greater than the length of the string value, LSET left-justifies the value in the buffer. That is, LSET adds spaces to the right end of the string until the string is the same length as the field.

If the length of the field is less than the length of the string value, LSET copies only enough characters to fill the field and ignores the remaining characters.

Figure 17-5 shows how the LSET statement places a string in a field.

```
FIELD 1, 20 AS patientName$
LSET patientName$ = "Robert Anderson II"
```

R	o	b	e	r	t		A	n	d	e	r	s	o	n		I	I		

```
LSET patientName$ = "Robert Lloyd Anderson II"
```

R	o	b	e	r	t		L	l	o	y	d		A	n	d	e	r	s	o

Figure 17-5.
The LSET statement with fields.

Using LSET with string variables

When the first parameter to LSET is a string variable (not a field name), LSET performs a different task. Because the length of the variable is not set by a FIELD statement, LSET uses the current length of the string variable to calculate the justification it will perform.

If the current length of the string variable is greater than the length of the value specified in the second parameter, LSET left-justifies the value. That is, LSET adds spaces to the right end of the string value until the string is the same length as the string variable.

If the current length of the string variable is less than the length of the value specified in the second parameter, LSET copies only enough characters to fill the string variable and ignores the remaining characters.

You can determine the current length of a string variable by using the LEN function. (See the LEN entry in Chapter 5, "Strings," for details.)

Figure 17-6 shows how the LSET statement works with string variables.

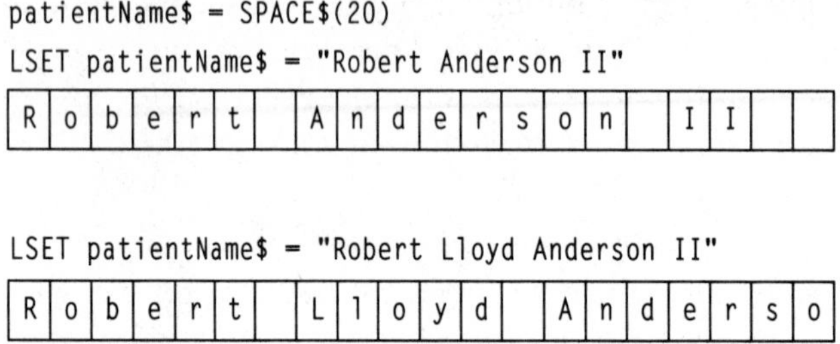

Figure 17-6.
The LSET statement with string variables.

Using LSET with record variables

The usual means of assignment (the equal sign or LET) can't copy record variables defined by different TYPE...END TYPE statements. To copy different record variables, you must use the LSET statement. However, the LSET statement merely copies from one record variable to another—it doesn't left-justify the data. (See the TYPE...END TYPE entry in Chapter 1, "Types and Variables," for details.)

When you use LSET in this way, the two parameters to LSET must both be record variables. The LSET statement copies as many bytes as it can from the record variable specified in the second parameter into the record variable specified in the first parameter. For example, if the length of the second record variable is 40 bytes and the length of the first is 30 bytes, LSET copies only 30 bytes from the second to the first. Because the LSET statement copies individual bytes to a record variable, the values of the elements of the record variable are not accurately copied unless the elements of the record variable to which bytes are being copied have the same type and location within that record variable as they have in the second record variable.

The following program segment demonstrates the use of LSET with record variables:

```
TYPE Type1
    x AS INTEGER
    y AS LONG
    z AS DOUBLE
END TYPE

TYPE Type2
    x AS INTEGER
    y AS LONG
END TYPE

DIM a1 AS Type1, a2 AS Type2

a1.x = 100
a1.y = 10000
a1.z = 100.1

a2.x = 200
a2.y = 200000

LSET a1 = a2
PRINT a1.x, a1.y, a1.z
```

After the LSET statement is executed, *a1.x* equals 200, *a1.y* equals 200000, and *a1.z* equals 100.1. Because the record variable *a2* has fewer bytes than the record variable *a1*, the value of *a1.z* does not change.

Comments

Remember that you must convert numeric values to strings before you place them in a field defined by a FIELD statement. (See the MKD$, MKDMBF$, MKI$, MKL$, MKS$, and MKSMBF$ entries for details.)

Tips

Using the FIELD and LSET statements to access random-access files can be a long and complicated procedure. If you are using QuickBASIC version 4.0 or later, use record variables as an easier alternative for performing random-access file I/O.

Compatibility

QuickBASIC 2.0, QuickBASIC 3.0, PowerBASIC, GW-BASIC, BASICA, and QuickBASIC for the Macintosh

Because these versions of BASIC don't include the TYPE...END TYPE statement, they don't support the use of LSET with record variables.

Example

See the CVD entry for a program that uses the LSET statement to place strings into fields that will be stored in a random-access file.

LTRIM$

See also: RTRIM$

QB2	■ QB4.5	✲ PowerBASIC
QB3	■ ANSI	GW-BASIC
■ QB4	■ BASIC7	MacQB

Purpose

The LTRIM$ function returns a copy of a string expression without leading spaces (spaces on the left). You use the LTRIM$ function to format data in which leading spaces would either cause misaligned output or be misinterpreted as literal characters.

Syntax

LTRIM$(*string*)

string is any string expression.

Usage

```
PRINT #1, LTRIM$(description$)
```

Writes the variable *description$* without leading spaces to the file associated with file number 1.

Description

Because some names (such as those of devices, directories, and filenames) must be used literally, QuickBASIC provides the LTRIM$ function to let you delete extra spaces that might have been inserted by the user or the program. The LTRIM$ function accepts any string expression and returns the same string without leading spaces. The string expression can also contain the concatenation operator and string functions such as MID$, LEFT$, or RIGHT$.

Comments

The LTRIM$ function removes only spaces from the beginning of a string; it leaves other white-space characters, such as tab or null characters. To manually remove all white-space characters, you can use the following function:

```
FUNCTION NewLTrim$ (stringVar$)   ' check each character
    FOR i% = 1 TO LEN(stringVar$) ' start at the beginning
        SELECT CASE ASC(MID$(stringVar$, i%, 1))
            CASE 0, 9, 32         ' if a null, tab, or space character, do nothing
            CASE ELSE             ' found first character
                NewLTrim$ = MID$(stringVar$, i%)
                EXIT FUNCTION
        END SELECT
    NEXT i%
    NewLTrim$ = ""                ' string is all white space
END FUNCTION
```

Compatibility

PowerBASIC

PowerBASIC supports the use of a second parameter to the LTRIM$ function. This parameter specifies a string that LTRIM$ removes from the beginning of the string. LTRIM$ removes occurrences of this match string until it encounters a character that does not match. If you use the keyword ANY before the match string in the call to LTRIM$, the function removes any occurrences of the characters in the match string from the beginning of the string.

Example

The following program uses the LTRIM$ and RTRIM$ functions to delete the leading and trailing spaces from lines in a text file.

```
CLS
PRINT "This program deletes leading and trailing spaces from each line of "
PRINT "a file and writes the resulting lines to another file."
PRINT

LINE INPUT "Enter name of input file:  "; filename$
LINE INPUT "Enter name of output file: "; output$

OPEN filename$ FOR INPUT AS #1
OPEN output$ FOR OUTPUT AS #2

DO UNTIL EOF(1)
    LINE INPUT #1, inputLine$
    PRINT #2, LTRIM$(RTRIM$(inputLine$))
LOOP

CLOSE
```

MKD$

See also: CVD, CVDMBF, DOUBLE, FIELD, MKDMBF$

✲ QB2	■ QB4.5	■ PowerBASIC
■ QB3	ANSI	✲ GW-BASIC
■ QB4	■ BASIC7	■ MacQB

Purpose

The MKD$ function converts a double-precision number to an 8-byte string. The MKD$ function complements the CVD function. You use the MKD$ function to convert a double-precision number to a string that will be assigned to a field defined by the FIELD statement.

Syntax

MKD$(*number*)

number is any numeric expression in the range –1.7976931D+308 through 1.7976931D+308.

Usage

```
LSET amountDue$ = MKD$(265.98)
```

Places the string representing the double-precision value 265.98 into the field *amountDue$*.

Description

Many versions of BASIC do not let you store numeric values in random-access files; you must convert numbers to strings before storing them and then convert them back to numbers when you read the file. (QuickBASIC 4.0 introduced the TYPE...END TYPE statement, which enables you to store numeric values.) The MKD$ function converts a double-precision value to an 8-byte string. Note that the specified number can be any numeric expression; MKD$ converts the number to double precision.

The MKD$ function returns a value that you must either assign to a variable or use in an expression. Usually, you use MKD$ in an LSET statement, as in the following example:

```
LSET cost$ = MKD$(1006.99)
```

Comments

If you specify the command-line switch /MBF, QuickBASIC assumes that the value that MKD$ converts is a number in Microsoft Binary format. (See the MKDMBF$ entry for details.) Otherwise, the MKD$ function converts a number in IEEE format.

Compatibility

QuickBASIC 2.0, GW-BASIC, and BASICA

QuickBASIC version 2.0, GW-BASIC, and BASICA do not support the IEEE formatting of floating-point values. Because these versions of BASIC use only Microsoft Binary format, the value converted by the MKD$ function is in Microsoft Binary format.

Example

See the "Example" section in the CVD entry.

MKDMBF$

See also: CVD, CVDMBF, DOUBLE, FIELD, MKD$

QB2	■ QB4.5	✲ PowerBASIC
■ QB3	ANSI	GW-BASIC
■ QB4	■ BASIC7	MacQB

Purpose

The MKDMBF$ function converts a double-precision number in IEEE format to an 8-byte string containing the number in Microsoft Binary format. The MKDMBF$ function complements the CVDMBF function. You use the MKDMBF$ function to convert a double-precision number to a string that will be assigned to a field defined by a FIELD statement.

Syntax

MKDMBF$(*number*)

number is any numeric expression in the range –1.7976931D+308 through 1.7976931D+308.

Usage

```
LSET amountDue$ = MKDMBF$(265.98)
```

Places the string representing the double-precision value 265.98 into the field *amountDue$*.

Description

Many versions of BASIC do not let you store numeric values in random-access files; you must convert numbers to strings before storing them and then convert them back to numbers when you read the file. (QuickBASIC 4.0 introduced the TYPE...END TYPE statement, which enables you to store numeric values.) The MKDMBF$ function converts a double-precision value to an 8-byte string. Note that the specified number can be any numeric expression; MKDMBF$ converts the number to double precision.

The MKDMBF$ function returns a value that you must either assign to a variable or use in an expression. Usually, you use MKDMBF$ in an LSET statement, as in the following example:

```
LSET cost$ = MKDMBF$(1006.99)
```

Compatibility

PowerBASIC

PowerBASIC supports the MKMD$ function, which performs the same task that the MKDMBF$ statement does in QuickBASIC 4.5.

Example

See the "Example" section in the CVD entry.

MKI$

See also: CVI, FIELD, INTEGER

■ QB2	■ QB4.5	■ PowerBASIC
■ QB3	ANSI	■ GW-BASIC
■ QB4	■ BASIC7	■ MacQB

Purpose

The MKI$ function converts an integer number to a 2-byte string. The MKI$ function complements the CVI function. Use the MKI$ function to convert an integer number to a string that will be assigned to a field defined by the FIELD statement.

Syntax

MKI$(*number*)

number is any numeric expression in the range –32768 through 32767.

Usage

```
LSET age$ = MKI$(19)
```

Places the string representing the integer value 19 into the field *age$*.

Description

Many versions of BASIC do not let you store numeric values in random-access files; you must convert numbers to strings before storing them and then convert them back to numbers when you read the file. (QuickBASIC 4.0 introduced the TYPE...END TYPE statement, which enables you to store numeric values.) The MKI$ function converts an integer value to a 2-byte string. Note that the specified number can be any numeric expression in the range for integers (–32768 to 32767). MKI$ converts the number to an integer.

The MKI$ function returns a value that you must either assign to a variable or use in an expression. Usually, you use MKI$ in an LSET$ statement, as in the following example:

```
LSET squareFeet$ = MKI$(256)
```

Comments

Because the CVI and MKI$ functions operate on integer values and not floating-point values, the /MBF command-line option has no effect on them.

Example

See the "Example" section in the CVD entry.

MKL$

See also: CVL, FIELD, LONG

QB2	■ QB4.5	PowerBASIC
QB3	ANSI	GW-BASIC
■ QB4	■ BASIC7	■ MacQB

Purpose

The MKL$ function converts a long-integer number to a 4-byte string. The MKL$ function complements the CVL function. You use the MKL$ function to convert a long integer to a string that will be assigned to a field defined by the FIELD statement.

Syntax

MKL$(*number*)

number is any numeric expression in the range –2147483648 through 2147483647.

Usage

```
LSET population$ = MKL$(225102963)
```

Places the string representing the long-integer value 225102963 into the variable *population$*.

Description

Many versions of BASIC do not let you store numeric values in random-access files; you must convert numbers to strings before storing them and then convert them back to numbers when you read the file. (QuickBASIC 4.0 introduced the TYPE...END TYPE statement, which enables you to store numeric values.) The MKL$ function converts a long-integer value to a 4-byte string. Note that the specified number can be any numeric expression in the range for long integers (–2147483648 through 2147483647) MKL$ converts the number to a long integer.

The MKL$ function returns a value that you must either assign to a variable or use in an expression. Usually, you use MKL$ in an LSET statement, as in the following example:

```
LSET mem$ = MKL$(131072)
```

Comments

Because the CVL and MKL$ functions operate on integer values and not floating-point values, the /MBF command-line option has no effect on them.

Example

See the "Example" section in the CVD entry.

MKS$

See also: CVS, CVSMBF, FIELD, MKSMBF$, SINGLE

✲ QB2	■ QB4.5	■ PowerBASIC
■ QB3	ANSI	✲ GW-BASIC
■ QB4	■ BASIC7	■ MacQB

Purpose

The MKS$ function converts a single-precision number to a 4-byte string. The MKS$ function complements the CVS function. You use the MKS$ function to convert a single-precision number to a string that will be assigned to a field defined by a FIELD statement.

Syntax

MKS$(*number*)

number is any numeric expression in the range –3.402823E+38 through 3.402823E+38.

Usage

```
LSET wholesale$ = MKS$(ourCost!)
```

Places the string representing the value of *ourCost!* into the field *wholesale$*.

Description

Many versions of BASIC do not let you store numeric values in random-access files; you must convert numbers to strings before storing them and then convert them back to numbers when you read the file. (QuickBASIC 4.0 introduced the TYPE...END TYPE statement, which enables you to store numeric values.) The MKS$ function converts a single-precision value to a 4-byte string. Note that the specified number can be any numeric expression; MKS$ converts the number to single precision.

The MKS$ function returns a value that you must either assign to a variable or use in an expression. Usually, you use MKS$ in an LSET statement, as in the following example:

```
LSET cost$ = MKS$(1006.99)
```

Comments

If you specify the command line option /MBF, QuickBASIC assumes that the value MKS$ converts is a number in Microsoft Binary format. (See the MKSMBF$ entry for details.) Otherwise, the MKS$ function converts a number in IEEE format.

Compatibility

QuickBASIC 2.0, GW-BASIC, and BASICA

QuickBASIC version 2.0, GW-BASIC, and BASICA do not support the IEEE formatting of floating-point values. Because these versions of BASIC use only Microsoft Binary format, the value converted by the MKS$ function is in Microsoft Binary format.

Example

See the "Example" section in the CVD entry.

MKSMBF$

See also: CVS, CVSMBF, FIELD, MKS$, SINGLE

QB2	■ QB4.5	✲ PowerBASIC
■ QB3	ANSI	GW-BASIC
■ QB4	■ BASIC7	MacQB

Purpose

The MKSMBF$ function converts a single-precision number in IEEE format to a 4-byte string containing the number in Microsoft Binary format. The MKSMBF$ function complements the CVSMBF function. You use the MKSMBF$ function to convert a single-precision number to a string that will be assigned to a field defined by a FIELD statement.

Syntax

MKSMBF$(*number*)

number is any numeric variable or numeric expression in the range –3.402823E+38 through 3.402823E+38.

Usage

```
LSET amountDue$ = MKSMBF$(265.98)
```

Places the string representing the single-precision value 265.98 into the field *amountDue$*.

Description

Many versions of BASIC do not let you store numeric values in random-access files; you must convert numbers to strings and then convert them back to numbers when you read the file. (QuickBASIC 4.0 introduced the TYPE...END TYPE statement, which enables you to store numeric values.) The MKSMBF$ function converts a single-precision value to a 4-byte string. Note that the specified number can be any numeric expression; MKSMBF$ converts the number to single precision.

The MKSMBF$ function returns a value that you must assign to a variable or use in an expression. Usually, you will use MKSMBF$ in an LSET statement, as in the following example:

```
LSET cost$ = MKSMBF$(1006.99)
```

Compatibility

PowerBASIC

PowerBASIC supports the MKMS$ function, which performs the same task that the MKSMBF$ statement does in QuickBASIC 4.5.

Example

See the "Example" section in the CVD entry.

NAME

See also: CHDIR

■ QB2	■ QB4.5	■ PowerBASIC
■ QB3	ANSI	■ GW-BASIC
■ QB4	■ BASIC7	✲ MacQB

Purpose

The NAME statement changes the name or the location of a file. You use the NAME statement to let your program efficiently manage files.

Syntax

NAME *oldfilespec* AS *newfilespec*

oldfilespec is the existing filename. It can also include a pathname.

newfilespec is the new filename for the file. It can also include a pathname.

Usage

```
NAME "CUSTOMER.DAT" AS "OLD-CUST.DAT"
```

Renames the file CUSTOMER.DAT as OLD-CUST.DAT.

```
NAME "\CONFIG.SYS" AS "\BIN\OLDCONFIG.SYS"
```

Moves the file CONFIG.SYS from the root directory to the directory \BIN and changes the name of the file to OLDCONFIG.SYS.

Description

Like the DOS RENAME command, the QuickBASIC NAME statement changes the name of a file on a disk. The NAME statement can also move a file from one directory to another directory on the same drive. However, NAME cannot rename directories.

The two parameters to NAME must be string constants or expressions that contain a filename, which can be preceded by a pathname. If the pathname of the new name is different than that of the old name, NAME moves the file to the specified directory and, if the filename is different, renames the file.

Errors

The NAME statement doesn't physically transfer a file's data; it merely changes DOS's directory information about the file. If the two parameters do not both use the same drive, QuickBASIC displays a "Rename across disks" error message.

If the file to be renamed doesn't exist, QuickBASIC returns a "File not found" error message; if the new file name already exists, QuickBASIC returns a "File already exists" error message.

You must close an open file before you use the NAME statement to rename or move it. If the file to be renamed is currently open, QuickBASIC displays a "File already open" error message.

Compatibility

QuickBASIC for the Macintosh

QuickBASIC for the Macintosh uses the following syntax for NAME:

NAME *oldfilespec* AS *newfilespec*[, *type*]

type is the new file type that you can specify for the new name *newfilespec*. For example, all files saved as text from the QuickBASIC environment are of type TEXT. Files created by QuickBASIC that are applications have the type TEXT. You can specify any type in the NAME statement to change the type.

Example

The following program uses the NAME statement to make a backup copy of an existing file before overwriting it with new data.

```
CLS
ON ERROR GOTO ErrorHandler                ' branches to ErrorHandler for errors

NAME "REPORT.RPT" AS "REPORT.BAK"         ' if file exists, rename it

OPEN "REPORT.RPT" FOR OUTPUT AS #1        ' open file for output

PRINT #1, "REPORT.RPT"
PRINT "Information has been written to the file REPORT.RPT"
CLOSE
END

ErrorHandler:
    SELECT CASE ERR
        CASE 53
            PRINT "REPORT.RPT not found. No backup has been made."
            RESUME NEXT
```

(continued)

continued

```
        CASE 58
            KILL "REPORT.BAK"
            PRINT "Old backup file has been replaced by new one."
            RESUME
        CASE ELSE
            ON ERROR GOTO 0
    END SELECT
```

OPEN

See also: CLOSE, FREEFILE, IOCTL, OPEN COM

✲ QB2	■ QB4.5	■ PowerBASIC
✲ QB3	■ ANSI	✲ GW-BASIC
■ QB4	■ BASIC7	✲ MacQB

Purpose

The OPEN statement opens a file or device so that the program can perform input and output operations with the file or device. The OPEN statement prepares a file that will be either read from or written to. You must use OPEN before using a QuickBASIC I/O statement such as GET, PUT, PRINT #, or INPUT #, for example.

Syntax

New syntax:

OPEN *file* [FOR *accessmode*] [ACCESS *access*] [*lock*] AS [#]*filenum* [LEN = *reclen*]

Traditional syntax:

OPEN *mode*, [#]*filenum*, *file*[, *reclen*]

file is the name of the file that will be opened.

accessmode is a keyword that specifies the way the program will use the file. It can be one of the following keywords: INPUT, OUTPUT, APPEND, RANDOM, and BINARY.

access is a keyword that specifies the kind of access that the program will have to the file being opened. It can be one of the following keywords: READ, WRITE, or READ WRITE.

lock is a clause that specifies the kind of access other programs can have to an open file. It can be one of the following clauses: SHARED, LOCK READ, LOCK WRITE, or LOCK READ WRITE.

filenum is the number (in the range 1 through 255) that is associated with the file. It is used to access the file.

reclen is the length of each record in a sequential or random-access file. It must be in the range 1 through 32767.

mode is a single letter that specifies the way the program will use the file. It can be one of the following letters: I, O, A, R, or B.

Usage

```
OPEN "A:STUFF.DAT" FOR INPUT AS #1
```

Opens the sequential file STUFF.DAT on drive A: as file number 1 and specifies that data will be read.

```
OPEN "CONFIG.DAT" FOR RANDOM ACCESS READ AS #12
```

Opens the random-access file CONFIG.DAT as file number 12 and specifies that data will be read.

```
OPEN "REPORT.TXT" FOR APPEND ACCESS WRITE AS #1
```

Opens the sequential file REPORT.TXT as file number 1 and specifies that data be written to the end of the file.

```
OPEN "INFO" FOR INPUT ACCESS READ LOCK WRITE AS 1
```

Opens the sequential file INFO as file number 1 and specifies that data will be read. The LOCK clause prevents other processes from opening INFO and writing data.

```
OPEN "D:\PATIENTS.DAT" FOR RANDOM ACCESS READ WRITE LOCK WRITE AS #3 LEN = 1024
```

Opens the random-access file PATIENTS.DAT on the D: drive. The current process can read from or write to the file, but other processes are prevented from opening the file for writing. This file was opened as file number 3, and each record in the file is 1024 bytes long.

Description

Before you can read to or write from a file, you must first open the file. OPEN allocates and initializes a buffer for that file. A *buffer* is an area in memory in which QuickBASIC places data that is read from and written to a file. Reading information from a disk is a slow, mechanical process; therefore, QuickBASIC holds blocks of data in the buffer so that they can be accessed more quickly. The OPEN statement can also communicate with DOS and a local area network to set access mode and file locking, thus allowing several QuickBASIC programs to access the same files.

The file to be opened must be specified by a string constant or expression that contains a DOS or QuickBASIC device or filename. Note that you can precede a filename with a drive name or directory name or both, according to DOS file conventions. See Table 17-5 for a list of valid QuickBASIC device names.

The LEN clause in the OPEN statement, which is optional, lets you specify either the length, in bytes, of records in the file or the size, in bytes, of QuickBASIC's buffer for that file. For random-access files, the LEN clause specifies the number of bytes in each record of the file; if omitted, the length by default is 128 bytes. QuickBASIC ignores the LEN clause for binary files. For sequential files, the LEN clause specifies the size (in bytes) of the buffer QuickBASIC uses when reading from or writing to the file; 512 bytes is the default size. Specifying a larger buffer speeds up I/O operations. However, QuickBASIC allocates a little more than the specified number of bytes from the available memory, so you must determine whether increases in speed are worth the additional memory that the buffer requires. If the file is a character device, QuickBASIC ignores the length because the buffer of a character device is always 1 byte and cannot be changed.

Device	Description
CONS:	Console; screen output and keyboard input
KYBD:	Keyboard; keyboard input only
SCRN:	Screen; screen output only
COM*n*:	Communications port *n*; input and output
LPT*n*:	Parallel printer port *n*; input and output

Table 17-5.
QuickBASIC devices.

The FOR clause

In the new OPEN syntax, you specify the access mode by using a FOR clause with one of the following keywords: INPUT, OUTPUT, APPEND, RANDOM, or BINARY.

In the traditional OPEN syntax, you specify the access mode by specifying the first letter of one of the new syntax keywords (I, O, A, R, or B). If you use the traditional syntax, you must specify an access mode.

Table 17-6 lists the definitions of the access modes. If you omit the FOR mode clause when using the new syntax, QuickBASIC opens the file for random access.

New syntax	Traditional syntax	Description
INPUT	I	Sequential input
OUTPUT	O	Sequential output
APPEND	A	Sequential output to the end of the file
RANDOM	R	Random-access I/O (default mode) to any record position
BINARY	B	Binary I/O to any byte position

Table 17-6.
Access modes specified by the FOR clause.

When you open a file using the keyword BINARY in the FOR clause, variables can be read from and written to any byte position in the file regardless of the file's internal structure. (See the GET and PUT entries for details about binary mode I/O.)

If a file consists of ASCII text entered on separate lines or separated by spaces or commas, use the INPUT keyword in the FOR clause to open the sequential file for accessing the contents. With input mode, the data in a file can be unstructured and of different types (numeric and text) because the I/O routines INPUT # and LINE INPUT # read the file and make the necessary conversions (from ASCII characters to numeric variables, for example). (See the INPUT # and LINE INPUT # entries for details about input mode I/O.)

Specify the keyword OUTPUT in the FOR clause to create a sequential file. The data written to a file opened for output can be unstructured and of different types. (See the PRINT # and WRITE # entries for details about output mode I/O.)

Specify APPEND to open a sequential file to which you need to add information. When you open a file using APPEND, any data you write to the file appears at the end of the file; the original data remains untouched. Otherwise, append mode is the same as output.

Specify RANDOM in the FOR clause to open a random-access file that stores records of data that have the same structure. These records can be defined by either a FIELD statement or a TYPE...END TYPE statement. You can access any record in a random-access file directly; you don't have to start a search at the beginning of the file to find the record. (See the GET and PUT entries for details about random mode I/O.)

The ACCESS clause

In a networked, multi-tasking, or multi-user environment, in which different processes can access the same file at the same time, it is important to clearly define the privileges a process has to each file. For example, if one process is making changes to a database, that process needs both read and write privileges. If another process is printing a report based on the data in that database, that process needs only read privileges.

The ACCESS clause can include one of the following keywords: READ, WRITE, or READ WRITE. These specify that the file is to be opened for reading only, for writing only, or for both reading and writing. ACCESS READ WRITE is valid only for files opened with the keywords RANDOM, BINARY, or APPEND in the FOR clause.

ACCESS works only if the program is run under DOS version 3.0 or later.

If the process that opens a file denies read access, any attempt by another process to open that file with ACCESS READ or ACCESS READ WRITE results in the runtime error message "Permission denied." If the process that opens a file denies write access, any attempt by another process to open that file with ACCESS WRITE or ACCESS READ WRITE results in the runtime error message "Permission denied."

If you don't specify an ACCESS clause with a random-access or binary file, QuickBASIC makes three different attempts to open the file—one with an implicit ACCESS READ WRITE clause, the next with an implicit ACCESS WRITE, and the final attempt with an implicit ACCESS READ. If a file-sharing conflict arises with another process, the next attempt is made. If all three attempts fail, QuickBASIC returns a "Permission denied" error message.

The lock clause

In a networked, multitasking, or multiuser environment, in which different processes can access the same file at the same time, it is important to clearly define the privileges all processes have to a file. The lock clause of OPEN notifies the operating system which access privileges any other process can use for the file. For example, if the lock clause is LOCK READ, no other process can access the file with read privileges. Table 17-7 lists the keywords you can specify in the lock clause.

Lock clause	Description
(Default)	No other process can open the file.
SHARED	Any process can open the file in any mode.
LOCK READ	No other process can open the file by using an ACCESS READ clause; no other process can already have ACCESS READ privileges.
LOCK WRITE	No other process can open the file by using an ACCESS WRITE clause; no other process can already have ACCESS WRITE privileges.
LOCK READ WRITE	No other process can open the file by using an ACCESS READ WRITE clause; no other process can already have ACCESS READ WRITE privileges.

Table 17-7.
Network-access lock definitions.

Errors

If you use the OPEN statement with the INPUT keyword (or I) and the file does not exist, QuickBASIC displays a "File not found" error message. In any other mode (specified by OUTPUT, APPEND, RANDOM, or BINARY), if you use the OPEN statement and the file does not exist, QuickBASIC merely creates the file with a length of 0 bytes; no error message is displayed.

If a program uses an OPEN statement with the ACCESS clause under versions of DOS earlier than 3.0, QuickBASIC returns an "Advanced feature unavailable" error message.

Tips

Because each open file buffer uses available memory space, always close a file when you no longer need it.

Warnings

If you use a user-defined function or a DEF FN function as a parameter to any QuickBASIC I/O statement, that function must not use an I/O statement itself; such use can cause unpredictable results.

When you open a file with the APPEND keyword, the ACCESS clause, if used, must be READ WRITE, not merely WRITE; the OPEN statement must have read privileges to be able to find the end of the file.

Compatibility

QuickBASIC 2.0, QuickBASIC 3.0, GW-BASIC, and BASICA

The BINARY keyword in the FOR clause of the OPEN statement is not supported in these versions of BASIC, which support only sequential and random-access files.

QuickBASIC for the Macintosh

QuickBASIC for the Macintosh does not support the BINARY keyword in the FOR clause or the ACCESS and lock clauses. Also, QuickBASIC for the Macintosh does not report an error if it can't find a file; instead, it opens a dialog box and requests the user to locate the file.

Example

The following example, which uses three OPEN statements, converts a text file to hexadecimal and octal formats.

```
OPEN "INPUT.DAT" FOR INPUT AS #1
OPEN "HEX.DAT" FOR OUTPUT AS #2
OPEN "OCTAL.DAT" FOR OUTPUT AS #3

DO UNTIL EOF(1)
    LINE INPUT #1, text$        ' get a line
    PRINT text$

    PRINT #2, text$,
    FOR x = 1 TO LEN(text$)
        PRINT #2, HEX$(ASC(MID$(text$, x, 1))); " ";    ' print the hex value
    NEXT
    PRINT #2,

    PRINT #3, text$,
    FOR x = 1 TO LEN(text$)
        PRINT #3, OCT$(ASC(MID$(text$, x, 1))); " ";    ' print the octal value
    NEXT
    PRINT #3,
LOOP

CLOSE                           ' close all open files
```

Suppose, for example, that INPUT.DAT contains the following data:

```
Hello, this is a test...
```

Then, after you run the above program, the file HEX.DAT contains

```
Hello, this is a test...    48 65 6C 6C 6F 2C 20 74 68 69 73
20 69 73 20 61 20 74 65 73 74 2E 2E 2E
```

and the file OCTAL.DAT contains

```
Hello, this is a test...    110 145 154 154 157 54 40 164
150 151 163 40 151 163 40 141 40 164 145 163 164 56 56 56
```

PRINT

See also: INPUT #, PRINT, PRINT # USING, PRINT USING, WRITE #

■ QB2 ■ QB4.5 ■ PowerBASIC
■ QB3 ■ ANSI ■ GW-BASIC
■ QB4 ■ BASIC7 ■ MacQB

Purpose

The PRINT # statement writes unformatted data to a sequential file. You can use the PRINT # statement to add text and numbers to a sequential file.

Syntax

PRINT #*filenum*, [*expr* [{;|,}] ...]

filenum is the file number of the open sequential file to which you are writing data.

expr is a numeric or string expression that contains the value to be written to the file; you can specify several expressions, separating them with semicolons or commas.

If you use a semicolon between two expressions, the second expression will be written immediately after the first one. If you use a comma between two expressions, the second expression will be written in the next print zone. (Each print zone is 14 characters in length.) A semicolon or comma at the end of the statement keeps the file pointer on the same line of the file so the output of the next PRINT # statement begins on the same line.

Usage

```
PRINT #1, customerName$
```

Writes the value of the string variable *customerName$* to the file opened as file number 1.

```
PRINT #5, "Today's date is "; DATE$
```

Writes a string constant and the value returned by the DATE$ function to the file opened as file number 5.

Description

Sequential file output is useful for creating files that users can view or edit, such as report or mail-merge files. In QuickBASIC, you can use the PRINT # statement to write characters to a sequential output file. Note that the file to which you will write data must have been previously opened by using the OUTPUT or APPEND keyword in the OPEN statement.

The value written to the file can be specified by either a constant (quoted text or a constant defined by CONST) or an expression of any simple type, such as an array element, a record element, a simple variable, or a mathematical or string expression that uses QuickBASIC functions. If you do not specify any values in a PRINT # statement, PRINT # writes a blank line to the file.

The PRINT # statement writes data to the file exactly as PRINT writes data to the screen. If you need to read a file later, you must insert delimiters (such as a carriage-return/linefeed pair, spaces, or commas) between data items.

Writing numeric values

If a parameter to PRINT # is any type of numeric variable or expression, PRINT # writes the value of that variable or expression to the file. When PRINT # writes numbers to a file, it inserts a space after each number. PRINT # also precedes positive numeric values with a space and negative numeric values with a minus sign.

If the parameter is an integer or long-integer variable or expression, PRINT # writes the value of that variable or expression to the file, using as many digits as necessary to represent the number. Except as specified in the previous paragraph, no extra leading spaces or zeros precede the value when it is written to the file. Figure 17-7 illustrates this procedure.

```
PRINT #1, 100

. . .|   | 1 | 0 | 0 |   |. . .


PRINT #1, -9523

. . .| - | 9 | 5 | 2 | 3 |   |. . .
```

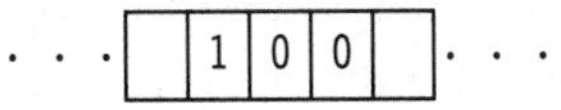

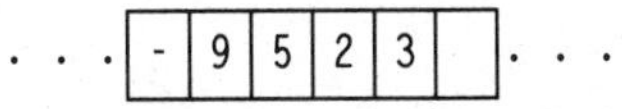

Figure 17-7.
Using PRINT # to write integers to a file.

If a parameter to PRINT # is a single-precision or double-precision variable or expression, PRINT # writes the value of that variable or expression to the file, using as many digits as necessary to represent the number. If QuickBASIC can represent the value of a single-precision number in seven or fewer digits (plus the decimal point) without loss of accuracy, PRINT # writes the value to the file in fixed-point format; otherwise, PRINT # writes the single-precision value in scientific notation. If QuickBASIC can represent the value of a double-precision number in 16 or fewer digits (plus the decimal point) without loss of accuracy, PRINT # writes the value to the file in fixed-point format; otherwise, PRINT # writes the double-precision value in scientific notation. Figure 17-8 on the following page illustrates this procedure.

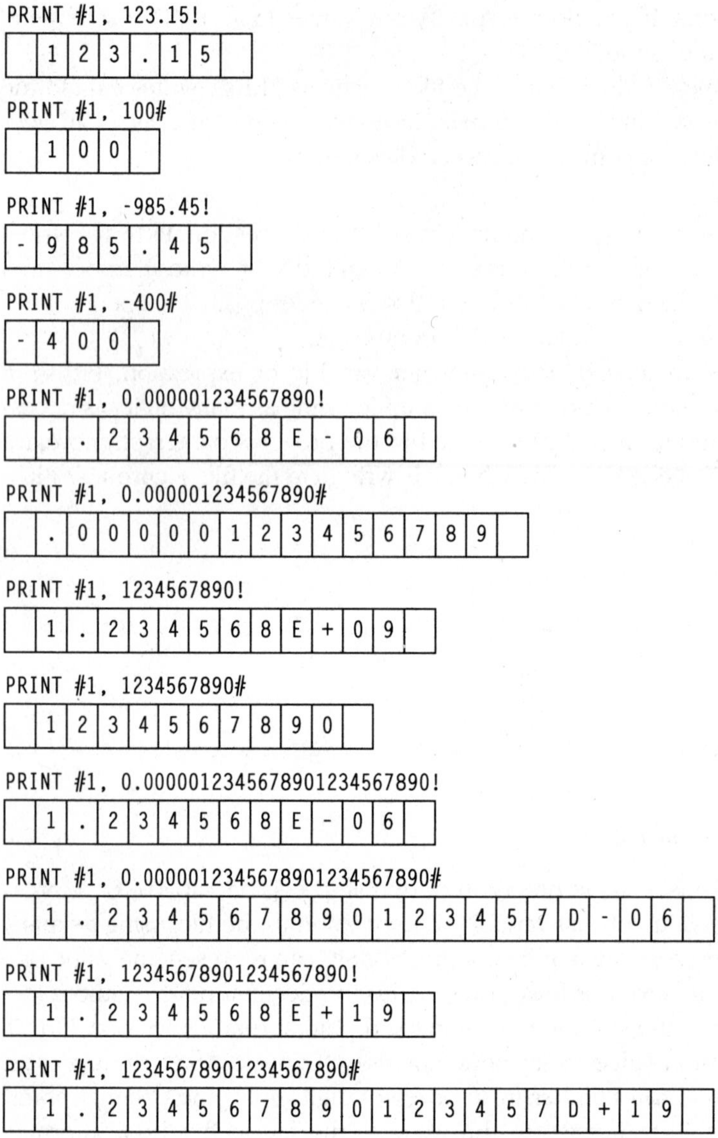

```
PRINT #1, 123.15!
```

	1	2	3	.	1	5	

```
PRINT #1, 100#
```

	1	0	0	

```
PRINT #1, -985.45!
```

-	9	8	5	.	4	5	

```
PRINT #1, -400#
```

-	4	0	0	

```
PRINT #1, 0.000001234567890!
```

	1	.	2	3	4	5	6	8	E	-	0	6	

```
PRINT #1, 0.000001234567890#
```

	.	0	0	0	0	0	1	2	3	4	5	6	7	8	9	

```
PRINT #1, 1234567890!
```

	1	.	2	3	4	5	6	8	E	+	0	9	

```
PRINT #1, 1234567890#
```

	1	2	3	4	5	6	7	8	9	0	

```
PRINT #1, 0.0000012345678901234567890!
```

	1	.	2	3	4	5	6	8	E	-	0	6	

```
PRINT #1, 0.0000012345678901234567890#
```

	1	.	2	3	4	5	6	7	8	9	0	1	2	3	4	5	7	D	-	0	6	

```
PRINT #1, 12345678901234567890!
```

	1	.	2	3	4	5	6	8	E	+	1	9	

```
PRINT #1, 12345678901234567890#
```

	1	.	2	3	4	5	6	7	8	9	0	1	2	3	4	5	7	D	+	1	9	

Figure 17-8.
Using PRINT # to write single-precision and double-precision numbers to a file.

Comments

PRINT # cannot write entire arrays or record variables; you must use PRINT # for each array element or each record element. For example, you need to use a FOR...NEXT loop to print an entire array, as in the following program segment:

```
FOR i% = 1 TO 50
    PRINT #1, array$(i%)
NEXT
```

If you use commas to separate parameters, PRINT # inserts spaces in the file to position the next tab stop. Because this can waste disk space, however, it is better to use semicolons between numeric values and quoted commas between string variables, as in the following example:

```
PRINT #1, stringVar$; ","; numericVar%; dollarVar#
```

Errors

If you use an array or a record variable as a parameter, QuickBASIC displays a "Type mismatch" error message.

Tips

To speed up sequential file output, you can increase the size of the buffer by using the LEN clause in the OPEN statement of a file. However, remember that an increased buffer size reduces the available memory for the program.

Example

The following program uses the PRINT # statement to write the contents of the 80-by-25-character text screen to a sequential file.

```
OPEN "SCREEN.DAT" FOR APPEND AS #1

FOR y% = 1 TO 25
    FOR x% = 1 TO 80
        PRINT #1, CHR$(SCREEN(y%, x%));
    NEXT x%

NEXT y%

PRINT #1, STRING$(80, 196)
PRINT #1, "This screen was written on "; DATE$; " at "; TIME$; "."
PRINT #1, STRING$(80, 196)

CLOSE
```

PRINT # USING

See also: INPUT #, PRINT, PRINT #, PRINT USING, WRITE #

■ QB2	■ QB4.5	■ PowerBASIC
■ QB3	■ ANSI	■ GW-BASIC
■ QB4	■ BASIC7	■ MacQB

Purpose

The PRINT # USING statement writes formatted data to an open sequential file, just as PRINT USING writes formatted data to the display. (See Chapter 8, "Simple I/O.") You can use PRINT # USING to write numbers and text to a file that will, for example, be used to fill in specific portions of a form.

Syntax

PRINT *#filenum*, USING *templateString*; [*expr*[; *expr*...]][{ ; ¦ , }]

filenum is the file number of an open file to which data will be written.

templateString is either a string constant or a string variable. It can contain literal text, which is printed unchanged, and one or more special formatting characters (described in the PRINT USING entry in Chapter 8, "Simple I/O") that determine how the variables or expressions following the template string are to be printed.

expr is a numeric or string expression that contains the value to be written to the file; you can specify several expressions by separating them with semicolons. A comma at the end of the statement causes the file pointer to remain on the current line of the file and to move to the next print zone. (Each print zone is 14 characters in length.) A semicolon at the end of the statement causes the file pointer to remain on the current line, positioned immediately after the most recent character written.

Usage

```
PRINT #1, USING "######"; numVar%
```

Writes six digits of the contents of the variable *numVar%* to file number 1.

```
PRINT #1, USING "Processing record ##### of ##### records"; currentRec%; totalRecs%
```

Writes two 5-digit formatted numbers, *currentRec%* and *totalRecs%*, which are surrounded by text, to file number 1.

```
PRINT #1, USING "Pay to the order of !. !. &"; firstName$, middleName$, lastName$
```

Writes two single-character strings and a variable-length string to file number 1.

Description

One of the challenges of programming is to create programs that generate functional and attractive output. QuickBASIC's PRINT # USING statement lets you format file output.

The PRINT # USING statement writes data to a file exactly as PRINT USING writes data to the screen. If you must later read the file as a sequential file opened with the keyword INPUT, you must insert delimiters between data items. (For a complete list of formatting characters, see the PRINT USING entry in Chapter 8, "Simple I/O.")

Comments

The PRINT # USING statement cannot write entire arrays or record variables; you must use a separate PRINT # USING statement for each array element or each record element.

Errors

If you use an array or a record variable as a parameter, QuickBASIC returns a "Type mismatch" error message.

Tips

To speed up sequential file output, you can increase the size of the buffer by using the LEN clause in the OPEN statement of a file. However, remember that an increased buffer size reduces the available memory for the program.

Example

The following program uses the PRINT # USING statement to write data to a file that might later be printed onto checks.

```
CLS
DEFINT A-Z              ' define variables as integer by default

file = FREEFILE                        ' get next available file number
OPEN "CHECKS" FOR APPEND AS #file      ' open the file for additional output

DO
    PRINT
    PRINT "When you're finished, press Enter."
    PRINT

    LINE INPUT "Enter payee's first name:  "; first$
    IF first$ = "" THEN EXIT DO          ' quit if user presses Enter
    LINE INPUT "Enter payee's middle name: "; middle$
    LINE INPUT "Enter payee's last name:   "; last$
    INPUT "Enter amount to be paid:   ", amount!

    PRINT #file, "The Acme Novelty Company", , , DATE$   ' commas specify tabs
    PRINT #file, : PRINT #file, : PRINT #file,           ' skip three lines

    PRINT #file, "Pay to the order of: "
    PRINT #file, USING "!. !. \               \ "; first$; middle$; last$;
    PRINT #file, USING "               **$#,###,###.##"; amount!

    dollars& = FIX(amount!)              ' calculate the number of whole dollars
    cents = (amount! - dollars&) * 100   ' calculate the number of cents
```

(continued)

continued

```
    PRINT #file, USING "#,###,### and ##/100 dollars"; dollars&; cents
    PRINT #file, : PRINT #file, : PRINT #file,
    PRINT #file, , , "Jill Acme, President"
    PRINT #file, : PRINT #file, : PRINT #file,
LOOP

CLOSE #file
```

PUT (File I/O)

See also: FIELD, GET (File I/O), INPUT #, LINE INPUT #, OPEN, TYPE...END TYPE

✲ QB2	■ QB4.5	✲ PowerBASIC
✲ QB3	✲ ANSI	✲ GW-BASIC
■ QB4	■ BASIC7	✲ MacQB

Purpose

The PUT statement writes information to a random-access or binary file from fields defined by a FIELD statement or from record variables defined by a TYPE...END TYPE statement.

Syntax

PUT [#]*filenum*[, [*position*][, *variable*]]

filenum is the file number assigned to a file in an OPEN statement.

position is the number of the record (in random-access files) or byte (in binary files) at which writing data begins (in the range 1 through 2147483647).

variable is the variable that contains the data to be written to the file.

Usage

```
PUT #1, 1
```

Writes the contents of the fields associated with a random-access file to the first record in the file opened as file number 1.

```
PUT 1, , info
```

Writes the record variable *info* to the next record in a random-access file.

```
PUT #1, 128, patientType
```

If file number 1 is associated with a binary file, this statement writes the contents of the variable *patientType* to the file, beginning at byte number 128. If file number 1 is associated with a random-access file, this statement writes the contents of the record variable *patientType* to record number 128.

Description

You can use the PUT statement to write simple variables or entire records to a random-access or binary file.

When you use the PUT statement with a random-access file, you can specify the number of the record at which writing begins. Each record consists of the number of bytes specified in the LEN clause of the OPEN statement. The first record number in a file is record number 1. If you do not specify a record number, PUT writes the record after the one used in the most recent GET or PUT operation or after the record specified in the most recent SEEK statement.

When you use PUT with random-access files, you can specify any variable whose size in bytes is no larger than the record length specified when you opened the file. Specify a variable that matches the structure of the file's records.

If you use the PUT statement with a binary file, you can specify the number of the byte at which writing begins. The first byte in a file is byte number 1. If you do not specify a byte number, PUT writes the byte after the one used in the most recent GET or PUT operation or after the byte specified in the most recent SEEK statement.

The variable that you specify for a binary file parameter can be of any type and length. The PUT statement writes the number of bytes contained in the variable.

If you use the PUT statement when the record for the file has been defined by a FIELD statement, you cannot specify a variable. QuickBASIC returns a "FIELD statement active" error message if you do specify a variable. To write values to the file, you must first assign the values to the fields of the record by using the LSET or RSET statement. Then use PUT without a variable to write the values to the file.

Warnings

Because the maximum size of a record in a file is 32,767 bytes, the maximum size of the variable in a PUT statement to a random-access or binary file is also 32,767 bytes.

If the specified variable is a variable-length string, PUT precedes the data in the string with a 2-byte header that specifies the length of the string. Therefore, each variable-length string extends the length of a record by 2 bytes. Note that this occurs in QuickBASIC versions 4.00b and later. This might cause a problem if you must share data files with a program written in an earlier version of QuickBASIC. To prevent this, used fixed-length strings in your GET and PUT statements.

Compatibility

QuickBASIC 2.0, QuickBASIC 3.0, ANSI BASIC, GW-BASIC, BASICA, and QuickBASIC for the Macintosh

QuickBASIC versions 2.0 and 3.0, ANSI BASIC, GW-BASIC, BASICA, and QuickBASIC for the Macintosh do not support the TYPE...END TYPE statement. Because of this, you cannot specify a record variable in a PUT statement. In these versions of BASIC, PUT works only with records defined by the FIELD statement.

PowerBASIC

PowerBASIC does not support the TYPE...END TYPE statement. Because of this, you cannot specify a record variable in the PUT statement. In PowerBASIC, PUT works with random-access files containing records defined by the FIELD statement or the MAP statement. To read binary files in PowerBASIC, you must use the PowerBASIC PUT$ statement.

Example

The following program uses the GET and PUT statements to update a file that contains the user's color choices for the screen.

```
TYPE ConfigType
    normal AS INTEGER                ' color of box internal area
    highlight AS INTEGER             ' color of letter highlight
    inverseHighlight AS INTEGER      ' color of the inverse of letter highlight
    inverse AS INTEGER               ' color of highlight bar
    help AS INTEGER                  ' color of help line
    cursorNormal AS INTEGER          ' cursor size when overstriking
    cursorInsert AS INTEGER          ' cursor size when inserting
END TYPE

DIM config AS ConfigType             ' define the record variable config

OPEN "CONFIG.DAT" FOR BINARY AS #1   ' open the file

GET #1, 1, config                    ' read current configuration information

CLS
PRINT "Enter new colors."
PRINT

PRINT "Normal color = "; config.normal;
INPUT "  Change to: ", config.normal

PRINT "Highlight color = "; config.highlight;
INPUT "  Change to: ", config.highlight

PRINT "Inverse highlight color = "; config.inverseHighlight;
INPUT "  Change to: ", config.inverseHighlight

PRINT "Inverse color = "; config.inverse;
INPUT "  Change to: ", config.inverse

PRINT "Help color = "; config.help;
INPUT "  Change to: ", config.help

PRINT "Overstrike cursor size = "; config.cursorNormal;
INPUT "  Change to: ", config.cursorNormal
```

(continued)

continued

```
PRINT "Insert cursor size = "; config.cursorInsert;
INPUT "  Change to: ", config.cursorInsert

PUT #1, 1, config                    ' write the information to the file
CLOSE

END
```

RESET

See also: CLOSE, END, SYSTEM

■ QB2	■ QB4.5	■ PowerBASIC
■ QB3	ANSI	■ GW-BASIC
■ QB4	■ BASIC7	■ MacQB

Purpose

The RESET statement closes all open files and writes the data in the corresponding buffers to the appropriate file or device. You can use RESET at the end of your program to be sure all files are closed before the program ends.

Syntax

RESET

Usage

```
PRINT "All tasks have been completed."
RESET
```

Displays a shutdown message, clears all data from the current file buffers, and then closes all open files.

Description

The RESET statement closes all open files and clears any data still in the file buffers that were allocated by the OPEN statement. The RESET statement works the same as the CLOSE statement without any parameters.

Comments

The RESET statement (and the CLOSE, END, and SYSTEM statements) clears pending I/O by writing the contents of the current file buffers to the appropriate file or device; however, RESET doesn't execute a PUT statement to update a file containing fields (defined by FIELD) to a random-access file. Therefore, if you have changed any fields, you must execute a PUT statement to add the changes to the file before executing the RESET statement.

Example

The following program uses the RESET statement to close all files when the user quits the program.

```
OPEN "FIRST" FOR INPUT AS #1
OPEN "SECOND" FOR INPUT AS #2
OPEN "THIRD" FOR OUTPUT AS #3
OPEN "GARFIELD.DAT" FOR APPEND AS #7

INPUT "Do you want to quit the program?"; yesNo$

DO
    IF UCASE$(LEFT$(yesNo$, 1)) = "Y" THEN
        RESET
        END
    END IF
LOOP
```

RSET

See also: FIELD, LSET, MKD$, MKDMBF$, MKI$, MKL$, MKS$, MKSMBF$, PUT (File I/O)

■ QB2 ■ QB4.5 ■ PowerBASIC
■ QB3 ■ ANSI ■ GW-BASIC
■ QB4 ■ BASIC7 ■ MacQB

Purpose

The RSET statement puts the value of an expression or a variable into a specified field of a random-access file's buffer. RSET also right-justifies this expression or variable. RSET can also be used to right-justify any string variable.

Syntax

RSET *var* = *expr*

var and *expr* must both be strings.

Usage

```
RSET address$ = "123 PARK ST."
```

Right-justifies the string constant "123 PARK ST." and places it into the *address$* field if *address$* is the name of a field defined by a FIELD statement. If *address$* is a string variable, RSET only right-justifies it within the current length of *address$*.

```
RSET amtDue$ = MKD$(total#)
```

Places the string representation of the contents of *total#* variable into *amtDue$*, which can be either the name of a field defined by a FIELD statement or a string variable.

Description

The FIELD statement allocates a special storage buffer when it defines the record for a random-access file. Because of this special allocation, you cannot use the equal sign (=) or the LET statement to assign values to the fields defined by the FIELD statement. Instead, you must use the LSET or RSET statement to make the assignment. Note that you can also use RSET with string variables.

Using RSET with fields

When you specify a field name as the first parameter in an RSET statement, the RSET statement copies the value of the second parameter (which must be a string) into the location in a random-access buffer allocated for the specified field.

If the length of the field is greater than the length of the string value, RSET right-justifies the value in the buffer. That is, RSET adds spaces to the beginning of the string until it is the same length as the field.

If the length of the field is less than the length of the string value, RSET copies only enough characters to fill the field and ignores the remaining characters.

Figure 17-9 shows how the RSET statement places a string in a field.

```
FIELD 1, 20 AS patientName$
RSET patientName$ = "Robert Anderson II"
|   |   | R | o | b | e | r | t |   | A | n | d | e | r | s | o | n |   | I | I |

RSET patientName$ = "Robert Lloyd Anderson II"
| R | o | b | e | r | t |   | L | l | o | y | d |   | A | n | d | e | r | s | o |
```

Figure 17-9.
The RSET statement with fields.

Using RSET with string variables

When the first parameter to RSET is a string variable (not a field name), RSET performs a different task. Because the length of the variable is not set by a FIELD statement, RSET uses the current length of the string variable to calculate the justification it will perform.

If the current length of the string variable is greater than the length of the value specified in the second parameter, RSET right-justifies the value. That is, RSET adds spaces to the beginning of the string value until it is the same length as the string variable.

If the current length of the string variable is less than the length of the value specified in the second parameter, RSET copies only enough characters to fill the string variable and ignores the remaining characters.

You can determine the current length of a string variable by using the LEN function. (See the LEN entry in Chapter 5, "Strings," for details.)

Figure 17-10 shows how the RESET statement works with string variables.

```
patientName$ = SPACE$(20)
RSET patientName$ = "Robert Anderson II"
```

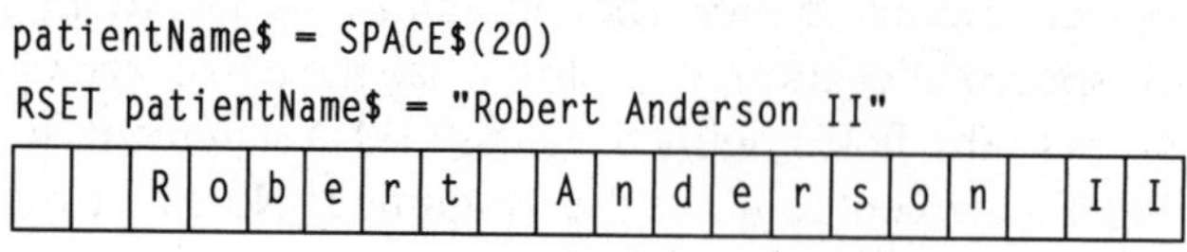


```
RSET patientName$ = "Robert Lloyd Anderson II"
```

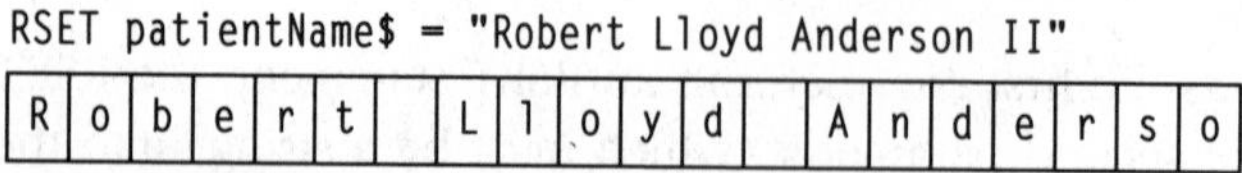

Figure 17-10.
The RSET statement with string variables.

Comments

Remember that you must convert numeric values to strings before you place them into a field defined by a FIELD statement. (See the MKD$, MKDMBF$, MKI$, MKL$, MKS$, and MKSMBF$ entries for details.)

Tips

Using the FIELD and RSET statements to access random-access files can be a long and complicated procedure. If you are using QuickBASIC version 4.0 or later, use record variables as an easier alternative for performing random-access file I/O.

Example

The following program uses RSET to right-justify user input. It writes job titles and people's names to a file, positioning the job title on the left side and the corresponding name on the right. The program then displays the contents of the file.

```
OPEN "CREDITS.TXT" FOR OUTPUT AS #1

DO
    job$ = SPACE$(40)
    person$ = SPACE$(40)

    LINE INPUT "Job title:     "; jobTitle$
    IF jobTitle$ = "" THEN EXIT DO
    LINE INPUT "Person's name: "; personName$
    PRINT

    LSET job$ = jobTitle$
    RSET person$ = personName$
    PRINT #1, job$; person$          ' write the information to the file
LOOP UNTIL jobTitle$ = ""
```

(continued)

continued

```
CLOSE #1

OPEN "credits.txt" FOR INPUT AS #1

DO UNTIL EOF(1)
    LINE INPUT #1, credit$          ' display the contents of the file
    PRINT credit$
LOOP
CLOSE #1
```

RTRIM$

See also: LTRIM$

QB2	■ QB4.5	✲ PowerBASIC
QB3	■ ANSI	GW-BASIC
■ QB4	■ BASIC7	MacQB

Purpose

The RTRIM$ function returns a copy of a string expression without trailing spaces (spaces on the right). You use the RTRIM$ function to format data in which trailing spaces would either cause misaligned output or be misinterpreted as literal characters.

Syntax

RTRIM$(*string*)

string is any string expression.

Usage

```
PRINT #1, RTRIM$(description$)
```

Writes the variable *description$* without trailing spaces to the file associated with file number 1.

Description

Because some names (such as those of devices, directories, and filenames) must be used literally, QuickBASIC provides the RTRIM$ function to let you delete extra spaces that might have been inserted by the user or the program. The RTRIM$ function accepts any string expression and returns the same string without trailing spaces. The string expression can also contain the concatenation operator and string functions such as MID$, LEFT$, or RIGHT$.

Comments

The RTRIM$ function removes only spaces from the end of a string; it leaves other white-space characters, such as tab or null characters. To manually remove all white-space characters, you can use the following function:

```
FUNCTION NewRTrim$ (stringVar$)
    FOR i% = LEN(stringVar$) TO 1 STEP -1          ' check each character
        SELECT CASE ASC(MID$(stringVar$, i%, 1))  ' start at the end
            CASE 0, 9, 32       ' if a null, tab, or space character, do nothing
            CASE ELSE           ' found first character
                NewRTrim$ = LEFT$(stringVar$, i%)
                EXIT FUNCTION
        END SELECT
    NEXT i%
    NewRTrim$ = ""              ' string contains only white-space characters
END FUNCTION
```

Compatibility

PowerBASIC

PowerBASIC supports the use of a second parameter to the RTRIM$ function. This parameter specifies a string that RTRIM$ removes from the end of the string. RTRIM$ removes occurrences of this match string until it encounters a character that does not match. If you use the keyword ANY before the match string in the call to RTRIM$, the function removes any occurrences of the characters in the match string from the end of the string.

Example

The following program uses the RTRIM$ function to delete the trailing spaces from user input.

```
CLS

LINE INPUT "Enter your first name:  "; first$
LINE INPUT "Enter your middle name: "; middle$
LINE INPUT "Enter your last name:   "; last$

PRINT
PRINT "Pay to the order of: "; RTRIM$(first$); " ";
PRINT LEFT$(middle$, 1); ". "; RTRIM$(last$)
```

SEEK (Function)

See also: GET (File I/O), OPEN, PUT (File I/O), SEEK (Statement)

QB2	■ QB4.5	PowerBASIC
QB3	ANSI	GW-BASIC
■ QB4	■ BASIC7	MacQB

Purpose

The SEEK function returns the number of the current record or byte position in a file. You can use SEEK, for example, to determine how close the current record is to the end of the file.

Syntax

SEEK(*filenum*)

filenum is the file number of an open file.

Usage

```
PRINT "The current file position is"; SEEK(1)
```

Displays the current file position for the file opened as file number 1.

Description

The value that the SEEK function returns for random-access files is the number of the next record that will be read from or written to when you use the PUT and GET file I/O statements. Note that the first record in a file is record number 1.

If the file is a sequential or binary file, the SEEK function returns the byte number at which the next I/O operation (such as a PUT or a GET statement) will take place. Note that the first byte in a file is byte number 1.

Comments

The largest value the SEEK function can return is 2147483647 because that is the largest file that QuickBASIC and DOS support.

Warnings

The SEEK function returns 0 when used with the QuickBASIC SCRN:, KYBD:, CONS:, COM1:, COM2:, LPT1:, and LPT2: devices. The SEEK function returns meaningful values only when it is used with files.

Example

The following program uses the SEEK function to determine which record is current in a random-access file.

```
TYPE Planets                        ' type definition for planet information
    nam AS STRING * 20              ' name
    diameter AS LONG                ' diameter
    perihelion AS DOUBLE            ' orbital point closest to sun
    aphelion AS DOUBLE              ' orbital point farthest from sun
    highTemp AS SINGLE              ' highest surface temperature
    lowTemp AS SINGLE               ' lowest surface temperature
    yearDiscovered AS INTEGER       ' year discovered
END TYPE

DIM planet AS Planets               ' define a variable of type Planets

CLS
OPEN "SOL.DAT" FOR RANDOM AS #1 LEN = 50    ' open the data file
```

(continued)

continued

```
FOR planetNum% = 1 TO 9
    PRINT : PRINT : PRINT

    SEEK #1, planetNum%                     ' move to the correct record
    GET #1, , planet                        ' read the record
    PRINT "Planet number"; SEEK(1) - 1      ' display the record number

    PRINT : PRINT "Information about planet "; planet.nam
    PRINT STRING$(79, 45): PRINT

    ' get information from the user if the record is empty
    IF planet.nam = STRING$(20, 0) THEN
        INPUT "Name"; planet.nam
        INPUT "Diameter (km)"; planet.diameter
        INPUT "Perihelion (km)"; planet.perihelion
        INPUT "Aphelion (km)"; planet.aphelion
        INPUT "Highest temperature"; planet.highTemp
        INPUT "Lowest temperature"; planet.lowTemp
        INPUT "Discovered in"; planet.yearDiscovered
        PUT #1, planetNum%, planet          ' write the information to the file
        PRINT : PRINT "Information saved": PRINT : PRINT
    ELSE                                    ' display the information
        PRINT "Diameter is"; planet.diameter; "kilometers."
        PRINT "Perihelion is"; planet.perihelion; "kilometers."
        PRINT "Aphelion is"; planet.aphelion; "kilometers."
        PRINT "Highest temperature is"; planet.highTemp; "degrees."
        PRINT "Lowest temperature is"; planet.lowTemp; "degrees."
        PRINT "Discovered in"; planet.yearDiscovered; "."
    END IF
NEXT

CLOSE
```

SEEK (Statement)

See also: GET (File I/O), OPEN, PUT (File I/O), SEEK (Function)

QB2	■ QB4.5	■ PowerBASIC
QB3	ANSI	GW-BASIC
■ QB4	■ BASIC7	MacQB

Purpose

The SEEK statement sets the current position in an open file. The current position is the location at which the next I/O operation (such as a GET or a PUT operation) will take place.

Syntax

SEEK [#]*filenum*, *position*

filenum is the file number of an open file.

position is the number of the record or byte that you want to move to within the file. It must be in the range 1 through 2147483647.

Usage

```
OPEN "FILE.DAT" FOR RANDOM AS #1
SEEK 1, 128
```

Sets the current position for the file opened as number 1 to record number 128.

```
OPEN "FILE.DAT" FOR BINARY AS #1
SEEK 1, 128
```

Sets the current position for the file opened as number 1 to byte number 128.

```
OPEN "FILE.DAT" FOR RANDOM AS #1
SEEK 1, SEEK(1) - 200
```

Sets the current position for the file opened as number 1 to the previous position (returned by the SEEK function) minus 200 records.

Description

QuickBASIC's GET and PUT file I/O statements let you omit which record or byte in the file to read from or write to; if you do not specify a record or byte number, the statement reads from or writes to the current position in the file. The current position is updated to the next location in the file after a read or write operation. You can use the current position to access files sequentially, should you need to. However, the SEEK statement lets you change the current file position to any other record or byte. After you execute the SEEK statement, the next I/O operation that doesn't include a specific record number is performed at the new location.

The specified position for a random-access file is the record number that will become the current position. The first record in a file is record number 1. The specified position for a sequential or binary file is the byte number that will become the current position. The first byte in a file is byte number 1.

Comments

QuickBASIC ignores the SEEK statement if the *filenum* parameter is the file number of the SCRN:, KYBD:, CONS:, COM1:, COM2:, LPT1:, or LPT2: QuickBASIC device.

The example program for the SEEK statement in the QuickBASIC Advisor (the online help system in QuickBASIC 4.5) contains an error in its call to the SEEK statement. The program opens a random-access file, reads records, and then calls the SEEK statement to move the current position back a record. The program calls SEEK by using the following statement:

```
SEEK #1, SEEK(1) - LEN(RecordVar)
```

However, for random-access files, you specify the record number to which you would like to move, not the byte number as used in the above statement. The correct call to SEEK is shown in the following statement:

```
SEEK #1, SEEK(1) - 1
```

Errors

If you specify a position that is less than or equal to 0, QuickBASIC returns a "Bad record number" error message.

Tips

If you specify a position that is beyond the end of the open file, the next PUT statement extends the size of the file, filling the space between the most recent byte or record and the new position with random values. It is better, however, to extend a file by writing blank records one at a time.

Example

The following program uses the SEEK statement to change the current position to a specific record in a random-access file.

```
TYPE Planets                        ' type definition for planet information
    nam AS STRING * 20              ' name
    diameter AS LONG                ' diameter
    perihelion AS DOUBLE            ' orbital point closest to sun
    aphelion AS DOUBLE              ' orbital point farthest from sun
    highTemp AS SINGLE              ' highest surface temperature
    lowTemp AS SINGLE               ' lowest surface temperature
    yearDiscovered AS INTEGER       ' year discovered
END TYPE

DIM planet AS Planets               ' define a variable of type Planets

CLS
OPEN "SOL.DAT" FOR RANDOM AS #1 LEN = 50    'open the data file

DO
    PRINT : PRINT : PRINT
    INPUT "Information about which planet"; planetNum%    ' get a record number

    ' exit if user presses Enter or planetNum% out of range
    IF planetNum% < 1 OR planetNum% > 9 THEN EXIT DO

    SEEK #1, planetNum%                         ' move to the correct record
    GET #1, , planet                            ' read the record

    PRINT : PRINT "Information about planet "; planet.nam
    PRINT STRING$(79, 45): PRINT
```

(continued)

continued

```
        ' get information from the user if the record is empty
        IF planet.nam = STRING$(20, 0) THEN
            INPUT "Name"; planet.nam
            INPUT "Diameter (km)"; planet.diameter
            INPUT "Perihelion (km)"; planet.perihelion
            INPUT "Aphelion (km)"; planet.aphelion
            INPUT "Highest temperature"; planet.highTemp
            INPUT "Lowest temperature"; planet.lowTemp
            INPUT "Discovered in"; planet.yearDiscovered
            PUT #1, planetNum%, planet        ' write the information to the file
            PRINT : PRINT "Information saved": PRINT : PRINT
        ELSE                                  ' display the information
            PRINT "Diameter is"; planet.diameter; "kilometers."
            PRINT "Perihelion is"; planet.perihelion; "kilometers."
            PRINT "Aphelion is"; planet.aphelion; "kilometers."
            PRINT "Highest temperature is"; planet.highTemp; "degrees."
            PRINT "Lowest temperature is"; planet.lowTemp; "degrees."
            PRINT "Discovered in"; planet.yearDiscovered; "."
        END IF
    LOOP

    CLOSE
```

UNLOCK

See also: LOCK, OPEN

■ QB2	■ QB4.5	PowerBASIC
■ QB3	ANSI	✲ GW-BASIC
■ QB4	■ BASIC7	MacQB

Purpose

The UNLOCK statement lets other network programs access a shared file or sections of that file. You use UNLOCK to let other programs share a file or a portion of a file that was previously locked during a critical I/O operation.

Syntax

UNLOCK [#] *filenum*[, {*record* ¦ [*start*] TO *end*}]

filenum is the file number of an open file.

record is the number of the record or byte to be unlocked.

start and *end* are integers that specify a range of records or bytes to be unlocked.

Usage

```
UNLOCK #1
```

Unlocks the entire file opened as file number 1.

```
OPEN "VENDORS.DAT" FOR RANDOM AS #4
:
UNLOCK #4, 10
```

Unlocks record 10 of the random-access file opened as file number 4.

```
OPEN "TRANS.DAT" FOR BINARY AS #2
:
UNLOCK #2, TO 512
```

Unlocks bytes 1 through 512 of the binary file opened as file number 2.

Description

You use UNLOCK with programs that will be used in a network environment in which several users or processes share the same files. After you use the QuickBASIC LOCK statement to prevent conflicts that can occur when different programs try to access the same data simultaneously, you must use the UNLOCK statement to release the locks on the file.

In a random-access file, you specify the numbers of the records to be locked. The first record in a file is always record number 1. In a binary file, you specify the bytes to be locked. The first byte in the file is always byte number 1. You can unlock individual records or bytes only in binary or random-access files; with sequential files you can unlock only the entire file.

Comments

You must use the LOCK and UNLOCK statements in *exactly* matching pairs. That is, you cannot combine the UNLOCK statements of more than one LOCK statement to form an "equivalent" UNLOCK statement; you must instead use UNLOCK statements that correspond exactly to the original LOCK statements. For example, the two statements

```
LOCK #3, 1 TO 10
LOCK #3, 11 TO 20
```

require the two UNLOCK statements

```
UNLOCK #3, 1 TO 10
UNLOCK #3, 11 TO 20
```

You cannot simply combine the two UNLOCK statements into the single statement

```
UNLOCK #3, 1 TO 20
```

Note that QuickBASIC lets you issue the above single UNLOCK statement without returning an error; however, the statement has no effect, and the 20 bytes or records remain locked.

Errors

If you specify the UNLOCK statement before you use the LOCK statement, QuickBASIC returns a "Permission denied" error message.

Tips

If you must use QuickBASIC with networks other than IBM PC Network and MS-Network, consider using a third-party file manager that supports other popular networks. See Appendix C, "Third-Party Add-Ons," for information about third-party file manager products.

Warnings

Microsoft supports QuickBASIC only on IBM PC Network, MS-Network, and compatible systems. Although limited success has been reported using other networks, such as Novell and 3Com, problems can occur.

If you lock a file and then either lose power or reboot your computer before you execute the matching UNLOCK statement, data in the locked file might be lost. To minimize the danger of losing data, use LOCK to lock records only as long as necessary.

Compatibility

GW-BASIC and BASICA

GW-BASIC supports the LOCK and UNLOCK statements. BASICA does not.

Example

The following program uses the LOCK statement to guarantee that no other program can access the file CONFIG.DAT while the program is running. Before the program ends, it releases its lock on the file by issuing the matching UNLOCK statement.

```
TYPE ConfigType
    normal AS INTEGER               ' color of box internal area
    highlight AS INTEGER            ' color of letter highlight
    inverseHighlight AS INTEGER     ' color of the inverse of letter highlight
    inverse AS INTEGER              ' color of highlight bar
    help AS INTEGER                 ' color of help line
    cursorNormal AS INTEGER         ' cursor size when overstriking
    cursorInsert AS INTEGER         ' cursor size when inserting
END TYPE

DIM config AS ConfigType            ' define the record variable config

CLS
PRINT "Enter new colors."
PRINT

OPEN "CONFIG.DAT" FOR BINARY ACCESS READ WRITE LOCK WRITE AS #1  ' open file

LOCK #1                             ' lock the entire file
GET #1, 1, config                   ' read the current configuration information

PRINT "Normal color = "; config.normal;
INPUT "  Change to: ", config.normal
```

(continued)

continued

```
PRINT "Highlight color = "; config.highlight;
INPUT "  Change to: ", config.highlight

PRINT "Inverse highlight color = "; config.inverseHighlight;
INPUT "  Change to: ", config.inverseHighlight

PRINT "Inverse color = "; config.inverse;
INPUT "  Change to: ", config.inverse

PRINT "Help color = "; config.help;
INPUT "  Change to: ", config.help

PRINT "Overstrike cursor size = "; config.cursorNormal;
INPUT "  Change to: ", config.cursorNormal

PRINT "Insert cursor size = "; config.cursorInsert;
INPUT "  Change to: ", config.cursorInsert

PUT #1, 1, config                   ' write the information to the file
UNLOCK #1                           ' unlock the entire file

CLOSE #1

END
```

WIDTH (File I/O)

See also: LPOS, LPRINT, POS (File I/O), PRINT, TAB

■ QB2	■ QB4.5	■ PowerBASIC
■ QB3	ANSI	■ GW-BASIC
■ QB4	■ BASIC7	✲ MacQB

Purpose

The WIDTH (File I/O) statement sets a maximum line width for sequential files. You can use the WIDTH statement, for example, to limit the line lengths in a file containing a report.

Syntax

WIDTH {#*filenum* ¦ *device*}, *width*

filenum is the file number of an open sequential file.

device is a string expression that specifies the name of a QuickBASIC device.

width is the desired width (in characters) of a line for either *filenum* or *device*.

Usage

```
WIDTH #1, 40
```

Sets the width of the specified file to 40 characters.

```
WIDTH "CONS:", 32
```

Sets the width of the QuickBASIC device CONS: to 32 characters.

Description

Usually, you write data to sequential files without formatting. However, you can use the WIDTH statement to prevent text from being written beyond a specified right margin. The WIDTH statement accomplishes this by wrapping any long line to the next line. Figure 17-11 illustrates the effects of a WIDTH statement.

```
WIDTH, #1, 25
sample$ = "ABCDEFGHIJKLMNOPQRSTUVWXYZABCDEFGHIJKLMNOPQRSTUVWXYZABCDEFGH"
PRINT #1, sample$
```

```
A B C D E F G H I J K L M N O P Q R S T U V W X Y
Z A B C D E F G H I J K L M N O P Q R S T U V W X
Y Z A B C D E F G H
```

Figure 17-11.
The use of the WIDTH statement.

Using the WIDTH statement with a filename lets you set the line width for an opened file or for a QuickBASIC device opened as a file. This is, in fact, the only way to change the line width of a file. Note that the file or device opened as a file must be open before you issue the WIDTH statement.

Using the WIDTH statement with a device name lets you set the line width for a QuickBASIC device. You cannot use the WIDTH statement to affect a DOS device. Note that WIDTH does not effect output to the device until the next time you open it.

Errors

If the specified device is not a QuickBASIC device (CONS:, SCRN:, LPT*n*:, or COM*n*), QuickBASIC returns an "Illegal function call" error message.

Compatibility

QuickBASIC for the Macintosh

Most of the Macintosh screen and printer fonts are proportional. (Different letters require different amounts of horizontal space.) Therefore, the line length specified by WIDTH depends on which font is in use.

Example

The following program creates a report whose lines do not exceed 80 characters.

```
OPEN "SALES.RPT" FOR OUTPUT AS #1           ' open report file
WIDTH #1, 80                                ' set line width to 80

PRINT #1, "Sales report as of "; DATE$      ' print heading

FOR region% = 1 TO 30
    PRINT #1, USING "Region ##: "; region%;  ' print line heading

    salesAmt% = RND * 50                    ' calculate fictitious sales
    FOR i% = 1 TO salesAmt%
        PRINT #1, "* ";                     ' write the graph to the file
    NEXT
    PRINT #1,                               ' move to next report line
NEXT                                        ' move to next region

CLOSE
```

WRITE

See also: INPUT #, PRINT #

■ QB2	■ QB4.5	■ PowerBASIC
■ QB3	ANSI	■ GW-BASIC
■ QB4	■ BASIC7	■ MacQB

Purpose

The WRITE # statement writes delimited, unformatted data to a sequential file. You can use the WRITE # statement to quickly write data to a file so that it can be easily read by the INPUT # statement.

Syntax

WRITE # *filenum*[, *expr* [, *expr*]...]

filenum is the file number of a currently open file.

expr is a numeric or string expression that contains the value to be written to the file. Separate multiple entries with commas.

Usage

```
WRITE #1, customerName$, customerAddress$, customerPhone$
```

Writes the values of three string variables (each separated by commas and enclosed in quotation marks) to the file opened as file number 1.

```
WRITE #2, patientName$, patientBirthday%, pastDueAmount#
```

Writes the values of three variables to the file opened as file number 2; the value of *patientName$* is enclosed in quotation marks in the file, and all the values are separated by commas.

Description

The QuickBASIC file input statement INPUT # requires that data be formatted and delimited. If you use the PRINT # statement to write data to a file, you must explicitly include spaces, quotation marks, or commas for delimiters. This can be difficult to enter and to read, as you can see in the following example:

```
PRINT #2, CHR$(34); patientName$; CHR$(34); ","; birthday%; ","; pastDueAmount#
```

You can perform the same operation with the following simpler and more readable WRITE # statement:

```
WRITE #2, patientName$, birthday%, pastDueAmount#
```

The specified file number is the number associated with the file to which the data will be written. Note that the file must have been opened as a sequential file by using the keyword OUTPUT or APPEND in the OPEN statement.

The value written to the file can be specified by a constant (quoted text, a numeric value, or a constant defined by CONST) or by an expression of any simple type, such as an array element, a record element, a simple variable, or a mathematical or string expression that uses QuickBASIC functions. If you don't use parameters in a WRITE # statement, the statement writes a blank line to the file.

When the WRITE # statement writes data to a file, it uses the least amount of space, while still allowing the INPUT # statement to later read what was written. As shown in Figure 17-12, WRITE # encloses string variables in quotation marks. Unlike the PRINT # statement, however, WRITE # writes numeric variables to the file without leading or trailing space. It writes negative numeric variables to the file with a preceding minus sign. Unlike the PRINT # statement, WRITE # inserts commas between all variables in the file. Figure 17-12 illustrates the actions of the WRITE # statement.

```
patientName$ = "Doe, John"
birthday! = 12170
pastDueAmount# = 150.25
```

"	D	o	e	,		J	o	h	n	"	,	1	2	1	7	0	,	1	5	0	.	2	5

Figure 17-12.
Using WRITE # to write to a file.

After writing the last specified value to the file, the WRITE # statement inserts a newline character in the file. Therefore, the next WRITE # or PRINT # statement writes data to the next line in the file. Unlike the PRINT # statement, the WRITE # statement always writes a newline character.

Comments

The WRITE # statement does not have a corresponding WRITE # USING statement to provide formatted output. If you must format data, use the PRINT # USING statement.

Because the WRITE # statement encloses strings in quotation marks, the INPUT # statement cannot correctly read strings that have been written to the file by using WRITE # and that already have quotation marks in them. If you need to read strings that include quotation marks, use the LINE INPUT # statement instead.

Example

The following program uses the WRITE # statement to write the contents of the current screen to a file; the program encloses each line in quotation marks so that you can later use the INPUT # statement to read the file one line at a time.

```
OPEN "SCREEN.DAT" FOR APPEND AS #1

FOR y = 1 TO 25
    screenLine$ = ""

    FOR x = 1 TO 80
        screenLine$ = screenLine$ + CHR$(SCREEN(y, x))
    NEXT

    WRITE #1, screenLine$
NEXT

WRITE #1, STRING$(80, 196)
WRITE #1, "This screen was written on ", DATE$, " at ", TIME$
WRITE #1, STRING$(80, 196)

CLOSE
```

SECTION IV

DEVELOPMENT

CHAPTER 18

DOS and Program Management

Introduction

QuickBASIC includes many commands and functions that help you control the interaction between your program and the DOS environment. For example, the program management routines discussed in this chapter let you perform the following operations:

- Use any of several methods to exit a QuickBASIC program
- Pass control to a second program (either a QuickBASIC source program or an executable file)
- Examine QuickBASIC's copy of the DOS environment and change or add to the variables in it
- Create, change to, or remove a disk directory
- Delete files from a disk
- Run the DOS command processor, execute any DOS commands or other programs, and then resume execution of a QuickBASIC program
- Send control instructions to or receive them from a device driver

Table 18-1 lists the QuickBASIC program-management statements and functions in alphabetic order.

Statement or function	Description
CHDIR	Makes the specified directory the current (default) directory.
CLEAR	Reinitializes (clears) all program variables; can also set the size of the QuickBASIC stack, which maintains data during subroutine and procedure calls.
: (Colon)	Separates multiple statements on the same program line.
COMMAND$	Returns the arguments of the command line that was used to run the current program.

Table 18-1. *(continued)*
QuickBASIC program-management statements and functions.

Table 18-1. *continued*

Statement or function	Description
END	Ends a program and closes all open files. If you execute END from within the QuickBASIC environment, control returns to that environment; otherwise, control returns to the operating system.
ENVIRON	Adds, removes, or changes an environment variable.
ENVIRON$	Returns the value of QuickBASIC's copy of a DOS environment variable.
IOCTL	Sends a control string to a device driver.
IOCTL$	Receives a status string from a device driver.
KILL	Deletes a disk file; can use DOS wildcards.
MKDIR	Creates the specified directory on a disk.
REM	Begins a comment (remark) line. A single quotation mark also begins a comment line or begins a comment at the end of an executable statement.
RMDIR	Removes a directory from a disk. The directory must not contain any files.
RUN	Restarts the current program (optionally, from a specified line number) or runs another program; however, the second program cannot access data from the first.
SHELL	Runs a copy of COMMAND.COM, the DOS command processor, with which you can run any DOS command or program (memory permitting).
STOP	Ends execution of the QuickBASIC program. If you execute STOP from within the QuickBASIC environment, open files are left open and control returns to that environment; otherwise, all files are closed and control returns to the operating system.
SYSTEM	Ends execution of the QuickBASIC program and returns control to the operating system. If you execute SYSTEM from within the QuickBASIC environment, control returns to that environment.

The Statement Separator and Comments

You can place several QuickBASIC statements on the same program line; merely separate the statements with a colon (:). Generally, putting several executable statements on the same line makes your code harder to read. Sometimes, however, putting multiple statements on one line makes your code easier to read, such as when you use multiple PRINT statements to force blank lines in a display:

```
PRINT : PRINT : REM skip two lines
```

This line includes two PRINT statements and a REM (remark, or comment) statement that explains the purpose of the line. Using a single quote mark symbol (') is a shorthand method for specifying a comment, as in the following statement:

```
PRINT : PRINT ' skip two lines
```

Note that you don't need to use a colon in front of a quoted comment on a line that contains executable statements. A comment introduced by a single quotation mark or by

REM can occupy a complete line by itself, but if a comment follows executable code on the same line, the comment must be preceded either by single quotation mark or by a colon and the REM keyword.

Exiting a QuickBASIC Program

QuickBASIC implicitly calls the END statement after the last statement in a program. END closes all files and terminates the program. You can insert END statements in any part of your program to exit the program, as shown in the following program segment:

```
DO
    DisplayMenu
    INPUT ans$
    IF UCASE$(ans$) = "X" THEN END
    IF UCASE$(ans$) = "A" THEN AddFile
LOOP
```

This loop executes END only if the user inputs "x" or "X." Note that the keyword END is also used with the statements DEF FN, FUNCTION, IF, SELECT CASE, SUB, and TYPE...END TYPE to indicate the end of these structures or definitions.

The END statement is similar to the STOP and SYSTEM statements. One difference, however, is that END closes all open files regardless of whether you execute the program from the QuickBASIC environment or from DOS. STOP leaves files open when you run the program from the QuickBASIC environment, but it closes files when you run the program from the command line. The SYSTEM statement performs identically to END.

If your program executes END, STOP, or SYSTEM while running in the QuickBASIC environment, control returns to that environment. If your program is running as a compiled executable file, control returns to the operating system.

Running Programs and Using DOS Commands in a Program

Both the CHAIN and RUN commands can be used to run a second program from a QuickBASIC program. CHAIN lets the second program access any variables declared in a COMMON statement; RUN does not. RUN, on the other hand, can either start a second program or restart the current program from the beginning or at a specified line number. CHAIN and RUN can run only BASIC source files from the QuickBASIC environment; they can run only executable files from a stand-alone executable program. (See the CHAIN and RUN entries for details about these statements.)

If you want your program to use a DOS command or run a batch file, you can specify the command or the batch file's name in a call to the SHELL statement. The SHELL statement exits the program, runs the DOS command processor

COMMAND.COM, performs the specified task, and then returns to the program. If you don't specify a command or batch file in a call to SHELL, it exits the program and runs the command processor until the user enters the EXIT command.

Reinitializing Variables and Setting Stack Size

The CLEAR statement sets all numeric variables and numeric array elements to 0, sets all string variables and string array elements to the null string (""), and closes all files. If you execute a CLEAR statement before you use RUN, you can restart a program with a clean slate.

CLEAR also clears the stack and can also set its size. The stack is the area in memory that QuickBASIC uses to store the contents of variables used in subroutine and function calls. For example, the statement

```
CLEAR , , 8000
```

reinitializes all variables and sets the stack to 8000 bytes. (The default for QuickBASIC is 2048 bytes.) You might need to increase the size of the stack if your program has many deeply nested subroutines or procedures or if you use recursive procedures (subprograms or functions that call themselves). You cannot use CLEAR within a procedure or subroutine. The stack maintains the location to which the procedure or subroutine must return, so after CLEAR erases the stack, the procedure or subroutine can't return control to the statement that called it.

Accessing the Command Line

The COMMAND$ function returns the command-line arguments that were specified when the program was invoked. For example, consider the following 1-line program:

```
PRINT "The command-line arguments are ";COMMAND$
```

You can compile this program, which is called GETCOM.BAS, and then run it from the command line with arguments as shown in the following statement:

```
C>GETCOM /a /b /c SOMEFILE
```

The program then displays the following message:

```
The command-line arguments are /a /b /c SOMEFILE
```

The */a*, */b*, and */c* arguments might be switches used to specify a task for your program, and *SOMEFILE* might be the file that your program will process. The sample program in the COMMAND$ entry demonstrates how to assign the command-line arguments to a string variable and then parse the string (split it into meaningful segments).

Reading and Setting Environment Variables

QuickBASIC programs can obtain and modify information about the DOS environment. The environment is an area of memory that DOS copies into the data area of a QuickBASIC program when it runs. The copy consists of a series of variables associated with strings of information. The most familiar environment variable is the PATH variable, which contains the names of the directories that DOS will search for executable files. For example, the following command assigns several directories to the PATH variable:

```
PATH=C:\DOS;C:\QB45;C:\WORD;C:\EXCEL
```

QuickBASIC provides a statement and a function that interact with your program's copy of the environment. The ENVIRON statement replaces the information in a DOS environment variable. For example,

```
ENVIRON "PATH=C:\ACCT;C:\TEMP"
```

changes the value of the PATH variable to *C:\ACCT;C:\TEMP*.

The ENVIRON$ function in QuickBASIC returns the value of an environment variable. The statement *ENVIRON$(1)* returns the first variable and its value, *ENVIRON$(2)* returns the second one, and so on. Thus, if PATH is the third variable in the environment, the statement

```
PRINT ENVIRON$(3)
```

displays *PATH=C:\ACCT;C:\TEMP*

Or, you can use a variable name with the ENVIRON$ statement to retrieve the value of the specified variable. The following statement displays the same string the previous example did:

```
PRINT ENVIRON$("PATH")
```

Remember that your QuickBASIC program receives only a copy of the original DOS environment; any changes specified in ENVIRON statements do not change the original DOS environment, which is restored when your program completes execution. However, if your program runs another program with the CHAIN or RUN command or the SHELL statement, the new program receives a copy of your program's environment, including any changes or additions you've made. (See the ENVIRON entry for suggestions about how to prevent "Out of memory" errors that occur because of the limited size of the DOS environment.)

Communicating with Device Drivers

The IOCTL ("I/O control") statement sends a string of instructions to a device driver, which is a special program that DOS installs in memory (usually by means of a DEVICE statement in the CONFIG.SYS file). The program interprets instructions for a specific device (such as the printer, communications port, or mouse) and translates them into the low-level instructions that the hardware uses. In turn, you can request that the device driver report the status of the device (for example, whether the printer is ready to accept more text). When you specify the file number associated with an open device, the IOCTL$ statement returns the corresponding status report if the device supports IOCTL instructions. Unfortunately, most devices (including the common devices LPT1, LPT2, COM1, COM2, and so on) are not designed to accept IOCTL instructions.

Managing Files and Directories

QuickBASIC provides many statements that let users manage files; Chapter 17, "Files," discusses most of these. QuickBASIC provides three statements that let users manage directories: MKDIR creates a directory, CHDIR changes the current directory, and RMDIR removes a directory. These statements are similar to their DOS counterparts; however, you can't abbreviate them as you can in DOS. All the QuickBASIC file-related and directory-related statements accept valid DOS pathnames of up to 128 characters. (Some earlier versions of BASIC limit pathnames to 63 characters.)

Related Reading

Lesser, Murray. *Advanced QuickBASIC 4.0: Language Extension with Modular Tools.* New York, N.Y.: Bantam Computer Books, 1988.

Prata, Stephen, with Harry Henderson. *The Waite Group's Microsoft QuickBASIC Primer Plus.* Redmond, Wash.: Microsoft Press, 1990.

CHDIR

See also: MKDIR, RMDIR, SHELL, SYSTEM

■ QB2	■ QB4.5	■ PowerBASIC
■ QB3	ANSI	■ GW-BASIC
■ QB4	■ BASIC7	■ MacQB

Purpose

The CHDIR statement changes the current directory. You can use CHDIR to change the default directory for file-related commands (such as OPEN or CHAIN) so that the program doesn't have to specify a full directory path.

Syntax

CHDIR *directory*

directory is a string expression of no more than 63 characters that specifies a new directory or directory path.

Usage

```
TEMPDIR$ = "C:\TEMP"
CHDIR tempdir$
```

Changes the current directory on the C drive to the directory specified in the string variable *tempdir$*.

```
CHDIR "C:\ACCT\DATA"
```

Changes the current directory on the C drive to the directory specified in the string literal.

Description

DOS maintains a current directory for each drive in the system. The current directory is the default that DOS and QuickBASIC use if you don't specify path information in a command. For example, if the current directory on drive C (the current drive) is TEMP, the FILES statement lists the contents of the directory C:\TEMP.

Note that DOS keeps track of both the current drive and the current directory on each drive. Changing the current directory on a drive does not change the current drive. For example, if the current drive is A, the statements

```
CHDIR "C:\TEMP"
FILES
```

change the current directory on the C drive but they list the current directory of drive A, not that of C:\TEMP. You cannot change to a new drive by using the CHDIR statement. To change the current drive from within a BASIC program, you must use the SHELL statement, as in the statement *SHELL "C:"*.

Your programs should not assume you are using a particular drive or directory; instead, they should set the current drive and directory explicitly.

Comments

The QuickBASIC CHDIR statement is similar to the DOS CHDIR command; however, there are two differences. First, QuickBASIC does not recognize the abbreviation CD. Second, if you do not specify a directory when you enter CHDIR at the DOS prompt, DOS returns the name of the current directory; using the QuickBASIC CHDIR command without a parameter results in an error message.

Errors

If you specify in the CHDIR statement a path that doesn't exist, QuickBASIC displays a "Path not found" error message. If you specify an expression that is not a string, QuickBASIC returns a "Type mismatch" error message. If you do not specify a parameter, QuickBASIC returns an "Expected: expression" error message.

Example

The following program prompts the user for a directory path and then uses a CHDIR statement to make that the current directory. A FILES statement then displays the contents of the specified directory.

```
INPUT "Enter the directory to which you want to change: ", dir$
CHDIR dir$      ' change the current directory

' display the contents of the directory
PRINT "*** Listing of files in "; dir$; " ***": PRINT
FILES
```

CLEAR

See also: DECLARE, DIM, ERASE, FRE, REDIM

✲ QB2	■ QB4.5	✲ PowerBASIC
✲ QB3	ANSI	✲ GW-BASIC
■ QB4	■ BASIC7	✲ MacQB

Purpose

The CLEAR statement reinitializes all program variables (setting numeric values to 0 and strings to the null string, ""), clears the stack, closes all files, and can change the size of the stack. (The stack holds the data used for procedure and subroutine calls.) You might use CLEAR to increase the stack size if a program has procedures that are recursive or deeply nested, or that include many parameters and automatic variables.

Syntax

CLEAR [, , *stack*]

stack is the number of bytes (in the range 0 through 65535) to be allocated for the stack used by the program. Note that you must always precede *stack* with two commas.

Usage

```
CLEAR
```

Reinitializes all variables, clears the stack, and closes all open files.

```
CLEAR , , 1024
```

Reinitializes all variables, clears the stack, closes all open files, and sets the stack size to 1024 bytes.

Description

The main use of the CLEAR statement is to reinitialize all variables (including array elements) to 0 (for numeric values) or to the null string (for string values). In a program that traps an error normally considered fatal (perhaps involving the corruption of data), you can use the CLEAR statement to clear all (potentially incorrect) variable values; you can then restart the program from the beginning with a clean slate. (You might also do this in a game, to begin a new game upon request.) Note that CLEAR closes all open files.

Do not use CLEAR simply to reinitialize arrays and other variables later in the program because CLEAR reinitializes *all* variables, not only the ones you want to reuse. You can use the ERASE statement to reinitialize specific arrays without affecting other variables.

You can also use CLEAR to change the size of the stack used by your program. In this case, be sure to call the CLEAR statement at the beginning of your program, before you dimension arrays or initialize other variables, because CLEAR reinitializes all variables. QuickBASIC adds the amount of stack space it requires and the amount of stack space you specify to compute the size of the entire stack. The default size of the stack is 2048 bytes. When you run programs in the QuickBASIC environment, the stack size remains at the most recently specified value until you run a different program.

Errors

If you use CLEAR in a subroutine, QuickBASIC displays a "Return without GOSUB" error message. If you use CLEAR in a procedure, QuickBASIC returns an "Illegal function call" error message when you run the program.

In QuickBASIC 4.0 and Microsoft BASIC 6.0, in a compiled program that is not stand-alone, CLEAR does not correctly restore the DATA for a READ statement. Instead, when QuickBASIC encounters the first READ statement after a call to CLEAR, it returns a "Syntax error" error message. You can correct this by inserting a RESTORE statement after CLEAR. This problem does not occur in programs run from within the QuickBASIC environment and does not occur in QuickBASIC 4.5 or Microsoft BASIC 7.0.

Warnings

Do not use CLEAR outside module-level code because the statement clears the values currently on the stack (even if you don't specify a stack size). If you use CLEAR in a procedure or subroutine, QuickBASIC clears the return address from the stack, and the procedure or subroutine can't return to the statement that called it. For the same reason, do not use CLEAR in an event-handling routine. Also, do not use CLEAR in a loop (such as a FOR statement) because it sets the value of the counter variable to 0.

Compatibility

QuickBASIC 2.0 and QuickBASIC 3.0

When you specify a stack size in the CLEAR statement supported by QuickBASIC versions 2.0 and 3.0, you must specify the number of bytes for the entire stack, not merely the number of bytes for the program. The minimum stack size for these versions of BASIC is 512 bytes.

PowerBASIC

PowerBASIC does not support the use of any parameters with the CLEAR statement. You cannot, therefore, specify the size of the stack by using the CLEAR statement.

GW-BASIC, BASICA, and QuickBASIC for the Macintosh

GW-BASIC, BASICA, and QuickBASIC for the Macintosh support a parameter to CLEAR that specifies the number of bytes in the data segment of memory, where the program and data are stored. Place this parameter immediately to the left of the parameter specifying the stack size.

Example

The following program shows how to use the CLEAR statement at the beginning of a program to set the size of the stack. The program uses the recursive function *Factorial#* to calculate the factorial of a number (the product of all of the values from 1 through the number). The program calls the FRE function with the parameter –2 so that the function returns the amount of space currently available on the stack. Note that the stack space decreases with each recursive call to the *Factorial#* function.

```
DECLARE FUNCTION Factorial# (num%)

INPUT "Change stack size (y/n) "; ans$
IF UCASE$(ans$) = "Y" THEN
    INPUT "Stack size: ", size
    CLEAR , , size
END IF

PRINT "Stack space available "; FRE(-2); " bytes."

INPUT "Factorial of what number "; number%
fact# = Factorial#(number%)
PRINT "Factorial of "; number%; " is "; fact#
```

(continued)

continued

```
FUNCTION Factorial# (num%)
    PRINT "Stack space left: "; FRE(-2)
    IF num% = 0 THEN
        Factorial# = 1
    ELSE Factorial# = (num% * Factorial#(num% - 1))
    END IF
END FUNCTION
```

: (Colon)

See also: DATA, REM

■ QB2	■ QB4.5	■ PowerBASIC
■ QB3	■ ANSI	■ GW-BASIC
■ QB4	■ BASIC7	■ MacQB

Purpose

The colon (:) separates BASIC statements on one line of source code.

Syntax

statement : *statement* [: *statement*...]

statement is any valid QuickBASIC statement.

Usage

```
FOR customer% = 1 TO numCustomers%
    PRINT custInfo(customer%).custName: PRINT custInfo(customer%).street
    PRINT custInfo(customer%).city: PRINT custInfo(customer%).zip
NEXT customer%
```

Uses the colon to place multiple PRINT statements on one line.

Description

If you use more than one statement in the same line of code, you must separate the statements by using a colon. Although you don't need to add spaces before or after the colon, they can make the code easier to read. The QuickBASIC editor adds spaces for you.

If you use a BASIC interpreter, such as BASICA, putting several statements on the same line reduces the memory used by line numbers. Because most BASIC programmers now use BASIC compilers such as QuickBASIC and don't use line numbers, this consideration is no longer relevant. However, placing more than one statement on a line can speed program execution slightly. If you are writing a program in which speed is a factor, you might want to experiment with multiple-statement lines.

Using more than one statement on a single line often makes code harder to read. In particular, it obscures the operation of branching and looping statements. Because of this, use the colon cautiously. You can more clearly reveal the structure of a loop, its conditions, and the statements affected by using block statements and indention.

Comments

The QuickBASIC 4.5 editor does not let you enter a line more than 256 characters long; however, it accepts longer lines loaded from disk files. If you complete a line created outside the QuickBASIC editor with an underscore character (_), then QuickBASIC combines that line and the one that follows into a single line, no matter how long it is. Note that you cannot use the underscore character to continue a REM or DATA statement.

The colon can also be used in a program to signify that the word preceding it is a line label.

Errors

When you create an executable file from within the QuickBASIC environment, QuickBASIC adds underscores to lines more than 256 characters long so that no errors occur. But if you use the command-line compiler, BC.EXE, and if a line exceeds 256 characters in length and is not continued with an underscore, QuickBASIC displays a "Line too long" error message when you compile the program.

Example

The following example illustrates the use of multiple statements on a program line. In this program, the second PRINT statement on some program lines makes the text double spaced; including the second PRINT statement on the same line makes the listing more compact without sacrificing readability.

```
TYPE Information
    custName AS STRING * 20
    street AS STRING * 15
    city AS STRING * 15
    zip AS INTEGER
END TYPE

numCustomers% = 15
DIM custInfo(numCustomers%) AS Information

PRINT "Customer Mailing List": PRINT  ' double-spaced
PRINT "=====================": PRINT
PRINT TAB(8); DATE$: PRINT
PRINT "---------------------": PRINT

FOR customer% = 1 TO numCustomers%
    PRINT custInfo(customer%).custName: PRINT custInfo(customer%).street
    PRINT custInfo(customer%).city: PRINT custInfo(customer%).zip
NEXT customer%
```

COMMAND$

See also: ENVIRON, ENVIRON$

■ QB2	■ QB4.5	■ PowerBASIC
■ QB3	ANSI	GW-BASIC
■ QB4	■ BASIC7	MacQB

Purpose

The COMMAND$ function returns a string containing the arguments in the command line that invoked the program. You can use the COMMAND$ function to display the initial conditions, options, or values that the user specified when starting the program.

Syntax

COMMAND$

Usage

```
file$ = COMMAND$
KILL file$
```

Assigns the filename specified on the command line to the variable *file$* and then deletes that file.

Description

The COMMAND$ function returns a string that contains everything the user typed on the command line (except the program name) to run the program. COMMAND$ changes all lowercase letters to uppercase and removes any leading blanks. The maximum number of characters returned by COMMAND$ is 124. By searching the returned string for specific arguments, such as filenames, a program can use information that the user entered to set options, assign source and destination files, or perform any other specific task.

To test a program that uses command-line arguments from the QuickBASIC environment, you can choose the Modify COMMAND$ option from the Run menu and enter the arguments you want to pass to the program's command line. You can also specify the command-line arguments when you start QuickBASIC by using on the QB command line the /CMD switch followed by the arguments. Until you change these parameters or exit QuickBASIC, a COMMAND$ statement used in any program in the QuickBASIC environment will return these arguments.

Example

The following program calls the subprogram *GetArgs*, which receives a string array that will hold the command-line arguments, a variable indicating the maximum number of arguments, and a variable that will contain the number of arguments found by the *GetArgs* subprogram.

The program calls the subprogram, which examines the string returned by COMMAND$ character by character, separating the string into individual arguments and storing the arguments in the array. The main program prints the values stored in the array and then uses a FOR loop to prompt the user to confirm deletion of each specified file.

```
DEFINT A-Z
DECLARE SUB GetArgs (args$(), maxArgs, argsFound)

CLS
maxArgs = 10                    ' maximum of 10 command-line arguments
found = 0                       ' number of arguments found
DIM comline$(1 TO maxArgs)      ' array to hold the arguments

GetArgs comline$(), maxArgs, found        ' get command-line arguments

PRINT "Number of command-line arguments found: "; found
IF found = 0 THEN PRINT "You must enter at least one filename!": END

PRINT "Command-line arguments are: ";
FOR arg = 1 TO found
    PRINT comline$(arg); " ";
NEXT arg

PRINT
FOR file = 1 TO found
    delete$ = comline$(file)
    PRINT "Delete "; delete$; " (y/n)";
    INPUT ans$
    IF UCASE$(ans$) = "Y" THEN KILL delete$
NEXT file

SUB GetArgs (args$(), maxArgs, argsFound) STATIC
    CONST TRUE = -1, FALSE = 0

    argsFound = 0:              ' the number of arguments found
    in = FALSE                  ' flag indicating character is part of an argument

    cmdline$ = COMMAND$         ' get the command-line arguments
    comLength = LEN(cmdline$)

    FOR char = 1 TO comLength             ' check one character at a time
        char$ = MID$(cmdline$, char, 1)   ' get next character
        IF (char$ <> " " AND char$ <> CHR$(9)) THEN ' check if not space or tab
            IF NOT in THEN    ' check whether already in an argument
                IF argsFound = maxArgs THEN EXIT FOR
                argsFound = argsFound + 1          ' found a new argument
                in = TRUE
```

(continued)

continued

```
            END IF
            ' add the character to the current argument
            args$(argsFound) = args$(argsFound) + char$
        ELSE                    ' character is a space or tab
            in = FALSE
        END IF
    NEXT char
END SUB
```

END

See also: FUNCTION, GOSUB... RETURN, GOTO, IF, SELECT CASE, SUB, TYPE...END TYPE

■ QB2	■ QB4.5	■ PowerBASIC
■ QB3	■ ANSI	✲ GW-BASIC
■ QB4	■ BASIC7	■ MacQB

Purpose

The END statement terminates a QuickBASIC program. The END keyword can also end a type, function, or subprogram definition or a block statement.

Syntax

END

Usage

```
PRINT "This is a very short program."
END
```

Terminates program execution at the second line.

Description

The END statement closes all open files and ends execution of a QuickBASIC program. After the program ends, control passes to the environment in which the program was run. If the program was run from the QuickBASIC environment, an END statement returns you to that environment; from there you can edit the program or run it again. If the QuickBASIC program is a compiled executable file run from the command line, END returns control to DOS, which displays the DOS prompt.

If your program includes subroutines, place an END statement between the main program and the first subroutine; this prevents the subroutine from being executed inadvertently. QuickBASIC executes an implicit END statement at the end of every program. Because of this you need not use an END statement as the last statement. The END statement can, however, enhance the readability of the program.

Compatibility

PowerBASIC

PowerBASIC allows you to specify a return expression as a parameter in a call to the END statement. END passes the value of the expression to the program that called the PowerBASIC program. The value should usually be the value of a DOS error code.

GW-BASIC and BASICA

In GW-BASIC and BASICA, the END statement returns control to the command level. The program remains in memory; you can execute any lines after the END statement by using a CONT (continue) statement, or you can restart the program by using the RUN statement.

Example

The following program uses two END statements. The one inside the loop causes the program to exit immediately if the user responds to the prompt by typing the letter Y.

```
CONST MILETOKILO = 1.61
PRINT "This program converts from miles per hour to kilometers per hour."
DO
    INPUT "Do you want to stop? "; ans$
    IF UCASE$(ans$) = "Y" THEN END
    INPUT "How fast are you driving (in miles per hour) "; mph
    PRINT "That's "; mph * MILETOKILO; " kilometers per hour."
LOOP UNTIL mph = 0
PRINT "You're out of gas!"
END
```

ENVIRON

See also: ENVIRON$, SHELL

■ QB2	■ QB4.5	■ PowerBASIC
■ QB3	ANSI	■ GW-BASIC
■ QB4	■ BASIC7	MacQB

Purpose

The ENVIRON statement either changes the value of an environment variable or adds an entry to the program's copy of the DOS environment (a list of systemwide variables and their values that QuickBASIC makes available to every running program). You can, for example, use ENVIRON to change information (such as a directory search path) for a program run from the current program by using RUN or for DOS commands executed by a SHELL statement.

Syntax

ENVIRON "*varname*=[*text* ¦;]"
ENVIRON "*varname* [*text* ¦;]"

varname is a string that identifies the environment variable. To assign a value to the variable, follow the name with an equal sign or a space; then specify *text*, which is the variable's value.

If you use a semicolon in place of text or if you don't specify any text, ENVIRON deletes the variable from the environment.

Usage

```
ENVIRON "PATH=C:\QB45;C:\QB45\TEST;C:\ACCT\TEST"
```

Changes the value of the PATH environment variable in the QuickBASIC copy of the environment.

```
ENVIRON "SOURCE= "
```

Deletes the environment variable SOURCE from the QuickBASIC copy of the environment.

Description

DOS maintains a memory area that contains several variables your programs might need to access. These variables include PATH, the list of directories that DOS searches for executable files; COMSPEC, the location and name of the command processor; and PROMPT, the string of characters that DOS uses for its prompt. Each of these variable names is associated with a string that contains its value. To display a list of the currently defined environment variables, type SET at the DOS prompt.

When a QuickBASIC program runs, it receives a copy of the DOS environment, that is, a list of the variables and their values. The ENVIRON statement lets you change the values of the variables and add or delete variables. Remember that this is only a copy of the DOS environment: You will see when you exit QuickBASIC that the original DOS environment is unchanged. However, changes your program makes are passed to any programs run from the program and are inherited by other programs you run in the QuickBASIC environment.

Comments

By default, the environment is usually small (128 or 256 bytes), so using the ENVIRON statement frequently generates an "Out of memory" error message. You can expand the DOS environment by using the DOS SHELL command in your CONFIG.SYS file. For example, the command

```
SHELL=C:\DOS\COMMAND.COM /p /e:512
```

places the COMMAND.COM command processor in memory *(/p)* and sets a maximum environment size of 512 bytes *(/e:512)*. This feature was introduced in MS-DOS version

3.1. In MS-DOS 3.1, you specify not the number of bytes as you do in MS-DOS versions later than 3.1 but rather the number of 16-byte "paragraphs" in the environment; therefore, the MS-DOS 3.1 version of the above statement is

```
SHELL=C:\DOS\COMMAND.COM /p /e:32
```

This statement does not in itself prevent "Out of memory" error messages because a QuickBASIC program receives only a copy of the actual environment, not the full space allocated in the MS-DOS SHELL command. You cannot increase the amount of memory used by the copy. Before running your QuickBASIC program, however, you can use the DOS SET command to allocate a "dummy" variable, as the following example shows:

```
SET EXPAND=123456789012345678901234567890
```

Your program can then create available space in its copy of the environment by deallocating this variable as follows:

```
ENVIRON "EXPAND=;"
```

The space is then available for new environment variables and values.

Errors

If the environment cannot be expanded to include a new variable (or a longer value for an existing variable), QuickBASIC displays an "Out of Memory" error message. If the parameter you specify with ENVIRON isn't a string (if, for example, you forgot to enclose it in sets of quotation marks), QuickBASIC returns a "Type mismatch" error message.

Example

The following program changes the PROMPT environment variable and displays the new prompt and the changed environment list.

```
CLS
PRINT "Current environment is: "
SHELL "SET"     ' display the current environment

PRINT "Changing the prompt: "
ENVIRON "PROMPT=Type 'exit' to return to BASIC ==>"
SHELL           ' run the command processor with the new prompt

PRINT "This is the modified environment: "
SHELL "SET"     ' display the modified environment
```

ENVIRON$

See also: ENVIRON, SHELL

■ QB2	■ QB4.5	■ PowerBASIC
■ QB3	ANSI	■ GW-BASIC
■ QB4	■ BASIC7	MacQB

Purpose

The ENVIRON$ function returns the value of the specified DOS environment variable.

Syntax

ENVIRON$({*var* ¦ *num*})

var is the name of an environment variable.

num is an integer that specifies the position of the variable you want in the list of environment variables.

Usage

```
PRINT ENVIRON$("PATH")
```

Displays the value of the environment variable PATH, which specifies the current search path.

```
env$ = ENVIRON$(3)
```

Assigns to the variable *env$* the environment variable (and its value) that is third in the environment variable list.

Description

The ENVIRON$ function returns the value of the specified environment variable. ENVIRON$ accepts either the name of an environment variable or a number representing a position in the environment variable list. The function is case sensitive, so *ENVIRON$("PATH")* returns the search path, and *ENVIRON$("path")* returns a null (empty) string (unless your environment includes a variable called *path*).

If you specify a number that is greater than the number of variables in the environment, ENVIRON$ returns a null string.

Comments

Remember that the environment examined by ENVIRON$ is the copy of the DOS environment that the program receives; it differs from the original DOS environment if you introduced changes by using the ENVIRON statement.

Errors

If you specify a name in ENVIRON$ that isn't a string, QuickBASIC displays a "Type mismatch" error message.

Example

The following program first uses ENVIRON$ in a loop to list all the variables in the environment. Note that the test for the null string terminates the loop after the last variable is listed. The second part of the program accepts an environment variable name from the user and then displays the value of the variable if the variable exists.

```
CLS
var = 1
DO WHILE (ENVIRON$(var) <> "")
    PRINT var; ": "; ENVIRON$(var)
    var = var + 1
LOOP

DO
    PRINT : PRINT "Type 'q' to quit or "
    INPUT "the name of a variable to examine: "; varName$
    IF UCASE$(varName$) = "Q" THEN END
    PRINT varName$; " ";
    IF ENVIRON$(varName$) = "" THEN
        PRINT "is not defined"
        ELSE PRINT "is "; ENVIRON$(varName$)
    END IF
LOOP
```

IOCTL

See also: IOCTL$

■ QB2	■ QB4.5	■ PowerBASIC
■ QB3	ANSI	✲ GW-BASIC
■ QB4	■ BASIC7	MacQB

Purpose

The IOCTL ("I/O Control") statement sends an instruction string to a device driver that supports such instructions. You might use IOCTL to initialize a modem or to send instructions to the mouse.

Syntax

IOCTL [#] *filenum*, *string*

filenum is the file number used in the OPEN statement that opened the device as a file.

string is a string that contains an instruction that is meaningful to the device driver; it must be enclosed in a set of quotation marks and cannot exceed 32767 characters.

Usage

```
OPEN "SCANNER" FOR OUTPUT AS #4
IOCTL #4, "READPAGE"
```

Opens the device driver of a scanner so that it can receive output and then sends it a command.

Description

DOS supports any device driver that accepts IOCTL instructions. A device driver is a memory-resident program that translates the general instructions for a device (such as a printer, disk drive, or mouse) into the specific instructions that the hardware can use. Built-in drivers, such as LPT1 and COM1, do not support IOCTL instructions; however, you can replace the built-in drivers with enhanced drivers that do support IOCTL. If the driver in question supports IOCTL, its documentation should list the valid instructions. Note that most device drivers do not support IOCTL instructions.

You must first install the device driver (usually by using a DEVICE statement in the CONFIG.SYS file) and then open it with an OPEN statement in your program before you can use the IOCTL statement to send it instructions.

Errors

If the specified driver does not support IOCTL instructions, QuickBASIC displays an "Illegal function call" error message.

Compatibility

GW-BASIC and BASICA

The maximum number of characters allowed in a string in GW-BASIC and BASICA is 255. Because of this, an instruction string in an IOCTL statement can be only up to 255 characters long.

Example

The following example demonstrates the use of IOCTL. It assumes that you have installed a driver named MYDRIVER.SYS, which can handle IOCTL instructions.

```
OPEN "C:\SYS\MYDRIVER.SYS" FOR OUTPUT AS #1     ' open device driver as a file
IOCTL #1, "BLOCK"          ' use block mode
IOCTL #1, "1024"           ' use a block length of 1024 bytes
IOCTL #1, "READ 4"         ' read four blocks
IOCTL #1, "SEND"           ' send the data
CLOSE                      ' close the driver
```

IOCTL$

See also: IOCTL, OPEN

■ QB2	■ QB4.5	■ PowerBASIC
■ QB3	ANSI	■ GW-BASIC
■ QB4	■ BASIC7	MacQB

Purpose

The IOCTL$ function returns status information from a device driver that supports IOCTL instructions. You can use IOCTL$, for example, to receive the status of a modem or mouse.

Syntax

IOCTL$([#] *filenum*)

filenum is the file number used in the OPEN statement that opened the device as a file.

Usage

```
OPEN "MODEM" FOR OUTPUT AS #1
PRINT IOCTL$(#1)
```

Opens the MODEM device driver and displays status information returned by the device driver.

Description

A device driver is a memory-resident program that translates general instructions for a device (such as a printer, disk drive, or mouse) into the specific instructions that the hardware can use. You can use the IOCTL$ function only with drivers that support IOCTL instructions.

An installed device driver that supports IOCTL can supply status information in the IOCTL$ function. The device driver usually supplies status information concerning an instruction sent with the IOCTL statement. (See the device-driver documentation for details about the status information that the device driver returns.) Note that most device drivers do not support IOCTL instructions.

You must first install a device driver (usually by using a DEVICE statement in the CONFIG.SYS file) and then open it with an OPEN statement in your program before you can use the IOCTL$ function.

Errors

If the specified device driver does not support IOCTL instructions, QuickBASIC returns an "Illegal function call" error message.

Example

The following program assumes that you have installed a driver called MYDRIVER.SYS. It first opens the device as file number 1. If IOCTL$ returns a 0, the driver is not yet ready to receive input.

```
OPEN "C:\SYS\MYDRIVER.SYS" FOR OUTPUT AS #1    ' open the device driver

IF IOCTL$(#1) = 0 THEN     ' driver returns 0 if it is not enabled
    PRINT "Driver not enabled"
    END                    ' exit the program
ELSE
    ' use the driver
END IF

CLOSE #1
```

KILL

See also: FILES, RMDIR

■ QB2	■ QB4.5	■ PowerBASIC
■ QB3	ANSI	■ GW-BASIC
■ QB4	■ BASIC7	■ MacQB

Purpose

The KILL statement deletes a file and frees the space it occupied. You use KILL as you use the DOS DEL or ERASE command—to free space when a disk is full or to delete old files.

Syntax

KILL *filespec*

filespec is a string variable or constant that specifies the file or files to delete; *filespec* can include the wildcards, ? and *, to specify a group of files.

Usage

```
KILL "CONFIG.DAT"
```

Deletes the file CONFIG.DAT in the current directory.

```
KILL "*.DAT"
```

Deletes all files with the extension DAT in the current directory.

```
KILL "A:\DATA\TEST*.*"
```

Deletes all files on drive A in directory DATA that begin with the letters TEST.

Description

The KILL statement deletes files; the required string variable or constant specifies the file or files to delete. Note that the filename portion can include the wildcard characters, ? and *. The wildcard character ? matches any character in the same position in the filename. The wildcard character * matches one or more characters in the filename.

If you omit a drive name from the file specification, KILL uses the current drive. If you omit a pathname, KILL uses the current directory of the current drive.

Comments

You can use wildcards only in the filename of the file specification. QuickBASIC doesn't recognize wildcards in the directory, drive name, or pathname.

Errors

You can delete only closed files with the KILL statement. If you try to delete an open file, QuickBASIC displays a "File already open" error message. KILL deletes only files; use the RMDIR statement to delete empty directories.

If the file specification does not match any file, QuickBASIC returns a "File not found" error message. If you specify the letter of an external drive that does not have a disk inserted, QuickBASIC displays a "Disk not read" error message. If the specified disk does not exist, QuickBASIC returns a "Device unavailable" error message.

Tips

The KILL statement, like the DOS commands DEL and ERASE, doesn't actually delete a file; it merely erases the information DOS uses to keep track of the file. Several commercial utility programs can recover deleted files if you have not overwritten the area of the disk where it was stored. To ensure security so that no one can recover the data, open the file before you delete it, and overwrite the contents with blanks.

Warnings

Unlike the DOS DEL command, the QuickBASIC KILL statement will not prompt you if you are about to delete the entire contents of a directory. A single KILL statement can erase an entire directory! KILL can also delete the currently running program file, so be careful when using this statement in your programs.

Example

The following program uses FILES to display the directory the user specifies and then uses KILL to delete all the files in the directory.

```
DO
    PRINT "Enter the pathname of a directory whose files you want to delete."
    PRINT "Press Enter to quit."
    LINE INPUT fileSpec$

    IF fileSpec$ = "" THEN EXIT DO

    PRINT
    FILES fileSpec$ + "\*.*"          ' display the files in the directory
    PRINT

    LINE INPUT "Delete these files? (Y/N) "; yesNo$
```

(continued)

continued

```
    IF UCASE$(yesNo$) = "Y" THEN
        KILL fileSpec$ + "\*.*"         ' delete the files in the directory
        PRINT "All files in the directory "; fileSpec$; " have been deleted."
        PRINT
        PRINT
    END IF
LOOP UNTIL fileSpec$ = ""
```

MKDIR

See also: CHDIR, RMDIR

■ QB2	■ QB4.5	■ PowerBASIC
■ QB3	ANSI	■ GW-BASIC
■ QB4	■ BASIC7	MacQB

Purpose

The MKDIR statement creates the specified directory. You can use MKDIR to let the user make a new directory from within your QuickBASIC program and store it anywhere on disk.

Syntax

MKDIR *directory*

directory is a string expression of no more than 127 characters that specifies the subdirectory to be created.

Usage

`MKDIR "TEMP"`

Creates TEMP, a subdirectory of the current directory.

`MKDIR "C:\ACCT\TEMP"`

Creates TEMP, a subdirectory of the ACCT directory, on drive C.

Description

The MKDIR statement works like the DOS command MKDIR. It creates a new directory on the specified disk. Note that MKDIR creates the directory as a subdirectory of the current directory unless you specify a pathname.

Be sure to trap errors that occur with the MKDIR statement so that the user will know whether the directory could not be created because it already exists or because a file has the same name. (See the ON ERROR GOTO entry in Chapter 9, "Trapping and Errors.")

Note that you cannot shorten the QuickBASIC statement MKDIR to MD as you can the DOS command MKDIR.

Errors

If you specify a directory that already exists or if a file has the same name as the directory, QuickBASIC returns a "Path/File access error" error message. If you specify an expression that is not a string, QuickBASIC returns a "Type mismatch" error message.

Example

The following program prompts the user for a directory name and then attempts to create the directory. It prints an error message if the directory already exists or there is already a file by that name.

```
ON ERROR GOTO Errorhandler     ' set up error trapping

INPUT "Directory to create: "; dir$
MKDIR dir$                     ' attempt to create the directory
END

Errorhandler:
    errNum = ERR
    IF errNum = 75 THEN
        PRINT "Unable to create directory "; dir$
        PRINT "Directory already exists or "
        PRINT "there's already a file with that name. "
    END IF
    RESUME NEXT
```

REM

See also: $DYNAMIC, $STATIC

■ QB2	■ QB4.5	■ PowerBASIC
■ QB3	■ ANSI	■ GW-BASIC
■ QB4	■ BASIC7	■ MacQB

Purpose

The REM statement lets you include a comment in a program. You can use a single quotation mark in place of the keyword REM. A comment is a nonexecutable statement that describes or explains the operation of a program. REM can also introduce a metacommand (a special instruction to the compiler), such as $DYNAMIC.

Syntax

[REM | '] *comment*

comment is text that has any combination of characters. If you use the REM keyword, a comment that follows an executable statement on the same line must begin with a colon; spaces before and after the colon are optional.

Usage

```
REM Perform the operation each day of the week
FOR day% = 1 to 7
    CALL Total(sales(day%))        ' call the subprogram Total
NEXT day%
```

The first comment explains the purpose of the section of code; the second describes the action of a line of code.

Description

The REM statement introduces a remark, description, explanation, or metacommand in your program. QuickBASIC ignores text—except a metacommand—that follows the keyword REM or single quotation mark until you begin a new line. To add a remark to an executable statement, follow the statement with a colon and then begin the REM statement:

```
CALL Tree : REM catalog the hard disk
```

Note that you can also use a single quotation mark instead of a colon and the REM keyword:

```
CALL Tree ' catalog the hard disk
```

In a program that uses line numbers, you can use a REM statement as the destination line for a GOTO or GOSUB statement. Execution continues at the first executable statement after the REM statement.

Warnings

To include a comment within a DATA statement, you must use REM rather than a single quotation mark: QuickBASIC treats a single quotation mark as part of the data.

Do not confuse the single-quote comment character with a set of double quotation marks. A double quotation mark indicates a string character.

Example

The following program includes comments by using the REM statement and the single quotation mark.

```
REM this program displays the string "Hello" 50 times

FOR i% = 1 TO 50
     PRINT "Hello";     ' display the string
NEXT i%

END
```

RMDIR

See also: CHDIR, FILES, KILL, MKDIR

■ QB2	■ QB4.5	■ PowerBASIC
■ QB3	ANSI	■ GW-BASIC
■ QB4	■ BASIC7	MacQB

Purpose

The RMDIR statement removes a directory from a disk. The directory cannot contain any files.

Syntax

RMDIR *directory*

directory is a string expression of no more than 127 characters that specifies the subdirectory to be deleted.

Usage

```
RMDIR "C:\ACCT\TEMP"
```

Removes the TEMP subdirectory from the ACCT directory on drive C.

```
RMDIR dir$
```

Removes the directory specified by the value of the string variable *dir$*.

Description

The RMDIR statement deletes a directory that contains no files; it works in the same way as the DOS RMDIR command, except that you can't use the abbreviation RD in QuickBASIC. If your program creates a directory to store temporary files that hold intermediate steps in processing, for example, you can use RMDIR to remove the directory when your program no longer needs the files. First you must delete the temporary files by using the KILL statement. Then you can remove the directory by using RMDIR.

Errors

If the directory you specify in the RMDIR statement does not exist, QuickBASIC returns a "Path not found" error message. If the specified directory is not empty, QuickBASIC displays a "Path/File access error" error message. This error also occurs if you specify the name of a file rather than a directory. If you don't specify a string in the RMDIR statement, QuickBASIC displays a "Type mismatch" error message.

Example

The following program lets the user remove a directory. The program uses the ON ERROR GOTO statement to trap for the "Path/File access error" error message, which usually indicates that the directory isn't empty. The error handler asks the user whether he or she wants to remove the files. Note that the program does not distinguish between a nonempty directory and a file. If the user enters the name of a file, the KILL statement fails, and QuickBASIC returns a "Path not found" error message, so it is not necessary to make a distinction between a nonempty directory and a file.

```
ON ERROR GOTO Errhandler  ' set up error trapping

INPUT "Name of directory to remove: "; dir$
RMDIR dir$                ' attempt to remove the directory
END

Errhandler:
    errNum = ERR
    PRINT "Error number: "; errNum
    SELECT CASE errNum
    CASE 75               ' the directory probably contains files
        PRINT dir$; " isn't empty."
        PRINT "Do you still want to remove it?"
        PRINT "(All files in the directory will be deleted.)"
        INPUT ans$
        IF UCASE$(ans$) = "Y" THEN
            delDir$ = dir$ + "\*.*"    ' construct a path containing wildcards
            KILL delDir$               ' delete all files in the directory
            RESUME                     ' try removing directory again
        END IF

    CASE 76               ' the directory was not found
        PRINT dir$; " was not found."
    CASE ELSE
        ON ERROR GOTO 0   ' disable error trapping
    END SELECT
    RESUME NEXT
```

RUN

See also: CHAIN, CLEAR, GOTO, SHELL

✲ QB2	■ QB4.5	✲ PowerBASIC
✲ QB3	ANSI	✲ GW-BASIC
■ QB4	■ BASIC7	✲ MacQB

Purpose

You can use the RUN statement either to restart the current program from the beginning or from a specified line number or to run a second program. You can use RUN, for example, to restart a program after an error or to run a series of self-contained programs that don't need to share variables.

Syntax

RUN [*line* ¦ *file*]

line is the line number in the current program at which execution restarts.

file is a string expression of no more than 127 characters that contains the name of the program to be loaded into memory and run.

Usage

```
RUN 100
```

Restarts the current program at line 100.

```
RUN "ENDGAME"
```

Loads the ENDGAME program into memory and runs it.

```
RUN "C:\ACCT\CALC.COM"
```

Runs the CALC.COM program.

Description

The RUN statement transfers control either to the current program (at the beginning or at a specified line number) or to another program. Note that control does not return to the program that executed the RUN statement. If you specify a line number, RUN acts like a GOTO statement except that it closes all open files and clears all variables. In effect, RUN reruns the current program from the specified line. If you use RUN without a parameter, the current program executes from the beginning. You cannot use a non-numeric line label as the target of a RUN statement.

You can also use RUN to execute another program, beginning at the first line of the program. If the other program isn't in the current directory, you must specify its location by including a pathname. If you want to run the other program from the QuickBASIC environment, the specified program must be a QuickBASIC source file. QuickBASIC assumes that the program has the extension BAS, so you don't need to specify the extension.

If you execute RUN from a compiled program (an executable file run from DOS), QuickBASIC assumes that the specified program is another file with the extension EXE, so you don't need to specify the extension. To run a program that has a different extension, you must specify the extension.

Programmers today rarely use the RUN statement to run a second program because the CHAIN statement is much more versatile. It lets you run a second program, maintain open files, and access any variables specified by a COMMON statement—these are great advantages when you use a group of related programs.

Comments

RUN cannot run a DOS batch file. To run a batch file you must use the SHELL statement.

RUN does not let you preserve or share variable values from the original program. It also closes all open files, so be aware that the second program might need to reopen them.

Errors

If the program you specify in the RUN statement does not exist, QuickBASIC returns a "File not found" error message. If the line number you specify does not exist or is not in module-level code, QuickBASIC returns a "Label not defined" error message.

Compatibility

QuickBASIC 2.0 and QuickBASIC 3.0

QuickBASIC versions 2.0 and 3.0 return an "Illegal function call" error message if you execute a RUN statement in an event-handling subroutine. This occurs because a RUN statement clears the return address from the stack.

PowerBASIC

You cannot specify a line number as a parameter to the RUN statement in PowerBASIC. If you want to use RUN to restart the current program, you can restart it only from the beginning.

GW-BASIC, BASICA, and QuickBASIC for the Macintosh

These versions of BASIC support the R parameter in the RUN statement. When placed in the RUN statement immediately after the filename of the program to be run, the letter R specifies that all open files will remain open for the next program.

Example

The following program is the "front end" of an application program; it uses RUN to run the program PLANNER.BAS after displaying instructions (if the user requests them).

```
CLS
PRINT "Welcome to Project Planner."
INPUT "Do you need instructions (Y/N)"; ans$

IF UCASE$(ans$) = "Y" THEN
     PRINT "Instructions for using PLANNER.BAS"
     PRINT "More instructions...": PRINT
     PRINT "Press any key to continue..."
     ans$ = INPUT$(1)    ' wait for keypress
END IF
RUN "PLANNER.BAS"        ' assumes file in same directory
END
```

```
' PLANNER.BAS
CLS
PRINT "*** PLANNER MAIN MENU ***"
PRINT "Rest of PLANNER program runs here."
```

SHELL

See also: CHAIN, ENVIRON, RUN

■ QB2	■ QB4.5	■ PowerBASIC
■ QB3	ANSI	■ GW-BASIC
■ QB4	■ BASIC7	MacQB

Purpose

The SHELL statement lets you run a DOS command (or any executable or batch file) from a QuickBASIC program. In effect, the SHELL statement adds all the capabilities of DOS to QuickBASIC. For example, although no QuickBASIC command lets you format a disk, you can use the SHELL statement to call the DOS FORMAT command.

Syntax

SHELL [*command*]

command is a string expression containing a command that DOS can execute. Without parameters, SHELL runs the DOS command processor; the user must type EXIT on the command line to resume execution of the program.

Usage

```
SHELL "FORMAT B:"
```

Formats the disk in drive B from a QuickBASIC program; the DOS command FORMAT issues its usual prompts.

```
cmd$ = "DIR " + file$ + " /p"
SHELL cmd$
```

Executes the DOS command line contained in the variable *cmd$*.

Description

The SHELL statement runs a copy of the DOS command processor, COMMAND.COM, which inherits the DOS environment used by the current QuickBASIC program. SHELL is therefore equivalent to the DOS command COMMAND with the /C switch. Any commands in the specified string following the keyword SHELL are passed to DOS as though you had typed them at the DOS command line.

If the SHELL statement specifies a command that does not have an extension, DOS looks first for a command file with the extension COM, then for an executable file with the extension EXE, and finally for a batch file with the extension BAT. Unless you specify a pathname, DOS assumes the file is in the current directory. However, if the environment includes a PATH environment variable, DOS also searches the specified directories for the file.

Although the DOS command or program that you run with SHELL does not have direct access to the variables in your QuickBASIC program, you can convey information to the command or program by setting variables in the environment (discussed in the ENVIRON entry) or by specifying options in the SHELL statement's command string.

Note that DOS, not QuickBASIC, reports (or records) any errors caused by the command.

Errors

Because SHELL passes control to DOS, most errors (such as "File not found") are reported by DOS, not QuickBASIC. (See your DOS documentation for an explanation of DOS errors.) If you specify a parameter in SHELL that is not a string, QuickBASIC returns a "Type mismatch" error message.

Warnings

Because a QuickBASIC program remains in memory when it executes a SHELL statement, you cannot run a program by using SHELL if the program uses more than the available amount of memory. DOS returns an "Insufficient memory" error message if there is not enough memory for the program.

Example

The following program provides a menu of several DOS commands that the program performs on request. The user must enter E to exit the program. The inner loop (around the menu) displays the menu until the user enters a valid character.

Note how the command line to be used with each SHELL statement is constructed. Because the statements *SHELL "DIR file$"* and *SHELL "DIR ";file$* are invalid, you must build the command string by concatenating the DOS command with the string that is input by the user. Note that you sometimes need to add spaces: For example, you must add a space between the DOS COPY command and the source filename and between the source and target filenames.

```
DO              ' outer loop--loop until user enters E
    DO          ' inner loop--loop until user enters a valid letter
        CLS
        PRINT "Access DOS from BASIC to: "
        PRINT "V)iew a file"
        PRINT "D)irectory"
        PRINT "P)rint a file"
        PRINT "C)opy a file"
        PRINT "E)xit the program"
        INPUT choice$
        choice$ = UCASE$(choice$)
    LOOP UNTIL INSTR("VDPCE", choice$) <> 0
```

(continued)

continued

```
    CLS
    SELECT CASE choice$
    CASE "V"
        INPUT "View what file "; file$
        cmd$ = "MORE <" + file$
        SHELL cmd$
    CASE "D"
        INPUT "See which directory "; dir$
        cmd$ = "DIR " + dir$ + " /p"
        SHELL cmd$
    CASE "P"
        INPUT "Print what file "; file$
        cmd$ = "PRINT " + file$
        SHELL cmd$
    CASE "C"
        INPUT "File to be copied: ", source$
        INPUT "Copy to what file: ", dest$
        cmd$ = "COPY " + source$ + " " + dest$
        SHELL cmd$
    CASE "E"
        END
    CASE ELSE
       PRINT "Invalid Command: "; choice$
    END SELECT

    PRINT : PRINT "Press any key to continue"
    ans$ = INPUT$(1)
LOOP
```

STOP

See also: END

■ QB2	■ QB4.5	■ PowerBASIC
■ QB3	■ ANSI	✲ GW-BASIC
■ QB4	■ BASIC7	■ MacQB

Purpose

The STOP statement terminates a QuickBASIC program.

Syntax

STOP

Usage

```
PRINT "Executing first line"
STOP
```

Terminates the program after executing the PRINT statement.

Description

The STOP command stops execution of a program. When used within the QuickBASIC environment, STOP leaves files open and returns control to the QuickBASIC environment. When used within a compiled program, STOP closes all files and returns control to DOS. STOP is the same as END, except that STOP (when used within the QuickBASIC environment) leaves open files open, and END closes them.

The STOP command is used in earlier versions of BASIC as a debugging tool that lets you set a breakpoint at which the program will stop and return you to command mode. After you perform any debugging task you want, you can resume execution following the line containing the STOP statement. QuickBASIC 4.5 includes a powerful interactive debugger that is much easier to use for setting breakpoints, examining variables, and tracing program flow.

STOP is also used with various event-trapping statements to suspend trapping for the specified event. (For more information, see the following entries: KEY(n) ON/OFF/STOP, PEN ON/OFF/STOP, PLAY ON/OFF/STOP, STRIG ON/OFF/STOP, TIMER ON/OFF/STOP, and UEVENT ON/OFF/STOP.)

Compatibility

GW-BASIC and BASICA

In GW-BASIC and BASICA, the STOP statement returns control to the command level without closing any open files. The program remains in memory; you can execute any lines after the STOP statement by using a CONT (continue) statement, or you can restart the program with the RUN statement.

Example

The following program executes three assignment statements that use the RND function; when control reaches the STOP statement, the program terminates. Note that the fourth assignment statement isn't executed unless you run the program from within the QuickBASIC environment and then choose the Continue command from the Run menu to complete the program.

```
first = INT(3 * RND) + 1
second = INT(3 * RND) + 2
third = INT(3 * RND) + 3
STOP
fourth = first + second + third
```

SYSTEM

See also: END, SHELL, STOP

■ QB2	■ QB4.5	■ PowerBASIC
■ QB3	ANSI	■ GW-BASIC
■ QB4	■ BASIC7	■ MacQB

Purpose

The SYSTEM statement closes all open files and terminates a QuickBASIC program.

Syntax

SYSTEM

Usage

```
PRINT "This program is running in the QuickBASIC environment."
SYSTEM
```

Returns control to the QuickBASIC environment.

Description

The SYSTEM statement ends execution of a QuickBASIC program and removes the program from memory. If you run the program as a compiled, executable file or you run the program by specifying the program and the /RUN option when you start QuickBASIC, control returns to the operating system. However, if you run the program in the QuickBASIC environment, control returns to the environment. (If you enter a SYSTEM statement in QuickBASIC's Immediate window, QuickBASIC terminates and returns you to the operating system.)

The END and SYSTEM commands operate identically in QuickBASIC. (Both statements are supported for compatibility with GW-BASIC and BASICA.) The STOP statement is the same as END, except that STOP (when executed in the QuickBASIC environment) leaves open files open.

The SHELL statement is similar to SYSTEM because it exits QuickBASIC and invokes the operating system. However, SHELL does not remove the QuickBASIC program from memory, and the program continues executing after the command in the SHELL statement finishes executing or after the user types EXIT at the DOS prompt.

Example

The following program demonstrates that the SYSTEM statement returns control to the environment from which the program is run. If you run this program from within the QuickBASIC environment, it returns control to that environment. If you compile the program and run it as an executable file, it returns control to DOS.

```
PRINT "Program now running."
PRINT "Program still running";
FOR i% = 1 TO 10
    PRINT ".";
    SLEEP 1
NEXT i%

SYSTEM
```

CHAPTER 19

Port and Memory

Introduction

This chapter discusses how QuickBASIC programs can access the information stored in your computer's memory. It also shows you how to communicate directly with the computer hardware by using the memory outside the normal address space—the set of input/output channels known as ports. Table 19-1 lists QuickBASIC's port and memory statements and functions in alphabetic order.

Statement or function	Description
BLOAD	Loads a block of memory stored in a file into memory at an absolute address
BSAVE	Saves a block of memory to a disk file
FRE	Returns the amount of available stack space, string space, or memory
INP	Returns the byte at the specified port
OUT	Sends a byte to the specified port
PEEK	Returns the byte at the specified address
POKE	Writes a byte to the specified address
SETMEM	Specifies the amount of memory allocated for the far heap
WAIT	Waits for a specific signal to be read from the specified port

Table 19-1.
Port and memory statements and functions.

Memory

Several QuickBASIC statements and functions let you reference data stored at a specified address in your computer's memory. The PEEK function, for example, returns the contents of the byte at the specified location; the CALL ABSOLUTE statement lets you execute a machine-language program that begins at the specified address in memory. Note that these statements require the address to be an integer in the range 0 through 65535, so you can access a block of memory that contains only up to 64 KB. Each block of memory is called a segment. The QuickBASIC data segment, DGROUP, is one of the segments that you can access.

Your computer probably has considerably more than 64 KB of memory. IBM PCs and compatible computers can have up to 640 KB of random-access memory and

384 KB of memory dedicated to the video display, disk-drive controller, and ROM BIOS programs. Therefore, you can access as much as 1 MB (1024 KB) of memory.

Addressing Memory

You can specify any address in memory by using two 16-bit numbers: the segment and the offset. The number of the segment specifies the block of memory to be accessed; the number of the offset specifies the location of the address within the block of memory. Because the segment and offset are both 16-bit numbers, programmers often write addresses as two 4-digit hexadecimal values separated by a colon. For example, the address at segment 15, offset 145, is expressed as 000F:0091.

Each segment in memory begins at a paragraph boundary. (A paragraph is a block of 16 bytes.) Because of this, the 1 MB of address space in the PC can be divided into 65,535 possible segments. Any segment larger than 16 bytes, of course, will overlap the segments beginning at the next and subsequent paragraph boundaries.

QuickBASIC Programs in Memory

QuickBASIC uses a single 64-KB segment, DGROUP, to hold all the simple variables that a program uses. This 64-KB segment limit is the main factor that limits the size of your programs. Only complex variables, such as huge arrays, dynamic numeric arrays, and dynamic arrays of fixed-length strings, are given their own segments outside of DGROUP.

QuickBASIC uses DGROUP to contain the program stack, which stores temporary variables and the return addresses of subroutines. QuickBASIC also uses the code segment, which contains the program's statements.

Figure 19-1 shows how a QuickBASIC program is stored in memory. The program in the figure represents the simplest example—a stand-alone executable file created by the command-line compiler, BC.EXE, with the /O switch specified. If the program were an executable file that used the runtime library BRUN45.EXE, additional code would occupy the top of memory (above the far heap and communication buffers). When you run programs in the QuickBASIC environment, this space holds the Quick library (if a library is loaded).

Accessing Memory

QuickBASIC provides statements that let you examine and change memory directly. The PEEK function returns the value of the byte at a specified address, and the POKE statement lets you load a value into the byte at a specified address. The address, in both cases, is an unsigned integer value in the range 0 through 65535 that corresponds to the offset of the byte, which is measured from the beginning of the current segment. Because a byte consists of 8 bits, POKE can load only values in the range 0 through 255 into memory, and PEEK can return only values in the same range.

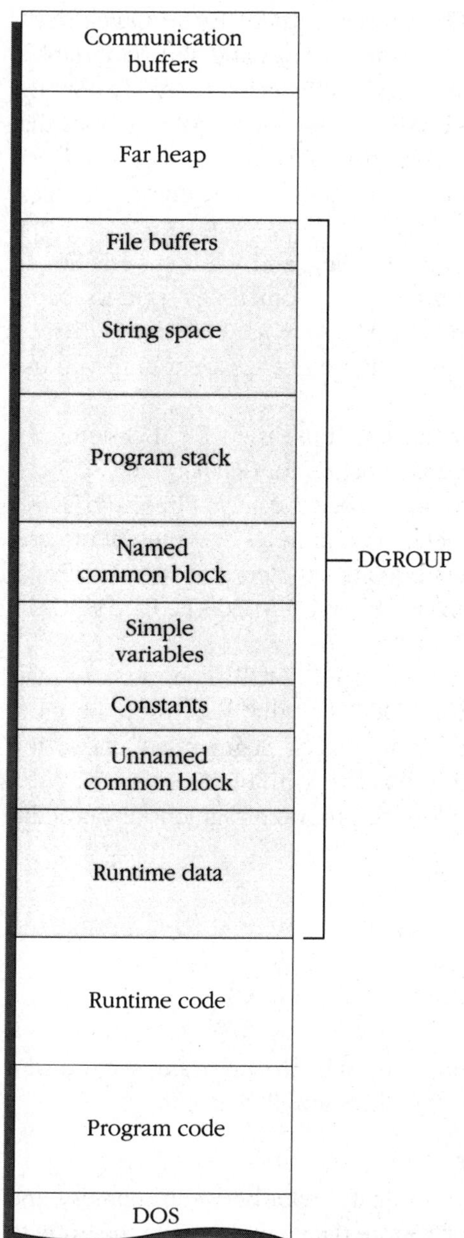

Figure 19-1.
Memory map of a QuickBASIC program.

Unless otherwise specified, PEEK and POKE access DGROUP, the QuickBASIC data segment. (See Figure 19-1.) Because DGROUP stores strings and simple variables, PEEK and POKE let you read or modify these objects directly as long as you know the location at which they are stored. Indeed, QuickBASIC supports a pair of functions that return this information: the VARPTR function returns the offset address of a numeric variable, and the SADD function does the same for a string. (See these entries in Chapter 20, "Mixed Language," for details.)

Of course, QuickBASIC offers easier ways of reading and loading variables in DGROUP than by using PEEK or POKE. Although PEEK is sometimes used to load a machine-code routine into a string (discussed in the CALL ABSOLUTE entry in Chapter 20, "Mixed Language"), the benefits of PEEK and POKE are not apparent until you use them outside the DGROUP data segment.

To access memory outside of DGROUP, you must first use the DEF SEG statement to select a new segment. (See Chapter 20, "Mixed Language," for details.) DEF SEG can specify any segment (0 through 65535) in the address space; because PEEK and POKE can address any offset within a full 64-KB segment, you can read or write data to any location in memory. The new segment you select becomes the current segment for all statements and functions that use absolute memory addresses—BLOAD, BSAVE, CALL ABSOLUTE, PEEK, and POKE.

Which areas of memory can you access outside of DGROUP? The memory map shown in Figure 19-1 includes the memory outside DGROUP that your program uses. (Be careful, however, about changing memory in the stack segment.) Outside the memory used by your program are areas that you can access with PEEK and POKE used by DOS and the ROM BIOS. For example, the following program fragment displays the release date of your computer's ROM BIOS:

```
DEF SEG = &HFFF0
romDate$ = ""
    FOR i% = 0 TO 7
        romDate$ = romDate$ + CHR$(PEEK(&HF5 + i%))
    NEXT i%
PRINT romDate$
```

For other examples of addresses outside the memory used by the program, see the DEF SEG entry in Chapter 20, "Mixed Language," and the PEEK and POKE entries.

Loading and Saving Blocks of Memory

QuickBASIC provides two statements that let you transfer data between memory and disk. If, for example, your program uses an array to store data, you can save the array to a disk file by using the BSAVE command. The next time you execute the program, you can reload the array into memory by using the BLOAD command.

Perhaps the most common use for BLOAD and BSAVE is to load and store screen images. To BSAVE, the video buffer is exactly the same as any other part of memory. You can use BSAVE to capture a graphics screen your program has created and store it in a disk file; you can later retrieve the screen by using BLOAD. The BLOAD and BSAVE entries include sample programs that let you load and save graphics displays in any screen mode.

The Far Heap

QuickBASIC also stores data in an area of memory above DGROUP. This area, called the "far heap," contains large variables such as huge arrays, dynamic numeric arrays, and dynamic arrays of fixed-length strings, each array occupying a segment of its own. The far heap (shown in Figure 19-1) uses the memory remaining after all other segments have been allocated.

Usually, QuickBASIC performs all the operations in the far heap for you, assigning memory from it when you dimension a new array and releasing memory back to it when you erase the array. However, if you use mixed-language procedures in your programs, problems can arise. Although QuickBASIC maintains its own arrays, it doesn't free memory for arrays created by a program in another language. Therefore, if your mixed-language routine needs memory from the far heap for any reason, you will have to use the SETMEM function to free the memory yourself.

Use SETMEM to change the number of bytes in the far heap. If the parameter is a negative number, that amount of memory is released; if it is positive, that amount of memory is requested from the operating system. However, SETMEM must release memory the first time you use it because when DOS starts your program it allocates all available space for the far heap of your program.

The FRE function lets you examine your program's use of memory. If you specify –1 as the function's parameter, FRE returns the number of bytes available in the heap, which is the area of memory used to hold all variables. (The heap is described in two parts. The near heap is the section of memory that contains strings and simple variables. As described earlier, the far heap stores huge arrays, dynamic numeric arrays, and dynamic arrays of fixed-length strings.) If you specify a parameter of –2, FRE returns the number of available bytes in the program stack. If you use any other number or a string as the parameter, the function returns the available string space. If you specify a string, FRE compacts the free string space into a single block of memory before returning the amount of available string space.

Ports

In addition to memory that holds data and active programs (including DOS and the ROM BIOS), your computer has an additional section of memory, which you can access from within QuickBASIC. This is the 64-KB block of memory used by hardware ports, which is outside the normal PC address space but which nevertheless can be read from and written to by your programs.

When you communicate by using a port, you are reading and writing to this block of memory. The INP function and the OUT statement are the same as PEEK and POKE, except that before they access a port address, they send a signal on the system bus to indicate the address is not in normal PC address space, but is the number of a port.

A port is an input/output (I/O) channel through which a hardware device sends information to your program and receives instructions in return. Hardware devices include the processor's support chips, the keyboard, disk controller, video adapter, math coprocessor, and so on. Every hardware device in your system is associated with one or more ports. Even so, because there are 65,536 port addresses available, many are not used. Table 19-2 lists the port addresses of the most common hardware devices.

Port address	Device description
000H–01FH	Direct memory access (DMA) controller
020H–03FH	Programmable interrupt controller
040H–05FH	Programmable interval timer
060H–06FH	Keyboard controller
070H–07FH	Real-time clock (PC/XT and PS/2 Model 30) CMOS configuration RAM (PC/AT and other PS/2s)
0A0H	NMI mask register (PC, PC/XT, and PS/2 Model 30)
0C0H–0CFH	Complex-sound generator (PCJr and Tandy 1000)
0E0H–0EFH	Real-time clock (PC/AT and PS/2 series)
0F0H–0FFH	Math coprocessor
1F0H–1F8H	Hard-disk controller
200H–207H	Game controller (joystick)
278H–27FH	Third parallel printer
2F8H–2FFH	Second serial port
300H–31FH	Prototype card
320H–32FH	Hard-disk controller (PC/XT and PS/2 Model 30)
360H–363H, 368H–36BH	PC network controller
378H–37FH	Second parallel printer
3A0H–3A9H	Bisynchronous adapter (mainframe link)
3B0H–3BBH	Monochrome Display Adapter (MDA); also used by EGA and VGA in monochrome video modes
3BCH–3BFH	First parallel printer port
3C0H–3CFH	Enhanced graphics adapters (EGA and VGA)
3D0H–3DFH	Color graphics adapters (CGA and MCGA); also used by EGA and VGA in color video modes
3F0H–3F7H	Floppy-disk controller
3F8H–3FFH	First serial port

Table 19-2.
Major I/O port addresses on PC systems.

The OUT statement writes a byte of information to a port address; the INP function returns the current setting of a port. The WAIT statement waits for a specific signal to be read from a port. If you have installed a data-acquisition device in your computer, such as a bar code reader, the WAIT statement can pause execution until that device is ready to transmit data. The INP function and the OUT and WAIT statements are rarely used in everyday programming because the higher-level QuickBASIC I/O statements and functions let you control system devices indirectly. Nevertheless, these statements let you program hardware at its lowest level whenever the need arises.

Related Reading

Davies, Russ. *Mapping the IBM PC and PCjr.* Greensboro, N.C.: Compute! Books, 1988.

Norton, Peter, and Richard Wilton. *The* New *Programmer's Guide to the IBM PC & PS/2.* 2d ed. Redmond, Wash.: Microsoft Press, 1988.

BLOAD

See also: BSAVE, DEF SEG, VARPTR, VARSEG

■ QB2	■ QB4.5	✲ PowerBASIC
■ QB3	ANSI	✲ GW-BASIC
■ QB4	■ BASIC7	MacQB

Purpose

The BLOAD statement loads a memory-image file created by the BSAVE statement into memory at a specified location. Because BLOAD retrieves files faster than any other method does, you can use the statement to load screen images that cannot be created quickly by QuickBASIC graphics statements.

Syntax

BLOAD *name*[, *offset*]

name is the name of the device or file that contains the memory image. *name* can include a directory path and drive name and can be either a string literal enclosed in quotation marks or a string expression.

offset is the address, in the current segment, at which the file is loaded. *offset* is a numeric expression in the range 0 through 65535. If you omit this parameter, the file is loaded into the segment and offset address from which it was saved.

Usage

```
BLOAD "BARCHART.IMG"
```

Loads a memory-image file into memory at the same address at which it was saved.

```
DEF SEG = freeSeg%
BLOAD mcFile$, &H400
```

Selects the memory segment specified in the integer variable *freeSeg%* and then loads a memory-image file into offset 1024 (400H) in that segment.

Description

QuickBASIC provides two commands that let you transfer memory-image files between disk and memory. A memory-image file is a file of binary data—an exact, bit-for-bit copy of a block of memory that can contain anything held in memory, such as an array of data or a screen image. The BSAVE statement saves a memory-image file to disk, and BLOAD loads it back into memory. By default, BLOAD restores the copy into the area of memory from which it was saved; however, you can also load the copy into any other part of memory. Because BLOAD uses a single binary read to transfer the entire file from disk to memory, it is faster than other file-retrieval methods.

In addition to loading memory-image files from disk, BLOAD can accept data from other input devices. For example, your program can use BLOAD to receive binary data from a remote computer: Merely specify the serial port (either COM1: or COM2:) as the source device and be sure that your modem is set to receive 8-bit data. Note that the incoming data must be in BLOAD file format, with the file header telling QuickBASIC how much data is to be received.

BLOAD file header

Files loaded by the BLOAD statement use a common header format that always begins with the hexadecimal number FDH (253 decimal), which identifies a file as a memory-image file. The next 4 bytes contain the segment and offset address of the block of memory from which the file was saved. If you use the BLOAD statement without specifying an offset, QuickBASIC uses this address to restore the file to memory. However, if you specify an offset value, BLOAD loads the file, beginning at that offset, into the segment specified by the last DEF SEG statement. The last 2 bytes in the header contain the length of the file, in bytes. Figure 19-2 shows the memory-image file header format.

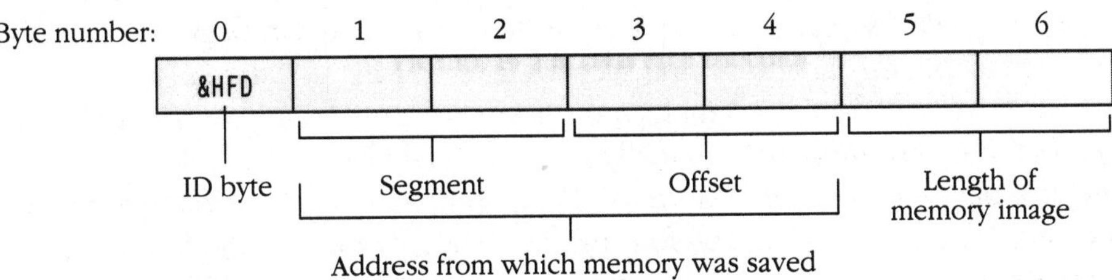

Figure 19-2.
The memory-image file header format.

The memory image itself begins immediately after the file header and is terminated by the Ctrl-Z character (ASCII 26), which is the standard DOS end-of-file marker. Because only 2 bytes are provided to hold the length of the file, the largest image that you can save in a single file is 64 KB, or one full segment.

Warnings

QuickBASIC does not check to see whether the addresses specified in a BLOAD statement are free for your program to use; consequently, the image file you load might overwrite other programs or even the operating system itself.

When loading graphics images, be sure that the current screen mode is the same as the one in which the image was saved; otherwise, the display will not be correct.

Compatibility

PowerBASIC

PowerBASIC offers two ways to specify the address to which BLOAD loads the data from a file. You can specify an offset in the current segment, or you can specify a 20-bit number in the range 0 through 1048575 (1 MB) that is an absolute address in the 1 MB of memory accessible to your program. Note that to use 20-bit addressing, your program must first execute the statement

```
DEF SEG = 0
```

This method lets you load data across segment boundaries.

GW-BASIC and BASICA

In GW-BASIC and BASICA, BLOAD is often used to load machine-language routines at a fixed offset address in the BASIC data segment. This is possible because the CLEAR command in these versions of BASIC can protect part of the data segment, thus preventing any variables from overwriting the loaded routine. Because QuickBASIC does not let you reserve memory in the data segment, however, do not use this technique. In fact, you never need to use this technique, because you can store machine-language routines in libraries or link them directly to your program.

Example

To load previously saved CGA graphics screens, simply use BLOAD with the name of the file you want to reload; the original BSAVE command stored the segment and offset address of your screen buffer in the file header. Loading EGA and VGA screens is more difficult because each screen requires four BSAVE files—one for each bit plane that these video adapters use. The following subprogram uses BLOAD to load the four files that form an EGA or VGA color graphics display. (See the "Example" section in the BSAVE entry for the program that originally saved the image.)

The four bit planes used by EGA and VGA graphics adapters are mapped into the same segment of video memory. The four planes (blue, green, red, and intensity) control the appearance of the pixels on the graphics screen. (See the SCREEN (Statement) entry in Chapter 11, "Graphics," for a description of all screen modes.)

This program uses the port at address 3C4H, which is the EGA and VGA address register. The program first writes the value 2 to the port to enable the data register at port 3C5H to set the currently addressable bit plane. The program then selects one bit plane at a time by writing the values 1, 2, 4, and 8 to port 3C5H.

See the OUT entry for details about writing to hardware ports.

```
SUB VGALoad (title$) STATIC
    SHARED screenMode AS INTEGER

    IF LEN(title$) > 8 THEN title$ = LEFT$(title$, 8)
    IF screenMode% > 6 THEN
        IF screenMode% = 13 THEN
            BLOAD title$ + ".GRA"    ' load the only bit plane
        ELSE
            FOR i% = 0 TO 3
                OUT &H3C4, 2          ' enable port
                OUT &H3C5, 2 ^ i%     ' set the currently addressable bit plane
                BLOAD title$ + ".BP" + CHR$(49 + i%)    ' load the bit plane
                IF i% = 1 AND screenMode% = 10 THEN EXIT FOR
            NEXT i%
        END IF
    END IF
END SUB
```

BSAVE

See also: BLOAD, DEF SEG, SCREEN (Statement), VARPTR, VARSEG

■ QB2	■ QB4.5	✲ PowerBASIC
■ QB3	ANSI	■ GW-BASIC
■ QB4	■ BASIC7	MacQB

Purpose

The BSAVE statement transfers a memory image to a disk file or device. You can use BSAVE to save complex screen images created by graphics statements.

Syntax

BSAVE *name, offset, bytes*

name is a string expression that contains the name of the device or file to which the memory image is to be saved; it can include a directory path and a drive name.

offset is the address, in the current segment, at which the block of memory to be saved begins; *bytes* is the length of the block of memory. *offset* and *bytes* are numeric expressions in the range 0 through 65535.

Usage

```
DEF SEG = &HB800
BSAVE "PICTURE.DAT", 0, 16384
```

Selects the video segment for computers that use a color adapter and writes a 16-KB screen image to the file PICTURE.DAT. Copying starts at offset 0 in the segment.

Description

Use BSAVE to transfer an exact copy of an area of memory to a memory-image file on disk. A memory-image file is a file containing binary data—an exact, bit-for-bit copy of a block of memory that can contain anything held in memory, such as an array of data or a screen image. You must specify the name of the file to which you want to save the memory image, the file's starting address in memory, and the number of bytes to be transferred. If the file does not already exist, BSAVE creates it. Use the BLOAD statement to reload the file into memory.

You specify in a BSAVE statement only the offset of the address at which you want copying to begin. To copy from a segment other than the default data segment, DGROUP, you must first change segments by calling the DEF SEG statement. To save from the beginning of a segment, use an offset of 0.

The sum of the specified offset and number of bytes should not be greater than 65,535 (the number of bytes in a segment). If the total exceeds this number, QuickBASIC will not report an error, but when BSAVE reaches the end of the segment it will wrap around and copy bytes from the beginning of the specified segment.

BSAVE is useful for saving screen displays, and it works equally well with text mode and high-resolution graphics. To use BSAVE for this purpose, you must know the segment address of video memory used by the display adapter you are using and the size (in bytes) of the screen image in the various screen modes. Table 19-3 lists this information.

Screen mode	Segment	Page size (in bytes)	Number of pages	Remarks
0	B000H	4096	1	MDA and Hercules
	B800H	4096	4	80-column text
	B800H	2048	8	40-column text
1	B800H	16384	1	320 by 200, four colors
2	B800H	16384	1	640 by 200, two colors
3	B800H	32768	1	Hercules only
11	B800H	65536	1	VGA and MCGA
13	B800H	65536	1	VGA and MCGA

Note: Computers with a CGA adapter and a monochrome monitor use the video buffer segment address B800H, not B000H.

Table 19-3.
Address and size of the display buffer in QuickBASIC screen modes.

The screen modes that can be used only by EGA and VGA adapters support a different scheme of addressing video memory which uses bit planes. See the sample program in the "Example" section for a method of saving EGA and VGA screens.

Tips

A memory-image file can store numeric and fixed-length string arrays more quickly than a random-access or binary disk file. Because QuickBASIC processes a random-access file one record at a time and a binary file one value at a time, it requires more time to load or save a random-access or binary file than a memory-image file, which QuickBASIC reads or writes in a single pass.

The following program segment uses BSAVE to save a single-precision array:

```
elements& = UBOUND(table!) - LBOUND(table!) + 1  ' number of elements in array
bytes& = elements& * 4                           ' number of bytes in array

DEF SEG = VARSEG(table!(0))                      ' switch to array's segment
BSAVE "TABLE.IMG", VARPTR(table!(0)), bytes&     ' save array on disk

DEF SEG     ' restore default data segment
```

You can then use the BLOAD statement to load the array back into memory.

Compatibility

PowerBASIC

PowerBASIC offers two ways to specify the address from which BSAVE copies data. You can specify an offset in the current segment, or you can specify a 20-bit number in the range 0 through 1048575 (1 MB) that is an absolute address in the 1 MB of memory accessible to your program. Note that to use 20-bit addressing, your program must first execute the statement

```
DEF SEG = 0
```

This method enables you to save data across segment boundaries.

Example

Saving screen images created in the screen modes used only by EGA and VGA adapters is complicated because BSAVE must create four files to store each bit plane that these video adapters use. The following subprogram extracts each bit plane from the EGA or VGA video buffer and uses BSAVE to save it to a file.

The four bit planes used by EGA and VGA graphics adapters are mapped into the same segment of video memory. The four planes (blue, green, red, and intensity) control the appearance of the pixels on the graphics screen. (See the SCREEN (Statement) entry in Chapter 11, "Graphics," for a description of all screen modes.)

This program uses the port at address 3CEH, which is the EGA and VGA port. The program first writes the value 4 to the port to enable the data register at port 3CFH to set the currently addressable bit plane. The program then selects one bit plane at a time by writing the values 1 through 3 to port 3CFH. (See the OUT entry in this chapter for details about writing to hardware ports.)

```
' subprogram to save EGA and VGA screens from video memory
SUB VGASave (title AS STRING) STATIC
    SHARED screenMode AS INTEGER  ' current screen mode
    IF LEN(title$) > 8 THEN
        title$ = LEFT$(title$, 8)
    END IF
    SELECT CASE screenMode%       ' video buffer sizes
        CASE 7
            bytes& = 8000
        CASE 8
            bytes& = 16000
        CASE 9, 10
            bytes& = 28000
        CASE 11, 12
            bytes& = 38400
        CASE 13
            bytes& = 64000
```

(continued)

continued

```
        CASE ELSE
            bytes& = 0
    END SELECT

    IF bytes& THEN
        DEF SEG = &HA000            ' video buffer segment
        IF screenMode% = 13 THEN
            BSAVE title$ + ".GRA", 0, bytes&
        ELSE
            FOR i% = 0 TO 3
                OUT &H3CE, 4        ' enable port
                OUT &H3CF, i%       ' set the currently addressable bit plane
                BSAVE title$ + ".BP" + CHR$(49 + i%), 0, bytes&
                IF i% = 1 AND screenMode% = 10 THEN EXIT FOR
            NEXT i%
        END IF
        DEF SEG
    END IF
END SUB
```

FRE

See also: DIM, $DYNAMIC, ERASE, $STATIC

✲ QB2	■ QB4.5	✲ PowerBASIC
✲ QB3	ANSI	✲ GW-BASIC
■ QB4	■ BASIC7	✲ MacQB

Purpose

The FRE function returns the amount of available stack space, string space, or memory. You can use FRE to determine whether your program has enough space to perform a task that requires a large amount of memory.

Syntax

FRE (*number*)

or

FRE (*string*)

If *number* is –1, the FRE function returns the amount of memory available in the heap; if it is –2, FRE returns the amount of available stack space; if you use any other numeric value, FRE returns the size of the next block of unused string space. If you specify *string*, FRE first compacts unused string space into the largest possible block and then returns the amount of available string space.

Usage

```
PRINT FRE(-1)
```

Displays the amount of memory available in the far heap.

```
IF FRE(-2) < 256 THEN PRINT "Stack space is running out!"
```

Checks the available space in the stack and warns the user if the stack is smaller than 256 bytes.

Description

The FRE function returns the number of bytes available for use in one of three areas of memory that QuickBASIC uses to store data for your program: the heap, the stack, and the string space. The heap, which is the memory that QuickBASIC uses to hold all variables, is divided into two parts. The near heap is the section of memory that contains strings and simple variables. The far heap stores huge arrays, dynamic numeric arrays, and dynamic arrays of fixed-length strings. The stack stores temporary variables and the return addresses of subroutines and functions. The string space is the part of the near heap that holds the values of variables containing strings.

The value that FRE returns depends on the parameter specified in the function call. If you specify –1, FRE returns the number of bytes available in the heap. The parameter –2 directs FRE to return the number of available bytes in the stack. If any other number or string is specified, FRE returns the amount of available string space.

If you specify a string as a parameter, FRE compacts the free string space into a single block of memory before returning the amount of available string space. Compaction clears the string space of all strings that are no longer in use and combines all fragmented portions of the string space. Many versions of BASIC have a sophisticated string memory-management system that continuously performs compaction, so you will probably not have to use FRE with a string variable. Early versions of BASIC do not perform this task, however, so using FRE in these versions is an important memory-management task.

Note that FRE used with the parameter –2 (for stack space) returns reliable results only when a running program executes it. Although you can execute *FRE(–2)* from the immediate window, the results will not be accurate.

Compatibility

QuickBASIC 2.0 and QuickBASIC 3.0

QuickBASIC versions 2.0 and 3.0 do not support the parameter –2 (to return the amount of available stack space) with the FRE function. FRE can only be used to return the amount of string space or heap space and to compact the string space.

PowerBASIC

In PowerBASIC if you use a string or the value 0 as the parameter to the FRE function, FRE returns the size of the largest possible block of available string space. You can also use FRE with the parameters –1 and –2 to determine the available space in the heap and the stack, but you cannot use the function with a parameter of any other numeric value to find the size of the next block of unused string space as you can in QuickBASIC version 4.5.

GW-BASIC and BASICA

You can use the FRE function in GW-BASIC only to return the amount of available string space. In BASICA, the FRE function can return only the number of bytes available in the data segment. In both of these versions of BASIC, you can use FRE to compact the string space.

QuickBASIC for the Macintosh

QuickBASIC for the Macintosh supports the parameters –1 and –2 in the same way that QuickBASIC version 4.5 does. However, if you specify any other number or a null string, FRE in QuickBASIC for the Macintosh returns the number of bytes available in the data segment.

Example

The following program dimensions various kinds of arrays and then uses the FRE function to examine the changing amounts of available memory.

```
REM $DYNAMIC            ' make all arrays dynamic
DECLARE SUB MemAvail ()

CLS
MemAvail                ' show available memory
DIM array%(15000)       ' dynamic array of integers
PRINT "After defining a dynamic array of 15000 integers:"
MemAvail

DIM strArray$(1000)   ' dynamic variable-length string array
PRINT "After defining a dynamic array of 1000 variable-length strings:"
MemAvail

FOR i% = 1 TO 1000
    strArray$(i%) = "Test string"
NEXT i%
PRINT "After filling the array:"
MemAvail

DIM dynString(1000) AS STRING * 10     ' dynamic fixed-length string array
PRINT "After defining a dynamic array of 1000 fixed-length strings:"
MemAvail

FOR i% = 1 TO 1000
    dynString(i%) = "Test"
NEXT i%
PRINT "After filling the array:"
MemAvail
```

(continued)

continued

```
REM $STATIC
SUB MemAvail
    PRINT "Total heap space available: "; FRE(-1)
    PRINT "Total string space available: "; FRE(0)
    PRINT
END SUB
```

INP

See also: OUT, WAIT

■ QB2	■ QB4.5	■ PowerBASIC
■ QB3	ANSI	■ GW-BASIC
■ QB4	■ BASIC7	MacQB

Purpose

The INP function lets your program read a byte of data from a specified I/O port.

Syntax

INP(*port*)

port is the address of the specified port and is an integer in the range 0 through 65535 (or 0 through FFFF in hexadecimal).

Usage

```
PRINT INP(&H3B5)
```

Displays the value returned by the status register at port 949 (3B5H), which is the status register for the MDA, the Hercules adapter, and the EGA and VGA in monochrome modes. Any value other than 255 indicates that a monochrome display is installed.

```
IF INP(&H3D5) <> 255 THEN PRINT "Color adapter is installed"
```

Port 981 (3D5H) is the status register used by the CGA and by the EGA and VGA in color modes. If the value returned is 255, a monochrome display is installed.

Description

The central processor in the PC communicates with support chips and hardware devices by means of a series of ports. Ports are input/output (I/O) channels through which information passes between the CPU and the device it is controlling; QuickBASIC associates one or more hardware port with each device. QuickBASIC provides statements and functions that handle most hardware-related tasks. However, if you want to program your display adapter at a low level or if your computer uses a digital scanner or other nonstandard device, INP and its companion statement, OUT (discussed in the OUT entry), let you control the device without having to use an assembly-language routine.

The IBM PC and compatible computers allocate port addresses 0 through 3FFH to system hardware; however, not all of these addresses are actually used. Furthermore, because many ports are write only, INP does not always return meaningful data. Table 19-2, in the tutorial section, lists the port addresses associated with the major system devices. Before experimenting, however, consult your computer's technical reference manual for up-to-date information about ports.

INP reads data 1 byte at a time; therefore, each call to INP returns a value in the range 0 through 255. Many input ports require you to first write to another port associated with the device so that you can select which data item will be returned. For example, you can retrieve a pair of 8-bit random numbers by writing the value 0 to the system's timer control port at the address 43H and then reading the timer port (at address 40H) twice:

```
OUT &H43, 0
rand1% = INP(&H40): rand2% = INP(&H40)
```

The two values returned by INP in this example are the upper and lower bytes of a single 16-bit number; therefore, you need to read the port twice to retrieve the entire number.

Tips

The INP function requires an integer argument, and QuickBASIC integers are signed, with a range of –327678 through 32767; therefore, you cannot easily use integer variables with INP to access addresses above offset 32767. Note that INP converts any constant greater than 32767 and any long-integer, single-precision, or double-precision value to a 2-byte integer. See the PEEK entry in this chapter for a user-defined function (called *SInt%*) that converts a long integer to the equivalent signed integer so that you can use it with INP. However, if you use hexadecimal numbers, you don't need to perform this conversion.

The data that INP reads from a port is often "bit encoded"—each bit contains a different piece of information about that device's status. The DEF FN entry in Chapter 4, "Procedures," includes a collection of sample functions that can read or set the individual bits of an integer variable. These functions let you examine the information returned by INP more easily.

Warnings

Because port addresses are hardware-specific, using INP and the OUT statement limits the portability of your programs to computers that have the same hardware configuration as yours. Moreover, because these statements directly manipulate the system hardware, writing incorrect data to a port can "lock up" the computer.

Example

PC/AT and PS/2-series computers store configuration data in RAM that is stored in CMOS circuits. This RAM can be read through hardware port 71H. The following program reads configuration information and reports the number and type of fixed disks installed in the system. Note that the program writes a byte to address 70H so that the byte that the INP function reads contains the required information.

```
CLS
OUT &H70, &H12                  ' specify required information
diskType% = INP(&H71)           ' read fixed-disk data
PRINT diskType%
cDrive% = diskType% \ 16        ' drive C is specified in the first 4 bits
dDrive% = diskType% MOD 16      ' drive D is specified in the second 4 bits

IF cDrive% THEN
    PRINT "Fixed disk C is type"; cDrive%
ELSE
    PRINT "Fixed disk C is not installed"
END IF

IF dDrive% THEN
    PRINT "Fixed disk D is type"; dDrive%
ELSE
    PRINT "Fixed disk D is not installed"
END IF
END
```

OUT

See also: INP, WAIT

■ QB2	■ QB4.5	■ PowerBASIC
■ QB3	ANSI	■ GW-BASIC
■ QB4	■ BASIC7	MacQB

Purpose

The OUT statement sends a byte of data to a specified I/O port.

Syntax

OUT *port*, *byte*

port is the address of the specified port and is an integer in the range 0 through 65535 (or 0 through FFFF in hexadecimal).

byte is a value in the range 0 through 255.

Usage

```
OUT &H70, &H12
```

Writes the byte &H12 to the CMOS RAM port address. This prepares the port for obtaining a specific value with the INP function.

Description

A port is an input/output (I/O) channel through which a program can directly control a hardware device. Usually you don't need to access specific ports, because QuickBASIC provides statements and functions that handle most hardware-related tasks. However, if you want to program your display adapter at a low level or if your computer uses a scanner or other nonstandard device, OUT and its companion function, INP (discussed in the INP entry), let you control the device without having to use an assembly-language routine.

The IBM PC and compatible computers allocate port addresses 0 through 3FFH to system hardware; however, not all of these addresses are actually used. Furthermore, many ports are read only, so you cannot always use OUT. Table 19-2, in the tutorial, lists the port addresses associated with the major system devices. Before experimenting, however, consult your computer's technical reference manual for up-to-date information about the ports. Remember that OUT writes data 1 byte at a time; therefore, the value you send to the port must be in the range 0 through 255.

Tips

The OUT statement requires an integer argument for the address parameter, and QuickBASIC integers are signed with a range of –327678 through 32767; therefore, you cannot easily use integer variables with OUT to access addresses above offset 32767. Note that OUT converts any constant greater than 32767 and any long-integer, single-precision, or double-precision value to a 2-byte integer. See the PEEK entry for a user-defined function (called *SInt%*) that converts a long integer to the equivalent signed integer so that you can use it with OUT. However, if you use hexadecimal numbers, you don't need to make this conversion.

Many devices expect the data you write to their control port to be bit encoded—each bit contains a different programming instruction. See the DEF FN entry in Chapter 4, "Procedures," for sample functions that let you set the individual bits of an integer variable you send to the OUT statement.

The programming examples listed in the reference manuals for many hardware devices are usually written in assembly language, which can treat two adjacent 8-bit ports as a single 16-bit port. Although the QuickBASIC OUT statement can write only 8-bit values (in the range 0 through 255) to I/O ports, you can duplicate the effect of assembly-language code by writing to two successive ports. The following statements, for example, write values to the color graphics adapter ports:

```
OUT &H3D4, 12
OUT &H3D5, 5
```

Port 3D4H is the port used by the CGA and MCGA video adapters and by EGA and VGA video adapters in color modes. Writing the value 12 to port 3D4H enables the start address register of the data port, which is located at address 3D5H. If you write the value 5 to the enabled register at 3D5H, a screen mode 9 graphics display scrolls upward one row.

Warnings

Because port addresses are hardware specific, using the INP function and OUT limits the portability of your programs to computers that have the same hardware configuration as yours. Moreover, because these statements directly manipulate the system hardware, writing incorrect data to a port can "lock up" the computer.

Example

If the EGA and VGA adapters have enough memory, they can store more than one screenful of information at a time; QuickBASIC lets you use the SCREEN statement to switch between these screen pages. The hardware itself, however, allows much finer control of the display; in fact, by programming the adapter's start address registers directly, you can specify the position of the visible part of the video buffer to the nearest pixel. The following subprogram draws a design on the screen and then lets the user press the arrow keys to move the screen contents in any direction. The subprogram uses the OUT statement to scroll the screen.

```
DECLARE SUB PanDisplay (x%, y%)

CONST FALSE = 0, TRUE = NOT FALSE

SCREEN 9
LINE (0, 0)-(639, 349), 9, BF                ' draw the design
VIEW SCREEN (40, 25)-(600, 325), 0, 15
CIRCLE (319, 174), 150, 14: PAINT (319, 174), 14, 14

' initialize variables
x% = 0: y% = 0
esc$ = CHR$(27)
leftArrow$ = CHR$(0) + CHR$(75): rightArrow$ = CHR$(0) + CHR$(77)
upArrow$ = CHR$(0) + CHR$(72): downArrow$ = CHR$(0) + CHR$(80)

DO
    DO
        keyStroke$ = INKEY$
    LOOP WHILE keyStroke$ = ""
    pan% = TRUE
    SELECT CASE keyStroke$                   ' calculate new x- or y-coordinate
        CASE leftArrow$
            IF x% > 0 THEN x% = x% - 1
        CASE rightArrow$
            IF x% < 79 THEN x% = x% + 1
```

(continued)

continued

```
        CASE upArrow$
            IF y% > 0 THEN y% = y% - 1
        CASE downArrow$
            IF y% < 22 THEN y% = y% + 1
        CASE ELSE
            pan% = FALSE
    END SELECT
    IF pan% THEN PanDisplay x%, y% * 5     ' move the display
LOOP UNTIL keyStroke$ = esc$
END

' set display window coordinates
SUB PanDisplay (x%, y%) STATIC
    OUT &H3D4, 12: OUT &H3D5, y%           ' scroll screen vertically
    OUT &H3D4, 13: OUT &H3D5, x%           ' scroll screen horizontally
END SUB
```

PEEK

See also: DEF SEG, POKE, SADD, VARPTR

■ QB2	■ QB4.5	✲ PowerBASIC
■ QB3	ANSI	■ GW-BASIC
■ QB4	■ BASIC7	✲ MacQB

Purpose

The PEEK function returns the contents of the specified memory address in the current segment. You can, for example, use PEEK to find the current hardware configuration of the system.

Syntax

PEEK(*address*)

address is an integer expression in the range 0 through 65535 that specifies the offset of the byte you want to examine in the current segment of memory.

Usage

```
PRINT PEEK(16384)
```

Prints the value contained in the byte at offset 16384 in the current segment.

```
byte% = PEEK(&HF000)
```

Assigns the contents of address F000H to the integer variable *byte%*. Note that you can specify addresses in either hexadecimal or decimal notation.

```
DEF SEG = videoSeg%
offSet% = (row% - 1) * 160 + (col% - 1) * 2
character% = PEEK(offSet%)
```

Reads the ASCII value of a character on the video display after you specify both the segment address of video memory and the screen row and column position of the character. (Note that the video memory segment is B000H for monochrome displays and B800H for color displays.)

Description

The PEEK function lets you directly examine data in memory. This data might be variables used by your program, characters on the screen, or information provided by the BIOS or DOS. You can use the DEF SEG statement to specify the memory segment you want PEEK to read from. If you do not define a new segment, QuickBASIC uses DGROUP, the default data segment. (See the DEF SEG entry in Chapter 20, "Mixed Language," for details about changing the default segment.)

PEEK returns a value in the range 0 through 255, the contents of a single byte of memory. However, if you want to read a value other than a single character, you need to read the contents of two or more contiguous memory addresses. An integer, for example, is stored in 2 adjacent bytes, the least significant byte (LSB) preceding the most significant byte (MSB). The MSB is the number of times the integer value can be divided by 256, and the LSB is the remainder of this division. The number 1000, for example, would be stored in memory as shown in Figure 19-3.

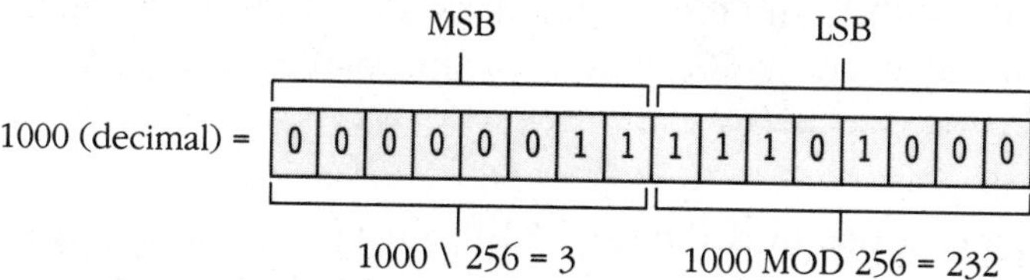

Figure 19-3.
How QuickBASIC stores the number 1000.

Therefore, to obtain the value of the integer that begins at the address specified by the variable *loc%*, you need to use the following statement:

```
intValue% = PEEK(loc%) + (PEEK(loc% + 1) * 256)
```

Tips

The PEEK function requires an integer argument, and QuickBASIC integers are signed, with a range of –32768 through 32767; therefore, you cannot easily use integer variables with PEEK to examine addresses above offset 32767. Note that PEEK converts any constant greater than 32767 and any long-integer, single-precision or double-precision value to a 2-byte integer. The following function converts a long-integer variable to the equivalent signed integer so that you can use it with the PEEK function:

```
FUNCTION SInt% (n&) STATIC
    SInt% = -((n& > 32767) * (n& - 65536)) - ((n& < 32768) * n&)
END FUNCTION
```

Now, to display the byte at the address specified by the value in the long-integer variable *offset&*, you can issue the statement:

```
PRINT PEEK(SInt%(offset&))
```

However, if you use hexadecimal numbers, you don't need to make this conversion. The following statements do not produce an error:

```
offset& = &HFFFF
PRINT PEEK(offset&)
```

Compatibility

PowerBASIC

PowerBASIC offers two ways to specify the address that PEEK accesses. You can specify an offset in the current segment, or you can specify a 20-bit number in the range 0 through 1048575 that is an absolute address in the 1 MB of memory accessible to your program. Note that to use 20-bit addressing, your program must first execute the statement

```
DEF SEG = 0
```

This method lets you access data across segment boundaries.

In addition to PEEK, which accesses memory and returns a byte value, PowerBASIC also provides the PEEKI, PEEKL, and PEEK$ functions. PEEKI returns a 2-byte value, PEEKL returns a 4-byte value, and PEEK$ returns a specified number of bytes as a string.

QuickBASIC for the Macintosh

Because the CPU in the Macintosh is not divided into 64-KB segments, you must specify in the PEEK function in QuickBASIC for the Macintosh the absolute address of the byte you want to examine. Possible addresses are in the range 0 through 2147483647 in decimal and 0 through FFFFFFFFH in hexadecimal; however, the address you specify must correspond to a physical location in memory for the value returned to be meaningful.

In addition to PEEK, which returns a byte value, QuickBASIC for the Macintosh also provides the PEEKW and PEEKL functions, which return the word (2-byte) and double-word (4-byte) values stored at the specified address.

Example

A program that will be used on different computers might need to determine what type of hardware a system has installed. It can easily find this information on an IBM PC compatible because the ROM BIOS in those computers maintains a 2-byte "equipment list" in low memory. The following program uses PEEK to read the equipment list and then displays its contents.

```
DECLARE FUNCTION SInt% (num&)
DECLARE FUNCTION BitTest% (number%, bit%)
DEF SEG = &H40          ' change default segment to low memory

lowByte = PEEK(&H10)  ' get least significant byte of equipment list
hiByte = PEEK(&H11)   ' get most significant byte of equipment list
equipment% = SInt%(lowByte + (hiByte * 256))   ' form equipment list

DEF SEG                 ' change default segment to DGROUP
flag$ = STRING$(16, "0")
FOR i% = 15 TO 0 STEP -1
    IF BitTest%(equipment%, i%) THEN    ' extract each bit
        MID$(flag$, 16 - i%, 1) = "1"
    END IF
NEXT i%

' display equipment list
CLS : LOCATE 1, 1
PRINT "F E D C B A 9 8 7 6 5 4 3 2 1 0"
PRINT STRING$(32, CHR$(196))
FOR i% = 1 TO 16: PRINT MID$(flag$, i%, 1); " "; : NEXT
PRINT : PRINT STRING$(32, CHR$(196))

LOCATE 7, 1
PRINT "ROM BIOS equipment list at 0040:0010"
PRINT
PRINT "0:   Floppy drives installed?"
PRINT "1:   Math coprocessor installed?"
PRINT "2-3: Original PC motherboard RAM "
PRINT "4-5: Initial video mode "
PRINT "6-7: Number of floppy drives"
PRINT "9-B: Number of serial ports"
PRINT "C:   Game adapter installed?"
PRINT "E-F: Number of parallel printers"
END

FUNCTION BitTest% (number%, bit%)
   ' extract a bit from the number
    BitTest% = -SGN(number% AND 2 ^ bit%)
END FUNCTION

FUNCTION SInt% (num&)
    SInt% = -((num& > 32767) * (num& - 65536)) - ((num& < 32767) * num&)
END FUNCTION
```

POKE

See also: DEF SEG, PEEK, SADD, VARPTR

■ QB2	■ QB4.5	✲ PowerBASIC
■ QB3	ANSI	■ GW-BASIC
■ QB4	■ BASIC7	✲ MacQB

Purpose

The POKE statement writes a byte of data to a specified memory address in the current segment. You can use POKE, for example, to set the status of the Ctrl key.

Syntax

POKE *address, char*

address is an integer expression in the range 0 through 65535 that specifies the offset of the address to which you want POKE to write in the current memory segment.

char is the integer value in the range 0 through 255 to be written to the specified address.

Usage

```
POKE 4096, 127
```

Writes the value 127 into the byte at offset 4096 in the current segment.

```
POKE &HC000, ASC("A")
```

Writes the character A into offset C000H in the current segment. Note that you can specify addresses in either hexadecimal or decimal notation.

```
keyBuff% = &H1A
DEF SEG = &H40
POKE keyBuff%, PEEK(keyBuff% + 2)
```

Copies the contents of one byte into another byte. (Note that these addresses used by PEEK and POKE are in the BIOS data segment and contain pointers to the start (&H1A) and end (&H1C) of the keyboard type-ahead buffer. In effect, these statements empty the keyboard buffer.)

Description

The POKE statement inserts a single byte of data (a value in the range 0 through 255) into a specified address. The effect of this operation depends on the address you write to. Often, POKE simply stores a character in an unoccupied area of memory. Some addresses, however, are used by your computer for specific purposes; writing to these locations gives instructions to the hardware. For example, if you are using a color monitor, the contents of the screen are stored in memory in segment B800H; writing to the addresses in that area of memory displays characters on the screen. (The corresponding address for computers with monochrome monitors is segment B000H.)

You can use the DEF SEG statement to specify the memory segment you want POKE to write to. If you do not define a new segment, QuickBASIC uses DGROUP, the default data segment. (See the DEF SEG entry in Chapter 20, "Mixed Languages," for details about changing the default segment.)

If you want to write any value other than a character, you need to write to two or more contiguous memory addresses. An integer, for example, is stored in two adjacent bytes, the least significant byte (LSB) preceding the most significant byte (MSB). The MSB is the number of times the integer value can be divided by 256, and the LSB is the remainder of this division. The number 1000, for example, would be stored in memory as shown in Figure 19-4.

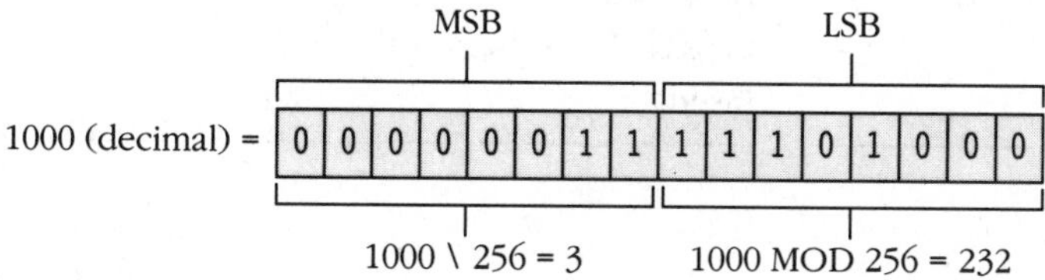

Figure 19-4.
How QuickBASIC stores the number 1000.

Therefore, to store an integer in memory, you need to use POKE twice, as shown in the following statements:

```
POKE byte%, intValue% MOD 256
POKE byte% + 1, intValue% \ 256
```

Tips

The POKE statement requires an integer argument, and QuickBASIC integers are signed with a range of –32768 through 32767; therefore, you cannot easily use integer variables with POKE to access addresses above offset 32767. Note that POKE converts any constant greater than 32767 and any long-integer, single-precision, or double-precision value to a 2-byte integer. See the PEEK entry for a user-defined function (called *SInt%*) that converts a long integer to the equivalent signed integer so that you can use it with POKE. However, if you use hexadecimal numbers, you don't need to make this conversion.

The PC ROM BIOS records the status of the Shift keys and the Ctrl, Alt, Caps Lock, Num Lock, Scroll Lock, and Insert keys at location 0040:0017 (segment 40H, offset 17H) in memory. You can direct your programs to access these keys by using POKE to send a byte to that address. To do so, you must first switch to the BIOS data segment by using the following statement:

```
DEF SEG = &H40
```

You can then turn on, turn off, or toggle the specified key by using one of the following statements:

POKE &H17, PEEK(&H17) OR *key%*	Turns the key on
POKE &H17, PEEK(&H17) AND (255 - *key%*)	Turns the key off
POKE &H17, PEEK(&H17) XOR *key%*	Toggles the key status

Table 19-4 shows the possible values of *key%*, which is the bit value that specifies a key:

Key	Value of key%	Key	Value of key%
Right Shift	1	Scroll Lock	16
Left Shift	2	Num Lock	32
Ctrl	4	Caps Lock	64
Alt	8	Insert	128

Table 19-4.
The possible values of key%.

Use the DEF SEG statement to restore QuickBASIC's data segment.

Warnings

When using POKE be careful not to overwrite any addresses used by DOS or other resident programs; doing this might cause your program to "crash" or your computer to "lock up."

Compatibility

PowerBASIC

PowerBASIC offers two ways to specify the address to which POKE writes. You can specify an offset in the current segment, or you can specify a 20-bit number in the range 0 through 1048575 (1 MB) that is an absolute address in the 1 MB of memory accessible to your program. Note that to use 20-bit addressing, your program must first execute the statement

```
DEF SEG = 0
```

This method lets you write data across segment boundaries.

In addition to POKE, which writes a 1-byte value to memory, PowerBASIC also provides the POKEI, POKEL, and POKE$ statements. POKEI writes a 2-byte value, POKEL writes a 4-byte value, and POKE$ writes a string of any length.

QuickBASIC for the Macintosh

Because the CPU in the Macintosh is not divided into 64-KB segments, you must specify in the POKE statement in QuickBASIC for the Macintosh the absolute address of the byte to which you want to write. Possible addresses are in the range 0 through 2147483647 in decimal and 0 through FFFFFFFFH in hexadecimal; however, the address you specify must correspond to physical memory.

In addition to POKE, which lets you write a byte value, QuickBASIC for the Macintosh also provides the POKEW and POKEL functions, which let you write word (2-byte) and double-word (4-byte) values into memory at the specified address. For these last two statements, you can specify only an even value for the address.

Example

Some programming languages let you return a status code to the operating system when a program finishes executing. Although QuickBASIC does not provide such a feature, the following program demonstrates a trick that lets your program return commands. The program uses POKE to insert the text of a DOS command into the keyboard type-ahead buffer, so the command is executed as soon as the program stops running. (You can substitute your own DOS command, but it must be no more than 15 characters long, including the carriage return.)

```
buffer$ = "CLS" + CHR$(13) + "DIR /W"      ' DOS commands to enter

buffer$ = LEFT$(buffer$, 14) + CHR$(13)    ' use only 15 characters
length% = LEN(buffer$)                     ' length of command
DEF SEG = &H40              ' BIOS data segment
head% = &H1A                ' buffer head pointer
tail% = &H1C                ' buffer tail pointer
start% = &H1E               ' type-ahead buffer

' fill the even bytes with characters from buffer$
' the odd bytes are reserved for keyboard scan codes
FOR i% = 1 TO length%
    POKE start% + (i% - 1) * 2, ASC(MID$(buffer$, i%, 1))
NEXT i%

POKE tail%, start% + (i% - 1) * 2          ' set new tail pointer
POKE head%, start%          ' set new head pointer
DEF SEG                     ' restore segment
END
```

SETMEM

See also: CLEAR, FRE

QB2	■ QB4.5	PowerBASIC
QB3	ANSI	GW-BASIC
■ QB4	■ BASIC7	MacQB

Purpose

The SETMEM function changes the amount of memory allocated for the far heap and returns the number of bytes in the far heap. Use SETMEM to make memory available for mixed-language routines that need to use space in the far heap. For example, if a C function in your library needs memory to sort a file, you must free enough bytes from QuickBASIC's storage to allow the function to work.

Syntax

SETMEM(*bytes*)

bytes is an integer expression that indicates the number of bytes of memory you want to reallocate. If *bytes* is negative, SETMEM frees memory allocated to QuickBASIC; if it is positive, SETMEM allocates additional memory to QuickBASIC. If *bytes* is 0, SETMEM only returns the number of bytes in the far heap.

Usage

```
PRINT SETMEM(0)
```

Displays the number of bytes in the far heap without changing the current size.

```
heapSize& = SETMEM(-10240)
```

Releases a 10-KB block of memory.

```
heapSize& = SETMEM(farData&)
```

Requests an additional block of memory, the size of which is contained in the variable *farData&* (assuming that *farData&* contains a positive value).

Description

When a QuickBASIC program starts, DOS allocates to it all the free memory in the system, regardless of the actual program size. If you intend to link your program with mixed-language procedures that require memory of their own, you first need to free some of QuickBASIC's memory. The SETMEM function lets you do this. It also lets you reallocate the memory to QuickBASIC when the function finishes operating.

SETMEM acts on the far heap, the area of memory used by QuickBASIC to store dynamic arrays and other data objects that are stored in separate segments. You cannot use SETMEM to modify the amount of memory allocated to QuickBASIC's data segment, DGROUP, which is always set at 64 KB. Nor can you use SETMEM to change the stack size; use the CLEAR statement to do that.

After SETMEM changes the amount of allocated memory, it returns the number of bytes in the far heap. If the function cannot allocate the entire number of bytes you specify, it allocates as many as possible; however, it does not return an error message. To be sure that you have reserved sufficient memory, compare the size of the far heap before the function call with the size returned by the function. To check the current far heap size, call SETMEM with a parameter value of 0.

The SHELL statement also attempts to release memory from the far heap so that it can load the command processor or the application you specify. If you have reserved too much memory for other data or procedures, SHELL cannot do so. After it finishes (or fails), SHELL returns to QuickBASIC any memory the program was first allocated. (See the SHELL entry in Chapter 18, "DOS and Program Management," for details.)

Example

The following program shows you how QuickBASIC manages far memory. The program builds a dynamic array of integers, fills it with random data, and then uses SETMEM to free enough memory for a copy to be made. An assembly-language procedure uses the freed memory to perform the copying. When the procedure returns, the original program checks to see whether the copy is accurate before restoring the allocated memory. To run this program in the QuickBASIC environment, specify the following QB command line:

```
QB SETMEM.BAS /L QB.QLB
```

```
DECLARE SUB ABSOLUTE (sSeg%, sOff%, length%, dSeg%, address%)
' $DYNAMIC                        ' make all arrays dynamic

RANDOMIZE TIMER                   ' set a random seed for RND
code$ = SPACE$(64)                ' will hold the machine code
arraySize% = 1000                 ' size of source array
DIM source(arraySize%) AS INTEGER    ' define the source array

FOR i% = 0 TO arraySize%          ' fill array with random numbers
    source(i%) = RND * arraySize%
NEXT i%

bytes% = arraySize% * 2           ' array size in bytes
oldHeap& = SETMEM(0)              ' save original heap size
heapSize& = SETMEM(-bytes% * 2) ' free memory for the array copy

IF oldHeap& - heapSize& < bytes% THEN
    PRINT "MEMORY ALLOCATION FAILURE--NOT ENOUGH MEMORY"
    BEEP: PRINT "Can't continue.": STOP
END IF

testSum& = 0                      ' set up for checksum test
FOR i% = 1 TO 64                  ' load machine code into code$
    READ a$
    byte% = VAL("&H" + a$)
    testSum& = testSum& + byte%
    MID$(code$, i%, 1) = CHR$(byte%)
NEXT i%

READ checkSum&
IF testSum& <> checkSum& THEN   ' check for typing errors in DATA statements
    PRINT "CHECKSUM ERROR--DATA VALUES INCORRECT"
    BEEP: PRINT "Can't continue.": STOP
END IF

ABSOLUTE VARSEG(source(0)), VARPTR(source(0)), bytes%, target%, SADD(code$)
```

(continued)

continued

```
IF target% <> 0 THEN            ' check whether array was copied accurately
    DEF SEG = target%
    FOR i% = 0 TO arraySize% - 1
        byte% = PEEK(i% * 2) + PEEK(i% * 2 + 1) * 256
        IF byte% <> source(i%) THEN
            PRINT "ARRAYS NOT IDENTICAL!": BEEP: EXIT FOR
        END IF
    NEXT i%
    IF i% = arraySize% THEN
        PRINT "ARRAYS ARE IDENTICAL - EXPERIMENT SUCCESSFUL"
        PLAY "T240 03 L8 D# F G L8 B- P8 L8 G L2 B-"
    END IF
    DEF SEG                     ' restore data segment
ELSE
    PRINT "UNABLE TO ALLOCATE MEMORY!": BEEP
END IF

heapSize& = SETMEM(bytes% * 2)  ' restore original heap
END

DATA   55, 8B, EC, 06, 56, 57, 8B, 5E, 08, 8B, 1F, 53, B1, 04, D3
DATA   EB, 59, B4, 48, CD, 21, 72, 19, 8E, C0, 33, FF, 8B, 5E, 0A
DATA   8B, 37, 1E, 8B, 5E, 0C, 8B, 07, 8E, D8, FC, F3, A4, 1F, 8C
DATA   C0, EB, 02, 33, C0, 8B, 5E, 06, 89, 07, 5F, 5E, 07, 5D, CA
DATA   08, 00, 00, 00, 6718
```

WAIT

See also: INP, OUT

■ QB2	■ QB4.5	■ PowerBASIC
■ QB3	✲ ANSI	■ GW-BASIC
■ QB4	■ BASIC7	MacQB

Purpose

The WAIT statement reads data from a specified hardware port and suspends program execution until a specified bit pattern is read. You can use WAIT to pause execution until a device is ready for a particular event to take place. For example, if the program is part of an EPOS (Electronic Point-of-Sale) system, it might wait for the cash register to signal that it is ready for the next customer.

Syntax

WAIT *port*, *andExpr*[, *xorExpr*]

port is the address of the port to be monitored; it can be an integer expression in the range 0 through 65535.

andExpr is an integer value that is used as an operand in a logical AND operation with the byte read from the port. You can also use the integer value *xorExpr* as an operand in a logical XOR (exclusive OR) operation with the byte that is performed before the AND operation. Program execution continues only when the result of these operations is a nonzero value.

Usage

```
WAIT &H60, 127
```

Polls the port at address 60H until the top bit of the byte read is set.

```
WAIT device%, 1, 1
```

Polls the port specified by the variable *device%* until bit 0 of the byte read is not set.

Description

The WAIT statement is most useful in real-time programs that let you communicate with other computers. For example, if you are writing a program that links your PC to another computer, you need to monitor the hardware port that connects the computers; otherwise, you might lose data.

WAIT suspends execution until the specified output port returns a byte of a specified bit pattern. Whenever you execute a WAIT statement, QuickBASIC reads a byte from the specified port and performs an AND operation with the logical expression specified in the second parameter. For example, if you want program execution to pause until the sixth bit of the byte read is set, you specify the value 32 in the second parameter. This masks all bits but the sixth one. If WAIT reads the value 183 from a port, the AND operation masks the sixth bit, as follows:

```
WAIT port%, 32
```

```
        1 0 1 1 0 1 1 1  = 183
    AND 0 0 1 0 0 0 0 0  =  32
    -----------------------
        0 0 1 0 0 0 0 0  =  32
```

Because the result of this operation is nonzero, WAIT completes and the program resumes execution.

To reverse the logic of the test—to wait until the sixth bit is *not* set—you can perform a preliminary XOR operation with the byte read by including a third parameter in the call to WAIT. You can use the XOR operation to toggle one or more bits, reversing their current settings. Again, suppose the byte read from a port is 183. If you then use 32 as the value for both the second and the third parameters of WAIT, the statement performs the following operations.

```
WAIT port%, 32, 32
```

	1 0 1 1 0 1 1 1 = 183		1 0 0 1 0 1 1 1 = 151
XOR	0 0 1 0 0 0 0 0 = 32	AND	0 0 1 0 0 0 0 0 = 32
	1 0 0 1 0 1 1 1 = 151		0 0 0 0 0 0 0 0 = 0

Note that the WAIT statement does not return a value. If you need to read the information that the port is transmitting, use the INP function. (See the INP entry.)

Warnings

If the specified bit pattern does not occur at the port being polled (for example, if a remote computer fails to reply to your message), WAIT remains in an endless loop. If this happens, you can regain control only by rebooting the computer.

Compatibility

ANSI BASIC

The ANSI WAIT statement has several versions, none of which reads hardware ports. WAIT DELAY pauses execution for a specified number of seconds; WAIT TIMER waits for a specified time on the system clock; and WAIT EVENT suspends the program until another program in a multitasking environment passes a signal. WAIT EVENT has a TIMEOUT clause that enables the original program to resume if it doesn't receive the signal within a specified amount of time.

Example

The following program uses the WAIT statement to pause program execution until the printer connected to the first parallel port is on line. Because the sixth bit of the byte at address 3BDH is 0 when the printer is ready, the call to WAIT uses the number 32 in the second and third parameters.

```
CLS
PRINT "Be sure that your printer is ready."
WAIT &H3BD, 32, 32             ' wait until first parallel printer is ready
PRINT "Now printing a message."
LPRINT "QuickBASIC Bible", DATE$, TIME$; CHR$(12)
```

CHAPTER 20

Mixed Language

Introduction

Although QuickBASIC is powerful and rich in built-in features, it is not well suited for certain programming tasks. FORTRAN, for example, is better adapted for applications that must perform specialized scientific calculations and intensive number-crunching. C has a wealth of functions for manipulating and moving large blocks of memory, and assembly language produces the fastest and most efficient code for low-level applications and for controlling the PC hardware.

With QuickBASIC, however, you can call on the resources of another language whenever your program requires them. If you need special string-handling functions, for example, you can add a C library. If you want to write data directly to the screen, you can call an assembly-language routine. QuickBASIC lets you use procedures from other languages so easily that they become extensions of QuickBASIC itself.

Table 20-1 contains an alphabetic listing of QuickBASIC's mixed-language statements and functions.

Statement or function	Description
CALL (Non-BASIC procedures)	Executes a routine contained in an external module or library
CALL ABSOLUTE	Executes a machine-language routine that begins at an absolute address in memory
CALL INT86OLD, CALL INT86XOLD	Call a DOS or BIOS interrupt service; provided for compatibility with previous versions of QuickBASIC
CALL INTERRUPT, CALL INTERRUPTX	Call a DOS or BIOS interrupt service using a user-defined record structure
DECLARE (Non-BASIC procedures)	Defines the parameters and calling convention used by a routine contained in an external module or library
DEF SEG	Defines the current segment in memory for functions and statements that use absolute addresses
SADD	Returns the offset address of a string variable in the current segment in memory
VARPTR, VARPTR$	Return the offset address of a variable in the current data segment
VARSEG	Returns the segment address of a variable

Table 20-1.
Mixed-language statements and functions.

External Routines

This section discusses the method for storing routines (functions and procedures) in separately compiled modules that you can link to QuickBASIC programs and then execute by using the CALL (Non-BASIC procedures) statement. It also explains the DECLARE statement, which lets you define how parameters are passed to external routines and describes how to store modules in link libraries and Quick libraries so that your collection of routines is organized efficiently. If you maintain your modules in libraries, you can call routines written in any Microsoft language.

If you have been programming for some time (in QuickBASIC, GW-BASIC, or some other language), you probably have a large collection of useful routines that you use again and again in the programs you write. For example, you might have created special functions that check for specific files, that handle user input in a convenient way, or that clear selected areas of the screen.

To avoid typing the same code in every program, you can store standard routines in a separate file and then use the $INCLUDE metacommand to merge the file with each new program. The following statement merges the code contained in ROUTINES.BI into the program:

```
' $INCLUDE: 'ROUTINES.BI'
```

This method has a few drawbacks, however. For example, you cannot use subprograms or function definitions in files merged by using $INCLUDE. Furthermore, because included files can contain only BASIC source code, you cannot use them to add routines written in other languages to your QuickBASIC programs.

An alternative method lets you use QuickBASIC subprograms and functions as well as routines written in other programming languages: You compile these routines as separate modules and then use the Link program to link to your program only the modules that you need. If you write your programs with the QuickBASIC editor, you know that QuickBASIC treats each subprogram and user-defined function as a separate program. For example, if you include the statement

```
DEFINT A-Z
```

at the beginning of your main program, QuickBASIC copies this statement to the beginning of every subprogram or user-defined function definition you create. By copying the environment to each module, QuickBASIC makes the modules independent of the rest of the program. Therefore, even if you remove the main program code, you can use the BC.EXE command line compiler to compile each subprogram or user-defined function as the object file of a stand-alone program. If, for example, you want to compile the subprogram *PANEL* (which is found in the sample program in the CALL (BASIC procedures) entry) as a separate module, merely save the subprogram as a file and then compile it by using the following command:

```
BC /O PANEL.BAS;
```

The command-line compiler compiles the routine stored in the file PANEL.BAS and produces the object file PANEL.OBJ. Note the semicolon at the end of the command line. If you don't include it, the compiler asks you to supply the name of the object file and the source listing. The semicolon directs the compiler to use the defaults for these options.

The /O switch directs the compiler to create an object file that can be linked to stand-alone programs. You can omit this option if you use PANEL.OBJ only with programs that use the QuickBASIC runtime module BRUN45.EXE.

Before you can use PANEL.OBJ in another program, you must link it to that program using the Microsoft Object Linker, LINK.EXE. To link PANEL.OBJ to MAINPROG.OBJ, for example, use the following command line:

```
LINK MAINPROG PANEL;
```

Notice that MAINPROG itself must be compiled to an object file with BC.EXE before you can use the above command line. (The linker assumes the OBJ extensions, so you do not need to type them.) Once again, the semicolon directs the linker to use the default options. The call to the linker creates a single executable program named MAINPROG.EXE.

Non-BASIC Programs

Using the linker to include more than one object file in a program works equally well with routines that are written in other Microsoft programming languages, including C, FORTRAN, Pascal, and Macro Assembler (MASM). First you must convert the routine into an object file by using the compiler supplied with the language it was written in. For example, the QuickC sample program COPYBLOK.C, in the CALL (Non-BASIC procedures) entry, should be compiled with the QuickC command-line compiler by using the following command:

```
QCL /Ox /AM /Gs /c COPYBLOK.C
```

For a full explanation of the QuickC command-line switches, see the QuickC manual. Note the /AM switch, which selects the medium memory model. You must specify this switch if you intend to link a QuickC program to a QuickBASIC program. QuickBASIC always uses the medium memory model.

The above QCL command line produces the object file COPYBLOK.OBJ. You can then link this file to a QuickBASIC program exactly as you link more than one QuickBASIC object file:

```
LINK MAINPROG PANEL COPYBLOK;
```

This command links the QuickBASIC subprogram *Panel* and the C function *CopyBlock* (the function contained in COPYBLOK.C) to the main module, thereby making MAINPROG.EXE a true mixed-language program.

The DECLARE Statement

Before you can actually use *CopyBlock* and *Panel* in your QuickBASIC program, you must declare them at the beginning of the program, as follows:

```
DECLARE SUB Panel (switch%, row%, col%, rows%, cols%)
DECLARE SUB CopyBlock CDECL (s1%, o1%, s2%, o2%, BYVAL bytes%)
```

The DECLARE statement defines the number and type of parameters a routine will use. You can also use the CDECL keyword in the DECLARE statement to specify that QuickBASIC must use the C calling conventions when it passes the parameter to a routine. The BYVAL keyword, when used in the DECLARE statement, indicates that QuickBASIC must pass the value contained in a variable instead of passing the variable's address in memory, which is the default. (For a complete list of the DECLARE options, see the DECLARE (Non-BASIC procedures) entry.) Note that if the routine you declare returns a value, you must replace the keyword SUB with the keyword FUNCTION in the DECLARE statement.

After you declare a routine in this way, you never need to specify CDECL or BYVAL again. In fact, the CALL keyword itself becomes optional, so you can use the *CopyBlock* routine to copy one array to another simply by calling the statement:

```
CopyBlock 21185, 0, 22954, 0, 10000
```

Although *CopyBlock* is written in a language other than QuickBASIC, it becomes, in effect, an extension of QuickBASIC and can be used like any other QuickBASIC statement.

When you use the QuickBASIC environment editor to write subprograms and user-defined functions, QuickBASIC generates DECLARE statements for you. You must, however, write your own DECLARE statements for your linked routines, so it is a good idea to store those DECLARE statements in an external file that you can merely insert into a new program. Better still, you can use the $INCLUDE metacommand to merge with the main program the file that contains the DECLARE statements, as in the following statement:

```
' $INCLUDE: 'DECLARE.BI'
```

Using $INCLUDE is valid with a file containing DECLARE statements even though it isn't with files containing the subprograms or user-defined functions themselves.

Libraries

Linking object modules directly to your program works well when you are using only a few such routines. As your collection grows, however, you will find that typing the name of each module on the linker command line becomes cumbersome; you will also have trouble organizing the object modules so that all the ones you need are in the proper disk directory for the linker. Some languages provide a utility program called MAKE, which helps you build programs from multiple modules; QuickBASIC lets you store your routines in libraries.

A library is simply a collection of object modules. It lets you consolidate all your routines into a single file instead of having dozens of object modules cluttering up your disks. You might find it more convenient to create several libraries, each containing a different category of routines. For example, one library might contain the routines for drawing complex graphics. Another might contain the routines that perform file I/O. QuickBASIC actually uses two types of libraries—link libraries, which the LINK.EXE program uses when you build stand-alone executable programs, and Quick libraries, which the QuickBASIC environment uses.

Link Libraries

Microsoft provides the Library Manager program, LIB.EXE, as part of the QuickBASIC package. You can use this program to combine object files into a link library. For example, to combine the previous example routines into a link library, issue the following command:

```
LIB MIXED.LIB + PANEL + COPYBLOK, MIXED.CAT;
```

After you use the above command, your current directory includes two additional files—MIXED.LIB and MIXED.CAT.

MIXED.LIB is the link library. You can specify any valid filename for the library in the command line; however, you must use the extension LIB.

The MIXED.CAT file contains information similar to the following:

```
PANEL.............PANEL           _CopyBlock........COPYBLOK
PANEL             Offset: 00000010H  Code and data size: f6H
  Panel
COPYBLOK          Offset: 000001f0H  Code and data size: 112H
  CopyBlock
```

MIXED.CAT includes a listing of the names of each module and routine in the library. As your collection of routines and libraries grows, you will find these "catalog" files useful for locating specific routines.

To build a program that uses routines in a link library, you must use the linker to give the program access to the library. For example, to use the routines from MIXED.LIB in the MAINPROG program, enter the following linker command:

```
LINK MAINPROG,,,MIXED.LIB;
```

This produces an executable file that contains exactly the same code as does the executable file created with the command

```
LINK MAINPROG PANEL COPYBLOK;
```

You must still include the appropriate DECLARE statements in the MAINPROG program to define the routines that you will call. Because LINK.EXE uses from the library only those modules that contain the routines you have declared, using libraries can decrease the size of your program. If your library contains many routines, LINK.EXE includes in your program only the required modules and ignores the rest. This prevents the final program from containing unnecessary code.

LIB.EXE can do more than create new link libraries; it includes options that let you add, replace, or delete modules from existing libraries. (See the QuickBASIC documentation for a complete description of this program.)

Quick Libraries

Link libraries store routines used by stand-alone programs. However, you can also build Quick libraries, which let you use library routines in the QuickBASIC environment.

You can store exactly the same object modules in a Quick library as you can in a link library. You do not, however, use the LIB.EXE program to build a Quick library; you must use LINK.EXE instead. For example, to create a Quick library called MIXED.QLB that contains the same object modules as the sample link library MIXED.LIB, use the following command line:

```
LINK /QU PANEL COPYBLOK, MIXED.QLB,, BQLB45.LIB;
```

The /QU switch directs the linker to produce a Quick library instead of an executable file. BQLB45.LIB is a support library that LINK.EXE uses to build the Quick library; this QuickBASIC library must be in the current directory when you issue the above LINK command. Note that you can also create a Quick library from the QuickBASIC environment. Load the source files that you want in the library into the environment, and then choose the Make Library command from the Run menu.

After you build the Quick library, you must load it and the program that will use it into the QuickBASIC environment. In the example, you start QuickBASIC with the command:

```
QB MAINPROG.BAS /L MIXED.QLB
```

Remember that the source code of the program that will call routines in the Quick library must include the appropriate DECLARE statements to access them.

Loading Machine-Language Routines into Variables

QuickBASIC provides another method of using non-BASIC routines. You can load a machine-language routine (which is a routine that has been translated into an executable format) into a QuickBASIC variable and execute it by using the CALL ABSOLUTE statement. This method, first used by GW-BASIC and BASICA, is retained in QuickBASIC so that you can easily port routines written for those languages to QuickBASIC. Loading machine-language routines is not as useful as using mixed-language libraries because it limits you to using machine-language routines. CALL ABSOLUTE is also more difficult to use because you must convert the machine-language code into QuickBASIC DATA statements before you can load the code into a variable. (See the following section, "Converting Machine Language into DATA Statements," for details.)

CALL ABSOLUTE is an external routine, not one of QuickBASIC's built-in statements. Therefore, you must link the library that contains it to any program that needs to use it. Note that you can link either a link library or a Quick library.

QuickBASIC includes CALL ABSOLUTE in two predefined libraries—QB.LIB (the link library) and QB.QLB (the Quick library). If you want to build a stand-alone executable program that uses CALL ABSOLUTE, you must link it by using the command

```
LINK MAINPROG,,,QB.LIB;
```

To use CALL ABSOLUTE in a program run from the QuickBASIC environment, you must load it by using the command

```
QB MAINPROG.BAS /L QB.QLB
```

(QB.LIB and QB.QLB also contain the object modules for two other external routines—CALL INTERRUPT and CALL INT86OLD.)

As with other external routines, you must declare CALL ABSOLUTE in your program before you can execute it. QuickBASIC provides the necessary DECLARE statement in the file QB.BI. Merge it with your program by using the $INCLUDE metacommand as follows:

```
' $INCLUDE: 'QB.BI'
```

After you include the DECLARE statement, you can call the CALL ABSOLUTE statement as you would any other QuickBASIC statement. You can omit the keyword CALL, as in the following statement:

```
ABSOLUTE address%
```

address% is the address in memory of the variable that contains the assembly-language program.

QuickBASIC provides two functions to help you determine the address of a variable: VARPTR, which returns the address of a numeric variable, an array, or a fixed-length string; and SADD, which returns the address of a variable-length string.

The address returned by these functions is the offset of the specified variable in its memory segment. If you load the machine-language routine into a string, the offset completely describes the address of the routine because QuickBASIC always stores strings in the default data segment, DGROUP. In this case, you can execute the loaded routine by using the statement

```
ABSOLUTE SADD(routine$)
```

If you load the routine into an array, use the address returned by VARPTR for the array's first element; that is, use the following statement to retrieve the address:

```
address% = VARPTR(codeArray%(0))
```

However, because QuickBASIC doesn't store dynamic arrays in DGROUP, you must change to the proper memory segment before you call the routine. The VARSEG function returns the segment address of a variable, and the DEF SEG statement lets you set that address as the current segment. To execute a machine-language routine that has been loaded into a dynamic array, use the following statements:

```
DEF SEG = VARSEG(codeArray%(0))
ABSOLUTE VARPTR(codeArray%(0))
```

Each element of an integer array can hold 2 bytes of machine code, so when you dimension the array, you need to use only half the number of subscripts as the number of bytes in the routine. Use the POKE statement to load the code directly into the memory occupied by the array, as demonstrated in the following program segment:

```
DEF SEG = VARSEG(codeArray%(0))   ' change to the correct segment
offSet% = VARPTR(codeArray%(0))   ' find beginning of the array

FOR i% = 0 TO 30
    READ byte%
    POKE offSet% + i%, VAL("&H" + byte%)
NEXT i%

DATA   55, 8B, EC, 06, 1E, 57, 56, 2E, C7, 06
⋮
```

Although using CALL ABSOLUTE is probably the most memory-efficient method of loading a non-BASIC routine, you must be careful when you load an array or string and call the routine. In particular, you must be sure that QuickBASIC does not move the variable before you call the routine. You can prevent this from happening by using dynamic arrays to hold the routine; because QuickBASIC places dynamic arrays in their own segments outside of DGROUP, they never move.

Converting Machine Language into DATA Statements

To use your machine-language routines with the CALL ABSOLUTE statement, you must convert them into DATA statements that can be used in your QuickBASIC program. One way to convert a routine is to load it into a debugging program such as Debug or Microsoft CodeView and then copy the byte values from the display into DATA statements in your program. However, the following program provides a better way of making the conversion. It reads a file that contains machine language and translates each byte into QuickBASIC DATA statements that you can then merge into your program. The program also calculates a checksum value that your loading routine can use to detect incorrectly typed data and then places the value by itself in the last DATA statement.

```
' BIN2DATA.BAS - translates binary files into DATA statements
binFile$ = "ROUTINE.COM"                ' change to machine-language filename
dataFile$ = "HEXDATA.INC"

OPEN binFile$ FOR BINARY AS #1 LEN = 1
OPEN dataFile$ FOR OUTPUT AS #2

DIM byte AS STRING * 1

dataLine$ = "DATA   "
count% = 0: checkSum& = 0

DO UNTIL EOF(1)
    GET #1, , byte
    checkSum& = checkSum& + ASC(byte)
    dataLine$ = dataLine$ + RIGHT$("0" + HEX$(ASC(byte)), 2)
    count% = count% + 1
    IF count% < 15 THEN
        dataLine$ = dataLine$ + ", "
    ELSE
        PRINT #2, dataLine$
        dataLine$ = "DATA   "
        count% = 0
    END IF
LOOP

IF count% > 0 THEN
    dataLine$ = LEFT$(dataLine$, LEN(dataLine$) - 2)
    PRINT #2, dataLine$
END IF

dataLine$ = "DATA   " + STR$(checkSum&)
PRINT #2, dataLine$
CLOSE
END
```

Interrupts

QuickBASIC provides several ways in which you can access external routines. The methods described so far assume that you've written code in another programming language or that you're using a third-party software library. However, another method gives you access to a built-in library containing hundreds of useful routines—all absolutely free and already written. These routines are built into your computer, and you access them by using interrupts.

An "interrupt" is a signal to the microprocessor that a task must be performed. When an interrupt occurs, the processor immediately suspends the current task and jumps to a routine that is designed to manage the event that triggered the interrupt; this routine is called an "interrupt handler." After the handler executes the required operation, control returns to the next instruction in the suspended task.

The PC family of processors permits 256 different interrupts (numbered from 0 through 255). Some of these are allocated to hardware devices: Every 54.936 milliseconds, for example, the timer generates interrupt number 8, which executes a subroutine that updates the system clock and the date and time flags. Most interrupt numbers, however, are reserved for software interrupts that can be generated by the CALL INTERRUPT statement.

You call an interrupt handler in QuickBASIC by specifying an interrupt number, not by specifying its address. At boot up, the BIOS writes the addresses to an interrupt vector table at the beginning of memory. When you issue an interrupt, the processor simply looks up the table entry for that interrupt number and then jumps to the corresponding address. Because different computers have different hardware configurations and use different versions of DOS and BIOS, the addresses in this table vary from machine to machine. However, because the interrupt numbers themselves do not change, programs that use them are portable between all computers in the PC family.

When you issue an interrupt, the processor performs the following actions:

1. Saves on the stack the flags register, the current code segment (CS), and the instruction pointer (IP).
2. Looks up the address of the handling routine in the Interrupt Vector Table, beginning at memory location 0000:0000. (Because each table entry is 4 bytes long, the correct entry can be found by multiplying the interrupt number by 4.)
3. Loads into the CS:IP registers the segment and offset address of the interrupt-handling routine, thus transferring control to that routine.
4. Executes the codes of the handling routine until the processor encounters an IRET (return from interrupt) instruction.
5. Restores from the stack the original instruction pointer, code segment, and flags register and continues execution with the instruction that follows the original interrupt call.

CALL INTERRUPT

You can use the CALL INTERRUPT statement to generate software interrupts from your QuickBASIC program. Like CALL ABSOLUTE, CALL INTERRUPT is an external routine stored in the libraries QB.LIB and QB.QLB.

Before you can use CALL INTERRUPT in a stand-alone executable program, you must link the library that contains it to your program with a command such as the following:

```
LINK MAINPROG,,,QB.LIB;
```

To use CALL INTERRUPT in the QuickBASIC environment, you must load the Quick library QB.QLB when you start QuickBASIC:

```
QB MAINPROG.BAS /L QB.QLB
```

In both cases, you must include in your program the file containing the DECLARE statement for CALL INTERRUPT. Before any executable statements, enter the following statement:

```
' $INCLUDE: 'QB.BI'
```

QB.BI also contains the definition of *RegType*, a special variable type that holds the values that are set in the CPU registers (shown in Figure 20-1 on the following page) when the interrupt call is made. The following TYPE...END TYPE statement is the definition of *RegType*:

```
TYPE RegType
    ax AS INTEGER
    bx AS INTEGER
    cx AS INTEGER
    dx AS INTEGER
    bp AS INTEGER
    si AS INTEGER
    di AS INTEGER
    flags AS INTEGER
END TYPE
```

Because most functions accessed with an interrupt also return values in registers, you must dimension two variables of type *RegType*. One variable holds the values passed to the interrupt, and the other holds the values returned. You can use the following statement to dimension the variables:

```
DIM inRegs AS RegType, outRegs AS RegType
```

Each *RegType* element corresponds to a CPU register, so you refer to each element by the name of the appropriate register. For example, to load the value 1000 into the BX register and then call a DOS interrupt, use the following code:

```
inRegs.bx = 1000
INTERRUPT &H21, inRegs, outRegs
```

Note that including the DECLARE statement in QB.BI declares a CALL INTERRUPT statement; therefore, you do not need to use the CALL keyword. Note also that most programmers use hexadecimal numbers when referring to interrupts; so the above statement refers to interrupt 21H instead of 33, its decimal equivalent. However, CALL INTERRUPT accepts either notation.

You must access any of the more than 100 DOS services through interrupt number 21H. For example, function number 0EH (14 decimal) lets you specify which disk drive is the current drive. To use the function, you must specify the function number in AH (the upper byte of the AX register) and the drive number in DL (the lower byte of the DX register) and then call interrupt 21H.

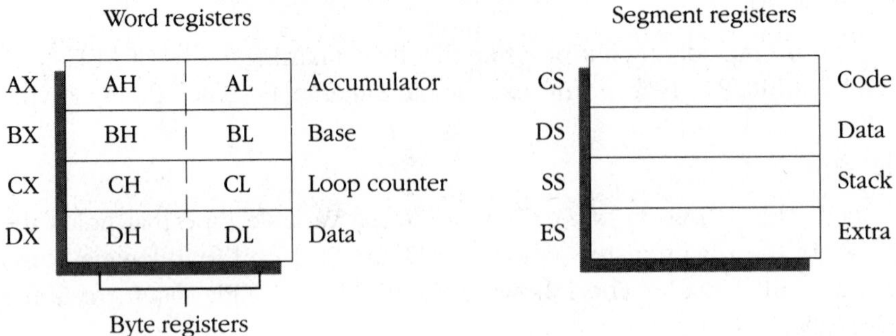

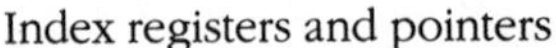

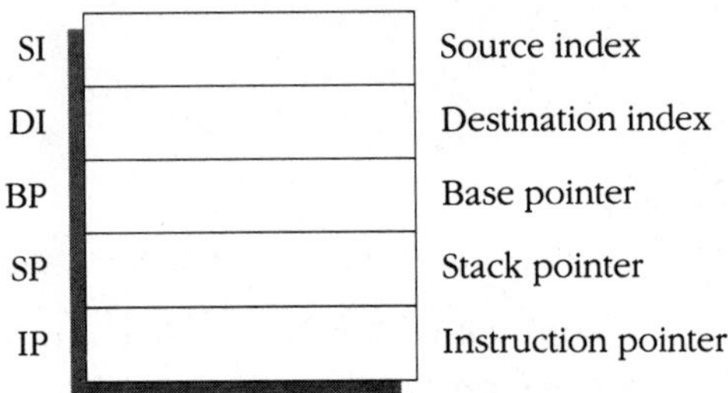

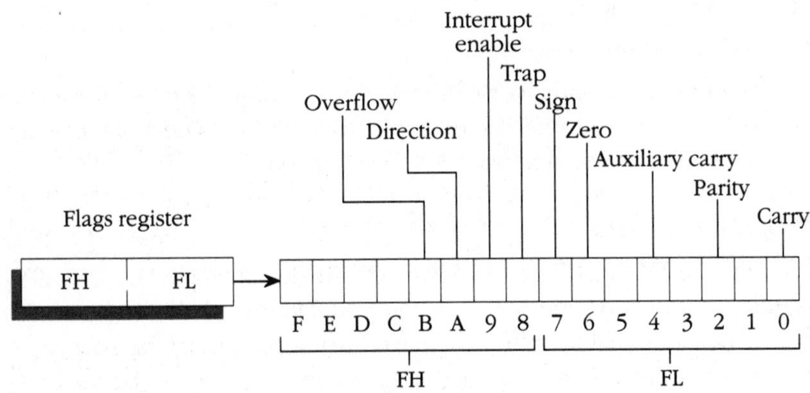

Figure 20-1.
The CPU registers.

If you need to set only the upper byte of a 2-byte register by using decimal numbers, you must multiply by 256 the value you want to place in the register:

```
inRegs.ax = (14 * 256)
```

Using hexadecimal numbers, however, simplifies the procedure. Simply follow the hexadecimal value you want to place in the high byte with two zeros to fill the low byte:

```
inRegs.ax = &HE00
```

Disk drives are numbered as follows: A = 0, B = 1, C = 2, and so on. To select drive C, you would load DX with the value 2:

```
inRegs.dx = 2
```

In this case, using a decimal number is simpler.

Now, issuing interrupt 21H as follows makes drive C the default:

```
INTERRUPT &H21, inRegs, outRegs
```

Function 0EH returns the number of logical drives in your system. Because this number is returned in the AL register and the function number (which you set) is contained in AH, you must remove the high byte of AX to obtain the correct return value:

```
drives% = outRegs.ax MOD 256
```

(The programs in the following section contain several examples of interrupt calls. For more information about these functions, see the "Related Reading" section at the end of this tutorial.)

CALL INT86OLD

In addition to CALL INTERRUPT, QuickBASIC provides a similar statement, CALL INT86OLD, to provide compatibility with earlier versions of BASIC.

CALL INT86OLD is similar to the INT86 routine included in QuickBASIC versions 2.0 and 3.0; it lets you easily convert programs written in those versions of the language. With CALL INT86OLD, you pass register values to and from a routine in integer arrays, not in variables of the user-defined data type *RegType*. Although the same functions available through CALL INT86OLD are available through CALL INTERRUPT, the latter statement is now the preferred one for calling interrupt functions.

Interrupt Services

Not every interrupt has its own handler. Some are dedicated to hardware devices that your computer might not have—a network controller, for example. Others are reserved for future use. However, two sets of interrupt services are common to all PCs that run DOS—those provided by the PC BIOS and those provided by DOS itself.

The BIOS services use several interrupts, each of which performs a set of functions related to a particular hardware device. Table 20-2 lists the BIOS interrupts.

Interrupt number	**Description**
05H	Print-screen service; invoked when Shift-PrtScrn is pressed on the keyboard, but can also be called from a program
10H	Various video display services; includes functions for selecting text and graphic modes, setting cursor size and location, scrolling parts of the screen, and outputting text and graphics to the display
11H	Equipment-list service; returns the system's equipment-list configuration
12H	Memory-size service; returns the installed memory size (not including extended memory)
13H	Low-level disk services; includes functions for reading, writing, and formatting absolute disk sectors
14H	Serial-communications services; includes functions that initialize and read the status of an RS232 port or send and receive characters
15H	Cassette functions in PC; includes multitasking and extended-memory functions in the AT and PS/2 series
16H	Keyboard services; includes functions that read keyboard status, flags, and keypresses
17H	Printer services; includes functions for checking printer status, initializing the parallel port, and sending output to the printer

Table 20-2.
PC ROM-BIOS interrupt services.

You access all DOS interrupt services through interrupt 21H (33 decimal). This one interrupt supports more than 100 functions (as of DOS 4.0). To select a particular function, you merely call interrupt 21H and specify the appropriate function number in the AH register.

Many of these DOS and BIOS services, of course, are duplicated by existing QuickBASIC statements and functions (which themselves call the BIOS or DOS interrupts). Even so, many routines that QuickBASIC does not provide directly are useful, and you can access them by using the CALL INTERRUPT statement.

Related Reading

Craig, John Clark. *Microsoft QuickBASIC Programmer's Toolbox.* Redmond, Wash.: Microsoft Press, 1988.

Duncan, Ray. *Advanced MS-DOS Programming, 2nd ed.* Redmond, Wash.: Microsoft Press, 1988.

Duncan, Ray. *IBM ROM BIOS: Programmer's Quick Reference.* Redmond, Wash.: Microsoft Press, 1988.

Duncan, Ray. *MS-DOS Functions: Programmer's Quick Reference.* Redmond, Wash.: Microsoft Press, 1988.

Lafore, Robert, *The Waite Group's Microsoft C Programming for the IBM.* Indianapolis, Ind.: Howard W. Sams & Co., 1987.

Norton, Peter, and Richard Wilton. *The* New *Peter Norton Programmer's Guide to the IBM PC & PS/2.* 2d ed. Redmond, Wash.: Microsoft Press, 1988.

The Waite Group. *MS-DOS Developer's Guide.* Indianapolis, Ind.: Howard W. Sams & Co., 1989.

The Waite Group. *MS-DOS Papers.* Indianapolis, Ind.: Howard W. Sams & Co., 1988.

CALL (Non-BASIC procedures)

See also: CALL ABSOLUTE, DECLARE (Non-BASIC procedures)

✲ QB2	■ QB4.5	✲ PowerBASIC
✲ QB3	ANSI	✲ GW-BASIC
■ QB4	■ BASIC7	✲ MacQB

Purpose

The CALL statement transfers control to a procedure. The procedure can be a subprogram written in QuickBASIC with the SUB statement, or it can be a non-BASIC procedure stored in an external library. (For information about calling QuickBASIC subprograms, see the CALL entry in Chapter 4, "Procedures.") This entry describes how to call non-BASIC procedures and discusses the special keywords that let CALL execute the procedures properly.

Syntax

[CALL] *procedure* [(][[{BYVAL ¦ SEG}] *arg* [AS *type*][, ...]][)]

or

CALLS *procedure* [(*arg* [AS *type*][, ...])]

procedure is the name of the procedure to be executed; it can be as many as 40 characters long.

arg is a valid QuickBASIC variable, constant, or expression to be passed to the called program. You can include a type-declaration character with a variable, or you can use the AS keyword with *type* to define its type.

The BYVAL keyword directs QuickBASIC to pass the actual value of an argument to the program. (Most C routines require this.) If you don't specify BYVAL, QuickBASIC passes the address of the argument as an offset in DGROUP, QuickBASIC's data segment. The SEG keyword directs QuickBASIC to pass both the segment and offset of the address of an argument. The segment and offset combination is called a "segmented," or "far," address.

The CALLS variant stipulates that all arguments be passed as far addresses, exactly as if you had used the SEG keyword with each argument. You cannot specify BYVAL in a CALLS statement.

Usage

```
DECLARE SUB FastPrint (r%, c%, m$, a%)
FastPrint row% + 1, 10, "HELLO!", 78
```

Declares and calls the non-BASIC procedure *FastPrint*. Because the prototype for *FastPrint* has been declared, you don't have to use the CALL keyword and the parentheses around the argument list.

```
CALLS FortranProg(num AS LONG, den AS LONG)
```

Calls a FORTRAN routine that requires two long-integer arguments. Because the CALLS statement is used, both arguments are passed as far addresses.

Description

CALL (BASIC procedures) and CALL (Non-BASIC procedures) are very similar. What distinguishes them from each other are the special keywords, BYVAL and SEG, that CALL (Non-BASIC procedures) provides to make the calling process conform to the conventions of the non-BASIC language being called. You don't need to use these keywords when you call QuickBASIC subprograms by using CALL (BASIC procedures) because that statement uses the default conventions of QuickBASIC.

You must declare all non-BASIC procedures before you call them. (See the DECLARE entry in Chapter 4, "Procedures.") After you declare a procedure by using DECLARE, the keyword CALL is optional; you can call the procedure merely by naming it. However, if you omit CALL, you must also omit the parentheses around the argument list. Because the CALLS statement is a special case of CALL, you must include the CALLS keyword.

Current versions of all Microsoft programming languages use the same format for the object modules and libraries that they produce. Therefore, when you link the individual modules of an executable program, QuickBASIC can use them as if they were originally written in QuickBASIC. The Microsoft linker merely establishes references to the named procedures so that the CALL statements can find them.

By default, QuickBASIC always passes arguments to external procedures as near references. This means that it passes the addresses of the variables in the argument list as offsets from the beginning of QuickBASIC's default data segment, DGROUP. During this process, QuickBASIC evaluates expressions and constants and converts them into temporary variables. If you are passing dynamic numeric arrays and dynamic arrays of fixed-length strings that are not stored in DGROUP, you must use the SEG keyword, which directs QuickBASIC to include the segment part of the address as well as the offset. The BYVAL keyword specifies that QuickBASIC will pass the argument's actual value and not its address. You do not normally use BYVAL or SEG in a CALL statement. The correct place to specify BYVAL and SEG is in a DECLARE statement, as shown in the following statement:

```
DECLARE SUB Sort (BYVAL index AS INTEGER, SEG ray() AS LONG)
```

If you specify how arguments are passed in the DECLARE statement, you have to do it only once. Then, in the CALL statement, you need to include only the names or values of the arguments. In fact, even the keyword CALL is optional. If you omit the CALL keyword, be sure to also omit the parentheses surrounding the argument list.

The only time you must use BYVAL or SEG in a CALL statement is when you want to override the calling convention that you previously declared.

Comments

A side effect of the CALL statement occurs when the called procedure changes the parameters you pass to it. By default, QuickBASIC passes the addresses of the variables; therefore, any changes to the variables are transferred back to the QuickBASIC program that called the procedure. When you pass variables by value with BYVAL, however, QuickBASIC passes only the contents of the variables to the procedure. The original variables are unaffected by the actions of the called procedure.

Before QuickBASIC 4.0 introduced the BYVAL clause, you could simulate passing a procedure's parameters by value by enclosing the variables in parentheses. In the following statement, for example, the variable *original%* is passed by value:

```
CALL Convert(result&, (original%))
```

The use of parentheses around *original%* directs QuickBASIC to evaluate the variable as an expression. This forces QuickBASIC to create a temporary variable to hold the contents of *original%*. Therefore, it is the address of this temporary variable that is passed to *Convert*, not the address of *original%* itself. This ensures that any changes made to the argument within the routine are made only to the temporary variable and are not passed back to the calling program.

This technique still works with CALL in QuickBASIC 4.5; however, because the BYVAL keyword passes variables by value, you do not need to use it.

Errors

If you call an assembly-language routine that has not been declared public in the original assembly-language source code, QuickBASIC returns a "Symbol not defined" error message. This does not apply to procedures written in C, Pascal, or FORTRAN, which are public by default.

Tips

The name of the procedure your QuickBASIC program calls is usually the same as the name of the external procedure. However, you might prefer to use another name—especially if the procedure is written in FORTRAN, which limits a procedure name to 6 characters. QuickBASIC lets you substitute a different name (of as many as 40 characters) by specifying an ALIAS clause in the matching DECLARE statement.

Compatibility

QuickBASIC 2.0 and QuickBASIC 3.0

QuickBASIC versions 2.0 and 3.0 do not support the use of the keywords SEG or BYVAL in the CALL statement. To pass a segmented (far) address, you must instead use the CALLS statement. You can only simulate passing by value by placing parentheses around a parameter.

PowerBASIC

PowerBASIC lets you merge machine-language procedures into a program by using the $INLINE metacommand. You can write assembly-language code in your PowerBASIC source code directly, as hexadecimal byte values, or you can specify the name of a separately assembled COM file that will be merged with your program when it runs. In both cases, a CALL statement executes the routine just as it does any other subprogram.

GW-BASIC and BASICA

Some versions of GW-BASIC include the CALLS statement to transfer control to routines written in FORTRAN. The CALL and CALLS statements in these versions differ from those in the QuickBASIC version: these statements in GW-BASIC and BASICA require you to specify the external procedure's address (as you do in CALL ABSOLUTE) rather than its name. In GW-BASIC and BASICA, you must also use DEF SEG to set the current segment to that of the called procedure before you execute it. QuickBASIC does not require this.

QuickBASIC for the Macintosh

QuickBASIC for the Macintosh lets you call either procedures written in assembly language or procedures that are stored in "resource libraries." Although superficially similar to Quick libraries, resource libraries are not compatible with their MS-DOS equivalents. To call a resource library procedure from Macintosh QuickBASIC code, simply name it and specify its arguments; the CALL keyword is not required.

You can also use CALL to access many of the low-level graphics, text, and mouse routines built into ROM. For example, the following statement selects Monaco, a monospace font, as the default font for text output:

```
CALL TEXTFONT(4)
```

Note that QuickBASIC for the Macintosh does not support the use of the keywords BYVAL and SEG.

Example

Among the many functions Microsoft QuickC provides is the powerful *_movedata* function, which lets you quickly copy blocks of data between any two locations in memory. The following mixed-language program uses the QuickC function *CopyBlock*, which calls *_movedata*, to copy the contents of one array to another. You need to use QuickC to compile the QuickC module that contains *CopyBlock*.

First compile the QuickC file COPYBLOK.C, which contains *CopyBlock*, with the following command:

```
QCL /Ox /AM /Gs /c COPYBLOK.C
```

This command line produces the object file COPYBLOK.OBJ, which you can link directly to a QuickBASIC object file by using the LINK program. You can also use the object file to build a Quick library or a link library. To create a link library, use the LIB program. To create a Quick library called CPROCS.QLB, use the following command:

```
LINK /QU COPYBLOK,CPROCS.QLB,,BQLB45.LIB
```

Now you can use the *CopyBlock* function in a QuickBASIC program when you load the Quick library with QuickBASIC or when you link either the object file or the link library with the object file containing your QuickBASIC program.

```
' CALL.BAS
DECLARE SUB CopyBlock CDECL (seg1%, off1%, seg2%, off2%, BYVAL bytes%)

CLS
DIM a1(1 TO 100) AS INTEGER, a2(1 TO 100) AS INTEGER

FOR i% = 1 TO 100: a1(i%) = i%: NEXT     ' fill the first array
bytes% = 200                             ' the number of bytes in the array

' copy the contents of the first array to the second by calling CopyBlock
CopyBlock VARSEG(a1(1)), VARPTR(a1(1)), VARSEG(a2(1)), VARPTR(a2(1)), bytes%

' print the contents of the second array
FOR i% = 1 TO 100: PRINT a2(i%); : NEXT
END
```

```
#include <memory.h>

/* COPYBLOK.C */
/* copies a block of data from one location in memory to another */
void CopyBlock(*seg1, *off1, *seg2, *off2, bytes)
    unsigned int *seg1, *off1, *seg2, *off2, bytes;
    {
    movedata(*seg1, *off1, *seg2, *off2, bytes);
    }
```

CALL ABSOLUTE

See also: CALL (Non-BASIC procedures), DECLARE, DEF SEG, SADD, VARPTR, VARSEG

■ QB2	■ QB4.5	✲ PowerBASIC
■ QB3	ANSI	✲ GW-BASIC
■ QB4	■ BASIC7	✲ MacQB

Purpose

The CALL ABSOLUTE statement executes a machine-language routine that has been loaded into a variable at an absolute address in memory. Although this statement lets you use routines developed for earlier versions of BASIC, the preferred method for accessing machine-language routines in QuickBASIC is by using the CALL statement (discussed in the CALL (Non-BASIC procedures) entry).

Syntax

[CALL] ABSOLUTE[(][*var*...] *address*[)]

The CALL keyword in the CALL ABSOLUTE statement is optional; however, if you omit it, you must declare ABSOLUTE as a subprogram and you must omit the parentheses around the argument list.

var is one or more optional variables supplied as parameters to the machine-language routine.

address is a valid QuickBASIC expression or variable name that evaluates to an integer value that is the offset of the called routine in the currently defined segment.

Usage

```
CALL ABSOLUTE (&HF000)
```

Transfers control to a machine-language routine in memory at offset 61440 (F000H) in the current segment.

```
DECLARE SUB ABSOLUTE(score AS INTEGER, address AS INTEGER)
ABSOLUTE hiScore%, SADD(mCode$)
```

Transfers control to a machine-language routine that has been loaded into the string *mCode$*. The routine requires one argument, *hiScore%*. Because this routine has been declared, the CALL keyword and the parentheses are omitted.

Description

Most programmers who move to QuickBASIC from an earlier version of BASIC already have a collection of useful machine-language routines. These routines might enhance the display, speed up slow-moving sections of code, or perform an operation that is difficult to do in BASIC. The CALL ABSOLUTE statement lets you port machine-language routines developed under BASIC to QuickBASIC programs without extensively modifying those routines.

CALL ABSOLUTE is not a built-in QuickBASIC statement; to use it, you must either load the Quick library QB.QLB into the QuickBASIC environment or link your program with the link library QB.LIB when you build an executable program from the command line. (Both QB.QLB and QB.LIB are included on the QuickBASIC distribution disks. See the tutorial section for details about how to link external libraries to your QuickBASIC programs.)

You must declare ABSOLUTE as an external subprogram before any of the executable statements in your program. Microsoft includes a declaration in the file QB.BI, which you can place at the head of your program by using the $INCLUDE metacommand:

```
' $INCLUDE: 'QB.BI'
```

The file QB.BI also includes prototypes and type declarations for other QuickBASIC external procedures (such as CALL INTERRUPT and CALL INT86OLD). If your program doesn't use any of these other statements, you can reduce the size of the final program by omitting the $INCLUDE metacommand and replacing it with the appropriate DECLARE statement, as shown in the following statement:

```
DECLARE SUB ABSOLUTE (address AS INTEGER)
```

Furthermore, the prototype declaration in QB.BI makes no provision for passing parameters to your machine-language procedure; therefore, if the procedure expects arguments, you must edit the DECLARE statement so that it includes parameter declarations as follows:

```
DECLARE SUB ABSOLUTE (arg1 AS INTEGER, arg2$, address AS INTEGER)
```

The two additional parameters to CALL ABSOLUTE are separated by commas. Note that the parameter that contains the address must always be the last item in the argument list.

Each dynamic array is stored in its own segment in the far heap. So if your program uses a machine-language routine stored in a dynamic array, you must use the VARSEG function to find the array's segment and then use the DEF SEG statement to change the current segment.

CALL ABSOLUTE provides a degree of compatibility with earlier versions of BASIC, which often use the BLOAD statement to load machine-language files into an absolute address in memory. Now that QuickBASIC lets you link machine-language support modules directly to your programs and provides the CALL (Non-BASIC procedures) statement to let you access them, this technique is no longer necessary. CALL (Non-BASIC procedures) is now the preferred method of invoking any kind of external routine.

Errors

If you use CALL ABSOLUTE to access a string variable that holds a machine-language routine, do not declare it as a fixed-length string. If you try to use the SADD function to return the address of a fixed-length string, QuickBASIC returns a "Fixed-length string illegal" error message.

Compatibility

PowerBASIC

The PowerBASIC argument syntax for CALL ABSOLUTE is the same as it is in GW-BASIC and BASICA:

CALL ABSOLUTE *address* [(*var*...)]

Unlike other languages, PowerBASIC accepts only integer variables as arguments.

PowerBASIC provides the SUB INLINE statement, which lets you insert machine language directly into the program source code.

GW-BASIC and BASICA

GW-BASIC and BASICA use the CALL statement (without the ABSOLUTE keyword) to execute machine-language routines. However, the syntax of CALL differs from that of CALL ABSOLUTE. For CALL, you must first specify the address of the called routine and then list the arguments in parentheses, as shown in the following syntax line:

CALL *address* [(*var*...)]

The statement is functionally identical to CALL ABSOLUTE in QuickBASIC.

QuickBASIC for the Macintosh

Like QuickBASIC 4.5, QuickBASIC for the Macintosh uses the CALL statement to access both BASIC subprograms and machine-language subroutines. However, it does not support the ABSOLUTE keyword, and the syntax of CALL is the same as that in GW-BASICA—the address precedes the argument list:

CALL *address* [(*var*...)]

Note that the variable *address* must be either a long integer or a floating-point value, because Macintosh memory addressing is based on the Motorola 68020 and 68030 microprocessors, both of which can directly specify addresses with 32 bits of precision. You do not need to work with segments and offsets.

Example

QuickBASIC runtime errors commonly occur when a program tries to send output to a printer that has run out of paper or is not on line. The following program uses a machine-language routine that is stored in an array and used with CALL ABSOLUTE to test the printer status prior to output; the program then takes appropriate action if the printer is not available.

To run this program in the QuickBASIC environment, use the command

```
QB CALLABS.BAS /L QB.QLB
```

To compile the stand-alone version, use the following commands:

```
BC /O CALLABS;
LINK  CALLABS,,,QB.LIB;
```

```
DECLARE SUB ABSOLUTE (argument AS INTEGER, address AS INTEGER)

' $DYNAMIC                           ' make all arrays dynamic

DIM mCode(0 TO 11) AS INTEGER       ' dimension array for routine
printer% = 1                        ' 1 = LPT1:, 2 = LPT2: etc.
testSum& = 0                        ' set up for checksum test

DEF SEG = VARSEG(mCode(0))          ' set the array segment
offSet% = VARPTR(mCode(0))          ' get the array address
RESTORE Code

FOR i% = 0 TO 23                    ' read each machine-code byte
    READ byte%
    testSum& = testSum& + byte%
    POKE offSet% + i%, byte%        ' load the byte into the array
NEXT i%

READ checkSum&
IF testSum& <> checkSum& THEN       ' check for typing errors
    PRINT "CHECKSUM ERROR!!!"
    BEEP: PRINT "Can't continue"
    STOP
END IF

ABSOLUTE printer%, offSet%          ' execute the routine
DEF SEG                             ' restore default segment

IF printer% = 144 OR printer% = 208 THEN      ' indicates printer is ready
    PRINT "The printer is ready for output."
ELSE
    PRINT "The printer is not ready for output."
END IF
END

' machine-language routine data bytes and the checksum
Code:
    DATA &H55, &H8B, &HEC, &H8B, &H5E, &H06, &H8B, &H17
    DATA &H4A, &HB4, &H02, &HCD, &H17, &H8A, &HC4, &HB4
    DATA &H00, &H89, &H07, &H5D, &HCA, &H02, &H00, &H00
    DATA 2300
```

CALL INT86OLD, CALL INT86XOLD

See also: CALL INTERRUPT, DECLARE

✲ QB2	■ QB4.5	✲ PowerBASIC
✲ QB3	ANSI	GW-BASIC
■ QB4	■ BASIC7	MacQB

Purpose

The CALL INT86OLD and CALL INT86XOLD statements call DOS and BIOS interrupt services in a way that is compatible with earlier versions of BASIC.

Syntax

[CALL] INT86OLD [(]*intNum*, *inRegs()*, *outRegs()*[)]
[CALL] INT86XOLD[(]*intNum*, *inRegs()*, *outRegs()*[)]

The CALL keyword is optional; however, if you omit it, you must declare either INT86OLD or INT86XOLD as a subprogram and you must omit the parentheses around the argument list.

intNum is an integer in the range 0 through 255 that specifies the number of the software interrupt to be called.

inRegs is an integer array of either 8 elements (CALL INT86OLD) or 10 elements (CALL INT86XOLD) that contains the values to be set in the CPU registers when the interrupt handler begins execution. *outRegs* is the corresponding integer array that holds the CPU register values when the interrupt finishes executing; it has 8 elements in INT86OLD and 10 elements in INT86XOLD.

Usage

```
CALL INT86OLD(&H10, inRegs%(), outRegs%())
```

Calls a BIOS video interrupt service with CPU registers specified by the array *inRegs*.

```
INT86XOLD 33, segRegsIn%(), segRegsOut%()
```

Calls a DOS service with CPU registers specified by *segRegsIn%* loaded. (Note that you can use either decimal or hexadecimal numbers to specify the interrupt number.)

Description

INT86OLD and INT86XOLD are not built-in QuickBASIC statements; they are external procedures. So before you can use them, you must either load the Quick library QB.QLB into the QuickBASIC environment or link your program with the link library QB.LIB when you build an executable program. (Both QB.QLB and QB.LIB are included on the QuickBASIC distribution disks. See the tutorial section for details about how to link external libraries to your QuickBASIC programs.)

To use the statements, your program also must declare INT86OLD and INT86XOLD before any executable statements. The QuickBASIC file QB.BI includes prototype declarations that you can append to the beginning of your program by using the $INCLUDE metacommand:

```
' $INCLUDE: 'QB.BI'
```

The QB.BI file also includes prototypes and type declarations for other external procedures (such as CALL INTERRUPT and CALL ABSOLUTE). If your program doesn't use any of these other statements, you can reduce the size of the final program by omitting the $INCLUDE metacommand and replacing it with the appropriate DECLARE statement, which is one of the following:

```
DECLARE SUB INT86OLD (intNum AS INTEGER, inRegs(1) AS INTEGER,_
            outRegs(1) AS INTEGER)
DECLARE SUB INT86XOLD (intNum AS INTEGER, inRegs(1) AS INTEGER,_
            outRegs(1) AS INTEGER)
```

CALL INT86OLD and CALL INT86XOLD let your programs generate software interrupts. Interrupts are discussed more fully in the tutorial section. In general, you can access all the low-level services provided by DOS and the BIOS by assigning values to the CPU registers and then issuing the appropriate interrupt number. For programs written in QuickBASIC 4.0 or 4.5, use the CALL INTERRUPT function, which uses variables of the user-defined type, *RegType*, to pass register values. This is the currently preferred method of accessing interrupt services.

In the second argument of CALL INT86OLD, you pass an 8-element integer array that contains the values to be loaded into the registers prior to the interrupt. In the third parameter, you pass another 8-element array, which holds the register settings after the interrupt is finished executing.

CALL INT86XOLD is functionally identical to CALL INT86OLD, but the second and third parameters must each contain 10 elements. CALLINT86XOLD lets you handle interrupts that accept or return values in the (infrequently used) segment registers DS and ES. (See Table 20-3.)

Entry value	**Register**	**Exit value**
inRegs(1)	AX	outRegs(1)
inRegs(2)	BX	outRegs(2)
inRegs(3)	CX	outRegs(3)
inRegs(4)	DX	outRegs(4)
inRegs(5)	BP	outRegs(5)
inRegs(6)	SI	outRegs(6)
inRegs(7)	DI	outRegs(7)
inRegs(8)	Flags	outRegs(8)
inRegs(9)	DS*	outRegs(9)
inRegs(10)	ES*	outRegs(10)

* INT86XOLD only

Table 20-3.
Relationships between CALL INT86OLD and CALL INT86XOLD arrays and CPU registers.

The interrupt service you call determines which registers are changed by the call. Many of the services are described in the tutorial section; you can also see The Waite Group's *MS-DOS Developer's Guide* for a complete list and for details about how to use them.

Comments

You do not need to use different array pairs for CALL INT86OLD and CALL INT86XOLD. It is usually more convenient to use the same 10-element array for both functions; CALL INT86OLD simply ignores any values set in elements 9 and 10 of the first array and fails to return the DS and ES segment registers in elements 9 and 10 of the second array. You can even use the same array to hold both the entry and exit values without generating errors or unpredictable side-effects. However, use the same array only if you do not need to preserve the register settings made at entry into the interrupt handler.

Errors

The only internal error checking that QuickBASIC performs with the CALL INT86OLD and CALL INT86XOLD statements is to test whether the interrupt number is in the range 0 through 255. If it is outside this range, QuickBASIC doesn't call the interrupt, and the statement returns with the interrupt number parameter containing –1 and the second array parameter unchanged. QuickBASIC doesn't verify the existence of the interrupt service you call, nor does it check to see whether the registers are correctly set for an existing service. Be careful. Calling interrupts randomly can crash your program or even reformat your hard disk!

Tips

You can use CALL INT86XOLD for both types of interrupt—those that accept or return values set in the segment registers (DS and ES) and those that do not—so you never need to use CALL INT86OLD. Simply be sure to assign a value of –1 to elements 9 (DS) and 10 (ES) of the first array to force the interrupt to use the default settings for these registers, not the values supplied in the array. This makes CALL INT86XOLD operate exactly as CALL INT86OLD does.

Compatibility

QuickBASIC 2.0 and QuickBASIC 3.0

The CALL INT86OLD and CALL INT86XOLD statements are directly equivalent to the CALL INT86 and CALL INT86X statements in QuickBASIC versions 2.0 and 3.0. However, in versions 2.0 and 3.0 you must pass in the parameter list the addresses of the arrays that contain the register values.

PowerBASIC

The PowerBASIC function that is equivalent to INT86XOLD resembles QuickBASIC's CALL INTERRUPT statement

CALL INTERRUPT *intNum*

However, in PowerBASIC, you don't need to use arrays to hold the register values. PowerBASIC maintains an internal buffer that stores registers before and after a CALL INTERRUPT or CALL ABSOLUTE call. You can read this buffer by using the REG function and write to the buffer by using the REG statement.

Example

Early versions of MS-DOS and PC-DOS did not include many of the facilities that we now take for granted in our programs. DOS 1, for example, did not allow subdirectories, and file-sharing was not added until version 3.10. The following program uses CALL INT86OLD to test the current operating system version number so that a program can determine what facilities it supports.

To run this program in the QuickBASIC environment, use the command

```
QB INT86OLD.BAS /L QB.QLB
```

To compile the stand-alone version, use the following commands:

```
BC /O INT86OLD;
LINK INT86OLD,,,QB.LIB;
```

```
' $INCLUDE: 'QB.BI'

' assign register names to the array subscripts they represent
CONST AX = 1, BX = 2, CX = 3, DX = 4, BP = 5
CONST SI = 6, DI = 7, FLAGS = 8

DIM inRegs(1 TO 8) AS INTEGER, outregs(1 TO 8) AS INTEGER

inRegs(AX) = &H3000                  ' DOS function 48 - get version number
CALL INT86OLD(&H21, inRegs(), outregs())

minor% = outregs(AX) \ 256           ' calculate minor version number
major% = outregs(AX) MOD 256         ' calculate major version number
IF major% = 0 THEN major% = 1        ' DOS 1.0 does not include this function
version$ = LTRIM$(RTRIM$(STR$(major%))) + "." + LTRIM$(RTRIM$(STR$(minor%)))

PRINT : PRINT
PRINT "This program is running under DOS "; version$
END
```

CALL INTERRUPT, CALL INTERRUPTX

See also: CALL INT86OLD, CALL INT86XOLD, DECLARE

✲ QB2	■ QB4.5	✲ PowerBASIC
✲ QB3	ANSI	GW-BASIC
■ QB4	■ BASIC7	MacQB

Purpose

The CALL INTERRUPT and CALL INTERRUPTX statements call a DOS or BIOS service by using a user-defined record structure. You can use these statements to call, for example, BIOS functions to scroll sections of the screen, to test whether the printer is ready for output, to read and write complete disk sectors, or to direct DOS to find, move, or manipulate files.

Syntax

[CALL] INTERRUPT [(]*intNum*, *inRegs*, *outRegs*[)]
[CALL] INTERRUPTX [(]*intNum*, *inRegsX*, *outRegsX*[)]

The CALL keyword is optional; however, if you omit it, you must declare either INTERRUPT or INTERRUPTX as a subprogram and you must omit the parentheses around the parameter list.

intNum is an integer in the range 0 through 255 that specifies the number of the software interrupt to be called.

inRegs, a variable of type *RegType*, contains the values to be set in the CPU registers when the interrupt handler begins executing. *outRegs*, a variable of type *RegType*, holds the CPU register values when the interrupt finishes executing.

inRegsX and *outRegsX*, variables of type *RegTypeX*, contain the CPU register values when you use CALL INTERRUPTX.

Usage

```
CALL INTERRUPT(&H16, inRegs, outRegs)
```

Calls the BIOS keyboard interrupt, 16H.

```
INTERRUPTX &H21, inRegsX, outRegsX
```

Calls DOS service 21H and uses the segment registers. Note that because the CALL keyword and the parentheses are omitted, the procedure must have been previously declared.

Description

DOS and the BIOS provide hundreds of useful functions and services that you can access with software interrupts. The CALL INTERRUPT and CALL INTERRUPTX statements in QuickBASIC give you easy access to these services. Interrupts signal the CPU to suspend the current program and execute a special routine designed to handle the event that triggered the interrupt; such routines are called "interrupt handlers." Interrupts can be caused by system events (for example, when a hardware device needs attention) or by software (for example, when an assembly-language program issues an INT instruction and the number of an interrupt handler). Most software interrupts require that you specify values in one or more CPU registers to control the way that the handling routine performs its task. When the interrupt handler finishes, the CPU resumes the suspended program.

INTERRUPT and INTERRUPTX are not built-in QuickBASIC statements. They are external procedures; therefore before you can use them, you must either load the Quick library QB.QLB into the QuickBASIC environment or link your program with the link library QB.LIB when you build the executable program. Both QB.QLB and QB.LIB are included in the QuickBASIC distribution disks.

To use either the INTERRUPT or INTERRUPTX statement, your program must declare it before any executable statements. The QuickBASIC file QB.BI includes prototype declarations that you can append to the head of your program with the $INCLUDE metacommand:

```
' $INCLUDE: 'QB.BI'
```

QB.BI also includes prototypes for other external procedures (such as CALL INT86OLD and CALL ABSOLUTE). If your program doesn't use any of these statements, you can reduce its final size by omitting the $INCLUDE metacommand and replacing it with the appropriate DECLARE statement, as shown in the following statements:

```
DECLARE SUB INTERRUPT(intNum AS INTEGER,  inRegs AS RegType,_
            outRegs AS RegType)
DECLARE SUB INTERRUPTX(intNum AS INTEGER, inRegs AS RegType,_
            outRegs AS RegType)
```

Before you do this, however, you also need to provide the definition of the structure *RegType* or *RegTypeX*, both of which are included in QB.BI.

The following TYPE...END TYPE statement defines *RegType*:

```
TYPE RegType
    ax AS INTEGER
    bx AS INTEGER
    cx AS INTEGER
    dx AS INTEGER
    bp AS INTEGER
    si AS INTEGER
    di AS INTEGER
    flags AS INTEGER
END TYPE
```

Note that the elements of *RegType* have the same names as the CPU registers to which they correspond.

You must explicitly dimension variables of type *RegType* for use in CALL INTERRUPT and variables of type *RegTypeX* for use in CALL INTERRUPTX. Each element of *RegType* or *RegTypeX* represents a specific CPU register. Some interrupts require that you load values into specific elements of the variable of type *RegType* or *RegTypeX* before you call the interrupt. In addition, many BIOS and DOS interrupt services also return values, which you can read from the appropriate element of the second variable of type *RegType* or *RegTypeX* when the interrupt exits.

The only difference between CALL INTERRUPT and CALL INTERRUPTX is that you can use CALL INTERRUPTX system calls that accept or return values in the (infrequently used) segment registers DS and ES. CALL INTERRUPT ignores any values in these registers. The file QB.BI contains the definition of type *RegTypeX*, which is equivalent to *RegType* with two additional elements: *ds* and *es*.

The registers that are set or returned by the call vary with the interrupt service you are calling. Many of the more useful services are described in the tutorial section and in The Waite Group's *MS-DOS Developer's Guide*.

Errors

The only internal error checking that QuickBASIC performs for CALL INTERRUPT and CALL INTERRUPTX is to test whether the interrupt number is in the range 0 through 255. If it is outside this range, QuickBASIC doesn't call the interrupt, and the statement returns with the interrupt number parameter containing –1 and the second variable of type *RegType* or *RegTypeX* unchanged. QuickBASIC doesn't verify the existence of the interrupt service you call, nor does it check to see whether the registers are correctly set for an existing service. Be careful. Calling interrupts randomly can crash your program or even reformat your hard disk!

Tips

You don't need to use the structures *RegType* and *RegTypeX* in the CALL INTERRUPT and CALL INTERRUPTX statements; you can make programs simpler and shorter by creating your own header file to replace QB.BI. The header file might look like the following.

```
' QBI.BI - custom header file for QuickBASIC INTERRUPT calls
' define the type needed for INTERRUPT and INTERRUPTX
    TYPE RegType
        ax    AS INTEGER
        bx    AS INTEGER
        cx    AS INTEGER
        dx    AS INTEGER
        bp    AS INTEGER
        si    AS INTEGER
```

(continued)

continued

```
        di    AS INTEGER
        flags AS INTEGER
        ds    AS INTEGER
        es    AS INTEGER
    END TYPE
' generate a software interrupt, loading all but the segment registers
DECLARE SUB INTERRUPT(intNum AS INTEGER, inReg AS RegType, outReg AS RegType)
' generate a software interrupt, loading all registers
DECLARE SUB INTERRUPTX(intNum AS INTEGER, inReg AS RegType, outReg AS RegType)
```

Of course, you still need to link your program with QB.LIB (or QB.QLB, in the environment), but now you need only supply one structure, *RegType*, to both functions. CALL INTERRUPT ignores any values set in elements 9 and 10 of the first variable of type *RegType* and fails to return the segment registers in elements 9 and 10 of the second variable of type *RegType*. You can even use the same structure to hold both entry and exit values without generating errors or unpredictable side effects; however, do this only if you do not need to preserve the register settings made at entry.

You can use INTERRUPTX for both types of interrupt—those that need values set in the segment registers (DS and ES) and those that do not—so you never need to use CALL INTERRUPT. Simply be sure to assign a value of –1 to the *ds* and *es* elements to force CALL INTERRUPTX to use the default settings for these registers, not the values supplied in the structure. This makes CALL INTERRUPTX operate exactly like CALL INTERRUPT.

Warnings

The QuickBASIC manual does not mention that QB.BI actually contains separate data types for INTERRUPT and INTERRUPTX. *RegType*, as defined in QB.BI, contains elements for eight registers—AX through Flags. However, *RegType*, as listed in the manual, adds elements for the DS and ES registers and is actually named *RegTypeX* in QB.BI. Therefore, if you use ' $INCLUDE: 'QB.BI' in your program and then use variables of type *RegType* to set values in the *ds* and *es* elements that are reserved for segment registers, QuickBASIC displays an "Element not defined" error message.

Compatibility

QuickBASIC 2.0 and QuickBASIC 3.0

QuickBASIC versions 2.0 and 3.0 use the statements CALL INT86 and CALL INT86X for interrupt calls. Because user-defined types were not the supported in QuickBASIC until version 4.0, in versions 2.0 and 3.0 you must pass register values in integer arrays. QuickBASIC versions 4.0 and 4.5 offer these functions as CALL INT86OLD and CALL INT86XOLD to preserve compatibility with earlier versions of BASIC.

PowerBASIC

The PowerBASIC syntax for calling interrupts is from that of QuickBASIC:

CALL INTERRUPT *intNum*

You don't need to use variables to hold the register values. PowerBASIC maintains an internal buffer that stores registers before and after a CALL INTERRUPT or CALL ABSOLUTE call. You can read this buffer by using the REG function and write to the buffer by using the REG statement.

Example

Although the QuickBASIC CLS statement can clear the entire video display, no statement clears only a specified, rectangular section of the screen. The BIOS, however, offers several methods of doing this through interrupt 10H. The following program calls a BIOS interrupt to clear the screen from the current cursor position to the end of the line (or to the right edge of the screen).

In this program, the subprogram *ClearEnd* calls two of the subservice provided by BIOS video interrupt 10H. (You select a subservice by placing its number in AH, the high byte of the AX register.)

To clear the screen to the end of the line, use subservice 9, which writes a string of ASCII characters to the display, beginning at the current cursor position. Because the ASCII code of the characters to be written must be passed in AL, the low byte of AX, *inRegs.ax* must contain two values: 09H for the subservice and 20H for the ASCII value of the space character. When combined, these values produce the value 0920H, which the program places in *inRegs.ax*.

BIOS subservice 9 also requires you to specify the color, or attribute, of the character in the BX register and the number of times the character is to be repeated in the CX register.

Unfortunately, subservice 9 does not wrap text output past column 80 to the next screen line, so it cannot clear to the end of the entire display. However, the sample program uses subservice 7, which clears a rectangular area of the screen when the low byte of AX, which is AL, is set to 0.

In subservice 7, BH (the high byte of the BX register) controls the color, or attribute, of the cleared area. The CX and DX registers define the row and column coordinates of the upper left and lower right corners of the rectangular area to be cleared. (Note that you have to adjust the values slightly because the BIOS numbers screen rows and columns start from 0, not 1 as they do in QuickBASIC.) You can clear to the end of the bottom line without causing the display to scroll upward.

To run the sample program in the QuickBASIC environment, use the command

```
QB INTRUPT.BAS /L QB.QLB
```

To compile the stand-alone version, use the following commands:

```
BC /O INTRUPT;
LINK INTRUPT,,,QB.LIB;
```

```
' $INCLUDE: 'QB.BI'

DECLARE SUB ClearEnd (clr%, switch%)

DIM SHARED inRegs AS RegType, outRegs AS RegType

COLOR 0, 7: CLS
KEY OFF
LOCATE 24, 30: PRINT "Press a key to clear.";
LOCATE 5, 1, 1: PRINT "Clear to the end of the line. >";
r$ = INPUT$(1)
ClearEnd 0, 0
LOCATE 9, 1, 1: PRINT "Clear to the end of the screen. >";
r$ = INPUT$(1)
ClearEnd 0, 1
LOCATE 10, 1
END

' clear to the end of the line or display
SUB ClearEnd (clr%, switch%) STATIC
    attribute% = (16 * clr%) + 15
    inRegs.ax = &H920                  ' blanks (ASCII 32)
    inRegs.bx = attribute%             ' background color
    inRegs.cx = (80 - POS(0)) + 1      ' number of characters
    INTERRUPT &H10, inRegs, outRegs    ' call the BIOS service
    IF switch% THEN                    ' if nonzero, clear to end of display
        inRegs.ax = &H700              ' clear the panel
        inRegs.bx = attribute% * 256   ' background color
        inRegs.cx = CSRLIN * 256       ' begin at the next row
        inRegs.dx = &H184F             ' end at row 25, col 80
        INTERRUPT &H10, inRegs, outRegs  ' call the BIOS service
    END IF
END SUB
```

DECLARE (Non-BASIC procedures)

See also: CALL (Non-BASIC procedures)

QB2	■ QB4.5	✲ PowerBASIC
QB3	✲ ANSI	GW-BASIC
■ QB4	■ BASIC7	MacQB

Purpose

The DECLARE (Non-BASIC procedures) statement defines how non-BASIC procedures in support modules are called from QuickBASIC module-level code. Use DECLARE to specify the name of an external routine, the types of variables passed to it as arguments, and the method by which the variables are passed.

Syntax

DECLARE [FUNCTION|SUB] *Name* [CDECL][ALIAS "*PublicName*"][(*parameters*)]

FUNCTION indicates that the procedure is a function, which returns a value; SUB indicates that the procedure is a subprogram, which does not return a value.

Name is an identifier of up to 40 characters that names the procedure to be called.

CDECL is a keyword specifying that the arguments to the procedure will be passed according to the C language calling conventions.

ALIAS is a keyword that is followed by *PublicName*, the name of the procedure in the external module. When ALIAS is used, *Name* can be any name you want to use in place of *PublicName* in your program for the external procedure.

parameters is an optional list of parameters that uses the following syntax:

([{BYVAL|SEG}] *var* [AS {*type*|ANY}], ...)

BYVAL is a keyword that specifies that the parameter *var* will be passed as a value instead of as an address (that is, by reference). *var* must be numeric when you use BYVAL.

SEG is a keyword that specifies that the parameter *var* will be passed by far reference instead of by near reference; that is, QuickBASIC passes the segment and offset of the address of the variable instead of passing only the offset.

type is the type of the parameter used by the external procedure. You can specify INTEGER, LONG, SINGLE, DOUBLE, STRING, or a user-defined type. You can also specify the type by appending a type-declaration character to the variable name.

ANY is a keyword that lets you pass a variable of any type. You cannot specify ANY with a variable passed by value.

Usage

```
DECLARE SUB PrtScrn ()
```

Declares a subprogram called *PrtScrn*. The empty parentheses indicate that *PrtScrn* requires no parameters.

```
DECLARE SUB HelpMate (context%, topic$)
```

Declares a subprogram called *HelpMate*. QuickBASIC passes the address of *context%* and the address of the string descriptor for *topic$* as offsets when the program calls *HelpMate*.

```
DECLARE SUB AnyThing (number%, placeMarker AS ANY, text$)
```

Declares a subprogram called *AnyThing*. The second argument passed to *AnyThing* is followed by the AS ANY clause, which disables type-checking for this parameter.

```
DECLARE FUNCTION SquareRoot! ALIAS "SQRT" (SEG Number!)
```

Declares a function called *SquareRoot!*, which calls a function that has a different name (*SQRT*) in the module that contains it. The ALIAS clause enables QuickBASIC to find the correct module. The single-precision argument *Number!* is passed as a far reference; the SEG keyword specifies that QuickBASIC send both the segment and offset parts of the address.

Description

The DECLARE (Non-BASIC procedures) statement defines a non-BASIC procedure. It specifies the name of the procedure and the parameters that must be passed to it. It can also be used to specify the method that QuickBASIC uses to pass the parameters.

If the called procedure returns a value, declare the procedure as a function rather than as a subprogram. Append an explicit type-declaration character (%, &, !, #, or $) to the name to specify the type of the value a function returns. If the called procedure does not return a value, declare the procedure as a subprogram.

When QuickBASIC passes variables to an external procedure, the program pushes them onto the stack in the order in which they appear in the parameter list; thus it reads the arguments from left to right. A function written in C, however, expects arguments to be passed in reverse order, from right to left. The CDECL keyword directs QuickBASIC to pass the arguments in the order that a C function expects. CDECL also causes QuickBASIC to convert the procedure name (or alias, if one is used) to lowercase and to append an underscore as the first character. The result corresponds to the C convention for function names.

QuickBASIC allows names of as many as 40 characters for subprograms and functions; other languages are not so generous. You can use a longer name in the module-level QuickBASIC code by specifying the new name in the declaration, followed by the keyword ALIAS and the shorter, public name of the external program.

QuickBASIC provides several clauses that let you specify how to pass arguments to the called procedure. By default, QuickBASIC passes variables by near reference; that is, it passes the address of the variable, which is offset from the beginning of DGROUP (QuickBASIC's default data segment). To pass either a dynamic numeric array or a dynamic array of fixed-length strings, which QuickBASIC always stores outside of DGROUP, you can use the SEG clause; this passes both the segment and offset of the variable's address.

Errors

If you call an external procedure with a variable whose type differs from the one in the corresponding position in the DECLARE argument list, QuickBASIC returns a "Parameter type mismatch" error message. If the procedure expects more or fewer arguments than those listed in the DECLARE statement, QuickBASIC returns an "Argument-count mismatch" error message.

Tips

If you do not include an argument list in the DECLARE statement, you can still pass parameters to a called procedure. However, none of the variables that you send to the CALL statement will be checked for type, and the call will use the default method of passing, that is, by near reference. This lets you make a call using a varying number of arguments—a valid operation if the external procedure supports it.

Compatibility

ANSI BASIC

ANSI BASIC uses the keyword DECLARE for declarations of numeric types and data structures used for communications. ANSI BASIC does not support a statement that performs the same task as the DECLARE statement does in QuickBASIC version 4.5.

PowerBASIC

In PowerBASIC, the DECLARE statement is used to declare functions and subprograms contained in object and unit files. PowerBASIC does not support the keywords CDECL, ALIAS, BYVAL, SEG, or ANY with the DECLARE statement.

Example

QuickBASIC 4.5 provides the SLEEP statement, which causes a program to pause for either a specified number of seconds or until a key is pressed. However, if you want to specify delays that are more precise than the nearest second, you can use the BIOS routine that updates the system timer a constant 18.2 times per second, regardless of the speed of the computer's CPU. The following program uses an assembly-language procedure that pauses for a specified number of $\frac{1}{18.2}$-second timer ticks before returning control to the main program. You can store the procedure in a library or link it as an object file to a stand-alone program. Note that the DECLARE statement defines the way the procedure is called from the QuickBASIC program.

```
DECLARE SUB Pause (BYVAL ticks AS INTEGER)

DO
    CLS : LOCATE 10, 1, 1
    PRINT "How many seconds to pause <enter -1 to quit> ";
    INPUT seconds!
    PRINT
    SELECT CASE seconds!
        CASE IS < 0
            EXIT DO
        CASE IS > 1800
            PRINT "OUT OF RANGE!": BEEP
```

(continued)

continued

```
        CASE ELSE
            ticks% = seconds! * 18.2
            PRINT "Started at  : "; TIME$
            Pause ticks%     'call the assembly-language procedure
            PRINT "Finished at : "; TIME$
    END SELECT
    PRINT : PRINT "Press any key to continue.";
    r$ = INPUT$(1)
LOOP
END
```

```
; DECLARE.ASM - waits for the specified number of ticks to pass.
;
; Assemble by using the Microsoft Macro Assembler version 5.x
; For use with Microsoft BASIC 6.0 and QuickBASIC 4.x
;
        Public  Pause
        .Model Medium
        .Code

Pause   proc    far
        push    bp                      ; save base pointer
        mov     bp,sp                   ; establish stack frame
        push    es                      ; save extra segment
        mov     cx,[bp+6]               ; number of ticks to wait
        cmp     cx,1                    ; abort if 0 or negative
        jb      Egress
        mov     ax,40h                  ; point ES to BIOS data at segment 0040
        mov     es,ax
        mov     ax,es:[6Ch]             ; get initial tick count
Idle:
        push    ax                      ; save last count
        mov     ax,es:[6Ch]             ; get new count
        pop     dx                      ; restore last count
        cmp     ax,dx                   ; has it changed?
        je      Idle                    ; no, try again
        loop    Idle                    ; repeat for each tick
Egress:
        pop     es                      ; clean up the stack
        pop     bp
        ret     2                       ; return to QuickBASIC
Pause   endp

        end
```

DEF SEG

See also: BLOAD, BSAVE, CALL ABSOLUTE, PEEK, POKE, VARPTR, VARPTR$, VARSEG

■ QB2	■ QB4.5	■ PowerBASIC
■ QB3	ANSI	■ GW-BASIC
■ QB4	■ BASIC7	MacQB

Purpose

The DEF SEG statement specifies the segment to be used by QuickBASIC statements and functions that directly address memory. PC chip architecture divides memory into 64-KB areas; each is defined by the address at which it starts, which is called its segment number. You use DEF SEG to set the current segment address for subsequent PEEK functions and BLOAD, BSAVE, CALL ABSOLUTE, and POKE statements.

Syntax

DEF SEG [= *segment*]

segment is any constant, integer variable, or expression that evaluates to a number in the range 0 through 65535. If you omit *segment*, QuickBASIC uses the default data segment, DGROUP.

Note that because the largest signed decimal integer is 32767, hexadecimal numbers are often used to set the segment value.

Usage

```
DEF SEG = &HB800
```

Sets the current segment address to the video display buffer in systems using a Color Graphic Adapter (CGA).

```
DEF SEG
```

Resets the current segment to the QuickBASIC default data segment, DGROUP.

Description

Several QuickBASIC statements and functions let you reference data stored at an absolute address in your computer's memory. The PEEK function, for example, returns the contents of the byte at a specified location; The CALL ABSOLUTE statement executes a machine-language program stored at a specified address. These statements and functions require that the address be an integer in the range 0 through 65535, which is a value specifying a location in a 64-KB block of memory. One such block of memory is the default data segment, DGROUP.

Your computer has considerably more than 64 KB of memory. IBM PCs and compatible computers can have as much as 640 KB of random access memory, as well as 384 KB of memory dedicated to the video display, disk drive controller, and the programs in BIOS that control low-level computer operations. Therefore, you can directly access up to 1 MB (1024 KB) of memory. Figure 20-2 depicts the memory map of an IBM PC or compatible computer, showing the relative positions of various parts of memory.

Only data stored above segment 9FFFH and below segment 0060H are at fixed locations in memory. Absolute addresses of programs, device drivers, and resident programs vary with the version of DOS used, the number and type of TSR programs loaded, and the amount of RAM installed.

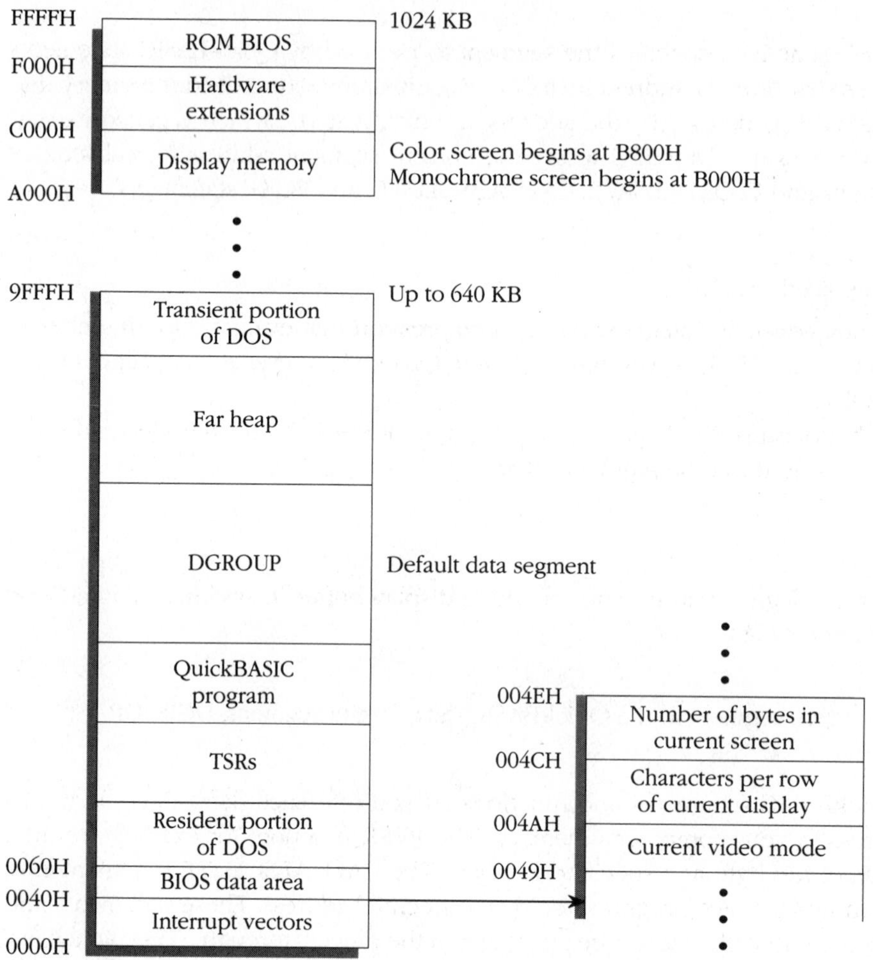

Figure 20-2.
Memory map of an IBM PC showing the relationships of various segments.

To access a segment in the 1024 KB of addressable memory, you must first specify the starting address of a 64-KB block. The starting address is called the "segment address." For example, you might need to access the memory external to DGROUP to load (using the BLOAD statement) a graphics-image file directly into the video-display buffer. DEF SEG lets you specify the 64-KB segment in which this operation will take place. Until you issue another DEF SEG statement, QuickBASIC interprets any address you specify in a PEEK function or a BLOAD, BSAVE, CALL ABSOLUTE, or POKE statement as an offset of this segment. Specifying a different segment does not disrupt your program unless you write over memory being used by the operating system, by QuickBASIC, or by the program itself.

Comments

Although DEF SEG lets you access memory anywhere within the normal 1024-KB address space, QuickBASIC does not provide statements or functions that let you access any extended or expanded memory your computer might have. However, several third-party libraries and utilities contain routines that permit QuickBASIC programs to use extended or expanded memory. (See Appendix C, "Third-Party Add-Ons.")

Errors

If you specify a segment address outside the range 0 through 65535, QuickBASIC returns an "Illegal function call" error message and does not change the current segment.

Warnings

Be careful when using addresses in your QuickBASIC programs. A program that uses data or buffers at specific memory addresses might not work on all PC-DOS or MS-DOS computers. The Tandy Model 2000, for example, uses a floating display segment whose address depends on the amount of memory installed. All IBM PC/XT, AT, PS/2, and compatible machines, however, maintain the addresses discussed in this entry.

Example

To help you better understand DEF SEG, let's examine how you might use the BIOS data area in low memory, beginning at segment 0040H. This area contains the keyboard buffer, information about the status of installed equipment, and information about the video display.

The following program uses the information in the BIOS data area to write text from QuickBASIC directly to the bottom line of the computer screen without causing the screen to scroll. The program first checks the BIOS data area to see whether the program is running on a computer with a monochrome display or on a computer with a color display; this lets you determine which segment of memory to send output to. To perform this check, the program uses DEF SEG to set the current working segment to the BIOS data area, which starts at 40H.

The program also checks the screen dimensions, defined in the BIOS data segment, to determine whether the display is in 40-column or 80-column mode and whether the number of screen rows is 25, 43, or 50. This information lets you calculate the offset address (in video memory) of the bottom row of the screen.

Finally, the program sends text to the display; however, first it uses DEF SEG again to set the correct video segment. Note that each character output requires 2 bytes of video memory, one for the ASCII code of the character and the other for its display attribute, or color.

```
DEF SEG = &H40                    ' set segment to BIOS data area
IF PEEK(&H49) = 7 THEN            ' check video mode
    videoSegment% = &HB000        ' mode 7 indicates a monochrome display
ELSE
    videoSegment% = &HB800        ' any other mode indicates a color display
END IF

columns% = PEEK(&H4A) + (PEEK(&H4B) * 256)  ' get screen width
bytes% = PEEK(&H4C) + (PEEK(&H4D) * 256)    ' get screen size
rows% = bytes% \ (columns% * 2)             ' calculate number of rows
offSet% = (columns% * (rows% - 1)) * 2      ' get last row

DEF SEG = videoSegment%                     ' set segment to video memory
FOR i% = 0 TO columns% - 1
    POKE offSet% + (i% * 2), ASC("*")       ' write a character
    POKE offSet% + (i% * 2) + 1, 78         ' write an attribute
NEXT i%
DEF SEG                                     ' restore the DGROUP segment
SLEEP 3
END
```

SADD

See also: LEN, PEEK, POKE, VARPTR, VARPTR$

QB2	■ QB4.5	✲ PowerBASIC
QB3	ANSI	GW-BASIC
■ QB4	■ BASIC7	■ MacQB

Purpose

The SADD function returns the offset of a string expression within the DGROUP data segment. You can use SADD to pass strings to routines written in other programming languages.

Syntax

SADD(*string*)

string is any QuickBASIC variable-length string variable, including an element of a variable-length string array. It cannot be a fixed-length string, nor can it be part of a user-defined type.

Usage

```
address% = SADD(code$)
```

Assigns the address of the string *code$* to the variable *address%*.

```
CALL Scan(SADD(a$), LEN(a$))
```

Passes the address and length of *a$* to a non-BASIC procedure called *Scan*, which is located in a separately compiled support module.

Description

Sometimes you need to find the exact address, in memory, of a QuickBASIC string. You might, for example, have loaded a machine-language routine into a string and need to pass the string's address to the CALL ABSOLUTE statement. The VARPTR statement does not return the address of a variable-length string, only a pointer to the string descriptor. The SADD function, however, returns the address.

SADD, which stands for "string address," returns a near pointer to the address in memory of the first byte of the specified string variable. The integer value that SADD returns is the address of the string as an offset from the beginning of DGROUP, QuickBASIC's default data segment, in which all variable-length strings are stored.

Because DGROUP is the default data segment when a QuickBASIC program begins executing, you do not need to obtain a separate segment address for a variable-length string when you refer to its absolute address in memory.

Errors

You cannot use the SADD function to return the address of a fixed-length string. If you try to do so, QuickBASIC returns a "Fixed-length string illegal" error message. To obtain the address of a fixed-length string, use the VARPTR statement. (See the VARPTR, VARPTR$ entry for details.)

Warnings

QuickBASIC allocates storage in the DGROUP data segment dynamically. If you create a new string variable, change the size of an existing string, or use a string inside a function or expression, QuickBASIC might change the address of this or other variables. To avoid this, your program should use the address returned by SADD immediately; if it doesn't, QuickBASIC might move the string, making the returned address incorrect.

Non-BASIC procedures that manipulate QuickBASIC strings should not change the length of the strings passed to them. Doing so will almost certainly disrupt QuickBASIC's internal pointers, causing unpredictable (and often fatal) errors.

Compatibility

PowerBASIC

PowerBASIC does not include the SADD function. Instead, it supports the STRPTR function, which returns the offset address of a string expression, just as SADD does in QuickBASIC. In addition, PowerBASIC includes the STRSEG function, which returns the segment address of a string expression.

Example

One of the most useful QuickBASIC graphics statements is PCOPY, which lets you copy the contents of the current display to another video page, from which it can later be restored. Unfortunately, only screen modes 7 and higher support PCOPY; thus programmers using CGA-equipped computers cannot access this function.

The following general-purpose routine copies the contents of a graphics screen into a string variable and restores the display when required to do so. To ensure maximum speed, the program uses a machine-language routine to execute the copying process; note that both the routine and the display are stored in strings within the default data segment. The SADD function returns the calling address of the machine-language routine and also returns the address of the string that holds the screen image.

To run this program in the QuickBASIC environment, use the command

```
QB SADD.BAS /L QB.QLB
```

To compile the stand-alone version, use the following commands:

```
BC /O SADD;
LINK  SADD,,,QB.LIB;
```

```
DECLARE SUB ABSOLUTE (offset%, length%, switch%, address%)

buffer$ = SPACE$(&H4000)      ' holds screen contents
code$ = SPACE$(103)           ' holds machine language

' load machine-language routine into the string
RESTORE MCode
FOR i% = 1 TO 103
    READ a$
    MID$(code$, i%, 1) = CHR$(VAL("&H" + a$))
NEXT i%

' draw a changing pattern on the screen, copy the screen contents
' into buffer$ when the user presses a key
SCREEN 1
RANDOMIZE TIMER
```

(continued)

continued

```
LINE (0, 0)-(319, 199), 1, BF       ' draw a filled box the size of the screen
VIEW (32, 4)-(289, 196), 0, 2       ' reduce the size of the graphics screen
xLimit% = 253: yLimit% = 190
signA% = 0: version% = 1: x1% = 0: y1% = 0
rate% = INT(RND * 3) + 2            ' set the rate of change
colors% = INT(RND * 3) + 1

DO WHILE INKEY$ = ""
    IF x1% <= 0 THEN x1% = 0: changeX% = signA%
    IF y1% <= 0 THEN y1% = 0: changeY% = signA%
    IF x1% >= xLimit% THEN x1% = xLimit%: changeX% = -signA%
    IF y1% >= yLimit% THEN y1% = yLimit%: changeY% = -signA%
    IF signA% <= 1 THEN signA% = 1: signB% = 1
    IF signA% >= rate% THEN signA% = rate%: signB% = -1

    x2% = 255 - x1%: y2% = 191 - y1%
    IF version% = 1 THEN
        LINE (x1%, y1%)-(x2%, y2%), colors%, B    ' draw the outline of a box
        version% = 2
        LINE (x1%, y1%)-(x2%, y2%), 0             ' draw a black diagonal line
        LINE (x1%, y2%)-(x2%, y1%), 0
    ELSE
        LINE (x1%, y1%)-(x2%, y2%), 15, B         ' draw the outline of a box
        LINE (x1%, y1%)-(x2%, y2%), colors%       ' draw a diagonal line
        LINE (x2%, y1%)-(x1%, y2%), colors%
        version% = 1
        colors% = INT(RND * 3) + 1                ' change color
    END IF
    x1% = x1% + changeX%
    y1% = y1% + changeY%
    signA% = signA% + signB%
LOOP

' save screen contents
ABSOLUTE SADD(buffer$), LEN(buffer$), 1, SADD(code$)

SCREEN 0
WIDTH 80: LOCATE 10, 23
PRINT "Press any key to restore the screen."
r$ = INPUT$(1)
SCREEN 1

' restore previous screen contents
ABSOLUTE SADD(buffer$), LEN(buffer$), 2, SADD(code$)
r$ = INPUT$(1): SCREEN 0
END
```

(continued)

continued

```
' data containing the machine-language routine
MCode:
    DATA   55, 8B, EC, 57, 56, 06, 1E, 8B, 5E, 08, 8B, 07, 3D, 00, 40
    DATA   73, 05, B8, FF, FF, EB, 3B, B9, 00, 20, BA, DA, 03, 8B, 5E
    DATA   0A, 8B, 37, B8, 00, B8, 8E, C0, BF, 00, 00, 8B, 5E, 06, 8B
    DATA   07, 3D, 02, 00, 74, 15, E8, 23, 00, 26, 8B, 05, 89, 04, 83
    DATA   C6, 02, 83, C7, 02, E2, F0, B8, 00, 00, EB, 09, E8, 0E, 00
    DATA   A5, E2, FA, B8, 00, 00, 1F, 07, 5E, 5F, 5D, CA, 06, 00, FA
    DATA   EC, A8, 01, 75, FB, EC, A8, 01, 74, FB, FB, C3, 00
```

VARPTR, VARPTR$

See also: DEF SEG, SADD, VARSEG

■ QB2	■ QB4.5	■ PowerBASIC
■ QB3	ANSI	✲ GW-BASIC
■ QB4	■ BASIC7	✲ MacQB

Purpose

The VARPTR function returns the offset address of a variable within its current memory segment. If you need to load a machine-language routine directly into memory, for example, you use VARPTR to find the address of the variable into which these statements can be loaded. The VARPTR$ function returns a string that contains the address of a variable. Use VARPTR$ in calls to DRAW or PLAY to execute substrings contained in variables.

Syntax

VARPTR(*var*)
VARPTR$(*var*)

var is any valid QuickBASIC variable. If the specified variable does not exist, QuickBASIC creates it before returning the address or the string containing the address.

Usage

`PRINT VARPTR(a!)`

Displays the address of the single-precision variable *a!* as an offset from the beginning of DGROUP, QuickBASIC's default data segment.

`offSet% = VARPTR(codeArray%(0))`

Assigns the offset address of the first element in the integer array *codeArray%* to the variable *offset%.*

`PLAY "X" + VARPTR$(cmd$)`

Plays the music dictated by the commands contained in the string variable *cmd$.*

Description

Every reference to a location in memory consists of two parts—the "segment," an integer value (in the range 0 through 65535) that specifies the 64-KB block of memory in which the object resides, and the "offset," another integer value (in the range 0 through 65535) that specifies the location of the object within that 64-KB segment. The VARSEG function returns the segment part of a variable's address; the VARPTR function returns the offset part of the address. The VARPTR$ function returns the offset part as a string.

Because QuickBASIC stores simple variables and strings in DGROUP, the default data segment, you need to use only VARPTR to address these variables. Dynamic numeric arrays and dynamic arrays of fixed-length strings, however, are stored in their own segments outside of DGROUP; therefore, you need to use both VARSEG and VARPTR to address them.

Note that when you use VARPTR (or VARSEG) to obtain the address of an array, you must specify an element number as well as the array name. Because array data is stored contiguously in memory, the address of an array's first element is actually the address of the entire array.

When you use VARPTR with a variable-length string, it does not return the address of the string itself; instead, it returns a pointer to a 4-byte string descriptor in DGROUP. The first 2 bytes of the descriptor hold the length of the string; the second 2 bytes hold the address of the string, which is offset from the beginning of DGROUP. You usually need to specify the string descriptor only for non-BASIC routines that you call from QuickBASIC. QuickBASIC programs themselves can obtain the same information more easily by using the LEN function, which returns the string length, and SADD, which returns the address of the first byte of the string.

A fixed-length string does not use a descriptor. When you use VARPTR with a fixed-length string, it works exactly like SADD, returning the offset address of the first byte of the string. (Note that you cannot use SADD with fixed-length strings.)

Tips

QuickBASIC stores numeric arrays differently for programs compiled as executable files than it does for programs run in the QuickBASIC environment. In an executable file, all static arrays are stored in DGROUP, so you need to use only VARPTR to address them. Dynamic arrays in an executable file are stored in separate segments, so you need to use both VARSEG and VARPTR to address them.

In a program run in the QuickBASIC environment, both static and dynamic arrays are stored in separate segments, so you must use both VARSEG and VARPTR to address them. The only exception to this is static arrays declared as COMMON; QuickBASIC stores these arrays in DGROUP.

To simplify your programming tasks, always use both VARSEG and VARPTR when specifying the address of a numeric array. This ensures correct results whether your program is running in the QuickBASIC environment or as an executable file at the DOS command line.

Note that QuickBASIC always stores arrays of variable-length strings in DGROUP.

Warnings

QuickBASIC allocates storage in DGROUP dynamically. If you create a new variable, change the size of an existing variable, or use a variable inside a function or expression, QuickBASIC might change the address of this or other variables. To avoid this, your program should always use the address returned by VARPTR immediately; if it doesn't, QuickBASIC can move the variable, making the returned address incorrect.

Compatibility

GW-BASIC and BASICA

GW-BASIC (but not BASICA) provides the following additional syntax:

VARPTR([#]*buffer*)

If you use this syntax, VARPTR returns the address of the first byte of a file buffer and lets you directly access data that has been read from the file associated with the buffer. This syntax is not supported by QuickBASIC. You can, however, use VARPTR in QuickBASIC to locate variables of user-defined types that have been assigned to file buffers with the GET and PUT statements.

QuickBASIC for the Macintosh

The VARPTR function supported by QuickBASIC for the Macintosh returns the absolute address of a variable as a long integer in the range 0 through 4294967296. The Macintosh's CPU is a 32-bit processor and does not use segmented addresses in memory. Therefore, QuickBASIC for the Macintosh doesn't include the VARSEG function.

QuickBASIC for the Macintosh also does not include the VARPTR$ function.

Example

QuickBASIC lacks a function that detects whether a particular file exists or not. If you try to open a nonexistent file, QuickBASIC either creates it by using a length of 0 bytes or, if it is opened for input only, reports an error. You can trap for these error conditions, but the error-trapping code is often clumsy.

The DOS services include several functions that return information about specified files. The following program uses a machine-language routine that can be incorporated into other programs. The routine queries DOS for the size (in bytes) of a specified file. The routine accepts a filename containing wildcard characters (* and ?); if you supply such a filename, it returns the summation of the sizes of all matching files. If the routine returns 0, the file does not exist.

In order to be as compact as possible, the following program uses an assembly-language routine stored in an array variable instead of a separately linked object module.

The program leaves empty the first 29 elements of the array that contain the machine language; those elements form a temporary disk transfer address and filename buffer. The actual code of the routine begins at element 30, and the value returned by the routine is assigned to element 1.

To run this program in the QuickBASIC environment, use the command

```
QB VARPTR.BAS /L QB.QLB
```

To compile the stand-alone version, use the following commands:

```
BC /O VARPTR;
LINK  VARPTR,,,QB.LIB;
```

```
' $DYNAMIC                        ' make all arrays dynamic

DECLARE SUB ABSOLUTE (filename AS STRING, address AS INTEGER)

DIM mCode(1 TO 70) AS LONG        ' array for the machine-language routine
DIM byte AS STRING * 2            ' holds each data item

DEF SEG = VARSEG(mCode(1))        ' set the array segment
offSet% = VARPTR(mCode(30))       ' address of the 30th element

' load the machine-language data bytes into the array
RESTORE
FOR i% = 0 TO 161
    READ byte
    POKE offSet% + i%, VAL("&H" + byte)
NEXT i%

CLS
PRINT "THIS PROGRAM REPORTS THE SIZE OF FILES YOU SPECIFY"
PRINT "-----------------------------------------------"
PRINT
PRINT "The filename can include a directory path and can"
PRINT "use the wildcard characters ? and *."
PRINT "The program returns the size of the file, in bytes,"
PRINT "or, if it finds more than one match, the summation"
PRINT "of the sizes of all the files. If the size returned is 0,"
PRINT "the file does not exist (at least not in the specified"
PRINT "directory)."
PRINT
PRINT "Enter the pathname (up to 64 characters) of the file,"
PRINT "or press Enter to quit."

DO
    LOCATE 14, 1: PRINT SPACE$(240);
    LOCATE 14, 1: INPUT "Pathname"; pathName$
```

(continued)

continued

```
    IF LEN(pathName$) > 1 AND LEN(pathName$) < 65 THEN
        ABSOLUTE pathName$, VARPTR(mCode(30))      ' call the routine
        LOCATE 16, 1: PRINT "Size = "; mCode(1)    ' display the size
        LOCATE 20, 1, 1: PRINT "Press any key to continue. ";
        r$ = INPUT$(1)
        LOCATE 20, 1: PRINT SPACE$(26);
    END IF
LOOP UNTIL pathName$ = ""
DEF SEG                           ' restore segment
END

' machine-language routine
    DATA  55, 8B, EC, 06, 1E, 57, 56, 2E, C7, 06, 00, 00, 00, 00, 2E
    DATA  C7, 06, 02, 00, 00, 00, 0E, 07, 8B, 5E, 06, 8B, 0F, 83, F9
    DATA  01, 72, 6F, 83, F9, 40, 77, 6A, 8B, 77, 02, BF, 33, 00, FC
    DATA  F3, A4, B0, 00, AA, 0E, 1F, B4, 2F, CD, 21, 2E, 89, 1E, 2F
    DATA  00, 2E, 8C, 06, 31, 00, BA, 04, 00, B4, 1A, CD, 21, BA, 33
    DATA  00, 33, C9, B4, 4E, CD, 21, 72, 2D, 2E, A1, 1E, 00, 2E, 8B
    DATA  16, 20, 00, 2E, A3, 00, 00, 2E, 89, 16, 02, 00, B4, 4F, CD
    DATA  21, 72, 15, 2E, A1, 1E, 00, 2E, 8B, 16, 20, 00, 2E, 01, 06
    DATA  00, 00, 2E, 11, 16, 02, 00, EB, E5, 2E, A1, 31, 00, 2E, 8B
    DATA  16, 2F, 00, 8E, D8, B4, 1A, CD, 21, 2E, 8B, 16, 02, 00, 2E
    DATA  A1, 00, 00, 5E, 5F, 1F, 07, 5D, CA, 02, 00, 00
```

VARSEG

See also: DEF SEG, SADD, VARPTR, VARPTR$

QB2	■ QB4.5	■ PowerBASIC
QB3	ANSI	GW-BASIC
■ QB4	■ BASIC7	MacQB

Purpose

The VARSEG function returns the segment part of a variable's address. You might use VARSEG, for example, to find the segment of a dynamic numeric array that you want to save on disk by using BSAVE.

Syntax

VARSEG(*var*)

var is any valid QuickBASIC variable name. If the specified variable does not exist, QuickBASIC creates it before returning the address.

Usage

```
PRINT VARSEG(a!)
```

Displays the segment part of the address of the single-precision variable *a!*. (This is also the segment address of DGROUP.)

```
segment% = VARSEG(codeArray%(0))
```

Assigns the segment of the first element in the integer array *codeArray%* to the variable *segment%*.

Description

VARSEG returns the segment occupied by any variable, thus enabling you to fully specify the variable's address. VARSEG returns an integer number that corresponds to the address of the segment containing the specified variable. If the specified variable is a simple numeric variable or a variable-length string, the returned value indicates the current setting of the DS register, which contains the segment address of DGROUP. Because DGROUP is QuickBASIC's default segment, you do not need to specify the segment part of the address when referring to data stored there. Usually all you need to specify is the offset from the beginning of the segment (which is returned by the VARPTR function).

If the variable is a dynamic numeric array or a dynamic array of fixed-length strings, VARSEG returns the segment address that QuickBASIC allocated to that variable. Your programs must specify both the segment (by using VARSEG) and the offset (by using VARPTR) of such a variable when passing its address.

Example

See the "Example" section in the VARPTR entry for a program that uses both VARPTR and VARSEG.

CHAPTER 21

Metacommands

Introduction

Strictly speaking, metacommands are not QuickBASIC statements at all. They merely give the QuickBASIC compiler—either the command-line compiler or the one used in the QuickBASIC environment—instructions about how to build a program. After the program is compiled, metacommands perform no other useful service; for this reason, they are always prefaced with the REM keyword or a single quotation mark so that they aren't confused with executable QuickBASIC statements.

QuickBASIC supports only three metacommands: $INCLUDE specifies an external source-code file that the compiler will insert into the program being compiled; $DYNAMIC and $STATIC determine when memory for subsequently dimensioned arrays is allocated. Table 21-1 summarizes the QuickBASIC metacommands.

Metacommand	Description
$DYNAMIC	Declares that QuickBASIC will allocate the memory for subsequent arrays at runtime
$INCLUDE	Specifies a source-code file that the compiler will insert into the program at the current line
$STATIC	Declares that QuickBASIC will allocate the memory for subsequent arrays at compile time

Table 21-1.
QuickBASIC metacommands.

Including Files

Merging files into programs by using the $INCLUDE metacommand helps you split programs into smaller, more manageable sections that you can write as separate modules and then combine when you compile the final program. This procedure keeps you from having to maintain large, unwieldy source code files. It also encourages you to develop more structured programs because it lets you store different functional modules in separate files.

Do not confuse files merged by $INCLUDE with the separately compiled object modules you can link to stand-alone programs that are compiled with the command-line compiler BC.EXE. $INCLUDE can merge only files containing QuickBASIC source code that was saved in ASCII format. The compiler simply "pastes" the source code into the QuickBASIC program, beginning at the line in which you placed the $INCLUDE metacommand.

Files specified in $INCLUDE can contain only statements that are executed as part of the module-level code; they cannot contain user-defined subprograms or functions. However, you can insert the DECLARE statements in these files to declare subprograms and functions.

$INCLUDE is the only QuickBASIC metacommand that requires an argument. To use this metacommand, follow $INCLUDE with a colon and then the argument, the name of the file you want to include. The following metacommand, for example, directs the compiler to merge the file BITS.BI into the program:

```
' $INCLUDE: 'BITS.BI'
```

By default, the compiler searches the current directory for the specified file. You can, however, store included files in another directory. The compiler will find the files if you set the DOS environment variable INCLUDE from the DOS command line or from your AUTOEXEC.BAT file. For example, use the command

```
SET INCLUDE=C:\QB45\INCLUDE
```

to direct the compiler to search the \QB45\INCLUDE directory for your included files.

You can also use the Set Paths command found in the Options menu in the QuickBASIC 4.5 environment to specify the directories that are searched for files. However, setting the INCLUDE environment variable in the DOS environment has two principal advantages—it is in effect when you use BC.EXE to compile from the DOS command line, and it works with all versions of QuickBASIC, not merely with version 4.5.

Array Storage

The $DYNAMIC and $STATIC metacommands tell QuickBASIC how to assign memory to the arrays that your program dimensions.

Static Arrays

You declare that all subsequent arrays will be static by using the $STATIC metacommand:

```
' $STATIC
```

For all subsequent, explicitly dimensioned arrays, the compiler will allocate storage space in memory as the program compiles. This allocation is fixed and cannot be changed as the program runs. Therefore, even if you use the ERASE statement on a static array, QuickBASIC merely reinitializes each element to 0 (or to a null string for a string array) instead of removing the array from memory altogether. The REDIM statement does not work with static arrays because the amount of memory allocated to such arrays cannot be changed.

Dynamic Arrays

You declare that all subsequent arrays will be dynamic by using the $DYNAMIC metacommand:

```
' $DYNAMIC
```

QuickBASIC allocates memory to dynamic arrays at runtime, so your program can change this allocation during execution. You can use the REDIM statement to reduce or increase the number of elements in an array, which changes the actual amount of memory the array uses, and you can also use the ERASE statement to completely free the memory allocated to the array.

Because the compiler assigns static arrays only once, the compiled program doesn't need to create or destroy them at runtime. Consequently, programs that use static arrays execute slightly faster than programs that use dynamic arrays. On the other hand, static arrays can waste memory because after you dimension them, their space cannot be freed for use by other variables.

Note that implicitly dimensioned arrays (arrays that are not defined in a DIM statement) are static arrays even if the program uses the $DYNAMIC metacommand. Arrays that are dimensioned with a variable or expression are always dynamic.

Using Multiple Metacommands

You can use the $STATIC and $DYNAMIC metacommands in the same program. All arrays dimensioned following a $STATIC metacommand are static until the compiler encounters a $DYNAMIC metacommand. Then all subsequent arrays are dynamic until the compiler encounters a $STATIC metacommand, and so on.

You can include more than one metacommand on one line by simply separating the metacommands with any amount of white space. Because compilation resumes immediately after the compiler merges a file specified in an $INCLUDE metacommand, you must specify $INCLUDE as the last metacommand on the line.

$DYNAMIC

See also: $STATIC

■ QB2	■ QB4.5	■ PowerBASIC
■ QB3	ANSI	GW-BASIC
■ QB4	■ BASIC7	MacQB

Purpose

The $DYNAMIC metacommand directs the compiler to allocate memory for storing numeric arrays and fixed-length string arrays while the program is running. This lets the program redimension or erase arrays during execution, allowing more efficient use of available memory.

Syntax

' $DYNAMIC

Note that $DYNAMIC is an instruction to the compiler, not an executable statement; therefore, you must preface it with a single quotation mark or the keyword REM. If you use $DYNAMIC on a line with other statements, it must be the last statement on that line (except for other metacommands sharing the same comment).

Usage

```
REM $DYNAMIC
```

Directs the compiler to make all subsequent arrays dynamic.

```
CLS: ' $DYNAMIC  $INCLUDE: 'FILELIST.INC'
```

Clears the screen, specifies that all subsequent arrays are dynamic, and merges the file FILELIST.INC into the program.

Description

If your program includes the $DYNAMIC metacommand, QuickBASIC doesn't allocate memory to arrays until the program starts executing. If you use $DYNAMIC, you can reassign array storage when program requirements change. You can change the size of an array by using the REDIM statement, or you can delete the array from memory by using the ERASE statement. (See the REDIM and ERASE entries in Chapter 6, "Arrays and Data," for details.)

The opposite of $DYNAMIC is the $STATIC metacommand, which forces QuickBASIC to allocate array space when the program is compiled. However, memory allocated to static arrays cannot be released or resized. Use the $DYNAMIC metacommand if you don't know in advance how big your arrays will be. If, however, you know how much array storage a program needs, then use $STATIC—your program will run faster. (See the $STATIC entry for details.)

Errors

If you include the metacommand $DYNAMIC without the REM keyword or a single quotation mark, QuickBASIC returns an "Expected: statement" error message.

Tips

Numeric arrays in a program that has been compiled as a stand-alone executable file are stored differently than they are in a program that is run in the QuickBASIC environment. In an executable file, QuickBASIC stores all static arrays with simple variables and strings in the default data segment DGROUP. To locate an element of a static array in memory, you need only use the VARPTR function to find its offset address within DGROUP. However, because a dynamic array is allocated its own segment outside DGROUP, you must specify both the segment and the offset part of the array's address to locate an element. Use the VARSEG function to return the segment of a variable. (See the VARPTR and VARSEG entries in Chapter 20, "Mixed Language," for details.)

When you run a program in the QuickBASIC environment, QuickBASIC assigns each array—whether static or dynamic—its own segment. The only exceptions to this are static arrays that you have declared COMMON and arrays of variable-length strings; QuickBASIC stores these in DGROUP as usual.

By using far pointers to locate an array in memory, you can avoid having to write separate versions for executable programs and programs run in the environment. Specify both the segment and the offset when you address numeric arrays.

$INCLUDE

■ QB2	■ QB4.5	■ PowerBASIC
■ QB3	ANSI	GW-BASIC
■ QB4	■ BASIC7	■ MacQB

Purpose

The $INCLUDE metacommand directs the QuickBASIC compiler to insert statements from an external file at a specific point in the program. This lets you split large programs into more manageable modules that you can develop and test separately and then assemble at compile time.

Syntax

' $INCLUDE: '*filename*'

Note that $INCLUDE is an instruction to the compiler, not an executable statement; therefore, you must preface it with a single quotation mark or the keyword REM. If you use $INCLUDE on a line with other statements, it must be the last statement on that line.

filename is the name of the source code file you want to insert. *filename* must be a string constant, not a variable or expression. *filename* can include a directory path and must be enclosed in single quotation marks; you must use a colon to separate *filename* from the $INCLUDE keyword.

Usage

```
REM $INCLUDE: 'STARTUP.BI'
```

Inserts the source-code file STARTUP.BI into the program being compiled. QuickBASIC first looks for the file in the current directory, and then it searches the directory specified by the DOS INCLUDE environment variable.

```
' $INCLUDE: '\PROGRAMS\PART1.BAS'
```

Loads the file PART1.BAS into the program being compiled. QuickBASIC looks for the file only in the PROGRAMS subdirectory.

Description

A file specified by the $INCLUDE metacommand must be a source-code file that is stored separate from the main program. It must be an ASCII file—not one in BASIC Quick-load format—and cannot contain subprograms or functions. With these restrictions, files specified by $INCLUDE can contain any QuickBASIC statements that can be used in module-level code.

QuickBASIC processes $INCLUDE metacommands only when it is compiling a program. If the compiler encounters an $INCLUDE metacommand, it stops processing the current file and loads the statements from the new file into memory. Then it compiles this code and inserts it into the main program at the line of the $INCLUDE statement. After QuickBASIC has compiled the included file, it resumes compiling the main program at the line following the one that contains $INCLUDE.

Included files can themselves contain $INCLUDE metacommands; in fact, you can nest files as many as 5 levels deep. By convention, QuickBASIC uses the extension BI to denote an included file, and many programmers use the extension INC instead; however, you can use any valid DOS filename and extension as the argument to $INCLUDE.

Errors

If you include the metacommand $INCLUDE without the REM keyword or a single quotation mark, QuickBASIC returns an "Expected: statement" error message.

$STATIC

See also: $DYNAMIC

■ QB2	■ QB4.5	■ PowerBASIC
■ QB3	ANSI	GW-BASIC
■ QB4	■ BASIC7	MacQB

Purpose

The $STATIC metacommand directs the compiler to allocate memory for storing arrays when the program is compiled, not when it is running. This lets your programs run faster but, because arrays cannot be redimensioned or deleted, can result in inefficient memory usage.

Syntax

' $STATIC

Note that $STATIC is an instruction to the compiler, not an executable statement; therefore, you must preface it with a single quotation mark or the keyword REM. If you use $STATIC on a line with other statements, it must be the last statement on that line (except for other metacommands sharing the same comment).

Usage

```
REM $STATIC
```

Directs the compiler to allocate memory for all subsequent arrays.

```
' $STATIC  $INCLUDE: 'VIDEO.BI'
```

Directs the compiler to allocate memory for all subsequent arrays and merges the file VIDEO.BI into the program.

Description

If your program includes the $STATIC metacommand, QuickBASIC allocates storage space to all explicitly dimensioned arrays when it compiles the program. (Explicit dimensioning means that you specify a specific number of elements in the DIM statement.) Arrays dimensioned by variables or expressions whose values are not known in advance are dynamic arrays, and QuickBASIC allocates memory for their storage after the program starts executing. Because QuickBASIC allocates memory for static arrays before a program starts, the running program doesn't have to waste time building arrays during execution; therefore, a program that uses static arrays executes faster than one that uses dynamic arrays.

Memory assigned to static arrays cannot be released or resized while the program is running. The REDIM statement cannot be used to change the number of elements in a static array, because the amount of memory allocated to the array cannot be changed. The ERASE statement does not free the memory used by a static array; however, it resets all the array's elements to 0 or to null strings.

If your program references an array that has not been explicitly dimensioned by a previous DIM or REDIM statement, QuickBASIC creates it with 11 elements (numbered 0 through 10). Such arrays, called implicitly dimensioned arrays, are always static, so you cannot redimension or erase them. You can use implicitly dimensioned arrays only in programs run in the QuickBASIC environment; in programs passed to BC.EXE, references to undimensioned arrays cause an error during compilation.

Do not confuse the $STATIC metacommand with the STATIC statement, which is an executable statement that preserves the value of procedure variables between calls. (See the STATIC entry in Chapter 4, "Procedures," for details.)

Errors

If you include the metacommand $STATIC without the REM keyword or a single quotation mark, QuickBASIC returns an "Expected: statement" error message.

Tips

Numeric arrays in a program that has been compiled as a stand-alone executable file are stored differently than they are in a program that is run in the QuickBASIC environment. In an executable file, QuickBASIC stores all static arrays in the default data segment DGROUP along with simple variables and strings. To locate an element of a static array in memory, you need only use the VARPTR function to find its offset address within DGROUP. However, because a dynamic array is allocated its own segment outside DGROUP, you must specify both the segment and the offset part of the array's address to locate an element. Use the VARSEG function to return the segment of a variable. (See the VARPTR and VARSEG entries in Chapter 20, "Mixed Language," for details.)

When you run a program in the QuickBASIC environment, QuickBASIC assigns all arrays—both static and dynamic—their own segments. The only exceptions to this are static arrays that you have declared COMMON and arrays of variable-length strings; QuickBASIC stores these in DGROUP as usual.

By using far pointers to locate an array in memory, you can avoid having to write separate versions for executable programs and programs run in the environment. Specify both the segment and the offset when you address numeric arrays.

CHAPTER 22

Debugging

A Sample Debugging Session

This tutorial documents an interactive debugging session with a sample program. Imagine that you created the file SORTFILE.BAS, listed below, which is intended to sort a fixed-length file in memory; however, SORTFILE.BAS contains several errors that prevent it from executing properly. You can use the QuickBASIC environment to find these errors and correct them.

```
' SORTFILE.BAS - sorts a fixed-length file
DECLARE FUNCTION SortFile% (path$, recLen%, offSet%, fieldLen%, sortErr%)

CONST FALSE = 0, TRUE = NOT FALSE

TYPE Element
    sKey AS STRING * 10
    recNum AS INTEGER
END TYPE

PRINT : PRINT "SORTFILE - Random-access file sorter": PRINT

' acquire information needed to sort a file
LINE INPUT "Enter pathname of file to be sorted  ? "; path$
LINE INPUT "What is the record length of the file? "; temp$
recLen% = VAL(temp$)
LINE INPUT "Define sort field - starting position? "; temp$
offSet% = VAL(temp$)
LINE INPUT "                  - length of field  ? "; temp$
fieldLen% = VAL(temp$)

IF SortFile%(path$, recLen%, offSet%, fieldLen%, sortErr%) THEN
    PRINT "File successfully sorted"
ELSE
    PRINT "Unable to sort file": BEEP
END IF
END

' sort the file in memory
FUNCTION SortFile% (path$, recLen%, offSet%, fieldLen%, sortErr%) STATIC
    sortErr% = FALSE
```

(continued)

continued

```
' find file length
OPEN path$ FOR RANDOM AS #1 LEN = recLen%
fileLen& = LOF(1)
CLOSE 1

' check whether sort is possible
records& = fileLen& \ recLen%        ' (first definition of records&)
IF (fieldLen% + offSet%) > recLen% THEN
    sortErr% = 1: EXIT FUNCTION
END IF
freeRam& = FRE(-1): wanted& = records& * 12
IF fieldLen% > 10 OR wanted& > freeRam& THEN
    sortErr% = 2: EXIT FUNCTION
END IF

' create a temporary file
tempFile$ = UCASE$(path$)
dotPosition% = INSTR(tempFile$, ".")
IF dotPosition% > 0 THEN
    tempFile$ = LEFT$(tempFile$, dotPosition%) + "TMP"
ELSE
    tempFile$ = tempFile$ + ".TMP"
END IF
cmd$ = "COPY " + path$ + " " + tempFile$ + " > nul"
SHELL cmd$

' prepare for sort
DIM array(1 TO records%) AS Element

OPEN path$ FOR RANDOM AS #1 LEN = recLen%
IF offSet% > 1 THEN                  ' define records for reading the file
    FIELD 1, offSet% - 1 AS dummy$, fieldLen% AS key1$
ELSE
    FIELD 1, fieldLen% AS key1$
END IF
FIELD 1, recLen% AS finalRec$
i% = 1

' fill the array with sort keys from the file
DO
    GET 1, i%
    LSET array(i%).sKey = key1$       ' put each sort key in the array
    array(i%).recNum = i%             ' put each record number in the array
    i% = i% + 1
LOOP UNTIL i% > records&

' perform the sort
partition% = records% \ 2
DO WHILE partition% > 0
    range% = records& - partition%
```

(continued)

continued

```
        DO
            swapped% = FALSE
            FOR i% = 1 TO range%          ' if necessary, swap array elements
                IF array(i%).sKey > array(i% + partition%).sKey THEN
                    SWAP array(i%), array(i% + partition%)
                    swapped% = i%
                END IF
            NEXT i%
            range% = swapped%
        LOOP UNTIL NOT swapped%
        partition% = partition% \ 2
    LOOP

    ' use the sorted array to sort the file
    OPEN tempFile$ FOR RANDOM AS #2 LEN = recLen%    ' open temporary file
    FIELD 2, recLen% AS tempRec$           ' define records for the file
    FOR i% = 1 TO records&
        GET 2, array(i%).recNum            ' get one record from the file
        tempRecVar$ = tempRec$             ' assign record to temporary variable
        LSET finalRec$ = tempRecVar$       ' assign temporary variable to field
        PUT 1, i%                          ' write field to the file
    NEXT i%

    CLOSE : KILL tempFile$                 ' delete temporary file
    SortFile% = TRUE
END FUNCTION
```

The following listing shows file SAMPLE.DAT, which contains the unsorted data you will use to test the program.

```
89/03/01 1549 C00003 ICIPA    1000      2.50 B000001
89/03/01 1645 C00008 AAC       500      5.80 B000002  S000030
89/03/01 1646 C00013 CWC       250      5.00 B000003  S000044
89/03/01 1648 C00011 ALMO      500     10.00 S000004  B000006
89/03/01 1649 C00002 QCLGA     180      1.92 B000005  S000017
89/03/01 1651 C00005 ALMO      500     10.00 B000006  S000004
89/03/02 1648 C00011 ALMO     1000     10.00 S000004A B000009
89/03/02 1701 C00007 WPL       200      3.65 S000007  B000072
89/03/02 1703 C00012 CIG       700      5.80 S000008
89/03/02 1704 C00006 ALMO     1000     10.00 B000009  S000004A
89/03/02 1705 C00003 ASD       300     17.00 S000010
89/03/03 1706 C00009 ALMO      500     10.00 B000011  S000004
89/03/03 2042 C00002 POSO      100      6.00 S000014  B000073
89/03/04 2044 C00012 BUD       500      3.00 B000015
89/03/04 2045 C00013 ALMO      300     10.00 B000016  S000004C
89/03/04 2046 C00014 QCLGA     180      1.92 S000017  B000005
89/03/04 2047 C00007 BAB       300       .75 S000018
89/03/04 2049 C00001 ALMO      500     10.00 B000019  S000004D
89/03/05 2050 C00011 CCYOA    1000      2.24 B000020  A000023
```

(continued)

continued

```
89/03/05 2051 C00020 WOIPA   1000      6.65 S000021
89/03/05 2052 C00019 WIM     5000      0.10 B000022
89/03/06 2053 C00021 CCYOA   1000      2.24 S000023  B000020
89/03/07 2053 C00021 CCYOA   2000      2.24 S000023A B000026
89/03/07 1648 C00011 ALMO     500     10.00 S000004D B000019
89/03/08 1648 C00011 ALMO    2000     10.00 S000004E B000028
89/03/08 2125 C00018 WPL     2000      3.75 S000024
89/03/10 2126 C00025 ERA     8000       .05 S000025
89/03/11 2128 C00026 CCYOA   2000      2.24 B000026  S000023A
89/03/11 2129 C00014 AUP      100      5.18 B000027  S000041
89/03/11 2130 C00015 ALMO    2000     10.00 B000028  S000004E
89/03/12 2131 C00015 WLW      400      3.69 B000029
89/03/12 2132 C00018 AAC      500      5.80 S000030  B000002
```

Before you begin, make a working copy of this data file so that if the program corrupts the data in the working copy, you have a backup of the original file. Name the working copy SAMPLE.TST.

Now load the program SORTFILE.BAS into the QuickBASIC environment. The best way to test the program is to try to run it. Press Shift-F5 (or choose Start from the Run menu) and see what happens.

You should now see a prompt in the Output window. The program seems to have compiled correctly; the QuickBASIC editor would have caught any syntax errors before letting you get this far. The program is now asking for data. In response to the first prompt, "Enter pathname of file to be sorted," enter SAMPLE.TST. Then, in response to the next prompt, enter 64, the length of each record in the file SAMPLE.TST. The program then prompts you for information about the sort field.

The program is designed to use any field of a file record as the sort key. Use the product code field in SAMPLE.TST, which starts at position 22 in the record and is 5 characters long. When you're finished responding to the prompts, your screen contains the following information:

```
Enter pathname of file to be sorted  ? SAMPLE.TST
What is the record length of the file? 64
Define sort field - starting position? 22
                  - length of field  ? 5
```

The program immediately produces an error. QuickBASIC reports the error in a dialog box and positions the cursor at the statement that caused the error. The dialog box, shown in Figure 22-1, informs you that when the program tried to dimension the array, a subscript was out of range.

Why do you get a "Subscript out of range" error message when the array is only now being dimensioned? To find the answer to this question, you must examine the array. It's a dynamic array, and you're using a variable to dimension it. Look at the contents of that variable, *records%*. Press Enter to clear the error message from the screen.

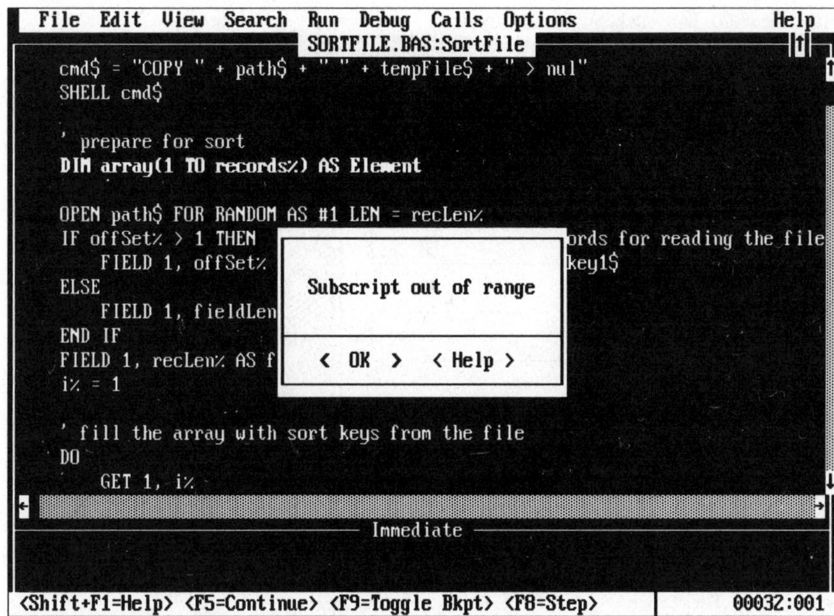

Figure 22-1.
The "Subscript out of range" error message.

QuickBASIC 4.5 introduces the Instant Watch function. To examine the contents of a variable, you need only place the cursor on it in the source code and press Shift-F9 (or choose Instant Watch from the Debug menu). For example, if you position the cursor on the variable *records%* and then press Shift-F9, you see the Instant Watch dialog box, which is shown in Figure 22-2.

The Instant Watch dialog box indicates the cause of the error. *records%*, which should contain the number of records in the file, actually contains the value 0. Press Esc to clear the Instant Watch dialog box from the screen, and look at the section of code that sets the value of *records%*.

Look a few lines above to the line that includes the comment *(first definition of records&)*; there's the error. The variable that holds the number of records is called *records&*, which is a long-integer variable:

```
records& = fileLen& \ recLen%        ' (first definition of records&)
```

Because you included an integer type-declaration character with the variable used to dimension the array, QuickBASIC assumed you were referring to a new variable and created *records%*. That's why *records%* was set to 0.

To correct the problem, move the cursor back to the DIM statement and retype *records%* as *records&*. QuickBASIC displays the message shown in Figure 22-3 as soon as you move the cursor off the line.

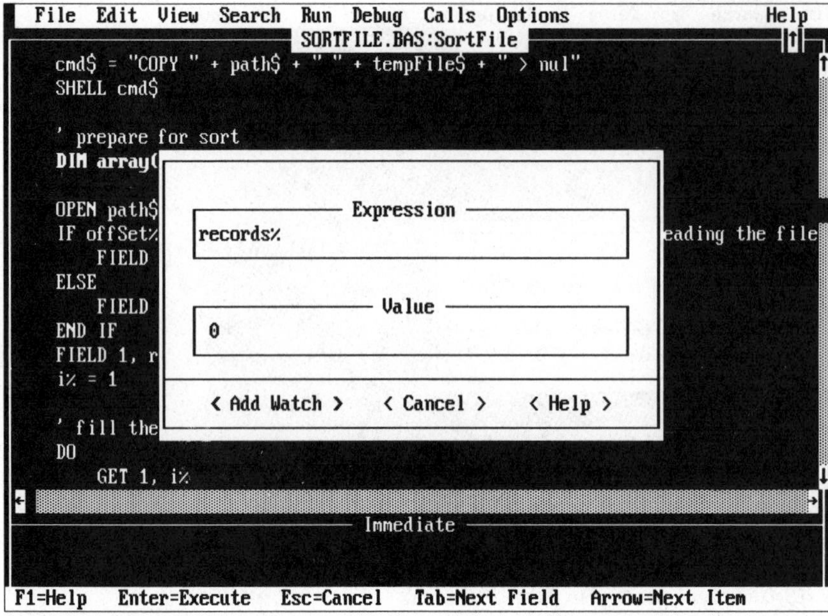

Figure 22-2.
The Instant Watch dialog box.

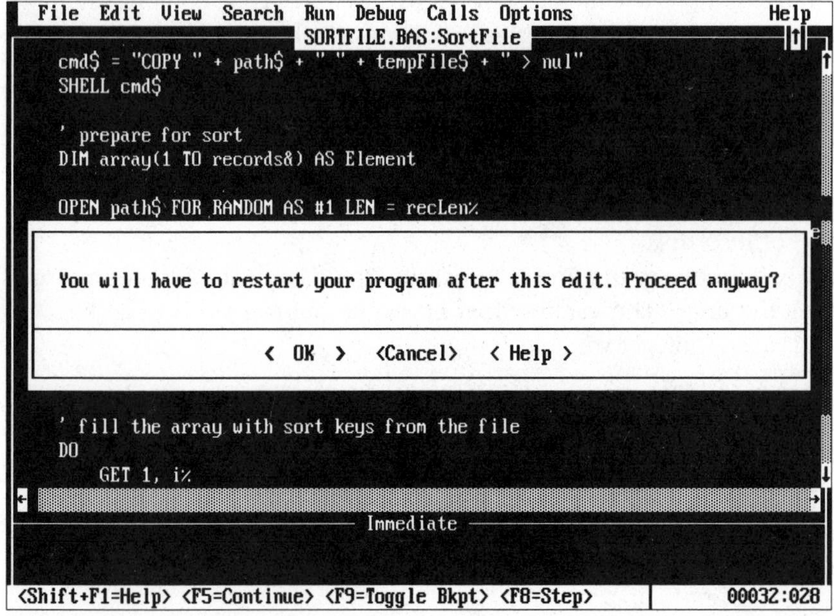

Figure 22-3.
The restart message.

The restart message tells you that the change you made affects the rest of the program, so you must restart the program if you want to maintain the change. Press Enter to accept the change and then press Shift-F5 to start the program from the beginning. After you reenter the parameters, the program displays the following message:

```
File successfully sorted
```

You're using the "quicksort" algorithm to sort the file; maybe the program is working already. Check the file and see whether it was sorted correctly.

You don't need to quit QuickBASIC in order to check the file. Merely start a secondary DOS shell from QuickBASIC and examine the file's contents. To do this, press Alt-F to open the File menu, and then press D to choose the DOS Shell command.

Now you are at the DOS command line. The quickest way to examine the file is to use the DOS TYPE command as follows:

```
TYPE SAMPLE.TST
```

The file is exactly the same as it was before. The program didn't sort the file at all. Return to QuickBASIC and see whether you can find out why. Enter the command EXIT and press any key to continue.

Notice that you're back in the program at the same point at which you left. The actual quicksort routine begins at the line following the comment *perform the sort*, which appears a few lines below your current position. Move the cursor to the routine, and see whether you can spot why it's not working.

The problem is not obvious, so you have to run the routine step by step to see whether you can see where it's going wrong. It would take too long to step through the entire program, so run the program at normal speed until it gets to the sort routine; then stop it.

You can do this by setting a "breakpoint." Perhaps the best place to stop would be at the top of the FOR...NEXT loop, which does the actual sorting. Move the cursor to that line and press F9 to set a breakpoint there. QuickBASIC highlights the line as shown in Figure 22-4 to indicate the program will pause when it reaches that line of code.

Now run the program to the breakpoint. Press Shift-F5 to start the program, and type the parameters again. The program then displays the following message:

```
File successfully sorted
```

What? Execution never reached the breakpoint. Evidently the program is not running the sort routine at all. Put the breakpoint somewhere else—immediately above the main sort loop. First press F9 again to clear the current breakpoint, and then move the cursor up a few lines, to the statement

```
DO WHILE partition% > 0
```

Press F9 to place a new breakpoint at that line. That is the beginning of the entire sort loop. The program must reach this statement.

Press Shift-F5 to start the program again. That breakpoint worked; the program stopped at the DO statement. Clear the breakpoint by pressing F9 again. Now step through the loop, one statement at a time, by pressing the F8 key.

What happened? Instead of moving into the loop, execution jumped directly to the statement after the final LOOP instruction. This is an entry-condition loop, with the test at the top, so somehow the test must have failed.

The loop executes only while the variable *partition%* contains a value greater than 0. Move back to the DO statement and check the actual value of the variable. Place the cursor on *partition%* and press Shift-F9 to open the Instant Watch dialog box again, as shown in Figure 22-5.

You can see that the value of *partition%* is 0. Now look at the previous line. The initial value of *partition%*, the partition size for the sort, is obtained by dividing the number of records by 2; however, you used the wrong type-declaration character for the variable *records%* again. It should be a long integer. Press Esc to clear the Instant Watch dialog box, and then move the cursor to *records%* so that you can edit it.

Wait. Have you made this same mistake anywhere else? Do a global search-and-replace operation to be sure you've fixed all occurrences of this particular error.

You perform a global search-and-replace operation by using the Change command in the Search menu. Press Alt-S to open the Search menu, and then press C to choose Change from this menu. As shown in Figure 22-6, QuickBASIC displays a dialog

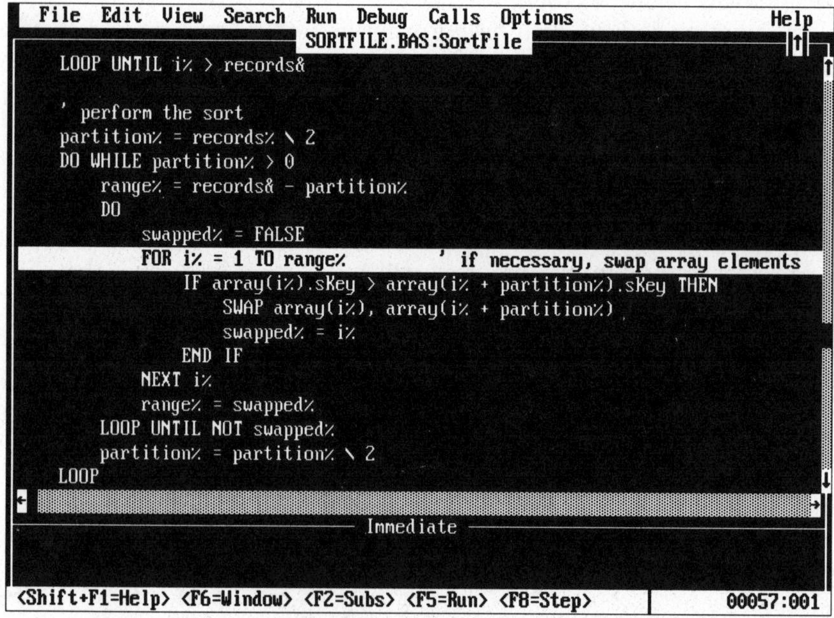

Figure 22-4.
Breakpoint set at the beginning of a FOR...NEXT loop.

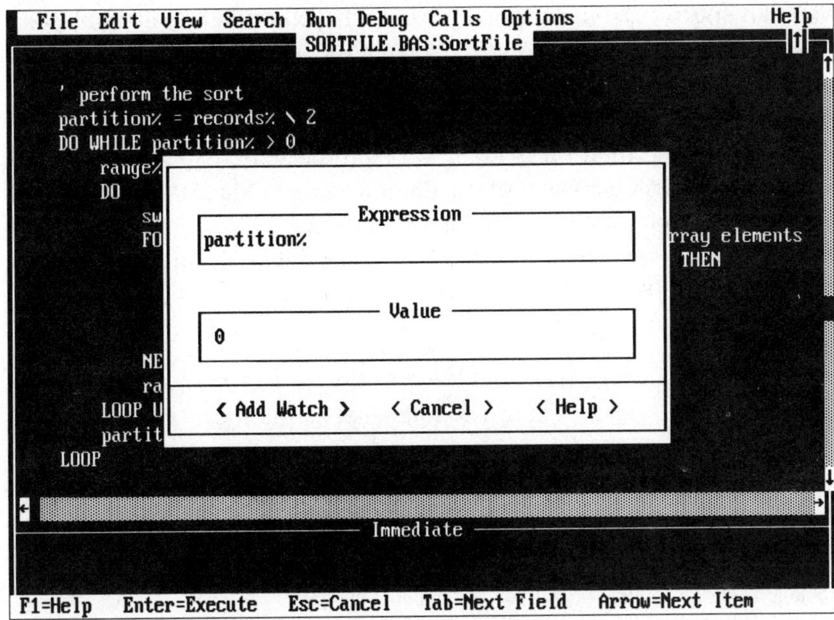

Figure 22-5.
Instant Watch dialog box for the variable partition%.

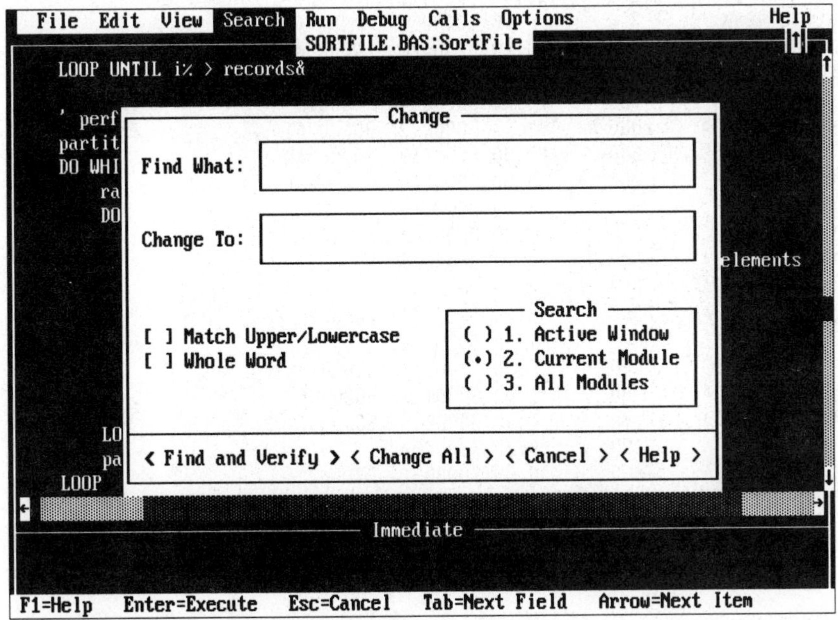

Figure 22-6.
Dialog box that specifies a global search-and-replace operation.

box in which you can specify the appropriate change. If your cursor is already positioned on the variable *records%*, QuickBASIC will place the variable name in the "Find What:" field. Otherwise, you will have to type it yourself. Once you specify what to find, press the Tab key to move to the "Change To:" field. Type *records&* as the name that will replace *records%*, and then press Enter to begin the search. QuickBASIC displays a dialog box when it finds *records%*. Press Enter to direct QuickBASIC to change the variable to *records&*. Good—it found only one occurrence of the error.

Try sorting the file again by pressing Shift-F5 to restart the program. The program reports:

```
File successfully sorted
```

The program took longer to run this time; did it work? Create a DOS shell by pressing Alt-F and then D and examine the file again. The following listing shows the contents of SAMPLE.TST:

```
89/03/01 1645 C00008 AAC       500      5.80 B000002  S000030
89/03/08 1648 C00011 ALMO     2000     10.00 S000004E B000028
89/03/12 2132 C00018 AAC       500      5.80 S000030  B000002
89/03/02 1648 C00011 ALMO     1000     10.00 S000004A B000009
89/03/01 1651 C00005 ALMO      500     10.00 B000006  S000004
89/03/02 1705 C00003 ASD       300     17.00 S000010
89/03/01 1648 C00011 ALMO      500     10.00 S000004  B000006
89/03/04 2045 C00013 ALMO      300     10.00 B000016  S000004C
89/03/02 1704 C00006 ALMO     1000     10.00 B000009  S000004A
89/03/11 2129 C00014 AUP       100      5.18 B000027  S000041
89/03/03 1706 C00009 ALMO      500     10.00 B000011  S000004
89/03/04 2047 C00007 BAB       300       .75 S000018
89/03/11 2130 C00015 ALMO     2000     10.00 B000028  S000004E
89/03/05 2050 C00011 CCYOA    1000      2.24 B000020  A000023
89/03/07 1648 C00011 ALMO      500     10.00 S000004D B000019
89/03/07 2053 C00021 CCYOA    2000      2.24 S000023A B000026
89/03/04 2049 C00001 ALMO      500     10.00 B000019  S000004D
89/03/02 1703 C00012 CIG       700      5.80 S000008
89/03/04 2044 C00012 BUD       500      3.00 B000015
89/03/01 1646 C00013 CWC       250      5.00 B000003  S000044
89/03/11 2128 C00026 CCYOA    2000      2.24 B000026  S000023A
89/03/01 1549 C00003 ICIPA    1000      2.50 B000001
89/03/06 2053 C00021 CCYOA    1000      2.24 S000023  B000020
89/03/10 2126 C00025 ERA      8000       .05 S000025
89/03/03 2042 C00002 POSO      100      6.00 S000014  B000073
89/03/04 2046 C00014 QCLGA     180      1.92 S000017  B000005
89/03/01 1649 C00002 QCLGA     180      1.92 B000005  S000017
89/03/05 2052 C00019 WIM      5000      0.10 B000022
89/03/05 2051 C00020 WOIPA    1000      6.65 S000021
89/03/12 2131 C00015 WLW       400      3.69 B000029
89/03/08 2125 C00018 WPL      2000      3.75 S000024
89/03/02 1701 C00007 WPL       200      3.65 S000007  B000072
```

At first glance the file appears sorted; however, on closer inspection, you can see that a few items are still out of place. The file has been partially sorted, but the program didn't quite finish the job. Restore the file to its original order by copying the backup file SAMPLE.DAT into SAMPLE.TST as follows:

```
COPY SAMPLE.DAT SAMPLE.TST
```

Enter the command EXIT to return to QuickBASIC. Now step through the sort again. Put the breakpoint back at the beginning of the DO statement so that when you restart the program it will pause at that point. Type F9 to create the breakpoint.

Before restarting the program choose the History On command from the Debug menu. When you do this, QuickBASIC records the last 20 statements that were executed; you can step backward and forward through statements by using the Shift-F8 and Shift-F10 key combinations. This might be handy if you overshoot the error. Choose History On from the Debug menu; Press Alt-D, then H. Now press Shift-F5 to start the program, and enter the data again. Good—execution stopped at the breakpoint. Press F9 to clear the breakpoint.

Now use the F8 key to step through the sort routine. Note that QuickBASIC highlights the current statement as you move through the program. The current statement is

```
DO WHILE partition% > 0
```

When you press F8, the cursor moves into the outermost loop. This loop should execute as long as the partition size is greater than 0, which it evidently is. Now the current statement is

```
range% = records& - partition%
```

This statement sets the sort range for the current pass through the file data in memory.

When you press F8 again, the cursor moves to the beginning of another loop. This repeats until all the out-of-sequence data in the current partition has been exchanged. The next statement is

```
swapped% = FALSE
```

This statement clears the swap flag and prepares for the next pass through the current partition.

Press F8 to move to the statement

```
FOR i% = 1 TO range%          ' if necessary, swap array elements
```

This statement is the beginning the innermost loop, which performs all the sorting.

Press F8 again. Now execution pauses at the following statement, which is the test that determines whether a pair of records needs to be swapped:

```
IF array(i%).sKey > array%(i% + partition%).sKey THEN
```

It would be useful if you could see what is in each record when it's tested. You could do this by selecting the Add Watch option from the Debug menu, but then you would have to type the names of the variables you want to watch. There's a quicker way. Move the cursor to the first variable, *array(i%).sKey*, and press Shift-F9 to display the Instant Watch dialog box, shown in Figure 22-7. Press Enter to select the "Add Watch" option. Note that the variable and its contents are now at the top of the screen. Do the same for the other variable, *array(i% + partition%).sKey.*

```
 File  Edit  View  Search  Run  Debug  Calls  Options                    Help
 SortFile array(i%).sKey: ICIPA
 SortFile array(i% + partition%).sKey: BAB
                          SORTFILE.BAS:SortFile
    LOOP UNTIL i% > records&

    ' perform the sort
    partition% = records& \ 2
    DO WHILE partition% > 0
        range% = records& - partition%
        DO
            swapped% = FALSE
            FOR i% = 1 TO range%          ' if necessary, swap array elements
                IF array(i%).sKey > array(i% + partition%).sKey THEN
                    SWAP array(i%), array(i% + partition%)
                    swapped% = i%
                END IF
            NEXT i%
            range% = swapped%
        LOOP UNTIL NOT swapped%

                              Immediate

<Shift+F1=Help> <F5=Continue> <F9=Toggle Bkpt> <F8=Step>          00058:017
```

Figure 22-7.
Variables in the Watch window.

Notice that the ASCII value of the first variable (ICIPA) is greater than that of the second variable (BAB); therefore, according to the logic of the program, the values of the two variables should have been exchanged. To see whether they were actually swapped, press F8 several times to execute and move through the IF statement.

Did you see the values change? The logic seems to be working correctly. However, step through the FOR...NEXT loop a few more times to be sure.

Continue to press F8 to move through the statements of the FOR...NEXT loop. AAC is less than ALMO, so they shouldn't have been swapped. They weren't.

CWC is larger than CCYOA, so they should have been swapped. They were.

Nothing appears to be wrong so far. Skip to the end of the FOR...NEXT loop and see whether execution continues to the next pass. You don't want to single-step through the entire execution of the loop waiting for this to happen, so speed up things a little by moving the cursor to the statement after the *NEXT i%* at the end of the loop and then pressing F7.

Pressing F7 executes the program at normal speed, from the next statement in sequence to the statement at the cursor. Now single-step again. The current statement is

```
range% = swapped%
```

This statement tells the program to sort through the same records that were exchanged last time. The program continues shuffling them until all are in order. (A pass is made without any swaps.)

Press F8 to move to the next statement:

```
LOOP UNTIL NOT swapped%
```

This should take you back to the top of the inner DO...LOOP. When you press F8 again, the cursor moves to the statement

```
partition% = partition% / 2
```

Something is wrong here: Execution dropped through the loop. This shouldn't have happened until *swapped%* equaled 0.

Place the cursor on the variable *swapped%*, and press Shift-F9 to display the Instant Watch dialog box.

The Instant Watch dialog box shows that *swapped%* contains the value 16—definitely a nonzero value. Why then did execution fall through the DO...LOOP statement? The program should have continued to loop until the variable *swapped%* became logically not true, or 0.

Is the test correct? See what NOT *swapped%* evaluates to; you can do this by setting NOT *swapped%* as a Watch expression. Press the shortcut key sequence (Alt-D, then A) to choose the Add Watch command from the Debug menu, type *NOT swapped%* in the dialog box, and then press Enter. The result is shown in Figure 22-8.

The problem is that QuickBASIC evaluates the expression as –17, which means *NOT swapped%* is true (nonzero). That's why execution fell through the loop.

The LOOP statement is currently repeating until *NOT swapped%* is true:

```
LOOP UNTIL NOT swapped%
```

This is quite different from repeating until *swapped%* is not true, which is what you want. How can you code it correctly? Reverse the logic, like this:

```
LOOP WHILE swapped%
```

Type the changed line. Before you run the program again, choose History Off; otherwise, the program will run very slowly when it begins executing. The History On option in the Debug menu is a toggle, so you use the same keystrokes to turn it off as you did to turn it on. Press Alt-D, and then H to disable history checking; press Shift-F5 to restart the program. Once again, the program reports

```
File successfully sorted
```

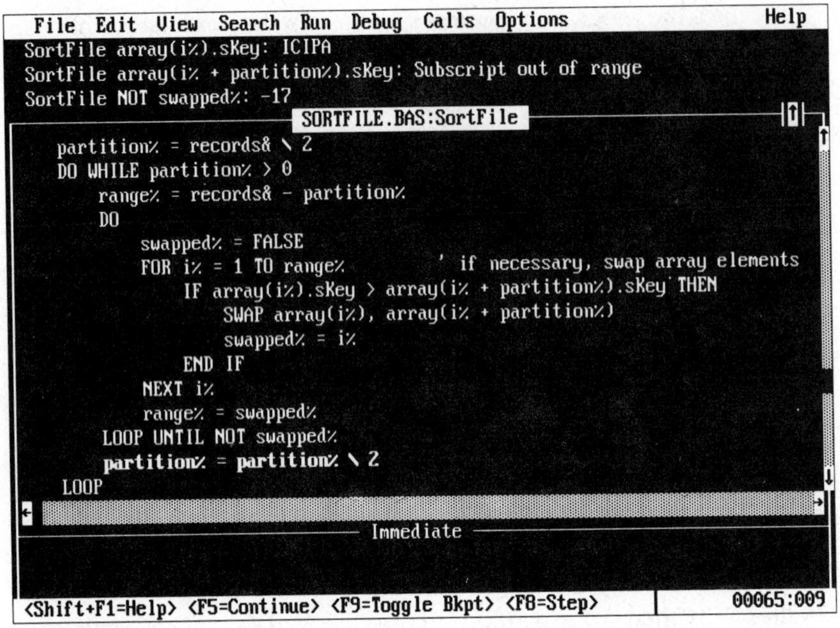

```
 File  Edit  View  Search  Run  Debug  Calls  Options                       Help
SortFile array(i%).sKey: ICIPA
SortFile array(i% + partition%).sKey: Subscript out of range
SortFile NOT swapped%: -17
                         SORTFILE.BAS:SortFile
    partition% = records& \ 2
    DO WHILE partition% > 0
        range% = records& - partition%
        DO
            swapped% = FALSE
            FOR i% = 1 TO range%           ' if necessary, swap array elements
                IF array(i%).sKey > array(i% + partition%).sKey THEN
                    SWAP array(i%), array(i% + partition%)
                    swapped% = i%
                END IF
            NEXT i%
            range% = swapped%
        LOOP UNTIL NOT swapped%
        partition% = partition% \ 2
    LOOP
                                Immediate

<Shift+F1=Help> <F5=Continue> <F9=Toggle Bkpt> <F8=Step>            00065:009
```

Figure 22-8.
The Watch expression demonstrating that NOT swapped% *is true.*

Check the file to see this for yourself. Press Alt-F, press D to create a DOS shell, and then use the DOS TYPE command to display the file again. The following listing shows the result of this sort:

```
89/03/01 1645 C00008 AAC        500      5.80 B000002  S000030
89/03/12 2132 C00018 AAC        500      5.80 S000030  B000002
89/03/08 1648 C00011 ALMO      2000     10.00 S000004E B000028
89/03/02 1648 C00011 ALMO      1000     10.00 S000004A B000009
89/03/04 2045 C00013 ALMO       300     10.00 B000016  S000004C
89/03/01 1651 C00005 ALMO       500     10.00 B000006  S000004
89/03/01 1648 C00011 ALMO       500     10.00 S000004  B000006
89/03/02 1704 C00006 ALMO      1000     10.00 B000009  S000004A
89/03/03 1706 C00009 ALMO       500     10.00 B000011  S000004
89/03/11 2130 C00015 ALMO      2000     10.00 B000028  S000004E
89/03/07 1648 C00011 ALMO       500     10.00 S000004D B000019
89/03/04 2049 C00001 ALMO       500     10.00 B000019  S000004D
89/03/02 1705 C00003 ASD        300     17.00 S000010
89/03/11 2129 C00014 AUP        100      5.18 B000027  S000041
89/03/04 2047 C00007 BAB        300       .75 S000018
89/03/04 2044 C00012 BUD        500      3.00 B000015
89/03/05 2050 C00011 CCYOA     1000      2.24 B000020  A000023
89/03/07 2053 C00021 CCYOA     2000      2.24 S000023A B000026
89/03/11 2128 C00026 CCYOA     2000      2.24 B000026  S000023A
89/03/06 2053 C00021 CCYOA     1000      2.24 S000023  B000020
89/03/02 1703 C00012 CIG        700      5.80 S000008
```

(continued)

```
89/03/01 1646 C00013 CWC        250        5.00 B000003  S000044
89/03/10 2126 C00025 ERA       8000         .05 S000025
89/03/01 1549 C00003 ICIPA     1000        2.50 B000001
89/03/03 2042 C00002 POSO       100        6.00 S000014  B000073
89/03/04 2046 C00014 QCLGA      180        1.92 S000017  B000005
89/03/01 1649 C00002 QCLGA      180        1.92 B000005  S000017
89/03/05 2052 C00019 WIM       5000        0.10 B000022
89/03/12 2131 C00015 WLW        400        3.69 B000029
89/03/05 2051 C00020 WOIPA     1000        6.65 S000021
89/03/08 2125 C00018 WPL       2000        3.75 S000024
89/03/02 1701 C00007 WPL        200        3.65 S000007  B000072
```

The program worked! The file is properly sorted in alphabetic order (using the product code field). You finally got all the bugs out of the program. Thank goodness for the QuickBASIC environment interpreter; this process would have taken quite a long time if you'd had to debug the program without it.

This tutorial session illustrated many of the tools that the QuickBASIC program environment provides to help you manage and debug your programs. The rest of this chapter discusses these facilities individually and in greater detail. It also includes several features the tutorial did not discuss.

Add Watch

QB2	■ QB4.5	■ PowerBASIC
QB3	ANSI	GW-BASIC
■ QB4	■ BASIC7	MacQB

Purpose

The Add Watch command in the Debug menu of the QuickBASIC environment lets you monitor a variable or expression while your program runs.

Selection

Keyboard

Press Alt-D to open the Debug menu. Because the Add Watch command is the first item in this menu, it is already chosen, as shown in Figure 22-9; merely press Enter to choose it. Or you can choose the command by pressing the shortcut key sequence Alt-D-A.

Mouse

Use the mouse to move the cursor to the Debug menu on the menu bar, and click the left button. When the Debug menu opens (as shown in Figure 22-9), move the cursor to the Add Watch command and then click the left button.

```
Debug
┌──────────────────────────────┐
│ Add Watch...                 │
│ Instant Watch...    Shift+F9 │
│ Watchpoint...                │
│ Delete Watch...              │
│ Delete All Watch             │
├──────────────────────────────┤
│ Trace On                     │
│ History On                   │
├──────────────────────────────┤
│ Toggle Breakpoint        F9  │
│ Clear All Breakpoints        │
│ Break on Errors              │
│ Set Next Statement           │
└──────────────────────────────┘
```

Figure 22-9.
The Debug menu.

Description

Choosing Add Watch displays a dialog box that prompts you to enter the variable you want to monitor. This is shown in Figure 22-10 on the following page. As each statement executes, QuickBASIC evaluates the variable and displays its current value in the Watch window, at the top of the screen. Note that you can also monitor an expression. For example, you can enter in the dialog box the following expression:

```
x& = 100
```

Instead of displaying the value of *x&* in the Watch window, QuickBASIC displays whether the expression is true or false. If the program you are debugging is producing incorrect results, the Watch window lets you continuously monitor important variables without having to stop the program to print them out. As the program runs, the variable or expression is reevaluated after each statement executes; if the value changes, QuickBASIC updates the display in the Watch window.

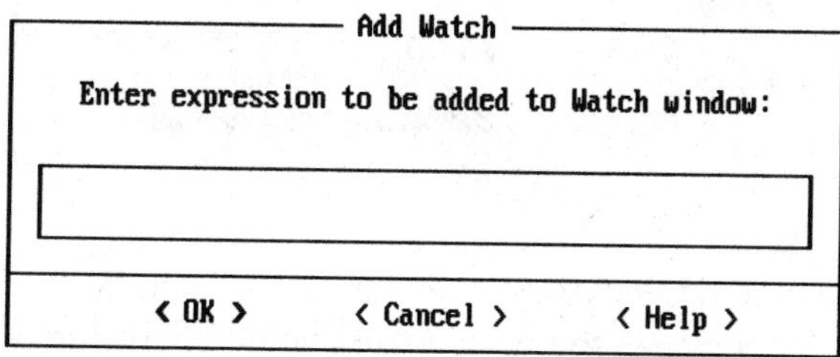

Figure 22-10.
The Add Watch dialog box.

The Watch window also displays the "context" of the variable or expression—the name of the module from which it was selected. This can be the module-level code, in which case the context is the program name, or it can be the name of a function or subprogram that appeared in the active Edit window when you entered the variable or expression.

If the code being executed does not have the same context as the expression does, QuickBASIC cannot evaluate it, and the Watch window reports that the expression or variable is "Not watchable." Even if the current module includes a variable of the same name as the variable you are monitoring, QuickBASIC ignores it because the context of the variables is different. Note that QuickBASIC displays the current context on the status line (at the bottom of the screen) while the program is executing.

Using watch variables and expressions slows program execution considerably because after each statement executes QuickBASIC must evaluate every specified variable. However, you use this feature only when you are testing or debugging a program, when the slower speed is usually not a problem.

Tips

In the Watch window, you might have trouble distinguishing between a null string, a string of blank spaces, and a string padded on the left with more blank spaces than the window can display.

To remedy this, you can add your own delimiters to the string you are monitoring. Because QuickBASIC lets you watch expressions as well as variables, you can easily specify the string by using the following expression:

```
"<" + watch$ + ">"
```

Then, even if the string *watch$* is full of blanks, you can see how long it is because the string is delimited by a less-than sign and a greater-than sign.

Or, if the string is likely to be padded on the left, you can merely specify only the unpadded part in the Watch window by using the following statement:

```
LTRIM$(watch$)
```

Break on Errors

QB2	■ QB4.5	PowerBASIC
QB3	ANSI	GW-BASIC
QB4	BASIC7	MacQB

Purpose

The Break on Errors command (introduced in QuickBASIC version 4.5) suspends error trapping in your program, so a runtime error causes the program to halt before the error handler gains control. This lets you examine the conditions that caused the error and to test the operation of the handler itself.

Selection

Keyboard

Press Alt-D to open the Debug menu. Break on Errors is the 10th item; use the arrow keys to choose the Break on Errors command, and then press Enter. (See Figure 22-9, in the Add Watch entry.) Or you can enter the shortcut sequence Alt-D-E.

Mouse

Use the mouse to move the cursor to the Debug menu on the menu bar, and click the left button. When the pull-down Debug menu opens, move the cursor to the Break on Errors command (shown in Figure 22-9) and then click the left button.

Description

The Break on Errors command is useful only if your program includes error trapping (that is, if it uses the ON ERROR GOTO statement to specify an error-handling subroutine). If a runtime error occurs after you choose Break on Errors, the program branches to the first statement in the error handler and then stops; QuickBASIC does not execute the error-handling code.

Break on Errors toggles stopping when an error occurs: Choose it once to enable it; choose it again to disable it. When enabled, the Break on Errors command is preceded by a bullet symbol in the Debug menu.

When the program stops, you can use the Immediate window or an Instant Watch window to examine the variables or expressions that might have caused the error. Choosing Break on Errors enables History On so that you can review the statements that triggered the error. (Press Shift-F8 to step backward through as many as 20 of the statements that preceded the error; press Shift-F10 to step forward to the line at which execution stopped.)

After you have found the cause of the error, you can restart the program by pressing F5. Note that you can also use the F8 key to single-step through the error handler. However, do not use the Set Next Statement command in the Debug menu to branch to another part of the program and then continue execution from there. Before you can do this, the program must execute the RESUME statement at the end of the error-handling subroutine so that QuickBASIC can clear the error and reenable trapping.

Clear All Breakpoints

See also: Toggle Breakpoint

QB2	■ QB4.5	✲ PowerBASIC
QB3	ANSI	GW-BASIC
■ QB4	■ BASIC7	MacQB

Purpose

The Clear All Breakpoints command cancels all set breakpoints and lets the program run without interruptions. You use Clear All Breakpoints after you have found and corrected all the bugs in your program.

Selection

Keyboard

Press Alt-D to open the Debug menu. The Clear All Breakpoints command is the ninth item; use the arrow keys to choose the Clear All Breakpoints command, and then press Enter. (See Figure 22-9, in the Add Watch entry.) Or you can enter the shortcut sequence Alt-D-C.

Mouse

Use the mouse to move the cursor to the Debug menu on the menu bar, and click the left button. When the pull-down Debug menu opens, move the cursor to the Clear All Breakpoints command (shown in Figure 22-9) and then click the left button.

Description

Breakpoints are markers that the QuickBASIC environment inserts into your code to cause the program to stop executing. The Clear All Breakpoints command instantly removes all the breakpoints that you set during a debugging session.

Note that Clear All Breakpoints has no effect on any watchpoints or watch expressions that you have enabled.

Compatibility

PowerBASIC

PowerBASIC supports the command Clear Breakpoints, which performs the same task as the QuickBASIC command Clear All Breakpoints.

Delete All Watch

QB2	■ QB4.5	✲ PowerBASIC
QB3	ANSI	■ GW-BASIC
■ QB4	■ BASIC7	■ MacQB

Purpose

The Delete All Watch command removes all variables and expressions from the Watch window and then closes the Watch window. Use Delete All Watch when you no longer need to monitor any variables or expressions.

Selection

Keyboard

Press Alt-D to open the Debug menu. The Delete All Watch command is the fifth item; use the arrow keys to choose the Delete All Watch command, and then press Enter. (See Figure 22-9, in the Add Watch entry.) Or you can enter the shortcut sequence Alt-D-L.

Mouse

Use the mouse to move the cursor to the Debug menu on the menu bar, and click the left button. When the pull-down Debug menu opens, move the cursor to the Delete All Watch command (shown in Figure 22-9) and then click the left button.

Description

The Delete All Watch command closes the Watch window and cancels all active watchpoints and watch expressions. Because the program no longer evaluates them, it subsequently runs at the normal speed, although any breakpoints that you have previously set remain in effect.

Compatibility

PowerBASIC

PowerBASIC supports the command Remove All Watches, which performs the same task as the QuickBASIC command Delete All Watch.

Delete Watch

QB2	■ QB4.5	■ PowerBASIC
QB3	ANSI	GW-BASIC
■ QB4	■ BASIC7	MacQB

Purpose

The Delete Watch command clears a variable or expression from the Watch window. Use Delete Watch to remove a variable or expression from the Watch window when you no longer need to monitor its value.

Selection

Keyboard

Press Alt-D to open the Debug menu. The Delete Watch command is the fourth item; use the arrow keys to choose the Delete Watch command, and then press Enter. (See Figure 22-9, in the Add Watch entry.) Or you can enter the shortcut sequence Alt-D-D.

Mouse

Use the mouse to move the cursor to the Debug menu on the menu bar, and click the left button. When the pull-down Debug menu opens, move the cursor to the Delete Watch command (shown in Figure 22-9) and then click the left button.

Description

Deleting a watchpoint or a watch expression with the Delete Watch command removes the variable or expression from the Watch window at the top of the screen. QuickBASIC no longer evaluates the expressions between statements as the program executes.

When you choose Delete Watch, QuickBASIC displays a dialog box that lists all current watch expressions and watchpoints. This is shown in Figure 22-11. Use the arrow keys to select the name of the expression to be deleted, and then press Enter to delete it. If you have a mouse, move the cursor to the appropriate expression name and double-click the left button.

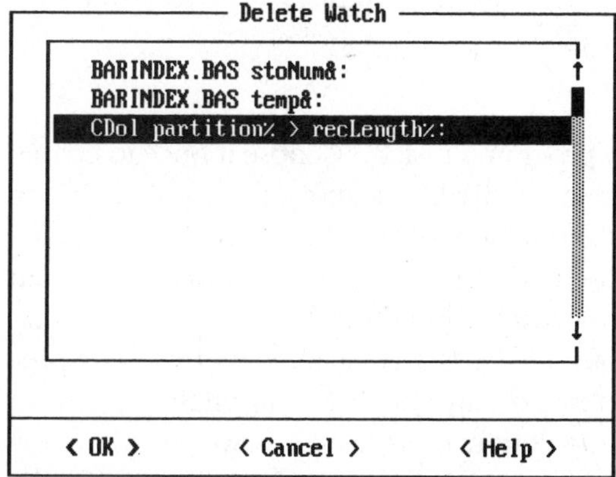

Figure 22-11.
The Delete Watch dialog box.

If you decide not to delete any variables or expressions, press Esc; this closes the Delete Watch dialog box without affecting the contents of the Watch window. You can also close the dialog box by choosing Cancel from the option list at the bottom of the Delete Watch dialog box. To do this, either use the Tab key to move the highlight to this option and then press Enter or use the mouse to position the cursor at the Cancel option and then click the left button. If you need help, select the Help option to display information about how to use Delete Watch.

History On

See also: Break on Errors, Trace On

QB2	■ QB4.5	PowerBASIC
QB3	ANSI	GW-BASIC
■ QB4	■ BASIC7	MacQB

Purpose

The History On command directs QuickBASIC to keep a record of the last 20 statements that your program executed. Whenever you interrupt the program, you can step backward and forward through these statements to examine the sequence of operations more closely.

Selection

Keyboard

Press Alt-D to open the Debug menu. History On is the seventh item; use the arrow keys to choose the History On command, and then press Enter. (See Figure 22-9, in the Add Watch entry.) Or you can enter the shortcut sequence Alt-D-H.

Mouse

Use the mouse to move the cursor to the Debug menu on the menu bar, and click the left button. When the pull-down Debug menu opens, move the cursor to the History On command (shown in Figure 22-9) and then click the left button.

Description

The History On command lets you record a program's history: Choose it once to enable the recording of statements; choose it again to disable statement recording. When enabled, the History On command is preceded by a bullet symbol in the Debug menu. QuickBASIC enables History On when you choose Trace On or Break on Errors from the Debug menu. (See the Trace On and Break on Errors entries.)

QuickBASIC records only the addresses of the last 20 statements that your program executed. It does not record the contents of any variables that might have been changed by those statements. The History On command is useful, however, when you need to see the sequence of statements that led to a runtime error or that made the value of a watchpoint true and caused the program to stop.

When the program is interrupted, QuickBASIC positions the cursor on the last statement that was executed. To step backward 1 statement in the previous 20 statements, press Shift-F8. The cursor moves only to those statements that executed; it skips any intervening statements.

After you have stepped backward through one or more statements, you can step forward through the same sequence of statements by pressing Shift-F10.

Tips

You can use History On to watch your program run in slow motion. If you begin a program with History On enabled but Animated Trace off, the display remains in the Output window instead of switching back to the Edit window every time a new statement executes. This greatly reduces execution speed, thus letting you watch in full detail the construction of a complex display.

Warnings

You can move forward and backward in the program only if you do not perform any other operation in the QuickBASIC environment after the program stops executing and before you press Shift-F8 or Shift-F10. For example, if you remove a breakpoint or add a watch expression, the history information is lost.

Instant Watch

QB2	■ QB4.5	PowerBASIC
QB3	ANSI	■ GW-BASIC
QB4	BASIC7	MacQB

Purpose

The Instant Watch command lets you examine the contents of a variable immediately; this saves you the inconvenience of adding the variable to the Watch window.

Selection

Keyboard

To examine a variable, either move the cursor to the variable in the program text and press Shift-F9, or enter the key sequence Alt-D-I.

Mouse

To examine a variable, move the mouse cursor to the variable, hold down the Shift key, and click the right button.

Description

When you choose the Instant Watch command, QuickBASIC displays a dialog box that contains the name of that variable as well as the variable's current value. This is shown in Figure 22-12.

You cannot change the variable in the expression field or assign it a new value. You can, however, add the expression to the Watch window so that you can monitor its value during program execution. To do so, select the Add Watch option at the bottom of the dialog box.

Choose the Cancel option to close the Instant Watch dialog box or choose Help to display information about the Instant Watch command. (You can also close the Instant Watch dialog box by pressing Esc.)

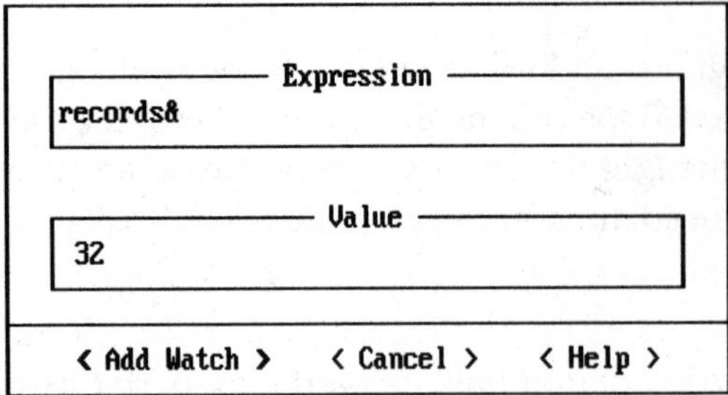

Figure 22-12.
The Instant Watch dialog box.

In addition to reporting the values of variables, the Instant Watch command can report the return value of any of QuickBASIC's built-in functions. For example, if you place the cursor on the keyword CSRLIN and press Shift-F9, QuickBASIC displays the Instant Watch dialog box containing the current row number of the cursor. Note that this is the row number of the cursor in the Output window (the window in which output from your program appears), not the cursor in the Edit window.

Tips

You can duplicate the effect of the Instant Watch command by using a PRINT statement in the Immediate window to return the current value of an expression. For example, you can enter the statement *PRINT CSRLIN* in the Immediate window to find the row position of the cursor. If you use the Immediate window, however, QuickBASIC displays the value in the Output window, thus overwriting your program display. Instant Watch does not overwrite data in the Output window.

Set Next Statement

QB2	■ QB4.5	PowerBASIC
QB3	ANSI	GW-BASIC
■ QB4	■ BASIC7	MacQB

Purpose

The Set Next Statement command lets you resume program execution (after temporarily interrupting it) at a statement other than the next in sequence. You can use this command to change the normal flow of execution or to examine the effect of alternative branchings in an IF or SELECT CASE statement.

Selection

Keyboard

Press Alt-D to open the Debug menu. Set Next Statement is the last item; use the arrow keys to choose the Set Next Statement command, and then press Enter. (See Figure 22-9, in the Add Watch entry.) Or you can enter the shortcut sequence Alt-D-S.

Mouse

Use the mouse to move the cursor to the Debug menu on the menu bar, and click the left button. When the pull-down Debug menu opens, move the cursor to the Set Next Statement command (shown in Figure 22-9) and then click the left button.

Description

The Set Next Statement command lets you select the first statement that will be executed when you restart the program after it was interrupted by a breakpoint, a watchpoint, or the Ctrl-Break key combination. QuickBASIC does not execute any code between the last statement executed and the new statement you specify. Therefore, you must set any variables that the new section of code requires.

To specify a new statement, use the arrow keys (or the mouse) to move the cursor to the appropriate program line, and then choose the Set Next Statement command from the Debug menu. The highlight that marks the current statement moves to the statement you have selected, and when you restart the program, execution will begin there. To resume execution, press F5; you can also use the F8 key to step through subsequent statements.

Warnings

Do not use the Set Next Statement command to continue execution after a runtime error has been trapped by the Break on Errors command. Before you can branch to another statement, the program must execute the RESUME statement at the end of the error-handling subroutine so that QuickBASIC can clear the error and reenable trapping.

Toggle Breakpoint

See also: Clear All Breakpoints

QB2	■ QB4.5	■ PowerBASIC
QB3	ANSI	GW-BASIC
■ QB4	■ BASIC7	■ MacQB

Purpose

A breakpoint is a location in your program at which you want execution to stop. You can set breakpoints either to suspend the program execution before it enters a critical section of code; or you can set them to stop the program after it has executed a procedure you want to test, which lets you examine the contents of any variables.

Selection

Keyboard

Press Alt-D to open the Debug menu. Toggle Breakpoint is the eighth item; use the arrow keys to choose the Toggle Breakpoint command, and then press Enter. (See Figure 22-9, in the Add Watch entry.) Or you can enter the shortcut sequence Alt-D-B. You can also press the F9 function key.

Mouse

Use the mouse to move the cursor to the Debug menu on the menu bar, and click the left button. When the pull-down Debug menu opens, move the cursor to the Toggle Breakpoint command (shown in Figure 22-9) and then click the left button.

Description

The Toggle Breakpoint command toggles a breakpoint: Choose it once to place a breakpoint at the line the cursor is on; choose it again to remove the breakpoint at the line the cursor is on. QuickBASIC highlights any line that contains a breakpoint.

When a program running in the QuickBASIC environment encounters a breakpoint, it stops immediately; it does not execute the statement in which the breakpoint is set. After the program stops, you can examine active variables or test the value of expressions either by issuing a PRINT statement in the Immediate window to display them or by entering them in the Watch window.

After you have tested the variables or expressions, you can resume program execution by pressing the F5 key. You can also use the F8 key to step through subsequent statements, one statement at a time. If the program is still stopped and you press F9 a second time to clear the breakpoint at the cursor, the program will not resume until you press F5. If your program contains more than one breakpoint, you can clear them all at once by choosing the Clear All Breakpoints command from the Debug menu. (See the Clear All Breakpoints entry.)

Trace On

See also: TROFF, TRON

QB2	■ QB4.5	■ PowerBASIC
QB3	ANSI	GW-BASIC
■ QB4	■ BASIC7	■ MacQB

Purpose

The Trace On command enables or disables program tracing in the QuickBASIC environment. When tracing is enabled, QuickBASIC selects each statement as it executes, displaying the statement in the environment's Edit window.

Selection

Keyboard

Press Alt-D to open the Debug menu. The Trace On command is the sixth item; use the arrow keys to choose the Trace On command, and then press Enter. (See Figure 22-9, in the Add Watch entry.) Or you can enter the shortcut sequence Alt-D-T.

Mouse

Use the mouse to move the cursor to the Debug menu on the menu bar, and click the left button. When the pull-down Debug menu opens, move the cursor to the Trace On command (shown in Figure 22-9) and click the left button.

Description

The Trace On command in the Debug menu toggles tracing: Choose it once to enable tracing; choose it again to disable tracing. When tracing is enabled, the Trace On command is preceded by a bullet symbol in the Debug menu.

Trace On turns on the "animated tracing" capabilities of QuickBASIC, which cause QuickBASIC to step through a program as it is executed. This gives you time to watch the details of program execution and lets you stop the program (by using Ctrl-Break) if it doesn't execute as you intended it to. Any watchpoints or breakpoints that were in effect before you chose Trace On will continue to stop execution at particular points in the program. As each statement executes, QuickBASIC highlights the line in which it appears in the Edit window; this lets you check whether the program is executing in the proper sequence. Any output that the program generates is directed to the Output window as usual; however, as soon as the output operation finishes, the display switches back to the Edit window.

Trace On enables History On (discussed in the History On entry), which enables QuickBASIC to keep a record of the last 20 lines executed by the program. If you stop the program at any stage during its execution, you can use this history to step backward (using Shift-F8) and forward (using Shift-F10) through those 20 statements.

Tips

The program itself can also enable and disable tracing—merely insert the statements TRON (trace on) and TROFF (trace off) at appropriate places in the program code. You can use these statements to restrict tracing to the section of the program in which you suspect bugs exist.

You can also enter TRON and TROFF directly in the Immediate window. However, doing this has exactly the same effect as does enabling or disabling Tracing from the Debug menu.

TROFF, TRON

See also: Trace On

■ QB2	■ QB4.5	✲ PowerBASIC
■ QB3	✲ ANSI	■ GW-BASIC
■ QB4	■ BASIC7	✲ MacQB

Purpose

The TRON statement activates the QuickBASIC Trace On command, which is used for debugging programs. When tracing is enabled, QuickBASIC highlights each statement as it executes. The TROFF statement disables line tracing.

Syntax

TRON
TROFF

Usage

```
TRON        ' enables tracing
FOR i% = 1 to range%
    IF array(i%) > array(i% + gap%) THEN
        SWAP array(i%), array(i% + gap%)
        swapped% = i%
    END IF
NEXT i%
TROFF       ' disables tracing
```

Enables tracing, executes a FOR loop, and then disables tracing.

Description

The TROFF and TRON statements help you monitor program execution in the QuickBASIC environment. They duplicate the effect of the Trace On command, which is found in the Debug menu. To ensure compatibility with code that was originally written in GW-BASIC or BASICA, QuickBASIC also supports these statements in stand-alone programs that were compiled with the /O switch. When tracing is enabled in a stand-alone program, the program displays the line numbers of statements as they execute. Because programs written in QuickBASIC usually use labels rather than line numbers, however, TROFF and TRON are no longer as useful as they were in earlier versions.

When executed in a program running in the QuickBASIC environment, TRON has the same effect as does choosing the Trace On command from the Debug menu. TRON turns on the animated tracing capabilities of QuickBASIC, which cause QuickBASIC to step through a program when it is executed. As each statement executes, QuickBASIC highlights it in the Edit window; this lets you check whether the statements are executing in the proper sequence. If any watchpoints or breakpoints are specified, they will stop execution at particular points in the program. You can also press Ctrl-Break to stop the program.

TROFF turns off animated tracing; however, the program continues to execute. When used together, TROFF and TRON help you isolate a section of program in which you suspect bugs exist.

Note that you can also enter TROFF and TRON in the Immediate window to toggle program tracing directly.

Errors

If you use TRON in a program that was compiled by using BC.EXE with the /D switch and it executes a statement that does not have an associated line number, the program displays the number of the nearest line that does contain a number. If the program contains no line numbers, the program stops and displays an error message with the following syntax:

No line number in module *XXXXXXXX* at address *SSSS:OOOO*
Hit any key to return to system

Because QuickBASIC lets you use meaningful labels (instead of line numbers) to mark branching points in your programs, TROFF and TRON are now seldom used in executable files.

Compatibility

ANSI BASIC

ANSI BASIC uses the statements TRACE OFF and TRACE ON to control program tracing. If TRACE ON is chosen, the program reports the line number of a branching statement and the line number to which the program branches; it also reports the line number of a statement that assigns a value to any variable and the value itself. You can direct this report to a file or a printer. In ANSI BASIC, tracing works only if the program previously executed a DEBUG ON statement.

PowerBASIC

When used in the PowerBASIC environment, TRON causes PowerBASIC to display program line numbers and labels in the trace window, not the output window.

QuickBASIC for the Macintosh

TROFF and TRON are available only in the QuickBASIC environment, where they operate exactly as they do in QuickBASIC for the PC. In QuickBASIC for the Macintosh, you can't use TROFF and TRON in compiled programs that are run outside the QuickBASIC environment.

Example

As stated in the "Description" section, TRON acts differently in a stand-alone executable program from the way it does in the QuickBASIC environment. The following program uses TROFF and TRON to report the line number of each statement as it executes. Compile this program by using the following commands.

```
BC /O /D TRON.BAS;
LINK TRON.OBJ;
```

Note that because you are not running this program inside the QuickBASIC environment, TRON cannot use the QuickBASIC feature that executes the program step by step. Instead, TRON prints the number of each line as it executes. You can toggle between TROFF and TRON by pressing any key; press the Esc key to quit.

```
100 CLS
110 counter& = 0
120 DO
130     counter& = counter& + 1
140     LOCATE 10, 10: PRINT counter&
150     r$ = INKEY$: IF r$ = CHR$(27) THEN EXIT DO
160     IF r$ <> "" THEN
170         IF trace% THEN
180             trace% = 0: TROFF           ' turn tracing off
190             LOCATE 11, 1: PRINT SPACE$(80);
200             LOCATE 10, 10
210         ELSE
220             trace% = -1: TRON           ' turn tracing on
230         END IF
240     END IF
250 LOOP WHILE 1
260 END
```

Watchpoint

QB2	■ QB4.5	PowerBASIC
QB3	ANSI	■ GW-BASIC
■ QB4	■ BASIC7	MacQB

Purpose

The Watchpoint command interrupts program execution when a specified condition is true. Watchpoints let you test to see whether a variable contains the values you expect it to.

Selection

Keyboard

Press Alt-D to open the Debug menu. The Watchpoint command is the third item; use the arrow keys to choose it, and then press Enter. (See Figure 22-9 in the Add Watch entry.) Or you can enter the shortcut sequence Alt-D-W.

Mouse

Use the mouse to move the cursor to the Debug menu on the menu bar, and click the left button. When the Debug menu opens, move the cursor to the Watchpoint command (shown in Figure 22-9) and then click the left button.

Description

The Watchpoint command allows you to specify a variable or expression that, when true, stops execution. Enter the variable or expression in the dialog box that appears when you select Watchpoint from the Debug menu. (See Figure 22-13.) After you press Enter, QuickBASIC displays in the Watch window at the top of the screen the specified variable or expression, including the "context" of the variable or expression and a message indicating whether it is false (zero) or true (nonzero). Thereafter, as the program runs, QuickBASIC reevaluates the expression after each statement is executed; if the expression becomes true (nonzero), the program stops. You must, of course, ensure that the expression is initially false; otherwise, the program will stop immediately. To resume program execution, press the F5 key.

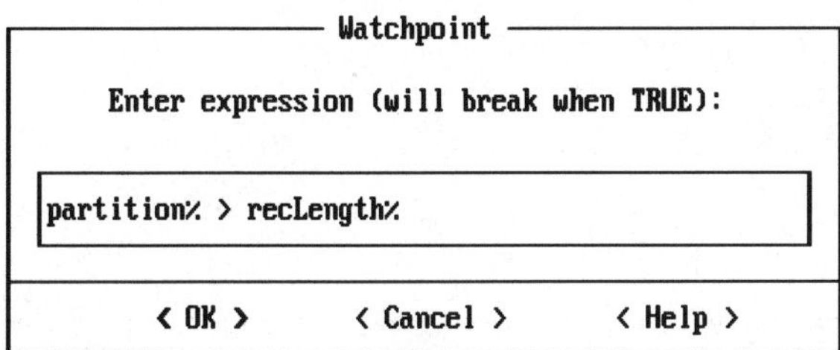

Figure 22-13.
The Watchpoint dialog box.

The "context" of a watchpoint is the name of the module from which it was selected. This can be the module-level code, in which case the context is the program name, or it can be the name of a function or subprogram that appeared in the active Edit window when you entered the watchpoint.

If the code being executed does not have the same context as the watchpoint, QuickBASIC cannot evaluate the watchpoint. The Watch window reports that the expression or variable is "Not watchable." Even if the current module includes a variable of the same name as the variable you are testing, Watchpoint ignores it because the context of the variables is different. Note that QuickBASIC displays the current context on the status line (at the bottom of the screen) while the program executes.

Using watchpoints slows program execution because after every statement QuickBASIC must evaluate every specified variable. However, you use this feature only when you are testing or debugging a program, when the slower speed is not usually a problem.

Note that you cannot use more than 8 watch expressions or watchpoints in one program.

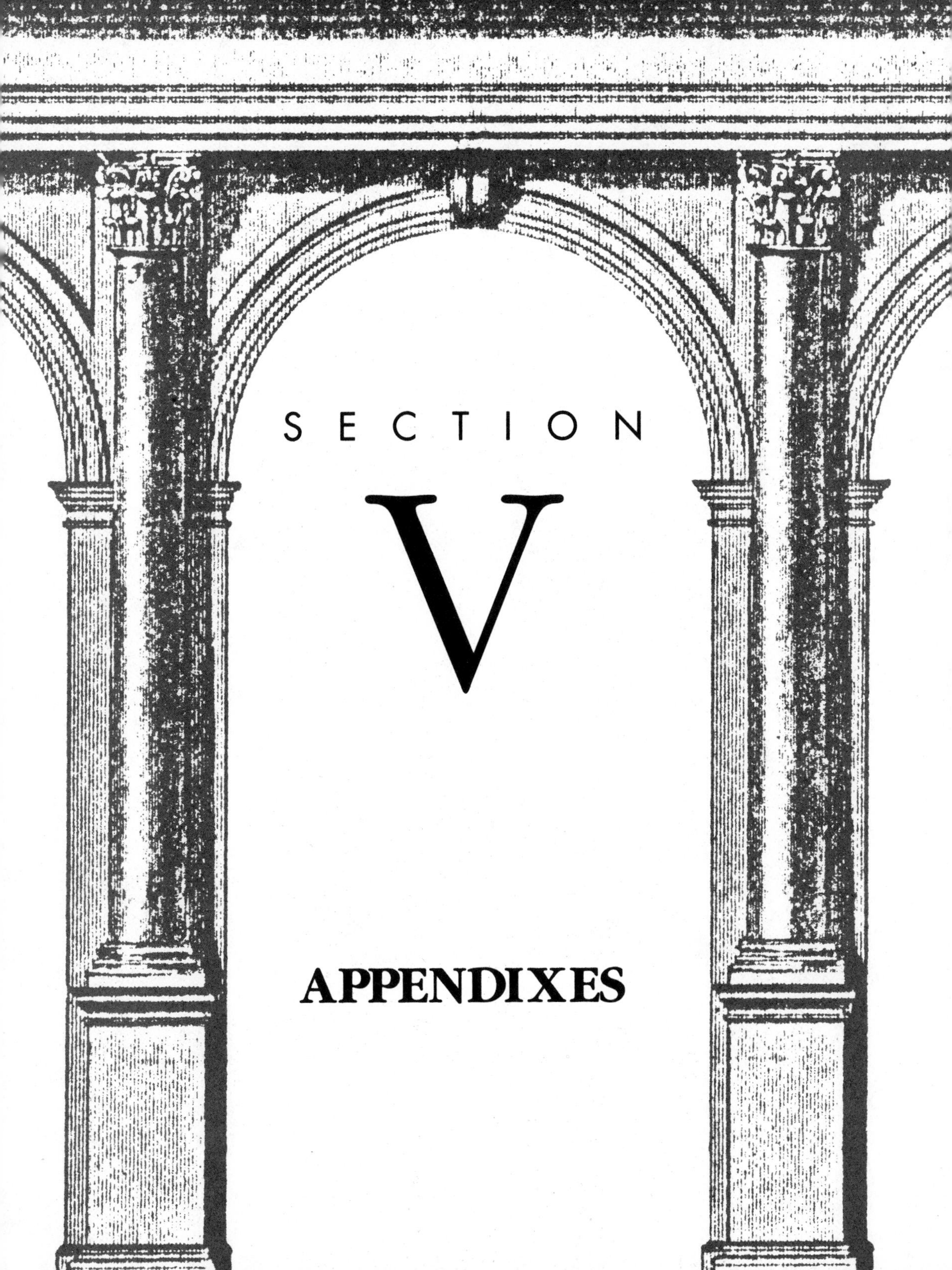

SECTION V

APPENDIXES

APPENDIX A

Microsoft KnowledgeBase

Selected Files from the Microsoft KnowledgeBase

Microsoft provides the usual customer-service channels as well as the Microsoft KnowledgeBase, a new level of technical support for QuickBASIC and other Microsoft products. Microsoft produced this database of text documents, called "articles," to clarify statements, functions, and other language features; to report bugs and offer possible workarounds; and to recommend programming practices for certain situations. Microsoft updates the database daily.

By scanning or downloading the articles in the Microsoft KnowledgeBase you'll learn a lot about programming in QuickBASIC. You'll also pick up tips, read insightful explanations, and learn problem solving from the people who understand the language at its deepest level.

The articles described in this appendix are only highlights of the more than 1000 articles available to users of CompuServe (GO MSKB) and GEnie. The articles are listed by title and document number and are grouped according to the chapters of this book.

Types and Variables

- Passing Variables to ON ERROR and ON Event Handlers. Article number: Q21863.
- How to Use User-Defined TYPEs with BTRIEVE Versions 4.1x. Article number: Q26493. Beginning with QuickBASIC 4.0 and BTRIEVE 4.1x, user-defined types can be used with this popular database facility.
- QuickBASIC Hangs Using User-Defined Record Greater than 64 KB. Article number: Q28050. User-defined types that require more than 64 KB are illegal; however, they are not trapped by QuickBASIC 4.0 or 4.00b and Microsoft BASIC 6.0 or 6.00b until runtime, when they make the system hang. Microsoft fixed the problem in QuickBASIC 4.5.
- "Out Of Memory"; Limits on Number of Variables in 4.00. Article number: Q31049. For QuickBASIC 4.0.

- Use ERASE to Reinitialize Array of User-Defined TYPE Records. Article number: Q31172. The article shows how to perform this operation with QuickBASIC 4.0 and later.
- How to Nest User-Defined TYPE Declarations in Compiled BASIC. Article number: Q31911.
- PUT User-Defined Type Versus FIELD, MKS in Random-Access File. Article number: Q38278. The article shows equivalent techniques and example code for QuickBASIC 4.0 and later.
- Passing Dynamic Array of User-Defined TYPE from QB to MASM 5.x. Article number: Q44409.

Flow Control

- FOR...NEXT Loop Can Execute Zero Times. Article number: Q22011. If the loop index is initially greater than the loop limit, the FOR loop won't execute at all.
- Cannot Use LONG Integer as FOR...NEXT Loop Counter in Editor. Article number: Q26481. This problem occurs in the QuickBASIC 4.0 environment; however, a loop with a long-integer counter works properly in executable files. Microsoft fixed the problem in QuickBASIC 4.00b.
- Using Long Integer as FOR Loop Index Fails with Negative STEP. Article number: Q27548. Microsoft fixed this problem in QuickBASIC 4.00b and Microsoft BASIC version 6.0.

Decisions and Operators

- Extra Spaces Added before ELSE with Each SAVE in QB Editor. Article number: Q26606. Microsoft fixed this problem in QuickBASIC 4.00b and Microsoft BASIC version 6.0.
- A GOTO Inside SELECT CASE Incorrectly Executes ELSE Block. Article number: Q31297. In executable files compiled with QuickBASIC 4.0, if a GOTO is executed from a SELECT CASE statement, when the GOTO is executed, any statements following CASE ELSE are also executed. Microsoft fixed this problem in QuickBASIC 4.5 and Microsoft BASIC 7.0.
- QB.EXE Editor Fails to Flag Extra ELSE Clause as Syntax Error. Article number: Q37319. This problem exists in QuickBASIC 4.0, 4.00b, and 4.5.
- Multiple CASE ELSE Allowed in QB.EXE; Causes Compile Errors. Article number: Q43901. This problem exists in QuickBASIC 4.0 and 4.5 and Microsoft BASIC 6.0 and 6.00b. The editor doesn't object to the second (or subsequent) CASE ELSE clause, but the first is always executed. The extra CASE ELSE clause will cause the compiler to return an error message. Microsoft fixed this problem in Microsoft BASIC 7.0.

Procedures

- "RETURN WITHOUT GOSUB" Error in Nested GOSUB. Article number: Q26001. This file contains example code demonstrating that when QuickBASIC returns from a nested GOSUB...RETURN statement and encounters a RETURN statement it produces an error message. Microsoft fixed this problem in QuickBASIC 4.00b and in Microsoft BASIC 6.0.
- QuickBASIC 4.x Procedure Name Followed By Colon Not Executed. Article number: Q30858. If you call a subprogram by name (without the CALL keyword), don't use a colon at the end of the name because QuickBASIC assumes the name is a line label.
- Using GOSUB, GOTO, ON Event GOSUB, ON ERROR GOTO in Modules. Article number: Q35143. This article describes which labels specified by these statements must be at the module level.
- LPRINT Forced to Screen Using OPEN in FUNCTION Procedure. Article number: Q37310. In general, don't perform I/O statements (such as PRINT) within a function that will be called from I/O statements. Such a function, when called from LPRINT, causes output to be displayed on the screen.
- Recursive FUNCTION Procedure Shouldn't Be STATIC in QuickBASIC. Article number: Q40413. A recursive procedure must create a series of temporary variables in order to work, so it cannot be declared static. This article corrects Microsoft's example factorial program found in the "Programming in BASIC" manual.
- Recursive Procedure Variables Not Saved When in COMMON. Article number: Q43930. Variables used in a recursive procedure that are declared in a COMMON statement do not retain values through recursive calls to the procedure.

Strings

- Explanation of String Space Garbage Collection; FRE Function. Article number: Q12337. This article explains how and when QuickBASIC reclaims string space and shows how to use the FRE function to force garbage collection.
- Length of Strings and String Descriptors. Article number: Q21836. This article explains that all QuickBASIC strings can have as many as 32,767 characters because each string has a 4-byte descriptor (with 2 bytes to contain the length); in GW-BASIC 3.2 and BASICA, however, strings have only 3-byte descriptors (with 1 byte to contain the length), so they are limited to 255 characters.
- LINE INPUT to Fixed-Length String Crashes QB.EXE Interpreter. Article number: Q27385. QuickBASIC 4.0 will hang if you use a fixed-length string variable as the input variable for a LINE INPUT statement. Microsoft fixed the problem in QuickBASIC 4.00b and Microsoft BASIC 6.0.

- EXE Can Hang Passing Dynamic String Array to Subprogram. Article number: Q27405. This problem does not occur when you compile programs from the QuickBASIC environment. Microsoft fixed the problem in QuickBASIC 4.00b and Microsoft BASIC 6.0.
- Out of String Space, Memory with Quick Library Can Hang QB. Article number: Q27544. If you've loaded a Quick library into the QuickBASIC environment and then run out of memory or string space, QuickBASIC might hang. Microsoft corrected this problem in QuickBASIC 4.00b and Microsoft BASIC 6.0.
- Fixed-Length String Illegal in FIELD: QB.EXE Wrongly Allows It. Article number: Q31506. You cannot use a fixed-length string in a FIELD statement (for use with random-access files). Although the BC.EXE compiler returns an error message in this case, the QuickBASIC editor does not warn you about the error. Microsoft fixed this in QuickBASIC 4.5.
- "Division By Zero" Dynamic, Fixed-Length STRING*1, 64 KB+ Array. Article number: Q38069. If you dimension a dynamic array of strings containing only one character to a size of 64 KB or larger, QuickBASIC returns a "Division by zero" error message. This problem exists through QuickBASIC 4.5 and Microsoft BASIC 6.00b but was corrected in Microsoft BASIC 7.0.
- FRE(–1), FRE("") Both Reduced by Run-Time String Allocation. Article number: Q41532. Because objects in the far heap (used for dynamic string allocation) can ultimately use space in the default data segment (DGROUP), the available space in the heap, reported by FRE(–1), is reduced accordingly as QuickBASIC stores variable-length strings or other variables in DGROUP. Similarly, objects in DGROUP can use space in the far heap.

Arrays and Data

- Reason for Unreadable Array Is QB.EXE in CALL to Quick Library. Article number: Q29934. When you pass a static array to a subprogram in a separately compiled source file, you must dimension the array in both the main source file and the subprogram source file. If you fail to do this and then compile from within the QuickBASIC environment, the data in the array might be unreadable. This problem occurs only in QuickBASIC 4.0 and Microsoft BASIC 6.0.
- Use ERASE to Reinitialize Array of User-Defined TYPE Records. Article number: Q31172. You can convert a large, user-defined record into an array and then use the ERASE statement to reinitialize all its fields quickly.
- "Duplicate Definition" on STATIC Array in Second CALL to SUB. Article number: Q31426. In a recursive subprogram or function (one that calls itself), you must avoid re-executing the code that dimensions a static array.

- Passing Array of TYPE or Fixed-Length Strings to SUBprogram. Article number: Q31557. You cannot pass an array of fixed-length strings directly to a subprogram or function. You can work around this by letting the subprogram access the array through a COMMON SHARED statement, by converting the array to an array of a user-defined type and then passing the array as that type, or by using a COMMON SHARED statement. This applies only to QuickBASIC 4.0, 4.00b, and 4.5, and Microsoft BASIC 6.0, and 7.0.
- "Overflow," "Subscript Out of Range," 32768+ Array Elements. Article number: Q32787. This article explains the situations that cause the most common array-related error messages.
- "Subscript Out of Range" DIM SHARED Dynamic Array in SUBprogram. Article number: Q33712. QuickBASIC returns a "Subscript out of range" error message if you attempt to dimension a dynamic array by using the $DYNAMIC metacommand and DIM SHARED statements at the module level (not the main module) of a program composed of subprograms (including libraries and Quick libraries). To work around the problem, dimension the array in the main module and pass it to the second module by using a COMMON SHARED statement.
- Cannot Pass More than 21 Dynamic Array Elements to Subprogram. Article number: Q34279.
- "Array Already Dimensioned" if 2nd DIM for Static Array in IF. Article number: Q35658. QuickBASIC processes DIM statements for static arrays at compile time even if the DIM statement is subject to an IF statement that would otherwise prevent it from being executed at runtime. If such a statement redimensions an array, QuickBASIC returns an "Array already dimensioned" error message.
- "Array Not Defined"; Must Dimension Array Above Its First Use. Article number: Q42474. Starting with QuickBASIC 4.0 and Microsoft BASIC 6.0, the statement that dimensions an array (that is not dynamically declared in a COMMON statement) must precede the first statement that refers to that array.
- Array in SUB Statement Doesn't Need Dimensions in Parentheses. Article number: Q47124. In QuickBASIC 3.0 and earlier, when you pass an array to a subprogram, you must specify the number of array dimensions in parentheses (such as *table(2)* for the two-dimensional array *table*). Starting with QuickBASIC 4.0 and Microsoft BASIC 6.0, you need only include empty parentheses (for example, *table*()).

Math

- Unexpected Result from CINT(.5) in QB87; IEEE Rounds to Even. Article number: Q23389. CINT rounds the fraction .5 to the nearest even integer; thus CINT(1.5) returns 2, but CINT(0.5) returns 0. (This even-number rounding also occurs with integer division assigned to an integer variable.) This behavior is consistent with

IEEE standards and applies to QuickBASIC 4.0 and 4.5, the coprocessor version of QuickBASIC 3.0, and Microsoft BASIC through version 7.0.

- RND and RANDOMIZE Alternatives for Generating Random Numbers. Article number: Q28150. This article describes the equation QuickBASIC uses to generate random numbers and lists sources of alternative methods.
- Converting Single to Double-Precision Produces Rounding Errors. Article number: Q33138. In QuickBASIC 3.0 and 4.0 and Microsoft BASIC 6.0, the CDBL function produces rounding errors when converting from single to double precision. This article recommends that instead of using CDBL, you convert the number to a string, append the # symbol, and then use VAL to convert the string back to a double-precision value.
- RANDOMIZE Statements Reseed but Don't Restart RND Sequence. Article number: Q36736. RANDOMIZE changes the seed for random numbers, but the next number you generate with RND will be at the current position in the new sequence rather than at the first number in the new sequence.

Simple I/O

- No Cursor Displayed in Graphics SCREENs 1, 2, 3, and 7 through 13. Article number: Q26088. The INKEY$ function displays a cursor only in screen mode 0.
- Colored Text in SCREEN 1 in QB Versions 2.x and 3.00, Not 4.00. Article number: Q26768. POKE statements used to change the color of text in versions of QuickBASIC earlier than 4.0 do not work in versions 4.0 and later; use the COLOR statement instead.
- How to INPUT Text without CTRL+BREAK Stopping Execution. Article number: Q37163. If you want to disable Ctrl-Break interrupts and handle events during input, avoid using the INPUT and LINE INPUT statements; instead, use the INKEY$ statement as shown in the article.
- LOCATE Must Place Cursor in VIEW PRINT Window or Line 25. Article number: Q38277. Despite the current VIEW PRINT setting, if the soft key display is off, you can access line 25 by using the LOCATE statement.

Trapping and Errors

- ERR Function Is Zeroed when It Is a Subprogram Watch Variable. Article number: Q27422. In QuickBASIC 4.0, using the ERR function as a watch variable inside a subprogram resets the value of ERR to 0 when an error trap occurs. Microsoft fixed this problem in QuickBASIC 4.00b.
- RESUME NEXT with Single-Line DEF FN RESUMEs Wrongly in QB.EXE. Article number: Q28037. An error in a single-line DEF FN function causes RESUME NEXT to return control to the wrong location in QuickBASIC 4.0 and Microsoft BASIC 6.0. Microsoft fixed this problem in QuickBASIC 4.5 and Microsoft BASIC 7.0.

- BASIC Example of CALL SetUEvent, ON UEVENT GOSUB Trapping. Article number: Q32164.
- CLEAR Resets ON ERROR GOTO and Turns Off Error Trapping. Article number: Q45451. After a CLEAR statement, you must execute an ON ERROR GOTO statement again to resume error trapping.
- ON TIMER Can Wrongly Trigger CALL SETUEVENT, ON UEVENT Trap. Article number: Q46182. You can't use timer and user-event trapping at the same time because after you call the SetUEvent statement all subsequent timer events trigger the UEVENT routine. This problem exists through QuickBASIC 4.5 and Microsoft BASIC 6.0. Microsoft fixed the problem in Microsoft BASIC 7.0.

Time

- DATE$, TIME$ in a Loop Can Push the System Time Backwards. Article number: Q25989. This problem occurs in MS-DOS versions 3.x when the date and time are repeatedly set in a loop.
- ON TIMER, then CHAIN, then TIMER ON Can Hang. Article number: Q27409. This problem occurred in QuickBASIC 4.0 and was fixed in QuickBASIC 4.00b and Microsoft BASIC 6.0.
- ON TIMER GOSUB Trapping Time Increments Smaller than 1 Second. Article number: Q37903. The shortest time that you can specify in a QuickBASIC timer event trap is 1 second. This article shows a technique for trapping events as often as every 1/30 of a second: use the ON PLAY statement to transfer control to a subroutine each time a short note (which might be silent) is played.
- TIME$ Problem in IF Statement at Midnight (24:00:00). Article number: Q44305. In the environment in QuickBASIC versions 4.0 and 4.5 and in Microsoft BASIC 7.0, the time 1/10 of a second before or after midnight can cause the TIME$ function to return an incorrect value.

Graphics

- Support for IBM EGA and Hercules Graphics Cards. Article number: Q21839. The EGA adapter is supported starting with QuickBASIC 2.0; Hercules is supported starting with 4.0. This article details all modes supported by these cards.
- How to Make MOUSE CALLs in Hercules Graphics Mode, SCREEN 3. Article number: Q30856. This article describes how you can make mouse calls in Hercules graphics mode. These calls change the shape of the cursor, detect the position of the cursor, detect mouse-button status, and so on.
- Create Your Own Non-ASCII Graphics Characters in CGA Graphics. Article number: Q35664. This article demonstrates how to define and use a RAM character set.

- Graphics GET and PUT Require Integer or LONG Array; Example. Article number: Q37308. If you do not use an integer or long-integer array with a GET or PUT statement, the resulting display will be distorted.
- How to Define Your Own Font in Graphics Mode for EGA or VGA. Article number: Q37343. This article shows how to define and use a RAM character set for EGA and VGA adapters.
- User-Defined Character Fonts for Hercules Graphics Mode. Article number: Q37475.
- Bibliography Reference for QuickBASIC: Graphics, Tutorials. Article number: Q37898. Lists useful books about computer graphics in general and QuickBASIC graphics in particular.
- QuickBASIC Program to Change the Mouse Shape in Graphics Mode. Article number: Q42587.
- Example of Graphics PUT on SCREEN 9 Using Bitmap DATA. Article number: Q43896.
- Graphics Algorithm Different in QuickBASIC Versus GW-BASIC. Article number: Q48058. QuickBASIC uses faster drawing techniques that can result in minor differences in appearance from displays generated with GW-BASIC.

Sound

- PLAY "X" Command Will Not Play More Than 16 Notes. Article number: Q22003. A PLAY statement that plays the notes specified in a string variable will play only 16 notes in QuickBASIC 2.0. Microsoft fixed this problem in QuickBASIC 2.01.
- PLAY "N0" First Note of Rest Clicks Speaker in QuickBASIC. Article number: Q22018.
- PLAY Commandstring Longer than 256 Characters Truncates Sound. Article number: Q26897. If you specify more than 256 characters in the command string for a PLAY statement in QuickBASIC 4.0, only as many commands are executed as the length exceeding 256. For example, in a string of 260 characters, only the first four commands are executed. This problem was corrected in QuickBASIC 4.00b and Microsoft BASIC 6.0. Note, however, that strings longer than 256 characters are not supported in versions earlier than QuickBASIC 4.0.

Light Pen and Joystick

- STICK Function Range Differs from BASICA. Article number: Q21887. The STICK function returns a smaller range of values in QuickBASIC than in BASICA. Therefore, your program should include a calibration routine that scales the values returned by STICK.

- Using PEN With Light Pen Instead of Mouse. Article number: Q21914. If you have a mouse driver installed, you must disable the driver with a call to mouse function 14 before you can use a light pen. Re-enable the driver with a call to mouse function 13.
- Using Joystick, STRIG(1) Incorrectly Returns 1, not −1. Article number: Q26895. In QuickBASIC 4.0 and Microsoft BASIC 6.0, when a joystick button is pressed, the STRIG function returns a 1 instead of a −1.
- PEN Function Returns Mouse Cursor Position in BASIC. Article number: Q32725. This article explains how you can use the PEN function to read the mouse position.
- PEN(5) Function in SCREEN 9 Only Returns 0 or 1 With Mouse. Article number: Q33044. In graphics screen modes 9, 10, 11, and 12, the PEN function returns a 0 or 1 rather than the *x*- and *y*- coordinates of the mouse cursor.

Keyboard

- Must Use A$=INKEY$ After SLEEP to Clear Keyboard Buffer. Article number: Q36397. This tip applies to QuickBASIC 4.0 (when the SLEEP statement was introduced), 4.5 and Microsoft BASIC 6.0 and 7.0.
- Example of Buffered Keyboard Input Using QuickBASIC. Article number: Q42949. This file shows you how to buffer and control keyboard input for applications (for QuickBASIC 2.0 and later).

Printer

- PRINT USING, LPRINT USING Decrease String Space. Article number: Q11319. The PRINT USING and LPRINT USING statements allocate a temporary string for formatting. (The small amount of space used seldom causes problems.)
- Faster Printing Disk File with SHELL "COPY X. PRN" vs. LPRINT. Article number: Q21851. Rather than reading individual lines from a disk file into a buffer and printing each line, you can use the SHELL statement to call the DOS COPY command to copy the file to the device PRN (the line printer). Of course, you can't control formatting when you use this method.
- Illegal Function Call Using LPRINT and SHELL. Article number: Q21970. In QuickBASIC versions 1.x and 2.0, QuickBASIC returns an "Illegal function call" or "Cannot find BRUN10.EXE" error message after you repeatedly use an LPRINT statement following a SHELL statement (such as in a loop). Microsoft fixed the problem in QuickBASIC 2.01.
- LPRINT Can Hang When Printer is Offline. Article number: Q25613. In QuickBASIC 2.x and 3.0, the system can hang if the printer is offline and you try to print by calling LPRINT. In QuickBASIC 2.x, a warm boot (Ctrl-Alt-Del) will

sometimes reset the system. This article supplies workarounds for early versions; Microsoft fixed the problem in QuickBASIC 4.0.

Communications Port

- Leaving Communications Port Lines ON Causes Problems. Article number: Q21788. In QuickBASIC 1.x, 2.x, and 3.00, if a program doesn't close communications lines when it exits, a subsequent program can have problems opening that port. In QuickBASIC 3.0, if a program exits after a "Device timeout" error occurs, the lines DTR and RTS are left on. QuickBASIC 4.0 and later versions clear these lines after a time-out, so the problem doesn't occur.
- Events to Either COM Port can Trigger Both Traps. Article number: Q21873. Microsoft fixed this problem in QuickBASIC 2.0.
- XON/XOFF Communications Protocol Not Supported in QuickBASIC. Article number: Q22019. No version of QuickBASIC or Microsoft BASIC supports the XON/XOFF handshaking protocol as part of the ASC option in the OPEN COM statement.
- "Device Unavailable" Error after OPEN COM1: then CHAIN. Article number: Q26475. Reopening the COM port in a chained-to program causes this error in QuickBASIC 4.0 and Microsoft BASIC 6.0. Microsoft fixed the problem in QuickBASIC 4.5 and Microsoft BASIC 6.00b.
- Serial Communications Port Not Restored after CTRL-BREAK. Article number: Q28147. This problem occurs in QuickBASIC 4.0 and Microsoft BASIC 6.0; Microsoft corrected it in QuickBASIC 4.5 and Microsoft BASIC 6.00b.
- Communications "Device Timeout": Increase CS and DS Time Limit. Article number: Q31432. If QuickBASIC returns a "Device Timeout" error message, try increasing the CS (Clear to Send) and DS (Data Set Ready) time limits in the OPEN COM statement.
- /C No Effect on Communications Receive Buffer in CHAINed Prog. Article number: Q32473. If you chain to a program that has a different buffer size (and the programs are compiled with the BRUN runtime module), the new program won't reset the buffer size. Compile both programs with the same /C command-line option.
- Communications (COM1:, COM2:) Receive Buffer Lost during CHAIN. Article number: Q34682. QuickBASIC clears the communications receive buffer when a program chains to another program; any data remaining in the buffer is lost. This problem occurs only in compiled executable programs in QuickBASIC 4.0 and 4.5 and Microsoft BASIC 6.0 and 6.00b. Microsoft fixed this problem in Microsoft BASIC 7.0.

- How to Solve Common QuickBASIC Communications Port Problems. Article number: Q39342. This article contains sample OPEN COM statements and offers advice for handling problems you might encounter.

Files

- INPUT# Does Not Input TABs. Article number: Q26081. The INPUT# statement reads the string returned from a TAB statement as a delimiter, so it does not insert tabs in the file.
- LINE INPUT#n Drops Null Characters from File; Use INPUT$. Article number: Q42669.
- How to Pipe (¦) Input into a QuickBASIC Program. Article number: Q46376. This article shows how to use the DOS (and OS/2) piping feature to send output from one program to a QuickBASIC program as input.

DOS and Program Management

- KEY, then CHAIN Causes "String Heap Corrupted." Article number: Q12026. In QuickBASIC 2.0, executing a CHAIN statement directly after a KEY statement causes an error. This problem was fixed in QuickBASIC 2.01.
- CLEAR Should Not be Used in Event Trap. Article number: Q12074. If you use the CLEAR statement in an event trap (code specified by an ON statement), QuickBASIC returns an "Illegal function call" error message.
- "String Space Corrupt" after CHAIN, CALLing User Library. Article number: Q21958. In QuickBASIC 2.0, QuickBASIC returns a "String space corrupt" error message when a chained-to program calls a program in a user library. Microsoft fixed this problem in QuickBASIC 2.01.
- ENVIRON Statement Produces "Out of Memory" Error Message. Article number: Q21963. The ENVIRON statement frequently produces an "Out of memory" error message due to the limited size of the DOS environment area. The article discusses how to increase the environment size.
- Using CLEAR Inside FOR...NEXT or WHILE...WEND loops. Article number: Q22032. Do not use the CLEAR statement inside a loop because CLEAR initializes the loop counter to the value 0, creating an infinite loop.
- 1040 Bytes Lost in Each CHAIN Compiled with BCOM. Article number: Q26084. This problem occurred in QuickBASIC 3.0 and was fixed in QuickBASIC 4.0.
- "Out of Memory," "Error R6005," with CHAIN/RUN in DOS 2.X. Article number: Q26677. This problem occurs only with DOS 2.x.
- "String Space Corrupt" with CHAIN, CLEAR, and KEY in QB 4.00. Article number: Q27395. In executable files developed in QuickBASIC 4.0, if you chain from a program that redefines a function key to a program that uses a CLEAR statement

and then redefines the same function key, QuickBASIC returns a "String space corrupt" error message. Microsoft fixed the problem in QuickBASIC 4.00b and Microsoft BASIC 6.0.

- CHAIN gives "Illegal Function Call" Error After CHDIR. Article number: Q28594. If you execute a CHAIN statement after a CHDIR statement, QuickBASIC might return an "Illegal function call" error message. This problem occurred in QuickBASIC 4.0 and Microsoft BASIC 6.0 and was fixed in QuickBASIC 4.00b and Microsoft BASIC 6.00b.
- CHAIN or RUN in Quick Library hangs QB.EXE Editor. Article number: Q28732. This problem occurred in QuickBASIC 4.0 and was fixed in QuickBASIC 4.00b and Microsoft BASIC 6.0.
- "RETURN without GOSUB" when ON ERROR and CHAIN in 4.00b. Article number: Q33621. In QuickBASIC 4.00b and 4.5 and Microsoft BASIC 6.0 and 6.00b, chaining to a program that uses ON ERROR GOTO can generate a "RETURN without GOSUB" error message unless you compile both programs with the same switches or you use the /O switch for the first program. This problem does not occur with programs executed from within the QuickBASIC environment. Microsoft fixed this problem in Microsoft BASIC 7.0.
- COMMON SHARED problem with Period in Variable after CHAIN. Article number: Q33622. If you use a period in a variable name (including an array name), QuickBASIC might not pass the variable to a chained program; this is more likely if the name without the period duplicates another variable name. This problem occurs in the QuickBASIC environment with 4.00b and 4.5, but it doesn't occur in QuickBASIC 4.0 or if you run the program from an executable file. QuickBASIC fixed this problem in Microsoft BASIC 7.0.
- CHAIN, RUN, and KILL Statements Do Not Use MS-DOS Search PATH. Article number: Q33736. The CHAIN, RUN, and KILL statements do not use the path specified in the DOS PATH environment variable; you must either use the current directory or specify the full pathname.
- CHAIN "RETURN without GOSUB" when Using ON ERROR GOTO and No /O. Article number: Q37483. If you chain from a program that does not trap errors with ON ERROR GOTO to a program that does, QuickBASIC might display a "RETURN without GOSUB" error when the program is compiled to use the BRUN4x.EXE runtime library. To correct this, either compile both programs with the /E switch (to support error trapping) or compile both programs with the /O switch (to make them stand-alone, executable files). Microsoft fixed this problem in Microsoft BASIC 7.0.
- CLEAR Resets ON ERROR GOTO and Turns Off Error Trapping. Article number: Q45451.

Port and Memory

- DEF SEG and PEEK Inside a FUNCTION Can Fail in QB Editor. Article number: Q27485. A PEEK function in a program in the QuickBASIC 4.0 environment can return old values rather than new values. This problem doesn't occur in executable files. Microsoft fixed the problem in QuickBASIC 4.00b and Microsoft BASIC version 6.0.
- How to Calculate Absolute Address; DEF SEG and PEEK Example. Article number: Q41531. The article explains how addresses are constructed in the PC from segment and offset and shows how you can calculate an absolute address.

Mixed Language

- QuickBASIC 4.x, BASIC 6.00 Can CAll C, FORTRAN, Pascal, MASM. Article number: Q21821. This article explains how you can call routines in these Microsoft languages from QuickBASIC.
- Passing Numeric Variables between BASIC and C by Far Reference. Article number: Q27324.
- Example Passing Near Numeric Variables between BASIC and C. Article number: Q27325.
- Passing BASIC Variable-Length String to C by Far Reference. Article number: Q27326.
- Passing COMMON Variables from BASIC to C by Far Reference. Article number: Q27327.
- Passing BASIC String Descriptor to C. Article number: Q31583.
- Example of Passing Fixed-Length Strings from C to BASIC. Article number: Q47348.
- Example of C Function Returning a String to BASIC. Article number: Q47756.
- Example of Passing Strings from C to BASIC. Article number: Q48207.

Metacommands

- "$INCLUDE File Access Error" Referencing Subdirectory with "." Article number: Q22039. QuickBASIC returns an error message if you use a directory name that includes a period in a path to an include file. Microsoft fixed the problem in QuickBASIC 2.01.
- "DECLARE Must Precede Executable Statements," Editing $INCLUDE. Article number: Q26487. In the QuickBASIC 4.0 environment, you can't edit an include file if the $INCLUDE statement occurs after an executable statement in the main program and the $INCLUDE file contains a call to an external routine (for example, in a library). Microsoft fixed this problem in QuickBASIC 4.00b and Microsoft BASIC 6.0.

- $INCLUDE with DATA Statements in SUB May Hang QB.EXE Editor. Article number: Q43791. Always place DATA statements at module level, never within subprograms or functions.
- Set Paths Menu in QB 4.50 Finds $INCLUDE and Library Files. Article number: Q45051. This new menu feature lets you specify the directories that QuickBASIC searches for executable, help, include, and library files.
- Reasons for "File Not Found" Error Using $INCLUDE Metacommand. Article number: Q50219.

Debugging

- Using Watch Variables in a CHAINed Program. Article number: Q23414. In QuickBASIC 3.0, chaining a program causes QuickBASIC to lose track of watch variables; therefore you cannot define new watch variables until you restart QuickBASIC. Microsoft fixed this problem in QuickBASIC 4.0, but you still must redefine watch variables after a program calls the CHAIN statement.
- "No Symbolic Information" Debugging QuickBASIC with CodeView. Article number: Q32498. This article explains how to avoid this error so that you can use the CodeView debugging application with QuickBASIC.

Note: You can find additional articles and examples in the CIS MSSYS Forum, QuickBASIC library; search under the keyword BAS2C.

APPENDIX B

CompuServe Files

Selected Files from CompuServe

This appendix lists some of the QuickBASIC and assembly-language source files available in the Microsoft Systems forum (GO MSSYS) and the Microsoft Software library (GO MSL) on the CompuServe Information Service (CIS). Many of these online treasures can be downloaded from CompuServe to your system. You'll find routines that create windows and menus, utilities that convert a program in one version of QuickBASIC to another, assembly-language routines that are quicker than the corresponding QuickBASIC commands, and even a library of math routines.

Unless otherwise specified, the following files are from the QuickBASIC data library in the MSSYS (Microsoft Systems) forum on CIS. Also, be sure to check the Microsoft Software library for files officially released by Microsoft. Various IBM and Macintosh programming forums contain additional files.

The following files are organized according to the chapters of this book, starting with general files that apply to QuickBASIC as a whole. Not all chapters are used to group these files because some general language features (such as IF statements) are used in nearly all programs, although no program features them in particular. Certainly, many new files will have been added by the time you see this book.

Note that many of these files are available on other online information services (such as GEnie and BIX) or on bulletin boards. In addition, many compiled BASIC programs (executable files) are also available. We have listed only source files here because of their value as examples for QuickBASIC programmers. The files with the extension ARC or ZIP are archived files that might contain the contents of more than one file. You must use utilities such as PKXARC and PKUNZIP to translate the archived files to their original form.

General

- ADVBAS.ARC. Contains routines that perform disk management, communications, mouse functions, string handling, array handling, window creation, and other tasks.
- BAS2QB.ARC. Converts unstructured BASIC programs into structured QuickBASIC programs.
- BAS2SB.ARC. Converts unstructured BASIC programs into structured QuickBASIC programs.

- FASTQL.ZIP. Speeds the creation of Quick libraries; for QuickBASIC 4.0 and later.
- MAKEQL.ZIP. Scans a QuickBASIC program and creates a Quick library of only those external routines that the program uses.
- QBAUTO. Compiles large sets of QuickBASIC source files; useful for large scale program development.
- QBMP40.ARC. Generates complete cross-reference listings of variables and procedures in a QuickBASIC program.
- QBSAMP.ARC. Provides several routines that solve various hardware problems involving printers and graphics displays.
- QB34MG.ARC. Converts a QuickBASIC 3.0 program to 4.0, replaces DEF FN statements with FUNCTION statements, and lets you split the program into separate modules.
- READRL.BAS. Enables QuickBASIC to read RLE Vidtex graphics files, which have the extension RLE.

Decisions and Operators

- DECIDE.BAS. Helps a QuickBASIC program quantify decisions.
- FUZZY.BAS. Enables QuickBASIC to use "fuzzy set theory" to make decisions based on nonspecific conditions.

Strings

- BASLNK.ARC. Provides suggestions for ways to develop list-processing facilities (a sophisticated extension of dynamic strings) in QuickBASIC.
- BASLNK.THD. Contains a discussion of string space and list management by QuickBASIC experts.
- DMENU.ARC. Writes a string to the video display in color; useful for menu bars.
- EDITOR.ARC. Contains an editor that lets you edit the strings your program uses.
- HLIGHT.ARC. Displays strings with substrings highlighted in color; useful for moving highlights in a menu and for similar tasks.
- NUVAL.ARC. Replaces the QuickBASIC VAL function; works with long-integer values.
- SOUNDE.ZIP. Provides routines that let you determine the SOUNDEX code for a string. SOUNDEX codes permit the matching of strings that are only approximately the same (having a misspelled or incomplete search string).
- TITLEG.BAS. Generates QuickBASIC and assembly-language source code for displaying a 5-row-by-5-column character string using the ASCII extended character set; for titles, banners, and so on.

Arrays and Data

- DATABA.ARC. Implements a menu-driven database with indexing and dynamic arrays in memory.
- QSORT.BAS. Sorts a one-dimensional or two-dimensional array of strings using a quicksort algorithm.
- SBSP2.PIT. Creates a MiniFinder-like window with the sorted contents of any string array; for Macintosh BASIC 3.0. (Shareware)
- SBSP3.PIT. Provides low-level utilities that include string handlers; for Macintosh BASIC 3.0. (Shareware)

Math

- BCDBAS.ARC. Provides a library of binary-coded decimal math routines; addition, subtraction, multiplication, and division are accurate to 80 significant digits. (Shareware: CIS, MSSYS forum, BASIC library)
- RANDI.ARC. Generates random integers; faster than the QuickBASIC RND function. (CIS, Microsoft Software library)
- TRIG.ARC. Defines versions of trigonometry functions that accept input in degrees rather than in radians (unlike the standard QuickBASIC trigonometry functions); also provides arcsine and arccosine functions. (CIS, MSSYS forum, BASIC library)

Simple I/O

- MYED.ARC. Provides a small text editor; can be memory resident. (Shareware)
- POPUPS.ZIP. Defines a pop-up windowing system; includes mouse support.
- PPWN20.ARC. Provides extensive routines that create and manipulate pop-up windows; excerpted from a shareware product.
- QBINKY.ARC. Provides full-screen field-editing routines for controlling user input.
- QBMENU.ZIP. Creates 1-line menus.
- SBSP1.PIT. Generates formatted text output (including multiple columns) for Macintosh BASIC 3.0. (Shareware)

Trapping and Errors

- ADLN15.ARC. Adds line numbers to a QuickBASIC program; lets you use the ERL function for trapping and pinpointing errors.
- CBSF20.ARC. Numbers source code lines; also creates a cross-reference list of variables and procedures.

- ERRLEV.ARC. Provides routines (in an object file) for setting the DOS ERRORLEVEL from a QuickBASIC program; useful for making utility programs that work with batch files.
- RTNCOD.ARC. Sets ERRORLEVEL codes.

Time

- QBDATE.ARC. Converts a date from string to integer and vice versa (including spelled-out versions of dates); assembly-language code.
- SYSTIX.ARC. Replaces the TIMER function with a long-integer version, which is faster because it requires no floating-point math.

Graphics

- BLACK1.ARC and BLACK2.ARC. Displays a rectangular grid "distorted by the gravity of a black hole"; a good illustration of graphics programming.
- EGASAV.BAS. Loads and saves EGA screens in screen modes 7 through 10.
- HRCDMP.ARC. Provides a utility to print screen dumps from a Hercules graphics screen to an Epson-compatible or HP Laserjet printer.
- IFS.ARC. Generates fractal images; uses a new, fast algorithm.
- PSETMA.ARC. Plots pixels for QuickBASIC; reportedly 30 percent faster than the QuickBASIC 4.0 PRESET and PSET statements.
- QBFONT.LST. Discusses and demonstrates how to use different fonts with systems that have QuickBASIC 4.0 or 4.5 and a Hercules graphics card.
- SCRSAV.ARC. Provides screen-save routines and screen-restore routines; includes assembly-language source and object code.
- VIDCMP.TXT. Lists the video cards that were tested for compatibility with QuickBASIC 4.5 prior to its release.
- VIDEO.ARC. Provides device-independent routines for color; includes adapter-type detection.

Light Pen and Joystick

No files were found for the light pen or joystick, but here are some window, mouse, and menu-related files.

- MICES.ARC. Implements selection bar menus styled after those used by Lotus Development Corporation; has mouse and keyboard support.
- MOUSE.ARC. Implements as many as 6 pull-down menus; menus remain down while the mouse button is pressed.
- POPMSE.ARC. Provides a set of routines that implement menu windows that support keyboard or mouse selection.

- QBMOUS.ARC. Demonstrates techniques for programming the mouse.

Keyboard

- EDIINP.ARC. Lets a user edit input on a single line.
- INT09.ARC. Provides a replacement keyboard-interrupt handler for use with hardware that doesn't work properly with QuickBASIC's built-in keyboard handler.
- QBUTIL.ARC. Provides various routines, including one that handles input from an enhanced keyboard.

Printer

- BCDBAS.ARC. Provides a library containing a function that formats a number according to the rules for PRINT USING (or LPRINT USING) so that you can assign the result to a variable for later use.
- BIGPRT.ARC. Demonstrates how to output large, block letters to the screen or to a printer.
- HRCDMP.ARC. Provides a utility to print screens from a Hercules graphics screen; supports Epson and HP LaserJet printers and includes a description of the Hercules graphics card memory.
- PINIT.ARC. Lets you initialize the printer port from a QuickBASIC program.
- PR.BAS. Provides an enhanced version of Microsoft's PRINT statement.
- PSOUT.TXT. Lets a QuickBASIC program output custom PostScript commands to the LaserWriter using AppleTalk; written in Macintosh BASIC 3.0. (CIS, MSSYS forum, Macintosh BASIC library)
- QBSAMP.ARC. Provides sample programs for sending Hercules graphics screens to Epson and HP Laserjet printers.
- SBSP1.PIT. Performs formatted printing on the Macintosh. (CIS, MSSYS forum, Macintosh BASIC library)

Communications

- DIALER.ARC. Demonstrates and describes MicroHelp's Stay-Res product, which lets you convert QuickBASIC programs into memory-resident utilities; the demonstration program displays a pop-up window and dials numbers on the modem.
- MSCOM1.TXT. Explains how to use the Apple modem with Microsoft QuickBASIC for the Macintosh.
- QBPRO6.ARC. Describes MicroHelp's communications library for QuickBASIC.

Files

- CRCTST.ARC. Demonstrates calculations of checksums (CRC); useful for communications routines and for verifying disk operations.

- DB.ARC. Reads a dBASE III file header and displays the record structure.
- FORMAT.BAS. Provides replacement routines for the PRINT USING and PRINT # USING statements that assign formatted data to a string variable rather than outputting it; you can then perform further formatting on the variable.
- INDEX.ARC. Provides subprograms that index and manage binary (B-tree) files.
- PD.ZIP. Provides a phone-directory program to demonstrate the editing of random-access database files.
- QBCOPY.ARC. Provides routines that copy files from within QuickBASIC programs; supports wildcards.
- QBDB3.ARC. Reads, writes, creates, and lists the structure of dBASE III files from QuickBASIC 3.0.
- QB4-BT.MSG. Provides demonstration routines for using QuickBASIC 4.0 with BTRIEVE.
- QB4INP.ARC. Provides input routines for numeric data types, for QuickBASIC 4.0 or later.

DOS and Program Management

- ASMDIR.ARC. Provides assembly-language and QuickBASIC routines that read DOS disk directories into a string array.
- ATDIR.ARC. Demonstrates the use of the DOS find first, find next, and other directory-related functions; uses the INTERRUPT and INTERRUPTX statements.
- CHNFIX.ARC. Fixes the problems that occur when a very small program chains to a large program in QuickBASIC 4.0 (using the command-line compiler BC.EXE) and Microsoft BASIC 6.0.
- DSKFLAG.ARC. Illustrates how to monitor disk space usage. (Shareware: CIS, Microsoft Software library)
- D-VER1.ARC. Generates a 2-column disk directory display with enhanced features.
- EXISTS.ARC. Determines whether a file exists.
- FASTQL.ZIP. Lets you build and list Quick libraries and extract routines from them.
- PCSYS2.EXE. Displays many system statistics (such as RAM allocation) using graphics displays.
- QBDIR.ARC. Reads DOS disk directories into a string array.
- WHEREA.BAS. Lets you determine in which directory a file resides.

Port and Memory

- IRQ.BAS. Demonstrates how to service hardware interrupts from QuickBASIC.
- QBBITS.ARC. Provides bit-manipulation routines (assembly-language source and object files) for QuickBASIC.

Mixed Language

- BASFOR.ARC. Provides sample programs that illustrate how to call FORTRAN routines from QuickBASIC.
- BASICC.ARC. Provides routines that pass variables between QuickBASIC and C.
- BASICF.ARC. Provides sample programs that call FORTRAN routines from QuickBASIC.
- BASPAS.ARC. Provides sample programs that illustrate how to call PASCAL routines from QuickBASIC.
- BASTOC.ARC. Provides sample programs that illustrate how to call C routines from QuickBASIC.
- C2QB.TXT. Provides sample programs that call QuickBASIC routines from a C program.

APPENDIX C

Third-Party Routines

Third-Party Add-Ons for QuickBASIC

At one time the only BASIC programmers were university students and novice hackers. Today, BASIC has evolved into QuickBASIC and Microsoft BASIC 7.0, systems used by professional programmers.

These languages include all the keywords you need to write any function; however, generating your own input routines, custom sorts, menu systems, and so on requires a lot of effort. These are not trivial tasks, and debugging the routines can consume many hours. You can save yourself a lot of trouble by supplementing your code with routines from QuickBASIC toolkits and libraries that are sold by independent, third-party developers. These libraries complement QuickBASIC's own keywords, extending the limits of the language to make it faster and more versatile. Some libraries offer complete interface packages; some packages include routines to use when writing TSR (terminate-and-stay-resident) programs in QuickBASIC; some individual routines augment BASIC by providing better error handling, more control over variables, and added features such as mouse support and menus.

Usually, your QuickBASIC program can call these third-party subroutines by using a simple statement such as *CALL LibRoutine(var).*

Third-party routines offer you many benefits: They save you development and debugging time; they help you avoid rewriting code for often-used operations; and they make your programs faster and smaller. They also make your programs more efficient because subroutine libraries are usually written in assembly language, Pascal, C, or a mixture of BASIC and one of these languages. The code has already been debugged, and most third-party vendors provide excellent technical support. Third-party routines also provide an educational benefit—many vendors include source code so that you can see how the routines are constructed.

This appendix provides an overview of some useful and interesting routines from the three most popular third-party routine vendors: Crescent Software, of Stamford, Connecticut; MicroHelp, Inc., of Roswell, Georgia; and Hammerly Computer Services, Inc., of Laurel, Maryland. Their offerings are grouped in the same functional categories as the rest of the topics in this book. The following sections discuss the most interesting routines and describe how to use them in your programs.

Types and Variables

As QuickBASIC compiles your programs, it creates the appropriate machine-language statements to handle all variable assignments and comparisons. In most cases, this code is very efficient and cannot be improved by add-on library routines. One exception, however, is QuickBASIC's handling of comparisons between different variables of a single user-defined type.

Comparing Variables of a User-Defined Type

QuickBASIC lets you freely compare numeric and string variables and then perform an action based on the result. However, you cannot compare variables of a user-defined type even if they are of the same type. If you execute the following statement, for example, QuickBASIC returns a "Type mismatch" error message:

```
IF typeVar1 = typeVar2 THEN PRINT "They are the same."
```

The only solution in QuickBASIC is to compare each field of the record variables separately; however, this quickly becomes cumbersome and generates unnecessary code:

```
IF typeVar1.intPart = typeVar2.intPart AND _
    typeVar1.sglPrec = typeVar2.sglPrec AND _
    typeVar1.dblPrec = typeVar2.dblPrec THEN PRINT "They are the same."
```

The QuickPak Professional package, from Crescent Software, provides a function that overcomes this limitation and is fully compatible with QuickBASIC's own comparisons. The *CompareT* function accepts three arguments—the two type variables being compared and their length, in bytes. *CompareT* simply compares all of the bytes in each variable, without regard to their meaning. The syntax is as follows:

CompareT%(*typeVar1*, *typeVar2*, *length*)

Overcoming the Size Barrier

The QuickPak Professional package also provides a new data type—very long integers. Very long integers have an impressive range: from –9223372036854775808 through +9223372036854775807. The routines *VLAdd*, *VLSub*, *VLMul*, and *VLDiv*, provided in QuickPak Professional, add, subtract, multiply, and divide very long integers.

The Mach 2 package, from MicroHelp, Inc., offers huge string arrays, which store a large number of strings more efficiently than QuickBASIC does. The *MhStore* procedure stores and retrieves huge string arrays, *MhOrder* sorts huge string arrays, *MhSrch* searches huge string arrays, and *MhEms* stores huge string arrays in LIM EMS memory.

Strings

QuickBASIC offers many advantages over other high-level programming languages, the most important being its support for variable-length strings. Unlike C and Pascal, which require the programmer to specify the length of all strings when writing the program, QuickBASIC lets you instead create strings as the program runs. Furthermore, a program can shorten, extend, or even erase strings if they are no longer needed. Unfortunately, the penalty for this luxury is that string operations in QuickBASIC are slower than in many other languages. Third-party routines let you overcome this obstacle.

Improving QuickBASIC's String Handling

String functions in QuickBASIC are generally slower than subroutines because memory is always allocated to hold the function's output. QB/Pro Volume 2, from MicroHelp, contains replacement routines for LEFT$, MID$, RIGHT$, and several related functions. Because these routines do not create new strings in memory, as their QuickBASIC counterparts do, they can operate more quickly. The following lines show the syntax for three of these routines:

CALL MhLeftString(*dest$*, *source$*, *numChars*)
CALL MhMidString(*dest$*, *destStart*, *numChars*, *source$*, *sourceStart*)
CALL MhRightString(*dest$*, *source$*, *numChars*)

Searching Backward for a Substring

QuickBASIC's INSTR function provides a fast way to determine whether one string occurs within another and, if so, where the substring begins. However, INSTR always searches from the beginning of the string, which precludes quickly finding the last occurrence of a character or substring.

QB/Pro Volume 2 includes the *MhBackwardInstr* routine, which serves the same purpose as INSTR except that it searches in a backward direction, beginning at the last element in the string. (The package includes a second, case-insensitive, version—*MhBackwardInstrNotSensitive.*) Searching backward is particularly valuable when you are parsing filenames to isolate the pathname from the rest of the name. Without this routine, you must use a FOR loop to step backward looking for a backslash as follows:

```
FOR x = LEN(filename$) TO 1 STEP -1
    IF MID$(filename$, x, 1) = "\" THEN       ' look for the last backslash
        path$ = LEFT$(filename$, x)           ' extract drive and path
        filename$ = MID$(filename$, x + 1)    ' extract the filename
        EXIT FOR
    END IF
NEXT
```

MhBackwardInstr lets you replace this loop with a single call such as:

```
CALL MhBackwardInstr(found, start, fileName$, "\")
```

In this example, the statement returns the position of the substring \ in *found; start* specifies where in the source string to begin searching (referenced from the end of the string); *fileName$* is the string you are searching within; and the backslash is the substring you want to locate.

Formatting a Value into a String Variable

QuickBASIC's PRINT USING statement is an extremely valuable feature of the language because it lets you round, format, and display values to a specified number of decimal places. Unfortunately, QuickBASIC provides no simple way to assign the formatted value to a string variable. QuickPak Professional contains the *FUsing* (formatted using) function, which returns a formatted string representation of a numeric value. You invoke *FUsing* by using the following syntax:

value$ = FUsing$(STR$(*number*), *mask$*)

FUsing accepts most of the formatting codes that PRINT USING supports, as the following table shows:

Character	Description
#	Represents a single numeric digit
.	Marks the position of the decimal point within a numeric field
+	Displays the sign of both positive and negative numbers
**	Fills any leading spaces with asterisks
$$	Appends a single dollar sign immediately to the left of the number
**$	Combines the effects of ** and $$
,	Inserts a comma in front of every third digit

Avoiding Errors Caused by ASC

One of the limitations of QuickBASIC's ASC function is that it generates an "Illegal function call" error message if you try to use it with a null string. The usual way to avoid this error is to include an extra test for a null string by using the LEN function.

QuickPak Professional provides the *ASCII* function to replace ASC, and it returns a value of –1 if the string is null. Thus you need not check to see whether the specified string is null.

Soundex Routines that Match Similar Strings

Mach 2 offers the *MhSndx* routine, which derives the "Soundex" code from a string. Soundex is an established technique that lets you compare two strings (such as names) to see whether they sound alike. *MhSndx* requires two parameters—the string to be examined and a 5-character string that receives the Soundex code, as the following statements show:

```
code$ = SPACE$(5)                   ' create room for the returned code
CALL MhSndx(work$, code$)           ' translate work$ to Soundex code
```

To use the subroutine, you must convert both strings to their Soundex equivalents and then use INSTR to see whether they are the same (or nearly the same), as shown below. If either string appears within the other one, the two strings sound alike.

```
code1$ = SPACE$(5)                 ' make room for the returned codes
code2$ = SPACE$(5)

CALL MhSndx(work1$, code1$)      ' convert both strings to Soundex
CALL MhSndx(work2$, code2$)
same = INSTR(code1$, code2$)     ' see whether code1$ is in code2$
IF same = 0 THEN same = INSTR(code2$, code1$)    ' check if code2$ is in code1$
```

Formatting Hexadecimal Numbers

QuickBASIC provides the HEX$ function to return the hexadecimal equivalent of any number. However, HEX$ returns only as many character positions as it needs to represent the number. If you need to print a group of hexadecimal values in a table, the necessary formatting can quickly get out of hand. QuickPak Professional includes the *QPHex$* function, which lets you specify the number of character positions to fill. This way, all values displayed at the same column position on the screen are lined up correctly.

Arrays and Data

Although QuickBASIC has many array-manipulation capabilities, some third-party routines can help you sort and search arrays as well as store string data outside of QuickBASIC's limited, 64-KB string memory. The subroutines in this section are merely a sampling of the many capabilities that these add-on packages provide.

Sorting Arrays

Mach 2 includes several assembly-language routines for sorting any type of data array in memory. You can, of course, sort and search arrays by using only QuickBASIC; however, assembly-language routines are much faster. The following lines show the syntax of the *MhISort*, *MhLSort*, and *MhSPSort* routines, which sort integer, long-integer, and single-precision arrays:

> CALL MhISort(*dataSeg*, *work$*, *offset*, *total*)
> CALL MhLSort(*dataSeg*, *work$*, *offset*, *total*)
> CALL MhSPSort(*dataSeg*, *work$*, *offset*, *total*)

dataSeg is the segment of memory that contains the first element of the array; *work$* is a temporary string that you must provide as a work space for the routine; *offset* is the address within the array at which to begin sorting; and *total* is the total number of elements to sort.

Bit Arrays

Many languages, such as C and Pascal, support "short" integer variables, which occupy only 1 byte of memory. The smallest variable that QuickBASIC can accommodate is an integer, which uses 2 bytes. QuickPak Professional contains routines for manipulating "bit" arrays that use only 1 bit per element. If your program needs only a simple true or false flag, using a conventional integer variable wastes 15 bits. One application for a bit array might be to flag which employees in a list of names are eligible for a raise. Another might indicate which records in a database file should be deleted. Using bit arrays lets you store a great deal of information in a small amount of memory.

DimBits dimensions a "bit" array, and *SetBit* and *GetBit* assign and retrieve individual bit elements. The routines store the elements in a string, which lets you easily dimension and erase the arrays. The calling syntax for these routines is shown in the following lines:

CALL DimBits(*array$*, *numElements*)
CALL SetBit(*array$*, *element*, *bit*)
value% = GetBit%(*array$*, *element*)

Storing String Array Data in Far Memory

One of the limitations of the IBM PC family of computers is its 64-KB size limit for variables and other data. Although QuickBASIC supports "huge" numeric arrays that can occupy all available DOS memory (up to 640 KB), string data is limited to a total of about 40 KB (less if a program uses many variables).

The Mach 2 package includes a complete set of routines for storing strings and very large string arrays in dynamic (far) memory (or even in expanded memory if it is present). (In this context, far memory is the memory located outside of QuickBASIC's default, 64-KB data segment.) These routines include *MhStringStore*, *MhStringInsert*, and *MhStringFetch*; other routines are provided to search and sort string arrays that reside in far memory. You might use these routines to store a large number of strings in a program such as a word processor, which must manipulate blocks of text, or a database, which uses strings to hold many records in memory at once. The calling syntax for these routines is shown in the following lines:

CALL MhStringStore(*arrayNum*, *element*, *lin$*, *errCode*)
CALL MhStringInsert(*arrayNum*, *element*, *lin$*, *errCode*)
CALL MhStringFetch(*chars*, *arrayNum*, *element*, *lin$*, *errCode*)

arrayNum is the array being accessed (0 through 19); *element* is the number of the string array element; *lin$* is the "near" string being stored or retrieved; and *errCode* indicates whether an error occurred.

Searching Arrays

Many applications need to be able to search string arrays quickly. QuickPak Professional includes several fast assembly-language routines that can search all or part of a string array, either distinguishing or ignoring capitalization. Because the routines can search without regard to capitalization, all possible matches are found. Routines are provided for performing both regular and fixed-length string searches that are either forward or backward and either case sensitive or case insensitive. You can also use the question-mark (?) wildcard character to match any single character. The calling syntax for two of these routines are as follows:

CALL Find2(*array$(start)*, *numElements*, *search$*)
CALL FindTB(*typeArray*(*lastElement*), *elementSize*, *numElements*, *search$*)

QuickPak Professional also includes routines that search any type of numeric array either for exact matches or for values that are equal to or greater than—or equal to or less than—a specific value.

Indexed Array Sorting

In many situations a program must present data in sorted order. However, sometimes you might want to access the array in sorted order without actually changing the array elements in memory. ProBas, from Hammerly Computer Services, includes routines that can manipulate an array of indexes (called pointers) containing the element numbers that correspond to those in the primary array. Note that sorting a table of integers (the integer indexes) is often faster than sorting the data. The following example shows the syntax of the ProBas *IPtrSort* routine, which performs an indexed sort on an integer array:

CALL IPtrSort(*dSegment*, *dOffset*, *pSegment*, *pOffset*, *count*)

dSegment and *dOffset* indicate where the primary data array is located in memory; *pSegment* and *pOffset* specify the index, or pointer, array; and *count* is the number of elements to consider in the sort. After the array has been sorted, you access each element by referring to its corresponding element in the index array, as the following program segment shows.

```
FOR x = 1 TO count              ' walk through the entire array
    PRINT array%(x)             ' display the original order
    PRINT array%(index%(x))     ' display the sorter order via the index
NEXT
```

Inserting and Deleting Array Elements

The only way you can use QuickBASIC commands to insert or delete a new element from an array is by using a FOR...NEXT statement. This is an extremely slow method, especially when many elements are involved.

QB/Pro Volume 1, from MicroHelp, includes several fast assembly-language routines that can insert or delete individual elements from any type of array. By using assembly language, these routines avoid the usual time-consuming overhead that QuickBASIC imposes and insert or delete the array element many times faster than an equivalent FOR...NEXT statement can. Two of these routines, *MhStringArrayInsert* and *MhStringArrayDelete*, are called with the following syntax:

CALL MhStringArrayInsert(*array$*(0), *total*, *insertElement*)
CALL MhStringArrayDelete(*array$*(0), *total*, *deleteElement*)

array$ is the name of the string array; *total* is the number of elements in the array, and *insertElement* or *deleteElement* is the number of the element to be inserted or deleted.

Sorting Based on More Than One Key

Sometimes you might want to sort an array based on more than one key. For example, you might first need to sort by a customer's last name, then by the last date a payment was made, and finally by the amount of money that is currently owed. QuickPak Professional includes the *KeySort* routine to let you sort a QuickBASIC array based on any number of keys. You must specify six pieces of information when calling *KeySort*—the array, the size of each element, the number of elements in the array, the type of data in each key, the sort direction (ascending or descending), and the number of sort keys. Because the number of sort keys will vary, the information about each key (the type of data in each key and the sort direction for the key) must be stored in a two-dimensional array. The calling syntax for *KeySort* is as follows:

CALL KeySort(*array*(*lowest*), *elSize*, *numEls*, *table*(1, 1), *numberOfKeys*)

Math

QuickBASIC provides a wealth of math capabilities suitable for both elementary calculations and sophisticated engineering problems. Third-party vendors, however, provide even more mathematical power. The following section describes a useful example.

A Spreadsheet Program in QuickBASIC

The SPREAD.BAS subprogram, from Crescent Software, provides a complete functional spreadsheet that you can incorporate into your own programs. This program has the "look and feel" of Lotus 1-2-3 and offers variable column widths, a resizeable window, cell editing, GOTO, and manual recalculation. Unlike 1-2-3, however, SPREAD is not a cell interpreter. That is, the user cannot enter or edit spreadsheet formulas; instead, spreadsheet formulas are hard-coded into the program.

You use six parameters to pass information between the main program and the spreadsheet subprogram. A two-dimensional string array contains the cell contents; each element holds the contents of one cell. A second two-dimensional string array holds the cell formatting information, which is a format string similar to those used in QuickBASIC's PRINT USING statement. The third array is a one-dimensional integer array, and it holds the column widths. The calling syntax is as follows:

CALL Spread(*cell$*(), *format$*(), *colWidth%*(), *wide%*, *high%*, *action%*)

wide% specifies the window width, and *high%* specifies the window height. *action* accepts one of three values: 1 preserves the original screen contents and displays a spreadsheet for the first time; 2 redisplays a worksheet (for example, to update the display when the user views a different range of cells); and 3 restores the original screen contents and returns immediately to the calling program.

Simple I/O

QuickBASIC provides a full complement of standard services for communicating with the outside world. Beyond simple "Teletype" output, BASIC lets you specify both foreground and background colors when printing to the screen. You can also read characters and colors from the screen directly to determine what a user typed. However, a few useful features are missing. For example, you can't create a "virtual" screen that is larger than the physical display. Furthermore, QuickBASIC provides no way to paint new colors on the screen without affecting the current text. Finally, some of QuickBASIC's screen-handling routines are slow because they call on the BIOS to do the real work. Third-party vendors have been quick to add these capabilities to their libraries of routines.

Virtual Screens

The ProBas library contains a complete collection of routines for manipulating "virtual screens." A virtual screen is an area of memory that is frequently accessed by using an array and in which a screen is composed in the background for later display. After you create a virtual screen, you can copy sections of it to the actual display screen. This lets you, for example, scroll a large display upward or downward and to the left or right anywhere on the actual physical display screen. You must use several separate, but related, routines to create and access virtual screens. Let's look at the more important ones.

To create a virtual screen, you must first dimension an array to hold the screen contents. A normal, 25-row-by-80-column screen array requires 4000 bytes (2000 integers), so you would dimension this array with 2000 elements as follows:

```
REDIM array(1 TO 2000)
```

Note that you must use REDIM instead of DIM so that QuickBASIC creates the array in far memory, which is outside the default, 64-KB string-data area. Next you call the following *DClear* routine, which is similar to the QuickBASIC CLS statement:

CALL DClear(VARSEG(*array*(1)), VARPTR(*array*(1)), *colr*)

In this example, you pass to *DClear* the segment and offset of the array as well as the color—to set the background color of the cleared display.

When you use the *DXQPrint* routine, writing text to a virtual screen is nearly as easy as writing the actual screen:

CALL DXQPrint(VARSEG(*array*(1)), VARPTR(*array*(1)), *x$*, *row*, *col*, *colr*)

Like *DClear*, *DXQPrint* requires the segment and offset of the array in memory; you must also specify the string to be printed, the virtual row and column, and a color. After you construct the screen in memory, you can display it by using the *DPutScreen* routine, as follows:

```
CALL DPutScreen(VARSEG(array(1)), VARPTR(array(1)), uLRow, uLColumn, _
    lRRow, lRColumn, page, screenMode)
```

Set *screenMode* to –1 for the fastest display time; set it to 0 to prevent interference (often called "snow") on CGA adapters. *uLRow* and *uLColumn* specify the coordinates of the upper left corner of the displayed screen. *lRRow* and *lRColumn* specify the lower right corner. *page* is the video page onto which *DPutScreen* writes.

Nondestructively Painting the Screen

QuickPak Professional includes several routines that paint new colors on all or a portion of the display screen. *PaintBox* can paint any rectangular area of the screen; merely specify the upper left and lower right corners of the rectangle, the color to use, and the appropriate video page as follows:

```
CALL PaintBox(uLRow, uLColumn, lRRow, lRColumn, colr, page)
```

Two additional versions of *PaintBox* are also provided: *PaintBox0* uses less code when you don't need multiple screen pages, and *MPaintBox* contains additional logic to handle a mouse cursor. It is important to avoid painting over a mouse cursor so that the screen is not disturbed when you subsequently move the mouse.

Browsing Through a String Array

Scrolling the display screen is not necessarily the most efficient way to let a user view large amounts of text. QuickPak Professional includes a unique routine, *APrint*, that lets you scroll an entire string array upward or downward and to the left or right without having to scroll the screen manually.

Using *APrint* to display part of an array is similar to using MID$ to display part of a string. You must specify the first character to display, how many characters to display, a starting element number, and a number of elements, as the following syntax shows:

```
CALL APrint(array$(firstEl), numEls, firstChar, numChars, colr, page)
```

APrint also accepts a display color and a video page number. As with all the routines in QuickPak Professional, using –1 for *page* specifies the current page. Likewise, using –1 for *color* directs *APrint* to use the current screen colors. The following example is a complete "string array browsing" routine:

```
firstEl = 1                 ' start by displaying element 1
firstChar = 1               ' begin with the first character in each string
DO
    LOCATE 1, 1
    CALL APrint(array$(firstEl), 25, firstChar, 80, 7, -1)

    DO
        x$ = INKEY$                     ' get a key
        IF x$ = CHR$(27) THEN END       ' end if user presses Esc
    LOOP UNTIL LEN(x$) = 2              ' wait until user presses an extended key

    SELECT CASE ASC(RIGHT$(x$, 1))      ' get the extended-key code
        CASE 80                         ' down arrow
            firstEl = firstEl + 1
        CASE 72                         ' up arrow
            IF firstEl > 1 THEN firstEl = firstEl - 1
        CASE 75                         ' left arrow
            IF firstChar > 1 THEN firstChar = firstChar - 1
        CASE 77                         ' right arrow
            firstChar = firstChar + 1
        CASE ELSE
    END SELECT
LOOP
```

Reading Characters from the Screen

Although QuickBASIC provides the SCREEN function for reading characters and colors from the display screen, it is slow. The Mach 2 package contains the *MhRscr* routine, which can read several characters from the screen at once and copy them into a string variable. *MhRscr* requires five parameters, as shown in the following syntax line:

CALL MhRscr(*text$*, *page*, *row*, *column*, *numChars*)

text$ is the string that will receive the screen contents; note that you must initialize it to a length sufficient to hold the text; *page* specifies which display page to read from; *row* and *column* indicate where on the display to begin reading; *numChars* specifies the number of characters to process. If you don't initialize *text$* to a length at least equal to *numChars*, QuickBASIC returns a "String space corrupt" error message.

Trapping and Errors

QuickBASIC uses error-trapping statements to handle errors that occur when a program runs. However, many programmers avoid using error trapping because it makes a program run slowly and increases the program's size. Indeed, the primary purpose of many of the following third-party routines is to avoid using error trapping. Besides the adverse effect error trapping with QuickBASIC statements has on most programs, it is often inconvenient to use. The following alternative methods are available through third-party routines.

Determining Whether a Printer or a Communications Port is Ready

One of the most frustrating programming chores a programmer has to face is handling printer errors efficiently. Although QuickBASIC's error trapping can trap an error generated by the printer after the error occurs, it is usually much simpler to determine whether or not the printer is online before you begin printing. The Toolbox, from MicroHelp, contains a pair of BASIC functions—*LptStat* and *ComStat*—that do exactly that. *LptStat* reports the status of a specified parallel printer, and *ComStat* does the same for a serial printer. The following short example shows a typical use of these routines in context. Note that you must call the Toolbox *ComPortAddress* function before you can test the communications port.

```
IF LptStat(1) THEN                ' test parallel printer port 1
    PRINT "The printer isn't ready!"
END IF

address = ComPortAddress(2)       ' get the address of port 2
IF ComStat(address) THEN          ' test port 2
    PRINT "Please turn on your serial printer."
END IF
```

Determining Whether a Disk Drive is Ready

QuickPak Professional provides a pair of assembly-language functions that report whether a disk drive is ready for reading, writing, or both. *ReadTest* reports whether the drive has a disk in it and the door is closed, and *WriteTest* verifies that the disk is not write protected.

You can use these functions with QuickBASIC's NOT operator. Both *ReadTest* and *WriteTest* return –1 if the disk drive is ready and 0 if it is not. *NOT –1* returns 0 (false), and *NOT 0* returns –1 (true). Using NOT in this manner often helps make your programs more readable.

Date and Time

QuickBASIC date and time statements let your programs set and read the DOS system date and time, but not much else. Sophisticated spreadsheet programs such as Lotus 1-2-3 and Microsoft Excel include several functions for performing calculations based on elapsed time and number of days between two dates. These are useful, for example, when you need to calculate a payroll for hourly employees or estimate mortgage payments. However, when QuickBASIC lacks a function, third-party vendors are quick to offer solutions.

Date Arithmetic

QuickPak Professional offers a suite of functions for determining the number of days between two dates. Related functions return the day of the week for any specified date as well as spelled-out versions of months and days. Of course, all these routines account for leap years as they perform their calculations.

Date2Num accepts a date in string form (*mm-dd-yy* or *mm-dd-yyyy*) and returns an equivalent "serial number" integer value. One important benefit of converting dates into integer values is that they require less storage space. That is, a date such as "05-19-1990" is reduced from a 10-character string to only 2 bytes. Use *Date2Num* as shown in the following example:

```
serial = Date2Num%(DATE$)
```

A complementary routine, *Num2Date*, converts the integer representation of a date serial number back into a string that QuickBASIC can display.

Two other functions, *Date2Day* and *Num2Day*, return a weekday as a number (1 through 7) from either a string or date integer, as shown in the following example:

```
dayNumber = Date2Day%(DATE$)        ' convert from a string
dayNumber = Num2Day%(serial)        ' convert from an integer
```

Finally, the *DayName$* and *MonthName$* functions return the name of a day or month spelled out in English; you can use them as shown in the following example:

```
PRINT 'Today is '; DATE$; 'and it is a '; DayName$(Weekday%(DATE$))
```

Julian Conversions

With the Toolbox package you can convert dates to and from Julian dates and calculate the number of days between dates. Some useful routines are *ToJulian*, which converts U.S.-format dates to Julian dates; *FromJulian*, which converts Julian dates back to U.S.-format dates; and *DateDiff*, which calculates the difference between two dates.

Graphics

One of QuickBASIC's most powerful features is its extensive set of graphics statements, which can be used to draw circles and boxes and perform tiling and painting. Its DRAW statement includes a sublanguage that lets you create connecting lines in any direction and in any color. QuickBASIC's graphics statements also support nearly all the currently available display adapter types. One problem, however, is that no function exists for determining which type of adapter is connected to the system. This information is important because a program must know which graphics screen mode to use, as well as the range of screen pixels that it can address. You can insert an ON ERROR GOTO statement before using the SCREEN statement to detect whether the specified mode is invalid; then use a loop to try each possible screen mode until a valid one is initiated. This approach is shown in the following program segment:

```
ON ERROR GOTO Retry

FOR x = 13 TO 1 STEP -1      ' start with the highest resolution
    fail = 0                 ' set the fail flag to false
    SCREEN x                 ' attempt to switch to the mode
    IF NOT fail THEN EXIT FOR  ' exit loop because switch successful
NEXT

' place the program's graphics statements here

END
Retry:
    fail = -1                ' set the fail flag to true
    RESUME NEXT              ' continue to the next mode
```

The problem with this approach is that it adds code and slows program execution by using error trapping.

Setting and Reading the Current Video Mode

The Mach 2 package includes the *MhDisplay* routine, which determines the type of adapter installed, the number of rows and columns available on the screen, and the current video mode. Knowing the current adapter is especially valuable if you do graphics programming because it helps you avoid the "Illegal function call" error message that QuickBASIC displays when you try to switch to an illegal screen mode. You call *MhDisplay* by using the following syntax:

CALL MhDisplay(*mode, columns, rows, egaMemory, displayType*)

Printing Graphics Screen Images

One of the most difficult programming chores is transferring a graphics screen image to a dot-matrix or laser printer. Although the Epson (dot-matrix) and Hewlett-Packard (laser) printers have each created a widely accepted standard, they in fact use very different methods for accepting graphics images. QuickPak Professional includes the *ScrnDump* routine, which lets you print the current screen image on either type of printer. *ScrnDump* accepts the following three parameters: a printer resolution (specified in dots per inch), a printer number, and a special "translate" option. The routine uses the following syntax:

CALL *ScrnDump(dpi, lptNumber, translate)*

dpi is a string parameter that can be a null string ("") to indicate a dot-matrix printer, or "075", "100", "150", or "300" to specify the resolution of a laser printer. The printer number is either 1, 2, or 3. *translate* is either 0 or 1. The value 0 directs *ScrnDump* to print the screen as solid black on the paper, regardless of the actual colors being displayed; 1 directs *ScrnDump* to use different "hatching patterns," based on the current colors. (If you were to print a pie chart, for example, each portion would be shown with a different pattern.)

Managing PCX-Format Graphics Image Files

Although QuickBASIC provides a wealth of graphics statements and features, it includes no direct way to save EGA and VGA images to a disk file. (You can use BSAVE to save EGA and VGA screens, but using that method requires special OUT commands, and it creates four separate files.) You might want to save screens so that you can exchange graphics data with popular "paint" programs. Most business graphics packages support a standard file format known as PCX. This standard not only provides a well-defined structure for such files, but it also compresses images to 30 to 50 percent of their original size, thus saving space in memory. When you consider that a full VGA graphics screen can occupy as many as 153,600 bytes, this is an important feature.

The ProBas library contains routines that let you load and save PCX-format files and determine the type of file before reading it from a disk. You must know the type of file because your program must be in the correct screen mode before it can load a graphics screen image file. In the following example, the first statement (*GetPCX*) reads the file header and returns information about the graphics image in the file. (The *uLeft* and *lRight* parameters indicate where on the screen the original image was located.) The second statement specifies the correct video mode, and the third statement loads and displays the file.

```
CALL GetPCX(fileName$, uLeftX, uLeftY, lRightX, lRightY, mode, errCode)
SCREEN mode
CALL ShowPCX(fileName$, uLeftX, uLeftY, errCode)
```

Sound

One of QuickBASIC's most appealing features is its extended support for music and sound. Indeed, the PLAY statement includes a complete "sublanguage" that lets you specify tones and tempo in musical, rather than programming, terms. However, this capability comes at a price—using a single SOUND statement in a QuickBASIC program adds about 11 KB of code to the size of the executable file. The PLAY statement is even worse, adding more than 14 KB of code. Because these commands can operate in the background (that is, the tones can continue to play while your program executes other statements), QuickBASIC must use a lot of internal code to implement them. Therefore, this is a natural area in which add-on packages can improve upon existing QuickBASIC features.

Reducing the Size of the Sound Routines

QuickPak Professional contains two sound routines that greatly reduce the overhead added to your programs (compared with the effect of QuickBASIC's SOUND and PLAY statements). The first, *QPSound*, is a replacement for the SOUND statement that adds only 49 bytes to your program. The major difference between *QPSound* and SOUND (besides size) is that *QPSound* does not return to your program until the tone is completed. *QPSound* accepts the same arguments as SOUND does:

CALL QPSound(*frequency*, *duration*)

frequency is the pitch in Hertz (cycles per second); *duration* is the length, in approximately eighteenths of a second, of the tone.

The second routine, *Chime*, creates one of 10 attention-getting sounds. Because QuickPak Professional provides the assembly-language source code of all its routines, you can easily use an assembler to add other sound effects by editing and extending the data table used by *Chime*. The following brief example plays all the *Chime* sound effects:

```
FOR x = 1 TO 10
    CALL Chime(x)
NEXT
```

Mouse Routines

Because QuickBASIC has no provisions for adding mouse support to a program, each third-party vendor has developed its own routines and methods for implementing these services. In general, the routines are similar and provide the same types of services. The primary differences are in form rather than in function. For example, QB/Pro Volume 4, from MicroHelp, contains eight predefined graphics cursor shapes as simple calls with no parameters; however, QuickPak Professional lets you define any shape but requires slightly more programming effort.

Detecting the Presence of a Mouse

Before your program calls any mouse services, you must determine whether a mouse is present and whether the mouse driver has been installed. With QuickPak Professional you can use the *InitMouse* function as follows:

```
IF InitMouse% THEN PRINT "A mouse is installed on this PC"
```

InitMouse also resets the various mouse parameters (motion sensitivity, for example) to their default values.

Reading the Mouse Buttons and Cursor Position

Other important services include reading the mouse cursor location and determining which, if any, buttons are currently pressed. The Mach 2 package includes the *MhMouseStatus* routine, which performs these operations and is called using the following syntax:

CALL MhMouseStatus(*status*, *leftButton*, *rightButton*, *column*, *row*) *status* is the "raw" button information, bit encoded to reflect which buttons are currently pressed. That is, if bit 0 is set, then button 1 is being pressed; if bit 1 is set, then button 2 is being pressed. The *leftButton* and *rightButton* variables hold the same information; they are nonzero if the corresponding button is pressed when the routine is called. *column* and *row* contain the mouse cursor location.

Restricting the Mouse Cursor Travel

One useful mouse routine lets you restrict the mouse cursor to a specified area of the screen. The ProBas library includes the *SetMouseRange* routine (for text mode) and the *MMSetRange* routine (for graphics modes).

Keyboard

There are a few situations in which QuickBASIC's keyboard-handling routines are not sufficient. Two important shortcomings are the lack of a comprehensive text input and editing routine and a function to test whether a key is in the keyboard buffer without actually removing it from the keyboard buffer. All the third-party vendors discussed in this appendix address these and other limitations; the following sections discuss their routines in detail.

Input and Editing Routines

QuickBASIC provides four statements that accept user input through the keyboard—INKEY$, INPUT, INPUT$, and LINE INPUT. However, QuickBASIC lacks many capabilities that modern applications need. Perhaps the most important of these is the ability to accept an entire string of input and to restrict that string to a specified length. To be most useful, an input routine must also let the user insert and delete characters or abandon entry by pressing either Esc or a function key. The third-party vendors provide input-editing routines and let the user either enter a string for the first time or edit an existing string. Examine the following *MhInput* routine, which is contained in Mach 2:

```
CALL MhInput(default$, colr, cursNormal, cursInsert, fillChar, lin, _
        column, page, extendedTerm, ctrlTerm, allowCtrlChars, kShift, _
        kScan, kAscii, response$, errCode)
```

As you can see, this routine gives you complete control over the editing process. You provide a default string, editing color, a code to indicate the shape of the cursor in normal and insert modes, a row and column for the beginning input field, the video display page to use, flags to indicate whether extended or control keys should terminate input, the scan and ASCII codes for the most recent key pressed, and a string to receive the edited text. *MhInput* assigns an error code to the final variable if you made a mistake in any of the other parameters.

The next syntax example outlines the QuickPak Professional *Editor* procedure:

CALL Editor(*ed, activeLength, keyCode, numOnly, capsOn, normColor,* _
editColor, row, column)

The first parameter (*ed*) provides both a default response and the returned text. The parameter *activeLength* returns the length of the data that was entered. *keyCode* reports the most recent key pressed; *numOnly* tells *Editor* to accept only numbers; *capsOn* capitalizes all text; *normColor* and *editColor* are the text colors after and during editing; and *row* and *column* indicate where to place the input field. Preloading *keyCode* with a column number causes editing to begin at the specified position.

Preloading Characters into the Keyboard Buffer

Mach 2 includes the routine *StuffKey*, which lets you insert characters into the keyboard buffer as if they had been entered manually. This lets you add macro capabilities to your programs or even run command and batch files. The calling syntax for *StuffKey* is

CALL StuffKey(*text*)

To run a batch file, for example, simply assign the name of the file to the variable *text*, and then immediately end your program. This way, the filename will already be in the keyboard buffer, exactly as if the user had entered it. Because you also need to "press" the Enter key, you must append ASCII character 13 to the filename, as follows:

```
CALL StuffKey(text$ + CHR$(13))
```

Detecting Keys Without Disturbing the Keyboard Buffer

Sometimes you might need to know whether a character is present in the keyboard buffer without actually removing it. For example, if your program will be running extensive database reports, you can display a message such as "Press Esc to stop the report." Then you need only check the keyboard periodically for the Escape character. You can't use INKEY$ to check the buffer because it removes the character from the buffer, which prevents the user from entering other valid characters in advance.

Mach 2 includes the *MhInstat* routine to solve this problem. *MhInstat* returns information about the next key in the keyboard buffer without removing the character from the buffer. You call *MhInstat* by using the following syntax:

CALL MhInstat(*kShift, kScan, ascii*)

After you call *MhInstat*, *kShift* contains which, if any, shift keys were pressed; *kScan* holds the keyboard scan code; and *ascii* contains the character's ASCII value. The *kShift* parameter is bit coded so that 0 indicates no Shift keys, 1 is the right Shift key, 2 is the left Shift key, 4 is a Ctrl key, and 8 is an Alt key. You can combine these codes by using the OR operator to detect multiple modifiers. For example, 4 OR 8 equals 12, so if *kShift* equals 12, both the Ctrl and Alt keys are pressed.

Printer

QuickBASIC supports input and output for all the PC's resources. You can send text to the printer installed as LPT1: either by using the LPRINT command or by opening the device named LPT1: as a file and then using the PRINT # statement. Indeed, it is common to assign to a string variable the name LPT1:, SCRN:, or a filename so that you can use the same block of code to output data to any of these devices. That is, a program might prompt the user for a report destination, for example, and the appropriate output device would be specified simply by assigning the device name to a single string. However, third-party add-ons can further extend QuickBASIC's output capabilities.

Manipulating the DOS Print Spooler

QB/Pro Volume 4, from MicroHelp, includes seven routines that let your programs fully control the PRINT.COM spooler program, which is packaged with DOS. The PRINT command is a useful addition to DOS because it lets an application print one or more documents in the background. That is, a user can run PRINT from the DOS command line and then immediately begin working with another application. Because PRINT is a TSR (terminate-and-stay-resident) program, the printing process continues while the subsequent program does something else.

A PC can do only one thing at a time. However, the PRINT statement uses a technique known as "time-slicing" whereby it receives control periodically for a few milliseconds. (To do this, PRINT chains itself into the system timer interrupt.) Therefore, each time PRINT receives control, it sends a portion of text to the printer and then returns control to the foreground application. PRINT.COM provides a number of important and useful capabilities, and the routines in QB/PRO Volume 4 let you fully exploit all of them.

For example, the *MhSpoolCheck* routine, which uses the following call syntax, reports whether or not the PRINT program has been installed:

CALL MhSpoolCheck(*installed*)

If *MhSpoolCheck* assigns the variable *installed* a nonzero value, PRINT has already been installed and your program can use any of the other *MhSpool* routines.

MhSpoolAddFile lets you add to the current list (queue) of text files that are to be printed. Merely call *MhSpoolAddFile* and specify the name of the file to be printed and a variable that will contain an error code, which indicates whether an error occurred:

CALL MhSpoolAddFile(*fileName*, *errCode*)

As with all the QB/Pro Volume 4 routines, *fileName* must be a valid DOS filename. Therefore, you must manually append a CHR$(0) character to the end of the name as shown in the following statement:

```
fileName$ = fileName$ + CHR$(0)
```

In DOS parlance this is called an "ASCIIZ" string because it ends with a zero byte that identifies the end of the string.

The next routine, *MhSpoolKill*, deletes all the currently pending filenames from the PRINT queue. *MhSpoolKill* accepts a single parameter, which contains an error code if an error occurs:

CALL MhSpoolKill(*errCode*)

If *errCode* contains –1 after a call to *MhSpoolKill*, the PRINT.COM program has not been installed. The value 0 indicates that the operation was successful, and the value 9 indicates that the spooler was busy.

Another routine, *MhSpoolRemoveFile*, lets you remove a file from the print queue. You call this routine as follows:

CALL MhSpoolRemoveFile(*fileName*, *errCode*)

fileName is the ASCIIZ name of the file you want to remove, and the value of *errCode* indicates whether the operation was successful. If *errCode* is 2, for example, the specified file was not present in the PRINT queue; if *errCode* is 12, the specified filename was too long.

Printing Without Requiring ON ERROR GOTO

QuickPak Professional includes the *BLPrint* routine, which lets you access any parallel printer directly. Although QuickBASIC can print to any physical device without assistance, if the printer is turned off or is offline, the program displays an error message. *BLPrint* lets you bypass QuickBASIC's normal error handling by sending the text through the PC's BIOS. You call BLPrint as follows:

CALL BLPrint(*lptNumber*, *text*, *characters*)

lptNumber is either 1, 2, or 3, indicating which printer to use; *text* is the string to be printed; and *characters* contain the number of characters that were successfully printed. If *characters* contains a –1, the entire line was printed without error. Otherwise, *characters* holds the number of characters that were actually printed. This lets your program resume printing even if the printer was disconnected in the middle of a line. The following program segment shows how to recover from a printer error. Note that if you need to print an entire string array, the statements between the DO and LOOP keywords should be placed within a FOR...NEXT statement.

```
DO
    BLPrint lptno, work$, characters    ' print the text string
    IF characters <> -1 THEN            ' anything except -1 indicates an error
        PRINT "Fix the printer and press a key";
        k$ = INPUT$(1)
        ' calculate how much to reprint
        work$ = RIGHT$(work$, LEN(work$) - characters)
    END IF
LOOP UNTIL characters = -1
```

Communications

One of QuickBASIC's most powerful features is its ability to implement fully "interrupt-driven" communications by using the OPEN COM statement. With interrupt-driven communications, characters coming through the COM port are always processed—even if the program is performing another operation. For example, your program might be waiting for a keystroke in a menu subprogram at the same time a remote terminal sends a character. In that case, the modem generates a hardware interrupt, thus causing the program to stop what it is currently doing and instead deal with the incoming character stream.

The statement *OPEN "COM1:1200,N,8,1"* is equivalent to hundreds of lines of assembly-language code. (In fact, some versions of QuickBASIC include a special object file, NOCOM.OBJ, that you can link with a program to remove support for communications; the resulting programs are therefore much smaller.) In some situations, the communications routines provided with QuickBASIC fall short of the programmer's needs. One example is QuickBASIC's need to use error trapping to check for errors in communications. Many programmers prefer to avoid error trapping whenever possible because trapping increases program size and slows execution. Another limitation is that after a serial port has been opened, you cannot change its baud rate and other parameters without first closing the port. This makes it impossible to switch to a different baud rate or parity protocol, for example, in the middle of a session.

Replacing QuickBASIC's OPEN COM Statement

QB/Pro Volume 6, from Microhelp, contains a complete replacement for QuickBASIC's communication-handling statements. It includes routines for opening any or all of the PC's four serial ports, reading and writing data, and detecting errors that are likely to occur during transmissions. It also includes routines for handling the XMODEM and YMODEM communications protocols and several sample "terminal" programs. The following listing shows the steps you need to create a fully functional communications program.

```
DECLARE SUB ErrorHandler ()
DEFINT A-Z
PRINT "Press Esc to end this program."

port = 2                                  ' use COM2:
CALL MhComBuffer4a(port, eCode)           ' 4-KB transmit and receive buffer
IF eCode THEN ErrorHandler                ' test for errors

' open the port at 2400 baud, no parity, 1 stop bit, 8 data bits
CALL MhOpenComPort(port, 2400, 0, 1, 8, eCode)
IF eCode THEN ErrorHandler                ' test for errors
```

(continued)

continued

```
DO
    ' display all incoming data and send all keystrokes
    CALL MhGetRecvStatus(port, charsInBuffer, eCode) ' check receive buffer
    IF eCode THEN ErrorHandler                        ' test for errors

    IF charsInBuffer THEN                             ' new data has arrived
        lin$ = SPACE$(100 + charsInBuffer * 2)        ' holds incoming data
        CALL MhGetData(port, lin$, length, eCode)     ' read from receive buffer
        IF eCode THEN ErrorHandler                    ' test for errors
        IF length THEN                                ' if lin$ is not empty,
            PRINT LEFT$(lin$, length);                ' then print its contents
        END IF
    END IF

    keyPress$ = INKEY$                                ' test for user keystrokes
    IF keyPress$ = CHR$(27) GOTO EndProgram           ' end if user presses Esc
    CALL MhSendData(port, keyPress$, eCode)           ' transmit the character
    IF eCode THEN ErrorHandler                        ' test for errors
LOOP

EndProgram:
    CALL MhCloseComPort(port, eCode)                  ' close the COM port
    END

SUB ErrorHandler
    PRINT
    PRINT "Error code "; eCode; "has occurred."
    END
END SUB
```

File I/O

Although QuickBASIC's error trapping statements are useful, they have several unfortunate drawbacks. First, and perhaps foremost, error trapping requires that you specify a new location in the program to which execution will branch when an error occurs. A typical error-handling routine might, for example, display a message telling a user to insert a disk in the drive and then press any key to continue. For large and complex programs, this means you must not only handle the error but also figure out what caused the error. The error-code variables returned by the QB/Pro Volume 6 routines let you simply identify errors at the point in the program at which they occurred. Furthermore, when a program uses error trapping, it becomes noticeably larger and slower. Therefore, many programmers avoid QuickBASIC's method of handling errors.

Enhancing QuickBASIC's File Handling

All the third-party libraries discussed in this appendix address the error-trapping downfalls by including routines that replace QuickBASIC's file-handling statements with ones that let you determine whether an error occurred. In particular, the libraries include additional routines for opening and closing files and for reading and writing strings and numeric data.

Eliminating Error Trapping

To eliminate the need for error trapping, all the third-party packages discussed in this appendix contain routines that entirely replace QuickBASIC's file statements with new routines. These routines open and close files and read and write data to those files. In all cases, enhancements make these routines more versatile than their QuickBASIC counterparts; for example, one of their specialized features lets you read and write entire arrays and display screens.

Using the ProBas library as an example, you open a file with the *FOpen* routine by using the following syntax:

CALL FOpen(*fileName*, *readWrite*, *sharing*, *handle*, *errCode*)

readWrite lets you specify whether the file is opened for reading (input), writing (output), or both. *sharing* lets you open the file for network access and allow other applications read access, write access, or neither. If the file is opened successfully, *handle* will contain the handle value assigned by DOS that you will use for subsequent access to that file. *errorCode* will contain one of six possible values after *FOpen* completes:

Value	Description
0	No error
2	File not found
3	Path not found
4	No handle available
5	Access denied
15	Invalid drive

After you open a file, you can read and write data by using any of several routines. In each case, however, you must specify the handle that was assigned by DOS.

The remainder of the section discusses several examples that use the ProBas library. *DFWrite* writes an entire integer array to a file; all you need to do is specify the location in memory of the array and the number of bytes it contains. The following program segment uses *DFWrite* and prints the error code if an error occurs:

```
segment = VARSEG(array(0))
offset = VARPTR(array(0))
CALL DFWrite(handle, segment, offset, numBytes, bytesWritten, errCode)
IF errCode THEN PRINT "Error: "; errCode
```

The *SFRead* routine reads data into a string from a file; the string length specifies the number of bytes to be read. *SFRead* returns in the third parameter the number of bytes that were actually read, so the program can check whether it tried to read past the end of the file.

```
st$ = SPACE$(20)                               ' set the number of bytes to read
CALL SFRead(handle, st$, bytesRead, errCode)    ' read from the file
```

QuickPak Professional uses an approach different from that used in the ProBas library. The *FLInput* routine reads characters to a carriage return in the file and then returns a string of the correct length. Rather than require a separate "error" parameter, errors are handled by two assembly-language functions—*DOSError* indicates that an error occurred and *WhichError* reports which one:

```
CALL FOpen(fileName$, handle)                   ' open the file
st$ = FLInput$(handle, SPACE$(80))              ' read a single line
IF DOSError% THEN PRINT "Error: "; WhichError% ' test for an error
```

The QuickPak Professional routines translate DOS error codes into QuickBASIC error codes. That is, a "File not found" error message is returned as the number 53.

The Mach 2 package includes routines that handle file I/O and management more directly. Useful routines include: *MhFile*, which opens, creates, and closes files; *MhRwsub*, which reads and writes sequential and random-access files; and *MhDir*, which retrieves and sets the current directory, creates a directory, and removes a directory. *MhFind*, like QuickBASIC's FILES statement, can retrieve files based on a wildcard specification; however, *MhFind* can also assign the matching files QuickBASIC variables for further use. *MhRlb* removes leading blanks from a string expression and is a faster machine-language replacement for LTRIM$.

Network Files

The Development Products Division of Novell, Inc., produces many professional development tools that complement the Novell Netware network operating system. One of these tools, *Btrieve*, is a data-record management system that can store, retrieve, and update the data in your files. *Btrieve*, unlike many of QuickBASIC's own file I/O statements, works with many networks, and it indexes the data so that you can immediately access any record in your file.

Program Control

QuickBASIC offers many statements that interface with DOS. One of the most valuable of these is the SHELL statement, which lets your program temporarily invoke a copy of the DOS command processor and run another program or issue a DOS command. However, add-ons can improve even this capability.

When you use the QuickBASIC's SHELL statement, your program remains in memory while the second command processor runs. If your program is large or if it uses many dynamic arrays that occupy a lot of memory, very little memory is left for the program or command that SHELL must execute.

An Improved SHELL Command

QB/Pro Volume 3 (called SuperShell), from MicroHelp, contains a complete replacement for the SHELL statement. The replacement includes several enhancements, the most important being that it can release nearly all the memory occupied by the current QuickBASIC program. Also, when you use the replacement to specify a message, the message does not scroll off the screen. Other clever enhancements include a constant display of the current time or date and the ability to retrieve the DOS ERRORLEVEL variable returned by the program running in the new shell. This package contains even more capabilities; the following discussion, however, focuses on only the most important features.

In order to provide as much memory as possible to DOS, SuperShell lets you store your program's code and data in either expanded (EMS) memory or in a disk file. By default, SuperShell uses expanded memory for storage. You can, however, avoid using expanded memory by first calling the *MhIgnoreEms* routine.

If expanded memory is not available, you can specify the name of a file that SuperShell creates to hold the program: Simply call *MhSetDiskFile* before you call the *MhShell* routine:

```
CALL MhSetDisk(fileName$, errCode)
```

When you finally call the *MhShell* routine, specify the name of the program to be executed and any optional command line parameters:

```
CALL MhShell(program$, cmdLine$, errorLevel, errCode)
```

Note that to execute internal DOS commands, such as DIR or VER, you must first run the COMMAND.COM program and specify the /c (command) parameter. This lets you pass the DOS command in the *cmdLine$* variable. Also note that your program must prefix the DOS command with the command's length. The following example, provided in the SuperShell manual, shows this procedure in context:

```
program$ = "C:\DOS\CHKDSK.COM" + CHR$(0)   ' ASCIIZ name of the program
cmdLine$ = "A:/F"                          ' the command line arguments
length$ = CHR$(LEN(cmdLine$))              ' create string of the length
cmdLines$ = length$ + cmdLine$ + CHR$(13) ' add the "Enter" character
CALL MhShell(program$, cmdLine$, errorLevel, errCode) ' invoke the shell
```

Finding Your Program's Data Files

Although DOS provides the PATH environment variable for locating an executable file you want to run, it does not provide such a facility for finding data files. This can be a serious problem when your program needs to access data files that are not in the current directory. For example, if your program is in a directory listed in the PATH environment variable, it is possible that the user might start your program from another directory. In that case, your program needs some way to determine where its data files are located.

QuickPak Professional contains a function named *ExeName*, which returns the full pathname of the currently running program. Therefore, your program can know from which directory it was loaded even if that directory is not the current one. *ExeName* is a function that you call by using the following syntax:

fullName$* = *ExeName$

In this case, *fullName$* is assigned the full name of your program—the drive letter, path, and filename. You can then use a simple FOR...NEXT statement to move backward through the string and find the path and drive letter. After you know the path, you can easily access the data files in that directory.

(Note that *ExeName* requires DOS version 3.0 or later; it returns a null string, "", if used with DOS 2.x.)

Extending QuickBASIC's DOS Capabilities

As powerful as QuickBASIC is for conventional file operations, it lacks several important DOS services. For example, it doesn't let you directly obtain the current disk drive and directory. Several third-party vendors include these and other useful DOS extensions; however, each package implements its extensions in a different way.

Determining the Current Drive and Directory

Mach 2 uses the *MhDir* routine to replace QuickBASIC's directory-handling statements and provide additional functionality, such as letting you change, create, and remove directories. Other routines let you determine the current drive or directory. For example, you call *MhDir* with a number that represents the drive, the name of the directory, and an error code parameter. The following two examples call *MhDir* with different *operation* codes as the first parameter. The first obtains the current default drive, and the second returns the current directory.

```
operation = 1                         ' specify the default drive service
CALL MhDir(operation, drive, dir$, errCode) ' call the routine

operation = 2                         ' specify the current directory service
drive = 1                             ' specify drive A
dir$ = SPACE$(65)                     ' make room to hold the returned name
CALL MhDir(operation, drive, dir$, errCode) ' call the routine
stringEnd = INSTR(dir$, CHR$(0))                ' find the end of the string
dir$ = "\" + LEFT$(dir$, stringEnd - 1)         ' keep the part you need
```

Compare that with the *GetDrive%* and *GetDir$* functions contained in QuickPak Professional. Because these are functions, they return the information directly, so you don't have to preassign string space:

```
drive = GetDrive%           ' get the current drive as an ASCII value

drive$ = CHR$(GetDrive%)    ' get the current drive as a string

curDir$ = GetDir$("")       ' get the directory for the current drive

drive$ = "a"                ' get the current directory for drive A
curDir$ = GetDir$(drive$)
```

Loading and Saving Large Blocks of Data

One of the slowest operations a QuickBASIC program can perform is saving or loading a numeric array from a file. QuickPak Professional provides several routines for loading and saving arrays, including huge arrays that can span more than one segment.

FGetAH and *FPutAH* accept a filename, the index of the starting array element, the size of each array element, and the number of elements. You call them by using the following syntax:

CALL FPutAH(*fileName*, SEG *array*(*start*), *elementSize*, *numberElements*)
CALL FGetAH(*fileName*, SEG *array*(*start*), *elementSize*, *numberElements*)

You cannot use these routines with string arrays because QuickBASIC does not store conventional string arrays in contiguous memory locations. However, *FastSave* retrieves all the elements of a single string array and saves them on disk in a single operation; the complementary *FastLoad* routine can reload the array later. These routines are typically 10 times faster than the QuickBASIC PRINT # and INPUT # statements.

Exceeding the DOS Limit of 15 Open Files

Although QuickBASIC lets you specify any file number between 1 and 255, DOS limits your program to only 15 active (opened) files at one time. If you create a large database that must access many individual data files, this can be an unfortunate limitation. QB/Pro Volume 4 includes a useful routine that lets a program open as many as 251 files at one time. However, *MhExtraFiles* requires DOS 3.0 or later; you call this routine by using the following syntax:

CALL MhExtraFiles(*numFiles*, *errCode*)

Changing the DOS SEEK Location in a File

Like all the third-party companies discussed in this appendix, ProBas provides several low-level routines for manipulating files and avoiding QuickBASIC's built-in statements. For example, *FSetLoc* sets the current file location to anywhere in the file, and *FSetEnd* seeks the end of the file.

Note that when you manipulate files by calling DOS directly, as these routines do, you must remember to specify the file handle that DOS assigns.

Changing the Length of a File

Deleting records from a database file can be difficult because you can't directly shorten a file's length. The usual practice involves reading each record one by one and then writing to another file only those records that you want to save. However, your disk must have enough free space to hold a second copy of the entire file. QuickPak Professional includes a routine called *ClipFile*, which truncates (or extends) a file to a new length. *ClipFile* accepts two arguments—the name of the file and a new length, as shown in the following syntax line:

CALL ClipFile(*fileName*, *newLength*)

Sorting a Disk File

Although all the third-party vendors discussed in this appendix provide routines that sort arrays, sorting an entire data file that might not fit into available memory is more difficult. QuickPak Professional includes a routine that sorts a random-access file on any number of sort keys, in either ascending or descending order. To accommodate the varying amount of information (based on the number of keys you specify), *FileSort* uses an array to hold a table of record offsets and data types.

Rather than actually reorder the information in the file, *FileSort* creates a second, parallel file that contains a series of long-integer record numbers. Therefore, you can access the primary file in sorted order by referring to the data in the index file. Note that you can also specify starting and ending record numbers to facilitate sorting only a portion of the file, as shown in the following syntax line:

CALL FileSort(*fileName*, *index*, *first*, *last*, *table()*, *recLength*)

Port and Memory

One of QuickBASIC's greatest strengths is its memory handling, which doesn't burden the programmer with many low-level details. In particular, QuickBASIC lets a programmer freely access dynamic arrays in far memory. Contrast that to the same operation in C and Pascal, in which you must manually allocate memory and then refer to individual elements by using pointers that hold the element addresses. However, QuickBASIC does not include support for accessing extended and expanded memory.

Extended memory is available on PCs equipped with an 80286 or later microprocessor. It is the area of memory that extends beyond the 1-MB address limit imposed by the earlier 8088 and 8086 microprocessors. In general, programs rarely use extended memory because no standard exists for identifying which areas of memory are in use. For example, if your program is accessing a RAM disk in extended memory, it might accidentally overwrite files or other information already stored there.

Expanded memory, on the other hand, follows an established protocol developed jointly by Lotus, Intel, and Microsoft. Expanded memory is a hardware technique that swaps multiple banks of external memory with existing memory within the PC's 1-MB address space.

For example, many expanded-memory drivers use the 64-KB segment beginning at &HD000:0000 as the common area for all memory access. All expanded-memory accesses are routed through an expanded-memory manager (EMM), which is usually loaded as a device driver specified in the DOS CONFIG.SYS file. A complete discussion of accessing extended and expanded memory is beyond the scope of this appendix; however, the following sections show that because of the complexity involved in saving and retrieving data using expanded memory, third-party add-on packages have helped fill an important void.

Accessing Expanded Memory

The expanded-memory device driver provides many separate services. Unfortunately, after the device driver is installed you can access these services only by using assembly language or, in QuickBASIC, the CALL INTERRUPT statement. Furthermore, these device drivers always allocate memory in 16-KB blocks, so expanded memory is most useful for storing entire data arrays or display screens. It is not useful for storing individual variables or short strings.

QuickPak Professional contains several routines to simplify storing data in expanded memory. Many of these routines store entire arrays; however, several are also provided to access individual elements. Other, related services return the total amount of expanded memory installed, the amount currently available, and a status code for the most recent EMS operation. The rest of this section examines a few of the more important of these routines.

Array2Ems and *Ems2Array* let you easily store and retrieve an entire array in a single operation. *EmsGet1El* and *EmsSet1El* provide access to individual elements in expanded memory; *EmsNumPages* indicates the total installed expanded memory; and *EmsPagesFree* returns the number of 16-KB memory pages currently available. As with many of the QuickPak Professional routines, functions are used, when appropriate, to reduce the number of parameters passed. This section shows the correct calling syntax for each of these routines. Like DOS, the EMS driver assigns a handle to a block of memory when it first allocates memory. The calling program then uses that handle whenever it needs to access data stored in the allocated memory. Consider the following calling syntax lines:

CALL Array2Ems(*array*(*first*), *elementSize*, *numElements*, *handle*)
CALL Ems2Array(*array*(*first*), *elementSize*, *numElements*, *handle*)

The *Array2Ems* and *Ems2Array* statements use the same number and type of parameters to specify where the array is located in near memory and to determine how large the array is. In these syntax lines, *array(first)* is the first element in the array or the first element in the portion being stored. (You don't need to save an entire array—you can specify any contiguous elements.) *elementSize* indicates the size of each element in bytes; that is, you would specify 2 for an integer array, 4 for a long-integer or single-precision array, or 8 for a double-precision array. If you are saving an array of fixed-length strings or user-defined types, you specify the size of each element. *numElements* is the number of elements to consider, and *handle* is the variable that stores the handle number that the EMS manager assigns to the block of memory. The *Array2Ems* statement assigns the handle number to the *handle* parameter; when you retrieve the array later with *Ems2Array*, you must specify the same handle number.

The *EmsGet1El* and *EmsSet1El* routines let you store and retrieve individual elements by copying them to and from a variable of the same type in near memory. Call these routines by using the following syntax lines:

CALL EmsGet1El(*variable, elementSize, elementNumber, handle*)
CALL EmsSet1El(*variable, elementSize, elementNumber, handle*)

For example, to replace element 1000 of an integer array in expanded memory, you use *EmsSet1El* as follows:

```
CALL EmsSet1El(value%, 2, 1000, handle)
```

Likewise, to retrieve element 2000 from a single-precision array, you use the following statement:

```
CALL EmsGet1El(variable!, 4, 2000, handle)
```

QuickPak Professional also contains *EmsNumPages* and *EmsPagesFree*. The *EmsNumPages* function returns the number of pages available in expanded memory. *EmsPagesFree* returns the number of pages not currently in use. Each page contains 16,384 bytes.

Accessing Extended Memory

ProBas contains four routines that manipulate extended memory. *GetExtM* returns the total amount of extended memory that is installed; *ExtMem* tells how much of that memory is currently available; and *ExtPut* and *ExtGet* store and retrieve data there. Call *GetExtM* with the following syntax:

CALL GetExtM(*kBytes*)

In this example, GetExtM assigns *kBytes* the total number of 1024-byte blocks that are installed.

Like *GetExtM*, *ExtMem* returns a value in kilobytes. *ExtMem* reports the number of 1024-byte blocks that are available:

CALL ExtMem(*kBytes*)

The *ExtPut* and *ExtGet* routines each require five parameters, which have the same meaning for both routines. Call the routines with the following syntax:

CALL ExtPut(*segment, offset, position, words, errCode*)
CALL ExtGet(*segment, offset, position, words, errCode*)

segment and *offset* specify where in near memory the data is located, and *position* indicates where in extended memory it is to be stored or retrieved. (Note that this parameter is a long integer so as to accommodate the large range of possible addresses.) *words* specifies how many words (a "word" being 2 bytes) are to be moved, and *errCode* indicates whether the memory access was successful.

APPENDIX D

QuickBASIC for the Macintosh

QuickBASIC for the Macintosh

Microsoft QuickBASIC for the Macintosh includes many of the features found in QuickBASIC for the IBM PC, but it also takes advantage of the Macintosh's unique interface, including the mouse, menus, sophisticated screen display, and the powerful Macintosh Toolbox library.

QuickBASIC programmers must be aware of the differences between QuickBASIC for the Macintosh and QuickBASIC for the PC when they port programs between environments. This appendix presents an overview of Macintosh-exclusive QuickBASIC commands as well as a summary of the DOS QuickBASIC commands that work differently from their Macintosh counterparts.

QuickBASIC for the Macintosh includes over 40 exclusive keywords that take advantage of the Macintosh's unique interface and operating system. Table D-1 lists these statements and functions. Table D-2 lists the statements and functions supported exclusively by QuickBASIC for the PC.

Math Differences

One of the biggest differences between PC and Macintosh versions of QuickBASIC is that QuickBASIC for the Macintosh comes in two different versions on the distribution disks. Each version supports a different internal storage format for floating-point numbers. The QuickBASIC decimal version (BCD format) does not round double-precision numbers, so it is best for applications that calculate dollar-and-cent values. The QuickBASIC binary version supports the IEEE (Institute of Electrical and Electronics Engineers) international standard and is more appropriate for scientific applications because it provides 80-bit precision. The binary version also performs calculations more quickly than its decimal counterpart because the internal BCD math routines are less efficient than the binary routines. Note that these two versions handle CINT differently. (See the CINT entry in Chapter 7, "Math.") QuickBASIC for the Macintosh supports the MKSBCD$ and MKDBCD$ functions, which convert single-precision or double-precision numbers in binary format into file buffer strings in decimal format. CVSBCD and CVDBCD translate them from strings in decimal format to numbers in binary format.

Interface element	Statement or function
Menus	MENU (Statement) MENU (Function) MENU ON/OFF/STOP MENU RESET ON MENU GOSUB
Dialog Boxes	DIALOG DIALOG ON/OFF/STOP ON DIALOG GOSUB
Windows	WINDOW
Buttons	BUTTON (Statement) BUTTON (Function)
Mouse Control	MOUSE MOUSE ON/OFF/STOP ON MOUSE GOSUB
User Input	EDIT$ EDIT FIELD
Graphics	PICTURE (Statement) PICTURE$ (Function) PICTURE ON/OFF PTAB
Screen	LCOPY SCROLL

Interface element	Statement or function
Toolbox Library	ToolBox
Program Control	BREAK ON/OFF/STOP CONT ON BREAK GOSUB SYSTEM (Function)
Math Conversions	CVDBCD CVSBCD MKDBCD$ MKSBCD$
Memory Control	PEEKL PEEKW POKEL POKEW
File Manipulation	FILES$ LIBRARY LIBRARY CLOSE LOAD MERGE
Sound	SOUND RESUME SOUND WAIT WAVE

Table D-1.
Statements and functions supported exclusively by QuickBASIC for the Macintosh.

Topic	Statement or function
Variables and Types	COMMON SHARED CONST TYPE...END TYPE
Flow Control	DO...LOOP
Procedures	DECLARE FUNCTION STATIC
Strings	LCASE$
Arrays and Data	REDIM
Simple I/O (Text and Cursor)	VIEW PRINT
Trapping and Errors	ERDEV ON UEVENT GOSUB UEVENT ON/OFF/STOP
Time	SLEEP
Graphics	COLOR DRAW PAINT PALETTE, PALETTE USING PCOPY PMAP SCREEN (Function) SCREEN (Statement) VIEW
Sound	ON PLAY GOSUB PLAY (Function) PLAY (Statement) PLAY ON/OFF/STOP
Lightpen and Joystick	ON PEN GOSUB ON STRIG GOSUB PEN ON/OFF/STOP PEN STICK STRIG STRIG ON/OFF/STOP
Keyboard	KEY KEY(*n*) ON/OFF/STOP ON KEY(*n*) GOSUB
Communications Port	COM ON/OFF/STOP ON COM GOSUB OPEN COM
Files	ACCESS CVDMBF CVSMBF FILEATTR FREEFILE LOCK LTRIM$ MKDMBF$ MKSMBF$ RTRIM$ SEEK (Function) SEEK (Statement) UNLOCK
DOS and Program Management	COMMAND$ ENVIRON ENVIRON$ IOCTL IOCTL$ MKDIR RMDIR SHELL
Debugging	Add Watch Break on Errors Clear All Breakpoints Delete All Watch Delete Watch History On Instant Watch Set Next Statement Toggle Breakpoint Trace On Watchpoint
Port and Memory	BLOAD BSAVE INP OUT SETMEM WAIT
Mixed Language	CALL ABSOLUTE CALL INT86OLD CALL INTERRUPT CALLS DEF SEG VARSEG VARPTR$

Table D-2.
Statements and functions supported exclusively by QuickBASIC for the PC.

The Interface

Much like QuickBASIC for the PC environment, QuickBASIC for the Macintosh environment has an interface that includes pull-down menus, mouse control, dialog boxes, and buttons. QuickBASIC for the Macintosh includes several keywords that allow you to directly control these elegant features in your programs.

Menus

QuickBASIC for the Macintosh includes statements that let you create customized menus on the Macintosh. The MENU statement creates new menu bar options and menu items. You can even use a ToolBox statement to add command-key equivalents to the menus. The MENU RESET statement restores the default menu. These menus conform to the Macintosh menu interface and therefore highlight selected menu items. The MENU function and the MENU ON/OFF/STOP and ON MENU GOSUB statements let you set up sophisticated menu event trapping. QuickBASIC for the Macintosh uses the same event-interrupt structure as does QuickBASIC for the PC. These powerful features let you bypass all the complex draw and trapping commands you'd need to create and use menus in QuickBASIC for the PC.

Dialog Boxes and Windows

The concept of dialog boxes helped the Macintosh computer set the standard for letting users enter complex information easily. The DIALOG function in QuickBASIC for the Macintosh returns values that correspond to the status of buttons, edit fields, and windows. The DIALOG ON/OFF/STOP and ON DIALOG GOSUB statements enable your program to perform dialog-box event trapping.

The WINDOW function and statement provide total control of as many as 16 screen windows. Windows can be of different sizes or types, active, in the background, or even redirected to a graphic printer. You also use the WINDOW statement to create a dialog box. These easy-to-use statements and functions make creating windows and dialog boxes easy and encourage you to program in a modular fashion. You would require a virtual arsenal of statements in QuickBASIC for the PC to duplicate their operations; however, you can find similar commands in third-party libraries.

Buttons

Most Macintosh interfaces use buttons extensively. The BUTTON statement creates a button and enables or disables existing buttons. The BUTTON function returns the status of a specified button. These commands simplify the process of receiving information from the user.

Mouse Control

QuickBASIC for the Macintosh offers mouse event-trapping routines that let your program trap user input and direct program control to a subroutine. The ON MOUSE GOSUB and MOUSE ON/OFF/STOP statements detect mouse clicks and drags, thus enabling QuickBASIC to handle highlighted screen selections. Although QuickBASIC for the PC does not include mouse control routines, many third-party vendors offer these types of mouse routines. (QuickBASIC programmers using a PC can also find mouse commands in the *Microsoft Mouse Programmer's Reference.*)

User Input

Two powerful routines in QuickBASIC for the Macintosh, the EDIT$ function and the EDIT FIELD statement, let you use rectangular fields for user input that allow the user to edit the entered text. The user can manipulate selected text with the Macintosh's standard Cut, Copy, and Paste commands. Programs using these commands and the mouse commands are generally intuitive and easy to learn.

Graphics and Screen

The PICTURE statements and PICTURE$ function let you easily draw pictures using QuickBASIC statements and library routines, save entire screen images to the Clipboard or to files, and even embed a picture within another picture. These commands work well in conjunction with the QuickBASIC for the Macintosh SCROLL statement. In comparison, scrolling with QuickBASIC for the PC is a tedious and complicated affair.

The LCOPY statement prints the current screen to an ImageWriter printer.

Note that QuickBASIC for the Macintosh has no commands to control color because it predates Macintoshes that support color.

Program Control

QuickBASIC for the Macintosh and for the PC use the same method of event handling. However, a few statements unique to QuickBASIC for the Macintosh help control program flow and safeguard your programs. The ON BREAK GOSUB and BREAK ON/OFF/STOP statements let you trap "break" events. These commands can be used to disable, enable, or suspend the trapping of Macintosh's key combination Command-. (period), which interrupts program flow. The CONT statement resumes program execution after a break or a STOP statement, and it is especially useful for debugging.

Unrelated but just as handy is the SYSTEM function, which lets your program access information about the system (such as what kind of Macintosh the program is running on).

Memory Control

QuickBASIC for the Macintosh offers customized variations of the POKE and PEEK statements that work with words (2-byte values) and double words (4-byte values). The PEEKL, PEEKW, POKEL, and POKEW statements manipulate values of single and double words in specified memory locations. For example, PEEKW returns the word (2 bytes) at a specified memory location. The POKEL statement places a double word (4 bytes) in memory.

File Manipulation

QuickBASIC for the Macintosh adds a few file-manipulation commands—some advanced, some primitive—that simplify programming immensely. The LIBRARY and LIBRARY CLOSE statements let you easily access as many as eight libraries at one time, including the Toolbox Library. (The Toolbox Library puts the Macintosh's features at your command.) You can also use a compiler such as Macintosh Programmer's Workshop Pascal to create your own machine-language libraries.

The FILES$ function conveniently displays a standard Macintosh file dialog box to simplify file selection. The LOAD statement loads a file from disk, and the MERGE statement appends a file to a program in memory. The last two statements work only in the QuickBASIC environment; $INCLUDE is the compiler metacommand equivalent of the MERGE statement.

Sound

The Macintosh is a versatile instrument for manipulating sound. It boasts multiple voices, which give you powerful control for sculpting soundwaves, and it even lets you store and replay music in stereo. You can synchronize sounds and store them in a buffer for later use. Even its sound-interfacing capabilities are impressive: PCs are limited by small speakers and restrictions that make importing and exporting sound difficult; Macintosh computers can import any sounds, store them in resources, and even send them directly to stereos, videotape recorders, and MIDI-compatible musical instruments. A few QuickBASIC statements for the Macintosh make programming multi-voice sound easy. If you want to create harmony, you must use the WAVE statement to define for each voice the waveform of a cycle sound wave. The waveform defines the timbre of the sound output by the Macintosh.

The SOUND WAIT and SOUND RESUME statements let you synchronize multiple voices. The SOUND WAIT statement saves all sound statements in a queue until you execute a SOUND RESUME.

Calling the Toolbox

QuickBASIC for the Macintosh gives you the ability to directly access the Macintosh's Toolbox, which lets you handle resources, icons, scroll bars, and some of the Macintosh QuickDraw routines. The compiler used by QuickBASIC for the Macintosh provides the Toolbox library, which gives you control over such elegant features as font size and typeface, the QuickDraw "pen," background patterns, the cursor, and alert and dialog boxes.

The QuickBASIC ToolBox statement lets you access Macintosh ROM routines that are not included in the Toolbox library. The *QuickBASIC for the Macintosh* documentation contains over 100 pages of information about how to call routines from the Toolbox library and from ROM.

Statements and Functions Not Supported by QuickBASIC for the Macintosh

Several statements and functions supported by QuickBASIC 4.5 for the PC have no equivalent in QuickBASIC for the Macintosh; some perform differently. It is important that you know these differences if you are planning to port your QuickBASIC program from one platform to another. Significantly, QuickBASIC for the Macintosh does not include the debugger, user-defined data types (defined with the TYPE...END TYPE statement), and user-defined functions (defined with the FUNCTION statement). It does not let you create dynamic arrays, nor does it give you direct programming control of the communications and printer ports. Also, although QuickBASIC for the Macintosh offers event trapping for a mouse, it does not permit event trapping for a joystick or light pen. QuickBASIC for the Macintosh also doesn't support color graphics. Table D-2 lists all the QuickBASIC 4.5 statements that do not exist in QuickBASIC for the Macintosh. Use the statements with caution if you plan to port your QuickBASIC program from the PC to the Macintosh. For more details, refer to specific entries throughout the reference sections in this book.

Keyword Differences

Refer to the compatibility boxes at the beginning of each entry in this book for differences between statements and functions supported by QuickBASIC for the PC and those supported by QuickBASIC for the Macintosh.

APPENDIX E

Statements Specific to OS/2 in Microsoft BASIC Compiler Versions 6.0 and 7.0

The Microsoft BASIC Compiler (but not QuickBASIC 4.5) supports the OS/2 protected mode. There are two important features of this mode that affect BASIC programs. First, more than one program can be running at the same time. These programs (called "processes") can communicate with each other or share data while running. Microsoft BASIC Compiler versions 6.0 and 7.0 provide a set of statements that take advantage of some of these features. These statements are summarized in Table E-1. Note that some of the statements also work in real mode (the mode also used by DOS), but others work only in protected mode (the mode available only in OS/2).

Second, unlike DOS, OS/2 controls all program access to memory and to the hardware devices. (If it didn't, one program's output could garble another's, or one program could corrupt memory belonging to another program.) Because of this, several BASIC statements and functions are either not available or work differently in protected mode. These differences are summarized in Table E-3 on page 885.

Statement or function	Description
ON SIGNAL GOSUB	Specifies an event-trapping subroutine for a protected mode signal
OPEN PIPE:	Connects input or output to another program by using a pipe
SHELL	Executes another program without suspending the current program
SIGNAL ON/OFF/STOP	Enables, disables, or suspends trapping for protected-mode signals sent between programs
SLEEP	Suspends execution of a BASIC program (also works in real mode)

Table E-1.
BASIC statements and functions for OS/2.

Protected-Mode Signals

OS/2 provides a set of signals that programs executing concurrently in protected mode can send to one another. When you call an ON SIGNAL GOSUB statement, you specify the signal to which you want the program to respond and specify the subroutine that will be executed when the signal is received. Table E-2 lists the signal values that you can specify.

Number	Signal name	Description
1	SIG_CTRLC	User interrupt (Ctrl-C)
2	SIG_BROKENPIPE	Pipe connection broken
3	SIG_KILLPROCESS	Program terminated
4	SIG_CTRLBREAK	User break (Ctrl-Break)
5	SIG_PFLG_A	Interprocess communication, process flag A
6	SIG_PFLG_B	Interprocess communication, process flag B
7	SIG_PFLG_C	Interprocess communication, process flag C

Table E-2.
Protected-mode signals.

For example,

```
ON SIGNAL(3) GOSUB ProcEnd
```

specifies that control will branch to the subroutine *ProcEnd* when another program (perhaps spawned from your program with the SHELL statement) terminates.

Signals 5 through 7 set flags that let you direct your program to communicate with other programs. To set the flag, you use the OS/2 function DOSFLAGPROCESS.

Similar to other event-trapping statements, SIGNAL ON enables signal trapping; SIGNAL OFF turns off trapping; and SIGNAL STOP suspends trapping but "remembers" a subsequent signal when trapping is re-enabled with another SIGNAL ON statement.

Starting a New Program

In QuickBASIC, only one program can be running at a time, so if your program executes another program by using the SHELL statement, the original program suspends or terminates. In OS/2 in protected mode, however, you can use the SHELL function to start another program without suspending or terminating the current one. You use SHELL with the following syntax:

processID = SHELL(*commandString*)

commandString specifies the name of the program you want to execute and any options for its command line, and *processID* is a numeric variable that holds the OS/2-process ID number of the new program.

Statement or function	Differences in OS/2 protected mode
BLOAD	Must write to an address that the program has permission to access.
BSAVE	Must copy from an address that the program has permission to access.
CALL	Can call both OS/2 functions and dynamic-link libraries. (You should include DOSCALLS.BI in your source file.)
CALL ABSOLUTE	Must specify an address that the program has permission to access.
CALL INT86, INT86X, INT86OLD, INTERRUPT	Not available in OS/2 protected mode. (Call the appropriate OS/2 function instead.)
COLOR	Ignored in screen mode 1 under OS/2 protected mode.
DEF SEG	Must refer to a selector that will generate addresses that will be valid at runtime.
INP	Not available in OS/2 protected mode. (Call the appropriate OS/2 function instead.)
IOCTL, IOCTL$	Not available in OS/2 protected mode. (Call the appropriate OS/2 function instead.)
ON PEN GOSUB, ON PLAY GOSUB, ON STRIG GOSUB	Not available in OS/2 protected mode.
OUT	Not available in OS/2 protected mode.
PALETTE, PALETTE USING	Not available in OS/2 protected mode.
PEEK	Must refer to an address for which your program has read permission.
PEN	Not available in OS/2 protected mode.
PLAY	Not available in OS/2 protected mode.
POKE	Must refer to an address for which your program has write permission.
SCREEN	Only screen modes 0 through 2 are available in OS/2 protected mode; multiple screen pages are not supported.
SETMEM	In OS/2, returns a dummy value only.
SOUND	Not available in OS/2 protected mode.
STICK	Not available in OS/2 protected mode.
STRIG	Not available in OS/2 protected mode.
VARSEG	Returns the selector of the specified variable or array.
WAIT	Not available in OS/2 protected mode. (Use SLEEP instead.)

Table E-3.
BASIC statements and functions that are unavailable or work differently in OS/2.

Suspending Execution of a Program

The SLEEP statement is followed by the number of seconds for which the program should suspend execution. Execution resumes when this amount of time has elapsed, the user presses a key, or an event whose trapping is enabled occurs. You can use SLEEP to leave a program in memory (but not have it use any processor time) until higher-priority programs have finished executing.

Using a Pipe

The OPEN PIPE: statement starts another program and creates a data connection, called a "pipe," between your program and the second program. This enables the programs to send data to and receive data from each other. For example, a text-formatting program can send data to a printing program while both continue to run. Use the following syntax:

OPEN "PIPE:*commandString*" [FOR *mode*] AS [#] *filenumber*

commandString specifies the name of the program you want to run and any options for its command line. *filenumber* is a BASIC file number that OPEN assigns to the interprocess connection. (This lets you use PRINT to send data to the other program and use INPUT to retrieve data from it.) The FOR clause is optional; *mode* can be INPUT (sequential input) or OUTPUT (sequential output). Specifying these options makes the pipe allow one-way random access; if you omit the option, the file is opened for two-way random access. (Note that OS/2 does not buffer pipe input and output.)

APPENDIX F

Error Messages & Error Codes

QuickBASIC Error Messages

Errors can occur during any of five stages of program development:

- When you start QuickBASIC or the BC.EXE compiler from the command line
- While you edit or compile a program
- While QuickBASIC links a program to create an executable file
- While a program runs
- While you use the QuickBASIC library utility to create, combine, or otherwise manipulate program libraries

The format of error messages varies with the version of QuickBASIC (or BASIC) that you are using and with the part of QuickBASIC that is running. GW-BASIC and BASICA provide brief messages or error codes with no online Help system. Earlier versions of QuickBASIC often provide more informative messages, but not full Help. QuickBASIC version 4.5, however, displays complete online Help to explain errors that arise during editing, compiling, and linking or running a program from within the QuickBASIC environment. This appendix provides a handy alphabetic and numeric listing and explanation of each error. You will find it especially helpful if you are using a version of QuickBASIC earlier than version 4.5 or if you are compiling, linking, or running a version 4.5 program outside the QuickBASIC environment (from the DOS command line).

Invocation Errors

These errors occur when you run QuickBASIC (QB.EXE) or the command-line compiler (BC.EXE) from the DOS command line. The most common errors result from using incorrect option switches.

Syntax and Compile-time Errors

Beginning with version 2.0, QuickBASIC has a built-in editor. QuickBASIC versions 4.0 and 4.5 have a "smart" editor that incorporates all syntax rules and that parses your program code as you enter it. When you attempt to move the cursor off the current program line, the editor checks the syntax and notifies you of any error, such as missing function parameters, invalid variables, or unclosed parentheses. The error dialog box that appears displays a brief error message and lets you access Help, which explains the error in more detail. This Help system is convenient, but it isn't available in versions of QuickBASIC earlier than 4.0, nor is it available if you are using BC.EXE to compile from the command line.

Runtime Errors

Some errors don't occur until a program is actually executed—for example, when an array index goes out of bounds, or when the program attempts to divide by 0 or runs out of stack space. If QuickBASIC detects an error while a program is running from the environment in QuickBASIC version 4.5, it displays an error box containing online help. Earlier versions of QuickBASIC provide more descriptive error messages than do GW-BASIC and BASICA, but no further help is available on line. In all versions of Quick-BASIC, if you run a program from outside the QuickBASIC environment (from an executable file) and an error occurs, only the following brief message is displayed:

Error *errno* in *module_name* at address *segment*:*offset*

errno is the error number, *module_name* is the filename of the program module, and *segment*:*offset* is the complete address within the compiled code at which the error occurred.

If you specify debugging-related switches (/D, /E, or /W) on the BC.EXE command line, the message appears in the following form:

Error *errno* in line *lineno* of module *module_name* at address *segment*:*offset*

The additional *lineno* parameter is the number of the line at which the error occurred.

Not all errors have error numbers, but most runtime errors do. Therefore, your ON ERROR GOTO statements can easily trap these errors to provide a safe and graceful way of handling them. The QuickBASIC ERR statement returns the error number, or code, of the preceding error. You specify an error code in the ERROR statement to simulate the error corresponding to the code. Table F-1 lists the error codes and their descriptions.

The following section lists all invocation, compile-time, and runtime errors in alphabetic order. Because these types of error messages share a common format, this list is easy to use as a reference. Each error message is printed in boldface and is followed by the error type (invocation, compile time, or runtime). An explanation of the error follows, sometimes with suggestions for correcting it. (Remember that QuickBASIC 4.5 notifies you of many compile-time errors before you actually compile the code.) Finally, if the error message has an error number, or code, it is shown in parentheses.

Code	Description
2	Syntax error
3	RETURN without GOSUB
4	Out of DATA
5	Illegal function call
6	Overflow
7	Out of memory
9	Subscript out of range
10	Duplicate definition
11	Division by zero
13	Type mismatch
14	Out of string space
16	String formula too complex
19	No RESUME
20	RESUME without error
24	Device timeout
25	Device fault
27	Out of paper
39	CASE ELSE expected
40	Variable required
50	FIELD overflow
51	Internal error
52	Bad file name or number

Code	Description
53	File not found
54	Bad file mode
55	File already open
56	FIELD statement active
57	Device I/O error
58	File already exists
59	Bad record length
61	Disk full
62	Input past end of file
63	Bad record number
64	Bad file name
67	Too many files
68	Device unavailable
69	Communications-buffer overflow
70	Permission denied
71	Disk not ready
72	Disk-media error
73	Advanced feature unavailable
74	Rename across disks
75	Path/File access error
76	Path not found

Invocation, Compile-time, and Runtime Errors

Advanced feature unavailable. Compile-time or runtime. You tried to use a feature that isn't available in this version of QuickBASIC or the version of DOS on your system. Check your documentation. (73)

Argument-count mismatch. Compile-time. You specified the wrong number of arguments to a subprogram or function. Compare the subprogram or function call with the header line or declaration of the subprogram or function.

Array already dimensioned. Compile-time or runtime. You used more than one DIM statement with a static array. This error also occurs if you use an OPTION BASE statement after dimensioning any array. Check the type of the array (static or dynamic) and the position of your OPTION BASE statement (if any).

Array not defined. Compile-time. You referred to an array with more than 10 elements without having first defined (dimensioned) it. (It is good practice to define all arrays, even those with fewer than 10 elements, but QuickBASIC doesn't force you to do so.) If the array isn't defined anywhere, add an appropriate DIM statement. If the array is in another module, use the appropriate statement (such as COMMON, SHARED, and so on).

Array not dimensioned. Compile-time. This message is similar to the preceding error, but it occurs when you run BC.EXE from the command line. You didn't dimension an array that you used in your program. BC.EXE displays this message as a warning and does not abandon compilation, but be sure to fix the error to prevent potential problems.

Array too big. Compile-time. You tried to dimension a static array that exceeds either 64 KB or the amount of space available in the default data segment (DGROUP). Reduce the size of the array, reduce other DGROUP data requirements (such as for strings), or declare the array to be dynamic so that it will be stored in the far heap.

AS clause required. Compile-time. You originally declared a variable by using an AS clause (for example, AS STRING) and then specified that variable in a DIM, REDIM, SHARED, or COMMON statement without including the AS clause.

AS clause required on first declaration. Compile-time. You referred to a variable name with an AS clause but did not include an AS clause in the original declaration. Add the appropriate AS clause to the declaration.

AS missing. Compile-time. The statement you used requires the AS keyword (for example, *OPEN "Filename" FOR OUTPUT AS #1*).

Asterisk missing. Compile-time. You tried to declare a fixed-length string but omitted the asterisk before the number of characters. Such a declaration should read STRING * *chars*.

Bad file mode. Runtime. You tried to do one of the following:

- Use a PUT or GET with a sequential file. (54)
- Execute an OPEN statement with a file mode other than I, O, or R. (54)
- Use a FIELD statement with a file not opened as a random-access file. (54)
- Output to a file that was opened as a sequential-access file for input. (54)
- Read from a file that was opened as a sequential-access file for output or for appending. (54)
- Use an include file previously saved in the default compressed format. (Load the file into the editor and resave it as text.) (54)
- Load a binary program that has been corrupted. (54)

Bad file name. Runtime. The filename you specified violated one of the rules for DOS files (illegal characters, name too long, and so on). This message might also occur if you introduce a syntax error in an OPEN statement, such as by omitting quotation marks around the filename. (64)

Bad file name or number. Runtime. Either you tried to refer to a filename or file number that was not specified properly in an OPEN statement or you used a number that is out of range. (52)

Bad record length. Runtime. You specified a record in a GET or PUT statement whose length does not match the record length originally specified in the OPEN statement. (59)

Bad record number. Runtime. You used a record number less than or equal to 0 in a GET or PUT statement. (This message occurs if, for example, you forgot to initialize a variable.) (63)

BASE missing. Compile-time. You used the word OPTION without following it with the keyword BASE.

Binary source file. Compile-time. You tried to compile a binary (compressed-format, object, or compiled-code) file rather than an ASCII source file. If you want to compile a BASICA source file, you must first save it by using the ,A option. (This error also occurs if you try to use the /ZI or /ZD CodeView option with binary source files.)

Block IF without END IF. Compile-time. You began writing a block-style IF statement but didn't end it with END IF. (Any IF statement that has no statement on the line following the keyword THEN is considered a block IF statement.)

Buffer size expected after /C:. Invocation. You must specify a buffer size with the /C switch. (See the tutorial section in Chapter 16, "Communications Port," and the OPEN COM entry for details.)

BYVAL allowed only with numeric arguments. Compile-time. You can specify only numeric variables with the BYVAL clause in a call to an external routine.

/C: buffer size too large. Invocation. You specified with the /C switch a buffer size of greater than 32,767 bytes.

Cannot continue. Runtime. Stops program execution during debugging because you made a major change while editing. Choose either Start or Restart from the Run menu to run the program from the beginning.

Cannot find file (*filename*). Input path:. Invocation. QuickBASIC couldn't find the Quick library or utility that it needed. Either specify the correct pathname or press the Ctrl-C key combination to return to the DOS prompt. (Note: before running QB.EXE or BC.EXE, you can set the LIB environment variable in the DOS environment to the path that contains your user library, Quick library, or link library. If, for example, you specify *SET LIB=C:\QB45\LIB*, then QB.EXE, BC.EXE, LINK.EXE, and LIB.EXE will look in the specified directory for the libraries they need.)

Cannot generate listing for BASIC binary source files. Invocation. You tried to compile a binary source file by using the BC.EXE command-line compiler, but you used the /A switch. Remove the /A switch from the command line and then recompile.

Cannot start with 'FN'. Compile-time. You can't begin the name of a variable, subprogram, or function defined by FUNCTION with the letters FN. You can use these letters only for functions defined with the DEF FN statement.

CASE ELSE expected. Runtime. The variable that controls a SELECT CASE statement has a value that doesn't correspond to any of the defined cases. Check to see whether invalid values are being generated for the control variable, define a case that specifies that value, or insert a CASE ELSE statement to handle such values. (39)

CASE without SELECT. Compile-time. The keyword CASE at the start of a SELECT CASE statement must be preceded by the keyword SELECT.

Colon expected after /C. Invocation. There must be a colon between /C and the buffer size (for example, /C:1024).

Comma missing. Compile-time. The syntax of the statement in question requires a comma. (See the entry for the statement or use QuickBASIC's online Help system to remind yourself of the syntax.)

COMMON and DECLARE must precede executable statements. Compile-time. You must place COMMON or DECLARE statement before any executable statements. Statements that define variables or compiler conditions or introduce comments (COMMON, DEF*type*, DIM, OPTION BASE, REM, TYPE) are not executable statements. (DIM for static arrays is not executable; however, DIM for dynamic arrays is executable.) Metacommands (for example, $DYNAMIC) are also not executable.

COMMON in Quick library too small. Compile-time. You have specified more common variables in your module than are available in the Quick library.

COMMON name illegal. Compile-time. You used an illegal name for a named common block. Check to see whether you used a reserved word or included an illegal character in the name.

Communications-buffer overflow. Runtime. The communications receive buffer overflowed. Try increasing the buffer size by using the /C command-line switch, increasing the value specified in the RB parameter in the OPEN COM statement, checking the buffer more frequently (by using the LOC function) to detect potential overflow, or reading the buffer more often by using the INPUT$ function. (69)

CONST/DIM SHARED follows SUB/FUNCTION. Compile-time. You placed a CONST or DIM SHARED declaration after a subprogram or function definition. Be sure to place these declarations at the beginning of the file. This message is a warning of potential trouble although your program might execute correctly.

Control structure in IF...THEN...ELSE incomplete. Compile-time. You used an unmatched LOOP, END IF, END SELECT, NEXT, or WEND statement within a single-line IF statement. Do not branch into a control structure without entering the control structure at its beginning.

Data-memory overflow. Compile-time. You used too much memory for static array elements, strings, or other variables. Make your arrays dynamic if that is possible. You can also conserve memory by omitting debugging switches. If all else fails, divide your program into parts that can be chained together.

DECLARE required. Compile-time. You performed an implict subroutine or function call (by naming the subroutine or function directly in a statement rather than by using the CALL statement) and did not declare the subroutine or function before calling it.

DEF FN not allowed in control statements. Compile-time. You cannot define a function with a DEF FN statement inside a control structure (such as IF or SELECT CASE).

DEF without END DEF. Compile-time. You started defining a DEF FN function but did not end the definition with END DEF.

DEF*type* character specification illegal. Compile-time. You used an invalid type name with a DEF*type* declaration. The valid types are INT, SNG, DBL, LNG, and STR. You might have tried to define a DEF FN function without putting a space before the function name.

Device fault. Runtime. A device has signaled a hardware error; for example, a printer might have run out of paper. If this error arises during transmission to a communications port, it indicates that signals specified in the OPEN COM statement were not received within the allotted time. (25)

Device I/O error. Runtime. A device has signaled an I/O error, and the operating system could not recover from the error (could not continue writing, reading, and so on). (57)

Device timeout. Runtime. The program did not receive data or a signal from an I/O device within the allotted time. This usually occurs in communications using the serial ports. (24)

Device unavailable. Runtime. You attempted to access a device that is not on line, is not properly configured, or does not exist. (68)

Disk full. Runtime. You tried to send data to the disk as part of a PRINT, WRITE, or CLOSE operation, and there wasn't enough room on the disk for the data. (61)

Disk-media error. Runtime. The disk controller found a problem with the disk surface when attempting to read or write to the disk. You might be able to "lock out" the bad sector by using the DOS FORMAT command after you back up all the data you can recover. (72)

Disk not ready. Runtime. Either the disk drive has no disk in it or you left the disk-drive door open. (71)

Division by zero. Compile-time or runtime. The program encountered a divisor of 0. You might have forgotten to initialize a variable or have misspelled a variable name. (11)

DO without LOOP. Compile-time. Each DO statement must end with the LOOP keyword.

Document too large. Editor. You tried to edit a program or other document that was too large for the QuickBASIC editor. Split the document into smaller pieces and edit them separately; then compile from the command line with BC.EXE.

Duplicate definition. Compile-time or runtime. You are using an identifier that has already been defined. You can't use constants, variables, subprograms, or functions that have the same name. This message might also occur because you attempted to redimension a dynamic array by using a second DIM statement; use ERASE and DIM (or just REDIM) to redimension the dynamic array. (10)

Duplicate label. Compile-time. You used the same label (or line number) for more than one program line.

Dynamic array element illegal. Compile-time. You tried to use VARPTR$ with an element of a dynamic array. Because the address of such an element might change during program execution, you cannot reliably use its address.

Element not defined. Compile-time. You referred to a field in a user-defined type, but you did not define that field in the TYPE...END TYPE statement.

ELSE without IF. Compile-time. You used an ELSE clause without beginning the structure with an IF clause, or you deleted the IF clause.

ELSEIF without IF. Compile-time. You used an ELSEIF clause without beginning the structure with an IF clause, or you deleted the IF clause.

END DEF without DEF. Compile-time. You tried to end a function definition with END DEF without beginning it with a DEF FN clause, or you deleted the DEF FN clause.

END IF without block IF. Compile-time. You tried to end a block (multi-line) IF statement without beginning it with an IF clause, or you deleted the IF clause.

END SELECT without SELECT. Compile-time. You tried to end a SELECT CASE statement without beginning it with a SELECT CASE clause, or you deleted the SELECT CASE clause.

END SUB or END FUNCTION must be last line in window. Compile-time. You tried to add module-level code following a subprogram or function definition. Either return to the main module (using the View menu in the editor) or put the code in a new module.

END SUB/FUNCTION without SUB/FUNCTION. Compile-time. You tried to end a subprogram or function definition without beginning it with the SUB or FUNCTION keyword, or you deleted the SUB or FUNCTION keyword.

END TYPE without TYPE. Compile-time. You tried to end a TYPE...END TYPE statement without beginning it with a TYPE clause, or you deleted the TYPE clause.

Equal sign missing. Compile-time. The syntax of the statement that prompted this message requires an equal sign (for example, in an assignment statement).

Error during QuickBASIC initialization. Invocation. Usually this means there isn't enough memory in your system to load both QuickBASIC and the Quick library you specified. Try either removing unnecessary memory-resident programs or reducing the size of the Quick library. This error might also occur if your machine is not completely IBM compatible.

Error in loading file (*filename*)—Cannot find file. Invocation. You tried to redirect input from a file to QuickBASIC from the command line, but the file wasn't in the specified location.

Error in loading file (*filename*)—Disk I/O error. Invocation. You tried to load a file into QuickBASIC, but there was a problem with the disk drive (for example, the door was open).

Error in loading file (*filename*)—DOS memory-area error. Invocation. You tried to load a file into QuickBASIC, but QuickBASIC found that part of the memory needed by DOS was overwritten (possibly by an incorrect assembly-language routine or by a POKE statement).

Error in loading file (*filename*)—Invalid format. Invocation. You tried to do one of the following:

- Load a Quick library that was created under a previous version of QuickBASIC
- Use a file that was not converted into a Quick library by the environment's Make Library command or by the /QU option with LINK
- Load a stand-alone link library rather than a Quick library

Error in loading file (*filename*)—Out of memory. Runtime. An operation required more memory than was available (for example, for allocating a file buffer). Try to reduce the memory used by DOS buffers, memory-resident programs, or device drivers; or try to make large arrays dynamic rather than static. Reducing the amount of text in the QuickBASIC editor also frees some memory.

EXIT DO not within DO...LOOP. Compile-time. You used an EXIT DO statement outside a DO...LOOP statement.

EXIT not within FOR...NEXT. Compile-time. You used an EXIT FOR statement outside a FOR...NEXT statement.

Expected: *item*. Compile-time. The syntax of the statement in question requires the *item* specified (for example, a closing parenthesis or a comma). If you are unsure of the correct syntax, look up the statement in the online Help system or in this book.

Expression too complex. Compile-time. You created an expression that has too many elements or whose elements are too deeply nested. The expression might require too many temporary strings for holding string literals. Try to simplify the expression, such as by assigning strings to variables and by using the variables rather than the literal strings in the expression.

Extra file name ignored. Invocation. You specified too many files on the command line when running BC.EXE; QuickBASIC ignored the last file name.

Far heap corrupt. Compile-time. Either a memory-resident program conflicted with QuickBASIC or a POKE statement or non-BASIC routine inadvertently modified one of QuickBASIC's internal memory locations.

FIELD overflow. Runtime. You tried to use the FIELD statement to specify more bytes than the record length of a random-access file. (50)

FIELD statement active. Runtime. You tried to specify a record variable in a GET or PUT statement, but the file being used had space allocated with a FIELD statement. GET and PUT cannot be used with a record variable that was specified in a FIELD statement. (56)

File already exists. Runtime. You tried to specify a file in a NAME statement, but the name specified is the same as that of an existing file or directory on the current disk. (58)

File already open. Runtime. You tried to open a file for sequential output, but the file was already open; or you tried to use KILL to delete an open file. (You must close the file before using KILL.) (55)

File not found. Runtime. In a program run from the QuickBASIC environment, you referred to a nonexistent file in a FILES, KILL, NAME, OPEN, or RUN statement. (53)

File not found in module *module-name* at address *segment:offset*. Runtime. In a program run from an executable file, you referred to a nonexistent file by using a FILES, KILL, NAME, OPEN, or RUN statement. (53)

File previously loaded. Compile-time. You tried to load a file that is already in memory.

Fixed-length string illegal. Compile-time. You tried to pass a fixed-length string to a subroutine or function. Use a variable-length string instead.

FOR index variable already in use. Compile-time. You tried to use the same index variable in more than one FOR loop in a set of nested FOR loops.

FOR index variable illegal. Compile-time. You used a variable other than a simple numeric variable as the index variable in a FOR loop.

FOR without NEXT. Compile-time. You started a FOR loop and did not end it with a NEXT clause.

Formal parameter specifications illegal. Compile-time. You made an error in a subprogram or function parameter list. You might have specified the wrong number or type of parameters.

Formal parameters not unique. Compile-time. You cannot use the same name more than once in a parameter list.

Function already defined. Compile-time. You tried to define a function that is already defined elsewhere.

Function name illegal. Compile-time. You tried to use a reserved keyword as the name of a user-defined function.

Function not defined. Compile-time. You tried to use a user-defined function before you defined or declared it.

GOSUB missing. Compile-time. You started an ON *event* statement, but did not follow it with the keyword GOSUB (for example, ON COM GOSUB).

GOTO missing. Compile-time. You started an ON ERROR statement but did not follow it with the keyword GOTO.

GOTO or GOSUB expected. Compile-time. The syntax in question requires a GOTO or GOSUB statement.

Help not found. Editor. QuickBASIC was unable to provide help because program errors prevented it from constructing a variable table for your program. Press F5 to display the line that caused the error.

Identifier cannot end with %, &, !, #, or $. Compile-time. You tried to use one of these type specifiers at the end of a user-defined type name, a subprogram name, or a name used in a COMMON statement.

Identifier cannot include period. Compile-time. Names of user-defined types and names of record elements cannot contain periods. A period, when used with record variables, can separate only the record name and the element name (for example, *address.street*). You also cannot use a period if the part of the name before the period matches the name of an existing variable defined with the clause AS *user-defined-type*. In general, avoid using periods to separate parts of variable names; instead, use mixed-case descriptive names (for example, *streetAddress*).

Identifier expected. Compile-time. You used an incorrect identifier (such as a number or a reserved keyword) where QuickBASIC expected a valid identifier.

Identifier too long. Compile-time. You tried to use an identifier more than 40 characters long.

Illegal function call. Runtime. Usually this means that you passed an out-of-range parameter to a math or string function. (For example, you specified a negative number with the SQR function.) Other examples include array subscripts that are too large or are negative (unless the array was properly specified with a TO clause), negative record numbers, or invalid or nonexistent devices in I/O statements. (5)

Illegal in direct mode. Compile-time. You tried to use a statement in the Immediate window that can be used only in a program.

Illegal in procedure or DEF FN. Compile-time. The statement in question cannot be used inside a FUNCTION, SUB, or DEF FN statement.

Illegal number. Compile-time. QuickBASIC expected a number, but you included non-numeric characters (such as most letters or punctuation).

Illegal outside of SUB, FUNCTION, or DEF FN. Compile-time. You can use the statement in question only in a FUNCTION, SUB, or DEF FN statement, not in module-level code.

Illegal outside of SUB/FUNCTION. Compile-time. You can use the statement in question only in a SUB or FUNCTION statement, not in module-level code.

Illegal outside of TYPE block. Compile-time. You can only use an AS clause in the form *name* AS *type* inside a TYPE...END TYPE statement.

Illegal type character in numeric constant. Compile-time. You used an inappropriate type-declaration character (%, &, !, #, or $)—for example, 1.34%.

$INCLUDE-file access-error. Compile-time. QuickBASIC was unable to find the include file you specified in an $INCLUDE metacommand.

Include file too large. Compile-time. You tried to include with the $INCLUDE metacommand a file that was too large. Split the file into smaller files.

Input file not found. Invocation. The compiler could not find the source file you specified when you ran BC.EXE from the command line.

INPUT missing. Compile-time. The syntax of the statement in question requires the keyword INPUT.

Input past end of file. Runtime. You tried to read past the end of a file. Before reading, check the return value of the EOF function to see whether you have reached the end of the file. (62)

Input runtime module path. Runtime. QuickBASIC requires the runtime module BRUN45.EXE but could not find it. Specify the path in which BRUN45.EXE resides.

Integer between 1 and 32767 required. Compile-time. The statement in question requires a positive-integer argument.

Internal error. Runtime. A catchall message for errors that arise within QuickBASIC's runtime code. Report any of these errors to Microsoft by using the Product Assistance Request form included in your QuickBASIC documentation. (51)

Internal error near *xxxx*. Compile-time. Report these errors to Microsoft, as in the previous entry.

Invalid character. Compile-time. Your source file contains an invalid character. You might have inadvertently inserted a control character, or you might be using a file from a word processor or editor that uses formatting codes. A source file can contain only ASCII characters.

Invalid constant. Compile-time. The expression you tried to assign to a constant is invalid. Numeric expressions can contain numeric constants or literals and any arithmetic operators except exponentiation (^). A string expression assigned to a constant must always be a single string literal.

Invalid DECLARE for BASIC procedure. Compile-time. You used a DECLARE statement with the ALIAS, CDECL, or BYVAL keyword to declare a BASIC subprogram or function. You can use these keywords only with a non-BASIC procedure.

Label not defined. Compile-time. You specified a line label in a GOTO or GOSUB statement, but the label doesn't exist in your program.

Label not defined: *label*. Compile-time. A GOTO statement referred to a nonexistent line label.

Left parenthesis missing. Compile-time. Either the syntax for the statement in question needs a left parenthesis or a REDIM statement tried to reallocate space for a variable that is not an array.

Line invalid. Start again. Invocation. You used an invalid character in the BC.EXE command line following a backslash (\) or a colon (:) in a path. Retype the line.

Line number or label missing. Compile-time. You used a statement (such as GOTO or GOSUB) that requires a line number or label, but you did not specify one.

Line too long. Compile-time. Your source code contains a line more than 255 characters long. You can use the underscore continuation character to create longer lines outside the QuickBASIC editor, but not within the editor.

LOOP without DO. Compile-time. You used the keyword LOOP, but you did not start the structure with the DO keyword.

Lower bound exceeds upper bound. Compile-time. In a DIM statement, the lower bound you specified for a dimension was greater than the upper bound—for example, *DIM temp(100 TO 50)*.

Math overflow. Compile-time. You tried to perform a calculation whose result was larger than can be represented in QuickBASIC's number format.

$Metacommand error. Compile-time. You incorrectly specified a metacommand; you might have spelled it wrong. With BC.EXE, this does not abort compilation. However, QuickBASIC ignores the metacommand, and this will probably cause the program to produce incorrect results.

Minus sign missing. Compile-time. The syntax of the statement in question requires a minus sign.

Missing Event Trapping (/W) or Checking Between Statements (/V) option. Compile-time. Your program contains an ON *event* statement that requires that you use one of these compiler options on the BC.EXE command line.

Missing On Error (/E) option. Compile-time. You tried to compile a program with BC.EXE that contains an ON ERROR GOTO statement. You must include the /E option in the BC.EXE command line.

Missing Resume Next (/X) option. Compile-time. You tried to use BC.EXE to compile a program that contains a RESUME, RESUME NEXT, or RESUME 0 statement. Add the /X option to the command line.

Module level code too large. Compile-time. Your module-level code exceeds QuickBASIC's internal limit. Convert some of the code into subprograms or functions.

Module not found. Unload module from program? Compile-time. QuickBASIC could not find the module that you specified, so it loaded an empty module. If you want to run the program anyway, enter the letter Y.

Must be first statement on the line. Compile-time. You tried to use another keyword in front of an IF, ELSE, ELSEIF, or END IF clause in a block IF statement. Only a line number or label can precede one of these clauses on the line.

Name of subprogram illegal. Compile-time. You either used a reserved keyword as the name of a subprogram or tried to use the same name for two different subprograms.

Nested function definition. Compile-time. You tried to insert a FUNCTION statement inside another FUNCTION statement or inside an IF statement.

NEXT missing for *variable*. Compile-time. You didn't use the NEXT keyword in a FOR loop. *variable* is the index variable of the loop in question.

NEXT without FOR. Compile-time. You used a NEXT keyword, but you didn't precede it with a FOR clause.

No line number in *module-name* at address *segment:offset*. Runtime. An ON ERROR GOTO statement was executed, but QuickBASIC couldn't find the line number in its internal table. You probably didn't specify the line number in your code; however, the line-number table might also have been corrupted by an incorrect POKE statement or an assembly-language routine. The program can't recover from this error.

No main module. Choose Set Main Module from the Run menu to select one. Compile-time. You have unloaded the main module, and you must load a main module again before you can run the program.

No RESUME. Runtime. The program ended while executing an error-handling routine. Insert a RESUME statement to return control from the error handler. (19)

Not watchable. Editor. You tried to specify in a watch expression a variable that is not accessible to the module, subprogram, or function currently in the View window. (For example, you might have specified a local variable in another subprogram.)

Numeric array illegal. Compile-time. You cannot use the VARPTR$ function to retrieve the address of a numeric array. (You can use only simple numeric variables and string arrays.)

Only simple variables allowed. Compile-time. You tried to use READ or INPUT with a user-defined type or an array of a user-defined type. (Elements of other arrays are acceptable. You can also read individual fields of a user-defined type one at a time.)

Operation requires disk. Compile-time. You specified a read or write operation that requires a disk device rather than a keyboard, printer, or communications device.

Option unknown: *option*. Invocation. You tried to use an option not recognized by BC.EXE.

Out of DATA. Runtime. You tried to execute a READ statement, but the DATA statements didn't contain any more items to be read. (You can use RESTORE to reread data items.) (4)

Out of data space. Compile-time or runtime. You ran out of space in QuickBASIC's default data segment (DGROUP), which contains static arrays, variable-length strings, and simple variables. Try to make arrays dynamic (including turning variable-length string arrays into dynamic, fixed-length string arrays), try to reduce buffers or the stack, use data types (such as integers) that don't require more space than necessary, or consider using alternative algorithms.

Out of memory. Invocation, compile-time, or runtime. An operation required more memory than was available (for example, the allocating of a file buffer). Try to reduce the memory used by DOS buffers, memory-resident programs, or device drivers; or try to make large arrays dynamic rather than static. Reducing the amount of text loaded into the QuickBASIC editor will also free some memory. (7)

Out of paper. Runtime. The printer is either out of paper or not turned on. (27)

Out of stack space. Runtime. Either the program contains too many active subprograms or functions or a recursive function has called itself too many times. You cannot trap this error.

Out of string space. Runtime. You ran out of space for static strings in the default data segment (DGROUP). Try using dynamic arrays of fixed-length strings. (14)

Overflow. Runtime. A program calculation exceeded the allowable range for integer or floating-point numbers. (6)

Overflow in numeric constant. Compile-time. You used a numeric constant that is too large for the type of number represented (for example, an integer greater than 32767).

Parameter type mismatch. Compile-time. You tried to call a subprogram or function with a parameter whose data type doesn't match the one defined in the parameter list.

Path not found. Runtime. You tried to execute an OPEN, MKDIR, CHDIR, or RMDIR statement with a path that DOS could not find. (76)

Path/File access error. Compile-time or runtime. During an OPEN, MKDIR, CHDIR, or RMDIR operation, DOS was unable to access the specified file using the path you specified. Check the pathname and (if you are trying to write to or delete a file) the file attributes. (75)

Permission denied. Runtime. You tried to write to a write-protected disk, or you tried to access a locked file on a network. (70)

Procedure already defined in Quick library. Compile-time. You loaded a Quick library that includes a subprogram or function whose name is already used in your program.

Procedure too large. Compile-time. A procedure is larger than QuickBASIC allows. Split the procedure into several smaller procedures.

Program-memory overflow. Compile-time. The compiled code for a module of your program exceeded 64 KB. Either split the module into two smaller modules or use the CHAIN statement to connect parts of your program.

Read error on standard input. Invocation. A system error occurred while BC.EXE was reading from the console or from a redirected input file.

Record/string assignment required. Compile-time. You used an LSET statement without specifying an assignment to a string or a record variable.

Redo from start. Runtime. The response to an INPUT statement provided the wrong number or type of data items. Retype the response, using the correct form.

Rename across disks. Runtime. You used a different drive designator when you tried to rename a file; QuickBASIC does not allow this. Copy the file to the new disk drive, and then use KILL to delete the original file. (74)

Requires DOS 2.10 or later. Invocation or runtime. In general, QuickBASIC requires that your system use DOS 2.1 or later.

RESUME without error. Runtime. You placed a RESUME statement outside an error-trapping routine. (20)

RETURN without GOSUB. Runtime. QuickBASIC executed a RETURN statement without having encountered a previous, unmatched GOSUB statement. (3)

Right parenthesis missing. Compile-time. The syntax of the statement in question requires a right, or closing, parenthesis.

SEG or BYVAL not allowed in CALLS. Compile-time. You can use the BYVAL and SEG keywords only in a CALL (Non-BASIC procedures) statement, not in a CALLS statement.

SELECT without END SELECT. Compile-time. You began a SELECT CASE statement but omitted (or misspelled) the END SELECT clause.

Semicolon missing. Compile-time. The syntax of the statement in question requires a semicolon.

Separator illegal. Compile-time. You used a character other than a semicolon or a comma as a delimiter in a PRINT USING or WRITE statement.

Simple or array variable expected. Compile-time. QuickBASIC requires a variable argument in the statement in question. You can use either a simple variable or an array.

Skipped forward to END TYPE statement. Compile-time. An error in a TYPE... END TYPE statement caused QuickBASIC to ignore the remaining statements in the type definition. Although compilation will continue, the program will probably not work correctly.

Statement cannot occur within $INCLUDE file. Compile-time. You tried to put a subroutine or function definition in a file included in your program by using the $INCLUDE metacommand. Use the Merge command in the File menu to insert the text of the file into the current module. You can also load the include file as a separate module, but you might need to insert SHARED statements to provide access to variables from the original module.

Statement cannot precede SUB/FUNCTION definition. Compile-time. Only a REM statement or DEF*type* statement can precede a subroutine or function definition.

Statement ignored. Compile-time. You used BC.EXE to compile a program that contains TRON and TROFF statements, but you didn't specify the /D option in the command line. The program will execute but might not function correctly. Recompile with the /D option.

Statement illegal in TYPE block. Compile-time. You can use only a REM statement or an *element* AS *typename* clause within a TYPE...END TYPE statement.

STOP in module *name* at address *segment:offset*. Runtime. The STOP statement you used in your program was executed.

String assignment required. Compile-time. You used an RSET statement without specifying an assignment to a string.

String constant required for ALIAS. Compile-time. You used a DECLARE (Non-BASIC procedures) statement with the ALIAS keyword, but you did not specify a string constant argument after ALIAS. Check to see whether you used a string variable.

String expression required. Compile-time. The syntax of the statement in question requires a string expression. You might have used a numeric variable or a numeric literal. Usually when QuickBASIC requires a string expression, you can use any combination of string variables, string constants, or string literals.

String formula too complex. Runtime. You used a string expression that was too long, or you specified more than 15 variables in an INPUT statement. Either assign part of the expression to a string variable and then use the variable in another expression or use two INPUT statements. (16)

String space corrupt. Runtime. This can be caused by one of the following problems:

- An assembly-language routine changed internal string pointers.
- An incorrect array subscript caused data to be changed outside the array. (Use the Produce Debug Code option to direct QuickBASIC to check array subscripts to ensure that they are within bounds.)
- An incorrect POKE or DEF SEG statement changed a string pointer or descriptor.
- Two chained programs contain mismatched COMMON declarations.

String variable required. Compile-time. The syntax of the statement in question requires a string variable, not a string literal or a numeric value.

SUB or FUNCTION missing. Compile-time. You specified a subprogram or function in a DECLARE statement, but the program contains no definition for the subprogram or function.

SUB/FUNCTION without END SUB/FUNCTION. Compile-time. You started a subprogram or function but didn't end the definition with an END FUNCTION or END SUB statement.

Subprogram error. Compile-time. This error is most likely to occur when you try to define a subprogram or function that is already defined in your program. Either try to insert a subprogram or function definition within another such definition or omit the END SUB or END FUNCTION statement.

Subprogram not defined. Compile-time. You called a subprogram that you haven't defined. You might need to load the program module or library that contains the definition.

Subprograms not allowed in control statements. Compile-time. You can't define a subprogram or function within an IF or SELECT CASE statement. (You can, of course, call a subprogram or function within a control statement.)

Subscript out of range. Runtime. The program tried to reference an array element beyond the defined subscript boundaries of the array. Also, you might have attempted to access an element of an undimensioned dynamic array (for example, if the array was erased), or you might have used an array that exceeded 64 KB in size and was not dynamic, or the /AH option was not used when you invoked QuickBASIC or BC.EXE. (9)

Subscript syntax illegal. Compile-time. A syntax error occurred in an array subscript specification (for example, you tried to use a string value for a subscript).

Syntax error. Compile-time or runtime. At compile time, this message usually indicates a typographical error or incorrect punctuation in a statement. The editor in QuickBASIC versions 4.0 and 4.5 reports these errors as soon as you move the cursor from the current line. At runtime, a syntax error usually indicates an improperly formatted item in a DATA statement. (2)

Syntax error in numeric constant. Compile-time. A numeric constant or literal contains invalid punctuation or other invalid characters.

THEN missing. Compile-time. You started writing an IF statement, but you forgot to include the THEN clause.

TO missing. Compile-time. Usually this means you tried to specify a range of array subscripts but omitted the TO keyword.

Too many arguments in function call. Compile-time. You tried to use more than 60 arguments when calling a function—an unlikely situation.

Too many dimensions. Compile-time. You tried to specify more than 60 dimensions in an array definition.

Too many files. Compile-time or runtime. At compile time, this error means that you tried to nest files included (by using the $INCLUDE metacommand) more than 5 levels deep. At runtime, this error means that your program tried to create a new file (with SAVE or OPEN) in a directory that already has 255 files in it. (67)

Too many labels. Compile-time or runtime. At compile time, this message means you used more than 255 line labels in an ON...GOSUB or ON...GOTO statement. At runtime in a compiled program, it means you used more than 59 labels in an ON...GOSUB or ON...GOTO statement.

Too many named COMMON blocks. Compile-time. You cannot use more than 126 named common blocks in a program.

Too many TYPE definitions. Compile-time. You cannot define more than 240 user-defined data types.

Too many variables for INPUT. Compile-time. You cannot specify more than 60 variables in an INPUT statement.

Too many variables for LINE INPUT. Compile-time. You cannot specify more than 1 variable in a LINE INPUT statement.

Type mismatch. Compile-time or runtime. You used the wrong type of variable for an operation. (For example, you can't use the LEFT$ function with a numeric argument or the ABS function with a string argument.) (13)

TYPE missing. Compile-time. You used the END TYPE clause but didn't include a preceding, unmatched TYPE clause. You might have inadvertently deleted that line.

Type more than 65535 bytes. Compile-time. A user-defined type cannot contain more than 64 KB of data.

Type not defined. Compile-time. You referred to another user-defined type within a TYPE...END TYPE statement, but the type you referred to is not defined in your program. You might need to load the module or library that contains the definition.

TYPE statement improperly nested. Compile-time. You cannot include a definition of a user-defined type within a subprogram or function.

TYPE without END TYPE. Compile-time. You started writing a user-defined type definition but did not end it with an END TYPE clause.

Typed variable not allowed in expression. Compile-time. You cannot use a record variable in the statement in question. You might have tried to pass a variable of a user-defined type to a subprogram or function.

Unexpected end of file in TYPE declaration. Compile-time. You embedded an end-of-file character in a user-defined type definition. If you use an editor that can search for control characters, search for and delete any Ctrl-Z characters.

Unprintable error. Runtime. No error message corresponds to the error code that was generated. You might have used the ERROR statement without including a defined error code.

Unrecognized switch error: "QU". Compile-time. You tried to create an executable file or a Quick library, but you used a version of the Microsoft Overlay Linker other than the one provided in the QuickBASIC package.

Valid options: [/RUN] file /AH /B /C:buf /G /NOHI /H /L [lib] /MBF /CMD string. Invocation. You tried to invoke QuickBASIC with an invalid option.

Variable-length string required. Compile-time. You tried to use a fixed-length string in a FIELD statement; QuickBASIC does not allow this.

Variable name not unique. Compile-time. You tried to define a variable as a user-defined type after the variable was used as a record variable.

Variable required. Compile-time or runtime. During compile time, you used an INPUT, LET, READ, or SHARED statement without specifying the name of a variable. At runtime, you used a GET or PUT statement that didn't specify a variable when used with a file opened in binary mode. (40)

WEND without WHILE. Compile-time. You used a WEND statement without a preceding, unmatched WHILE keyword. You might have inadvertently deleted that line.

WHILE without WEND. Compile-time. You started writing a WHILE statement but didn't end it with a WEND statement.

Wrong number of dimensions. Compile-time. You referred to an array element using a number of dimensions different from the number you specified in the array definition.

Linking Errors

The process of linking a QuickBASIC program involves combining object files and creating the appropriate calls to library subroutines needed by your program. This process is normally invisible to you when you compile a program from within the QuickBASIC environment. If an error occurs (for example, if a needed library is not available), QuickBASIC 4.5 displays an error box that lets you get online help. Earlier versions of QuickBASIC display a brief description of the error but provide no online help. However, in all versions, if you run the linker (LINK.EXE) from outside the environment, QuickBASIC returns only brief error messages. The following section lists all Link errors by error number.

There are three kinds of linker messages—fatal errors, nonfatal errors, and warnings. Fatal errors stop the linking process immediately. The fatal error message uses the syntax

location : fatal error L1*xxx* : *messagetext*

Nonfatal errors do not prevent the creation of the executable file, although the program is likely to have problems. The nonfatal error message uses the syntax

location : error L2*xxx* : *messagetext*

Finally, warning messages indicate possible problems (usually minor ones) but do not prevent the creation of the executable file. They use the syntax

location : error L4*xxx* : *messagetext*

Note that several linker messages refer to internal matters, such as group and segment definitions. The *Microsoft MS-DOS Programmer's Reference* and other detailed DOS programmer's reference books (such as *The Waite Group's MS-DOS Developer's Guide*) explain these matters. To correct some of the more obscure errors described below, you must be familiar with assembly-language programming concepts.

Link Errors by Error Number

Fatal Linker Errors

L1001 ***option*: option name ambiguous.** You didn't specify enough letters of a command-line option to let LINK.EXE know which option you wanted. For example, the option */N* generates this error because three different linker options begin with the letter N.

L1002 ***option*: unrecognized option name.** You specified a command-line option that does not exist.

L1003 /QUICKLIB,/EXEPACK incompatible. You tried to specify both the /QUICKLIB and the /EXEPACK options, but they can't be used together.

L1004 *option*: invalid numeric value. You used a non-numeric value with an option that requires a numeric value, or you used a number that was out of range for that option.

L1006 *option*: stack size exceeds 65535 bytes. You specified a value for the /STACKSIZE option that exceeded 64 KB, the maximum stack size.

L1007 *option*: interrupt number exceeds 255. You specified a number greater than 255 with the /OVERLAYINTERRUPT option. Only 255 user interrupt numbers are available.

L1008 *option*: segment limit set too high. You specified more than 3072 segments with the /SEGMENTS option.

L1009 *number*: CPARMAXALLOC : illegal value. You specified with the /CPARMAXALLOC option a number outside the range 1 through 65535.

L1020 no object modules specified. You didn't specify any object-file names, so LINK.EXE had nothing to link.

L1021 cannot nest response files. You specified a response file that includes another response file.

L1022 response line too long. A line in a response file was longer than 127 characters.

L1023 terminated by user. You pressed Ctrl-C or Ctrl-Break.

L1024 nested right parentheses. You incorrectly typed the contents specification of an overlay.

L1025 nested left parentheses. You incorrectly typed the contents specification of an overlay.

L1026 unmatched right parenthesis. You incorrectly typed the contents specification of an overlay.

L1027 unmatched left parenthesis. You incorrectly typed the contents specification of an overlay.

L1043 relocation table overflow. The program contained more than 32,768 long calls, long jumps, or other long pointers. Try to rearrange the program so you can use more short references.

L1045 too many TYPDEF records. An object module used more than 255 DOS TYPDEF records, which describe communal variables. This problem can occur only when you link to programs produced by the Microsoft FORTRAN Compiler or other compilers that support communal variables. Reduce the number of communal variables.

L1046 too many external symbols in one module. An object module has more than 1023 external symbols. Split the module (or the original source program) into smaller modules.

L1047 too many group, segment, and class names in one module. A compiled program module contained too many group, segment, or class names. Rewrite the module to use fewer such names, or split the module.

L1048 too many segments in module. An object module had more than 255 segments. Either split the module or combine segments.

L1049 too many segments. The program had either more than the default maximum number of segments (128), or more than the number specified in the /SEGMENTS command-line option. Increase the value for the /SEGMENTS option.

L1050 too many groups in one module. There were more than 21 group definitions (GRPDEF) in a single module. Either reduce the number of group definitions or split the module.

L1051 too many groups. The program defined too many groups, not counting DGROUP (the default data segment). Reduce the number of groups to fewer than 21.

L1052 too many libraries. You specified more than 32 libraries for linking. Either combine libraries, or rewrite the program to reduce the need for libraries.

L1053 out of memory for symbol table. The linker ran out of memory for the symbol table. (This limit varies with the total amount of free memory in the system.) Combine modules or segments and make new object files. Reduce the number of public symbols if possible.

L1054 requested segment limit too high. The linker ran out of memory for description tables of either the default number of segments (128) or the number of segments that you specified with the /SEGMENTS option. Specify a smaller number with /SEGMENTS.

L1056 too many overlays. The program defined more than 63 overlays. Combine the smaller or infrequently used overlays.

L1057 data record too large. An LEDATA record in an object module contained more than 1024 bytes of data. If a Microsoft compiler or assembler produced the module, contact Microsoft by using the Product Assistance Request form.

L1063 out of memory for CodeView information. You compiled too many object files with debugging information for the CodeView debugger. Turn off the Produce Debug Information option in the Make EXE File dialog box and then recompile.

L1070 segment size exceeds 64K. A segment contained more than 64 KB of code or data. Split your program code into smaller modules.

L1071 segment _TEXT larger than 65520 bytes. This error doesn't usually occur with QuickBASIC, but it might occur if you name a segment _TEXT and link it using the /DOSSEG option.

L1072 common area longer than 65536 bytes. The program had more than 64 KB of communal variables. Only a compiler that supports communal variables can create this type of program. Try using fewer communal variables.

L1080 cannot open list file. The disk or root directory was full. Remove unneeded files.

L1081 out of space for run file. The disk on which the executable file was being written was full. Either free more disk space or use a different disk.

L1083 cannot open run file. The disk or root directory was full. Remove unnecessary files.

L1084 cannot create temporary file. The disk or root directory was full. Remove unnecessary files.

L1085 cannot open temporary file. The disk or root directory was full. Remove unnecessary files.

L1086 scratch file missing. This was caused by an internal error with LINK. (Contact Microsoft by using the Product Assistance Request form.)

L1087 unexpected end-of-file on scratch file. You were using a floppy disk for the temporary linker files and removed the disk during linking. Restart the linker and leave the disk in the drive.

L1088 out of space for list file. The disk or root directory was full. Remove unnecessary files.

L1089 *filename*: cannot open response file. LINK couldn't find the specified response file. You might have typed the pathname incorrectly.

L1090 cannot reopen list file. You were using a floppy disk to hold the files generated by the linker, but you did not replace the disk with the original disk, which contains the list file, when requested to do so.

L1091 unexpected end-of-file on library. You were using libraries from a floppy disk, and you removed the disk before the linker finished reading the library.

L1093 object not found. The linker couldn't find one of the object files that you specified to be linked. You might have typed the pathnames incorrectly.

L1101 invalid object module. An object module had an invalid format. Try the link again; if the problem persists, contact Microsoft by using the Product Assistance Request form.

L1102 unexpected end of file. This error usually means that a library had an invalid format. Either try using a different copy of the library file or (if you have the source code) try re-creating the library with LIB.EXE.

L1103 attempt to access data outside segment bounds. A data record in an object module specified data extending beyond the end of the segment. If the object module was created using a Microsoft assembler or compiler, contact Microsoft by using the Product Assistance Request form.

L1104 *filename*: not valid library. A file you specified as a library to be linked was not a valid library. Either try a different copy of the library file or (if you have the source code) try re-creating the library with LIB.EXE.

L1113 unresolved COMDEF; internal error. Contact Microsoft by using the Product Assistance Request form and describe the circumstances that caused this error.

L1114 file not suitable for /EXEPACK; relink without. You specified the option /EXEPACK with a file for which packing would not be worthwhile. Run LINK.EXE again without the /EXEPACK option.

L1115 /QUICKLIB, overlays incompatible. You tried to use both the /QUICKLIB option and overlays. Use either one or the other.

Nonfatal Linker Errors

L2001 fixup(s) without data. A FIXUPP record occurred without a data record immediately preceding it. If the object file was created by a Microsoft compiler, contact Microsoft by using the Product Assistance Request form.

L2002 fixup overflow near *number* in frame seg *segname* target seg *segname* target offset *number*. This error can be caused by a group larger than 64 KB, the presence of an intersegment short jump or intersegment short call, the name of a data item conflicting with a data item in a library, or an EXTRN declaration in an assembly-language source file appearing inside the body of a segment. Revise the source file and then re-create the object file.

L2003 intersegment self-relative fixup at *offset* in segment *segname*. You tried to make a near call or jump to a far entry.

L2004 LOBYTE-type fixup overflow. A LOBYTE fixup generated an address overflow.

L2005 fixup type unsupported. A fixup type occurred that is not supported by LINK.EXE. This is usually a compiler error; if a Microsoft compiler or assembler was used, contact Microsoft by using the Product Assistance Request form.

L2011 *name*: NEAR/HUGE conflict. Conflicting NEAR and HUGE attributes were given for a communal variable. This error can occur only with object files produced by compilers that support communal variables, such as the Microsoft FORTRAN compiler.

L2012 *name*: array-element size mismatch. A far, communal array was declared with two or more different data types (such as integer and single precision), and the data types result in different element sizes. This error can occur only with compilers that support far communal arrays.

L2013 LIDATA record too large. A LIDATA record contains more than 512 bytes. If the program involved was compiled with a Microsoft assembler or compiler, contact Microsoft by using the Product Assistance Request form.

L2024 *name*: symbol already defined. A public symbol has been redefined. Delete all but one definition.

L2025 *name*: symbol defined more than once. You can specify only one definition per symbol. Delete any extra definitions.

L2029 unresolved externals. This message includes a list of symbols and the modules in which they occur. These symbols were referenced as external but were not defined anywhere in the modules or libraries linked by LINK.EXE. Check the spelling of the symbols.

L2041 stack plus data exceed 64K. The total size of the stack and the default data segment (DGROUP) cannot exceed 64 KB. Reduce the stack size if possible; reduce the amount of data stored in DGROUP if necessary. The linker checks for this error only if the /DOSSEG option is enabled. It is enabled by default by the library startup module.

L2043 Quick library support module missing. You did not specify (and so LINK.EXE could not find) the object module or library required for creating a Quick library. For QuickBASIC, you need to specify the library BQLB45.LIB.

L2044 *name*: symbol multiply defined, use /NOE. LINK.EXE has found a possible redefinition of a public symbol. This often results from your creating a symbol already in use in a library. Try to relink using the /NOEXTDICTIONARY option. Note that if error L2025 also occurs, a symbol has been redefined, so you will have to change a symbol name.

Linker Warnings

L4011 PACKCODE value exceeding 65500 unreliable. This is a warning that the Packcode segment size exceeds 65,500 bytes and therefore might be unreliable on the Intel 80286 microprocessor.

L4012 load-high disables EXEPACK. You tried to use the /HIGH and /EXEPACK options at the same time, so LINK.EXE disabled the /EXEPACK option. If you want the linker to pack the executable file, relink without the /HIGH option.

L4015 /CODEVIEW disables /DSALLOCATE. You tried to use the /CODEVIEW and /DSALLOCATE options at the same time, so LINK.EXE disabled /DSALLOCATE. If you want to use /DSALLOCATE, relink without the /CODEVIEW option.

L4016 /CODEVIEW disables /EXEPACK. You tried to use the /CODEVIEW and /EXEPACK options at the same time, so LINK.EXE disabled /EXEPACK. If you want the linker to pack the executable file, relink without the /CODEVIEW option.

L4020 *name*: code-segment size exceeds 65500. This message warns you that a code segment exceeds 65,500 bytes and therefore might be unreliable on the Intel 80286 microprocessor.

L4021 no stack segment. No stack segment was defined with a STACK combine type in the programs being linked. QuickBASIC does this automatically, but this problem can occur with an assembly-language program. Ignore this message if you intentionally omitted the stack definition from the assembly-language program. This message can also occur if you link with a version of LINK.EXE earlier than 2.4.

L4031 *name*: segment declared in more than one group. You declared a segment as belonging to two different groups. Correct the source file.

L4034 more than 239 overlay segments; extra put in root. The program designated more than 239 segments to be put in overlays. LINK.EXE put segments beginning with segment number 234 in the root (permanently resident) portion of the program.

L4045 name of output file is *name*. You did not specify the /QUICKLIB option early enough in the command line, so LINK.EXE used *name* instead for the name of the library.

L4050 too many public symbols for sorting. You specified the /MAP option, but the object files contained too many public symbols to execute the sort. In this case, LINK.EXE returns an unsorted list of public symbols.

L4051 *filename*: cannot find library. LINK.EXE could not find the specified link library. You probably typed an incorrect filename or specified the wrong path for the library.

L4053 VM.TMP: illegal filename; ignored. You used the reserved name VM.TMP as an object filename. Rename the file and relink.

L4054 *filename*: cannot find file. LINK.EXE could not find the specified file. You probably typed an incorrect filename or specified the wrong path for the file.

Library (LIB.EXE) Errors

Several errors can occur when you use LIB.EXE, the Microsoft QuickBASIC Library Manager. The error numbers consist of the letter U followed by four digits. The following section lists them in numeric order.

Library messages have one of the following formats:

{*filename* ¦ LIB}: fatal error U1*xxx*: *messagetext*
{*filename* ¦ LIB}: error U2*xxx*: *messagetext*
{*filename* ¦ LIB}: warning U4*xxx*: *messagetext*

A fatal error stops execution of LIB.EXE. Nonfatal errors or warnings let the operation continue; however, the resulting library will probably contain errors.

The following errors can occur when you run the LIB library management program.

U1105 page size too small. This error message usually indicates that you specified an invalid input library file. You might need to re-create the input library.

U1151 syntax error: illegal file specification. You specified a command operator (such as + or –) without immediately following it with a valid module name.

U1152 syntax error: option name missing. You used a slash (/) without an option name.

U1143 syntax error: option value missing. You specified the /PAGESIZE option without specifying a value.

U1154 option unknown. You specified an invalid option. As of the LIB.EXE program distributed with QuickBASIC version 4.5, only the /PAGESIZE option is supported.

U1155 syntax error: illegal input. You used a LIB.EXE command with incorrect syntax. (See Appendix G of the Microsoft QuickBASIC *Programming in BASIC* manual for proper syntax formats.)

U1156 syntax error. You used a LIB.EXE command with incorrect syntax. (See Appendix G of the Microsoft QuickBASIC *Programming in BASIC* manual for proper syntax formats.)

U1157 comma or new line missing. A comma or carriage return was missing from the command line. You might have caused this error by using a comma rather than a space to separate filenames and commands.

U1158 terminator missing. Your response to the "Output library" prompt or the last line in a response file did not end with a carriage return.

U1161 cannot rename old library. LIB.EXE usually renames the old version of the library being modified, by giving the library a BAK extension. This error occurs when an existing backup file had read-only protection and therefore could not be removed to accommodate the new back-up file. Change the protection on the backup file.

U1162 cannot reopen library. LIB.EXE could not reopen the old library after it was renamed with the BAK extension. This might be a disk error.

U1163 error writing to cross-reference file. The disk or root directory was full. Delete unneeded files.

U1170 too many symbols. There were more than 4609 symbols in the library file. Split the library into smaller libraries.

U1171 insufficient memory. LIB.EXE did not have enough memory to run. Try to remove resident programs or DOS features that occupy memory.

U1172 no more virtual memory. Note the circumstances of this error, and report it to Microsoft by using the Product Assistance Request form.

U1173 internal failure. Note the circumstances of this error, and report it to Microsoft by using the Product Assistance Request form.

U1174 mark: not allocated. Note the circumstances of this error, and report it to Microsoft by using the Product Assistance Request form.

U1175 free: not allocated. Note the circumstances of this error, and report it to Microsoft by using the Product Assistance Request form.

U1180 write to extract file failed. The disk or root directory was full. Delete unnecessary files.

U1181 write to library open file failed. The disk or root directory was full. Delete unnecessary files.

U1182 *filename*: cannot create extract file. Either the disk or root directory was full or the extract file already existed as a read-only file and could not be replaced with a new one. If necessary, remove the read-only protection on the extract file. If that is not the problem, delete unneeded files from the disk.

U1183 cannot open response file. LIB.EXE could not find the response file. You might have typed an incorrect filename or specified an incorrect path.

U1184 unexpected end of file on command input. You included an end-of-file character before the end of the information needed to respond to a prompt. (If this is in a response file, delete any Ctrl-Z characters that occur before the end of the response text.)

U1185 cannot create new library. Either the disk or root directory was full or the library file already existed as a read-only file and could not be replaced with a new one. If necessary, remove the read-only protection on the library file. If that is not the problem, delete unnecessary files from the disk.

U1186 error writing to new library. The disk or root directory was full. Delete unnecessary files.

U1187 cannot open VM.TMP. The disk or root directory was full. Delete unnecessary files.

U1188 cannot write to VM. Note the circumstances of this error, and report it to Microsoft by using the Product Assistance Request form.

U1189 cannot read from VM. Note the circumstances of this error, and report it to Microsoft by using the Product Assistance Request form.

U1190 interrupted by user. You pressed Ctrl-C or Ctrl-Break.

U1200 *name*: invalid library header. The input file you specified was not a library file or has been corrupted. Either try a different copy of the file or re-create the library from the appropriate source files.

U1203 *name*: invalid object module near *location*. You specified an invalid object module. Try recompiling the source code to generate a new object.

U2152 *filename*: cannot create listing. Either the disk or root directory was full or the listing file already existed as a read-only file and could not be replaced with a new one. If necessary, remove the read-only protection on the listing file. If that is not the problem, delete unnecessary files from the disk.

U2155 *modulename*: module not in library; ignored. LIB.EXE did not find the specified module in the input library. You might need to use a different library, or you might have specified the wrong module.

U2157 *filename*: cannot access file. LIB.EXE couldn't open the specified file. You might have typed an incorrect filename or specified the wrong path.

U2158 *libraryname*: invalid library header, file ignored. The input library had an invalid format. You might have specified a file that is not a library or one that has been corrupted. Try a different copy of the library; if that doesn't work, re-create the library.

U2159 *filename*: invalid format *hexnumber*; file ignored. The signature byte of the file was not a recognized type. (LIB.EXE currently recognizes Microsoft library,

Intel library, Microsoft object, or XENIX archive files.) The file might have been corrupted.

U4150 ***modulename*: module redefinition ignored.** You tried to add a module to a library that already had a module with that name, or you might have specified the same module more than once.

U4151 ***symbol*: symbol redefined in module *modulename*, redefinition ignored.** You defined the specified symbol in more than one module.

U4153 ***number*: page size too small; ignored.** You specified a value of less than 16 for the /PAGESIZE option.

U4155 ***modulename*: module not in library.** You specified a module to be replaced, but the module did not exist in the library.

U4156 ***libraryname*: output-library specification ignored.** You specified both a new library and an output library in the command line. You cannot do this unless one of the libraries already exists.

U4157 **insufficient memory, extended dictionary not created.** There wasn't enough memory available for LINK.EXE to create the extended dictionary for faster linking. The resulting library is valid, but it takes longer to create.

U4158 **internal error, extended dictionary not created.** Due to an internal error, LINK.EXE couldn't create the extended dictionary. The resulting library is valid, but it takes longer to create.

APPENDIX G

Control Codes

Ctrl-key combinations represent the first 32 ASCII codes, which originally controlled peripherals. Now the IBM PC also uses them to display special characters.

ASCII codes Dec	Hex	Control abbreviation and function		IBM character	DOS display
0	0	NUL	Null		^@[1]
1	1	SOH	Start of heading	☺	^A
2	2	STX	Start of text	☻	^B
3	3	ETX	End of text	♥	^C (Break)[2]
4	4	EOT	End of transmission	♦	^D
5	5	ENQ	Enquiry	♣	^E
6	6	ACK	Acknowledge	♠	
7	7	BEL	Bell	•	^G
8	8	BS	Backspace	◘	Backspace
9	9	HT	Horizontal tab	○	Tab
10	A	LF	Linefeed	◙	Linefeed
11	B	VT	Vertical tab	♂	^K
12	C	FF	Formfeed	♀	^L
13	D	CR	Carriage return	♪	Enter
14	E	SO	Shift out	♫	^N
15	F	SI	Shift in	☼	^O
16	10	DLE	Data link escape	►	Printer toggle[3]
17	11	DC1	Device control 1	◄	^Q (or Resume)
18	12	DC2	Device control 2	↕	^R
19	13	DC3	Device control 3	‼	Pause (or ^S)
20	14	DC4	Device control 4	¶	^T
21	15	NAK	Negative acknowledge	§	^U
22	16	SYN	Synchronous idle	▬	^V
23	17	ETB	End transmission block	↨	^W
24	18	CAN	Cancel	↑	^X
25	19	EM	End of medium	↓	^Y
26	1A	SUB	Substitute	→	^Z[4]
27	1B	ESC	Escape	←	\ (or ^[)[5]

(continued)

continued

ASCII codes		Control abbreviation		IBM	DOS
Dec	**Hex**	**and function**		**character**	**display**
28	1C	FS	File separator	∟	^\
29	1D	GS	Group separator	↔	^]
30	1E	RS	Record separator	▲	^^
31	1F	US	Unit separator	▼	^_

[1] Only by pressing F7; Ctrl-@ produces ^C (Break).

[2] Same as Break (Ctrl-Pause; on pre-101-key keyboards, Ctrl-Scroll Lock).

[3] Same as Ctrl-Print Screen (turns on and off echoing of screen characters to printer).

[4] Also by pressing F6; used as ASCII end-of-file marker.

[5] At the DOS command line, pressing the Esc key displays a backslash followed by a new, blank command line. However, the Escape character is often displayed as ^[.

APPENDIX H

ASCII Characters

ASCII	Dec	Hex	Control
	0	00	NUL (Null)
☺	1	01	SOH (Start of heading)
☻	2	02	STX (Start of test)
♥	3	03	ETX (End of text)
♦	4	04	EOT (End of transmission)
♣	5	05	ENQ (Enquiry)
♠	6	06	ACK (Acknowledge)
•	7	07	BEL (Bell)
◘	8	08	BS (Backspace)
○	9	09	HT (Horizontal tab)
◙	10	0A	LF (Linefeed)
♂	11	0B	VT (Vertical tab)
♀	12	0C	FF (Formfeed)
♪	13	0D	CR (Carriage return)
♫	14	0E	SO (Shift out)
☼	15	0F	SI (Shift in)
►	16	10	DLE (Data link escape)
◄	17	11	DC1 (Device control 1)
↕	18	12	DC2 (Device control 2)
‼	19	13	DC3 (Device control 3)
¶	20	14	DC4 (Device control 4)
§	21	15	NAK (Negative acknowledge)
▬	22	16	SYN (Synchronous idle)
↨	23	17	ETB (End transmission block)
↑	24	18	CAN (Cancel)
↓	25	19	EM (End of medium)
→	26	1A	SUB (Substitute)
←	27	1B	ESC (Escape)
∟	28	1C	FS (File separator)
↔	29	1D	GS (Group separator)
▲	30	1E	RS (Record separator)
▼	31	1F	US (Unit separator)

ASCII	Dec	Hex
<space>	32	20
!	33	21
"	34	22
#	35	23
$	36	24
%	37	25
&	38	26
'	39	27
(	40	28
)	41	29
*	42	2A
+	43	2B
,	44	2C
-	45	2D
.	46	2E
/	47	2F
0	48	30
1	49	31
2	50	32
3	51	33
4	52	34
5	53	35
6	54	36
7	55	37
8	56	38
9	57	39
:	58	3A
;	59	3B
<	60	3C
=	61	3D
>	62	3E
?	63	3F

(continued)

continued

ASCII	Dec	Hex
@	64	40
A	65	41
B	66	42
C	67	43
D	68	44
E	69	45
F	70	46
G	71	47
H	72	48
I	73	49
J	74	4A
K	75	4B
L	76	4C
M	77	4D
N	78	4E
O	79	4F
P	80	50
Q	81	51
R	82	52
S	83	53
T	84	54
U	85	55
V	86	56
W	87	57
X	88	58
Y	89	59
Z	90	5A
[	91	5B
\	92	5C
]	93	5D
^	94	5E
_	95	5F

ASCII	Dec	Hex
`	96	60
a	97	61
b	98	62
c	99	63
d	100	64
e	101	65
f	102	66
g	103	67
h	104	68
i	105	69
j	106	6A
k	107	6B
l	108	6C
m	109	6D
n	110	6E
o	111	6F
p	112	70
q	113	71
r	114	72
s	115	73
t	116	74
u	117	75
v	118	76
w	119	77
x	120	78
y	121	79
z	122	7A
{	123	7B
¦	124	7C
}	125	7D
~	126	7E
△	127	7F

ASCII	Dec	Hex
Ç	128	80
ü	129	81
é	130	82
â	131	83
ä	132	84
à	133	85
å	134	86
ç	135	87
ê	136	88
ë	137	89
è	138	8A
ï	139	8B
î	140	8C
ì	141	8D
Ä	142	8E
Å	143	8F
É	144	90
æ	145	91
Æ	146	92
ô	147	93
ö	148	94
ò	149	95
û	150	96
ù	151	97
ÿ	152	98
ö	153	99
Ü	154	9A
¢	155	9B
£	156	9C
¥	157	9D
Pt	158	9E
ƒ	159	9F

(continued)

continued

ASCII	Dec	Hex	ASCII	Dec	Hex	ASCII	Dec	Hex
á	160	A0	└	192	C0	α	224	E0
í	161	A1	┴	193	C1	β	225	E1
ó	162	A2	┬	194	C2	Γ	226	E2
ú	163	A3	├	195	C3	π	227	E3
ñ	164	A4	─	196	C4	Σ	228	E4
Ñ	165	A5	┼	197	C5	σ	229	E5
ª	166	A6	╞	198	C6	µ	230	E6
º	167	A7	╟	199	C7	τ	231	E7
¿	168	A8	╚	200	C8	Φ	232	E8
⌐	169	A9	╔	201	C9	Θ	233	E9
¬	170	AA	╩	202	CA	Ω	234	EA
½	171	AB	╦	203	CB	δ	235	EB
¼	172	AC	╠	204	CC	∞	236	EC
¡	173	AD	═	205	CD	φ	237	ED
«	174	AE	╬	206	CE	ε	238	EE
»	175	AF	╧	207	CF	∩	239	EF
░	176	B0	╨	208	D0	≡	240	F0
▒	177	B1	╤	209	D1	±	241	F1
▓	178	B2	╥	210	D2	≥	242	F2
│	179	B3	╙	211	D3	≤	243	F3
┤	180	B4	╘	212	D4	⌠	244	F4
╡	181	B5	╒	213	D5	⌡	245	F5
╢	182	B6	╓	214	D6	÷	246	F6
╖	183	B7	╫	215	D7	≈	247	F7
╕	184	B8	╪	216	D8	°	248	F8
╣	185	B9	┘	217	D9	•	249	F9
║	186	BA	┌	218	DA	·	250	FA
╗	187	BB	█	219	DB	√	251	FB
╝	188	BC	▄	220	DC	η	252	FC
╜	189	BD	▌	221	DD	^{2}	253	FD
╛	190	BE	▐	222	DE	■	254	FE
┐	191	BF	▀	223	DF		255	FF

Index

Special Characters

A

G

H

I

J

K

L

M

N

O

Q

R

T

U

V

W

X

Z

Robert Arnson has been programming for eight years in BASIC, Pascal, C, and FORTRAN. He has developed several large business applications for professional insurance and statement billing, using QuickBASIC versions 2.0 through 4.5 and BASIC compilers 6.0 and 7.0.

Christy Gemmell has been writing software professionally for nine years. His programs are used by stockbrokers, accountants, and direct-mail companies. He is a founding member of Qbug, the British QuickBASIC Users Group, and the author of the Assembly Language Toolbox for QuickBASIC, a shareware utilities package. He works for Arden Microsystems in Leicester, England. He has authored for British user-group magazines such as *80 Micro* several articles on computer topics and programs.

Harry Henderson is a freelance technical writer and editor. He writes documentation for a major software manufacturer and has coauthored many Waite Group books, including *Microsoft QuickC Programming* and the forthcoming *The Waite Group's Microsoft QuickBASIC Primer Plus*, published by Microsoft Press; and *Understanding MS-DOS*, 2d ed., *The Waite Group's Using PC-DOS*, and *UNIX Communications*, published by Howard W. Sams & Co.

Mitchell Waite is president of The Waite Group, a well-known developer of technical and computer books. He is also an experienced programmer, fluent in a variety of computer languages. Waite coauthored The Waite Group's bestselling *C Primer Plus, UNIX Primer Plus, BASIC Programming Primer, C: Step by Step*, and *The Waite Group's HyperTalk Bible*, all published by Howard W. Sams & Co.

The manuscript for this book was prepared and submitted to Microsoft Press in electronic form. Text files were processed and formatted using Microsoft Word.

Word processors: Judith Bloch and Debbie Kem
Principal proofreader: Jean Zimmer
Principal typographer: Ruth Pettis
Interior text designer: Darcie S. Furlan
Principal illustrator: Rebecca Geisler-Johnson
Cover designer: Thomas A. Draper
Cover photographer: Lisa Irwin
Cover color separator: Rainier Color Corporation

Text composition by Microsoft Press in Garamond with display type in Futura Bold, using the Magna composition system and the Linotronic 300 laser imagesetter.

Printed on recycled paper stock.

KEYWORDS, STATEMENTS, AND FUNCTIONS BY CATEGORY

Variables and Types

Flow Control

Decisions and Operators

Procedures

Strings

Arrays and Data

Math

Simple I/O

Trapping and Errors

Time (Timing, Date, and Time)

Graphics